Reason, History, and Politics

SUNY Series in Social and Political Thought

Kenneth Baynes, editor

Reason, History, and Politics

The Communitarian Grounds of Legitimation in the Modern Age

DAVID INGRAM

State University of New York Press

Published by
State University of New York Press

For information, address the State University of New York Press,
State University Plaza, Albany, NY 12246

Production by Bernadine Dawes • Marketing by Theresa Abad Swierzowski

Library of Congress Cataloging-in-Publication Data

Ingram, David, 1952–
    Reason, history, and politics : the communitarian grounds of
legitimization in the modern age / David Ingram.
        p. cm. — (SUNY series in social and political thought)
    Includes index.
    ISBN 0-7914-2349-2 (hc : acid-free paper). — ISBN 0-7914-2350-6
(pbk. : acid-free paper)
    1. Social sciences—Philosophy. 2. Community. 3. Postmodernism.
I. Title. II. Series.
H61.I533 1995
300—dc 20   94–28754
                                                            CIP

1 2 3 4 5 6 7 8 9 10

For Sabina

To
Marilyn and
Jarvy —
For sharing the joy
of parenting and so
much more...

With greatest affection...
David
4/22/95

Contents

Acknowledgments

The research that went into the composition of this book spans many years, and has benefited from the criticism and support of persons too numerous to mention. There are a few, however, who merit singular recognition. Jim Bohman, David Schweickart, Hans Seigfried, Ardis Collins, George Trey, Sara Waller, Liam Harte, and Bill Martin commented on earlier drafts of the book. Thanks also go to Femi Taiwo, Tom Carson, Paul Moser, Tom Sheehan, Seyla Benhabib, Larry May, and Bill Rehg, who along with my students helped me clarify its principal themes and arguments. Needless to say, my debt here extends to all my anonymous readers as well. However, I am most grateful to Julia Simon-Ingram, who has been my abiding teacher and critic these many years. Without her candid advice and support the book would be far less coherent—and certainly far less interesting to read—than it is. In addition to Clay Morgan, Ken Baynes, Bernadine Dawes, Judith Hoover, and all the other editors and assistants affiliated with SUNY Press who helped along the way, I would like to thank the University of Northern Iowa and Loyola University of Chicago for funding the many research leaves and grants that made this book project possible. Along with the NEH grant to participate in the 1990 Heidegger/Davidson Institute at the University of Santa Cruz, this support has been indispensable for bringing me into contact with different persons and ideas.

The following presses and journals have kindly consented to allow portions of my published research to be reprinted.

Chapter 1 contains excerpts of "Contractualism, Democracy, and Social Law: Basic Antinomies in Liberal Thought." It originally appeared in *Philosophy and Social Criticism* 17, no. 4 (Fall 1991): 265–96, and is reprinted with permission of the editor.

Chapter 4 contains portions of "The Retreat of the Political in the Modern Age: Jean-Luc Nancy on Totalitarianism and Community," originally published in *Research in Phenomenology* 18 (Fall 1988): 93–124; and "Foucault and Habermas on the Subject of Reason," in *The Foucault Companion*, ed. Gary Gutting (Cambridge: Cambridge University Press, 1994), reprinted by permission of the publisher.

Chapter 5 excerpts portions of "The Limits and Possibilities of Communicative Ethics for Democratic Theory," which originally appeared in *Political Theory* 21, no. 2 (May 1993), copyright © 1993 by Sage Publications, Inc. Reprinted by permission of Sage Publications, Inc.

Chapter 6 contains portions of "Dworkin, Habermas, and the CLS Movement on Moral Criticism in Law," originally published in *Philosophy and Social Criticism* 16, no. 4 (Fall 1991): 237–68. Reprinted by permission of the editor.

Chapter 7 contains portions of the following articles: "Legitimacy and the Postmodern Condition: The Political Thought of Jean-François Lyotard," published in *Praxis International* 7, nos. 3/4 (Winter 1987/8): 284–303 (permission to reprint granted by Blackwell publishers); "The Postmodern Kantianism of Arendt and Lyotard," published in *Review of Metaphysics* 41 (October 1988): 51–77 (permission to reprint granted by the editor); "Completing the Project of Enlightenment: Habermas on Aesthetic Rationality," published in Ronald Roblin, ed., *The Aesthetics of the Critical Theorists: Studies on Benjamin, Adorno, Marcuse, and Habermas* (Lewiston, N.Y.: Edwin Mellen Press, 1990). Reprinted by permission of the publisher.

Chapter 8 excerpts portions of the following articles: "The Copernican Revolution Revisited. Paradigm, Metaphor, and Incommensurability in the History of Science: Blumenberg's Response to Kuhn and Davidson," published in *History of the Human Sciences* 6, no. 4 (November 1993): 11–35; copyright ©1993 by Sage Publications, Inc. Reprinted by permission of Sage Publications, Inc.; and "Reflections on the Anthropocentric Limits of Scientific Realism: Blumenberg on the Legitimacy of the Modern Age," published in Thomas Flynn and Dalia Judovitz, eds., *Dialectic and Narrative*, (Albany: State University of New York Press, 1993). Permission to reprint granted by the publisher.

The author has translated all citations from foreign titles unless otherwise stated.

Introduction

these vain and futile declaimers go off in every direction, armed with
their deadly paradoxes, undermining the foundations of faith and anni-
hilating virtue

—Rousseau

We moderns labor under a rational regimen so total and dominant that
we forget that modernity once heralded an enlightenment of emancipation. This regimen—call it subjective reason (SR)—could not be more hostile to this noble purpose, since it permits only the cognitive evaluation of
means aimed at control.[1] More precisely, in calculating the efficient satisfaction of subjective needs, SR admits of a single rational end, namely
technological domination of an otherwise unpredictable environment. In
this sense SR is totalitarian; in its panoptic gaze, even human freedom
constitutes a chaotic force requiring discipline and control.

No wonder postmodern critics of science prefer to romanticize its
aesthetic qualities, the most important being predictive *indeterminacy*. If science is best described as a revolutionary movement in a permanent state
of *crisis*, then, they reason, its obsession with rigid control, as distinct from
flexible learning, is misguided. In fact, the crisis of determinacy, which
reflects a failure to explore more holistic, *less controlled*, forms of experimentation, is intimately related to another legitimation crisis: that of *skepticism*. SR is so totally absorbed in the task of efficient adaptation that it
cannot reflect on its own justification or rationale. Yet power cannot exist

1

for the sake of power alone. SR's legitimacy must therefore rest on an independent cognitive foundation: experience ordered and made consistent by formal logic. But it is precisely here—at the point where subjective experience meets objective reality—that SR reveals its cognitive poverty. For, by equating objective knowledge with beliefs whose ultimate justification resides in the sovereign subject's own certainty of what he or she has directly experienced, SR can account for truth as little as any other rational validity claim. As many critics of positivism have observed over the years, no belief claiming to be true, or *publicly* justifiable, conceivably follows from private experience. Nor does any norm or rule—including those of logic—since these too are by their very nature public. What makes them valid is less their correspondence with individual psychology than their general acceptance as useful methods of learning. Of course, this is not to deny that learning—especially when it aims at successful problem solving—depends on experience, specifically that of cause and effect. Here we encounter yet another crisis: the incapacity of SR to account for the *synthetic integrity* of causally ordered experience. Causal generalizations are not mere random correlations of contingently experienced events. To say that X caused Y is to say that X was necessary for Y: had X *not* occurred then Y would *not* have occurred. Since the logical form of a causal generalization is that of a *counterfactual* assertion, causal knowledge cannot be reduced to a *passive* recording of facts randomly associated by a lone observer. The logic of causal explanation follows more closely the logic of discovery rather than that of induction (abstraction). Discovery involves experimentally isolating necessary conditions through *active* interventions on the part of a *community* of scientists, who see and describe nature in the same way. Indeed, once we realize that causal knowledge is a communal achievement, predicated on a consensus regarding both the description of reality and its probable effects for later generations of co-researchers, it becomes increasingly apparent that reason is *communal*—depending on *intersubjective* collaboration and communication rather than on subjective experience. In short, it is *communicative* reason (CR), or free and impartial discussion, that provides the implicit *background* of *synthetic* conditions that make possible SR's *analytic* operations of abstraction, induction, and monological deduction.

Unfortunately, what I have here characterized as a superficial manifestation of reason—the partial and abstract method of formal logic and instrumental calculation—is now held up as its total and essential incarnation. So thoroughly has SR been ensconced in our popular imagination that appearance has supplanted essence in the nature of social reality; failure to realize the essence of reason—that is, failure to cultivate the conditions of open and impartial discussion at all levels of life—has encouraged the development of mechanistic and hierarchically managed techniques of social engineering whose implications for democratic community are frightening, to say the least. Yet it can hardly be denied that these implications follow as a matter of course from a culture of skepticism, domination, and disintegration. Today many of us—not just the *philosophes and littérateurs* against whom Rousseau railed—think that values lack rational foundation. Reduced to conflicting and variously weighted preferences, values fail to build a coherent, public mandate. Public reason, such as it is, shifts from democracy to administration. Consequently, just as in the workplace, managers—not citizens—assume unilateral responsibility for calculating costs, implementing decisions, and coordinating activities.

What I originally introduced as a three-pronged legitimation crisis affecting reason as a formal procedure of knowledge has here become a three-pronged legitimation crisis affecting modern society: *historical, political*, and *technological*. The crisis of skepticism, which extends to SR's incapacity to justify itself, is mirrored in modern society's failure to generate a democratic consensus requisite for legitimation of its laws. The crisis of synthesis, which reflects SR's incapacity to account for and produce coherent, lawful experience, is mirrored in that society's failure to establish the temporal coherence of its judicial decisions and existential commitments in a manner that is both historically continuous and revolutionary. Finally, the crisis of determinacy, which flows from SR's obsession with a disciplined predictability and control that remains elusive, finds parallel expression in a *carceral* society so mired in *technological domination* that it has lost the collective initiative and imagination to solve its environmental problems.

I submit that the *paradox* of reason as illegitimate and oppressive loses some of its force once we realize that SR is but a partial aspect of a richer CR. In realizing this, we understand why SR was falsely taken to be a complete and adequate basis for scientific knowledge by a positivist philosophy of science. And yet we can appreciate why stratified societies have nonetheless chosen to develop their political structures and technologies in ways that mimic SR's hierarchical logic of decision and control rather than CR's logic of democratic learning. For while considerations of formal simplicity and precision may explain why analytic philosophers continue to embrace SR—its shortcomings as a method of knowledge notwithstanding—very different factors enter into its popularity as a practical design for decision procedures and technologies.

A complete defense of these rather extravagant claims, including a fuller explanation of what I mean by SR and CR, will emerge only later on (notably in conjunction with my discussion of synthetic rationality in chapter 2 and my examination of communicative rationality in chapters 4, 5, and 7). However, a few—I am afraid, all too sketchy—indications of my intentions can be revealed in the remarks that immediately follow. First let me suggest how the question of rationality figures in the welfare state's current legitimation crises.

1. The most decisive fact about the welfare state is its intervention in the private sector in the name of a public—and ostensibly rational—interest: the self-realization of autonomous citizens as mainsprings for a more inclusive and rational democracy. Its regulatory arm not only oversees the safety, health, and education of the workforce, authorizes economic transfers, subsidies, and tax breaks targeted toward specific beneficiaries, but it ensures the conscionability and fairness of contracts in ways that belie the classical liberal ideology of contractual freedom and equality.

The moral basis legitimating this kind of interference is both liberal and communitarian. It is liberal insofar as it rectifies inequities in bargaining strength between employers and employees that severely constrain the latter's freedom to accept or reject contracts. It is communitarian insofar as it recognizes that individuals are responsible neither for contingencies of birth and upbringing that determine their capacities to compete nor for shifts in patterns of investment that determine their opportunities for gainful employment.

Supporting both sets of reasons is the recognition that capitalism itself has changed since the nineteenth century. As Durkheim and Marx pointed out, the functional exchange relationships definitive of capitalism make it *the* social form of production par excellence. This is even truer with the transition from an agrarian to an industrial—and now information-based—economy. Under a system composed of largely independent producers, the historical and contemporaneous contribution of the community to the social reproduction of life could be concealed behind the false facade of "self-made" individuals. With the advent of global capitalism and its dependence on computer technologies that rely on a highly specialized and educated workforce, this illusion all but evaporates. Recognition of the communitarian contribution and the contingent interlocking of individual destinies compels us to compensate victims of uneven economic growth and equalize educational opportunities and differential bargaining strengths of workers competing for scarce jobs.

Alas, the compensatory—and ultimately paternalistic—nature of the welfare state's attempt to ensure the social bases of autonomy and self-respect proves self-defeating. The communitarian no less than the liberal bemoans the interventionist state's violation of individual autonomy. And the former no less than the latter decries its overregulation of family, school, and local community. In short, both contend that this state produces disintegrative effects every bit as deleterious as the destabilizing mobilities and inequities of unregulated capitalism. However, in addition to being morally obtuse, welfare statism has shown itself to be almost as economically inefficient and politically dysfunctional as bureaucratic socialism and libertarian capitalism.

First, there are the familiar fiscal crises associated with policies aimed at maintaining stable economic growth. Then there are legitimation crises associated with changes in law and in the legislature's and judiciary's incapacity to justify their pronouncements to all segments of the population. These are magnified by real paradoxes of collective choice in tabulating votes and by economically based disparities in voter participation, representation, and strength. Finally, there are management crises affecting government's inability to engineer technological solutions to problems independently of local input.

Let us focus briefly on the legitimation problem. In my opinion, Rousseau was the first to have diagnosed its basis in reason. As he put it, "reason is what engenders egocentrism, and reflection strengthens it" (Rousseau 1987, 54). Resigned to the individualism of rational culture, he turned to the common interest each has in preserving his or her own life, liberty, and property as a basis for democratic solidarity. Yet, as his account of the social contract makes clear, this solution to the problem of political legitimacy is inherently ambiguous—wavering between liberal and communitarian interpretations of public reason. Does a law's coherence with universal *intuition* or *popular* acclaim make it a legitimate expression of rational interests?

Rousseau's insistence that laws be *formally* general in their subject matter and object so as to express a "universality of will" applicable to all without exception suggests he had the former in mind (161). This response anticipates Kant's account of the social contract, which presumes that even a "race of devils" would ascribe to a minimal principle of justice "allowing the *greatest possible human freedom* in accordance with laws by which *the freedom of each is made to be consistent with that of others*" (Kant 1927, A316/17–B373/74). This principle—intuited by each on his or her own—mandates the establishment of coercive laws preventing the violation of civil rights for mere utility's sake. The democratic intent of Kant's principle of self-determination notwithstanding, the thrust of *this* principle is to limit popular sovereignty vis-à-vis the protection of personal property.[2]

By contrast, the republican response allows that only a democratically assembled people can be the final judge in interpreting and deciding the extent of basic civil rights. For, even if these rights are grounded in reason, their generality would render them meaningless absent specification of their contribution to a *given* community's good. Here "public reason" is not limited to protecting negative liberty—or freedom from interference—as it is in Kant's account. Rather, it positively secures the satisfaction of common interests—valid, perhaps, for only a single community—that go beyond satisfying the consistency requirements of reason narrowly conceived.

But what community deliberates so impartially? Perhaps the intimate assembly of homogeneous and self-sufficient farmers extolled by Rousseau, who are made virtuous by patriotic sentiment. But since complex, pluralistic polities lack these kinds of citizens, consensus on the meaning and scope of basic rights seems highly unlikely. Our failure to resolve disputes about concrete rights generates a constitutional crisis that seems all but intractable given our "liberal" distinction between public reason and private interest. In short, the tension between judicial review and democracy—or between reason and will—underscores a deeper legitimation crisis besetting liberal society: the lack of rational consensus regarding policy aims and moral visions.

How do contemporary liberals and communitarians view this crisis? Following Kant, liberals think that reason commands the adoption of neutral rules for coordinating conflicting interests. However, since no interest is deducible from formal procedures of this sort, none is immanently rational or irrational. At best, we can speak of a rational *set* of interests transitively ordered and ranked so as to maximize arbitrarily chosen ends.

What are the problems with this view? First, far from being universal and impartial, toleration of conflicting ends is specific to circumstances of scarcity and plurality. Even if it were not partial with respect to certain circumstances and anthropological assumptions, its success in defining moral identity in terms of formal, *innate* capacities for rational choice would come at the expense of accounting for real, *social* motivation and identity.

Second, rationality remains captive to individualistic assumptions that continue to influence the theory and practice of liberalism long after the demise of libertarianism. Viewing value preferences as arbitrary determinants of subjective choice, public servants can only try to aggregate them as consistently and efficiently as possible. On this model of public reason, democracy at best functions as an economic mechanism for passively registering effective demand (monetary and organizational power converted into votes), not a moral vehicle for fairly and critically generating common interests requisite for bestowing legitimacy. Yet ever-recurrent budget crises prove that this mechanism fails to resolve conflicts as surely as it fails to protect against tyranny or maximize utility. Just as yesterday's pluralists today bemoan the hegemony of corporate powers that tyrannize over marginalized voting blocs, so today's economists rue the paradox of submaximal and inconsistent inputs. In the face of persistent domination, contradiction and conflict, is it any wonder that government by enlightened technocrats seems preferable to government by the people?

2. This book attempts a rhetorical rejoinder to this rhetorical question. It sketches an alternative account of public reason on communitarian—or more precisely, communicative—grounds. This task involves disentangling the liberal ideal of democratic consensus from distortions wrought by capitalism. In one sense, of course, capitalist democracy itself seems to be legitimated by a rational consensus. Its very structure rewards and promotes a kind of SR, namely, economic calculation aimed at short-term material gain. This rationality is a function of the material uncertainty generated by capitalism itself. The state and the general working population depend on private investment for tax revenues and wages, respectively. The uncertainty of this bottom line, coupled with the uncertainty of long-term political struggle and the high costs of coordinating it—not to mention the costs of gathering information necessary for political enlightenment generally—forces political agents to restrict their deliberations to the most narrow and self-centered, if also well-defined and practically fruitful, economic rationality (Cohen and Rogers 1983, chap. 3). Of course, the game of calculated interest is not played on an even field. Capitalists use their advantage in resources and concentrated numbers to acquire costly information and coordinate their lobbying efforts with relative ease, while producers and consumers rationally forgo the costly education and risky coordination required to protect themselves against these very same efforts. So the dairy industry gets its milk subsidy, along with an artificial increase in the market price of milk. To the isolated consumer who is worried about economically maximizing his or her increasingly scarce leisure time, the effort required to organize against a penny increase in the price of a quart of milk is not worth the time expended. And so capitalist democracy is rational in its own, *subjective* way, but hardly as a *communitarian* procedure for resolving long-term *public* interests.

Communitarians are thus the most vociferous critics of capitalist democracy and its discontents, which they naturally—but wrongly—attribute to liberal reason as such. Let us begin with Anglo-American varieties of communitarianism. Leaving aside their criticism of capitalism and focusing instead on their critique of liberal rationalism, a sympathetic, liberal critic can hardly endorse their attempt to salvage public spiritedness by replacing SR with shared traditions that encourage dogmatic patriotism and virtue at the expense of multicultural and multinational solidarity. To better appreciate their communitarian alternative to the kind of CR-based liberalism proposed here, we need to recall the problem of value skepticism. The problem of inferring values from facts is dispelled once we see that the validation of *any* nontrivial claim follows from its common acceptance.[3] To begin with, it makes no sense to say that factual claims have any special purchase on indubitable experience. As linguistic constructs, they bear no resemblance to the sensory givens to which they supposedly correspond. On the contrary, like value judgments they, too, are *interpretations* of experience. And the only way to validate an interpretation is to show that people do or would accept it upon discussing its merits rationally. *Intersubjective consensus* achieved under conditions of impartial discussion thus carries the burden of justification, not logical inference from *subjective* experience.

Now, a communicative account of argumentative justification is important for a communitarian reconstruction of *practical* reason. This becomes clearer when we examine the second problem of justification: the incapacity of SR to legitimate its own principles. The transcendental solution to this problem—exemplified in the Cartesian/Kantian tradition—involves deducing or intuiting a normative ground, or criterion of rationality, through self-introspection. The problem with this solution is that the perduring identity of the self—its unique personality no less than the rational faculties it shares with others—is taken for granted. Neither aspect of selfhood, however, is immediately present to consciousness without further presupposition. This presupposition is none other than the confirmation of self through mutual recognition by one's associates. *Who* we are is no doubt determined by our own personal life history, but that autobiography is recounted in terms of values, social roles, and ascriptions accepted as valid by the community at large.

To sum up, by defining self and community in terms of the maintenance of narrative identity, or a well-integrated life history in which part and whole mutually interpret one another in a *relatively harmonious consummation,* tradition-minded communitarians provide a kind of anthropological basis for public reason. Reason is primarily manifested in the day-to-day exchange of informal arguments whose common acceptance serves to rationally stabilize what are otherwise shaky dogmas. As such, it is the main vehicle for maintaining stable identity as well. Most importantly—and somewhat ironically—it means that we don't have to rely on patriotic or religious sentiment to transform people into virtuous communitarians. Rational communication alone requires of speakers that they respect—and care for—one another as unique individuals whose identities are also inextricably and solidaristically intertwined.

I will return to this point shortly. Before doing so I am afraid I will have to complicate matters by discussing a school of communitarian thought that directly challenges the rationality of reason as I have here reconstructed it. In sharp contrast to their Anglo-American counterparts, French communitarians view any political authority with alarm. Indeed, their objections to majoritarian tyranny, welfare paternalism, and ideologies projecting absolute ends of any kind (however thinly conceived) could easily be mistaken for similar objections proffered by classical liberals. Yet these postmodernists are decidedly communitarian in their belief that the technological apparatus of liberal society endangers pluralism. Stronger still, whereas Anglo-American communitarians include laws and norms among the goods requisite for maintaining a happy social identity, postmodern communitarians think they violate its inherent fluidity, indeterminacy, and open-endedness. Ironically, this last comment suggests that, for all their anticommunitarian posturing, postmodernists are the most communitarian of all. For, not only do they reject the atomistic individualism of classical liberalism, they reject notions of identity that do not cede primacy to the differential *relations* traversing linguistic interaction.

Postmodernists touch on a profound difficulty with tradition-based communitarianism. By acknowledging the primacy of differential relations they seem to be committed to denying the historical identity requisite for legitimating modern society. If we assume that medieval and modern worldviews are radically incommensurable—that is, that the core concepts of reason and reality on which they disagree cannot be translated into a language common to both—then there are no common criteria against which we can compare them. But unless we can make this comparison, we are in no position to justify modernity's legitimacy as *progressive*. And yet, if they *are* commensurable, so that the core concepts of the one can be literally translated without loss into that of the other, then they are not sufficiently distinguishable to justify the progression of one beyond the other.

The only way around this dilemma, I submit, is to reject the thesis that rational communication requires *literal* translatability instead of *metaphorical* paraphrase. To conceive rational argumentation in this manner—*aesthetically*—violates the formal logical canon of semantic univocity; two persons, say, can be said to argue rationally even if they do not literally intend the same thing by the same expression; and the conclusion they reach may be rational even if reached for very different reasons. What makes historical continuity and democratic community possible is thus the aesthetic capacity to fashion new metaphors that bridge *and* transform what otherwise appear to be incommensurable interpretations, worldviews, identities, and idioms. In fact, the concepts of market socialism, liberal communitarianism, rational indeterminacy, complex (decentered and differentiated) integrity, and postmodern legitimation defended in this book exemplify this sublime metaphoricity.[4]

What aesthetic rationality means in the context of my examination of CR and the problem of legitimation will be a topic for further discussion. Suffice it to say, although postmodernists have addressed the aesthetic dimension, they have done so in ways that either exaggerate the deconstruction of differences—in effect, rendering them entirely indeterminate—or multiply them to the point of reintroducing radical ruptures and incommensurabilities. However, if we reject the overly deterministic and unitary account of reasoning implicit in SR, the only acceptable alternative seems to be a *qualified* postmodern communitarianism. But how can relative plurality and indeterminacy be made compatible with political legitimacy?

3. SR assumes that legitimate decisions rest on a unique consensus: of the many ways a conflict might be consensually resolved, only one is right. Postmodernism denies this. My reconstruction splits the difference between these views. Once we accept the discursive structure of rationality, we must also accept its *reflexive* capacity to permit indefinite discussion about its own structural sense. Like SR, CR can be given a *formal* interpretation, or reconstruction of general rulelike competencies. In bridging what *appear* to be discrete spheres of understanding, speakers have an intuitive grasp of the deeper reciprocity binding them to their interlocutors. Perhaps in some highly mediated way the *bare* idea of universal human rights is as integral to the mutual openness and respect accompanying efforts at mutual understanding as it is to modern, postconventional notions of law.[5] Although I cannot defend the idea here, it seems correct to say that not only conceptions of formal logic but also conceptions of impartiality and inclusivity of the sort characteristic of CR underwrite all *genuine* efforts at mutual understanding, no matter what culture we are talking about. On the other hand, these efforts would be redundant if differences between interlocutors were effaced. Unlike SR, CR cannot be reduced to formal procedures, because its dialogic nature promotes endless *reflection* on its own concrete, practical sense; the differences that provoke reflection also produce conflicts in *substantive* interpretation (or judgment) about what reflection means.

As noted above, such differences are at the root of modern legitimation problems. Since persons living in pluralistic societies may have legitimate interests that won't be shared by all even after sincere attempts at consensual dialogue have been made, their aggregation will pose problems for any democratic regime. At best, we can hope that these differences will be mitigated in proportion to the rationality and inclusiveness of public debate, and that legislators and administrators responsible for deciding on policy goals will do so fairly.

In accordance with postmodern plurality and indeterminacy, "fairly" in this context can mean only one thing: the judicious balancing of competing criteria of justice. Citizens no less than judges must judge with *integrity*. Both confront the task of interpreting rights against the background of traditional precedents, policy aims, and the particularities of the situation being adjudicated. This interpretative exercise of judgment is itself aesthetic, in that it requires a certain sensibility (or sensitivity) with respect to fine, contextual discriminations as well as an intuitive knack for metaphorically mediating and harmonizing different perspectives and considerations of justice: distributive and procedural. Distributive justice, for example, must respect the "common understanding" a given society has regarding the meaning and distribution of goods. But in the modern democracies of the West our understanding of these matters is itself *complex* and open to multiple—sometimes conflicting—interpretations. Does need or money entitle one to basic medical care? Should market success determine one's political power? In raising the question of political power, one can scarcely ignore the competing standards of procedural justice at stake in regulating democratic processes. The communitarian's interest in insulating public opinion from the inegalitarian influence of money opposes the liberal's interest in retaining a marketplace of ideas and lifestyles in which unequal opportunities for participation inevitably develop. Do limits on campaign expenditures and contributions restrict the freedom of speech requisite for democratic dialogue or do they distribute it more fairly? Again, these questions raise further procedural concerns regarding the separation of powers, especially as this pertains to the proper role of the judiciary in preserving the integrity of democratic procedure itself.

The judicious mediation and balancing of distinct criteria of justice ultimately draw on different types of reasoning as well. Economic calculation of costs and benefits must be qualified by principled respect for moral rights; in turn, these rationales must be harmonized with an evolving interpretation of a people's traditionally and constitutionally based self-understanding of its own collective identity. Even the revolutionary changes in adjudication inaugurated by Reconstruction and the New Deal in American politics were marked by the imaginative grafting of new legal idioms onto older ones.

Americans should harbor no illusions about the success of this synthetic accomplishment. In reviewing the actual record one might well conclude that the rights of minorities, women, children, and workers have not fared as well as they might have under a different kind of democratic regime. On some occasions the courts have failed to extend constitutional guarantees to these groups in ways that could have enhanced their freedom and dignity; on others it has invoked such guarantees to stifle it. In my opinion, the courts have failed to live up to the popular mandate underlying the New Deal: not despotic paternalism but enhancement of those civil, political, and social rights requisite for bringing about a more just and inclusive democratic participation in all walks of life.

4. It is easy to see how questions of communication and identity intersect those of political and historical legitimation. Not so obvious is the relationship between CR and the third legitimation problem—the utility of reason with respect to human happiness and freedom. As noted above, comparative judgments of progress depend on communicative rationality. But what if such judgments reflect badly on the dehumanizing, antidemocratic effects of modern technology?

I shall argue that there are certain parallels between SR and mechanistic, hierarchical technologies designed for calculation and decision. However, I submit that information-based technologies designed for feedback learning and parallel processing actually augment human potentialities and democratic freedoms. This reference to the aesthetic fulfillment of reasonable, integrated personalities suggests yet another implication of CR. Rational societies *balance* and *integrate* cognitive (scientific-technological), moral, and aesthetic aspects of rational culture in ways that are globally enhancing.

Postmodernists deny this, of course. According to them, the dialectic of enlightenment—as Adorno and Horkheimer called it—is inherent in reason itself. Kant was the first to undertake a critique of this faculty. On one hand, by showing how cognitive reflection on the totality of objective conditions issues in self-referential paradox (antinomy), he initiated the end of premodern metaphysics and its dogmatic foundationalism. On the other hand, by showing how transcendental reflection on the totality of subjective conditions legitimates knowledge, morality, and taste as *distinct* deployments of reason, he placed in doubt their unity, thereby anticipating the postmodern rupture of reason with itself.

Following Max Weber, postmodernists reconceptualize this fragmentation as a *social* process. For Weber, the *cultural* value spheres of knowledge, morality, and aesthetics implicated in Kantian transcendental psychology acquire public institutionalization in scientific, legal, and artistic disciplines. These in turn anchor capitalist economy, bureaucratic administration, and private household. Cultural and social "rationalization" subjects the organic unity of traditional society to disenchantment in a manner no less rigorous than Kant's own critique of traditional metaphysics. Yet, from Weber's standpoint, rationalization can only assume the *unemancipated* form diagnosed by Nietzsche (Weber 1969, 144–48). Crushed between the millstones of technological efficiency and bureaucratic hierarchy on one side and amoral hedonism on the other, the vocational ethic of capitalism no longer commands autonomy but only ceaseless toil, authoritarian self-abnegation, and slavish consumption (Weber 1958, 79).

By confining rationality to "value-free" procedures of preference ranking, consistency testing, and instrumental calculation of the sort undertaken by individual utility maximizers, Weber was even less successful than Kant in extricating himself from the paradox of reason. Kant had hoped that the critique of cognitive reason—the restriction of its deployment to sense experience—would restore faith in moral reason. The romantic—and essentially communitarian—*counterdiscourse* that followed in its wake was much less hopeful. For Hegel—whose speculative philosophy culminates this discourse—the critical delimitation of theoretical and practical reason is emblematic of the very problem it ostensibly solves, and ultimately portends disastrous consequences for both science and morality.

Looking ahead to Weber and the twentieth century, he seemed to fathom the perverse affinity between totalitarianism and abstract individualism that would eventually emerge from the mass dynamics of modern society. In his opinion, the events culminating the Reign of Terror clearly attest to the moral impoverishment of a truncated enlightenment wherein utilitarian heteronomy and fanatical virtue—now secularized and emancipated from otherworldly religion—confront one another as opposed "moments" of reason. (Hegel 1977, paras. 582–95). Only the promise of reconciliation vouchsafed by dialectical reason, he thought, could redeem the spiritual and secular intentions of religion from rational diremption; only it could show how abstract morality and abstract need are sublated in the ethical community of a modern *Rechtsstaat.*

If postmodernists reject this speculative discourse, it is because they find its yearning for organic wholeness—reflected in Hegel's supreme estimate of state bureaucracy and corporate representation as placeholders of community—to be as potentially totalitarian as its emancipatory antithesis. However, since the dialectic of enlightenment sustains itself on reason's own self-diremption, only reason's self-reintegration can overcome it. Should we dismiss this dialectic as part myth—which I recommend we do—we must still account for the alienation and unfreedom accompanying technological regimentation. That neither modernists nor postmodernists do so stems from their continued reliance on narrow conceptions of reason.

Fortunately, we can retrieve aspects of idealism for reconstructing this notion. Hegel's account of identity as a reflexive relation to other is one such resource that can be given a true communitarian reading once it is detached from a Spirit-centered framework and translated into pragmatic categories of communicative action. When we see how strategic and instrumental types of action typically associated with science, technology, and decision theory only realize their potential reflexively, we might better appreciate the emancipatory legacy of materialism as well. Kant's notion of reflective judgment is another resource for reconstructing the community of reason. It accounts for metaphorical identifications—or family resemblances, to use Wittgenstein's phraseology—between types of discursive and nondiscursive reasoning that are otherwise incommensurable. Using this notion of judgment we can not only *explain* the *real* unity of CR, but we can *criticize* hegemonic imbalances between types of reasoning with reference to *possible* states of communal integrity.

Ultimately this will mean acknowledging the partiality of reason—and liberal democracy—vis-à-vis substantive notions of autonomy, equality, and human flourishing. Such notions are not neutral with respect to sects that breed intolerance or uncritical devotion to authority; nor are they neutral with respect to lifestyles that foster a lack of equal respect for one's fellow citizens. Indeed, they are incompatible with large-scale capitalist economies, since their fulfillment would require forms of technology, workplace democracy, community investment, and oversight that would undermine current forms of market behavior.

I have chosen to begin my defense of these claims by discussing the problem of political legitimation. Chapter 1 charts the history of liberal democratic theory and practice and examines its impact on various aspects of public law within the American setting. The tension between libertarian and communitarian strands of constitutional interpretation is shown to be unresolvable within the framework of SR. Drawing on Marx's critique of Hegel and Sandel's critique of Rawls, I argue that SR entails a split (or abstract) conception of political identity. The concluding section turns to Hegel's critique of SR to develop a richer, more reflective conception of knowledge and reality of the sort presupposed by Marx.

Chapter 2 relates Hegel's critique to contemporary debates in philosophy of science. The defense of holistic epistemology and relational ontology in science may seem tangential to the communitarian critique. However, once we see the limits of narrow notions of rationality in the hard sciences—something that Hegel's critique of abstract universals and deterministic notions of causality helps us to understand—we see their inadequacy in the human sciences as well.

My survey of philosophy of science defends this claim in relation to three separate points: first, that the logic of causal explanation and discovery is inherently interpretative and contextual—and thus depends on the synthetic achievements of transcendentally productive but empirically embodied social agents; second, that the logic of causal discovery and explanation in the human sciences further depends on the *reflexive* self-understanding of interpreter and agent; and third, that the communicative rationale undergirding science opens up new possibilities for the democratic application of information-based technology.

These points bear on the issue of postmodern legitimation in the following way. Contrary to empiricist philosophies of social science, which attempt to fix the reasons underlying social action in some causally determinate manner, the postempiricist philosophy of social science endorsed here embraces methodological pluralism. Such pluralism is the only satisfactory response to the causal and semantic indeterminacy of social phenomena. Despite their dependence on common norms of understanding, the specific rationales governing these methods gravitate around Kuhnian exemplars rather than logical constructions. Representing a distillation of successful cases, these *middle-range* (i.e., neither general nor local) paradigms entail criteria of explanatory adequacy that no longer aim at determinate prediction.

The upshot of this analysis is that reason and community are founded on normative structures whose concrete meaning remains at least partially indeterminate. Such indeterminacy, in turn, suggests several complementary paradigms—functional, hermeneutical, and game-theoretical—for studying problems of political legitimation.

These paradigms find articulation in different schools of communitarian thought. Chapter 3 discusses the Anglo-American schools. I here examine the tradition-based communitarianism of such diverse thinkers as Taylor, MacIntyre, and Walzer. I begin by discussing Rawls's notion of an overlapping consensus as one solution to the problem of legitimating overarching principles of justice within a pluralist setting. The failure of this liberal account of public reason to explain the rationality of political consensus leads me to consider two other kinds of consensual understanding: theoretical (based on radical translation of speech behavior) and practical (based on radical socialization into embodied speech habits). Both of them—the former represented by Davidson and Rorty, the latter by Dreyfus and MacIntyre—succumb to relativism. I conclude that only a dialectical model of interpretation of the sort elaborated by Gadamer—and qualified by Habermas—accounts for rational consensus and community.

The second half of the chapter explores the application of hermeneutical principles of coherence and perfectibility to problems of justice. My discussion of Walzer highlights the problematic notion of common understanding as it bears on a pluralistic interpretation of different spheres of justice. Concerns raised by Dworkin suggest a more porous—conflictual and indeterminate—interpretation of these spheres than Walzer seems to envisage. That Walzer himself presupposes unity of meaning within spheres and integrity between them can be explained, I argue, by his reliance on a teleological ideal of perfectibility implicit within hermeneutics itself. This ideal also functions in Taylor's discussion of the uneasy alliance between liberal and communitarian sources of identity in justifying a legal recognition of multicultural difference. Ultimately, it anticipates an *aesthetic* ideal of social integrity and reconciliation.

Besides problems of interpretative relativism and indeterminacy, communitarianism raises two other concerns: the tension between description and prescription and the integration of identity. To the extent that communitarianism is committed to *immanent*, culture-relative criticism *and* to the extent that abstract individualism accurately describes the contractual bonds of liberal culture, liberal *theory* cannot be criticized as a false, normative interpretation; however, to the extent that communitarianism rejects this theory's interpretation of liberal culture, liberal *culture* cannot be criticized as anticommunitarian. The only way out of this dilemma is to concede that liberalism contains a communitarian rationale that transcends its current theory *and* practice. As for the problem of identity, traditional communitarians tend to view cultures as self-contained, harmonious entities—their critique of abstract individualism notwithstanding. This is understandable given their hermeneutic point of departure. Interpreters are compelled to anticipate—however tacitly and tentatively—some coherent understanding of what their text means in its entirety. However, these *idealizing* assumptions function *ideologically* by covering over contradictions and bypassing covert, socioeconomic (functional) constraints.

Concern over holistic (or global) ideologies drives poststructuralists to reject hermeneutics. The varieties of poststructuralism discussed in chapter 4—descending from the deconstruction of sign systems and the genealogy of power relations—have this in common. The former—preeminently developed in the political philosophies of Derrida and Nancy—attempts to articulate the transcendental *essence* of political community. Such philosophy prescinds from both scientific description and normative prescription—categories of understanding that ostensibly collude with the totalitarian logic of modern technology. Instead it conceives the social bond in *aesthetic* terms—as a text or *literary* event of mythopoetic sharing and division *(partage)*.

The importance of the imaginary and symbolic in constituting the metaphorical alliances, semiotic identifications, and oppositions of hegemonic, democratic politics (as Laclau and Mouffe put it) should not be underestimated. Nor should those *asymmetrical* responsibilities toward friends, communal consociates, and significant others that Derrida and Nancy think are so basic to community. But to the extent that this responsibility signals a primary disruption (or decentering) of identity that extends to the reflexive—imaginary and linguistic—birth of selfhood itself (Lacan), one can question whether it precedes rather than follows communication based on the simultaneous adoption of *symmetrical* roles of speaker and respondent. Regardless of how one answers this question, there can be little doubt that the kinds of CR underwriting democratic forms of bargaining and consensual understanding imply moral reciprocity. Contrary to Derrida and Nancy, such a minimal form of moral rationality is not an impossible law that purports to logically deduce natural (moral) and legal duties from transcendent principles. Rather, it is the mundane conversation by which we democratically interpret and constitute any norm whatsoever.

In the second portion of the chapter I show how the genealogical communitarianism associated with Michel Foucault accounts for the scientific, technological, and normative dimension of liberal culture in a way that the deconstructive variety does not. Specifically, it shows how human sciences, strategies of governance, and other *rational* discourses produce a truth that is *also* a disciplinary technique.

There is much that is valuable in Foucault's genealogical critique of liberalism as a carceral culture. Foucault brilliantly dissects the dehumanizing aspects of technological society and its paradoxical connection to the humanistic rationale of self-empowerment. He also appreciates the way in which persons are shaped by normative traditions and strategic power relations. However, by bracketing the meaningfulness and validity of these social determinants, his genealogical descriptions sometimes seem indistinguishable from uncritical functionalist ones. Eventually he came to see the limits of this "happy positivism." His later hermeneutic genealogy even suggests a communitarian corrective to game theory and a strategic corrective to communication theory.

However, in at least one sense Foucault neglects the importance of communicative rationality in structuring social relations. This deficit is most apparent in his diagnosis of the dialectic of enlightenment. Foucault argues that reflection vacillates between two extremes, the one subjectivistic,

transcendental, and originary, the other objectivistic, empirical, and derivative. Failure to unify these aspects forces human science to progressively dehumanize humanity even as it strives to emancipate it.

Ironically, Foucault's own inability to escape this dialectic is borne out
by the ambiguity inherent in his genealogies, which waver between functionalistic and strategic accounts of social agency. Habermas shows us a
way out of this dilemma: Conceive reflection dialogically—not as a process
of subjective self-objectification but as a process of intersubjective communication.

Before turning to the third variety of postmodern communitarianism
associated with Lyotard's speech agonistics, I take up Habermas's attempt
to reformulate liberal theory in terms of discourse ethics. Chapter 5 addresses one aspect of this project: an examination of the limits and possibilities of consensus-oriented democracy for the legitimation of law. My
argument here consists of two strands. The first defends democracy against
well-known paradoxes of collective choice. The strategic pursuit of particular interests has a valid place in democratic theory, but one that must
be circumscribed by ethical considerations. The latter are articulated in
public debates over the common goods and values that properly comprise
a national identity. The second strand develops these points in a more
radical direction than Habermas's own proceduralist account. Here I make
a case for workplace democracy that draws on the substantive conditions
for exercising effective rights as well as the egalitarian potential of com-
puter-based "teledemocracy."

This argument takes issue with cognitivistic accounts of political rationality that assert that consensus on common interests is necessary for democratic legitimation. Despite mediating liberal and communitarian strands
of democratic thought, Habermas's own discourse ethic occasionally succumbs to this objection. At best, I argue, consensus regulates the reaching
of compromises between particular interest groups whose power cannot
always be equalized. In the final analysis, the principle of procedural equality
cannot suffice to legitimate democracy, since this principle itself is grounded
in a more complex mix of egalitarian values, the realization of which depends on the achievement of substantively just outcomes.

Chapter 6 takes up the second aspect of Habermas's theory of legitimation: the application of discourse ethics to adjudication. Habermas's position here is compared with that developed by Dworkin. As Dworkin
notes, the legitimacy of a decision cannot consist solely in its instantiation
of transcendent moral reason, but must also be a function of its compatibility with traditional precedent. Stated somewhat differently, the moral
rationality inherent in the meaning of positive law must achieve progres-

sive articulation in the course of reconstructing the *rational integrity* of legal traditions.

Dworkin's and Habermas's theories enable them to refute both positivistic and pragmatistic schools of jurisprudence while factoring traditional expectations and economic calculations into judicial decisions. My main disagreement with them is over their respective responses to interpretative conflict. Dworkin's belief that there is a *best* decision for every legal conflict must be qualified in a way that allows for more rational indeterminacy than he himself is willing to countenance. His—and to a lesser extent, Habermas's—ideal of a comprehensive judgment encompassing all points of view and relevant information underestimates what Critical Legal Studies (CLS) advocates correctly—albeit hyperbolically—characterize as the contradiction between liberal and communitarian paradigms. Likewise, Habermas's failure to entertain the possibility of a market socialism incorporating workplace democracy renders his own resolution of this contradiction enigmatic.

Habermas's attempt to frame the conflict of paradigms historically has, however, an advantage over Dworkin's tendency to impose hermeneutical continuity on the legal tradition as a whole. Bruce Ackerman illustrates this conflict well by viewing American constitutional history through the lens of Kuhn's account of scientific revolutions. At the same time, he shows how judges confront the synthetic task of forging new legal idioms out of older ones in a manner that is conducive to legitimating revolutionary paradigm shifts. Ultimately, this interpretation confirms Habermas's own hypothesis about the culmination of Western legal evolution by a reflexive (or synthetic) democratic paradigm. More importantly, perhaps, it anticipates the themes of revolutionary democracy and historical reoccupation of traditions occupying the remainder of my study.

Ackerman and Habermas remind us that in modern, pluralist societies "the people" only make their presence felt during those revolutionary crises when issues of moral principle and identity are at stake. In chapter 7 I examine one of the twentieth century's most ardent defenders of this revolutionary democracy. Hannah Arendt's notion of a democratic public sphere stresses the importance of revolving back to tradition in the revolutionary founding of generational identity. Most importantly, it shows how revolutionary acts of collective interpretation legitimate political reality through poetic disclosure and consensual praxis simultaneously. In this respect they anticipate the turn to aesthetic rationality that dominates the remainder of my book.

By focusing almost exclusively on the way in which political activity constitutes community, Arendt dismisses what is perhaps most distinctive about *modern* polity: its economic and administrative complexity. This feature of modernity poses a problem that she addressed in her last lectures on Kant's political philosophy: the problem of nihilism and totalitarianism. For Arendt, the only solution to this problem is *disinterested*, aesthetic judgment, understood as empathetic identification with humanity.

As noted above, such impartial judgment seems problematic—a point I develop further in discussing Lyotard's postmodern appropriation of Kant. According to Lyotard, the postmodern fragmentation of reason into disparate language games renders any talk of democratic consensus dangerously ideological. Unlike Arendt, his appreciation of the functional complexity of modern society leads him to postulate a permanent crisis of reflection, or paralogy, that prevents science, technology, politics, economics, and other rational systems from achieving stability and closure.

It is difficult to see how Kant's notion of reflective judgment could be relevant to this description of postmodern culture. Yet such a mediating faculty is necessary, Lyotard thinks, if one is to explain how conflict between incommensurable classes of utterances is possible. I argue that it is just as necessary for explaining the critical theorist's capacity to discriminate between hegemonic (unjust) and nonhegemonic (just) types of social interaction. In other words, the postmodern critic must appeal to a familiar liberal principle of tolerance—the agreement to disagree—in defending the autonomy of moral and aesthetic reason against the dominance of economic rationality.

Kant's notion of a *sensus communis* thus finds novel application in Lyotard's defense of postmodern political community. The indeterminacy of this idea requires that justice be judged in accordance with the narrative practices of local communities. However, it also stimulates the proliferation of new narrative practices and communities. So construed, political judgment is at once overdetermined—referring to multiple, conflicting contexts and criteria—and underdetermined with respect to our radical freedom to reflect.

Although I agree with Lyotard that no *single* criterion of legitimation dispenses justice without commission of a corresponding injustice, his tendency to privilege conflict and incommensurability over consensus and mediation runs counter to his own dialectical understanding of the essentially open and indeterminate nature of identity. Occasionally it leads him to dismiss the legitimation problem and condemn majoritarian democracy as tyrannical. Habermas's alternative account of aesthetic rationality rectifies this imbalance by conceiving reflective judgment as purposive with respect to the *integrity* of a rational and felicitous form of life. This notion also serves to counterbalance the cognitive one-sidedness of his own belief in the literal transparency of rational communication.

My final chapter uses communicative notions of aesthetic and functionalistic rationality to explain the *historical* legitimacy of the modern age in terms of its revolutionary break with, and progression beyond, its predecessor. The appraisal of revolution as a kind of *postmodern* rupture is examined through the lens of three debates. The first concerns the function of absolute foundations and final purposes in empowering and authorizing modern *political* revolutions. Modernists like Arendt hold that a qualified appeal to philosophical absolutes was necessary for legitimating the unprecedented notion of universal rights. Postmodern critics, by contrast, argue that the revolutionary mixing of philosophy and politics is ideological and illegitimate. Indeed, Derrida's and Lyotard's respective deconstructions of the most revolutionary documents of the Enlightenment—the American Declaration of Independence and the French Declaration of the Rights of Man and Citizen—purportedly show how their revolutionary declarations masked the radical incommensurability separating a contingent, political performance from a philosophical assertion of transcendent fact.

The second debate reexamines the concept of incommensurability as it functions in Kuhn's explanation of *scientific* revolutions. Responding to objections advanced by Davidson and Putnam, Kuhn argues that judgments of *relative* progress (e.g., that Copernicus advanced beyond Ptolemy) depend on conceiving rational communication metaphorically, not literally.

Addressing the Copernican revolution from another angle, the second debate—between Hans Blumenberg and secularization theorists—takes the question of progress one step further: the legitimation of the modern age in its entirety. Karl Löwith and other secularization theorists argue that the modern age is a continuation of preceding epochs, its claim to originality and progress merely reiterating prior eschatological themes within the Judeo-Christian tradition. Blumenberg, by contrast, insisted that a necessary condition for historiography as we know it—the postulation of *epochal* revolutions (breaks)—is intimately tied to our Cartesian heritage. Yet even he concedes that this heritage must be partially commensurable with preceding epochs in order to satisfy its own claim to legitimacy.

Many of Blumenberg's own studies on intellectual history attempt to spell out the nature of this continuity in terms of a *functional reoccupation*. This concept initially serves to justify a notion of identity that parallels similar transcendental arguments advanced by Davidson and Kant. However, it undergoes considerable mutation in Blumenberg's attempt to address the peculiar complementarity linking myth and reason in Western culture.

On one hand, Blumenberg follows Kuhn in appealing to the metaphorical nature of reason. On the other hand, he shares Nancy's belief in the rationality of myth and tradition as aesthetic sources for identity, community, and legitimacy. Ultimately, these two strands of thought come together in Blumenberg's theory that religion, politics, and science communicate with one another metaphorically to form, as it were, a complex community of literally incommensurable, yet mutually supporting, rhetorics of legitimation.

In the final analysis, the postmodern rejection of absolute foundations and final ends does not speak against the possibility of legitimating modernity so much as plead for its irrecusable relativity—its relative progressiveness, if you will. Blumenberg is certainly correct in holding that a prescientific tradition's capacity to legitimate scientific culture must be grasped in terms of a system of historical functions and not a dialogic transmission of substantive truths, as Gadamer would have it. Yet even this attempt to extend biological functionalism (natural selection) to the domain of culture—and thereby circumvent discursive justification—is one-sided, for it neglects the insufficiency of adaptability as a *normative* warrant for legitimacy. Hence I conclude that historical functionalism, too, must rest on CR, if for no other reason than the simple fact that even notions of relative progress derive their standards from ideals of discourse as mythological articles of existential faith.

To the reader who has patiently waded through the murky and labyrinthine passages of this all too densely argued introduction, I would like to offer a few final words of consolation. The chapters that follow will, I hope, reward him or her with clear, comprehensive, and well-integrated explanations of all that has gone before. *Reason, History, and Politics* culminates a decade of research spanning a wide spectrum of topics ranging from philosophy of science to contemporary debates over modernity. If perhaps I have cast my net too widely, it is owing less to a disregard for analysis and argument than to a deeply held Hegelian conviction that truth is comprehension that seeks comprehensiveness. I therefore make no apologies for the fact that the ontological and epistemological studies that form the heart and soul of this study draw their inspiration from German idealism. If this tradition has anything at all to teach us, it is that legitimation problems in the modern age can be understood only by surpassing the one-dimensional notions of analytical reason that have been inherited from positivism and neo-Kantianism. Hence the importance of historical narrative for my argument, which along with a commitment to hermeneutical and aesthetic holism, remains wedded to a judgment of integrity.

Although the chapters that comprise *Reason, History, and Politics* can be read as self-contained essays on specific figures and themes, they have been edited to form a coherent argument. Given the diversity of material they treat, their unity is perhaps less perspicuous than one might have hoped. Chapters 1, 3, 5, and 6 can be read as a separate and self-contained discussion of political legitimation, while chapters 2, 4, 7 and 8 are best understood as a series of more or less independent studies focusing on the legitimacy of science, technology, and modernity as a whole. To a certain extent, the arguments developed here are less analytical than dialectical—or, more precisely, dialogical. The very fact that some chapters *are* analytical might even evoke the impression of stylistic unevenness. Be that as it may, such unevenness reflects the principled conclusion of the book—namely, that formal and substantive modes of reasoning are essentially complementary. If—as I argue below—arguments are best conceived as conversations that take place against the background of narratives, then one can hardly avoid paying so much attention to debates and genealogies, even if doing so is less conducive to overall rigor and economy.

PART I

Reason, Community, and Science

Reason, Community and Science

1

Reason and Liberal Theory
A Communitarian Critique

My study departs from the premise that the theory and practice of liberal democracy embodies a narrow conception of rationality. This conception, I have argued, is not only wrong but deleterious, its effects ranging from nihilism to totalitarianism.

This chapter offers partial substantiation of these claims. I begin by sampling some of the major currents and proponents of liberal thought since its inception (sec. 1). Although it is neither exhaustive nor conclusive, this survey illustrates the extent to which SR has influenced liberal theory and practice. Among other things, it strongly suggests that democracies that embody SR are incapable of managing conflict and promoting public welfare. The result is increased bureaucracy and compromise.

The failure of bureaucratic planning to approximate economic rationality and welfare compromise to approximate moral rationality generates only one legitimation crisis, however. The other crisis pertains to the fundamental incoherence of a liberalism torn between competing ideas of rationality and democracy—the one predominantly libertarian, the other communitarian. I discuss the communitarian countertendency in detail in chapter 3; here, I attempt to show how it remains subordinate to the

27

dominant, libertarian strand. To illustrate this point I turn to debates between Federalists and antifederalist Republicans over ratification of the
Constitution. It is my contention that the history of constitutional interpretation up to the present can be seen as a continuation of this debate. In
support of this claim I recur to significant cases drawn from public and
private law (sec. 2).

I conclude by showing how the above tension gets mirrored in an
incoherent conception of rational agency, or selfhood. Liberalism's legitimation crisis is also an identity crisis. Marx's critique of one-sided political
emancipation gets at one aspect of this crisis: emancipated subjects acting
under precepts of SR are alienated from their own social and moral essence. Sandel's critique of deontological contractarian theories of the sort
advanced by Rawls gets at the reverse aspect: SR entails a notion of pure
moral autonomy whose distinguishing properties are relocated in the external agency of the state (sec. 3). These critiques suggest that SR fails as an
epistemological account of legitimation and as an ontological account of
agency. The last section takes an initial step toward reconstructing a more
satisfactory account of rational identity by reexamining Hegel's critique of
abstract identity (sec. 4).

1. SR has its political roots in the social contractarian tradition of Hobbes
and Locke. It was this tradition that first introduced a conception of public
law authorized by the confluence of private wills. The public reason informing this union instantiated the basic equality and freedom of human
beings oriented solely toward self-preservation. The moral domain—broadly
speaking, that aspect of the human condition encompassing desirable and
felicitous ends—was henceforth consigned to private predilection.

This subjectivizing of moral ends would have been inconceivable
within the tradition of natural law dating back to Aristotle.[1] That tradition
had imbued self-preservation with a rational impulse toward moral fulfillment. One's own happiness was thought to be organically dependent on
the happiness of all. Far from being a manifestation of the merely private,
desires ostensibly embodied—however imperfectly—the rational ends of a
naturally and divinely ordained hierarchy of being.

Although Aristotle believed that the precepts of morality were plain
to rational persons, he assumed that some persons—due to circumstances
of birth and education—were better equipped than others to perceive the
general good, and that they alone should be accorded the exclusive privilege of ruling. Thus his modest praise of restrictive forms of democracy

still echoes Plato's concern about the unstable, conflict-ridden mob rule that occurs whenever the masses come to power.[2]

Thomas Hobbes took issue with the elitist implications of this concept of moral reason but not with its antidemocratic bias. Writing in the aftermath of the scientific revolution inaugurated by Galileo and Bacon in the seventeenth century and constrained by the social realities of nascent capitalism, Hobbes repudiated teleological notions of reason and, in accordance with physical mechanism, held that passions—above all, the fear of death—determined behavior. Self-preservation continues to be the natural end of human endeavor in his theory but is drained of any moral significance.

Hobbes reasoned that, in a hypothetical state of nature, each person would have an *equal* and *unlimited* right to acquire whatever he or she deemed necessary for survival, either alone or in combination with others. Driven by their desire to assure themselves constant access to scarce resources, persons embark upon an insatiable quest for power that cannot but terminate in a war of all against all. Shorn of all operations but those of logical and causal inference and grounded in immediate experience of particulars, reason does not so much prescribe the ends of action as it does the means for maintaining action as such; it counsels us to seek peace whenever others are willing to do likewise. Reason is thus a slave to passion, calculating the shortest route to the long-term satisfaction of our most urgent desires.

Hobbes's account of rationality is problematic for reasons I have alluded to in the introduction. In the next chapter we will see why its reliance on SR renders it useless for explaining causal reasoning of any kind. Presently it suffices to note that Hobbes's version of practical reason (natural law) does not articulate an ideally just order replete with virtues to be emulated. At most it specifies the minimum steps that any group of enlightened egoists with conflicting interests must take in setting up institutions of law and order conducive to their mutual self-preservation. Each realizes that he or she must lay down his or her natural right to all things if others are willing to do likewise and, by majority consent, transfer it to a person or group of persons authorized to issue and enforce legally binding commands (Hobbes 1929, chaps. 14, 18).

Despite Hobbes's defense of natural equality, his contention that sovereign authority is above the law has not made him very popular with liberals. It is therefore not surprising that Locke has had a greater following among them. Locke stressed the importance of democratic procedures in the social contract, favored popular representation, and most importantly, implemented the private/public distinction in defending constitutionally limited government. Yet, notwithstanding his appeal to moral reason in establishing equal natural rights to property, his subsequent defense of a market-based economy with its attendant inequalities testifies to a rather different notion of rationality. For Locke no less than Hobbes, rationality consists in efficiently securing the means of preservation through ceaseless industry and calculated accumulation of wealth—capacities, he believed, that were possessed by some European men but not Africans, Native Americans, women, children, and wage laborers. This explains why, on Locke's account, the peaceable state of nature is fast reduced to a state of war once the Lockean provisos limiting the acquisition of property are made moot by the introduction of a money economy.[3] But as the Hobbesian example so amply attests, unsociable rationality seems a poor premise on which to hitch a defense of limited government. Thus, while Locke's moral principles may have justified constitutional democracy, his assumptions about differential capacities for economic rationality did not (Macpherson 1962, 232).

Today few contractarians appeal to natural law doctrines of the sort defended by Locke. Reasonable thinkers that they are, they prefer the secular versions worked out by Hobbes and Kant. Those, like David Gauthier, who have renewed the Hobbesian argument under the guise of game theory have not succeeded in explaining how agreements between self-interested persons who are tempted to make exceptions for themselves—especially under conditions of inequality and uncertain risk—could be morally binding. (Later on we will have occasion to discuss further the limits of rational choice and game-theoretic models of SR as applied to the explanation of social interaction and democratic rationality.)

Most contemporary contractarians opt for the deontological approach pioneered by Kant. I discussed the difficulty with this approach in my introduction: it locates moral reason in an empirically vacuous, transcendental subject. To avoid this problem, contemporary Kantians like Rawls attempt to reformulate the idea of a social contract in terms of formal procedure. Ironically, by placing less emphasis on metaphysical introspection of transcendental duties than on game-theoretical calculation based on empirically confirmable primary goods, this procedural version risks losing the singular advantage afforded by deontological theories, namely, the capacity to explain impartial moral incentives that transcend self-interest.

Thus, unlike Hobbesian game-theoretic explanations of justice, Rawls's deontological strategy of argumentation must qualify the strategic rationaltiy of his hypothetical contractors by building moral side constraints into the "original position" of collective choice as well as into the principles chosen, which articulate the "basic structure" of a society composed of rational agents who mutually respect one another's autonomy. In order to procure a result that any rational agent would accept, Rawls assumes that the contractors party to the original position are ignorant of the specific circumstances of their social situation as well as their own specific desires, values, and life plans. Detached from the unique capacities, traits, and motivations that comprise their unique identities, they are identified solely by the common rational faculty of free choice, whose single interest they seek to advance, regardless of whatever other interests they might have.

As we shall see in the conclusion of this chapter—if it is not already apparent—Rawls's reformulation of Kant may not succeed in extricating deontological contractarianism from metaphysical incoherence. Be that as it may, my present concern is over the impact this reformulation has on Rawls's theory of justice—specifically, its understanding of democracy. Rawls follows Kant in privileging individual autonomy—the basic capacity for rational choice—over social equality. Political inequalities stemming from these social inequalities must then be compensated by redistributive schemes that, as noted in the introduction, generate dependence, not autonomy.

To put the matter somewhat differently, Rawls's appeal to an individualistic conception of rationality that defines the moral and economic parameters of choice *prior* to collective deliberation gets reflected in his sharp distinction between the public sphere, consisting of such institutions as the Constitution and legal system, and the private sphere, consisting of the nuclear family and competitive market. To the former he assigns political rights, to the latter economic rights pertaining to distributive justice.

The distinction between political rights and economic rights, and the priority accorded to the former over the latter, reflects the former's privileged relationship to the conditions of rational choice stipulated in the original position.[4] Given its close proximity to an abstract conception of reason, the fair value of political liberty comes to mean something quite innocuous, namely, equal possession of voting rights and eligibility for office. Since formal political rights do not extend to the private sphere, they have no bearing on workplace hierarchies.[5] Hence the fair value of sharing in decisions of production and consumption that deeply affect one's autonomy and self-respect go unprotected.

To be sure, Rawls is deeply troubled by the impact of private property and wealth in skewing opportunities for informed and unconstrained participation in public discussion. He thus argues that constitutional government ought to "insure the fair value of political liberty for all persons" by securing the autonomy of political parties "with respect to private demands ... not expressed in a public forum and argued for openly by reference to a conception of the public good" (Rawls 1971, 226). Since he concedes that inequities in wealth and status undermine the fair value of political liberty by granting to some a greater influence in the shaping of public opinion (225), it seems that he should advocate even greater economic equality than his own difference principle will allow. Indeed, at one point he notes that property and wealth must be kept widely distributed in a society allowing private ownership of the means of production (225). But he never tells us how this redistribution might be effected within a capitalist system tolerating high levels of unemployment and social inequality. In the final analysis Rawls leaves us with the consoling thought that the low esteem and political impotence of those at the bottom of the social ladder might be offset by monetary compensations provided by the government. But welfare payments cannot redeem this loss of freedom and self-respect. As we will see, the paternalistic dependency fostered by the client-provider relationship simply undermines the autonomy requisite for political inclusion that redistribution ought to guarantee.

1.1 Despite its anti-utilitarian point of departure, Rawls's theory of justice is often praised for its inclusion of utilitarian calculation in moral reasoning, since it is precisely this feature that gives his deontological framework empirical substance. Hence it now seems appropriate for us to address this tradition's contribution—or lack thereof—in developing a democratic notion of public reasoning.

Utilitarianism saw itself as a bastion of rational—liberal and democratic—reform. If the aim of legislation is promotion of the greatest happiness for the greatest number, and if each person's happiness is to count as much as anyone else's, then, utilitarians concluded, the most rational regime must be elective representative government.

Although Bentham and Mill were both advocates of universal suffrage *in principle*, each eventually came out in support of a franchise limited to men possessing at least modest wealth and education.[6] They did so out of political expediency and the individualistic conviction that the primary justification for democracy was *protection* of private property against personal tyranny.[7] Both accepted the division between rich and poor as an unavoidable consequence of natural inequality, and so had strong reservations about extending the franchise to the lower, uneducated classes. By the same token they accepted the justice of private property because it conformed to reason as they understood it. Although the principle of diminishing utility favored a more equitable distribution of wealth, greed struck them as an all but irresistible incentive for optimizing aggregate utility. Given what they regarded as a *natural* propensity to acquire property—and thus a *natural* propensity to enter into contractual relations free from public constraint—it was rational that the happiness of most, if not all, persons be maximized by the production of more consumer goods, inequalities in distribution notwithstanding. Since such a system was clearly in the interest of the wealthy, the extension of the franchise to the poor became irrelevant.[8]

As a counterexample to the picture of utilitarian democracy depicted here, one is tempted to mention the reform efforts of John Stuart Mill, who along with T. H. Green, Bernard Bosanquet, F. H. Bradley, and other British idealists—and in opposition to his predecessors in the utilitarian tradition—subscribed to Humboldt's view that "the end of man . . . is the highest and most harmonious development of his powers to a complete and consistent whole."[9] Consonant with this romantic conception of human nature, the proper function of democracy, he maintained, should not be limited to protection of property. It should also include the broadest expression of political opinion, conducive to the *development* of all persons as responsible citizens without regard to class or gender.[10] Although Mill was clearly concerned about the communitarian conformism of Rousseauean democracy, he nonetheless evinced a sympathy for the older republican—and egalitarian—virtues. Indeed, in some respects his vision of democracy comports better with CR than Rousseau's. Rousseau thought that public debate marked a failure of citizens' capacity to inwardly perceive their common interests (Rousseau 1987, 204); occasionally, he suggests that communication itself is responsible for fomenting divisive factions (156). In sharp contrast to Rousseau and Bentham, Mill held that the simple aggregation of preferences ignores the discursive process by which preferences are rationally justified. Democracy should facilitate the critical alteration of preferences, not their passive representation.

Mill hoped that obstacles to universal suffrage, especially disparities in wealth and education that retard the development of the working class and generate conflict, might be remedied by replacing the existing regime of wage exploitation with a competitive system composed of worker cooperatives.[11] Yet so doubtful was he of the capacity of people to communicate rationally—to set aside their class interests for the sake of the common good—that he could not but affirm a stronger role for an impartial bureaucracy of elites educated in the mold of SR. And so his view of the educational function of the state in generating a common good is not so different from the antiliberal, Hegelian conception entertained by the British idealists. In the final analysis, the system of plural voting and appointed legislative commissioners that he proposed to offset the numerical advantage of the working class clashed with his vision of participatory, representative democracy.[12]

1.2 The rise of mass political parties in the twentieth century served to blunt the edge of class conflict and so disqualified Mill's worst fears. Yet it did so at the expense of abandoning his idealistic hope for a participatory democracy. To be sure, there were those like John Dewey, who continued to espouse the cause of participatory democracy. However, scientific rationalism and democratic pragmatism seemed ill-equipped to counteract the prevailing hierarchies of power. In endorsing the corporatist alliance between labor and capital that he saw emerging in the twenties and thirties, Dewey (1962; 1963) simply overestimated the egalitarianism of scientific culture as it functions within corporate capitalism.

Contrary to Dewey's expectations, it was the popular dissemination of hierarchical (foundationalist) and mechanistic conceptions of science—not the egalitarian, communicative, and adaptive intelligence he extolled—that proved decisive for democracy. Specifically, SR conspired with the emergence of the party system to engender a new phenomenon—*mass*, plebiscitary democracy—that provided the perfect vehicle for marshaling uncritical loyalty to the state. Mass democracy encouraged just that deferential respect for elites (technocrats, bureaucrats, and party leaders) so conducive to the aims of corporatism and class compromise.[13] And it gave the corporate managers of mass media (largely deregulated under the Reagan regime to allow for ever more hegemonic control by the wealthiest of elites) unprecedented opportunities for manufacturing consensus from the top down (Chomsky 1988).

Not surprisingly, the elitist and centrist tendencies in mass democracy found expression in economic theories of partisan politics. Those by Joseph Schumpeter (1943) and Anthony Downs (1957) are particularly noteworthy. According to these theories, competing elites arrayed in opposing political parties offer various assortments of goods to the electorate in exchange for votes. As Downs noted, when voters are evenly distributed along an ideological continuum, parties in a two-party system will move to the center; otherwise they will diverge from it. More disturbing for Downs was the implication, already well documented by Kenneth Arrow, that there is no rational decision procedure that can insure a fair aggregation for certain distributions of preferences.[14] This result was anticipated two centuries earlier by Marquis de Condorcet in his *Essai sur l'application de l'analyse à la probabilité des décisions rendue à la pluralité des voix* (1785). Condorcet noted the potential for multiple, cycling majorities in preference rankings involving the resolution of several issues in paired combinations or a single issue presenting more than two options. Since both of these conditions sometimes obtain, albeit more frequently in legislative agenda-setting contests than in elections, the fairness of majoritarian procedures is open to challenge, especially by permanent minorities, who feel that their vital interests have been sacrificed for the sake of satisfying a weak (or indeterminate) majority's less vital preferences (Barry 1979).[15] Indeed, Arrow's "Impossibility Theorem" (1951), which proved the fundamental irrationality of collective choice procedures, is confirmed by the failure of political parties to link voter preferences with policy outcomes, to provide clear-cut options, and to rise above accommodation to lobbies by elites. The democratization of mass parties in the United Kingdom and the United States during the seventies only partially remedied these difficulties, and was offset by countervailing tendencies strengthening the power of elites vis-à-vis the party rank and file.

Pluralists like Robert Dahl and Charles Lindblom defended the system in spite of its failure to satisfy principles of rational choice, arguing that mass parties generally permit vocal minorities to exercise some political influence in the form of voting blocs (Dahl 1956; Lindblom 1977; Berelson 1954). Given the irreducible plurality of opposing values and interests, the best that could be expected—so it was argued—would be *polyarchical* rule by minorities that encouraged stable economic growth through compromise.[16] Indeed, the argument was made that the system actually produces an optimal equilibrium of supply and demand, despite the fact that *effective* demand, itself largely orchestrated by the parties themselves, is primarily skewed in favor of the wealthy and educated.[17]

Notwithstanding their initial optimism, Dahl and Lindblom observed with increasing dismay the disequilibriating impact that economic corporations, government bureaucracies, and wealthy interest groups have on the democratic competition for power (Dahl 1982). To offset the veto power of economic corporations on government policies, Dahl advocated the extension of democracy to the workplace and the limitation of privatized government bureaucracies (Dahl 1985).

Recent trends in the evolution of mass parties during the last decade belie the optimism of pluralist theory. Mass parties have been weakened by their own internal dynamics, which compel them to ally themselves with the mass media. The ubiquitous visibility of media-anointed stars accounts for the capacity of incumbents and outsiders alike to generate campaign funds without relying on party support. Meanwhile the masses—having become increasingly disillusioned with the failure of parties to provide clear-cut alternatives—have redirected their loyalties toward other beneficiaries of media attention: special interest groups.[18]

Although pluralist theory is bankrupt as a description of democratic politics, it continues to function as a powerful ideology preserving the contractualist notion of democracy as a form of power-brokering among elites, whose market-simulating behavior ostensibly provides the checks and balances requisite for protecting minorities against hegemonic tyranny. Of course, neither political parties, plural interests, nor compromise policies as such are to blame for the rationality deficits plaguing mass democracy. I will argue in chapter 5 that the normative constraints of CR mitigate paradoxes of rational choice and majoritarian tyranny when suitably qualified. More to the point, as Jon Elster—no latecomer himself to rational choice theory—has recently observed, strategic calculations under conditions of SR are no substitute for democratic discussions about justice under conditions of CR.[19]

I will examine the strengths and weaknesses of rational choice theory in greater detail in chapters 2, 4, and 5. Its failure to offer a complete account of democratic legitimacy should not blind us to its partial validity in explaining a subordinate aspect of political rationality. At the same time, one ought not dismiss its deficient understanding of rational political agency, a shortcoming it shares with pluralist—indeed, most liberal—theories.[20]

Summarizing the preceding discussion, we may conclude that mainstream liberal theory and practice have evinced a decisive preference for conceptions of democracy embodying SR—a preference that is hardly surprising given liberalism's original and abiding interest in protecting individuals from state or publicly sanctioned tyranny. This preference, however, renders democracy incapable of satisfying its own legitimating conditions: not just resolution of conflict and coordination of action around shared values, goals, and strategies, but *also* protection against tyranny.

It therefore comes as no surprise that libertarians like William Mitchell (1983), who equate rationality with utility maximization, should argue that, in comparison to markets, democratic rule is both inefficient and unfair. According to him, the combination of monopolistic power and self-interest on the part of public servants and the combination of rational ignorance (as Cohen and Rogers put it) and self-interest on the part of the electorate conspire to encourage irresponsible fiscal behavior on the part of all. Elected officials interested in maintaining their popularity with voters are encouraged to tax and regulate rather than transfer existing funds, and so logrolling—creating new benefits for groups that feel slighted by the benefits received by others—and hence deficit spending go unchecked. Meanwhile, bureaucrats interested in expanding their programs are encouraged to ignore the marginal cost-benefit ratio of their services—a condition further abetted by their collusion with private suppliers, beneficiaries, politicians, and others who demand such services, and by the government's capacity to meet its budgetary needs through sale of bonds, printing additional money—in short, by incurring new debt, inflation notwithstanding.

Of course, it is wildly exaggerating to suggest, as Mitchell and other libertarian-minded thinkers do, that imperfect markets—with their externalities, consumer ignorance, advertising, monopoly, oligopoly, nonoptimal provision of public goods, and so forth—are fairer, more efficient, less coercive, and by comparison to the negative-sum game of democratic politics, generally beneficial for all. The reality, as Cohen and Rogers argue, is that both capitalist market and capitalist democracy are aspects of one and the same welfare state. Symbiotically interdependent, they both structure "rational" behavior in ways that facilitate the efficient satisfaction of short-term interests at the expense of the public good—this latter *in*efficiency facilitating as well majoritarian tyranny and bureaucratic despotism.

The legitimation crisis besetting liberal democracy is only half the story, of course. As we shall see in chapter 6, the crisis also extends to adjudication; a system of compromised legislation cannot but issue in a judicial practice lacking integrity. Since democracy remains key for legitimation generally, we will have to see whether a different model than the one I have just sketched is logically possible within liberalism. Such a model would have to comport with a rationale richer than that implied by SR; it would have to embody CR.

As noted above, there are democratic countertrends—exemplified, for example, in the writings of J. S. Mill and John Dewey—that approach a liberal communitarian vision based on CR. Instead of drawing on these utilitarian and pragmatic sources, however, I will attempt a more rigorous grounding of the communitarian vision based on Habermas's discourse ethic, which sees itself as a deontological alternative to contractarianism. Before taking up this topic in chapter 5, let me broadly explain why I think that the democratic communitarian alternative is not without standing in liberal society—in spite of the rather deficient way it exists there.

2. The two hundred years of American legal history illustrate well the tension between libertarian and democratic communitarian strands of liberal thought. The Founding is as good as any place to begin. It is worth recalling that the delegates attending the Philadelphia convention were attempting to salvage a confederation of states out of the debris of economic chaos. Besides disputes over tariffs, boundaries, currencies, and other issues affecting interstate commerce, the delegates were also distressed about the refusal of state and local municipalities to honor contracts and loans between bankers and indebted farmers. Shays's Rebellion, which liberated scores of debtors from prison and prevented foreclosures on land by the hated banking and commercial interests, transpired only a few months before the convention. Hence it is hardly inconsequential that many of the debates prior to the ratification of the Constitution centered around competing conceptions of public reason and contractual inviolability. These debates, in turn, expressed conflicting visions of democracy—the Republican vision was premised on premodern civic virtue; the Federalist vision, on modern commercial egoism. The former was exemplified in a yeoman democracy solidified by popular legislation of *common* mores and substantive notions of contractual equity; the latter, in a federal democracy that contained divisive commercial interests and moral passions by means of formal legal protections—including enforcement of contractual obligations as stipulated in Article I, Section 10 of the Constitution.

In working out their solution to the problem of pluralism, the Federalists were most concerned about protecting religious minorities and propertied classes from local democratic tyrannies dominated by envious levelers, desperate debtors, and other opponents of commerce. Federalism would prevent state legislatures from abrogating contracts and regulating interstate commerce. Indirect and virtual representation—bicameral establishment of an upper house of appointed senators, indirect election of the president, appointed judgeships, property qualifications for voting, and large, amorphous voting districts—would limit popular participation and strengthen the power of the propertied classes. Finally, the separation of powers would establish a system of mutual checks designed to thwart the influence of democratic legislatures in altering the Constitution.[21]

Underlying this vision, of course, was the notion that reason resided in experience—"the least fallible guide of human operations," as Hamilton put it in Federalist Paper No. 6. More precisely, to cite Madison, reason involved intuiting "the permanent and aggregate interests of the community" (*The Federalist*, No. 10). In contrast to this indubitable intuition of universal rights, popular assemblies were held to be breeding grounds for irrational passions. In the words of Hamilton, they were "subject to the impulses of rage, resentment, jealousy, avarice, and of other irregular and violent propensities" (*The Federalist*, No. 6).

If Federalists aspired to a liberal concept of the state that Madison himself insisted should remain "neutral between the different interests and factions,"[22] antifederalist Republicans aspired to a communitarian one. They clearly understood that the federal state was partial toward commercial interests and biased against participatory democracy. Federalists, of course, also subscribed to the principle of democratic legitimacy. But their belief in the doctrine of virtual representation enabled them to reconcile this principle with limited democracy. Hamilton stated it best when he said that the new government "will consist of proprietors of the land, merchants, and members of the learned professions, who will truly represent all those different interests and views of the community" (*The Federalist*, No. 36).

In the introduction I adverted to the paradoxical elitism of individualist conceptions of public reason. Locke's belief in differential rational capacities insinuated itself into eighteenth-century social contract theory, despite that theory's own original hostility toward elitist conceptions of teleological reasoning. The same paradox enters into the Federalists' theory of democracy, whose endorsement of virtual representation assumes that only some persons are capable of discerning the public good. Antifederalist Republicans, by contrast, were largely predisposed to a different view of reason, one that was inherently democratic. In short, they believed that virtue and knowledge of the public good could emerge only in political discussion. Like Montesquieu and Rousseau, Brutus felt that virtues of solidarity and mutual respect, not to mention consensus on the public good, required cultivation in a republic of limited size whose inhabitants were basically alike in "manners, sentiments, and interests." For, he noted, "in a large extended country it is impossible to have a representation, possessing the sentiments, and of integrity, to declare the minds of the people."[23]

To a certain extent what I just said about the Federalists' endorsement of democracy could be said of the Republicans' as well. Both were torn between locating the ground of legitimation in democracy on one side and individual reason on the other. For the communitarian Republican, however, the issue boiled down to a somewhat different question: Does the voice of reason reside in transient legislative majorities or in common legal traditions? As we shall see, the history of American constitutional interpretation has often been divided on just this question (Arthur 1989, 26). Indeed, alongside the liberal's appeal to transcendent moral intuition (natural law) one detects at least two other grounds for legitimating decisions: tradition (common law, case law, and ethical custom) and procedure (statutory law).

In subsequent chapters I will argue that each of these rationales plays a role in democratic legitimation. At this juncture, however, I would like to show how the Federalists' libertarian vision continues to dominate American constitutional interpretation, in spite of the democratic communitarian vision contained in key New Deal legislation. The point of this exercise is to suggest that the revolution inaugurated by the New Deal expanded certain areas of individual autonomy—namely, those rights to privacy, freedom of speech and association, and freedom of conscience deemed essential to the cultivation of political aptitudes—while limiting others pertaining to contract and property. In so doing, the New Deal appropriated the Federalist ideology of legal neutrality to justify a Republican vision of democracy.

2.1 The three main areas of public law that impinge on the integrity of a democratic system pertain to labor law (under the guise of public interest), procedural law (affecting campaign financing and congressional reapportionment), and social law.

For reasons that will soon become apparent, let us begin with labor law. During the Lochner era (named after a 1905 Supreme Court decision invalidating a New York law limiting bakery employees to ten-hour workdays and sixty-hour weeks) the Supreme Court upheld the contractual freedom of *men* by striking down federal and state laws regulating wages, hours, and work conditions.[24] This extreme deference to contractual freedom did not officially end until 1938, when Justice Harlan Fiske Stone ruled in footnote number 4 of *U.S. v. Carolene Products Co.* that courts would henceforth give a higher level of protection to personal rights like those contained in the First Amendment than to property rights:

> It is . . . unnecessary to consider whether legislation which restricts those political processes which can ordinarily be expected to bring about repeal of undesirable legislation, is to be subjected to more exacting judicial scrutiny under the general prohibitions of the Fourteenth Amendment than are most other types of legislation. . . . Nor need we enquire whether similar considerations enter into the review of statutes directed at particular religious or national or racial minorities . . . whether prejudice against discrete and insular minorities may be a special condition, which tends seriously to curtail the operation of those political processes ordinarily to be relied upon to protect minorities, and which may call for a correspondingly searching judicial inquiry. (Quoted in Ackerman1991, 128)

As Bruce Ackerman points out, *Carolene Products* initiated a veritable revolution by displacing the organizing core of the Constitution from the ideal of market freedom to that of egalitarian democracy. In effect, this undercut the classical liberal distinction between public and private law that supported inalienable property rights. It therefore also contravened the notion that private law rested on purely formal, rationally intuitable grounds that precede political agreements on substantive goods.

I will address the implications of this revolution for adjudication in chapter 6. Suffice it to say, the New Deal revolution underscores a new legitimation crisis. If the meaning of the Constitution cannot be eternally fixed by reference to some transparent and indubitable evidence, be it transcendent moral idea or original authorial intent, then a new legitimating rationale—one based on CR instead of SR—will have to be invoked to explain the legitimacy of changing interpretations.

As we shall see, it would be precipitous to see the peculiar change wrought by the New Deal as a subordination of the libertarian ideal as such to the principle of democratic community. Rather, the loss of contractual freedom under the New Deal—a freedom that had previously been invoked to justify (however inconsistently) the "political" right of newspapers to print what they wanted—had to be compensated for by a new libertarian doctrine. Because basic rights were now to be interpreted in light of specific political aims—that of securing public welfare—and because individuals had lost a right that had guaranteed them freedom in the marketplace of ideas, it was now necessary to extend the protection afforded by other rights to secure equal and effective political participation by all (Ackerman 1991, 125).

We might say that the New Deal redefined individual freedom and the libertarian ideal in terms of democratic self-determination. Lower standards of judicial scrutiny have been applied to limits on commercial speech, while higher ones have been erected to protect political speech. Due process has been strengthened in criminal proceedings to protect against arbitrary arrest and prosecution. And rights to privacy have been invoked to extend individuals' control over their personal lives. Indeed, when properly reconstructed, the Federalist (or libertarian) contribution to democratic communitarianism extends further than even the above list of rights.

This revolutionary filling of old libertarian bottles (or functions) with new social democratic wine will be the focus of my treatment of historical progress in chapter 8. However, to return to the example of labor law, it more often happens that the Federalist legacy comes back to obstruct democratic reform rather than further it. This obstruction can be clearly witnessed in the history of the Wagner Act of 1935.

The explicit aim of the Wagner Act was to promote industrial democracy as well as industrial peace, bargaining equity, economic recovery, and freedom of choice. Yet, with the exception of industrial peace, the goals stated above were undercut by the court's subsequent emphasis on contractualism and public interest doctrine. From 1937 to 1941 the courts refused to inquire into the substantive justice of labor contracts *(NLRB v. Jones and Laughlin Steel Co.)*, allowed employers to offer permanent positions to workers hired to replace striking employees *(NLRB v. Mackey Radio & Telegraph)*, and prohibited workers from threatening midterm work stoppages while permitting employers to unilaterally impose terms and conditions of employment upon concluding lawful negotiations to impasse *(NLRB v. Sands Manufacturing Co.)*.[25] The first of these rulings also redefined employee rights as public rights, thereby condoning bureaucratic intervention by the NLRB. Having subsumed labor law under the doctrine of public interest, this decision removed labor disputes from *democratic* oversight by the public at large. It instituted a corporatist solution that transferred power from rank-and-file workers to union leaders, redefined the union as a trustee of public interest, and thus restricted union activity to negotiating wage and benefits. While workers were denied the right to engage in sitdown strikes— a tactic that underscored their right to the means of production—they were also deprived of an effective voice within the union.

Subsequent decisions continuing up to and beyond the Taft-Hartley Act of 1947 repeatedly testified to a class compromise that was as hostile toward employee collective action as it was friendly toward long-range economic planning.[26] Thus, although the history of labor law in the United States bears witness to a willingness to implement industrial democracy, it does so inconsistently and in a highly truncated form. In the wake of the Reagan-Bush administration's insistence on using "cost-benefit" calculations to determine the scope of public interest doctrine, Justice Blackmun's candid remark that "Congress had no expectation that the elected union representative would become an equal partner in the running of the business enterprise" underscores the extent to which the old libertarian ideal of market autonomy continues to dominate.[27]

In chapter 5 I will offer a deeper philosophical justification for workplace democracy than that entertained by the Wagner Act. In general, recent Supreme Court decisions have been unfavorable to egalitarian democracy even at the level of partisan politics. For example, in *Buckley v. Valeo* (1976) the Court struck down two of the provisions of the Federal Election Campaign Act of 1971 that would have created fairer competition for media coverage by limiting the total amounts that candidates could spend in running for national office, including the amounts coming directly from their own pocketbooks. In justifying this decision, the Court held that such limits violated the First Amendment by restricting freedom of speech—in this instance, the dissemination of ideas. However, in a footnote the Court allowed that government could regulate the time, place, and method of speech by, for example, limiting the decibel levels on sound trucks. But in asserting that the latter restrictions limit only the "manner" and not the "extent" of speech, the Court not only argued speciously, it also discriminated against candidates whose main vehicle for disseminating their message is less formal and direct. As John Arthur notes, "[L]ess well-heeled candidates who must pass out leaflets, use sound trucks, and put up signs are subject to a variety of regulations designed to maintain peace and quiet, respect private property, or protect the beauty of a roadway ... [yet] the Court says, Congress cannot regulate those who can afford more expensive methods of communication, even if its purpose is to make the political process more fair and to focus debate on the merits of the candidate's position rather than the talents of her advertising agency" (Arthur 1989, 83). Arthur concludes that the unacknowledged reason underlying the Court's discrimination is *property*, or "the assumption that people should be allowed to spend their money as they wish" (84). Combined with the Court's upholding limits on individual campaign contributions—limits that have been rendered moot by PACs—this recrudescence of the older, libertarian version of a marketplace of ideas suggests—to cite Arthur again— "that, although it is unacceptable to buy a candidate, there's nothing wrong with buying an office" (84).

This is not the only area where the goal of democratic equality has been forfeited. There is the Court's resistance to aiding minorities in their struggle for fair representation. To cite a recent decision, *Shaw v. Reno* (1993), a 5–4 majority of the Supreme Court ruled unconstitutional North Carolina's attempt to comply with the Voting Rights Act of 1965 by gerrymandering the newly created 12th congressional district. In her majority opinion, Justice O'Connor held that North Carolina's attempt to procure minority representation through this device violated the equal protection clause of the Fourteenth Amendment. She argued, in effect, that equal protection extended to individuals, not to groups. In her opinion, the presumption that African-Americans "share the same political interests" (529), and that such interests can be assured adequate representation by apportioning districts based on their demographic distribution, undermines "the goal of a political system in which race no longer matters" (530).

Few would cavil with the desirability and justice of a color-blind protection of political rights as a *goal* to be striven for. But can a color-blind method of apportionment that protects only the *individual's* equal right to representation be just and workable in a society in which "race"—however socially constructed a category it might be—*still* matters? If the exclusionary logic of racism is essentially more insidious and systematic than other— religious and ethnic—forms of discrimination that once marred America's political landscape, and *if* its past and present effects can be compensated for and mitigated only by public policies aimed at erasing its systemic causes, must not the *groups* victimized by these effects be assured of the same political remedies now guaranteed to individuals? Even if we reject the notion of group rights as a dangerously blunt instrument for defending the legitimate use of otherwise suspect racial classifications in affirmative action remedies, and prefer instead to speak of individuals' rights as members of certain oppressed communities (or classes), the point remains the same. In neglecting the long history of confining African Americans to politically inconsequential ghettos surrounded by white majorities, the color-blind approach forgets that white racism is the reason why, despite their individual differences, an overwhelming number of African Americans living in those areas share *common* interests that can only be convincingly represented by members elected by their own community.

A careful study of this problem, I think, would show that racially based apportionment of voting districts, cumulative voting procedures, supermajoritarian ratification of proposals, rotation of executive offices, and other substantive remedies are necessary for combating white majoritarian tyranny. However, implementing these procedural changes will not be easy. One need only mention President Clinton's failed bid to appoint Lani Guinier to head the civil rights division of the attorney general's office in 1993 as a sober reminder of the obstacles facing reform. In part, the controversy generated over her nomination was fueled by her 1991 *Michigan Law Review* article, in which she argued that pluralist conceptions of democratic fairness—giving every individual the right to influence political bargaining through voting and interest-group affiliation—neglect the systemic inequalities in bargaining power between whites and nonwhites. More strongly, she argued that the election of nonwhites alone did not adequately address two other kinds of procedural injustice: the powerlessness of legislators from nonwhite districts in setting the legislative agenda and their powerlessness in influencing the passage of crucial pieces of legislation beneficial to their constituents. As she herself put it, for "those at the bottom, a system that gives everyone an equal chance of having their political preferences physically represented is inadequate" (Guinier 1991, 1135–36). To effect real policy changes in remedying systemic racism, she concluded, "a fair system of political representation would provide mechanisms to ensure that disadvantaged . . . groups also have a fair chance to have their policy preferences satisfied."

Aside from the problem of implementing a fair system of representation that would include all disadvantaged minorities, the use of group (or community) based schemes of apportionment—to take the most often cited remedy for combating white majoritarian tyranny—raises profound questions about the moral and philosophical interpretation of "equal protection." In what does democratic fairness consist? Democratic theorists allied with the so-called process (or procedural) school answer this question by appealing to the fairness of the rules governing the democratic "game" rather than to the fairness of its outcomes. Minimally, these rules mandate that each individual be given a single vote. However, more stringent models require the equal weighing of votes across geographic and demographic regions. According to the most stringent models, the influence voters have on campaign financing and, perhaps more importantly, the opportunities they have to shape public opinion (or the political agenda) should also be equal. In contrast to this position, democratic theorists such as Guinier, who are proponents of the outcome-based justification of democracy, contend that procedures guaranteeing individuals voting access, impact, and leverage are not necessarily fair if they still permit other, racially based inequalities to skew the outcomes in a way favoring a permanent, white majority/nonwhite minority balance of power.

It is easy to see how the distinction between procedural and outcome-based justifications of democracy maps on to the distinction between formal and substantive conceptions of due process. Justice O'Connor interprets the equal protection clause as an instance of procedural due process, which she believes accords with the color-blind, or rational neutrality, of justice. Guinier, by contrast, interprets it as an instance of substantive due process, or the assignment of a substantive right to have one's partial, policy preferences satisfied. In Guinier's opinion, the formal right to express one's preferences through voting does not sufficiently guarantee its effective exercise unless other mechanisms are present that ensure that voting will lead to a substantive representation of those preferences in legislative debates and outcomes.

My own view (see part 3) is that democratic procedural justice is dependent on the long-term production of equitable outcomes. Beyond showing that, I will argue that a substantive reading of the Fourteenth Amendment's due process clause is not fundamentally incompatible with a procedural reading, and may well follow from it. That unequals ought to be treated unequally in order to procure each individual (or group) his or her equal dignity under the law is readily distinguishable from the invidious principle of discrimination used to perpetuate the economic, political, and cultural inferiority of racial minorities. Even from a purely procedural standpoint, it is hardly obvious that racially based apportionment schemes are any less justifiable than other methods of assuring equitable power sharing (such as the nonproportional representation of state and regional interests in the Senate). However, to defend the impartiality of this communitarian view would require a mode of concrete philosophizing that privileges historical interpretation and sociological explanation over the abstract ratiocination favored by liberals like Rawls.

Another area that illustrates the continued dominance of the old libertarianism and the unfulfilled aspirations of democracy is welfare law. From the very beginning states and local municipalities were permitted broad discretion in establishing eligibility requirements, determining both quantity and quality of relief distributed and overseeing the behavior of clients. In the 1960s welfare was finally recognized as an entitlement; one no longer forfeited other constitutional rights in being an eligible recipient. However, during the 1970s and 1980s states were once again permitted to establish punitive ceilings in the dollar amount of stipends, to send caseworkers into homes, and to impose restrictive work requirements (workfare).

Thus, on one hand courts have interpreted the relationship between employers and employees, providers and clients, in accordance with contractual assumptions. Employees and recipients of aid do not have unqualified entitlements to work and welfare, because the latter are still under the private control of business and government. On the other hand, the law tacitly recognizes entitlements to work and welfare based on equity—rights that, in principle at least, cannot be exchanged or contractually forfeited.

Social law, then, ostensibly provides the material resources requisite for autonomous citizenship while functionally compensating for the weakness of the system within acceptable contractualist parameters. It thus faces a familiar dilemma: by processing "clients" through the contractual channels of bureaucratic administration, it defeats its own purpose—to foster autonomy, self-respect and democratic inclusion.

Moreover, the contradiction is spread over a two-tiered system of provisions skewed along gender lines (Pearce 1979). Unlike social security, disability pay, and medicare—social insurance schemes largely funded by the contributions of male wage earners and employers—Aid to Families with Dependent Children, welfare and Medicaid have been targeted at domestic households that are mostly (60 to 80 percent) headed by women. Whereas the former have been regarded as entitlements, the latter—funded by general tax revenues—have not, at least not entirely.

The fact that provisions drawn from public insurance schemes are regarded as full-fledged entitlements clearly indicates the contractualist assumptions embedded in this kind of aid. It thereby illuminates the peculiar kind of contradiction at the heart of unemployment and, to a lesser extent, disability compensation. Workers—mostly males—who have staked their identities as autonomous, dignified breadwinners are now placed in the position of having to accept monetary compensation for something that has no market-based monetary equivalent: their own self-respect. Their entitlement to compensation is based on something they no longer possess; lacking bargaining power, they cannot force the settlement of compensation in a way that would fully match what they are entitled to: a safe, fulfilling job. The situation is different in the case of welfare provisions. Women who accept this kind of aid know that their domestic labor is not legally protected and publicly recognized; they have therefore grown up with different expectations than men. However, if they feel the stigma of dependency less than men, they suffer worse for lack of legal status; they are truly clients, whose rights can be forfeited in return for aid. Because they have no clear right to the state's charity—and here the contractualist assumption of the state as a *private* agency controlling private capital is quite evident—they feel the contradiction of social legislation more directly.[28]

Of course, women *workers* also face forms of legal discrimination spared their male counterparts. The case of *Geduldig v. Aiello* (1974) illustrates this all too painfully. Here Justice Stewart ruled that California's exclusion of normal pregnancy from its list of disabilities warranting worker's compensation was constitutional on the grounds that some who would benefit from the exclusion—by paying lower premiums—are also working women. By parity of reasoning, of course, one could just as easily defend the constitutionality of excluding sickle-cell anemia from the list on the grounds that some blacks will benefit as well as whites. However, since this exclusion is clearly unconstitutional, one can only conclude that the lesser scrutiny accorded sex-based classifications—that they serve important state interests rather than compelling ones—reflects a deep-seated bias against those women who prefer nontraditional roles. To cite Arthur, "[I]t is not women who are pregnant and supported by men" who are punished by this ruling, "but working women who are also pregnant" (258).

It would be naïve to assume that the only obstacles facing women and other disenfranchised groups in America today are political. As Carol Pateman (1985) and other feminists have observed, the obstacles are also social and cultural, the oppression and subordination of women in home and workplace contributing to their oppression and subordination in the public and legal spheres as well. This might explain why the courts denigrate the testimony of rape victims, whose accounts of having refused consensual sex by the plainest of words, gestures, and acts are never enough to convince a judge or jury that an advance was sufficiently spurned. To make matters worse, most of us—not only women who have been "kept in their proper place"—lack the knowledge and wherewithal to initiate appeals on our behalf. Random shifts in appellate policy cannot be adequately absorbed, even by lawyers and caseworkers. Deprived of normal due process, poor citizens—and especially welfare clients—are denied the autonomy and respect accorded others. Ultimately, this loss stems from the contractual relationship that is imposed on the provider and client; as provider the state possesses the same discretionary powers over its resources as do owners of private property.[29] Thus the entitlements of welfare recipients amount to as much—and as little—as the rights of workers to collective bargaining.

In chapter 6 I will argue that one of the reasons for random shifts in appellate policy may be a legal system torn between conflicting approaches to constitutional interpretation—approaches that mirror the libertarian and democratic communitarian tendencies mentioned above. In the next section I examine these tensions in light of the deeper epistemological and ontological suppositions underlying liberalism. If I am not mistaken, liberalism's uncertainty of its own democratic identity—and hence its legitimation crisis—is duplicated in the identity crisis afflicting the liberal subject, whose rationality is at once subjective and communitarian.

3. Communitarians argue that the political injustices and legitimation crises indigenous to liberal society have their basis in deficient conceptions of rational moral identity. These conceptions—which I have assembled under the generic rubric SR—are taken to be overly abstract and thus empty of moral content.

The prototype for all criticisms of this sort is Hegel's critique of natural law—especially the deontological variety favored by Kant and Fichte. My main concern here will not be to discuss Hegel's specific critique of these and other (empirical) varieties of natural law. Instead, I will discuss two other communitarian critiques that draw implicitly or explicitly from Hegel—those by Marx and Sandel. The reason for this strategy is twofold: first, Hegel himself was viewed by Marx as a liberal of sorts; and second, it is Hegel's general view about rationality that is important for us, not his personal—and from our perspective, inadequate—application of it to political affairs.

Marx's critique of Hegel's philosophy of law is a convenient place to begin. Marx saw Hegel's philosophy as articulating the basic idea underlying any rational, modern state: the liberal idea of freedom, or universal emancipation. At the same time, he believed that Hegel's own understanding of this idea was—perhaps unavoidably—abstract and one-sided, but not untrue to the actual state of affairs emerging in Germany at that time and already realized in the United States. What Marx saw was a market society torn between the forces of egoism and conflict, on the one side, and bureaucratic order, on the other. But what makes this diagnosis especially pertinent for us is its understanding of the deeper crises underlying the ethical identity and legitimacy of this state.

To fully appreciate Marx's criticism, let us briefly review the main points of Hegel's political philosophy. As noted above, Hegel departs from a critique of natural law doctrines that treat reason and rights as residing in individuals prior to any political relationship. According to him, individuals obtain certainty of their identity as free subjects only through being recognized by others. The master-servant dialectic in the *Phenomenology* (1807) shows that this must be accomplished by externalizing oneself in the product of one's labor, an activity that divides the integral self into inner and outer aspects. The *Philosophy of Right* (1821) elaborates this idea further in terms of the notion of private property, understood as the embodiment of the owner's personality. Property is not merely a thing for *private* use, but *primarily* represents the medium through which a person's individuality and freedom is *publicly* recognized. Personal autonomy is thus confirmed in voluntary contracts involving the mutual exchange of property (Hegel 1952, para. 71).

Here, then, we see how Hegel uses a communitarian conception of selfhood to justify a classical liberal institution—private property. Later, Hegel argues that this institution presupposes a whole system of market exchanges, with its attendant division of labor, social inequality, and expansion of needs. But it is precisely at this juncture that Hegel's argument again turns communitarian. In and of itself, civil society remains inadequate as a basis for mutual recognition. First it is a society composed of particular interests that often conflict with one another. The freedom of one limits the freedom of the other; your right excludes mine. Second, since exchange sets up an external relationship between owners who are as indifferent to one another as Leibnizian monads, it alone does not suffice to guarantee a stable *ethical* identity above and beyond the random and contingent associations of buying and selling. Given the arbitrariness of market forces with their attendant crises, Hegel can find in civil society but a "show of rationality" (paras. 189, 245).

Far from protecting the integrity of the self as a distinct personality, the negative freedom afforded by liberalism actually undermines it. Although Hegel believed that conflicts of interest within civil society would be organized and thus partially contained by corporate institutions such as business and professional associations, he realized that their interaction would have to be regulated by laws reflecting a common, *national* will and identity. Thus Hegel's outline of a rational constitution is liberal in its respect for private property and political rights guaranteeing freedom of speech, association, conscience, and elective representation. It is communitarian, however, in its attempt to organize civil society rationally around national purposes (para. 255).

Hegel rejects the separation of powers doctrine and the system of checks and balances in favor of mutually integrated government functions. The penultimate guarantor of unity is the monarch, who ratifies the proposals and decrees of a supreme executive council. Some ministers are appointed to serve in the legislature as well, to further ensure representation of the government's interest. The legislature itself is divided into two houses (or estates), one representing commercial interests, the other agricultural interests. Representatives of the latter inherit their seats, since their stability and patriotism supports the government in its attempt to further common interests in opposition to conflicting business interests (para. 307). Only delegates representing these latter interests are elected, and only men who satisfy a property qualification are entitled to vote. Hegel dismisses "free unrestricted election" on the grounds that public opinion can only become a vehicle of rational enlightenment if it is carefully shaped by public education and filtered through a system of corporate representation (paras. 301–16).

Given Hegel's contempt for public opinion and his fear that civil society will degenerate into a "battlefield" of particular interests, it is hardly surprising that he locates the heart of communitarian sentiment in an impartial government bureaucracy. In effect, this move mirrors the general tendency of liberal democratic theory noted earlier. As we shall see in chapter 5, it also reflects a bias built into SR—that public reason is the privileged domain of educated administrators who alone possess the insight to perceive the public's true interests.

Now Marx was keenly aware of the irony of Hegel's bureaucratic communitarianism. He contrasts the bureaucratic *hierarchy of knowledge*, which he identifies with a personal, yet mechanical deference to formal rules, with democratic self-determination, which incorporates the substantive interests of the people into a truly unified knowledge and will (Tucker 1972, 20–24). Marx's critique thus probes beneath Hegel's bureaucratic communitarianism to its epistemological and ontological sources, which evince an unresolved tension between liberal and communitarian aspects.

Specifically, Marx argues that Hegel compromises his communitarian view of human nature when he tries to reconcile it with liberal society: "[T]he citizen of the state is separated from the citizen as a member of civil society [and] must therefore *divide up his own essence*" (Marx 1975, 143). More precisely, "[H]e lives in the *political community*, where he regards himself as a *communal being*, and in *civil society, where* he lives as a *private* individual, treats other men as means, degrades himself to the role of a mere means, and becomes the plaything of alien powers" (Tucker 1972, 32). Since the young Marx has exchanged his former idealism for Feuerbachian materialism, he does not think that *spiritual* identification with the nation constitutes the real communal essence of the individual but the latter's *material* identification with others as contributors to a social process of production.

Initially Marx thought that "only in unlimited voting, active as well as passive, does civil society actually rise to an abstraction of itself, to political existence as its true universal and essential existence" (Marx 1975, 189). However, by the time he wrote his essay on the Jewish question he decided that, no matter how progressive it might be, *political* (i.e., liberal) emancipation was essentially incompatible with *human* emancipation—or fulfillment of humanity's communitarian essence.[30]

On one hand Marx stressed the progressive nature of liberal reform. Liberalism dissolves feudal privileges and exclusions, thereby allowing individuals to freely develop their potentially communal, political natures. On the other hand, in failing to revolutionize these individuals—or as Marx citing Rousseau puts it, in failing to transform isolated, individual wholes into an association from which they derive their life and being (Tucker 1972, 46)—this reform allows them to "act after their own fashion," as *unfree* and alienated (45).

> It is a question of the liberty of man regarded as an isolated monad, withdrawn into himself . . . liberty as a right of man not founded upon the relations between man and man, but rather upon the separation of man from man . . . the practical application of the right of liberty is the right of private property. . . . It is the right of self-interest. . . . It leads every man to see in other men, not the *realization* but rather the *limitation* of his own liberty. (42)

Less than a year after he penned this remark Marx decided that the ultimate source of self-alienation resided in the dehumanizing, segmented, and mechanical forms of labor characteristic of capitalist forms of production. However, this in no way affected his general attitude toward political liberalism, which he continued to identify with bourgeois individualism, if not egoism.

Marx's notion of socialism as a transitional society linking capitalism and communism is developed in his *Critique of the Gotha Program* (1875). Under socialism, the means of production are in the hands of the workers and a spirit of cooperation reigns. Still, this society is "stamped with the birthmarks of the old society from whose womb it emerges. Accordingly, the individual producer receives back from society—after deductions have been made—exactly what he gives to it."[31] Bourgeois right, the right to receive in proportion to one's labor, now exists in a form in which "principle and practice are no longer at loggerheads." It is bourgeois right without exploitation, social domination, and alienation. However, the formal equality built into the notion still condones substantive inequality. "This *equal* right is an unequal right for unequal labor. It recognizes no class differences, because everyone is a worker like everyone else; but it tacitly recognizes unequal individual endowment and productive capacity as natural privileges. *It is therefore, a right of inequality, in its content, like every right"* (Tucker 1972, 530).[32]

Although the concept of right is still tied to privilege, and would thus be superseded in a higher Communist society, in which everyone would have what they need compatible with the full development of each, it is no longer opposed to sociality (531). It is, however, incompatible with complete emancipation from all privilege and conflict, because even rights to noninterference—for Marx individuality and independence are needs that should also be enhanced—come into conflict with rights to resources necessary for equal and effective participation.

By way of anticipating my later argument, we can, I think, see where Marx got it right—and where he got it wrong. He was only partially right about the relationship of political liberalism to economic liberalism. On the one hand, he exaggerated the dependency of the former on the latter, which he equated with capitalism. However, the abstract ideals of the former comprise a complex, evolving cultural legacy that extends beyond any of its concrete political and economic permutations, laissez-faire and welfare capitalism included. Indeed, the welfare state attests to this very fact in its own reliance on conflicting, libertarian and communitarian strands of liberal political legitimation—a contradiction, to be sure, whose ultimate resolution must await the end of capitalism. On the other hand, Marx so identified markets with capitalism, or with a transitional socialism still burdened with alienating relations of exchange, that he underestimated their possible communitarian transformation within a kind of market socialism.

Again, Marx was wrong about the rationality of a stateless society composed of individuals emancipated from every communal identity but their basic humanity. To be sure, Hegel's belief that the nation-state provides the outer limit for concrete communal identification seems less valid in today's complex global village than it was in the early nineteenth century—resurgent ethnic and nationalist strife notwithstanding. Thanks in part to multicultural influences, our *identities* have become fluid and decentered—in short, more susceptible to the kind of expansive reciprocity and openness characteristic of CR—even if our *political loyalties,* enflamed by memories of past ethnic struggle and fears of future reprisal, have not. Undoubtedly, for the vast majority of people experiencing the birthpangs of a postcolonial and postimperial world, identification with nationalism will eclipse any identification with postnational constitutional traditions. One can only hope that, by transforming our cultural identities into more expansive, mutually enriching traditions of learning, CR might strengthen necessary and productive political attachments even as it undermines those that foster insularity and aggressive nationalism. Improving on Marx's formulation, one might say that communicative rationalism—within and between sectarian communities—replaces global communism as the proper end of history.

The list of things Marx got right is perhaps more impressive. With some revision, his theory of alienated labor remains valid. Taylorism, we shall see, embodies a concept of efficiency that really is at odds with the efficient—and democratic—use of cybernetic technologies. Contrary to popular belief, economic rationality may well require workplace democracy. Second, Marx's critique of simple, ahistorical recipes of justice of the sort characterized by libertarian notions of desert opens the way for a more context-sensitive, pluralistic account of justice. As Richard Miller has forcefully argued, it is precisely Marx's repudiation of formal standards of equality grounded in abstract ideas of reason that underlies his deep suspicion of moralizing in general, be it utilitarian, procedural, or rights-based. Contrary to Marx, however, it is not social conflict alone that renders such moralizing approaches deficient, but social complexity—a complexity, I might add, whose immanent rationality Marx's own vision of communism directly challenges.[33] Finally, as I argue below, Marx is right that liberal theory and practice impose a split identity on individual's personalities. In so doing, they really do end up justifying the debasement of human beings to mere means, respect for individual autonomy and dignity notwithstanding.

3.1 Sandel's critique of Rawls in *Liberalism and the Limits of Justice* (1982) provides a good point of departure for systematically examining this charge. He makes much the same criticism of liberalism that Marx does, but in a somewhat inverted manner. Whereas Marx criticizes the way in which the liberal state appropriates the public ends of morality—thereby leaving individuals to pursue their private interests—Sandel criticizes the way in which the liberal state exploits individuals who are presumed to be autonomous and self-contained. Despite their differences, both Marx and Sandel criticize abstract conceptions of individualism by arguing that the rational basis for individual autonomy is participation in a democratic community.

Sandel's critique of Rawls's theory of justice—which he takes to be an exemplary reconstruction of *foundationalist* deontological theories—focuses on the residual, metaphysical aspects of Rawls's appeal to reason, aspects that issue in incoherent accounts of moral personality. The reader will recall that Rawls attempts to justify the rational impartiality of his principles of justice with respect to particular "thick" conceptions of the good. He does this by building a veil of ignorance into a hypothetical position of choice. To guide the contractors in their unanimous decision he also provides them with a list of primary goods, which empirical psychology and economics have determined to be goods that any rational person would want, regardless of his or her personal makeup and social situation.

According to Sandel, an argumentative strategy whose universal appeal depends on remaining impartial with respect to empirical goods cannot invoke them without begging important questions. The veil of ignorance renders Rawls's contractors virtually indistinguishable from one another, thereby rendering inexplicable the circumstances under which they are compelled to bargain: plurality and conflict (Sandel 1982, 30). Rawls himself concedes that consensus in the original position is guaranteed by abstracting from differences, hence reducing the contract to a single, rational choice. Rawls wants to provide a procedural, i.e., nonmetaphysical and nonpsychological, reconstruction of Kant's deductive, psychological approach; but we see that the notion of *pure*, procedural justice that ostensibly guarantees impartiality of choice corresponds to no conceivable contract (109).

If we assume that Rawls's "contractarian" theory of justice is really a cognitive deduction from subjectively intuited ends, then it succumbs to a new dilemma. On one hand, to ensure the universality of these ends, Rawls no less than Kant must locate them in subjects whose essential identity consists in just those "highest-order moral powers"—the capacity to determine, pursue, and revise one's own conception of the good life *and* the capacity to acknowledge and respect this same capacity in others—that inhere in all rational persons. These abstract, unconditional powers define an autonomy that, in Sandel's words, is "detached" from all content and "unencumbered" by prior determinations. Being empty of empirical content, these capacities would be incapable of generating substantive ends of any kind, including the "thin" conception of the good corresponding to Rawls's principles of justice (27 and 124).

Let's suppose, however, that Rawls deduces his principles from the empirical traits characteristic of persons living in liberal societies. When Rawls claims—as he now does—that the normative assumptions underlying the construction of the original position and its choice bias stand in a relationship of reflective equilibrium with respect to shared moral intuitions that form the basis for (as he now puts it) "model-conceptions" of "the moral person" and "the well-ordered society," he nowhere shows why these conventional intuitions should have any special claim on us.[34] Why should liberties *normally* protected in "the constitutions of the democratic states . . . which have worked so well" (Rawls 1982a, 6) exemplify liberties chosen in the original position?

Indeed, why assume as politically normative circumstances of plurality and *conflict* that lead *us* to consider justice the preeminent virtue—rather than, say, solidarity or friendship? If we respond to Sandel that the liberal democracy that presupposes these circumstances is better than less complicated societies—despite its flaws—then we must show why. Perhaps, following Habermas, we might argue that—owing to their marketplace of ideas—such societies make possible greater learning potential and hence adaptability. That argument, I shall claim, is a hard one to sustain; in any case, it is not one that Rawls even ventures to make.

Let us leave aside this problem. A more pressing question is this: Can an empirical inventory of the psychological preferences of persons living in liberal democracies yield a satisfactory account of neutral moral principles? The fact of conflict speaks against it—Rawls's speculation about "overlapping consensus" notwithstanding. Suppose, then, that we simplify the question further and ask whether, instead of many, just a single person, for example, a lone theoretician like Rawls, could integrate his own conflicting preferences into a well-ordered, principled identity. In this empirical model of the self we no longer assume a transcendental identity hovering above the flux of immediate preferences. If the self is just its momentary desires—a Humean bundle of ideas, as it were—then no such superordinate self exists that could accomplish such a feat of integration.

Somehow, the self that reflects on itself must avoid the Scylla of rational transcendence—or abstract identity—and the Charybdis of empirical situatedness, or concrete difference. Rawls tries to avoid this difficulty by building into his moral subject a capacity of reflection that mediates between abstract moral powers and contingent, personal attributes. Along with principles of rational choice, these "counting principles"—which consist of basic precepts of instrumental reasoning, or SR—guide, but do not determine, our selection of reasonable life plans. In the final analysis, Rawls concedes that "choice often rests on our direct self-knowledge not only of what things we want but also of how much we want them" (Rawls 1971, 417). But if our most fundamental desires are *given intensities* that we immediately intuit—no different, say, from the natural forces of our environment to which we must passively accede—then in what sense, asks Sandel, does Rawls's concept of reflection aid us in freely choosing *who* we want to be (Sandel 1982, 158)? In order for reflection to become self-reflection, i.e., *self*-knowledge (as opposed to knowledge of psychological states inessential to personal identity) *and* self-transformation, it must not be an external mediator, as it is in Rawls's instrumental account. It must be a movement of identity (unification) and nonidentity (critical separation) internal to both perduring self and its mutable psychological properties.

But that is not all. Unlike simple weighers of preferences, strong evaluators (to use Charles Taylor's expression) are not presumed to be self-contained repositories of preferences. The *integrity*—or critical unity *of* differentiation—implicit within the reflecting self presupposes a wider community of reflection. This community provides relatively stable and ordered values that gravitate around intersubjectively recognized traditions. It does so through the medium of communication itself—or CR, the medium of intersubjective reflection par excellence.

Thus deontological theories that construe individual identity and autonomy as givens that preexist community miss what is most distinctive about democratic politics: its capacity for furthering rational self-understanding and self-transformation. It remains to be seen whether all deontological theories of the Kantian variety fail in this respect. Habermas's attempt to develop a democratic discourse ethics suggests otherwise, but even that theory has to avoid reducing the normative thrust of CR to formal idealizations that merely replicate Kant's deductive transcendentalism.

For the time being, let us return to more urgent matters: the capacity of Rawls's theory of justice to accommodate the integrity and autonomy of citizens inhabiting liberal society. Given Rawls's strong deontological conception of moral identity, neither one's natural endowments nor one's socially acquired talents are attributes that one could be said to deserve, since they are not the product of one's own rational agency. Since they are not one's rightful possessions, one cannot be said to merit the benefits one obtains by means of them. These heteronomous conditions of agency are properly regarded as society's "common assets," which a just society should exploit to common, if unequal, advantage (Rawls 1971, 73–75, 101–4).

Here, Sandel observes, Rawls's metaphysics of moral agency undermines its own principle of justice. We noumenal agents are mere "guardians" of common assets whose social benefits the state can regulate in whatever way it sees fit. Indeed, given that the self has been "disencumbered" of these and all other possessions, whatever order is imposed on the concatenation of conflicting motivations and preferences must come from the state as the supreme administrative agency. Hence, like Hegel before him, Rawls ends up subordinating the autonomy and dignity of individual subjects to that of a supersubject—the state. But whereas Hegel postulated an identity between the two terms of this equation that made this subordination at least plausible, Rawls can only conceive the relationship instrumentally. Ironically, even basic elements of retributive justice would crumble under this instrumental logic, since criminality no less than civility are pooled among society's—not the individual's—liabilities and assets (Sandel, 1982, 90).

The point here is not that Rawls is wrong about natural and social talents being the product of forces—genetics and upbringing—that persons cannot be said to deserve. This Marxian point, I think, stands up against Nozick's Lockean claim that "it needn't be that the foundations of desert are themselves deserved, *all the way down*" (Nozick 1974, 225). For, even if persons have these undeserved foundations *legitimately*, as Nozick claims they do, they have them in virtue of their standing *in a community*. I do not mean to endorse Rawls here. A principle of distributive justice must respect the way individual choices determine just shares of advantages and liabilities. But that means—as I argue in chapter 6—that individuals must be accountable to the community for the social costs of their choices as well as for the social resources that make their choices possible. This position, advocated by Dworkin among others, allows for some redistribution of *our* assets and liabilities on the grounds that everyone ought to have equal basic resources; but it does so without—as in the case of Rawls's difference principle—violating our individual autonomy and self-respect. This is only possible *if* we assume that the community in question is an intrinsic end of ours and thus *constitutive of our innermost identity*.

Now, as Sandel himself notes, Rawls comes close to acknowledging this communitarian principle when he gives a fuller account of the kind of good a just community instantiates. Although it would appear that Rawls has in mind an instrumental (or sentimental) conception of community, in which community functions merely as a goal (or feeling) that preindividuated choosers might advance (or have), Sandel observes that Rawls occasionally writes as if community were more deeply constitutive of self-identity. He says, for example, that persons have "shared final ends," "share one another's fate," (Rawls 1971, 527), "participate in one another's nature," and are "realized in the activities of many selves" (565).[35]

This last comment, I think, provides a useful criterion for assessing the adequacy of Sandel's own critique of deontological theorizing. On one hand, Sandel appeals to community to ensure "some relative fixity of character" (Sandel 1982, 180). On the other hand, he does not want to fix this character relative to a single, overarching community—say, the nation—in the way that Hegel, Rawls, and Dworkin do. As he rightly observes:

> Each of us moves in an indefinite number of communities, some more
> inclusive than others, each making different claims on our allegiance,
> and there is no saying in advance which is *the* society or community
> whose purposes should govern the disposition of any particular set of
> our attributes and endowments. . . . In particular there would be no
> obvious reason why "more general social concerns" as such should in
> all cases defeat more local or particular concerns merely in virtue of
> their generality. (146)

These last comments, so troubling in light of recent multicultural confla-
grations here and abroad, are difficult to reconcile with the idea of community as a relatively fixed—or should we say self-contained—identity. It is
perhaps no exaggeration to say that Sandel here succumbs to the very logic
he criticizes in others. Self-contained communities, like self-contained individuals, ostensibly possess an identity prior to communicative involvement with others. If so, then the identity of persons inhabiting pluralistic
societies (or communities) is just as fragmented—or just as transcendent
and all-encompassing—as liberalism itself seems to imply. In order to escape
this dilemma, Sandel would have to explain how very different communities, with their incommensurable languages and worldviews, can communicate with one another at all. He would have to show what it is that
enables communication to function reflexively in preserving difference in
identity, or preserving indeterminacy (indefiniteness and fluidity) amid
determinacy (fixity).

   Hegel's reconstruction of the reflexive nature of explanation and identification is a first step in this direction. This deeper foray into epistemology
and metaphysics is necessary for two reasons. First, the political deficiencies of liberalism are of a piece with its metaphysics and epistemology.
Second, the concept of rationality undergirding this enterprise—SR—has
been equated with scientific reasoning and technological engineering in
all its manifestations. This concept not only dictates a false concept of scientific explanation, which produced a false concept of society, it also dictates
an antidemocratic—indeed, Platonic—vision of science and technology that
distorts liberal practice.

4. So far I have only alluded to Hegel's criticism of abstract individualism.
Now I would like to situate this criticism in light of his more sweeping
assessment of SR.

   In order to do this we must reexamine his critique of liberal theory. In
an essay on natural law written in 1802, Hegel shows how both empiricist

and formalist contractarian theories depart from the same foundationalist notions of rationality—notions that entail skepticism and dogmatism. Let us begin by paraphrasing Hegel's critique of the empiricist tradition. The reader will recall that the state of nature postulated by this tradition is an abstraction—one, as in the case of Hobbes, that ideally abstracts all social and political determinations from human nature in the raw, as it were. For Hegel as for Rousseau, Hobbes's abstract, passion-driven machine is neither natural nor human. Internally bereft of rational, moral content, it can but mirror the artificially constituted—acquisitive and competitive—personality traits cultivated in market societies. The same could be said of Locke's account of the naturalness of money, markets, private property, and inequality. A culturally relative, empirically verifiable account of rational acquisitiveness is introduced to supplement an overly abstract and essentially unknowable moral rationality conformable to divine command. Thus "the guiding principle for the *a priori* is the *a posteriori*" (Hegel 1975, 64).

Yet, Hegel ironically notes, formalistic natural law theories of the sort espoused by Kant and Fichte—and, as we have just seen, Rawls—are no less empiricistic and dogmatic. Kant, for instance, draws a sharp distinction between morality and legality. Law exists in order to regulate the unsociable behavior of persons driven by egoistic inclination—that is precisely why a "race of devils" would agree to a social contract in the first place. Equally formal and abstract, morality follows law in deriving its content from given needs (natural inclination) (64). Hence the classical liberal dichotomy—much excoriated by Marx and Sandel—between the transcendent self inwardly pursuing moral intentions and the empirical self outwardly pursuing selfish actions. By sundering moral reason and empirical inclination from their common root in ethical community—the concrete customs and virtues constitutive of identity—liberalism, Hegel concludes, must invest social order in oppressive laws that cease to reflect the living will and spirit of the people (130).

Before proceeding further with our discussion of Hegel, let us pause a moment to reflect on the epistemological correlate to this split ontology. First, since Hume, the standard assumption in logic has been that normative evaluations and prescriptions cannot be inferred from statements of fact. Because only factual statements are presumed to be publicly verifiable or falsifiable against the immediate, "indisputable" evidence of sensory experience, evaluations are reduced to expressions of subjective will and conscience. Morality thus derives its content from unquestioned needs and dispositions as factually given.

Second, as noted above, the foundationalist aspect of empiricist epistemology that makes the fact/value distinction so plausible depends on distinguishing *particulars*, or atomic facts that can be directly and indubitably *intuited* via sensory experience, from *universals*, or conceptual schemes, which (more or less) artificially organize (or classify) particulars. Since particular sensory stimuli are individuated in the *partes extra partes* of space and time, they remain essentially discrete and self-contained. So construed, an ontology composed of externally and contingently related particulars provides the perfect corollary to those emancipated monads Marx criticizes, who define their freedom and identity in terms of a legal possession that obeys the external machinations of the market.

To appreciate the radicalness of this abstraction of form and content, consider for a moment the holism postulated by premodern metaphysics. The latter departs from an enriched, teleological conception of nature. Concepts are not pragmatic or operational tools that relate externally to pregiven particulars, as nominalism holds; rather, they define the natural kinds that enable us to identify particulars in the first place. Moreover, such concepts (or essences) are at once descriptive and prescriptive. Natural kinds are *functionally* described relative to specific *ends* that can be more or less realized. Indeed, many of our concepts *are* of this sort; for example, we can infer that "X is a good watch" from "X runs on time." By parity of reasoning, we can infer from "X is a sea-captain" that "X ought to do the things expected of sea-captains" (MacIntyre 1981, 52). Such functionalism as this provided political theorists from Plato on with a moral realism capable of organically integrating nature, individual, and society.

No doubt, the basis for making such functional ascriptions needs clarification. Unless we want to buy into a metaphysics that fixes such ascriptions once and for all—a view that would require nothing less than a God's-eye view of eternal essences—we will have to provide a different, *hermeneutical* account of knowledge and reality. We should provide one in any case, for the alternative is a form/content distinction whose epistemological and ontological shortcomings are plain for all to see.

The prototype for the hermeneutical essentialism I will be defending in the next chapter is contained in Hegel's *Logik* (1812).[36] The *Logik* constitutes a *modern* defense of essentialism—one that moves within the ambit of subjectivity and historicity. For Hegel, Kant's insistence on retaining a form/content distinction hinders his account of individuation. Kant defends this distinction against Leibniz's doctrine of the identity of indiscernibles, which holds that we must turn to the internal conceptual determinations of a thing if we are to find the reason for its being the particular thing it is. If two things are conceptually indistinguishable, then they are identical. In point of fact, Leibniz does not think that there are indiscernible particulars, since part of the conceptual definition of a thing will refer to its spatio-temporal relationships to other things, and because God—creating the greatest plenitude of being with the most economical of means—ensures that no superfluous duplication occurs.

In the section of the *Critique of Pure Reason* that addresses concepts of reflection—or *comparative* concepts such as identity and difference, form and matter, inner and outer, agreement and opposition—Kant argues that Leibniz's rationalist account of identity is incoherent. Although Leibniz, like Kant, holds that spatiotemporal relations are *ideal*, he conceives them as confused sensible representations of conceptual relations. Hence he assumes that *analysis* of what is *thought* in the *concept* of a particular thing yields informative knowledge about that thing. This generates a number of problems.

First, the manner in which spatiotemporal phenomena are well founded remains enigmatic. There is no sufficient reason that explains how we get from immutable essences to mutable appearances, from form to matter, and so on (Kant 1927, A273/B329–A275/B331). Second, by wedding the idea of internal relations to the law of contradiction, Leibniz eliminates the category of interrelation altogether. Either a concept analytically contains another concept, in which case they are unrelated, or it does not, in which case they are again unrelated (A283/B339–A286/B342). To paraphrase the dilemma: The identity of each particular (monad) is defined through its internal relations with all other particulars. But since the analytic nature of conceptual relations (or propositions) implies that predicates are contained in their subjects, differentiation through relation to others paradoxically entails monism.

Kant's solution to this problem involves affirming a hard form/content distinction: conceptual relations on one side, sensible (spatiotemporal) relations on the other. Conceptual analysis alone does not extend our knowledge of objects and any attempt to do so is fallacious. Knowledge of thinghood in general involves *synthesizing* sensations into a unified spatio-temporal manifold by means of formal categories; knowledge of thinghood in its plurality—for example, of the difference between two drops of water whose *internal properties* are identical—involves *observation* and *comparison* within this manifold.

Now Hegel thinks that Kant's insistence on a hard form/content distinction in the reflective identification and differentiation of particular things generates absurdities of its own. The basis for saying, for example, that the leaves of a book are one unitary entity as opposed to a multitude of unrelated bits of paper is not that, in the former case, the sheets of paper ar somewhat more contiguous than in the latter (the leaves of my book can be scattered throughout my house and still be parts of the same thing). *Abstract* units do not *eo ipso* reveal any unifying principle at all (Hegel 1969, 490).

Even if discretely located concrete simples—for example, this patch of color—are visually distinguishable without reference to what they are, more abstract entities such as mass entities, theoretical constructs, and what Hegel calls concrete universals are not. Cultures and states, for example, cannot be distinguished in this manner, especially when there is disagreement between states (or cultures) as to which of them ought to occupy a certain territory. As Richard Rorty has persuasively argued, the presumption of Kantians like P. F. Strawson that such nonsubstantive entities are not individuals is indefensible without begging important questions.[37]

Perhaps the same could be said of Hegel's contrary view of the matter. Nevertheless, an indirect defense of it might begin with Hegel's own critique of the analytic/synthetic distinction and his parallel criticism of ontological atomism. Let's begin with the latter. As noted in my preliminary remarks on Hegel's critique of natural law, rationalism and empiricism are reverse sides of the same coin. According to Hegel, Leibniz can maintain the unique identities of particular things only by conceiving them as radically self-determining. This generates a paradox, since the properties that distinguish things are relational, referring to other things. As exclusive and self-contained, essential identity must somehow be maintained at the expense of its distinctive phenomenal properties. Leibniz can do this only by regarding individuals as *external* reflections of other things. In that case, however, the monad—considered solely from the perspective of its essential identity—is as undifferentiated as the bare surface of a mirror (Hegel 1969, 396, 446, 781). It is a bare particular, no different from Locke's *je ne sais quoi* or Hume's substance. Thus, rationalism and empiricism both end up bifurcating particular things into objective—but empirically unknowable—placeholders of identity, on one side, and merely subjective but phenomenally accessible properties, on the other (411–18).

This curious alliance between rational dogmatism and empirical skepticism has had its own defenders in twentieth-century analytic philosophy down to the present. The linguistic turn initiated by Frege reinstates nominalism in the form of a distinction between meaning and reference. Names denote particulars, general terms mean ideal contents. To be sure, no one maintained that reference could do without meaning. As Hegel noted in the *Phenomenology*—well before Wittgenstein wrote his *Philosophical Investigations*—pointing gestures accompanied by indexical expressions like "this" and "now" are no satisfactory substitute for definite descriptions (Hegel,

1979, 58–66).[38] Such descriptions, the analysts maintained, could be substituted for names without loss of truth or identity.

But what if the name in question (e.g., Earth) meant irreconcilably different things to different persons—"the center of the universe" to the Ptolemean, "the third planet from the sun" to the Copernican? If we think that rational disputation between the Ptolemean and Copernican about their ascriptions is possible—that is, that each can talk to the other about the *same* earth under conflicting descriptions—then this is because we think names rigidly designate apart from our descriptions. This Kripkean solution holds that reference is a function of the causal history of the name in question.

What is interesting about this solution is not its linking of identity with causation, but its quasi-nominalist distinction between reference and meaning. Without denying that reference and meaning can be partially dissociated in this manner—indeed, such dissociation will be useful when we discuss the possibility of cross-cultural communication in chapter 8— we must bear in mind that nothing here has been shown to disprove the necessary connection between referring and meaning in general. In Hegel's opinion, denial of this connection—and the corresponding acceptance of "bare particulars"—is incompatible with true causal explanations. If, as Hume thought, causal laws are simply shorthand for constantly observed, subjective associations of phenomena, they explain nothing about objects. Conversely, if they *reduce* phenomenal relations to essential ones on the old rationalist model, they are equally tautologous; to say that Y happens to X because it is the nature of Y to happen to it gets us nowhere (Hegel 1969, 712).

Hegel believed that Kant was right in rejecting these skeptical/dogmatic accounts. Causal necessity must involve a synthetic a priori relationship—a claim I will defend in further detail in chapter 2. For our present purposes it suffices to note that Hegel takes Kant's notion of synthetic a priori knowledge more seriously than Kant himself took it. If, as Kant maintained, intuitions without concepts are blind and concepts without intuitions are empty, then meaning and reference, reality and ideality, *and* essence and appearance are conceptually interconnected in a way that Kant's own form/content distinction fails to appreciate.

By claiming that the identity of things is a function of their essence, or internal conceptual constitution, Hegel seems to be reaching back to Leibniz. But the difference between them is striking. Whereas Leibniz and Kant think that all conceptual relations are analytical, Hegel does not. Accepting Kant's discussion of reason's antinomies while rejecting his form/content distinction, he defends the synthetic—or dialectical nature of rationality.

In contrast to the abstract identity of formal logic (A = A, "A tree is a tree"), the actual identification of phenomena is a synthetic activity that unites a manifold of diverse appearances under a distinct identity. Take, for instance, a tree as a unique growth process. A tree is *not* any one of its developmental stages taken singly, but neither is it something other than the *becoming* of these "moments."

Understood from the standpoint of subject-predicate logic, the synthetic nature of individuation forces us to concede that the subject and predicate of essential descriptions are related to one another under the opposed rubrics of difference and identity (Hegel 1969, 417–18, 431). A predicate *essentially* individuates a particular only by making use of determinations that are *not* what that particular is, precisely in order to say something informative about it in the first place. Thus Socrates both *is* and *is not* a man.

Is Hegel here guilty of conflating the "is" of *predication* with the "is" of *identity* as Russell accuses him of doing (Russell 1960, 130)? Is he only making the trivial claim that a *particular* (Socrates) is not identical to some *universal* (man), which is nevertheless truly predicated of it? The answer to this question depends on whether Socrates is a man only in the Russellian sense that a particular denoted by the name of "Socrates" just happens to be the existential placeholder of some predicate, in which case we are again committed to some version of the doctrine of bare particulars. Or perhaps "man" is analytically contained in the concept of Socrates, in which case the statement is uninformative. That might work with "Socrates is a man," but will it work with "$E = MC^2$"—assuming that this is an informative statement?[39]

As we know, Russell sought vigorously to eliminate paradoxes like the ones Hegel talks about from truth-functional logic. In particular, he was concerned to eliminate self-referential statements from the list of well-formed statements. He and Whitehead thought that the Liar's Paradox could be avoided by stipulating a hierarchical distinction between metalanguage and object language. For Hegel, on the contrary, truth is a reflexive process, not a decisive result. A logic geared toward learning rather than deductive inference must allow theory (metalanguage) and practice (object language) to mutually inform one another. As we shall see, this interpretative circle—which is also an ontological circle—is especially borne out in moral philosophy, where our attempt to apply and give content to the abstract ideas (metalanguage) regulating our conduct (object language) involves reinterpreting them in light of that conduct. It is manifested, however, in any argument conceived as a dialogue. For in this instance natural language—with its self-referential capacity for irony and indirect communication—serves as the common denominator for reflexively reinterpreting the theoretical languages that interpret it.

As recent debates about natural kinds and natural causes confirm, the problem of essentialism—and the problem of synthetic a priori knowledge—continues unabated. Since Hegel's account of the relationship between causality and identity is dialectical, it is also a fortiori holistic. There are two reasons for this. First, Hegel includes relational properties among the essential determinants of particular things. A total system of relational properties ultimately explains why something is what it is. As we shall see in the next chapter, the logic of causal discovery involves active and selective intervention in this system.

Second, essential descriptions contain concepts that are irreducible to brute particulars. To that extent their meaning must be specified, or determined, by reference to a total system of different meanings. Ontological categories of the sort treated in the *Logik* represent an extreme end of the spectrum.[40] This obscure masterpiece progressively specifies richer, more concrete conditions for the possibility of eliminating ambiguity, vagueness, and inconsistency in philosophical terminology.[41] However, even empirically saturated terms like color concepts derive their meaning in part from relations of similarity and difference vis-à-vis other such concepts.

All this amounts to a defense of structuralist linguistics. But unless we want to freeze the system of signifiers in some transcendental, ahistorical netherland, we will have to ground language in concrete contexts of writing, speech, and action. There are numerous places in Hegel's writings where he adverts to this broader linguistic context. However, as the examples of Heidegger and Wittgenstein amply attest, such contextualism has been invoked against essentialism—which brings us back to our initial question: How can Hegel defend essentialism against the onslaught of conventionalism and historicism?

In the remainder of this section I would like to briefly sketch a Hegelian response to this view, one that draws from the *Logik* (whether it is one that Hegel himself would subscribe to in all its details is irrelevant for my purposes). First, Hegel notes that not only philosophers but also ordinary persons are essentialists insofar as they make assertions that they believe to be universally true about things. Wittgenstein and Heidegger are no exception to this rule. Despite their anti-essentialism, both make essentialist claims about what language and being really are.

Second, to assume that such universal claims have only conventional justification is to presume that language communities are more parochial than they are. It is to assume, in short, that they are self-contained monads.

To the contrary, if Hegel is right, people necessarily identify and interpret their own cultures in light of their relationships to "alien" cultures. The other thus becomes a part of our own identity, for better or for worse.

On the other hand, by introducing historicality into the totality of essential relations and by acknowledging the essential finitude and contingency of identity vis-à-vis an indefinitely dense and extensive context of relationships, Hegel allows that individuation is infinitely indeterminate.[42] The reflexive relationship between individual and system is similar to the hermeneutical relationship between part and whole: each qualifies the other in ever deeper and richer circles of understanding. To concede this kind of indeterminacy need not commit us to subjectivism or relativism. For the *process* of reflection (or interpretation) may itself imply some general end toward which it aspires: openness and reciprocity with respect to the other, for instance.

These are promissory notes that will be redeemed in later chapters. For now, let me simply recapitulate the argument I have been developing in these last sections. I began by arguing that liberalism's identity crisis—its divided loyalty to libertarian individualism on one side and democratic communitarianism on the other—is duplicated within society and the individual. The public/private or state/civil society distinction finds parallel expression in the split personality of liberal subjects, who are seen as alienating their identifying properties to the state. For Marx, the egoistic member of civil society is an abstract, monadic individual whose identity comes from external possessions. Money is what mediates my relations to others. As Marx so felicitously put it in the *Economic and Philosophic Manuscripts* (1844): "The extent of the power of money is the extent of my power. Money's properties are my properties and essential powers—the properties and powers of its possessor. Thus what I *am* and *am capable* of is by no means determined by my individuality" (Tucker 1972, 103).

The reverse side of the individual property owner is the social citizen. For Marx, who follows Hegel in interpreting civil society through the eyes of political economy, the property owner is seen as primarily self-centered, while the state is viewed as the bastion of other-regarding ethical life. As Sandel correctly notes, deontological varieties of liberalism tend to reverse this order: the individual is posited as the bastion of moral autonomy over and against a politicized—potentially tyrannical—state. Yet both analyses agree on one important point: in both theory and practice, liberalism ends up externalizing the *social* properties of individual property owners (or moral agents) that properly define who and what they are. The properties are owned by the state, which assumes increased responsibility for coordinating life, educating citizens, and compensating for the lack of community, consensus, and social welfare at the level of civil society.

As we shall see in chapter 4, Hegel was the first in a long line of thinkers who feared that the fragmenting, disintegrative effects of liberal society might issue in its negation. Just as the abstract identity of mutually exclusive monads paradoxically entails monism, so too the abstract identity of mutually exclusive egos paradoxically entails totalitarianism. Hegel, of course, had the Reign of Terror in mind when he contemplated the dialectic of liberalism. But we today need not limit our understanding of totalitarianism to revolutionary movements that seek to revamp society from the top down in some violent manner. The growth of state bureaucracy and mass conformity—symptoms Tocqueville himself observed[43] upon visiting American in the 1830s—coupled with the growth of consumer alienation and corporate hierarchy should give us pause to rethink the freedom and individuality cultivated in our liberal society.

It is indeed ironic that Hegel himself embraced a bureaucratic solution to the problem of liberal anomie and that Marx himself could provide no alternative in its stead. In both instances there is a failure to radically rethink the relationship between public rationality and democratic politics. Hegel's demonstration of the community of reason still moves within the ambit of SR. The subject of reason is no longer the isolated individual, to be sure, but the *Geist* of a nation—or *God* (humanity) realizing its historical design behind the backs of historical agents. Hence the privileged status of philosophically trained civil servants like Hegel who have had the luxury of contemplating the meaning of history in general and its particular articulation in the spirit of the *Volk*. Marx, in the meantime, had early inklings of the democratic nature of public reason and saw its import for industrial democracy. However, his tendency to view self-realization primarily in terms of unalienated labor, that is, in terms of *a* subject reappropriating its expressively objectified laboring powers, still presupposes the same model of SR as Hegel's dialectic. His subsequent neglect of political life as a basis for mutual, rational self-realization rather than exclusionary class struggle provided his epigones with a model of emancipated society that stressed scientific management of industry rather than democratic resolution of conflict. In short, Marx underestimated the complexity and plurality of rationally organized economic systems, whose potential for flexible adaptation depends on an ongoing ethical debate over collective identity. The integrity of this *communitarian* debate requires precisely those *liberal* institutional guarantees—civil and political rights—that Marx so prematurely dismissed.

In the next chapter we will see how Hegel's original insight regarding the reflexivity of knowledge is rediscovered by twentieth-century philosophy of science. The importance of this rediscovery extends well beyond an adequate conception of knowledge. For if scientific and technological rationality is best conceived as a communitarian learning process conforming to CR, then its efficient deployment by no means dictates hierarchical instruments of reasoning aimed at determinate prediction, conclusive decision, and absolute control. Moreover, if accepting the reflexive nature of science and technology means conceiving it as a concerted, ongoing process of interpretation, then it also means accepting a certain degree of rational indeterminacy. This point becomes particularly important for understanding the *special* way in which social science and social reality are reflexive. For we will see that the social identity of individuals is doubly reflexive and indeterminate in a way that can only be captured using the model of communicative interaction.

2

Science and Technology
as Practical Reason

I have argued that the way philosophers and scientists have conceived reason—namely, in accordance with the model of SR—has influenced the way in which laypersons have conceived it as well. This in turn has affected their *actual* reasoning. The net effect for liberal democracy is painful to contemplate. Once values and goods are relegated to the status of personal preferences, democracy becomes a power struggle. Incapable of resolving conflicts efficiently and legitimately, the people end up ceding deliberation and decision to technically trained bureaucrats.

I submit that the only way to remedy this situation is to correct our accepted notion of public reason. Once people embrace the more robust notion of CR, they can begin to bring about a more rational—fairer and more efficient—democracy. One way to urge them in this direction is to show that SR fails as an account of reasoning in general. *If* CR explains learning and its methodical exemplification in natural science better than SR, then we will have taken a significant step toward justifying CR as a model of public reason as well.

But there are other reasons why we must address the rationality of science and technology. The legitimacy of liberal democracy hinges on that of science and technology. This is partly due to the decline of traditional authority in the wake of scientific enlightenment. In modern secular societies, states are expected to provide public goods and services as well as coordinate actions and resolve conflicts—functions that rely on scientific and technological expertise. That expertise, in turn, is the distillate of experimental learning processes and open discussions that only liberal democracies responsive to public needs seem to encourage. For problem solving on a large scale depends on the *general* attainment of critical aptitudes and technical education enabling concerted, well-informed, and imaginative discussion of moral and technical problems.

Of course, if science and technology ended up replacing traditional authority with a new kind of hierarchical regimentation, their very existence would oppose liberal democracy. In that case democrats might advocate returning to a simpler—preliberal and premodern—kind of society. This option would be attractive *if* SR fully captured the logic of science and technology.

Husserl saw that the "natural," objectifying attitude of a science caught in the grips of SR reduces even its *own* rationality to the status of a psychological fact lacking intersubjective validity (Husserl 1972). Unreflective and lost in the facticity of sense experience, science suppresses its deeper emancipatory intent and rationale: the aspiration toward responsible self-determination through progressive clarification and justification of presuppositions. Rejecting Husserl's attempt to effect this reflection within transcendental subjectivity, Heidegger argued for a more radical conclusion. For him, scientific objectification and technological domination are predestined by Western rationalism dating back to Plato. Since subjective "consciousness" itself represents the culminating achievement of this tradition, it is powerless to exercise any control over it (Heidegger 1978).

A reasonable skeptic will no doubt dispute the "metaphysical" presuppositions underlying Husserl's and Heidegger's divergent diagnoses of our scientific crisis. Perhaps, then, we can get clearer about the relationship between science, technology, and politics by sticking to more obvious facts. First, few people would deny that scientific knowledge, technical power, and political authority have been linked together since Plato wrote his *Republic.* Considering that modern science has understood itself on the model of SR, it is hardly surprising that its view of society as a mechanism or organism would dictate a peculiarly *ideological* figuration of this link as well. Portraying society as a static or harmonistic force operating beyond the conscious control of its members, it lends itself to conservatism in more ways than one. For, even if we conceive society as a predictable, law-governed domain susceptible to incremental alterations, those responsible for deciding the direction of change will be scientific and technological elites, not the general public. And because the rationality of ends extends beyond the ken of science, those that science serves will be those that happen to predominate. Thus, with the exclusion of moral and ethical questions from the list of scientifically relevant *political* issues, a public indoctrinated into the ideology of SR will tailor its deliberations around the sole remaining issue left undecided: which among several competing schools of economic and administrative expertise will most efficiently bring about stable growth as defined by the system.

The above ideology clearly depends on a specific view of science, nature, and society. The preference for scientific management presumes that social events are no less predictable than natural events, and hence are no less controllable. It presumes, in other words, that reality in general is governed by *determinate* causal laws that can be *logically* deduced from *well-founded* theories. In short, it identifies reason with SR.

Now in claiming that this view of science is ideological, I do not mean to suggest that it is without descriptive value. After all, the natural sciences *have* been remarkably successful in predicting determinate outcomes, the key to their success no doubt being a mathematical, experimental method that *does* to some very considerable extent abstract from the background context of shared theoretical values that guide it. Within the context of normal science (as Kuhn understands it) the communal commitments of a scientific paradigm *largely* remain hidden; in other words, they manifest themselves in the form of a *discipline*, or body of dogmas and habits, that each scientist has internalized in his or her subjectivity. Technology, too, must function predictably and efficiently. None of this, however, changes the fact that scientific revolutions—or shifts in paradigmatic commitments that inform scientific method—resolve themselves in the course of open, critical debate oriented toward consensus rather than by collective appeal to crucial (falsifying) experiments. Therefore it is hardly an objection to claim that SR—as a complete account of scientific rationality or as a technological design emphasizing monolithic decision and control over collective discovery and learning—functions ideologically. For if, as I shall argue, discovery, explanation, and technical application in natural science are rife with hermeneutic indeterminacy, then the emphasis on prediction and control that has hitherto prevailed in social science and technological design is misplaced and needs to be redirected elsewhere—toward democratic learning modeled on CR.

Of course, a *social* science modeled on the statistical and classificatory methods of natural science remains a powerful tool for social control, despite its limited predictive power. Positivists who conceive social science as a nomological enterprise equate rational action with habits of reasoning that are more or less *predictable*. Rational choice theorists who conceive it as a *probabilistic* science of strategic games equate it with maximizing utility in contexts of relative uncertainty and risk. Despite their differences, these attempts to define rational action have similar political consequences and weaknesses. Departing from a *methodological individualism* that abstracts from normative backgrounds and functional structures, they end up conceiving democracy as if it were a static, well-defined set of regular patterns (positivism) or an uneconomical method for maximizing utility (decision theory). Because democracy here comprises subrational—habitual or uneconomical—behavior, one might reasonably conclude that public reason can only reside in the utilitarian calculations and mechanical engineering of appointed technicians.

Now, it is my contention that the models of rational action that dictate this conclusion are false or overgeneralized. This becomes apparent when we see that the normative and functional backgrounds from which they abstract are necessary conditions for explaining most varieties of action. Contrary to these reductionist models, I argue that rational actors adopt multiple—strategic, normative, and communicative—perspectives. And they do so against the background of *individually* unintended but *socially* meaningful structures.

This background instantiates a dialectical rationality akin to that described in Hegel's *Logik*. What the latter calls a pure movement of reason here appears as a *hermeneutical circle* wherein part and whole mutually determine one another. Although such (con)textuality pertains to all human experience, it takes on a special significance for human science in general and political theory in particular. If the social structures that shape the identity of agents only exist in the form of shared meanings, then the identity of such structures in turn must be shaped by the conflicting interpretations of these very same agents. Since this self-interpretation is necessarily a social undertaking, it can only realize itself in *open* democratic discussion. Hence the *indeterminacy* of social phenomena.

The kind of social science appropriate for studying such phenomena will not be oriented toward determinate prediction and control, since it must itself reflect the reflexivity of its subject matter. It will be *critical*, however. Combining interpretation and explanation, it can further the cause of emancipation by enabling social agents to interpret, criticize and alter the very "mechanisms" that "determine" their behavior.

The preceding remarks are intended to situate the following foray into science, technology, and social action vis-à-vis my larger political concerns. The defense of critical social science against reductive approaches is intended to clarify the method(s) of philosophizing deployed in this book. Positivism is not just bad science; it is bad jurisprudence. Methodological individualism is not only false, but ideological. And SR is more than ideology, having permeated the very fabric of our democracy.

These are grand claims, to be sure. Hence a somewhat more detailed sketch of the argument I will be pursuing here may be useful. I will begin my argument by briefly examining the major tenets of SR undergirding positivist philosophy of science. Drawing on the work of postempiricist philosophers of science, I show how the foundationalism, logicism, and determinism of SR generate paradoxes that disappear only when we accept a dialectical paradigm of reason. Once we concede that the *counterfactual*—or ideal—reveals the factual, we must abandon logical atomism (the doctrine of bare particulars) for the less secure haven of holism. This entails identifying science with the synthetic—constructive and interpretative—accomplishments of a community of investigators. It also entails notions of rational learning and explanation shot through with historicity, contextuality, and indeterminacy (sec. 1).

Extending this analysis to social science, I argue that the hermeneutical indeterminacy and contextuality encountered in nature are magnified in the realm of human action. The identities of agents, actions, and institutions consist of implicitly understood meanings. This suggests an important limitation to formal models of teleological explanation of the sort proffered by von Wright and others: Reasons for acting cannot be reduced to intentions in the way that methodological individualism presupposes. Neither analytical nor abstract, the logical connection between meaning (reason) and action can only refer, as Hegel argues, to a *context* of interaction and interpretation. Thus, the extension of rational choice explanations beyond a core range of economic behavior to include voting and the like inevitably diminishes their explanatory power (sec. 2).

The logical connection argument establishes the interpretative manner in which agents' intentions, actions, and social structures mutually implicate—and thus identify—one another. My examination of Charles Taylor's defense of this view shows that such identity is *doubly* dialectical. Not only do individual actions and social institutions mutually interpret one another in the manner of a part/whole circle. But the meaning of one's own action depends on others who are in a position to understand it (sec. 3).

One such position—typically associated with functionalist social science—focuses on the unintended functions served by actions in maintaining systems. Not all critical theories are functionalist. But a correctly conceived functionalism merits serious consideration as a worthy candidate for such a theory, since it provides a critical counterbalance to the voluntarism and intentionalism of individualistic, action-theoretic approaches. Functionalism qualifies game theory by showing how preferences and choices—indeed, strategic reasoning as such—is prestructured by social norms and institutions. Most importantly, it explains how the unintended aggregate effects of individual actions are simultaneously functional and dysfunctional. Unqualified strategic rationality is socially irrational in that it undermines the stability of those moral norms and market structures that enable it to function in the first place. *Social* rationality, that is, the *implicitly presupposed* freedom and equality that enables each contractor to bargain with the other in good faith, is belied by a *strategic* rationality aimed at domination. This contradiction between different types of rational orientation mirrors the split personality of the liberal individual discussed in the previous chapter.

The preceding sections suggest that skillful technique no less than causal knowledge presupposes a holistic framework. The concluding section of this chapter therefore explores the possibility of a technological rationality geared towards learning rather than domination. Such a rationality first comes into its own with the advent of computers. That this potential remains unutilized is largely attributable to the dominance of SR in computer design. This dominance, in turn, reflects a managerial need for hierarchical control whose foundationalism, logicism, and determinism owes much to positivistic (or mechanistic) conceptions of science. It is my contention that only mechanical technologies need conform to this logic. Designed for purposes of communication rather than decision, computer technology could potentially redeem Marx's faith in the liberating potential of science, technology, and labor as vehicles of self-realization (sec. 4).

1. When Marx said that "natural science will in time subsume under itself the science of man, just as the science of man will subsume under itself natural science" (Tucker 1972, 91) he no doubt had in mind a unified science, but certainly not the kind envisaged by twentieth-century positivism. For it was the favorable reception of positivism—in particular, the *logical* positivism affiliated with the Vienna School—that in part led to the dominance of SR in the theory and practice of liberal democracy. However, before discussing positivism's version of the unified science thesis, let us first examine its philosophy of natural science.

Wittgenstein's *Tractatus* (1921) is generally regarded as one of the most significant documents setting forth the logical, ontological, and linguistic foundations for the positivist movement in general. Wittgenstein argued that the logical structure of language mirrors the ontological structure of reality. On this model, reality consists of objects, or simple elements, that are related to one another to form atomic facts. The elementary propositions of language, that is, those that are not reducible to complex disjunctions or conjunctions, are said to describe facts by combining names (undefinable terms that directly refer to particular objects) and concepts (predicates denoting general physicalistic properties or sensations). This structural isomorphism enables the truth or falsity of any elementary proposition, and therewith, the truth or falsity of any compound thereof, to be ascertained by simple comparison with reality.

In order to accommodate the theoretical complexity of modern science, logical positivists had to address the problem of bare particulars discussed in the previous chapter. In particular, they had to explain how formal systems consisting of general theoretical statements about nonobservable properties could be related to particular factual statements about observable sense qualia.

Now, formal systems are calculi consisting of basic elements and rules. The basic elements comprise primitive concepts and statements whose meanings are ostensibly equivalent to the empirical conditions that verify them. The rules of a system, by contrast, determine what counts as syntactically well-formed connections of elements, define the meanings of individual elements, and regulate the logical derivation of theorems and empirical hypotheses from axioms. Rules of logic, principles of mathematics, definitions, and other tautologous statements were thought to be analytically true, or true solely in virtue of the meanings of the terms contained in them; while theoretical principles and intermediary laws of a synthetic (i.e., informative) nature were thought to be true by simple correspondence with observed facts. These, in turn, functioned to causally explain or predict. Following the influential analysis proffered by Karl Popper, Carl Hempel, and Paul Oppenheim, it had been customary to think of causal explanations as *deducing* a description of some particular event E to be explained (the explanandum) from a description of a particular set of conditions C causally related to E, conjoined with an empirical generalization of the form, if C then E (the explanans).[1] This *covering law* model was later modified to allow for less deterministic—and thus less explanatory—forms of stochastic inference, in which the explanandum follows with a degree of probability greater than 50 percent but less than 100.[2]

As described above, positivism conforms to SR in three respects: it defines argumentation (justification) in terms of formal rules of deductive logic, it founds meaning and truth in direct observation, and it equates explanation with determinate causal prediction. These features of SR are all problematic.

To begin with, SR underestimates the indeterminacy and contextuality of causal explanation. It does so because it neglects the synthetic a priori contribution of agents who actively intervene in—and thus constitute—regularly functioning systems. This contribution—so decisive for Kant, Hegel, and later pragmatists—has consequences that extend to the very rationality of science as a communal *learning* process.

First let's examine the inability of positivism (or SR) to provide an adequate account of causal knowledge, conceived both as a logic of discovery (or learning) and as a logic of explanation (or rational justification). As a logic of explanation, the covering law model cannot distinguish between lawlike statements and statements denoting constant conjunctions of noncausally related events. The following example, mentioned by Rudolph Carnap, shows that the Humean conception of causality as a constant conjunction of successive events still raises paradoxes when explicated as an ordinary conditional of the sort definitive of a covering law.

(I)   Whenever iron is heated, the earth moves.
(II)   Whenever iron is heated, it expands.

II, unlike I, seems to explicate a real causal connection rather than a mere regularity or constant conjunction. As Roderick Chisholm and Nelson Goodman noted, in order to avoid collapsing the distinction between causal and noncausal regularities the former would have to be explicated as contrary-to-fact conditionals of the following type:

(III) If iron had been heated, then it would have expanded.[3]

The reason for this reformulation is simple. On the positivist model, causal connections refer to invariant relations that specify either necessary or sufficient conditions. Now in saying that the heating of iron caused its expansion we are saying more than that it was necessary for it. The heating was more than necessary—it actually sufficed to produce expansion. At the same time, it was not merely one among many factors that obtained in the world at the time of the heating that, taken together, proved sufficient. To say that the heating of iron caused it to expand implies that without the heating, the other factors would not have been sufficient to cause the expansion. In other words, the cause in question is one that is necessary for the other factors to be sufficient.

The major premise of a covering law explanation asserts only that the heating of iron (C) is sufficient for its expansion (E), that is, C then E. In order to capture the idea that the heating was also necessary for the expansion (E then C), one might think that a biconditional formulation would suffice (E if and only if C). But this formula will not work either, since causal laws assert one-way temporal relationships in which consequent effects cannot be understood as reciprocal causes of their respective antecedent conditions. From a commonsense perspective, it is counterintuitive to think of the expansion of iron as a cause of its heating. In order to preserve the asymmetry built into causal laws, one would have to reformulate the idea of a condition that is necessary for other factors being sufficient—an idea that cannot be reduced to any conjunction of ordinary conditionals. Only counterfactual conditionals approximate this idea inasmuch as they ascribe both necessity and sufficiency to the antecedent in an asymmetrical manner: If C had occurred, E would have also.

These difficulties directly relate to Hegel's critique of the tautologous nature of rationalist and empiricist explanations. As we noted in the previous chapter, this critique also touches on the epistemological vacuity, or nonreflexivity, of rationalist and empiricist logics of learning—a deficit often debated under the heading of the problem of induction. Hume showed that passive observation of discrete sense qualia can demonstrate only an *accidental* conjunction of C and E. It can record the contingent sameness of the past, but it can't prove that such sameness will obtain in the future. In telling us *how* things have happened but not *why* they must happen, it neither explains nor discovers anything.

Echoing Hegel and Kant, von Wright argues that causal necessity cannot be founded on passive observation but must be *actively* produced. The counterfactual form of causal laws already testifies to this productivity: If p were *done* to x, then q would occur. More precisely, we must consciously isolate causal relations through direct intervention in natural systems by actively suppressing or promoting certain influences. This intervention is both synthetic and a priori, since the intentional action that produces and activates a causal system cannot be described or explained physicalistically or causally.

I shall return to von Wright's intriguing defense of this claim below, for it has important consequences for the way in which we must conceive practical reason. For the moment, however, it suffices to note that von Wright's account of the role of intentional agency in producing causal systems entails a weaker form of necessity (determinism) than he seems to realize.

Adverting to the contextual nature of agent intervention, MacIntyre argues for a more radical conclusion than that drawn by von Wright: "[F]rom the fact that a particular cause produces a particular effect nothing whatsoever follows about how in general that effect can be produced" (MacIntyre 1976, 147). Following H. L. A. Hart's analysis of legal causes as decisive intervening factors, MacIntyre denies that causes must be necessary or sufficient conditions.[4] A court may validly determine that a patch of oil on a road was the cause of an accident, but this is not to say that *that* particular accident would not have happened but for that particular patch of oil. Had the patch of oil not been on the road another condition might have been present that could have caused the accident. Conversely, the patch of oil was not sufficient to bring about the action, since other factors had to be present as well, such as precipitation. That oil, not precipitation, is deemed to be decisive is because the former is identified as an extraordinary intervention vis-à-vis a relatively stable, hierarchically ordered system of relations, which in *this* case happens to include an atmospheric pressure conducive to condensation (144–45).

According to MacIntyre, causality is not a relationship between cause, effect, and law, but involves four interrelated terms: an intervening agent, a state of affairs that is interfered with by the intervention, the effect of the intervention, and the outcome that would have prevailed but for the intervention. On this reading, both what is interfered with and the interfering agency are to be understood as causes—and for two reasons. First, a cause is what makes a difference; what enables a person to successfully perform an act on some occasions and not on others. The discovery of causes is essentially the discovery of limitations to human action. Second, interfering causal *agents* achieve their effects in conjunction with *background* causal *agencies* and regularities. Some of these regularities might consist of sequences of sounds regulated by linguistic rules. Some might consist of covariant relations that cannot be broken by intervention, such as Boyle's law concerning the inverse relation obtaining between the pressure and volume of gases kept at constant temperatures. However, some regularities can be broken; the laws of Newtonian mechanics permit the prediction of particular events only so long as some narrow range of possible intervening factors does not occur that breaks the connection. In social science regularities of this type can be broken by a much wider range of intervening factors owing to the greater diversity and mutability of human actions (144–45). As a rule, social regularities cannot be specified independently of particular, causally efficacious interventions. Hence, the generalization that social class determines educational opportunity may or may not be causally relevant to the explanation of why a particular miner's son did not advance to university studies while his colleagues from wealthier families did.

I mention this case by way of anticipating some of the more intractable difficulties positivists have had in extending the covering law model to social science. MacIntyre's account shows that generalizations at best function as *background* assumptions for isolating decisive interventions rather than as premises from which causes can be deduced. Indeed, it explains why singular causal statements might not directly entail any generalizations. As Davidson remarks, reference to background generalizations "may mean that 'A caused B' entails some particular law involving the predicates used in descriptions 'A' and 'B,' or it may mean that 'A caused B' entails that there exists a causal law instantiated by some true descriptions of A and B" (Davidson 1968, 179). Proponents of the covering law theory assume the former to be the case. The example cited above, however, suggests that this possibility doesn't exist for at least one class of phenomena—social behavior. To cite Davidson, we need not assume that "there is any law connecting events classified as reasons with events classified as actions—the classifications may even be neurological, chemical, or physical."[5]

Significantly, a large portion of the causal explanations proffered by natural scientists also seem to be *heteronomic* in the sense described above. It is perfectly consistent to claim that smoking causes lung cancer in the absence of any law connecting these events under just *these* descriptions, so long as we can appeal to laws connecting specific chemical compounds in cigarette smoke, genetic and environmental factors, and so on, to the production of certain sorts of cellular mutation.

There is a more troubling problem with causal laws, however. There might be none that are necessary and universal. Positivists were willing to concede this in the case of social phenomena. It was thought that one might still explain such phenomena as the outcome of weaker tendencies, or probabilities. But if quantum mechanics tells us anything, it is that natural science is no less probabilistic than social science.

The contextuality—and thus indeterminism—of causal explanation has direct consequences for the communitarian nature of science. As Peirce noted, probability makes no sense at the level of individual choice or intervention since, as an ideal projection extended over an indefinite time and place, it has no bearing on the outcome of any given instance.[6] For this reason he concluded that scientific knowledge could only realize itself in the form of an ongoing *community* of investigators—one, moreover, whose scope has to be *ideally* extended through time and space. For only an ideal community could reach a "final true opinion" about probabilities that would make possible something like a fully deterministic explanation—and *identification*—of reality.

I will argue in chapter 5 that the idea of a final true consensus, although perhaps regulative for practitioners of normal science, is meaningless when applied to moral truth claims and the like. It suffices to note that Heisenberg's Uncertainty Principle already presumes that the investigators comprising our scientific community will measure probabilities from

incommensurable perspectives, thereby reaffirming the irrecusable contextuality and indeterminacy of explanation.[7]

1.1 Thus far I have argued that positivism's deterministic logic of explanation and discovery fails. It does so owing to its reliance on epistemic
foundationalism. However, it also fails because of its reliance on deductive
logic as the supreme exemplar of rational justification. Since these two
aspects of SR are complementary, criticism of the one will involve criticism of the other.

First, the deductive model of argumentation has been criticized by
Stephen Toulmin and others for its analytical sterility.[8] In most contexts
we try to substantiate our conclusions by drawing on *independently* established evidence, not by showing that they are analytically contained in
assumptions we take for granted. Our aim, after all, is to convince others.
That being the case, it seems more reasonable to focus on the formal rules
governing dialogic exchange rather than on those regulative for monologic
inference. This model of argumentation has the unique advantage of permitting value statements, which cannot be deduced from higher principles,
and counterfactual claims, which cannot be justified by induction, to be
justified by agreement. It thus enables us to breach the fact/value distinction: to the extent that an agreement has been reached under suitably rational conditions in which all are permitted to participate freely, equally,
and sincerely, those party to it ought to abide by the conclusion(s) reached.

Because the language in which the argument proceeds may be deemed
inadequate for expressing certain claims and the specific rules governing
rational conversation may be deemed inadequate for reaching true or valid
conclusions, processes of dialogic argumentation must be inherently reflexive in a way precluded by canons of formal logic. As I remarked in the
previous chapter, the distinction between metalanguage and object language postulated by Russell's theory of types is intended to avoid just this
reflexivity. Whether critically examining the adequacy of a given language
by means of that same language is paradoxical in the same way that a self-
referential negation is may well be academic, since we cannot stand outside the native language by which we come to understand other languages.
The critique of ideology—that is, of the social bias coloring our natural
language—must proceed immanently, by drawing on the semantic sources
of that same language. It matters not that we draw upon different cultures
to effect this critique, for our understanding of them will necessarily be
filtered through the lens of our own culture. To paraphrase Hegel: reason

is a dialectical process of indefinite reflection, not a final result. Rational learning cannot be conceived otherwise.

Once we accept that arguments possess a reflexive structure more conformable to CR rather than SR, foundationalism—the second aspect of SR endorsed by positivism—becomes otiose. Reality and meaning are no less a function of agreement than logical validity. Now, positivists rejected all coherence theories of truth of this sort. They assumed that abstract theoretical terms could be literally translated, at least partially if not wholly, into indubitable, first-person claims about immediately experienced sense data (protocol sentences). This enterprise failed for two reasons. As Peirce noted, the meaning of any object statement entails an indefinite number of *counterfactual* causal assertions about possible instrumental interventions and their accompanying sensory experiences.[9] And as Goodman proved, such assertions depend on whatever theory language is used to describe them.[10]

The inability to translate theoretical into observation language coincided with the breakdown of the time-honored distinction between analytic and synthetic knowledge. Quine (1963), for example, argued that the expression "P is analytically true" is tantamount to saying that "P is true by definition" or P is true by the synonymy, or mutual substitutability of subject and predicate terms. Since synonymy cannot be defined in an uncircular way, he concluded that analytic statements were true by conventional fiat, or stipulation.

If Quine's attack on the analytic-synthetic distinction showed that logical truths rest on factual convention, the failure of reductionism proved the reverse: there is no observation language which is not already *pre-interpreted* theoretically. Quine and Popper had already noted that values inform theories and theories inform scientific facts.[11] However, it was Kuhn's historical narration of scientific revolutions that seemed to deliver the death blow to the positivist conception of scientific progress, conceived as a cumulative growth in knowledge asymptotically approaching a final, true picture of reality.

According to Kuhn, not only are facts described in ways that invariably presuppose a prior conceptual framework, but the choice of theory during revolutionary periods of scientific crisis is determined by conventions of argumentation that have little to do with normal procedures of scientific experimentation. Kuhn observed (contra Popper) that anomalies that apparently falsify a hypothesis do not compel its abandonment unless they are deemed to be of crucial importance. As Duhem and Quine earlier noted, even when it has been determined that a crucial experiment yielding anomalous results is based on accurate measurements (a determination that is relative to the current state of technology) and that the problem resides in the law under consideration rather than in some auxiliary hypothesis, such results only lead to theoretical crises when alternative paradigms are available. These alternatives initially promise more than their predecessor, despite the initial modesty of their explanatory power.

Kuhn's discussion of the role of argumentation in persuading dissident scientists to "convert" to a new paradigm illustrates the way in which overlapping values shared by competing schools of thought are variously interpreted by them, so that "there is no neutral algorithm for theory choice, no systematic decision procedure which, properly applied, must lead each individual in the group to the same decision" (Kuhn 1970a, 200). The five "objective" criteria of choice mentioned by Kuhn—accuracy, consistency, scope, simplicity, and fruitfulness—may not be universal value orientations toward which all paradigm debates in the sciences gravitate (Kuhn 1977, 335). But even if they are, they cannot provide a discursive basis for resolving disagreements. They mean different things to practitioners of different paradigms and even to practitioners of subdisciplines within the same paradigm. This incommensurability, however, is compatible with a looser sort of unity—one based on the principle of metaphorical communication rather than on the formal logical canon of literal translation.[12]

Thus, contrary to the anarchistic view advanced by Paul Feyerabend, the *aesthetic judgment* favoring a revolutionary paradigm is neither spontaneous nor irrational, but reflexive (or comparative) in a manner that remains to be seen. The corpuscular language of classical physics used to describe the behavior of macrophenomena provided the requisite *analogue* used in describing the behavior of subatomic particles in quantum mechanics, despite the *literal* incommensurability between classical and quantum paradigms. Feyerabend's construal of the gestalt switch experienced by converts to a new paradigm on the model of child language acquisition, Piagetian developmental psychology, and the like overlooks this point, partly because it wrongly denies that such switches are examples of cross-cultural *learning* involving translation from one language to another. Hence, Feyerabend's appeal to Hegelian logic notwithstanding, it is rational dialogue (metaphoric paraphrase, reinterpretation, and synthesis) that accords with dialectics, not abstract contradiction.[13]

As we shall see, the metaphoricity of rational communication is also decisive for understanding the political and historical legitimacy of modern institutions. To anticipate my later defense of Kuhn, one could not grasp the *internal* rationale legitimating, say, the Copernican revolution without understanding how the metaphorical nature of scientific language enabled the Copernican to justify his worldview in light of expectations and questions generated within the radically different worldview of Ptolemean astronomy. Such *aesthetic* rationality not only explains how modern reason and premodern tradition serve to critically extend and legitimate the authority of the other, it also explains the dialogic encounter whereby each can learn from the other.

To summarize: we have seen how CR—not SR—best captures the synthetic, reflexive logic of scientific discovery and explanation. If science is neither foundationalistic, logocentric, nor deterministic, then it need not entail nihilism or objectivism.

Of course, to repeat what I said earlier, SR does faithfully capture the mathematical, analytical, and perhaps even—albeit less faithfully—experimental sides of scientific research. Yet leaving aside differences between pure and applied science, it is apparent that scientists themselves often overestimate the extent to which their research exclusively embodies SR. Thus, while canons of value freedom govern controlled observations in a way that approximates SR, they also function communicatively—as regulative ideas enjoining open discussion about basic paradigmatic commitments. One might object that as communicative ideals they regulate too weakly; for instance, it is hard to resist cynicism in light of the way gender and racial prejudices continue to determine the form and content of selected areas of research.[14] Compounding this bias—and perhaps indirectly related to it—are those *institutional* norms and social pressures under which scientists fund, conduct, and publish their research. Emanating from governmental agencies and commercial enterprises as well as from the competitive prestige and status hierarchies of the scientific community at large—these constraints belie the very idea of an open community of critics.

Be that as it may, this analysis at least suggests that science is not *necessarily* cut off from and opposed to the CR that properly describes the discursive resolution of *normal* scientific crises. Since it is not, we may assume that some of the values esteemed by its critics—such as freedom (to criticize), intersubjective reciprocity, epistemic holism, context-sensitivity, creativity, and preference for flexible learning over prediction and control—function in some regulative (albeit often subordinate) capacity there. And we may assume this without projecting—as Marcuse and others have done—the *radical* transformation of scientific rationality as I have here described it. In short, we can agree with Dewey and other pragmatists that scientific rationality as such is not opposed to liberal and communitarian democracy and may even be indispensable for it.

Still, as we shall see below, it would be precipitous indeed to extend the scientific method to social inquiry without further ado. The reason for this reservation is not that natural and social science deal with different ontological realms (nature versus "spirit," as Wilhelm Dilthey would have it) or that one offers causal explanations while the other only seeks to understand. Rather it is because they have deeper, anthropological *aims* that influence the methodological meaning of causal explanation.[15] Natural scientific explanations *approximate* prediction with intent to control. This dictates experimental procedures—controlled observation, measurement, replication, and so on, that *abstract* from the dense context of practical competencies and norms comprising an already understood but objectively nonthematizable *background*. It is this abstraction that enables an unchallenged *normal* science (in Kuhn's sense) to acquire the status of an orthodoxy (or consensual paradigm). But what is normative for natural science (even the more holistic and context-sensitive science advocated by feminists would incorporate considerable abstraction in its experimental method) would spell disaster for the social sciences. As Hubert Dreyfus correctly notes, the latter "are at best in the perpetual revolution and conflict of interpretations . . . when they are trying to account for *all* human behavior, even the pervasive background of cultural interpretation which makes action meaningful." Stated differently, social scientific explanations *approximate* interpretation with intent to criticize.[16] They typically show why some *past* act deviated from a normal, regular pattern of behavior or contradicted some other set of normative expectations. Either the act or the norm is judged to be subrational. And this lack of identity in turn reflects on the identity of the agent(s) whose actions are being explained. From the standpoint of methodology, since humans, unlike mere physical things, constitute their identities and actions through dialogic acts of mutual recognition (reflection), access to *these* data necessitates interpretation and reflection, which, in effect, *changes* them. This indeterminacy—or unpredictability—is more radical than that mentioned by Quine or Heisenberg, since the change in the data in turn changes the interpreter.

2. Now, positivists since Hobbes have struggled mightily against what they perceive to be the unscientific and irrational voluntarism informing such "metaphysical" accounts of moral life. Subsequently, they have attempted to view rational behavior the same way they view natural phenomena: as conformable to mechanistic laws. Their critics respond that rational behavior involves an intentional—not causal—relationship between reasons and actions, ends and means. I will argue that both positions are one-sided. Agents' practical reasons must be conceived as causes—and not just identifying descriptions—of their actions, otherwise social critique is pointless. Moreover, our conceiving them as such cannot preclude explaining them in terms of functional and physical mechanisms. Such a view, I believe, best comports with the complexity, contextuality, contingency, and indeterminacy of reflexive relationships as defended in Hegel's *Logik*.

Not surprisingly, positivists were more indebted to Mill's *Logic*, which extended the inductive method to moral as well as natural phenomena. Hempel's pioneering essay, "The Function of General Laws in History" (1942), refined Mill's position further by explicating the logic of social scientific explanations in terms of the covering law model (Hempel 1965). He proposed that historical events, such as the migration of farmers from the Dust Bowl to California in the 1930s, be explained by generalizations of the sort "populations tend to migrate to regions offering better living conditions" in conjunction with factual statements about how California offered these farmers better living conditions than the regions they were from (464). However, given the paucity of such explanations in actual historical and social scientific practice, Hempel allowed that most historians only offer "explanation sketches" based on generalizations that are either too widely confirmed and well known to bother mentioning or still premature and in need of further research and clarification. The failure to generate reliable predictions, Hempel added, could also be attributed to the statistical nature of such generalizations, which at most enable a probable, not a deductive, inference.

The first major attack on the Hempelian position was launched by William Dray in *Laws and Explanation in History* (1957). Dray argued—in a manner reminiscent of Hegel's own critique of rationalist and empiricist explanations—that true covering laws are either nonexplanatory descriptions of discrete events or nonexplanatory tautologies (i.e., definitions of rational behavior). In order for a behavioral law to provide sufficient explanation for a particular event, it would have to be either so general as to explain even the nonoccurrence of the event or so specific that only the single action in question could count as an instance of it. Thus, according to Dray, in order to explain why Louis XIV was unpopular, a defender of the covering law model like Popper would have to qualify his initial hypothesis (for example, that all rulers who act contrary to the interest of their subjects are unpopular) by adding that this law only holds true *whenever* the harm caused is sufficiently great (i.e., whenever the ruler in question wages a costly war, suppresses religious minorities, and maintains a costly retinue of courtiers). However, exceptions to this rule could be adduced that would again require the revision of this law to include specific policies that could only apply to the peculiar situation of Louis XIV. In this instance, the validity of the law would be purchased at the expense of its nomothetic generality. An alternate strategy, involving the subsumption of the event under trivial truths such as "Rulers who make their subjects very unhappy are unpopular," suffers from the opposite defect of procuring validity by fiat—reducing the law to an empty tautology that fails to relate the unpopularity of Louis XIV to the particular policies he followed (Dray 1957, 35, 102).

Popper and others questioned the force of this argument when applied to the explanation of those *fixed patterns* of behavior that comprise the subject matter of social—as distinct from historical—science.[17] The second half of Dray's book addresses this counterargument. Following Collingwood, Dray argued that any sufficient explanation of an action must refer to the agent's own purposes and rationale for acting. The social scientist no less than the historian looks for just that reason which—in the counterfactual, singular sense mentioned by von Wright, MacIntyre, and Davidson—caused the action to occur. Absent this necessary condition, the event would not have happened in *exactly* the way it did happen.

The question remains whether rational explanations constitute a unique logic of explanation. Hempel argued that such explanations would succeed in explaining why an actor A did X only if it afforded grounds for believing more than that it would have been rational for A to do X. This could be done if the maxims of rational conduct appealed to by Dray were reformulated as laws of human psychology. The revised covering law model of rational explanation would then take this form (Hempel 1965, 471).

1. A was in situation of type C.
2. A was a rational agent.
3. Schema R: In a situation of type C, any rational agent will do X.

---

4. Therefore A did X.

This emendation neglects to address the dialectic of abstract universal and concrete particular mentioned by Hegel and Dray. But there is another reason why the revision fails. As Dray pointed out, the *normative* generality of rational maxims—which leads us to expect certain kinds of behavior in certain circumstances—cannot be identified with the *empirical* generality of a covering law. For, Schema R would not be disconfirmed if A did *not* do X. It expresses a moral judgement of the form: "When in a situation of type $C_1 \ldots C_n$ the thing to do is X" (Dray 1957, 132). In short, it says that we *ought* to behave as others do, not that we *must*.

2.1 Now von Wright's formalization of rational explanations as practical (or teleological) syllogisms reveals a central weakness in all accounts that take *individual* agents' reasons for acting as sufficient. A practical syllogism explains why an action *a* occurred by showing that an actor *A* thought it necessary in order to bring about some other end *p* (von Wright 1971, 96). Inferences of this type, von Wright maintains, are distinctly teleological in nature and cannot be reduced to causal explanations. Though it may seem that they point to antecedent causes—indeed, we sometimes use them to show that an action occurred *because* of the actor's aims and beliefs—it is nevertheless clear that their fundamental structure is teleological in nature: "This happened in order that that should occur."

Taking account of factors that might invalidate the inference, von Wright gives us the following model of a practical inference (PI) (107).

1. From now on A intends to bring about *p* at time *t*.
2. From now on A considers that, unless he does *a* no later than at t, he cannot bring about *p* at *t*.

3. Therefore, no later than when he thinks time *t* has arrived, A sets himself to do *a*, unless he forgets about the time or is prevented.

Is this a sufficient explanation? Apparently not. We can imagine the extreme case of an assassin who intends to shoot a tyrant and aims his gun but does not fire, owing to an involuntary case of nerves. If a logical connection existed between intention and action, it would seem that we would have to conclude that the assassin did not intend to shoot after all. But supposing he did intend to shoot, his intention would not sufficiently explain his failure to act. Von Wright's critic could then say that something logically distinct from both the intention and the action—the nervousness—*caused* the action.

Weakness of the will *(akrasia)*, von Wright observes, need not pose a serious problem for PI, for in the vast majority of cases that are of interest to historians and social scientists the model is invoked *ex post actu*, to explain a past action rather than predict a future one (116). But this will not help. Chisholm gives the example of a man who, after intending to murder his uncle in order to inherit his wealth, kills him. Can we infer that he murdered him? Not if he did so accidentally. In that case, his intention would not have explained anything. Either it was not causally efficacious (the assassin could have fired the gun by accident owing to a sudden twitch in his finger) or it was causally efficacious in an unintended way (the intention to shoot could have produced the unintended twitch that caused the pull of the trigger).

PI can't function as both explanation and logical explication of action. Its ambiguity has thus led critics to reformulate it as a covering law explanation having as one of its premises the assertion that A is rational.[18] Yet this attempt amounts to reintroducing a variant of Hempel's Schema R, which no longer functions as an empirical law.

It seems that neither teleological nor covering law models suffice to explain actions. That norms of rational behavior function to explain some actions suggests that the distinction between reasons and causes is not as absolute as von Wright thinks. After all, we *expect* persons to behave rationally. It is not surprising, therefore, that when we encounter deviant behavior, we often look for supervening causal factors to explain it. These deviations may result from miscalculations or pathologies, but often they stem from critical—and rational—resistance to accepted norms. And these—to recall MacIntyre's discussion of this point—comprise a set of *background* conditions capable of being only partially and selectively thematized at any given moment.

The fact that norms often enter into our understanding of the causal efficacy of agents' reasons in the guise of *implicit preunderstanding* and not *explicit intention* suggests yet another reason why PI fails to explain certain actions: its instantiation of SR. PI evinces the logicism, determinism and foundationalism of SR in its presumption of an analytic connection between intention and action, on one hand, and the empirical verifiability of the reasons that explain *and* identify actions, on the other (von Wright 1971, 117). The importance of explicitly unintended but implicitly understood meaning shows why this reliance on SR frustrates both understanding and explanation. Clyde Kroeber's example of an aborigine who tries to heal his wound by carefully cleaning his knife illustrates the point I am trying to make. Without a broader narrative referring to the mythopoetic worldview in which the aborigine's medicinal magic functions—a worldview, be it noted, that is only partly reflected in the aborigine's explicit intentions—the knife cleaning remains inexplicable.[19] The totality of practical know-how and prepropositional understanding that makes up the aborigine's worldview must be narrated from the point of view of a virtual participant, such as an anthropologist, whose participation in the aborigine's culture is mediated by a certain reflective distance. This narrative no doubt draws on the everyday narratives that the aborigines tell themselves. But the practical, lived totality of meaningfulness indirectly implicated in these narratives—what neo-Hegelian communitarians like Charles Taylor believe constitutes the core of our identity—can never be completely narrated, and hence cannot be empirically verified (Taylor 1989, 29, 34).

2.2 Before discussing Taylor's argument I would like to examine another attempt to explain rational action in terms of individual intentions: rational choice theory. This theory is especially important to our study, since it has been used by some to justify the irrationality of democracy. What makes it so attractive to persons of positivistic bent is that, by explaining actions as outcomes of probabilistic calculations under uniquely specifiable conditions of risk and uncertainty, it incorporates contextuality and indeterminacy in a way the covering law model cannot. Yet like all theories that take SR as their basis, it cannot explain important instances of rational action.

Rational choice theory departs from a minimalist model of rationality that has at least this much in common with SR: the assumption that rationality consists in the (logical) consistency of beliefs and the transitivity of desires (i.e., preferring A to C if one also prefers A to B and B to C).[20] In addition to these formal limits, the theory assumes that it is rational to maximize one's utility—to choose, in other words, that action that best realizes one's utility *given* one's *subjective* preference rankings, beliefs, and available strategies. The theory also allows for additional complexity and contingency. *Game* theory factors in constraints imposed by the interdependent choices of others; multiple utility functions factor in multiple preference rankings that vary relative to different choice situations; and conceptions of bounded rationality factor in suboptimal notions of maximization, such as "satisficing" conditions and maxi-min rules, which maximize the best worst choice.[21]

No doubt the theory does explain a narrow range of rational behavior, most notably consumption and investment behavior constrained by prices. However, as Marx observed, it cannot explain how an aggregate of maximizing choices can yield a *stable* system of decision, since such choices tend to undermine the very market constraints that lend them determinacy. Nor can the theory explain voting, since the amount of time spent in gathering information, going to the polls, and so on seems disproportionately high in comparison to the miniscule chance of casting a decisive vote. Again, paradoxes involving the transitive ranking of group preferences discussed by Arrow and others (see chapter 1) compound the irrationality of democracy as a mechanism for choice.

I will address these paradoxes in more detail in chapter 5. Suffice it to say, there may be rational grounds for voting other than those countenanced by rational choice theory. In any case, the example of democracy raises a serious dilemma—familiar to us from our discussion of Hegel—that confronts rational choice explanations of actions lying outside the privileged domain of market transactions. Either they cannot locate an economic reason for a given action—in which case the action in question appears irrational and inexplicable—or they can, in which case the reason cited has nothing whatsoever to do with intentions of the agent that caused the action. Gary Becker's assertion that "a person decides to marry when the expected utility from marriage exceeds that expected from remaining single or from the additional search of a more compatible mate" is an example of this latter type of nonexplanation (Becker 1976, 10). As James Bohman remarks, "[T]his apparently lawlike statement has all the earmarks of a tautology. ... The theory was supposed to give an account of how reasons cause actions. Instead the theory searches for nonintentional maximizing motives and market mechanisms, making the rationality of the actors themselves less and less important as an explanatory condition" (Bohman 1992, 216).

Taking a somewhat different tack, Amartya Sen argues that rational choice theory gives too little structure to preference rankings.[22] Echoing Sandel's critique of the heteronomy of Rawlsian contractors, he contends that this theory cannot account for the *reflexivity* of choice, that is, the rational capacity to critically *judge* the worthiness of preference rankings in light of noneconomic (i.e., nonmaximizing) criteria. In order to exercise rational autonomy and stabilize one's preferences with respect to a structured identity, one would have to critically integrate them around values and norms that—as noted above—are irreducible to intentional objects of subjective desire. In his Storrs Lectures, Elster makes a similar point. Emphasizing the equal importance of moral argumentation and strategic bargaining in the American and French constitutional assemblies, he submits that rational communication in these instances sometimes required the delegates to not only refrain from asserting their personal preferences but to change them in accordance with the demands of justice and impartiality.

Elster's appeal to Habermas in making this argument anticipates the general direction of my own argument, namely, that democracy provides a public space for rational communication in which citizens freely and collectively shape their identities even while seeking to maximize their preferences.[23] For our present purposes, Elster's reference to CR as a condition for exercising rational choice forces us to confront the stubborn fact that "as soon as *reflexivity* is introduced, so is *indeterminacy*" (Bohman 1992, 218).

My remarks about structuration suggest that norms function to mitigate—not remove—this indeterminacy. Obviously, this is possible only if norms are not themselves objects of rational choice. Now, some norms—notably conventions that solve coordination problems—might be explained as outcomes of rational choice.[24] Driving on the left or right side of a road satisfies common preferences for stabilizing expectations about what others will do, namely, by regulating which side to drive on. However, not all conventions can be satisfactorily explained this way. Bohman's example of the conventional English spoken by the Irish testifies to a more sinister reason—imperialistic coercion.

More importantly, maximizing rationality can only explain why *some* norms are voluntarily adopted and adhered to. In many instances such rationality counsels against choosing mutually optimal strategies of cooperation. The Prisoner's Dilemma, which arises when rational maximizers choose suboptimal strategies of noncooperation to avoid worst case scenarios, exemplifies this problem. Attempts to explain how rational maximizers facing Prisoner Dilemmas would come to cooperate by adopting long-term views of their self-interest or by testing the trustworthiness of their opposing players through iterated plays over time are patently question-begging. Rational maximizers might rightly reason that repeated plays are too risky or suboptimal. Again, one's current long-term interests might diverge from one's future interests; or talk of long-term interest might simply be another way of saying that one ought to set aside one's narrow self-interest for the sake of adopting a moral point of view.

As the Free Rider Problem illustrates, even if rational maximizers solved their dilemma there would be no incentives for them to continue to cooperate. Beneficial cooperation over time would tempt rational maximizers to take advantage of others' willingness to forgo their self-interest—in other words, to enjoy the benefits of cooperation without incurring the corresponding costs. That is why Hobbes had to introduce coercion in his account of the social contract. To cite Bohman:

> [S]tability through rule following is inconsistent with the assumptions of rational choice theory . . . (it) is a consequence of rule following and is not caused by agents maximizing their own utility; nor is it an unintended consequence because the consequence itself is inconsistent with rational behavior in this sense. Once an order stable enough to permit repeated interaction is in place, then it can become clear that following rules in the long run may be utility maximizing for all agents (including themselves). (Bohman 1992, 222)

3. The preceding discussion shows that SR and its intentionalistic model of rational action fail to explain the normative structuration that is presupposed in framing any stable choice situation. But now we need to inquire further into the manner in which normative structuration explains intentional action. In his highly influential book, *The Idea of a Social Science and its*

Relation to Philosophy (1958), Peter Winch argued that it explained intentional action by constituting its meaning and identity. This version of the logical connection argument appeals to Wittgenstein's defense of the public, rule-governed nature of meaning. Wittgenstein held that the idea of a private language was nonsense, since it would be impossible for the inventor of such a language to know with certainty whether he or she were using an expression consistently. Consistent—or correct—usage only makes sense in light of publicly accepted rules (Wittgenstein 1952, 20). As Winch puts it, "[T]he notion of following a rule is logically inseparable from the notion of *making a mistake*" (Winch 1953, 32). The same applies to the meaning of action as well. We make sense of it by showing that it was the appropriate thing to do under the circumstances.

Winch's belief that rule, intention, and action are logically connected led him to conceive social scientific explanation as a species of conceptual analysis categorically distinct from causal explanation. I remarked earlier that such analysis seldom if ever suffices to explain action. Not only are some social actions *not* instances of following a rule correctly or incorrectly—MacIntyre's example of taking a walk being a case in point—but as ethnomethodologists never cease to remind us, the rules governing action sometimes allow so many exceptions and variations in force and application as to be indistinguishable from ad hoc inventions. Judging the causal impact of a given rule with respect to some action thus involves a rather fine discrimination of the sort that can only be obtained by participating in the language game in question.

This brings us back to the importance of understanding (*Verstehen*) in explaining action. Positivists allow that understanding may serve a valuable heuristic function in formulating causal hypotheses, but they deny it any role in the logic of explanation and confirmation. For them it consists in empathetically reconstructing an agents' subjective intentions on the basis of overt behavior. Thus, for Theodor Abel, a causal hypothesis linking the reduction of temperature to the lighting of fires acquires subjective plausibility once we understand it in terms of our own desire to seek warmth when feeling cold.[25]

One of the most influential criticisms of this notion of understanding is contained in Charles Taylor's seminal essay, "Interpretation and the Sciences of Man." According to Taylor, the meanings of actions cannot be reduced to actors' subjective beliefs and preferences as determined by empathetic introspection or question-and-answer surveys (Taylor 1977, 112–16). In addition to commonly shared beliefs and attitudes, there are also intersubjective meanings that underlie *and constitute* the practices about which we have subjective beliefs and attitudes.

Relying on the speech act theory of John Searle, Taylor argues that the institutional rules governing voting and bargaining are irreducible to formal rules regulating voting and bargaining procedures, such as direct versus indirect methods of electing chief executives. The institutional rules of voting and bargaining instead consist of *background distinctions* between free and forced choices, consensual and compromise resolutions, and so on that constitute the very meaning of the democratic process. One could neither understand nor explain the practice of negotiation in a Japanese village unless one knew that the word Americans translate as "bargaining" has a different sense for the Japanese than it has for us, one whose meaning is not bound up with the idea of contractual autonomy, self-interest, pressuring the opposition, and gaining a favorable advantage or balance of power (116–21). The same could be said of other common meanings that shape our collective identity as a nation, such as commitment to freedom. These meanings precede and condition our attempts to reach consensus on the specific claims that flow from them (121–23).

This raises an important question: If intersubjective meanings transcend the explicitly intended and empirically verifiable meanings of individual subjects, then what kind of understanding is necessary for grasping them? And, further, can such a procedure aspire to the level of value-free (or interpretation-free) objectivity characteristic of the natural sciences? Taylor's answer to this question rests on what he—following Hegel, Humboldt, and Gadamer—perceives to be the inherent *textuality* of meaning: "[J]ust as our color concepts are given their meaning by the field of contrast they set up, so that the introduction of new concepts will alter the boundaries of others, so the various meanings that a subordinate's demeanor can have for us, as deferential, respectful, cringing, mildly mocking, ironical, insolent, provoking, downright rude, are established by a field of contrast; and as with finer discrimination on our part, or a more sophisticated culture, new possibilities are born, so other terms of this range are altered" (107).

Now, social no less than literary texts must be understood through a circular process that requires interpreting the whole in terms of its parts and vice versa. This dialectic alone ensures that understanding is never complete. But incompleteness also supervenes through the situational character of understanding. The endeavor to understand the text in our own language, in ways that directly resonate with our selective and context-bound point of view, unavoidably fuses our own presuppositions to the meaning of the text. This *ontological* circle, as Gadamer puts it, renders futile any attempt to fix the text's meaning in terms of original authorial *intentions*; that attempt would only make sense if we could empathetically introspect such intentions in the conclusive, value- and context-free manner presupposed by foundationalism. On the contrary, the ontological circle ensures that the being and identity of the interpreter—no less than the being and identity (meaning) of the text interpreted—are continually altered in the course of interpretation. Hence the pathetic dialectic to which ethnomethodologists and postmodern anthropologists testify: to understand a culture exposes it to the *transformative* influence of the interpreter and his or her culture. As we shall see in chapter 3, the only way for the anthropologist to avoid the ethnocentric imposition of his or her beliefs is to risk them in mutual dialogue with the practitioners of the other culture. Hence, textual understanding must incorporate critical interpretation.

Taylor uses this hermeneutic insight to criticize not just action-oriented theories of explanation and understanding, but also those deontological and utilitarian moral theories that conceive practical reason as hedonistic calculation, consistency testing, or some other procedure of intentional deliberation. These theories simply ignore the contextual, interpretative nature of moral judgment that persists even in reflectively working through dilemmas. Such judgment, however, is less the outcome of rational procedure than substantive discrimination, character, and identity.

Like other social theorists who have been influenced by hermeneutics, Taylor puts great store in what Dilthey identified as the narrative (or textual) *unity* of personal identity. Contrary to Parfit and others influenced by empiricism, personal identity is irreducible to conscious role identifications and desires. Reducing identity in this manner would eliminate the historical continuity prerequisite for self-identification. For I identify myself—articulate *who* I am to myself and others—in terms of an autobiographical narrative extending back to my childhood and looking ahead to the completion and fulfillment of a life well lived (Taylor 1989, 48).

Taylor's focus on narrative identity as the pivot around which all moral reasoning revolves provides a welcome counterweight to the modern obsession with "*doing* the right thing." For, if practical reasoning only occurs against the background of "strong evaluations" whose nature reaches down to the very roots of our infinitely rich and dense identity, then *character*—not abstract ratiocination about formal principles and foundations—really determines our judgments and motivations. Yet Taylor is the last person who would "naturalize" our *mode of being* into something that merely supervenes externally in intentional action. Indeed, to say that our being is historical is to say that we sustain it—literally give it unity and purpose—through critically *re*interpreting it. Of course, this means that *others* too will interpret the meaning and identity of our existence differently than we do.

It is precisely this narrative dynamic—or ontological spiral—that explains why historical events cannot be predicted. "The success of prediction in the natural sciences," Taylor observes, "is bound up with the fact that all states of the system, past and future, can be described in the same range of concepts, as values, say, of the same variables" (105–12). Such stability is lacking in the domain of human affairs, since the identity of agents and their actions—and ultimately the social world in which they live—changes in accordance with their historical self-understanding. This explains the unreliability of social statistics. We cannot assume, for example, that the rise in reported instances of spousal rape indicates an increase in the incidence of this "deviant" behavior. The reason for this is not merely the greater willingness of women to report such behavior but the fact that what we today call "spousal rape" would have been classified as "conjugal intercourse" a few years ago. The change in classification is not merely nominal. For along with it comes a radical change in the very essence and valorization of the act—and so too the meaning of marital relations, spousal roles, and identities.

3.1 So far I have argued that the meaning and rationale of an action cannot be exclusively identified with subjective intentions. The normative background that implicitly structures our intentions must also be factored in. However, alongside these strata of meaning we must add the unintended *functions* that actions and norms serve in maintaining the social system.

Unlike subjectively intended and normatively implied meaning, this *latent* stratum of meaning is not one that social agents would recognize as fairly describing their intentions. For it consists of descriptions about the aggregate effects of behavior on society as a whole that can only be obtained statistically. The historical variability of statistical data discussed above obviously places considerable constraints on the validity of functional explanations. Since the latter depend on statistical correlations connecting individual actions under some intentional and normative description with some overarching social purpose that they serve to bring about and maintain, neither the boundary of the system nor its identifying goal (equilibrium) states can be empirically fixed.

This explains the error of functionalist explanations that conceive social systems on the model of biological organisms. Premised on SR, these explanations try to fix the boundaries and goal states of social systems vis-à-vis some empirically obvious—albeit vacuous and question-begging—characteristic, such as survival, social harmony, solidarity, stability, and so on. In general, empiricist varieties of functionalist explanation suffer from the same emptiness as nomological and rational choice explanations: many beliefs or practices could have fulfilled the same function differently—in which case none can be explained as necessary; or every belief or practice necessarily exists to fulfill some function, in which case none can be explained as *uniquely* decisive.

On the other hand, once we realize that empirical descriptions of *macro*-level processes such as systemic structures and goal states are not specifiable apart from interpretations of *micro*-level processes such as intentional actions, these defects can be overcome. For example, I might explain a capitalist's attempt to invest by pointing out that it—along with similar attempts by like-minded capitalists—*unintentionally* produces widespread competition that functions to sustain steady economic growth. This goal state *in turn* can be said to explain the intentional action that indirectly caused it; by *structuring* the increase in market shares it stimulated further investment. Because the goal state (economic growth) is not fully specifiable apart from the intentional activity of investment, the latter is a unique and necessary condition for bringing about the competition functional for sustaining it. This determination, however, is compatible with the indeterminate specification of those mechanisms that mediate micro- and macrophenomena. Hence investment activity serves different functions and even means different things depending on whether the market institutions are embedded in socialist or capitalist contexts (as I argue in chapter 5). Contrary to Elster and other critics of functionalism, the circularity implicit in this kind of rational explanation is no more vicious than that obtaining in any other kind of interpretation-dependent explanation.

The inclusion of functionalist explanations among the set of reasons accounting for rational action serves a critical purpose as well. The aggregated unintended consequences of individual actions may also function to bring about a *destructuration*—or *restructuration*—of the original equilibrium state of the system. We need only recall the instability of unregulated markets mentioned in conjunction with rational choice theory. As Marx noted, this structural crisis causes *disinvestment* among capitalists and *revolutionary* action among workers. Of course, the system only reaches this critical state when its destructuration is experienced as a rationality *and* identity crisis by individuals within that system. This crisis need not accompany cataclysmic depression and civil war. It suffices that the individuals in question experience a contradiction between the normative and functional rationales structuring their actions. Thus the equal autonomy constituting the normative meaning of contractual relations between employer and employee is belied by the coerciveness and inequality constituting their functional meaning.

To conclude: functionalist types of reason play as valid—and as limited—a role in assessing the practical rationality of social agents as strategic and normatively regulated types. As we shall see in chapter 8, functionalism can even be extended to the domain of history. Historical agents unintentionally produce and sustain patterns of questioning, systems of needs, and enduring sets of problems that take on a life of their own as anthropological constants, or formal structures, conditioning historical responses. This is one way actions inadvertently maintain historical identity; and it enables historians to account for continuities in reasoning spanning revolutionary breaks that are otherwise opaque to the agents themselves. Of course, if the preceding analysis is correct, the system of anthropological constants cannot determine historical change in the manner, say, of natural selection. Organic functionalism of this sort is vacuous and tends to perpetuate an ideological belief in fatalism.

This danger, as we shall see, is nowhere more apparent than in the field of technology, where the organic model of homeostatically regulated machinery has not led to the kinds of adaptive systems that are "user friendly" to democratic learning. Interestingly, our discussion of rational action suggests a more authentic notion of technique with vastly different implications. I noted above that the complete rationale underlying intentional action consists of an always implicit background of meaning. Some of this meaning is capable of being discursively explicated and interpreted in the form of propositions. Some of it, however, consists of skills, techniques, competencies, and other kinds of practical know-how whose criteria of success (or appropriateness) we understand intuitively, if at all. Thus, the retrospective explanation we offer in support of our moral and practical judgments never fully articulates the rich texture of discriminations that underlie them.

Heidegger's conception of understanding as *practical* involvement in a holistic field of tacitly understood assignments serves as a paradigm for this kind of rationale. His example of hammering illustrates the priority of practical context over theoretical abstraction. The meaning of the hammer, along with the meaning of the hammering and of the hammerer, extends well beyond the explicit intentions of an individual consciousness to include an implicit, corporeal awareness of an indefinitely vast, deep network of functions. The hammerer as *subject* standing over and against an intentional *object*—comprising the hammer as an inert substrate of measurable properties, the hammering as calculated motion, and the hammered as discrete materials and surfaces—is *derivative* of the hammering as unified process, situation, and event. Transparent, willful agency and the object on which it exerts its will first manifest themselves in the form of an isolable subject and object when a breakdown occurs in the unified *context* in which each interprets the other. They stand forth as foreground phenomena only against the background of a normally unproblematic totality of internal relations (Heidegger 1962, para. 15). Hence, technology as a medium of domination and subjective control presupposes a more holistic technique which, as we shall see, complements—and even completes itself in—communicative activity.

4. I suspect that the reason why liberals have been so blind to the dehumanizing effects of technological domination is because of their tendency to regard SR as formally neutral with respect to substantive values. So conceived, science and technology are means serviceable for good as well as evil, their structure remaining constant throughout variations in the societal context in which they find employment.

My account of the CR informing science suggests at least one challenge to this neutrality thesis. But the democratic values regulative for collective learning can be confined to scientific communities. Lysenkoist orthodoxy notwithstanding, relatively open and learned societies can exist within closed, totalitarian regimes of the sort typified by the former USSR, even if they cannot flourish there. Hence a qualified form of the liberal neutrality thesis might apply to science after all.

The situation with technology is more problematic, however. Unlike scientific rationality, technological design seems more susceptible to variable social constraints. If so, we might have to abandon the idea that technology, like science, evinces a single rational core.

I will argue that some technologies embody SR in their design—and thus prove especially functional for authoritarian or hierarchically managed societies—while others embody CR, which makes them better suited to democratic organizations. Following Andrew Feenberg's *Critical Theory of Technology*, let's distinguish three possible theories of technological rationality. As noted above, the *instrumental* (or liberal) theory defended by Weber regards any type of pure rationality—be it scientific, technological, or practical—as comprising logical, experimental, decisional, and discursive *procedures* that are *formally* neutral with respect to the values in whose service they might be deployed. By contrast, the *substantive* theory expounded by Heidegger, Foucault, and Ellul regards technological *rationality*—as distinct from *technique*—as incorporating a single end—the reduction of persons and things to objectified (quantified) resources subject to prediction, control, and domination—that structures all aspects of society. Interestingly, this theory accepts the liberal equation of science and technology with SR, but denies that SR is neutral with respect to the structure of social, cultural, and political life.

The third, *critical* theory of technological rationality defended by Feenberg and myself splits the difference between the two extremes mentioned above. It holds that the technical *elements* out of which technical designs are constructed are value-neutral, but not the designs (Feenberg, 1991, 81). Unlike the substantive theory, critical theory assumes that different technological designs—and thus different kinds of technological rationality—are possible that comport with different kinds of society. However, it agrees with the substantive theory in its identification of a dominant technological design whose embodiment of SR makes it especially suitable for sustaining authoritarian and hierarchical models of work and political administration. This design obeys what Michel De Certeau calls "the Cartesian gesture," the strategic calculation and manipulation of a potentially resistant "exteriority" from the isolated, circumscribed base of an interior "will and power."[26]

As we shall see, the design described above—let us call it the mechanical design—more or less succeeds in simulating the determinism, foundationalism, and logicism characteristic of positivist accounts of science. To cite Feenberg,

> [T]he scientific logic of classification and calculation is the metaphoric equivalent of the techno-logic of machinery. The input of data, the raw material, is worked over by the axiomatic of the system, yielding an output of truths, goods, or wealth. The identity of syllogistic-mathematical reasoning with mechanism inspired science and technology, and gave a distinctive practical aspect to modern Reason that culminates in the computer. (Feenberg 1991, 111)

It suffices to note that the critical theory of design rationality deviates from both liberal and substantive theories by insisting on technology's ambivalent effects with respect to democracy. Marx was doubtless the first critical theorist to appreciate this fact. He believed that labor and technology were more than instrumental means for procuring subsistence and constituted forms of communication, or social intercourse, through which persons express their identities and develop their powers. The technological rationalization of labor and machinery set in motion by capitalism augments—but does not realize—this potential. Although technological innovations introduced to lower costs competitively often require more skilled forms of labor and more social—because functionally differentiated—labor processes, they typically skew the distribution of skills and coordination responsibilities in a vertical direction—toward management and away from labor.

As noted in chapter 1, Marx came to regard alienated labor as *the* principal source of all alienation—social as well as political. The split subject of liberal society—whose social essence is contradicted by its monadic and egoistic existence—is not primarily exemplified by the self-interested subject of rights alienated from his social identity as citizen, but by the *de-skilled* assembly-line worker alienated from her humanity. The worker alienates her intelligence, sociality, and creative autonomy to managers and technical experts who coordinate her labor with other similarly segmented and atomized production units. Meanwhile she becomes an increasingly undifferentiated cog in a machine—lost in the mindless tedium of repetitious routine and bereft of that vibrant communication so necessary for reflectively integrating—indeed experiencing—herself as an identity perduring beyond the momentary present.[27]

Marx's ambivalence with respect to the technological rationalization effected by capitalism is mirrored in his own uncertainty regarding the emancipatory potential of technology generally. Now, it is customary to think of Marx as a naïve believer in technological determinism—and thus as an optimistic believer in the liberal view of technology. Yet his own views on the matter suggest otherwise. It is true that Marx sometimes says that socialist society appropriates—without necessarily revolutionizing—the technical means of capitalist production. And he also says that the unemployment and tendential fall in profit rates that inevitably destroy capitalism are caused by the latter's *misuse* of these means. On the other hand, there are Marx's own heartrending accounts about how the technical design of capitalist machinery cripples, fragments, and stultifies the workers who are forced to become its passive appendages.

Remarks scattered throughout such middle-period works as *The German Ideology* and *Grundriße* suggest that Marx envisaged a fundamentally different kind of technical design as prerequisite for democratic community—one abolishing the division between mental and manual labor. Prior to the development of postindustrial information-based technologies it was hard to conceive of this possibility, since technologies were all designed with the aim of perfecting an automated control system that operated independently of workers' more flexible but fallible responses. Even Marx came to believe that technically efficient production could provide few if any opportunities for individual self-development—hence his hope that by augmenting the productivity of such alienated forms of labor more leisure time would be available for truly ennobling pursuits. Ironically, rationalized labor would cease to be the vehicle for creative self-expression, communication, and reflexive learning that the early Marx—perhaps thinking of simple craft production—thought it should be.

We can scarcely blame Marx for not envisaging the democratic potential of modern computer technology. And yet this technology confirms rather than disproves Marx's own ambivalence toward technology in general. On one hand, it exhibits what Feenberg calls "the principle of the conservation of hierarchy" (Feenberg 1991, 92). This principle has come to define efficient production under capitalism. David Noble (1984, pt. 2) has shown, for example, that the introduction of numerical control in technology design—first using a "record/playback" system that facilitated the exact replication of a skilled worker's operations and then a digital system that replaced them altogether—retained its popularity despite failing to increase productivity or lower costs as expected, simply because it enabled technological elites to maintain better control over their unskilled workers (Feenberg 1991, 35). Computer record keeping and surveillance have not only perfected this control; they have extended it throughout all segments of that "carceral" society that Foucault and others have found to be definitive of rationalized political systems.

That the concept of computer programming should evoke the specter of authoritarian control is hardly surprising. After all, cognitivists in artificial intelligence research have sought to simulate the basic calculative and classificatory functions of SR in "serial computers" that mechanically process data input by means of syntactical rules. Such linear processing produces decisions efficiently and authoritatively—albeit in ways that sacrifice learning. Of course, researchers in the field of cybernetics tried to extend mechanistic concepts of feedback, homeostasis, and control to self-organizing systems in biology and neurology, as evidenced by their talk of genetic codes and programming. But these attempts failed to simulate the reflexivity characteristic of flexible adaptation.

Mechanistic designs had their heyday when technologies incorporated rigid controls, such as gearing and cams. Thus their efficient deployment required hierarchical management. But this limitation no longer applies to electronic information technology.[28] The reason for this can be glimpsed in the research of neoconnectionists in cognitive science. Neoconnectionists have jettisoned serial processing in favor of parallel processing as a proper model of how the mind works. The vast internal complexity of neural networks involved in such skills as visual recognition operates on the basis of a statistical memory that is reflexively altered through new feedback. Besides rejecting cognitive determinism, neurophysiologists have questioned the foundationalist model of knowledge definitive of SR, noting that symbolic representation occurs against a background of practical interventions that cannot itself be represented—a scientific confirmation of the Heideggerian account of technical know-how as contextually situated interpretation.[29]

We noted above that scientific rationality is best described as practical, holistic, and communitarian. Our discussion of computer technology as a simulation of cognition has led us to the same conclusion. For, once we realize that perfect representability, replicability, and determinacy are impossible technological goals to strive for in a complex world, learning to cope with failure contextually becomes paramount. With the accent on learning instead of planning we can begin to realize the communicative potential inherent in computer technology. This potential confirms the "principle of subversive rationalization" that Feenberg and others find so conducive to democratization (Feenberg, 1991, 92).

> A new field of "collaborative technologies" has emerged to adapt computer programs to the exigencies of application by workgroups. Instead of appearing as tools for individuals, programs are designed as "groupware" for use by a whole team. The social and technical dimensions of computerized activity are integrated here in a way that recalls Hirschhorn's communication theory of automated machinery and Zuboff's discussion of the textualization of work. (107)

The result of using computer technology as a medium of communicative learning is that it shapes rather than represents what we are. Instead of detaching us from community in the isolation of our monadic modules, it can reconnect us. But as Feenberg remarks, "[A] self-referential logic of action is needed to grasp a democratic process that would have as its goal not escape from community to a commanding position above it, but internal self-development in common with others" (133).

If the above account is right, then the prevalent notion—held even by social democrats like Habermas—that technological efficiency imposes unavoidable constraints on democratic legitimation needs to be questioned. Means-ends rationality may well be an unsurpassable dimension of modern industrialism, but the ends in question will determine what we consider to be efficient means. Mass media can inform as well as distort, and they can foster rational discussion of ends instead of manipulation by other means.

In summation, this chapter has attempted to show that SR, evincing though it may the kind of abstraction found in scientific method *qua* mathematical and experimental procedure, suppresses its own communicative (or paradigmatic) conditions of possibility. This abstraction (or suppression) finds actual incarnation in technologies designed for monological purposes of calculation and control. CR, by contrast, captures the communitarian spirit of scientific research as well as the logic governing certain cybernetic technologies—technologies that play an increasingly important role in our world economy. This means, however, that practical reason, as a complex reflection of diverse perspectives—strategic, normative, and functional—is inherently indeterminate. Whatever stability and identity we ascribe to it (and ourselves) will be the outcome of an ongoing process of narrative interpretation, or communication—within the individual and without.

We have only glimpsed the CR informing this process. Until we get a clearer idea about what it means and how it inheres in our speech and behavior, we will not have established its rightful priority. Nor will we have understood its democratic potential. This task of clarification will only be completed at the end of our long journey. The next few chapters discuss aspects of it. These aspects—interpretative, poetic, and pragmatic—touch on distinct but complementary features of the legitimation problem. The pragmatic dimension of communication foregrounds the problem of democracy. The interpretative and poetic dimensions foreground the problem of legal and critical judgment. Obviously, all these problems and dimensions interpenetrate one another.

The next chapter focuses on the hermeneutic dimension, specifically as it relates to Anglo-American communitarianism. The practical holism discussed in this chapter strongly supports this variety of communitarianism. However, it also seems to mire us in an ethnocentrism more characteristic of SR than CR. Representative of such ethnocentrism is Richard Rorty, who at times has recommended that we "settle back into the 'relativism' which assumes that our only useful notions of 'true' and 'real' and 'good' are extrapolations . . . from practices and belief."[30] Rorty's endorsement of cultural incommensurability illustrates one of the dilemmas posed by hermeneutic pragmatism for communitarianism. This logic of exclusion contradicts the Hegelian notion of community as comprised of distinct but commensurable individuals. Indeed, Rorty's recent distinction between poetic discourses of irony and scientific (pragmatic) discourses of liberal hope reinstates the liberal separation of private and public realms, subjective preferences and objective reasons, with a vengeance.[31] Meanwhile his acceptance of historicism undercuts the scope of critical reflection and identity formation requisite for traditional legitimation.

I cannot go into a more detailed discussion of Rorty's views here. However, my brief mention of them ought to prepare the reader for the task ahead of us. Clearly the problem of relativism is complicated and cannot be dealt with all at once. Hence I propose to deal with cultural relativism (multiculturalism or pluralism) in chapters 3 through 7, reserving the treatment of historical relativism for the concluding chapter. Presently we must explore further the tension between *tradition* as a *determinate*, well-circumscribed basis for hermeneutically constituted identity and *interpretation* as an *indeterminate*, open-ended process of communication.

PART II

The Subject of Reason: Varieties of Communitarianism

3

Anglo-American Communitarianism
and the Dilemmas of Social Critique

So far I have argued that CR provides a richer, more satisfactory explanation of science, technology, and social action. And yet, as my concluding remarks about Rorty attest, acceptance of this explanation comes at a steep price. CR entails hermeneutical holism and thus hermeneutical indeterminacy. It appears as if belief and action are so dependent on particular contexts for their reason and meaning that there are no shared, perduring standards of criticism.

The threat to communitarianism is obvious. Without such standards rational community is simply inconceivable. Yet even with them it remains problematic. For communitarians derive their critical standards from the liberal societies they inhabit—not from transcendent reason. Walzer, whose own communitarian philosophy follows this path of *immanent* criticism, formulates the quandary—which I have hitherto characterized as the problem of contextual holism—in the following way: If communitarians criticize liberal *ideology* for misrepresenting the *real*, communitarian nature of society, then they cannot criticize liberal *society*. Yet if liberal society really is as liberal ideology portrays it, then liberalism is not an ideology whose standards of meaning and reason could be criticized—at least not in the culture-immanent manner allowed by communitarians (Walzer 1990).

One way to escape this dilemma is to argue that liberal theory exaggerates or overlooks disintegrative practices in liberal society. In the former instance, a critical space opens up between theory and practice; in the latter it opens up between different theories (or practices).

In chapter 1, I explored this second possibility; conflicting types of liberalism reflect conflicting aspects of liberal society. Recently liberal theorists have come to this same recognition, but have done so in a manner aimed at blunting the communitarian critique. Instead of concluding that liberal society is hopelessly torn between conflicting principles of justice, Rawls presents his own principles of justice as possible candidates for consideration as consensual standards. In his opinion, they represent a middle ground wherein Lockean (libertarian) and Rousseauean (communitarian) *traditions* converge, the former stressing basic civil rights, the latter "equal liberties and values of public life" (Rawls 1993, 5). Thus, his theory of justice now approximates a qualified communitarian stance in three respects: it shows how libertarian and communitarian conceptions of justice complement one another; it justifies them as workable interpretations of commonly shared traditions; and it explains how even opposed *comprehensive* moral visions overlap, or converge, in underwriting this traditional consensus.

Does this turn to tradition signal a new and improved approach to immanent criticism? If so, does it avoid the conundrums of SR that we discussed in conjunction with Rawls's earlier attempt to ground principles of justice? Despite his hermeneutical turn, Rawls repeats the strategy deployed in *A Theory of Justice*: One begins by working out the principles of justice governing the basic structure of society from the standpoint of the original position and ends with a *pragmatic* defense of its workability, or acceptability vis-à-vis the peculiar moral psychology and pluralism pertinent to democratic political culture. Whereas the first stage *abstracts* from the conflicting, comprehensive religious, philosophical, and moral doctrines that comprise the full *moral identity* of hypothetical contractors, the second stage shows how they converge on an *overlapping consensus* supportive of the principles argued for.

Now, Rawls presents his notion of an overlapping consensus as a possible solution to the problem of pluralism. If successful it would show how immanent criticism is possible. Or rather, it would show how shared and perduring—and to that extent rational and transcendent—principles of justice might arise from particular, incommensurable traditions and their thick conceptions of the good. On one hand, he concedes that the diversity of conflicting comprehensive doctrines is a "permanent feature of the public culture of democracy" generated by the sheer freedom afforded by that culture (144). On the other hand, he allows that any *reasonable* compre-hensive doctrine and thus any reasonable conception of the *good* will gen-erate reasons—*not necessarily shared* by other such doctrines—supportive of the *abstract rights* and principles underwriting our *institutional identity* (30).

Rawls imagines such a consensus as a two-step process. Initially—per-haps after religious warfare and intolerance—a modus vivendi is reached that issues in a constitutional consensus. Such a consensus "is not deep and it is also not wide: it is narrow in scope, not including the basic structure but only the political procedures of democratic government" (159). It is also not strong, for if those who have consented should number them-selves among a dominant majority, they will be tempted to subordinate the provisions of the constitution to their own comprehensive doctrine (148). Over time, however, persons' comprehensive doctrines may loosen or become fragmented, while the advantages of publicly reasoned consti-tutional protections gain support as "freestanding." Debating policies in a public forum encourages persons to ground their moral opinions in more abstract principles that have a wider currency than the peculiar compre-hensive doctrines with which they identify; in the meantime, judges will also be required to articulate the unified meaning of constitutional provi-sions in terms of such principles. Finally, the *breadth* of an overlapping con-sensus—including agreement on substantive rights and principles of fair and equal opportunity and the satisfaction of basic needs—can be expected to arise from a rational desire to effect a cohesive union, in which all persons are guaranteed a certain level of education and material well-being requisite for participating as full-fledged citizens (166).

Rawls's notion of overlapping consensus explains the possibility of social cooperation based on traditional—not metaphysical—grounds. It does not, however, explain the possibility of community, much less a vibrant politi-cal culture expressive of public reason. Rawls is clear about the former point: *if* community is understood as an association whose unity rests on a comprehensive conception of the good, then it cannot be the overarching idea underlying a just democracy (146). He is less clear about the latter point. He himself argues that the possibility of an overlapping consensus—and thus of a political culture based on public reason—requires that persons appeal to just those political values, general beliefs, common forms of rea-soning, and scientific methods and conclusions that "others can reasonably be expected to endorse" (224–26). Such "gag rules," however,

> do not apply to our personal deliberations and reflections about politi-cal questions, or to the reasoning about them by members of associa-tions such as churches and universities, all of which is a vital part of

the background culture. Plainly, religious, philosophical, and moral considerations of many kinds may here properly play a role. But the ideal of public reason does hold for citizens when they engage in political advocacy in the public forum and thus for members of political parties and for candidates in their campaigns and for other groups who support them. It holds equally for how citizens are to vote in elections when constitutional essentials are at stake. (215)

Rawls is certainly right to allow religious, philosophical, and other substantive moral considerations to play a role in *informal* political discussions. Yet even if one concedes that formal parliamentary and court proceedings are less wide open in this respect, there are—as Dworkin and Elster have shown—no grounds for assuming that such considerations never ought to play any role there. The expectation appears even less reasonable when applied to voting. Indeed, it might have the perverse effect of lulling citizens into not reflecting too deeply about their most basic commitments. For once a belief is abstracted from the comprehensive doctrine and practical background in which it originally functioned, it ceases to be a deeply held conviction, having lost the very context from which its fuller meaning, purpose, and rationale derive. Related to this diminution of reflection is a more serious impairment in Rawlsian public reason, namely, its subjectivization of comprehensive doctrines. On one hand, public reason makes possible critical dialogue across different conceptions of the good in that it forces us to regard our own and other conceptions as mere interpretations rather than dogmas. On the other hand, it does this by bracketing the very truth claims accompanying our comprehensive doctrines that motivate us to engage in serious, transformative dialogue in the first place.

From a communitarian perspective, this ambivalence can be explained by the fact that Rawls's model of public reason subordinates the aim of political culture to that of justice, understood as fair social cooperation. It neglects the fact that democracy often involves debating policies designed to advance the substantive interests of specific groups, and that group-specific privileges of this sort first find articulation in discussions where comprehensive doctrines—and thus conflicting interpretations of an overlapping consensus—mutually inform one another. As our examination of Walzer and Taylor will confirm, these discussions over the respect and concern owed to groups as speech communities "solidified" by distinct—if also fluid and overlapping—identities, is also a struggle for recognition, justice, and integrity. Witness, for example, the struggle between French Quebecois and Canadian nationalists. Does Rawls really think that this struggle can be negotiated without the public articulation of specific goods and ways of life associated with conflicting comprehensive doctrines? Supposing he did not, could he allow its articulation if it impinged on the scope of formal constitutional rights?

As we shall see below, the question about basic rights is complicated by the fact that persons are owed respect not only as bearers of abstract rights but as members of discrete communities whose future survival—as a distinct locus of cultural identity and self-worth—is at stake. It is not clear whether Rawls's conception of public reason can requite this latter form of right. Perhaps he thinks that it need not, since, as he himself points out, justice as fairness is not neutral with respect to all comprehensive goods, *even* if they are reasonable. In any case, by splitting our identity into comprehensive and institutional, moral and political aspects, he leaves no room for politically adjudicating multicultural struggles for recognition. Consequently, he leaves no room for the kind of immanent criticism that works through the dialogical resolution of multicultural conflicts.

The communitarian critiques of liberal society discussed in section 1 below focus on this deficit. Although some are more willing to accommodate "liberal" conflict than others, all agree that conflicts regarding social identity and comprehensive conceptions of the good ought not to be privatized or excluded from political fora in the a priori manner demanded by SR. That part of our moral identity—and that part of our comprehensive vision of the good—which ought to remain outside of public reason must itself be negotiated *through* public reason. Otherwise, liberal democracy at best facilitates a modus vivendi among partial associations, not a moral community composed of mutually recognized subcommunities.

After discussing possible ways in which liberal society might accommodate communitarian reform, I turn next to the theoretical problem of justifying such reform (sec. 2). Communitarian responses to this problem generally fall somewhere between two extremes. One extreme—practical holism—tries to ground conceptions of virtue and value in the objective meanings constitutive of social practices. The other extreme—theoretical holism—eschews any grounding and instead reduces meaning and value to beliefs about observable behavior. Practical holists like MacIntyre tend to be traditionalist (or neo-Aristotelian) in bent; theoretical holists—here represented by Rorty—tend to be postmodern, but otherwise liberal and democratic. Despite their considerable differences, neither succeeds in establishing a viable notion of CR capable of generating shared, perduring standards of criticism.

The next section (sec. 3) examines a communitarian philosopher who does. Gadamer's hermeneutics reconstructs understanding as a dialogic "fusion of horizons." Implicit in this notion of understanding is an ideal expectation of coherence and perfect reasonableness that also implies a model of unconstrained communication, or CR. I argue—with Habermas—that this *procedural* ideal of justice serves as a criterion for questioning distorted communication, or ideology. Unfortunately, Gadamer's conservative interpretation of it exhibits the limits of a purely hermeneutic model of social critique unqualified by functionalist explanation.

Another problem with Gadamer's hermeneutics—one following again from his principle of perfectibility—is its understanding of community as a coherent, unified text. Although this problem has been the enduring focus of recent debates among French postmodernists, a number of Anglo-American communitarian thinkers have made it the predominant theme of their own work as well. Two of them—Walzer and Taylor—have attempted to redeem the plural, multicultural, and multivalent sources of good circulating in liberal society on a firmer, communitarian basis. On one hand, they deploy a strategy of accommodation (Warnke 1993, 112) that resonates more with the liberal principle of separateness and tolerance than it does with the communitarian principle of communicative integration. On the other hand, they appeal to a higher communal good that bears striking resemblance to Gadamer's own principle of perfectibility—and my notion of aesthetic rationality. This suggests a possible response to the question concerning the relative priority of universal individual rights vis-à-vis particular concrete goods. The hermeneutical expectation of coherence and perfectibility grounds ideals of justice (reciprocity) and integrity (solidarity) underwriting CR equally deeply.

1. I would like to begin my discussion of these issues by briefly recalling some highlights of the communitarian critique of liberal society. Now, Anglo-American communitarian critiques of liberal society are as numerous and diverse as the critics who proffer them. For convenience' sake, I shall simply focus on a few main figures who reflect some of this diversity. The spectrum ranges from traditional antimodernists, like MacIntyre, to liberal postmodernists like Rorty and Walzer. Those on one side of the spectrum believe that community and liberalism are incompatible under any description; those on the other side disagree. There are also thematically oriented communitarian critiques of liberal society—such as those emanating from socialist or feminist concerns—whose representatives span the entire range of this spectrum.

Let us begin with the traditionalist critique. MacIntyre's diagnosis of liberal society focuses on the dialectical affinity between radical individualism and bureaucratic collectivism that I discussed in the first chapter. In a culture dominated by *emotivism*, which reduces moral judgments to expressions of *personal* approval or disapproval, modern politics—to paraphrase Clausewitz—amounts to little more than "civil war carried on by other means" (MacIntyre 1981, 236). For MacIntyre this means that the difference between our Hobbesian state and its Stalinist counterpart is one of degree only. In the final analysis, Marxism and liberalism are but variations of a single culture. That culture—which extols emancipation through scientific enlightenment—destroys the fabric of tradition, thereby uprooting us from our very identity.

MacIntyre frames this *contradiction* in terms of a stark antithesis between the modern bureaucratic state and morality in general (1994, 316). The social contractarian elements of the modern liberal state comprise formal rights that presumably provide universally accepted ground rules regulating potential conflict. As we just saw in the case of Rawls, these rules of reason accommodate diverse conceptions of the good as well as the traditions that sustain them, but only by consigning them to the status of irrational, subjective preferences. Formal democratic procedures permit such goods to be aggregated and weighed, yet conflicts regarding the substantive meaning of these and other procedures, and thus ultimately between substantive goods themselves, can only be resolved by legal fiat. Ironically, then, the subjectivization of substantive conceptions of the good precludes just that form of rational dialogue necessary for testing the objective validity of those procedures designed to adjudicate conflicts in the first place (MacIntyre 1988, 344).

Of course, utilitarian and deontological strands of liberal morality do sometimes require that we test the rational coherence and instrumental efficacy of substantive traditions from a transcendent perspective. In this instance, however, liberalism stands in potential conflict to those patriotic virtues requisite for maintaining the state during times of war. Liberals make poor soldiers. Indeed, liberal morality makes poor citizens, since no appeal to abstract reason can *motivate* virtuous conduct in the absence of moral character shaped by tradition. For this reason, MacIntyre concludes that what Habermas calls "constitutional patriotism"—or loyalty to a country based on its institutionalization of *universal* civil and democratic rights— is incoherent (1994, 317).

To be sure, traditionalists like MacIntyre are not opposed to civil and democratic rights. They merely insist, following Edmund Burke, that their justification and scope be grounded in the *particular* conceptions of virtue and good that emanate from parochial tradition. For this reason, true patriotism is incompatible with nations that have disowned their *true* history, as was the case with the former USSR, or succumbed to reciprocal self-interest, as is currently the case with the United States (316).

Despite its resemblance to some of the points argued for in chapter 1, MacIntyre's gloomy prognosis of liberal society leaves modernists like myself without anything to pin our hopes on. At its most extreme it simply denies that moral virtue of any kind is possible in modern society. However, at other moments it asserts that at least some of the practices essential to liberal society *do* embody virtues, and that these, in turn, serve as linchpins for shared identity. Indeed, his own acknowledgment that the human good is radically heterogeneous—so that there is no rational principle for ranking, synthesizing, and choosing goods—suggests a condition of complexity and conflict more in tune with modernism than with traditionalism (MacIntyre 1981, 133).[1]

I will return to the problem of accommodating virtue within a modern society in chapters 4, 5, and 6. More recently MacIntyre has focused his discussion of conflict on a somewhat different set of issues revolving around the rational resolution of crises internal to traditions. Siding with Hegel against Rawls, he argues that the rationality of any tradition depends on working out its internal conflicts dialectically. In extreme cases, this tradition-immanent dialogue must assume the form of a cross-cultural dialogue between otherwise incommensurable traditions.

MacIntyre's account of rational dialogue as a counterweight to liberalism's reduction of traditional truth claims to subjective preferences is no doubt necessary for retrieving a model of consensual learning based on CR. But, as we shall see in chapter 5, such learning must be founded on liberal, democratic institutions in the manner proposed by Habermas. A variety of communitarianism tending in this direction—one, in my opinion, that recognizes the traditional authority underlying liberal values—may be found in the writings of Taylor and Walzer, who attempt to forge a modern communitarian vision that preserves significant aspects of enlightenment rationalism and liberalism.

Taylor's position is in fact very similar to my own. In his opinion, the story of "hypertrophy" advanced by MacIntyre and Weber—that rational emancipation undermines its own traditional raison d'être—is "too crude" because it fails to appreciate how *complexly* interwoven are the freedom, equality, and technological spirit *integral* to the modern identity (Taylor 1994, 57). Given this complexity, the proper aim of communitarian criticism, he avers, is to "rescue" these values "in their integrity" from distortions wrought by capitalism.

Now, Taylor argues that contemporary liberal society is in the throes of a legitimation crisis caused by the conflicting demands of capitalism and communal identity. This crisis is also an identity crisis, since the *instrumentalism* fueling capitalist growth itself constitutes an important component of our identity. More precisely, that identity is characterized by notions of autonomy, nature, and efficacy that have their distant sources in Greco-Roman and Judeo-Christian thought, but only recently evolved into their recognizably modern forms beginning around the seventeenth century. The first phase of this process, which culminated in the Enlightenment, gave rise to the notion of free human beings who find their purposes (or nature) *within* themselves. Along with humanistic inwardness, the privileging of everyday life over spiritual salvation marks a new concern with science and rational control (instrumentalism). The romantic celebration of free, creative expressivity and moral striving marks the second phase of our modern identity. Together these phases comprise four dimensions of the modern identity: freedom, equality, productivity, and sovereignty. In short, modern subjects understand themselves as bearers of equal rights who are also citizens and producers.

Liberal society seems to satisfy the needs of the modern identity; it provides us with the privacy and intimate community requisite for exploring our expressive needs, and it provides us with the economic growth requisite for satisfying our material needs, acquiring independence from nature, and realizing our aims. In fact, as Taylor notes, capitalism ends up suppressing the expressive side of our identity beneath the instrumental. And it does so in ways that violate our freedom, nature, and efficacy. Taylor here recites a litany of horrors familiar to Marxists: "These features of industrial society—the meaninglessness and subordination of work; the mindless lack of control of priorities; above all the fetishization of commodities—all represent a challenge to our image of ourselves as realized moderns determining our purposes out of ourselves, dominating and not being dominated by things" (66).

Taylor summarizes his indictment by noting that "the very success of the growth of consumption tends to discredit the importance attached to material gains; the increasing stress on the goal of self-fulfillment tends to fragment the family, which was previously its privileged focus; and the increased concentration and mobility of our society alienates us from government" (68). These effects become more widespread as Western capitalism assimilates exogenous cultures to the superficial but hegemonic identity of a uniform consumer society. Such cultural imperialism not only undermines the rich variety of traditions necessary for gaining a critical self-understanding of one's own tradition, but it also lays waste to local environments and nature, thereby eliminating another source of transcendent meaning and purpose.

Taylor concludes that "freedom of mobility has begun to destroy the very conditions, in family and citizen community, of the identity of freedom" in much the same way that our "efficacy as producers has come to threaten our efficacy as citizens" (70). Indeed, the statistical increase in disintegration—revolving around residential displacement, divorce and separation within the family, social standing, and political loyalty—shows to what extent Americans have become uprooted from family, community, and tradition. These "four mobilities" (as Walzer puts it) are at best ambiguous. Although they allow persons to escape from oppressive circumstances that prevent them from reshaping (and reintegrating) their identities, they also allow them to shed commitments and backgrounds necessary for stabilizing them (Walzer 1990).

As we shall see, Walzer's own concerns about capitalism are not fundamentally different from Taylor's. Both see it as hegemonic and destructive of liberal community, properly conceived. Thus, although they question the separation of public and private life—arguing, for example, that the private spheres of production and reproduction need to be democratized—they mostly stress the opposite danger—the invasion of the family and community by corporations and government bureaucracies.

By contrast, an important strand of communitarian feminism attempts to reverse this influence by seeking to domesticate state and economy. On one hand, due consideration is given to such facts as the so-called "feminization of poverty," the paternalism of welfare, the degradation of and violence against women, and other gendered effects of contemporary liberal society. On the other hand, consideration is also given to the manner in which patriarchy has migrated from the private to the public sphere. Again, coming from a rather different direction, some feminists—especially those influenced by the work of developmental psychologist Carol Gilligan—have suggested that the formal rights and judicial/administrative hierarchies anchoring the public culture of liberal society reflect a masculine bias that allows no voice to feminine virtues of caring and solidarity essential to nurturing. Hence it is argued that liberal society cannot aspire to a true democratic community unless it incorporates this domestic voice in its legal, political, and economic institutions (Benhabib 1992).

This last diagnosis has much to recommend it. Still it remains to be seen whether an ethic of care can be extended to public institutions riven by conflict.[2] Likewise, it remains to be seen whether it comprises a distinct type of postconventional morality or merely a suppressed aspect of a broader, nongendered morality.[3] If I am not mistaken the caring and solidarity constitutive of the public good—no less than the freedom and equality constitutive of individual rights—are values implicit in CR, in which case the oft-cited opposition between sentiment and reason that supposedly adheres in the distinction between an ethics of care and an ethics of justice will need to be reexamined.

All of this by way of anticipation. Needless to say, the recent spate of communitarian critiques has not been wanting in substantive proposals for reform. These can be grouped along a spectrum ranging from the conservative endorsement of traditional values and virtues compatible with capitalist economy to more radical reforms.

Emblematic of middle and extreme positions are the reform initiatives advanced by Galston, Sunstein, and Walzer. Galston's falls squarely within the conservative—but also progressive—range of reform proposals. Reconciled to the inevitable incompatibility of classical virtue—with its privileging of civic participation over private life—and liberal individualism, Galston seeks cultivation of just those cultural conditions necessary for fostering distinctly liberal goods and virtues. Since he is not really a communitarian, the substantive goods he thinks ought to be promoted in liberal society do not converge on a summum bonum, but gravitate around avoidance of cruelty and other evils (or vices, as Judith Shklar puts it), on one hand, and cultivation of civic capacities—instrumentalism, rationality, freedom, and so forth—on the other. Besides tolerance, liberal virtue, he remarks, demands adherence to a nonascetic work ethic, moderation and responsibility in managing one's life, familial fidelity, adaptability, and willingness to resolve conflict through open discussion. Complementing these *instrumental* virtues are those virtuous *ends* encompassing individual excellence, moral duty, autonomy, and dignity. Galston concludes that these cultural prerequisites are incompatible with spiraling budget deficits, poverty, welfare dependency, consumerism, family breakdown, "and the growing barbarization and tribalization of American life" (236). Yet, despite the fact that he thinks these problems are *structural,* his own recommendations for reform sound remarkably restrained: revitalization of a civic education that encourages dogmatic acceptance—not skepticism—of basic liberal democratic values; and endorsement of *functional*—as opposed to *intrinsic*—traditionalism, which esteems stable families and strong values grounded in religious faith or moral duty.

Although salutary, Galston's recommendations do not go far enough in addressing the structural problems of a market economy and the ancillary tensions between civic solidarity and personal perfection. The minimalist conception of the good he advocates is not appreciably different from Rawls's thin (or neutral) conception of the good, which he criticizes for being too thin. Indeed, he no less than Rawls wants to accommodate heterogeneous conceptions of the good life. Yet this liberal defense of tolerance, coupled with Galston's rationalist critique of "hierarchies of race, gender and ethnicity" (1991, 280), clashes with the parochial dogmatism of his "communitarian" vision, which extols two-parent families, religion-based moral virtue, and other traditional values. This contradiction is summed up in his insistence on inculcating an "unswerving belief in the correctness of one's own way of life" unsullied by that "respect for opposing points of view and ways of life" advocated by Amy Gutmann—a policy, one would think, that could hardly be more hostile to liberal open-mindedness and multicultural learning (253–54).[4]

More insightful in this respect are Sunstein's proposals for reform, which allow greater leeway for public coercion and government paternalism in removing just those *ideological* obstacles to the promotion of individual freedom and welfare that originate in traditional prejudices and economic constraints. The spirit of these proposals is best captured by Elster's own critique (1986) of instrumentalist views of democracy as a market simulator. Echoing Amos Tversky's objection that voters' choices conceal rather than reveal preferences—either because the most preferred options are deemed to be too risky or too unpleasant to implement, or because the preferences themselves are inherently defective—Elster contends that justice, not preference aggregation, ought to be the proper aim of democratic politics. The problem with counteradaptive preferences (I prefer X because it is rare or forbidden) and adaptive preferences (I prefer X because it is easily obtained or widely preferred) is that they violate the criterion of autonomous choice in being determined by extraneous and irrelevant factors. This irrationality is tolerable in a market in which only the consumer suffers for his or her defective preferences. In a democracy, however, others are made to suffer—unjustly—as well.

Sunstein agrees that liberal tolerance of "revealed" *subjective* preferences ("subjective welfarism") is misplaced when these preferences are not an expression of rational, autonomous choice (Sunstein 1991, 294). Preferences shaped by past conditioning, misinformation, and market pressures—rather than by sustained, critical deliberation in a political forum—do not have the moral standing of "interests" that democratic polities are compelled to acknowledge. Indeed, in Sunstein's opinion, democracies are obligated to override them if they conflict with the freedom and welfare of citizens. This applies in the case of addictions, prejudices and uninformed opinions shaped by unjust background conditions, narrow-minded or shortsighted pursuit of personal aims provoked by a market mentality, and general ideological aspirations intolerant of basic rights (299).

To remedy these distortions, Sunstein proposes legal reforms in four major areas of public life: (1) greater subsidies for high quality public broadcasting and increased regulation of commercial broadcasting; (2) "programs that attempt to respond to the deprivations faced by poor people—most obviously by eliminating poverty, but also through broad public education and regulatory efforts designed to make cultural resources generally available regardless of wealth" (301); (3) legal reclassification of "hate speech," gratuitous depictions of violence (in television entertainment, for example), and pornography in the same category as commercial speech, libel, and bribery; and (4) regulation of campaign expenditures combined with proportional and group representation "as a kind of second-best solution for the real-world failures of Madisonian deliberation" (306).

Although Sunstein's reforms are on the whole judicious, the paternalistic spirit in which they're proposed strikes me as altogether elitist and undemocratic. It matters whether public coercion is the outcome of democratic discussion regarding the collective reasonableness of preferences or of unilateral intervention by appointed elites. Sunstein himself no doubt favors the former of these procedures, but he seems to endorse as a pragmatic, "second-best solution to the real-world failures of Madisonian deliberation" the paternalistic remedies enjoined by the courts. However, unilateral judicial activism unsupported by popular political mandates is a poor substitute for democratic politics (witness, for example, the decline of the civil rights movement as a *political* force), and in any case has proven in recent years to be more of a hindrance to the implementation of the reforms Sunstein proposes.

More radical suggestions for democratic reform of the sort I will propose in chapter 5 have been advanced by Walzer. Despite his pessimism about the fate of participatory democracy in the West, Walzer's recent reflections on the communitarianism/liberalism debate suggest that the welfare state might still plumb the liberal *tradition* for associative bases that are otherwise absent in liberal theory and that are becoming increasingly moribund in liberal society. The strengthening of the Wagner Act, which actively fostered union organization in America during the Great Depression; the use of tax exemptions and matching grants to religious groups for purposes of establishing day care centers, nursing homes, hospitals, and so on; the passage of plant-closing laws designed to afford protection to local communities of work and residence; the strengthening of local governments through federal revenue sharing—these are steps that the welfare state could take to offset the fragmenting tendencies of voluntary association and the complementary growth of bureaucracy. The latter, in turn, would also further the kind of communitarian ethic defended by MacIntyre and other neo-Aristotelians, in that it would encourage "the development and display of civic virtue in a pluralist variety of settings" (Walzer 1990, 20).

I will return to Walzer's more detailed discussion of democratic reform—especially as it pertains to workplace democracy—at the conclusion of this chapter. Presently, we need to get a clearer understanding of how the interpretative basis of society discussed in chapter 2 sheds light on the moral premises underlying the communitarian critiques discussed above. The epistemological and metaphysical premises of communitarianism—the contextualism of belief and practice that it brings to bear against liberal rationalism, on one hand, and the socially situated nature of identity that it brings to bear against liberal subjectivism, on the other—are indeed established by the interpretative basis of society. However, these alone do not suffice to justify the priority of the good over the right or the priority of communal self-determination over individual choice.

The next section focuses on this problem by examining two extremes: a traditionalistic communitarianism emphasizing *practical* holism, and a postmodern communitarianism emphasizing *theoretical* holism. Despite their apparent differences, neither of these approaches excludes the other, and indeed they converge on roughly the same impasse: a recrudescence of a kind of SR whose relativism (or skepticism) obstructs rational critique.

2. Now, the two extremes I have in mind are Rorty's "ironic" liberalism and MacIntyre's dogmatic communitarianism. That hermeneutical holism alone fails as justification for a strong communitarian program is amply borne out by the former. Nonetheless, as we shall see, there is a sense in which Rorty's Deweyan liberalism—filtered through the lens of postmodern aestheticism—resonates with a notion of community possessing some critical content. I shall argue at the conclusion of this chapter that it is precisely this aestheticism that enables such communitarian criticism. However, Rorty's way of conceiving the aesthetic has the unfortunate and ironic consequence of subjectivizing it—in effect, detaching it from a public-based CR of the sort necessary for sustaining critical understanding. Diametrically opposed to this kind of subjectivism is MacIntyre's own traditional communitarianism. In my opinion, his account of practically embodied virtues provides a salutary counterbalance to Rorty's nominalism and historicism. Yet it remains as entangled in historicism as Rorty's own account. In truth, both philosophers waver between modern universalism, on one hand, and traditional parochialism or postmodern skepticism, on the other. Although it is tempting to dissolve relativism and skepticism by embracing a radical form of practical holism of the sort proffered by Dreyfus, this solution, it seems to me, promises more than it delivers. For, in the final analysis, practical understanding is always already articulated within a narrative self-understanding that aims at theoretical enlargement.

First let's look at Rorty's fascinating blend of liberal and communitarian, modern and postmodern themes. *Contingency, Irony, and Solidarity* (1989) takes as its point of departure Donald Davidson's philosophy of language. According to Rorty, Davidson's "nonreductive behaviorist" conception of language enables us to do without traditional conceptions of meaning, reference, expressivity, and intentionality (Rorty 1989, 15). There is certainly no doubt that Davidson's pragmatic holism reduces linguistic understanding to a form of radical translation that does Quine's one better. For on Davidson's account, "meaning" is just our best translation—relative to our own linguistic behavior—of the causes motivating the highly local and idiosyncratic linguistic behavior of others. Since "passing theories" of what others mean by their peculiar malapropisms and novel metaphors suffice for purposes of translation, we can dispense altogether with the idea of a language, understood as a system of normative conventions.

Rorty draws several important epistemological and ontological conclusions from this theoretical holism. The utter contingency of language as a context-specific tool privileges the aesthetic function of metaphorical *effect* over the cognitive function of *representation*. Truth "tokens" continue to function in language, but truth as a deep relationship to some nonlinguistic reality ceases to be meaningful. Rorty rightly concludes from this that scientific revolutions are, in the words of Mary Hesse, "metaphoric redescriptions" (Rorty 1989, 16). But his own take on what this means for an ontology of self and community deviates markedly from conventional communitarianism. Rorty agrees with Nietzsche that the "process of coming to know oneself, confronting one's contingency, tracking one's causes home, is identical with the process of inventing a new language—that is, of thinking up some new metaphors" (27). The only society capable of protecting and nourishing this metaphoric capacity is one that, in the illustrious tradition of liberalism extending from Mill to Dewey, permits "experiments in living." In short, it is none other than liberal democracy that creates the private space necessary for cultivating "strong poets" (to use Harold Bloom's phrase). Such a "poeticized culture" would require a high degree of irony and toleration. And since neither tradition nor reason are accepted as authoritative sources of ultimate truth, it would require the radical politicization—indeed, democratization—of all public matters.

Here we see both the strengths and weaknesses of Rorty's "liberal utopia" as a democratic communitarian project. Its strengths lie in its social democratic defense of inclusive, undistorted, free, and equal communication of the sort that Habermas and others have proposed. Its weakness lies in its "ethnocentrism," that is, its open rejection of the universal CR that Habermas and I think is necessary for justifying it.

Rorty is sympathetic to communitarian concerns in his conviction that "the forces unleashed by the Enlightenment have undermined the Enlightenment's own convictions" (56). However, unlike traditional communitarians—and radical critics like Adorno and Horkheimer—he rejects only the *rationalism* of the Enlightenment, not liberalism, much less capitalism. He sounds most communitarian when, citing Oakeshott and Hegel, he says that we ought to think of morality not as some abstract, universal principle, but as "the voice of ourselves as members of a community, speakers of a common language," whose principled reflection on common purposes remains bound to specific institutions and practices (59). He sounds most liberal, however, when he draws "a firm distinction" between the public and the private (93). As he so felicitously puts it, "My private purposes, and the part of my final vocabulary which is not relevant to my public actions, are none of your business" (97).

Surely no communitarian would cavil with the need for privacy. But the question is: Can one critically order one's private purposes apart from public discourse, and can the boundary separating private and public spheres be drawn independently of democratic political debate? To the former query Rorty responds: "Nothing can serve as a criticism of a person save another person, or of a culture save another culture . . . [since] our doubts about our own characters or our own culture can be resolved or assuaged only by enlarging our acquaintance" (80). Well and good. But Rorty's response to the second question is much murkier. Feminists who deny Rorty's claim that "sexual matters are of merely private concern" (196) would press for treating the private in a public, political way. For the private oppression of women—spousal battery and rape, exploitation of domestic labor, denial of women's *rights* to abortion, and so on—are clearly legal issues.

Let us assume that Rorty, as a good communitarian, agrees that the boundaries separating private and public spheres cannot be fixed a priori. There still remains the problem of how seriously his liberal will take public discourse. According to Rorty, the ideal liberal has jettisoned Enlightenment rationality in favor of radical nominalism and historicism. He or she will thus adopt an *ironic* stance toward the "metaphysics . . . woven into the public rhetoric of modern liberal societies" that requires taking the universal scope of our knowledge and moral claims seriously (82). Although we can still appeal to the "traditional metaphysical distinctions" of reason and logic, we will give them "a respectable ironist sense by sociologizing them—treating them as distinctions between contingently existing sets of practices, or strategies employed within such practices, rather than between natural kinds" (83).

The sociological approach to our communicative behavior is necessitated by Rorty's Davidsonian vision of language, which reduces the first-person, *normative* utterances persons speak when addressing one another within the *performative* (or interactive) mode to third-person, *factual* descriptions about linguistic causes and effects. But even Rorty concedes that this detached, onlooker attitude toward language is incompatible with the communitarian way we *participate* in it, namely as *actors* who have been *socialized* into communicatively constituted roles, expectations, and identities.

> But even if I am right in thinking that a liberal culture whose public rhetoric is nominalist and historicist is both possible and desirable, I cannot go on to claim that there could or ought to be a culture whose public rhetoric is *ironist*. I cannot imagine a culture which socialized its youth in such a way as to make them continually dubious about their own process of socialization. Irony seems inherently a private matter. (87)

Several uncommunitarian consequences follow from this behaviorist account of language. First, liberals who think behavioristically but interact with others dialogically are radically divided and alienated selves—Rorty describes them as "uprooted"—of the sort described in chapter 1. Second, as ironists they are radically detached from the kind of Socratic dialogue that Rorty himself thinks necessary for aesthetic and moral self-development. Third, behaviorist accounts of language entail a more radical ethnocentrism than even Rorty—himself an unabashed "bluff philistine" and ethnocentrist—countenances. To paraphrase Gadamer's critique of the historicism and nominalism of the romantic school of history: The detached standpoint bequeathed to Rorty and Davidson *via the Enlightenment* ends up fragmenting the historical and cultural landscape into *intrinsically* meaningless atoms of subjective expression or of brute behavior. The only way to "identify" with these facts for purposes of "understanding" is by *comparatively abstracting* the formal, universal core that they share with humanity at large. Rorty himself seems to appeal to such a positivistic method of induction when he says that *solidarity* with other persons remote from us is only possible by seeing their differences as "unimportant when compared with similarities with respect to pain and humiliation" (p. 192). But surely, beyond this merely *aesthetic* empathy we have for sentient beings as such we can *also* obtain a higher solidarity based on *mutual understanding*. Rorty agrees—as evidenced by his own Gadamerian talk of expanding horizons—without apparently realizing that his extensionalist account of language prevents him from doing so.

Last but not least, symptomatic of Rorty's conceptual behaviorism we find an odd instrumental complement to his celebration of the "radical diversity" of private purposes and the "radically poetic character of individual lives," namely, his belief in social engineering: "I want to see freely arrived at agreement as agreement on how to accomplish common purposes, e.g., *prediction* and *control* of the *behavior* of atoms or *people*, equalizing life-chances, decreasing cruelty" (67; my italics). Such instrumentalism, if it is not contradicted by the dynamic metaphoricity of interpretatively constituted social relations and self-understandings, is at least incompatible with the antibureaucratic, democratic thrust of Rorty's utopianism.

To summarize, Rorty—quite rightly, I think—wants to expand the range of "rational" communication (or argument) to include a strong aesthetic (metaphorical) and rhetorical dimension. In this respect his appeal to Kuhn and Dewey against Habermas is to be applauded. Where he goes astray is in opposing the aesthetic dimension to communicative rationality—an error that directly follows from his behaviorist conception of language. Indeed, as we shall see in chapter 8, it is only because Kuhn has an *intensionalist* account of linguistic meaning that he, not Davidson, can show how metaphor bridges radically incommensurable paradigms in a manner that explains the *internal rationale* and traditional legitimacy of scientific revolutions. In other words, the story of progress that Rorty, following Hans Blumenberg, wants to retrospectively tell about "all the things characteristic of your time of which you most approve, with which you most unflinchingly identify" can only be told if history is more than a succession of *contingent* gestalt switches (55).

2.1 The questions about relativism raised by Rorty's and Davidson's peculiar brand of theoretical holism will be addressed in my consideration of Gadamer below. Presently, I would like to turn my attention to the more practically oriented holism of MacIntyre and Dreyfus.

MacIntyre's practical communitarianism can be understood as a reaction to the sort of conceptual and instrumental behaviorism advanced by Rorty. In general, he thinks behaviorism and liberalism reflect the same rational formalism. Although he believes that predictive social science of the sort to which behaviorism aspires is doomed to shatter on the hermeneutic indeterminacy of social life, he nonetheless thinks that it provides just the necessary ideological underpinnings for bureaucratic social engineering.

At the same time, MacIntyre cannot be too complacent about hermeneutic indeterminacy, since it threatens to subjectivize and relativize the purposefulness of life in a decidedly anticommunitarian direction. His strategy, then, is to try to show how a teleological core of meaning is objectively embedded in the constitutive roles and norms of social *practice*. Having abandoned *natural* teleology, MacIntyre pins his hopes on the *ethos* that precedes, conditions, and *determines* the subjective intentions of individual actors.

On MacIntyre's model, individual actions draw their broader meaning from social practices that aim at achieving certain *goods*. Some goods, such as wealth, status, and power, are *external* to the practice in question in that they are procurable by other practices. Others, such as the nonmaterial rewards of excellence, are *internal* to the practice and require *virtue* in order to be obtained. Virtue functions both as a means for obtaining internal goods that benefit individuals and society as a whole *and* as a check on the institutional mechanisms that maintain practices through external rewards.

For MacIntyre, the reason why virtue ought to be pursued cannot be understood apart from the good it provides the individual. Although one could forgo the pursuit of internal goods attendant on performing an action, perform an action poorly or cynically, or decide badly in neglecting to perform certain practices altogether, one could not do so *and* also live a good life. For, "to ask 'What is good for me?' is to ask how best I might live out that unity and bring it to completion" (MacIntyre 1981, 203). Indeed, without the basic virtues common to any achievement of excellence—justice, truthfulness, and courage—the process of self-discovery, of learning about the proper balance of goods requisite for living a fully satisfying life, would be pointless.

Thus we have MacIntyre's classical solution to the problem of motivation afflicting modern, universalistic moral doctrines. It is important to notice here that one's good is not simply a function of engaging in virtuous *practices* but also involves living a life of *unity*. In short, one must *reflectively* integrate one's life into a coherent and complete *identity*. MacIntyre puts great store in the way in which our identities are constituted by the stories we tell about ourselves, for it is just this "narrative quest" that brings unity to our lives in the first place. Our autobiographies, however, are not mere subjective fabrication (fiction). The integrity and wholeness of a life well

lived relates internally to the shared histories of our community; the stories we tell about ourselves refer to the social roles we have adopted for
ourselves, and these, in turn, are defined in terms of historical traditions.

MacIntyre's virtue ethic thus contains a dual refutation of liberal subjectivism. First, specific virtues, values, and goods are prescribed by the
very nature of the specific social practices in which they function. The
latter, in turn, are legitimated by shared, narrative traditions. Second,
despite the differences in their traditions, practices, and virtues, all societies—including liberal ones, it seems—depend on the pursuit of justice,
truthfulness, and courage for their own well-being. Specific codes of justice, truthfulness, and courage may vary from culture to culture; but happy
societies, like happy individuals, possess integrated identities based on shared
traditions whose own integrity and legitimacy refer to their presumed truthfulness and justice.

The last point is particularly pertinent in light of the problem of relativism. As we noted at the outset of this chapter, if one adopts a strong
contextualist view of traditions, then their critical reinterpretation and preservation can only proceed immanently, by appeal to reasons acceptable
within the tradition in question. MacIntyre succumbs to this way of thinking when he says that a tradition is just a "historically extended, socially
embodied argument . . . precisely in part about the goods which constitute
the tradition" (207). But if MacIntyre is right in saying this, how could we
criticize "corrupt traditions" that lack virtues, or that prescribe vices and
meretricious goods?

Before examining MacIntyre's more recent response to this question,
let us look at an attempt to use practical holism for purposes of dissolving
the problem of relativism. Dreyfus argues that "when we understand another culture we come to share its *know-how and discriminations* rather than
arriving at agreement concerning which assumptions and beliefs are true"
(Dreyfus 1985, 235). Once we see that the meanings, purposes, virtues,
and goods constitutive of action are *prediscursive* in the manner suggested
by Heidegger's example of hammering, the infamous debate between moral
relativists and moral absolutists ceases to make any sense.

Extending this analysis to the communitarianism/liberalism debate,
Hubert and Stuart Dreyfus have recently suggested that the tendency among
developmental psychologists like Piaget, Kohlberg, and their followers (notably Habermas) to rank universalistic, deontological reasoning above contextual, ethical intuition needs to be reversed. On their phenomenological
account of skill acquisition, the explicit appeal to rules and principles occurs at the *beginning*—not the end—of moral education. Initially we learn
rules through learning examples. Later we learn to devise a plan of action,

consisting of a hierarchical decision procedure, based on an intuitively chosen, situational perspective (stage 3). At higher levels of *proficiency* and *expertise* (stages 4 and 5 respectively) dependence on detached planning wanes; we learn to respond immediately and intuitively (Dreyfus and Dreyfus 1990, 24–44).

The expert, then, is one who can dispense with any form of practical reasoning, including *phronesis*. In the event of novel situations that prove recalcitrant to past habits, the wise moral expert will still consult others for alternative solutions. But there is no need to privilege rational discussion over practical expertise in ethical matters. Indeed, the authors conclude that an ethic of *care* of the sort described by developmental psychologist Carol Gilligan, which contextualizes moral responses in light of the unique needs of individuals in specific situations, may provide a better account of postconventional morality than a deontological ethic of justice.

Now this position strikes me as an all too facile solution to the problem of relativism. To begin with, the authors themselves concede that demands for political justice require rational decisions and legitimating arguments. Hence they endorse a distinction between rule-governed reflection (morality) and concrete action (customary ethics). Presumably, the problem of relativism crops up only in the former, not in the latter. But the *Moralität/Sittlichkeit* distinction may be more problematic than it seems. It is far from obvious that virtuosity is as removed from choice as Dreyfus and MacIntyre think it is. MacIntyre may be right that the task of the moral virtuoso "may be performed better or worse independently of the choice of alternatives that he or she makes" but the *goods* internally related to this performance that lend it purpose and meaning are themselves subject to conflicting interpretations (MacIntyre 1981, 208). If so, the virtuous life comprises a narratively integrated whole whose constitutive goods reflect critical choices susceptible to discursive justification and criticism.

If choices and beliefs are as integral to internal goods and virtues as the above account suggests, then the potential for conflicting interpretations—and thus for relativism and skepticism—cannot be as easily dismissed as Dreyfus thinks. All of which takes us back to the question of practical reason: How can we tell when the goods and virtues esteemed by our culture are genuinely rational?

In *Whose Justice? Which Rationality?* (1988) MacIntyre answers this question with reference to periods of crisis in which traditions are compelled to break out of their parochial shells. Under normal conditions, "relevant beliefs, texts, and authorities" of a tradition are unquestioned, goods are unambiguously ordered, and the arena of social interaction is structured by well-defined social roles (141). Here practical rationality is primarily restricted to the *phronetic* exercise of sound judgment in the application of moral maxims. However, if unresolved normative conflicts, inconsistencies in the established system of belief, obstacles to application in the face of novel situations, or infiltrations of alien and incompatible belief systems should emerge within the moral tradition, more reflective types of practical reasoning will be required. Should these instabilities threaten the legitimacy of the tradition as a whole, practical reasoning will have to shed its parochial cloak by drawing on the revitalizing symbols of other traditions (398). Such intercultural dialogue succeeds in salvaging the crisis-torn tradition if it critically reinterprets it in such a way as to preserve *and* broaden its identity. In short, it succeeds only if it furnishes "a solution to the problems which had previously proved intractable," provides "an explanation of just what it was which rendered the tradition . . . sterile and incoherent," and "exhibits some fundamental continuity of the new conceptual and theoretical structures with the shared beliefs in terms of which the tradition of inquiry had been defined up to this point" (362).

It remains an open question whether the requirements of this last stage of practical reasoning do not entail something like the universal rationality MacIntyre seeks to discredit. Belief in universal reason, in his judgment, is as pernicious as cultural imperialism, or the illusion, held by Rawls, that "traditions with their own strong, substantive criteria of truth and rationality" can be translated into the superficial, "international languages of modernity" without loss or distortion (384). At the same time, he observes—against Rorty and others—that within our parochial traditions of reasoning we *necessarily* raise *unconditional* truth claims. How, then, can we *learn* from other traditions, whose criteria of truth and rationality are radically incommensurable with our own? How can we be persuaded to adopt the superior rationality of the novel tradition from the standpoint of our own diminished rationality?

MacIntyre suggests that dialogue between partially incommensurable traditions of rationality necessitates a *conversion* process, whereby one acquires a second language as if it were one's first. Double socialization into two "languages in use"—which are distinguished from the superficial international languages of modernity by their embeddedness in unique practical backgrounds—enables one to experience a *critical* distance (or difference) requisite for dialogue. Applied to the problem of cross-cultural learning, this comparative confrontation between particular traditions shows "where and in what respects utterances in the one (language) are untransportable into the other" (375). In other words, one adopts a principle of hermeneutic charity that is just the opposite of that adopted by Davidson and Rorty: instead of presuming that utterances in the alien language largely map onto utterances in one's own, one assumes just the contrary. For at issue here are also sententially irreducible *background practices*, not theories about what others "hold to be true."

Two objections arise at this juncture. First, the Davidsonian counter: Haven't we already transported an utterance from one language into another—either the target language or a third language—in showing *how* it is incommensurable? If so, then MacIntyre contradicts himself when, trying to show how biblical expressions written in Hebrew cannot be translated into English, he *paraphrases* them in English. Second, the language of conversion and double socialization suggests that one's immersion in a tradition is an all-or-nothing affair. If traditions are as particularistic as MacIntyre claims they are, then we are stuck in a familiar Hegelian dialectic. Going from one tradition to the other involves either a change or a split in identity. In neither case do we have an *expanded* identity of the sort characteristic of bilingual understanding *and* rational learning (Habermas 1991b, 216).

As we shall see in chapter 8, notions of *local* incommensurability of the sort defended by MacIntyre and Kuhn may have some validity after all. Although we cannot preclude *metaphorical* paraphrase as a basis for rational communication, it would be presumptuous to think that translation manuals can succeed where lived immersion in language leaves off. More importantly, as we shall see in our examination of Gadamer, the *fusion of horizons* that characterizes authentic understanding between different traditions already anticipates a universal notion of practical reason.

To conclude, MacIntyre no less than Rorty ends up in a kind of ethnocentric impasse. Conversion and assimilation are but reverse sides of the same coin; in both instances one remains enclosed in a parochial horizon of understanding. Moreover, this problem affects interpretative debate within a tradition as well as critical dialogue between traditions. As Georgia Warnke points out, "[T]he difficulty of translating, say, the fourteenth-century English of Lancashire into another period's or region's English-in-use and, hence, the difficulty of understanding its concerns will be the same as that of translating between a particular Irish-in-use and a particular English-in-use" (Warnke 1993, 120).

It is my contention that ethnocentrism is not preordained by the so-called limits of our parochial language. For the constraints imposed by the presuppositions of our language also provide possibilities—questions, themes, reference points, and so on—for exploring and opening up new horizons of meaning. Indeed, as I argue below, some of these constraints consist of *general* competencies requisite for sustaining communication in any language. These in turn ground—in an equiprimordial sense that remains to be seen—ideals of justice *and* the good life.

Ethnocentrism *is* preordained, however, by extreme forms of practical and theoretical holism of the sort entertained respectively by MacIntyre and Rorty. The conceptual behaviorism of the latter invites the radical translator to assimilate the meaning intended by the speaker to his or her own frame of reference. But when it comes to critical reflection on parochial prejudices, detached observation followed by monological translation is simply no substitute for *engaged* dialogue. Conversely, the lived experientialism of the former invites the radical convert to shed his or her native identity for immediate identification with the totally "other." Here again, participatory immersion unmediated by one's native culture is simply no substitute for *critically distantiated* dialogue. The failure of each of these options to strike the right hermeneutical balance between practical engagement and theoretical distantiation entails a meretricious aestheticism: concentration on either superficial (formal) resemblances or particular (intuitively felt) differences.

2.2 In the remainder of this section I would like to examine an account of critical understanding that combines engagement and distantiation in a way that resolves the problem of relativism *and* justifies the standpoint of ideology critique. The account I have in mind is developed in Gadamer's *Truth and Method* (1960). Now Gadamer's account of understanding as a kind of dialogue provides the basic model underlying Rorty's and MacIntyre's respective notions of rational, multicultural learning. The difference between them is that Gadamer sees understanding as a paradigm of *universal* reason.

One way to appreciate this difference is by noticing how much more closely Gadamer's account of dialogic learning accords with Hegel's own phenomenology of experience. For Hegel, *Bildung* denotes a process of cultivation, or education, whereby egoistic individuality is elevated to the moral plane of free, universal self-consciousness. What Gadamer finds attractive about this notion is not its identification with absolute knowledge—or some complete synthetic understanding of all possible historical worldviews—but just its *progressive openness for new experience* (Gadamer 1960, 336).

The *ideality* (or universality) of this self-consciousness does not consist of some ultimate—transparent and presuppositionless—understanding. It does, however, consist in understanding how we are affected by our own tradition, that is, how that tradition both furthers and obstructs understanding. The ideality of such historically affected consciousness *(Wirkungsgeschichtliches Bewußtsein)* also consists in appreciating how we ourselves contribute to the preservation of tradition. For only by taking the ideal truth claim of a distant tradition seriously—for example, by trying to apply it as a potentially reasonable and meaningful response to our present predicament—can we let it challenge our own preconceived notions of truth (343).

Both of these senses of effective history—affecting tradition and being affected by it—combine dialectically to create a third sense of ideality. Trying to understand the ideal meaning of a traditional text enables us to critically emancipate ourselves from those "prejudices" of our native tradition that are confining, or unproductive for understanding. This emancipatory ideal is the reverse side of an enlarging (or universalizing) ideal, which involves acquiring new presuppositions. The result is a kind of Hegelian synthesis, or fusion of horizons *(Horizontverschmelzung)* (289). Successful understanding issues in a mutual agreement *(Einverständnis)* between interpreter and text regarding some truth claim in a way that both preserves and alters their identities.

The conception of horizon—or space of possible meaningfulness—indicates the sense in which the constraining and liberating aspects of linguistic prejudices complement one another. Horizons open up a clear field of vision only insofar as they limit our vision. We expand our horizons by understanding new cultures, that is, by allowing the horizon opened up by those cultures to effect a shift in our perspective (288). But this shift is only incompletely captured by the synthetic notion of expanding one's horizons. For it also entails an alteration in one's general outlook—from one of ethnocentric denial of the other to universal respect for the *rights* of the other.

Contrary to MacIntyre—and to a lesser extent, Gadamer himself—it is this ethical notion of openness and reciprocity, not the notion of synthesis, that is decisive for rational understanding. For understanding, Gadamer notes, can only proceed by way of a Socratic dialogue—simulated or otherwise—between interpreter and text, speaker and listener, in which each remains open to what the other has to say. Thus Gadamer writes that "the experience of the 'thou' manifests the paradoxical element that something standing over against me asserts its own *rights* and requires absolute recognition and in that very process is understood" (xxiii; my italics).

We might summarize this discussion by saying that rational transcendence, or the anticipation of all-inclusive democratic dialogue, is implicit within *every* parochial frame of self-understanding. In the words of Gadamer, "The living idea of reason" cannot renounce the ideal of a general agreement grounded in "a shared life under conditions of uncoercive communication" (Gadamer 1971, 316). Hence the "end-thought of freedom" possesses a compelling evidentness that "one can as little get beyond [as] one can get beyond consciousness itself" (Gadamer 1976a, 37).

This teleological way of stating Gadamer's thesis might conflict with the purely descriptive, phenomenological manner in which he advances it—a problem, we saw, that affects most communitarian criticism. Be that as it may, Gadamer does not hesitate to sound the communitarian alarm in light of the theoretical implications of his hermeneutics. He tells us, for example, that the political reason that "vindicates again the noblest task of the citizen ... decision-making according to one's own responsibility" can "only be realized and transmitted dialogically" (Gadamer 1975a, 314). This experience, however, is contradicted by the fact that "even the opinions which form the patterns of social life and constitute the conditions for solidarity are today dominated to a great extent by the technical and economic organizations within our civilization" (Gadamer 1976b, 64).

As we shall see, Habermas's program of ideology critique draws its inspiration from precisely these sorts of reflections. Yet Habermas questions whether Gadamer's notion of critical dialogue strikes the right balance between theoretical and practical holism, participation, and critical distantiation. Part of the problem has to do with the way Gadamer conceives understanding as a "fusion of horizons." Gadamer insists that addressing the claims of tradition in fruitful dialogue involves granting them a certain authority—in effect, reversing the Enlightenment's "prejudice against prejudices." If understanding is equivalent to rendering meaningful, and if rendering meaningful is equivalent to rendering reasonable—that is coherent and applicable to the interpreter's own frame of reference—then it is hard to see how understanding could avoid reaffirming the authority of tradition (Gadamer 1960, 261).

Coupled with this conservative tendency is Gadamer's own privileging of consensus over emancipation and equality. In his social and political writings, he likens the traditional consensus that unites and harmonizes the different social strata of a community *(Gemeinschaft)* to the equilibrium *(Gleichgewicht)* of forces that secures the well-being of a biological organism (Gadamer 1976, 32). Language is here regarded as the ultimate medium of consensual solidarity—a "game of interpretation" in which "everyone is at the center"(32). The tendency of this line of thinking is to treat relations of authority and inequality—such as that between educator and pupil, scholar and layperson—as resting on a kind of tacit consent. It was for just these reasons that Gadamer objected to Habermas's extension of psychoanalytic ideology critique to the social arena. By refusing to play the language game of open disputation, the critic of ideology presumes the *dialogically untested* superiority of his or her own theoretical insight vis-à-vis the linguistic tradition. But this superiority is based on an unreasonable emancipatory expectation: that undistorted communication permits transparent, prejudice-free self-understanding.

In response to Gadamer, Habermas noted that the idea of unconstrained communication only justified a suspicion of everyday language in light of known distortions emanating from extralinguistic causes, namely, economic and political domination. In order to perceive such domination and explain its effects on language, one must adopt a theoretical posture eccentric to everyday understanding. In short, one must interpret the latent, functional meaning of speech and action in the manner argued for in chapter 2.

For our purposes, Habermas's invocation of psychoanalysis is somewhat misleading, since it implies that understanding follows from a theoretical explanation of causes, rather than vice versa. In that case the critical theorist—like the linguistic behaviorist and psychotherapist—would have reflected himself or herself out of any critical dialogue. However, if my analysis of functionalism in chapter 2 is correct, then a theoretical explanation of causes would originate in an internal dialogue with oneself and others—or rather, in the divided self-understanding of an identity in a state of crisis.

3. The problem of ideology suggests that the regulative presupposition underlying Gadamer's hermeneutics—the presumption that a text not only represents a coherent unity, but also that it asserts the whole truth (Gadamer 1975, 278)—needs to be qualified. In chapter 6 we will see that it is precisely this presumption of completeness and perfection *(Vorgriff auf Vollkommenheit)* that critical legal scholars find so troublesome about Dworkin's own legal hermeneutics. Must judges—let alone philosophers of law—always interpret the legal canon as if it were an instantiation of ideal justice just waiting to be correctly appreciated? Indeed, must they even interpret it as a unified whole?

Gadamer, I think, takes this presumption of coherence and perfectibility to an altogether unhealthy—if not ideological—extreme. It is one thing to view *texts* charitably, another to view one's own society that way. Yet we do find Gadamer interpreting linguistic communities as unified, perfect wholes. Hence his endorsement of Aristotle's strong communitarian vision of language as "the agreement on which human community, its harmony with respect to the good and proper, is founded" (1960, 408). The problem of ideology—not to mention the pluralism of goods and their interpretations—suggests, however, that talk of an *ontological* social consensus (or coherence) is misplaced when addressing the highly differentiated and stratified liberal societies of our modern epoch. If there is a sense in which consensus and coherence remain appropriate, it can only be *counterfactual*: specifying the ideal harmony and integrity (or good) of complex societies.

We find ourselves again confronted with the problem of hermeneutical indeterminacy and pluralism. The communitarian thinkers I address in this section accept this problem as setting limits to political interpretation. Unlike MacIntyre and Gadamer, they do not think that the rationality of a tradition or culture necessitates resolving its internal tensions. Like the good liberals that they are, they are willing to risk accommodating separate strands of interpretation or separate spheres of goods and criteria of justice. Whether they can defend this distinctly liberal notion of tolerance and justice without appeal to an ideal of the good life remains to be seen.

In *Spheres of Justice,*, Michael Walzer argues that an account of justice (rights) must be pluralist rather than reductive, complex rather than simple. Different principles of justice, he submits, apply to different kinds of goods. Stronger still, they draw their meaning and justification from goods whose own specific meaning and validity is relative to the *social understanding* that a given community has of itself. Since this understanding is constituted by shared practices, traditions, and language games that make up a relatively unified context, it can only be critically interpreted from within, by those who participate in (or identify with) it (Walzer 1983, 7–10).

Contrary to Rawls, there is no such thing as a universal list of primary goods applicable to all persons at all times that might be rationally deduced or empirically ascertained. Hence, there is no single principle of justice, such as the Difference Principle, regulating their distribution (15): the caste system is as just (or unjust) *within* Indian society as is the merit system, say, *within* American society—the one specifying equal opportunity through indefinite cycles of reincarnation, the other through individual achievement in a single lifetime (27).

In addition to making this contextualist point, Walzer argues that "every social good or set of goods constitutes, as it were, a distributive sphere within which only certain criteria and arrangements are appropriate" (10). Whereas one society might tie the distribution of public offices to merit and qualification, another might tie it to wealth, as a good procurable on the market. Walzer, for example, thinks that in a society like ours—where individuals have overlapping racial, ethnic, and religious identifications and no groups are granted special legal status—qualification for public offices and scarce vacancies in professional schools are generally understood to be reserved for those who have demonstrated the requisite skills and knowledge. Hence, contrary to Dworkin and others, he opposes affirmative action programs that factor in extraneous qualifications, such as race, in ways that violate the principle of individual merit (150). To take other examples, Walzer argues that Americans would largely agree (upon deeper reflection) that health and social security ought to be distributed in accordance with the criterion of need, money in accordance with free exchange, and primary education in accordance with strict equality.

There are two important points to be made with respect to this account of justice. First, it presumes that any complex society will order its distribution of goods in accordance with a complex scheme of justice. Second, it presumes that a corresponding scheme of equality will also be *complex* rather than *simple*, in that it will allow "many small inequalities" but not their multiplication across distinct spheres (17). Theories of justice that advocate simple equality attack social *domination* by first attacking the *monopoly* certain individuals have over certain dominant goods, such as money, that command a wide range of other goods. The problem with this approach is twofold: it requires extensive bureaucratic redistribution of the dominant good throughout all segments of society, and it requires that such redistribution remain permanently in effect, offsetting the voluntary exchanges that give rise to inequalities in the first place. In effect, this strategy creates a new problem of domination based on the monopolization of a new good—political power (16).

Since there is no workable solution to the problem of political monopoly under these provisions, Walzer proposes a different strategy: diminish the importance of monopoly by attacking the problem of dominance through the principle of blocked exchanges.

> In formal terms, complex equality means that no citizen's standing in one sphere or with regard to one social good can be undercut by his standing in some other sphere, with regard to some other good. Thus, citizen X may be chosen over citizen Y for political office, and then the two of them will be unequal in the sphere of politics. But they will not be unequal generally so long as X's office gives him no advantages over Y in any other sphere—superior medical care, access to better schools for his children, entrepreneurial opportunities, and so on. (19)

In Walzer's opinion, then, fairly large—even monopolistic—inequalities in the distribution of a single good might be compatible with complex equality. Income differentials, for example, are tolerable *up to a point* so long as they are prevented from having an adverse impact on the just distributional schemes governing other spheres. Walzer himself criticizes the way in which wealth and status in the United States are permitted to undermine the principle of equal opportunity in education and the principle of basic need in health and social security. Of course, failing to provide equal access to health care and education is not *inherently* unjust. However, *if* a community has decided to underwrite the social costs of health care and social security through Medicare and Medicaid programs, and *if* hospitals sometimes allocate medical treatment on the basis of charity and emergency need regardless of the patient's ability to pay for services rendered, then "to be cut off from the help they provide is not only dangerous but degrading" (89).

What makes Walzer's position so problematic is that "political power is always dominant" insofar as "it is used to defend the boundaries of all the distributive spheres, including its own, and to enforce the common understandings of what goods are and what they are for" (115). Defending the boundaries of distributive spheres will indeed require a bureaucratic state of some kind, though one less expansive than that based on simple equality. Hence, it is all the more important that the state be democratically accountable, and that its own power be constrained by a system of checks and balances.

Thus, unlike MacIntyre and Foucault, Walzer has no problem with bureaucracy per se or with hierarchies of administrative power based on expertise. What redeems this inequality in who decides the means and policies for implementing the general good is the existence of a vibrant public sphere that decides what the good is. To this end, Walzer thinks it essential that state power not be "colonized" by wealth, talent, blood or gender" (282).

More radical still, Walzer extends the principle of democratic sovereignty to include the workplace. Although the principle "What touches all should be decided by all" is not unconditionally valid, it does have special validity when applied to places of residence and work. George Pullman's unsuccessful attempt in the 1880s and 1890s to establish a company town illustrates the parallel between these two types of sovereignty. Pullman ruled this town the same way he ruled his factory: autocratically. The workers struck in 1894—as much against his factory autocracy as against his residential tyranny—and in 1898 the Illinois Supreme Court forced him to divest himself of his township, but not his factory holdings.

But is there really any difference between the two types of despotism exercised by Pullman? Walzer thinks not. Both the factory and the town were the product of Pullman's entrepreneurial activity; both were sustained by private investment (just as municipalities are sustained by bonds sold to outsiders); and both were characterized by voluntary membership. Our abhorrence of residential tyranny—say, by landlords over their tenants—

flows from our common affirmation of the *public* sovereignty exercised by a community over its residential assets just as it flows from our belief in the *private* sanctity of the individual at home with himself or herself; and it is this affirmation that applies here as well:

> The right to impose [factory] fines does the work of taxation; the right to evict tenants or discharge workers does [some of] the work of punishment. Rules are issued and enforced without public debate by appointed rather than elected officials. There are no established judicial procedures, no legitimate forms of opposition, no channels for participation or even protest. If this sort of thing is wrong for towns, then it is wrong for companies and factories, too. (301)

Walzer concludes his discussion by advocating privately owned worker cooperatives organized and regulated at national and local levels. But what is most interesting here is not his substantive recommendations for organization (about which he is very flexible), but his method of argumentation. By appealing to an analogical argument *instead* of a "common understanding" he belies his own self-proclaimed interpretative approach. I think he is right to do so; and I would argue that he should go further, by pointing out how the principle of democracy in general, and industrial democracy in particular, is more deeply entrenched in the formal and substantive conditions underlying CR (as I argue in chapter 5).

Walzer of course would reject this kind of deep, *theoretical* justification. Indeed, he has been adamant in his criticism of Rawls, Ackerman, Habermas, and other liberals who design ideal conversations as a way of philosophically predetermining the basic rights constitutive of a just society. In his opinion, not only do these attempts fail as proposals but they preempt the very democracy they seek to justify (Walzer 1989–90, 182–96). Preempting democracy, they also preempt justice, for democracy is the only basis in Western society for critically articulating the needs and values constitutive of a pluralistic communal identity and, therewith, the goods and rights appropriate to it.

Walzer may be right about democracy as the last court of appeal for the determination of rights. After all, even constitutions that entrench a basic schedule of rights as trumps against wayward democratic majorities cannot immunize judges who interpret them from the inevitable pressure of public opinion. Whether this is a fact to be regretted or appreciated will be the topic of a later discussion. In any case, we will see that there is more agreement among Walzer, Ackerman, and Habermas on the legitimate scope of mandated democratic majorities to reinterpret the meaning of basic rights than his own somewhat tendentious reading of these authors might suggest. (Ironically Walzer's own treatment of just and unjust wars [1977, 54] as well as his discussion of "the principle of mutual aid" [1983, 33] contains an endorsement of the universal rights "not to be robbed of life or liberty" [xv] and the natural duty to help others in distress.)

On the other hand, Walzer's failure to appreciate the function of "ideal conversations" in getting us to perceive the subtle distortions of public communication wrought by power and money weakens his own case for democracy. His tradition-based critique underestimates the extent to which inequalities in wealth and education can influence the democratic process even *after* the necessary blocked exchanges have been institutionally implemented. One cannot but agree with Walzer that some persons—most notably politicians—will have more influence on democratic debate simply owing to their superior skill and motivation (1988, 304). At the same time, however, one must acknowledge that the skills and motivations requisite for political participation are a function of educational opportunities contingent on financial status. Walzer's proposals for equal primary education and free access to higher education only partially remedy these inequalities, since they do not address patterns of discrimination that continue to influence admission to the best universities. Hence compensatory justice must also qualify the just distribution of goods.

Dworkin gets at the problem best when he observes that Walzer's own objection to affirmative action programs and private health care rests on a dogmatic "interpretation" of what our common understandings entail—one that overlooks *conflicts of interpretation* over the meanings of goods, their criteria for distribution, and their complex overlap. Lockean and Rousseauean interpretations of what justice requires—to anticipate Taylor's take on multicultural conflict—cannot be neatly assigned to discrete spheres of justice. Rather, as the examples of affirmative action, public health care, and production and distribution of commodities clearly attest, our understanding about what justice demands in each of these areas is itself divided along lines of class, gender, ethnicity, and occupation.

Once one rejects the idea of "fixed and preordained spheres of justice," then "some reflective basis for deciding which of our traditional distinctions and discriminations are genuine and which spurious" becomes necessary (Dworkin 1983, 114). Rawls's model of overlapping consensus suggests one such basis; Habermas's discourse ethics suggests another. Because of its instantiation of CR, the distinct advantage of the latter would reside in its founding a public space in which functional constraints and power relations can be articulated. It is not unreasonable to suppose that interlocutors confronting their own mutually constraining behaviors might be compelled at some point in their discussion to adopt a functionalist perspective on their economic interdependency, thereby seeing more clearly the need for an egalitarian national health policy than their own divided common sense would otherwise permit. In any case, I suspect that it is from such a perspective as this that Dworkin justifies affirmative action. Since functionalism diminishes individual contributions relative to social ones, a functionalist can be expected to expand qualifications for scarce positions to include, besides "merit," factors that lie outside the purview of sovereign individual accomplishments, such as handicaps due to past and present discrimination, ethnic, regional, and other biographical facts that suggest a likelihood of service to neglected communities, and so on.

There are several interpretative issues at stake here. First, Dworkin seems to conceive common understandings as agreements on subjective opinions, whereas Walzer, like Taylor, conceives them as constitutive of the very institutions and practices by which persons form opinions. Hence, Dworkin's appeal to different opinions about what justice in the sphere of medicine requires misses Walzer's point, namely that prior to any differences in opinion there are deeper, shared commitments to standards of justice. Second, however, Dworkin's objection might be directed against Walzer's *own* interpretation of this deeper meaning. Walzer does not admit that there can be conflicting interpretations of this understanding, because he assigns different conceptions of justice to different spheres. Finally, Dworkin's interpretation of our understanding of health care is based on a time-slice understanding of *current* practices, whereas Walzer's is based on a historical one—an approach, one would think, that would make him *more*, not *less*, amenable to affirmative action programs designed to compensate the victims of discrimination.

Both Dworkin and Walzer presume to offer an interpretation of our medical practice that is coherent and truthful to its most reasonable aspects. But this anticipation of completed meaning is itself incomplete, and remains relative to different *contexts* of interpretation. Given the fact that our subjective opinions do influence the way we understand our constitutive meanings and that choice of context—present-time-slice or historical narrative—and spatiotemporal horizons of interpretation are indeterminate, there may be no way to adjudicate the debate between Dworkin and Walzer *on purely hermeneutical grounds* (Warnke 1993, 24). Hence the need to resort to more global, functionalist forms of historical explanation.

But there is another interpretative issue at stake here. In his response to Dworkin, Walzer rightly defended himself against the charge of presuming "fixed and preordained spheres of justice" (Walzer 1983, 116). As he himself observes, the balancing of spheres of justice may require their mutual overlap or communicative interpenetration. Thus, he concedes that in modern India today the distribution of state jobs may necessitate something like affirmative action for untouchables balanced against the principle of merit (315). Yet despite his recognition of the conflictual, contingent, and dynamic nature of "our" understanding of these spheres, he himself presumes to have a privileged understanding of the right balance, or mix, of goods and distributive criteria within a given sphere and within society as a whole. So given his insistence on preserving the *autonomy* of distinct spheres of justice, he too must appeal to some more all-encompassing, *theoretical* account of justice beyond the conflicting, sphere-immanent accounts circulating in "our" common understanding.

Walzer's global concept of justice does not privilege the right over the good. Rather, like Plato's concept of justice, it bears a stronger resemblance to the good, understood as an ideally felicitous harmony among distinct spheres of justice. On this reading societies are susceptible to two sorts of *immanent criticism*: they may be deficient in institutionalizing a coherent scheme of justice; and particular spheres of justice internal to them may be deficient in satisfying their own distributional criteria.

Walzer's belief that the complex equality underlying this scheme is itself a good, so that modern, liberal democracies make for better overall human flourishing than premodern or totalitarian societies, must, I think, be understood in light of his hermeneutical commitments as well. As he puts it, "the autonomy of spheres will make for a greater sharing of social goods than will any other conceivable arrangement" (321). In the final analysis, it remains to be seen whether his commitment to an independent criterion of coherence is sufficient for establishing the health and integrity of a community's identity apart from other values, such as vitality (favored by postmodernists like Lyotard and Rorty) and reflective depth and maturity (favored by Gadamer and Habermas).[5]

3.1 The need to balance the pluralism, complexity, and indeterminacy of modern society with the unity and determinacy of traditional community has been a predominant theme of Charles Taylor's own liberal communitarian vision. What he adds to the equation is a profound respect for the aesthetic and experiential—above all, epiphanic (or religious)—dimension by which we integrate our lives. For underlying the communitarian critique of alienation and fetishism is a deep understanding of the harmonic telos underlying all life.

To appreciate Taylor's contribution we must recall our discussion of his interpretative account of personal identity in chapter 2, which served as a kind of counter to subject-centered, intentionalist explanations of action. This account was also directed against certain types of moral theories, namely, those *proceduralist* theories that take the *choice* of right or wrong *actions* as the sole problem of ethical theory. These theories undertake a double abstraction: they abstract the question of right conduct from the question of the good, and they abstract the reasons for moral choice—in the form of *basic* universal principles—from the finer qualitative discriminations embedded in the background practices and contexts of ethical life.

Taylor's critique of proceduralist ethics bears a striking resemblance to another Hegelian whose thought we have examined: Alasdair MacIntyre. Indeed he cites MacIntyre's account of the importance of "internal goods" and "narrative quests" in fleshing out an account of moral motivation. This Aristotelian account also endorses a hermeneutic principle of coherence and perfectibility: "We can speak of a single 'complete good' *(teleion agathon),* because our condition is such that the disparate goods we seek have to be coherently combined in a single life, and in their right proportions" (Taylor 1989, 77).

Taylor's point recalls Walzer's concern about preserving the autonomy of separate spheres of goods and justice. Sometimes he phrases this concern in terms of a need to balance our Lockean belief in individual rights and our Aristotelian belief in the priority of communal membership. Whereas the former distributes goods in accordance with the principle of individual contribution, the latter distributes them in accordance with the principle of equal sharing (Taylor 1985, 313). More recently, as we have seen, he phrases this concern in terms of a need to balance Lockean instrumentalism with Rousseauean expressivism. Here the problem involves reconciling different *sources* of modern self-identity.

Indeed, for Taylor the problem of modern identity revolves around two distinct but interrelated conflicts: between multicultural particularism and constitutional universalism, on one hand, and between the various sources of modern self-identity, on the other. The former problem arises out of the modern problem of recognition. Traditional hierarchies automatically accorded recognition based on unequal social standing, thereby guaranteeing a stable and dignified sense of self. By contrast, modern societies accord equal recognition to all, but only in the abstract. When it comes to procuring respect for our identities as unique *individuals*—detached from social roles and conventions—we moderns depend on the voluntary recognition of others (Taylor 1992, 28).

It is precisely this expressivistic idea of *inward* self-determination that informs Rousseau's concern about *authenticity*—being true to oneself rather than to the opinions of others. Beginning with Herder this idea is used to affirm the autonomy of one's native culture against cultural imperialism (31). Despite their apparent differences, Rousseau's and Herder's concerns exhibit the same dialectic: the very recognition that confers a stable, dignified, and autonomous sense of self threatens to rob it of its authenticity.

The lesson Taylor draws from this is taken directly from Hegel's account of the master/servant dialectic. Because recognition of one's *particular* individuality, no less than recognition of one's *universal* freedom and equality, comes from others—either "significant others" with whom we interact on an intimate basis or others we encounter in the public sphere—voluntary recognition of our inward worth and identity is something that we moderns must struggle for (36).

This struggle has been played out with greatest intensity in current debates over educational reform. The demand to expand the curriculum in a multicultural direction—when it is not made on behalf of broadening one's cultural horizons—stems from a prior commitment to recognize the equal value of different cultures. On one hand, this recognition has its basis in our belief in equal, universal rights: "Just as all must have equal civil rights, and equal voting rights, regardless of race and culture, so all should enjoy the presumption that their traditional culture has value" (68). Here the argument is made that multiculturalism shows equal respect to women and students of non-European provenance by recognizing the value of hitherto excluded texts by authors writing outside mainstream, male-dominated, Eurocentric culture. Not to recognize the value of these texts amounts to presenting a one-sided and potentially demeaning picture of them to the students who identify with them (65). On the other hand, this demand for recognition extends beyond the claim to universal equality, since it presumes that every culture has something *uniquely* worthwhile to teach us. Following Gadamer, Taylor presents this demand as an expectation—not a guarantee—that, by respecting the potential truth-claim of a culture, its difference, if not its truth, will force us to critically examine our own prejudices (72).

Now the uneasy manner in which respect for difference flows from respect for common humanity impinges on the conflict between the modern sources of identity in the following way. Whereas the Lockean, instrumentalist account of the modern self emphasizes what people have in *common*—capacities for reasoning and exercising free choice—the Rousseauean, expressivist account emphasizes what differentiates them as individuals. And whereas the former emphasizes a liberal politics of neutrality that recognizes one's common humanity through the guarantee of universal rights that apply equally to all—*regardless* of ethnic, racial, religious, and gender differences—the latter emphasizes a communitarian politics of difference that recognizes one's unique dignity through discriminatory rights that treat different people differently (38).

And so we have a conflict between two types of recognition and their respective approaches to dealing with discrimination and cultural difference: color- and gender-blind antidiscrimination laws versus color- and gender-sensitive "reverse" discrimination laws; and toleration of minority subcultures versus active intervention on their behalf. The problem of respecting multicultural differences is especially close to Taylor's own political concerns as a Canadian of mixed French and English ancestry. What is at stake in the demands for autonomy put forth by French Canadians and aboriginal peoples, in his opinion, is nothing less than the future *survival* of distinct cultures.

Quebec recently sought to procure this result by passing laws that prevented francophones and immigrants from sending their children to English-language schools, required businesses with more than fifty employees to be run in French, and outlawed the signing of commercial documents in any language other than French (52). This legislation seemed to violate the Canadian Charter of Rights, modeled after the American prototype, which provides for judicial review of legislation at all levels of government. In fact the signage law has been overturned by the Supreme Court of Canada, despite the fact that the Meech Lake amendment's recognition of Quebec as a "distinct society" made possible a less uniform review of Quebec's legislation (53).

Not surprisingly, many liberals saw this amendment as a violation of the nondiscriminatory provisions of the Charter. The procedural model of liberalism underlying this criticism disallows Quebec's language laws as partial attempts to further the substantive good of a particular community at the expense of individuals' rights with respect to the education of their children and the conduct of their businesses. Taylor's own solution to this problem involves acknowledging—as Rawls and many liberals have already done—that liberalism is itself "a fighting creed" and was therefore never neutral with respect to all conceptions of the good. In his opinion, therefore, liberalism need not preclude a modus vivendi between universal rights and multicultural privileges: "One has to distinguish the fundamental liberties, those that should never be infringed and therefore ought to be unassailably entrenched, on one hand, from privileges and immunities that are important, but that can be revoked or restricted for reasons of public policy—although one would need a strong reason to do this—on the other" (59).

Perhaps this is putting the opposition between universal individual rights and particular group privileges a bit too strongly. Finding Taylor's communitarian appeal to group rights both unnecessary and dangerous, Habermas argues that the liberal attribution of rights to individuals need not—and indeed cannot—bracket the cultural and historical context in which such rights are concretely debated and promulgated (Habermas 1994, 116). The democratic and juridical specification of actionable rights will perforce treat unequals unequally in order to assure their formal equality as individual citizens (113). Therefore nothing in the liberal model forbids racial, sexual, and group classifications from entering into the determination of how individuals' rights are to be equitably secured (129). By contrast, the communitarian concept of group rights positively threatens individual autonomy. A case in point is Taylor's apparent support of Quebec's education law, which pits the collective right of certain Quebecois to legally enforce the continual preservation of their culture against the individual rights of immigrant and francophone parents to educate their children in the language and culture they deem appropriate. This collective right does not follow from Taylor's principle that we owe all cultures equal respect on the presumption that they all have something to teach us; the force of that presumption in encouraging multicultural education remains whether we impose a monolithic language requirement or not (129). Nor does it follow from his principle of cultivating identity through dialogical openness. That principle runs counter to the dogmatic insulation of cultures and communities from individuals' needs to cultivate their identities freely, critically, and authentically. Indeed, as Habermas rightly notes, the fundamentalist (or essentialist) attempt to maintain a closed, ultrastable identity through such coercive means can even prove self-defeating:

> The ecological perspective on species conservation cannot be transferred to cultures. Cultural heritages and the forms of life articulated in them normally reproduce themselves by convincing those whose personality structures they shape, that is, by motivating them to appropriate productively and continue the traditions. The constitutional state can make this hermeneutic achievement of the cultural reproduction of lifeworlds possible, but it cannot guarantee it. For to guarantee survival would necessarily rob the members of the very freedom to say yes or no that is necessary if they are to appropriate and preserve their cultural heritage.(130)

Taylor's attempt to reconcile liberal universalism and communal particularism may be closer to the constitutional patriotism advocated by Habermas than Taylor would care to admit, since it can only succeed within a multicultural dialogue that goes beyond liberal tolerance and communitarian insularity. Mutual concern for preserving multicultural differences through selective privileges can be expected only if persons embrace the dynamic vitality of a complex identity vulnerable to transformative influences emanating from other cultures. Habermas is right to observe that this imperative becomes increasingly urgent given the *postnational* integration of national economies and the resulting impact that uneven development has on the global environment (Habermas 1992, 632)

As we noted above, for Taylor the conflict between multiculturalism and constitutionalism is itself part and parcel of a broader legitimation crisis. That crisis, in turn, touches on no fewer than three subsidiary conflicts: uncertainty and division concerning the three major traditional sources of modern moral identity and their respective constitutive goods, conflict between Enlightenment instrumentalism and romantic expressivism, and the conflict between the ultimate demands of morality and human fulfillment. The first aspect does not reflect any disagreement over the general demands of modern morality. Taylor agrees with Rawls that those living in Western democracies generally agree on the *general* values of freedom, equality, benevolence, inwardness, and the affirmation of ordinary life. Yet he observes that conflicts of interpretation arise over the concrete meanings attached to these values, and thus over ultimate sources and goods.

The conflict between theistic and humanistic sources of valuation offers a particularly poignant illustration of this problem. Theism and its secular counterparts (romanticism and naturalism) interpret all of creation as a community of communion with God's benevolent love *(agape)*. Its vision of community thus resonates with our belief in the essential goodness of nature, whose purposes transcend and limit those of humanity. Accordingly, deep ecologists and others inspired by it oppose the instrumental exploitation of nature for human purposes.

The second aspect of our legitimation crisis concerns the tension between "disengaged" instrumentalist and romantic expressive modes of humanism. As noted above, Taylor holds that the former has largely succeeded in suppressing the latter. The meaninglessness, atomization, and loss of freedom associated with modern consumer society reflects the polarization of liberal society into ascetic work and hedonistic consumption. The "iron cage" of which Weber spoke leaves no basis for morality; or rather, the modern procedural modes of morality that make their appearance are so detached from our concrete identities and motivations that they are incapable of resisting nihilism and cynical conformism.

The third aspect of our legitimation crisis concerns the antagonism between the ultimate demands of morality and natural fulfillment. Devotion to the "hypergoods" that give life meaning comes with a price: ascetic mutilation of self, family, and community in the name of some idea or ideology. The bottom line here as elsewhere is that "we end up relating to each other through a series of partial roles" (Taylor 1992, 502).

For Taylor, all these tensions revolve around a common denominator: the suppression of our originary theistic-romantic need for community and wholeness. Contrary to his and Walzer's earlier discussion of distributive principles, the need here cannot be met by balancing separate spheres of good. As long as these spheres are not also integrated—that is, as long as they do not communicate with one another—no community, and hence no integral identity, is possible. Taylor himself observes that the three domains (or sources) borrow from and influence one another. Moreover, there have been attempts to "straddle the boundaries" separating them—Marxism's "marriage of Enlightenment naturalism and romantic expressivism" being a case in point (496).

What Marx owes to romantic expressivism in general and German idealism in particular is summed up in Schiller's sixth *Aesthetic Letter*. That letter provides Taylor with a "picture of restored harmony within the person and between the people, as a result of 'decloisonnement', the breaking down of barriers between art and life, work and love, class and class, and the image of this harmony as a fuller freedom" (497). In Taylor's opinion, whatever hope remains for liberal community is bound up with tapping just this *aesthetic*, or *epiphanic, experience* (512). The latter, which can be opened up by art, philosophy, and criticism, establishes a *personal* resonance with a "cosmic order of meanings" that is no longer *publicly* accessible. For the only "order of argument" capable of demonstrating the proper unity, integrity, harmony, and health constitutive of *the* good must proceed "ad hominem," by way of sharing one's *way of experiencing* the world (505).

Something like this reconciliatory vision has inspired critical theory from its inception in German idealism down to the present day. But not all critical theorists have drawn inspiration from it in equal measure. Habermas for one has taken issue with the notion that "strong evaluations" have an objective (or cosmic) basis, accessible only through aesthetic "world disclosure." In this connection he cites Adorno's view that modern art has lost its objective, that is, authoritative, reconciliatory power. His own position, as we shall see, is premised on a categorical distinction between cognitive, moral, and aesthetic validity claims and their corresponding objective, social, and subjective "worlds." In accordance with this neo-Kantian scheme—which he, following Weber, takes to be the hallmark of cultural rationalization (or modernization)—philosophy's proper task is cognitive, the rational reconstruction of universal competencies for speaking and acting that ground procedural morality. In his opinion, philosophy would cease to live up to its postmetaphysical responsibilities if it accepted Taylor's recommendation. In seeking engagement with the good it would be indistinguishable from art itself; hence its "arguments" would be aesthetic and evaluative, not cognitive and reconstructive (Habermas 1991, 183–84).

Taylor's response to Habermas is already contained in his criticism of the latter's moral proceduralism. Habermas's acceptance of a strong differentiation of cognitive, moral, and aesthetic spheres prevents him from grounding his own critique of social reification. Such a strong differentiation consigns the aesthetic to the sphere of subjective pleasure and expressive authenticity. What is needed for criticism, however, is a conception of the aesthetic that illuminates a felicitous balance between this sphere and its cognitive and moral counterparts. Although Taylor allows that such illumination proceeds aesthetically, through *personal* resonance, he adds that "in full integrity, the enterprise is an attempt to surmount subjectivism" (Taylor 1989, 510).

Now I submit that Taylor and Habermas are both right, up to a point. Habermas is right when he defends a procedural account of moral *discourse* as intimately connected to universal presuppositions of rational speech; for such an account—whose ideal of justice is necessary for criticizing ideologies that perpetuate domination—follows from the hermeneutical principle of rational perfectibility. Taylor is right when he criticizes this notion as an incomplete account of moral rationality, for implicit in this principle is also a teleological ideal of integrity, solidarity, and well-being. Again, Habermas rightly emphasizes the differentiation of modern culture—or types of discursive reasoning, if you will—but Taylor rightly draws our attention to integrative countertendencies in the way we rationally experience and judge.

If the transcendence of hermeneutical practice toward theory teaches us anything, it is that *logical* distinctions—between justice and the good, rational argumentation and experience, justification and judgment, and formal reconstruction of universal procedure and critical interpretation of tradition—cease to designate hard and fast boundaries within the *integral* process of reflection. This *qualified* affirmation of Hegelian synthesis and Gadamerian perfectibility does indeed implicate a kind of aesthetic resonance, to use Taylor's expression, but in a reflexive manner—mediating public discourse and private dialogue—that still remains to be articulated.

As we shall see in chapter 7, Habermas himself toys with a notion of aesthetic rationality that bears striking resemblance to Taylor's. And he is driven to do so for much the same reason, namely, to ground the clinical judgment of social reification in an experience of life lived in full integrity. Because this judgment mediates between different types of validity and discourse, it necessitates a corresponding expansion of CR to include metaphorical resonances. Thus, despite Habermas's insistence on separating philosophy from art and aesthetic criticism, he himself concedes that the former shares the latter's capacity to metaphorically communicate an experience of our lifeworld that is not confined to cognitive discourse.

3.3 If we retrace the argument presented in this chapter it becomes apparent that the conception of aesthetic rationality that grounds the clinical judgment of social reification complements the conception of CR that grounds the critique of ideology. The idea of unconstrained, democratic dialogue implicit in the latter and the idea of felicitous integrity implicit in the former presented themselves as responses to the question posed by the problem of contextual holism: How is immanent criticism—or criticism rooted in community traditions and their diverse conceptions of the good— possible? Liberals like Rawls who have abandoned transcendent reason in favor of tradition as a basis for criticism give us one possible answer to this question: Immanent criticism is possible because the multiple, conflicting traditions (conceptions of the good) circulating in liberal society mutually complement one another. Most importantly, the libertarian tradition functions to check and balance the republican tradition and vice versa. Also, conflicting traditions converge in an overlapping consensus on more abstract, universal principles of justice that provide a quasi-transcendent rationale for criticism.

The problem with Rawls's account of immanent criticism is that it can neither explain how conflicting traditions critically check one another nor show how the resulting overlapping consensus produces a system of justice possessing overall integrity, as distinct from hegemonic accommodation. As for the former problem, we remarked that Rawls thinks it unnecessary for conflicting traditions to communicate with one another in order to justify principles of justice. Rather, each draws on parochial reasons immanent to its own monadic sphere to support the consensus in question. But how do we know that these reasons are rational—and not ideological—if incommensurable traditions cannot encounter one another in critical dialogue?

It seems that Rawls's "communitarian" revision of his theory remains mired in the SR that characterized *A Theory of Justice*. But there are other problems in addition to relativism and skepticism that plague Rawls's revision, and these concern his notion of public reason. If public reason requires that we bracket our comprehensive traditions, how can politics serve as a dialogical vehicle for the critical reform of our ethical identities? By focusing primarily on the liberal problem of social cooperation and its emphasis on bracketing our differences, hasn't Rawls tacitly favored one comprehensive tradition—the libertarian—over the other, republican one? And doesn't this bias reflect the unfelicitous hegemony of individual instrumentalism vis-à-vis communal expressivism that prevents current liberal societies from nurturing the democratic solidarity requisite for maintaining healthy, integral identity-formation?

As we saw, communitarian criticisms of liberalism find this lack of sustained communication between comprehensive traditions problematic. However, the extreme varieties of theoretical and practical holism that we initially examined were just as wanting in this area. The former, defended by Rorty, conceives communication on the model of radical translation. It requires that we assimilate the speech behavior of others to our own familiar, ethnocentric horizon of meaning. The latter, defended by Dreyfus and MacIntyre, conceives communication on the model of socialization. It requires that we transcend our native horizon of understanding and immerse ourselves wholly in the other's horizon.

Observational distance and participatory immersion are equally incompatible with critical dialogue; hence neither extricates us from SR. We accordingly sought a middle path between these extremes—one presented by Gadamer's philosophical hermeneutics. Yet here we observed an ambiguity in Gadamer's hermeneutical principle of an expected completion of meaning and truth that rendered his attempt to ground CR problematic. This principle can function uncritically, by leading us to overlook the real contradictions and ideological constraints operating in tradition. Gadamer's other way of interpreting the principle—as a projection of unconstrained and unlimited communication—avoids this ambiguity. As a *theoretical* outgrowth of communicative practice, the principle can serve as an idea of justice underwriting our criticism of tradition and language as a whole—at least (following Habermas) insofar as these are affected by economic constraints and forms of political domination.

The problem of conflicting interpretations suggests another kind of criticism, however. The communitarian criticism advanced by Taylor and Walzer is more pluralist than that proposed by MacIntyre and Gadamer, in that it doesn't privilege synthesis over accommodation. However, we saw that their attempt to accommodate separate spheres of justice and sources of identity also implies an idea of integrity that is grounded just as deeply in the hermeneutical principle of coherence and perfectibility as the idea of justice. This notion of the good—which guides the critique of social reification—introduces a new aspect of CR, namely, harmonious communication between rationalization complexes.

Our discussion of hermeneutics in this chapter has thus yielded two communitarian ideas requiring further examination: The idea of unconstrained dialogue establishes the procedural rationale justifying participatory democracy; the idea of communicative integrity establishes the aesthetic rationale underwriting critical judgment. In the theories of law and democracy developed by Dworkin and Habermas the two ideas converge: A system of legal rights that lacks integrity or ignores the expressive aims of democracy as a solidaristic process of identity-formation and self-realization will also lack legitimacy, and thus fall short of instantiating the good it esteems above all others—justice.

Before we pursue these ideas further, we must address the French communitarian critique of hermeneutic idealism. This critique cuts to the heart of the Anglo-American communitarianism discussed in this chapter. By departing from a more radical notion of the relational nature of community and identity, it effectively deconstructs both of these terms—along with the allied notions of subjectivity, rationality, and autonomy. The strategy governing this approach is familiar to us from our examination of the Gadamer/Habermas controversy: the "text" that underlies community is woven with mutually intertwined—but clashing—strands of meaning. The aim of interpretation is to demonstrate this fact in order to explode once and for all the ideology of coherence, completion, perfectibility, and identity.

We thus find ourselves once again confronted by the specter of radical hermeneutical indeterminacy that haunted our earlier discussion of science, technology, and social action. Postmodern French communitarians find consolation in such indeterminacy because it—rather than enlightened democratic consensus or romantic aesthetic harmony—ostensibly frustrates the modern, totalitarian trend toward closure. Yet it remains to be seen whether their mythopoetic model of social text—as an impersonal process of linguistic deconstruction—succeeds where the hermeneutical model fails. What becomes of community after the demise of dialectical reason, if not the return of the Subject?

4

French Communitarianism and
the Subjugation of Identity

I concluded the last chapter with a tentative endorsement of hermeneutics as a philosophical basis for communitarianism. What recommended hermeneutics for this function was its potential for meeting two needs: the equiprimordial grounding of the right and the good; and the avoidance of relativism and skepticism. Hermeneutics seemed to explain how the transcendent expectations of rational coherence, agreement, and perfectibility that guide the critique of ideology and reification arise within parochial contexts of practical understanding. At the same time, I observed that the *presumption* of rational coherence and perfectibility can function ideologically itself, by *limiting* criticism to the exposure of those prejudices that obstruct the restoration of the traditional text's (presumed) identity as rational, continuous, and coherent.

This is where French communitarians break with their Anglo-American counterparts. Although the latter talk about conflicting traditions and strands of identity, they generally presume that narrative unity describes the normal, that is, original, condition of historical, communal, and autobiographical "texts." French communitarians deny this. To understand why presupposes an appreciation of the deep philosophical differences separating the two schools.

To begin with, French communitarians question the very metaphysical assumptions about rationality that Anglo-American communitarians take for granted. Some Anglo-American communitarians—most notably MacIntyre and Taylor—do criticize SR from a hermeneutical standpoint. Yet, French communitarians contend that hermeneutics—and by extension CR—retains residues of SR operant within Hegelian dialectics as a whole. Even the ontological hermeneutics espoused by Heidegger and Gadamer seems deficient on this score. Being, language, and tradition here function in a manner analogous to Hegel's *Geist;* instead of the Cartesian subject as the *immutable* foundation underlying rational intuition, we have the macrosubject of historicality as the *ever-present* ground (*Grund* or reason) predestining the disclosure of truth.

Second, because of its radical questioning of rationalist metaphysics, French communitarianism is less congenial to the sorts of descriptive and prescriptive approaches to political philosophy characteristic of Anglo-American varieties. One is tempted to say that it is "transcendental" in the sense that it seeks to uncover the general structures (or conditions) underlying the possibility of knowledge, action, and subjectivity. More importantly, it construes these conditions in such a way that *prescriptions* about the right and the good seem inherently ideological, that is, illegitimate and potentially totalitarian.

Although many Anglo-American communitarians also undertake transcendental inquiries into the ontological preconditions for political community, they do so from a hermeneutical standpoint that seems (to them, at least) to be both descriptive of "common understandings" and prescriptive of basic communicative values—such as perfectibility, reciprocity, and integrity—that emerge within that *experience.* By contrast, the transcendental inquiry pursued by French communitarians is more radical, in that it goes beyond subjective experience in all of its forms—including the experience of dialogic encounter germane to intersubjectivity. More specifically, French communitarians deconstruct the subject of experience by showing that it is a *construct* that masks and distorts its own conditions of possibility. These conditions—of language and power—are at once impersonal (or objective) and heterogeneous. Inclining toward mutability, instability, and disunity, they *present* no ground for theorizing about justice or the good.

We might summarize this last difference accordingly: whereas Anglo-American communitarians are primarily concerned with overcoming the kinds of relativism and skepticism that vitiate *experience-immanent* criticism,

French communitarians are primarily concerned with overcoming ideologies of totality and subjectivity that suppress the *relationalism* of *experience-transcendent* deconstruction.

It is this emphasis on the relational *subtext* underlying subjectivity that explains why French poststructuralism is simultaneously communitarian and anticommunitarian. French poststructuralism is communitarian insofar as it rejects any form of subjectivism and individualism. Relational communicability—or communion with otherness—both underwrites and decomposes the surface effect (illusory appearance, or *Schein*) of stable, self-contained identity. Community here marks something like a permanent, if not originary, condition of excess and rupture, or an unrepresentable—and therefore unrealizable—practical idea in the Kantian sense.

But it is precisely such communitarian ideas as these that render poststructuralism anticommunitarian—indeed, *anarchic* in the original sense of the term. For, by repudiating any legitimate sense of identity, commonality, stability, origin, ground, and closure, they leave absolutely open any question regarding justice or public well-being.

The three varieties of French poststructuralist thought discussed in this book reflect—in my opinion—progressively radical stages of communitarian criticism. The *deconstructive* approach, developed by Derrida and Nancy, bears the strongest resemblance to the hermeneutical varieties discussed in chapter 3. It explicitly undertakes a transcendental exposition of community and subjectivity, and does so, moreover, from the *textual* standpoint of reading and writing. On this account, community retains a relationship to a kind of sharing, however unsettled and divisive.

The second, *genealogical* approach, developed by Foucault, has certain affinities with the critical, functionalist sociology discussed in chapter 2. What Habermas's program of ideology critique does for hermeneutics, it does for narrative deconstruction. In short, it is more radical than the deconstructive variety in that it explains textual meanings as illusory surface effects of more conflict-ridden technologies, economies, power relations, and other "material" (or embodied) interactions. It is also more historicist and nominalist than its deconstructive counterpart, and its appeal to the primacy of agonal power relations and strategic gaming is even less compatible with descriptive and prescriptive notions of community.

The third approach, developed by Lyotard, bears the strongest resemblance to my own, which takes as its point of departure the community of *speech* and judgment. This approach is more radical than the genealogical tracing of power relations in at least one sense: it exposes the latter's positivism with regard to norms and meanings. By taking seriously the norms and meanings informing local narrative practices, Lyotard's speech act theory provides a deeper link between the idea of community and a complex scheme of justice than even Walzer's own account of our shared understandings.

In this chapter we will examine the deconstructive and genealogical varieties of communitarian thought (exploration of Lyotard's critique of consensus and judgment will be postponed for later discussion of democracy and law). I contend that their bracketing of hermeneutics vitiates their criticism of totalitarian ideologies—those stemming from CR (or hermeneutics) as well as those stemming from SR.

This is apparent in their identification of technology and rationality with SR—a view that contradicts our earlier hermeneutical grounding of CR (sec. 1). Nancy argues against this analysis by pointing out that the hermeneutical anticipation of complete and perfectible meaning itself amounts to a kind of totalitarian ideology (sec. 2). Contrary to Gadamer and Anglo-American communitarians, tradition fails to provide a stable and continuous identity of meaning requisite for sustaining the truth and authority of texts. This applies as well to the narrative texture of community, which exists in a permanent state of crisis. The upshot of this anarchic view of community is a notion of political life devoid of any reference to autonomous agency and, one would suppose, any reference to a legal sphere composed of autonomous subjects. Following Derrida, Nancy argues that a communitarian ethic compatible with this insight commands textual interventions respectful of our *essential* responsibility to the Other—a responsibility that precedes any mutual recognition of rights and goods. Hence it is Nancy's contention that no system of rights or community of goods can claim legitimacy.

It may well be that this entire analysis depends on suppressing the basic reciprocity underlying communication. Even still, the psychoanalytic implications Nancy draws from it raise important questions about the patriarchal bias implicit in individuation and its relationship to authoritarianism and totalitarianism. For if Nancy's Lacanian take on identity is correct, selfhood originates and remains in a state of material dependence and self-exteriorization. In that case much depends on whether this inherently divided self—or self shared among a community of similar selves—is symptomatic of a particular social formation (liberal society, for instance) or paradigmatic of all forms of socialization (sec. 3).

I conclude that Nancy's questionable preference for this latter interpretation ultimately stems from his peculiar approach, which combines deconstruction and transcendental philosophy. Foucault's analysis of the aporias attending any transcendental philosophy recommends the adoption of more historically attuned methods (sec. 4). Unfortunately, his tendency to construe these methods positivistically prevents him from developing a coherent account of agency and action—a deficit that is only made good in his histories of sexuality.

Habermas, by contrast, shows why the problem of subjective agency must be reconceived in terms of a theory of communicative interaction. Yet despite its salutary invocation of democratic values, this theory lends itself to a mistaken impression that strategic power relations are somehow opposed to consensual communication. Following Foucault, I argue that this is not the case and, indeed, cannot be the case if we are to explain the possibility of political alliances.

1. Nancy's deconstruction of community takes off from a philosophical analysis of modern totalitarianism. The point of departure for his treatment of this issue is Heidegger's account of the affinity between Western metaphysics, on one hand, and modern conceptions of sovereignty, power, freedom, and subjectivity, on the other. Heidegger's account runs as follows: Beginning with Plato we find the visible world of transient appearance subordinated to an invisible world of immutable (self-identical) being. The loss of value suffered by the visible world is later reflected in modern rationalism (or SR), which replaces the immutability of Platonic Ideas with the certainty of the Cartesian *cogito*. With truth now defined as an identity of subject and object, the world of appearance ceases to be anything more than a mere object of consciousness, and later (as in German idealism) an ideal projection of objectifying, transcendental subjectivity. The culmination of this tradition in Nietzsche's philosophy witnesses the devaluation of both objective world and subjective ego as illusory effects—or mere instrumental values—of an originary, biological will to power.

It is here that the totalitarian implications of SR become evident. Because values and meanings are mere instrumentalities of arbitrary willing, SR cannot but lead to the total infusion of scientific strategies of prediction and control in economy, polity, society, and culture. Thus what was formerly meant by the political—public debate among equals over what constitutes the ultimate good of society—is increasingly marginalized, if not suppressed, as dysfunctional and dangerous. Consequently, suppression of the political is compelled by the totalitarian logic of global administration (Nancy and Lacoue-Labarthe 1981, 16–17).

Nancy hesitates to include Western democracy under the rubric of totalitarianism, despite the fact that his own Heideggerian predilections compel him to do so. Citing the views of Claude Lefort and Hannah Arendt, he notes that totalitarianism grows out of the anomic disintegration of liberal democracy. It seeks to contain this tendency by reorganizing public and private spheres of life around a stable, homogeneous *corps politique* similar to that formerly vested in the unitary will of the monarch, but founded on a communitarian—racial, ethnic, or national—ideology. In other words, it seeks to restore traditional authority by collapsing distinct political, legal, cultural, and economic spheres into a totally integrated and hierarchically administered identity.[1]

Nancy is well aware that liberal democracies seldom degenerate to this level of reaction. He is, however, cognizant of the trend toward bureaucratization discussed earlier. In this connection he cites Lyotard's analysis of capitalism as a cybernetic exchange system oriented toward stability and Arendt's lament over the victory of *animal laborans* (or welfare economics) over political action. These views will merit further discussion in chapter 7. Suffice it to say, Nancy is keenly aware of the technological manipulation of public opinion by mass media that makes modern liberal democracy a mockery of rational communication (Nancy 1983, 188–89).

It is precisely this withdrawal of *(retrait du)* political life that explains Nancy's own retreat from *(retrait du)* political philosophy as it is ordinarily understood. For Nancy no less than for Taylor and MacIntyre, political philosophy must eschew behavioral social science if it is to remain truthful to the nonempirical ethical phenomena constitutive of political life and avoid becoming an instrument of rational choice engineering. But, contrary to Taylor and MacIntyre, neither can it renew the classical project of prescriptive ethics without perpetuating the totalitarian logic inherent in foundational (or teleological) metaphysics.

What remains of political philosophy after these descriptive and prescriptive functions are removed? With explicit reference to Kant, Nancy allows that a kind of transcendental reflection may be possible that delimits the a priori conditions of political life—the essence of the political *(le politique)* as distinct from its empirical manifestations *(la politique)*. These conditions are inextricably connected to notions of freedom and community, and it is the business of the philosopher to reveal their proper signification absent any ideological distortions. This task requires a different kind of immanent criticism—one that deconstructs subjectivity, individuality, identity, rationality, totality, finality, and other metaphysical categories (196–98). It also requires a distinctly transcendental—and from the perspective of Anglo-American communitarianism, apolitical—idea of community. For it is Nancy's belief that, by confusing community with mundane, practical ideals of solidarity (and thereby succumbing to the allure of transcendental illusion), Hegelian, Marxian, and neo-Aristotelian varieties of communitarianism ostensibly risk the very totalitarianism they perceive in liberalism (Nancy and Lacoue-Labarthe 1981, 18, 24).

2. In order to understand the kind of deconstructive criticism Nancy thinks is necessary for authentic communitarian philosophizing—and thus to understand as well his concerns about Hegelian, Marxian, and neo-Aristotelian varieties of communitarianism—one must first understand his critique of hermeneutics. This critique draws its inspiration from Derrida's critique of *logocentrism*, or the primacy of spoken communication over writing as the proper paradigm for linguisticality.

By "logocentrism" Derrida means the view—familiar to us from our earlier examination of logical positivism in chapter 2—that there are "hard" (extralinguistic) facts and univocal meanings that can be (a) transparently intuited and (b) truth-functionally or definitively correlated with one another through the medium of language. According to this view, the determinate meaning and veracity of language is guaranteed solely by the immediate *presence* of a *complete* context of semantic reference. This context includes things and events referred to by the speaker as well as the speaker's own intentions—both of which can be fully presented through gesture and speech.

In comparison to this immediate *identification* of subjective thought (signified meanings), language (acoustic signifiers), and objective givens (immediate sense experience), *writing* seems both derivative and degenerative. Because written texts are detachable from their original context—hence, from the relatively univocal sense determined by the author's spoken declaration of his or her intentions—their meaning is likewise detachable (indeterminate and free-floating), varying from context to context. This lack of determinate meaning, Derrida tell us, is *wrongly* perceived to be privative and parasitic on an original fullness (presence) of meaning in speech.

Given this presumption, it is hardly surprising that Derrida should trace back to logocentrism the entire course of Western metaphysics from Plato on. Far from being an innocent prejudice, the "metaphysics of presence" implicit in logocentrism has functioned as a kind of political ideology, very similar to that diagnosed with respect to SR. For, in Derrida's opinion, logocentrism favors hierarchy and dominance, at least insofar as certain metaphorically related terms (presence, being, identity, truth, speech, rationality, masculinity) are given priority over their contraries (absence, nonbeing, difference, error, writing, fancy, and femininity).

Now Derrida points out—quite ironically—that the possibility of metaphorically relating and thus of "identifying" certain categories of terms already presupposes the inversion of this hierarchy. As Saussure had earlier shown, linguistic signifiers acquire their meanings through their differential relations with one another. This means—to recall the point of our earlier discussion of Hegel's logic—that the intrinsic identity (being, meaning, or essence) of some determinant individual is inextricably contaminated with alterity. Hence, there is no immediate perception of objects and no immediate understanding of meanings—no *presence*—that is not already metaphorically interpreted (or interrupted) by linguistic mediation, or *absence*. To cite Derrida,

> There is no phenomenality reducing the sign or the representer so that the thing signified may be allowed to glow finally in the luminosity of its presence. The so-called "thing itself" is always already a *representamen* shielded from the simplicity of intuitive evidence. The *representamen* functions only by giving rise to an *interpretant* that itself becomes a sign and so on to infinity.[2]

Derrida's "privileging" of writing, absence, and infinite interpretation must not be understood as just another metaphysical ideology—one that replaces the dominance of logocentrism with that of anarchy. Derrida does not advocate abandoning rational communication as a valid aim of political speech. Nonetheless he points out that whatever meaning obtains in rational communication is essentially fluid, since both the context of speech and the system of signifiers are unbounded and open to endless interpretation.

All this sounds very much like the ontological hermeneutics put forth by Heidegger and Gadamer. Like Gadamer, Derrida holds that to understand the meaning of a text as something true, reasonable, and perduring— that is, as identical across ever mutable, spatiotemporal contexts—is to understand it *differently*. At the same time, there appears to be a profound difference in the way he conceives this "event" (advent or *Ereignis*) of meaning. That both he and Gadamer view meaning as an event (or trace) shows the extent to which they agree that meaning is nonsubjective. Meanings are not (as Husserl argued) constituted by subjective intentions, be they transcendental or otherwise. Language—as movement of tradition or as open system of differential relations—transcends intentionality.

But what does this mean precisely? For Gadamer, it means that there is a continuous—potentially complete and perfectible—truth (meaning) awaiting to be completed, or made fully present (albeit in a different way each time it is interpreted). Hermeneutic objectivity and truth is made possible by the continuous efficacy of tradition as a common constraint on our subjective intentions. For Derrida, by contrast, it means that there is a permanent rupture in the system of differential sign relations, or absence of meaning that can never be completely filled or brought to consciousness. *Différance*—the neologism Derrida coined to describe the difference and deferral of meaning in writing—thus constitutes a counternotion to the Heideggerian view of language as a clearing for the advent (coming-to-presence) of Being.

The opposition between Gadamer's and Derrida's nonsubjectivist accounts of meaning is explicitly addressed by Nancy. Nancy does not expressly oppose Derrida to Gadamer. Instead, he invokes Heidegger's own opinion that every disclosure of Being implies a corresponding concealment, such that Being itself remains absent in discourse. According to Nancy, the problem with Gadamer's hermeneutics—especially its conception of the hermeneutical circle—is that it violates the ontological difference between Being and beings.

Qua ontological, the hermeneutical circle involves projecting a horizon of possible meaningfulness (Being), in terms of which particular beings are brought to thematic presence. Now, there are two ways to understand this horizon, each corresponding to distinct features of our historical consciousness of finitude or subjective limitation. One way—favored by Gadamer—identifies the horizon with traditional prejudices that act as familiar and shared *substantive constraints.* The other way—favored by Heidegger in *Being and Time*—identifies the horizon with our own mortality, which, by disrupting our familiar and shared reference points, opens up a new—potentially discontinuous and radically other—horizon of meaning (Nancy 1982, 30). Whereas the former grounds interpretation in particular prejudices—"beings" capable of being brought to thematic awareness—the latter opens up (exposes) this grounding to the abyss of nonmeaning (Being).

Like Habermas, Nancy thinks that Gadamer's appeal to tradition as a *substantively* rational basis guiding interpretation evinces a deeply conservative bias built into Hegelian dialectics generally. For Gadamer as for Hegel, the point of departure for dialectical logic is immediate identity, or—in Nancy's words—the "immediacy of the participation in a shared meaning" (17–21). Although this immediate and unproblematic understanding gets "suppressed" (or interrupted) owing to the passage of time, and so requires the interpretative bridging of cultural distance, it ends up getting "conceived into the final product" of interpretation as a restoration of substantial continuity and agreement. Thus, the event (advent) of successful interpretation always issues in a (re)appropriation *(Ereignis)* of a familiar—if somewhat altered—traditional identity.

We can paraphrase Nancy's objection in a somewhat different way: Gadamer assumes that there must be a prior agreement (identity) linking interlocutors, whether these be persons or traditions speaking to us from texts. At the very least there must be agreement on linguisticality, if not on a common language. Such sharing is what guarantees possible objectivity and truth. But why assume that tradition, language, and linguisticality involve a kind of sharing that makes objective truth possible? Doesn't the radical finitude inscribed in our anxious awareness of our eventual mortality ensure that my understanding of a "common tradition" will never completely coincide with the way others understand it? Stronger still, doesn't it entail that every understanding is a rupture with, rather than a continuation of, tradition?

If this *absence* of agreement and mutual understanding does not entail the absence of communication and community, it does suggest their fragility and incompleteness. This condition of emptiness and nihilism—which assumes even greater prominence in the modern age—may well be fueled by existential *Angst*, as Nancy seems to suggest. Indeed, as we shall see below, the singular virtue of deconstructive varieties of communitarianism— as distinct from their Anglo-American counterparts—is showing how ethical questions regarding identity, responsibility, and so forth *are* deeply personal and radically contextual in just this existential sense. Despite their nihilism, these deconstructive varieties are nonetheless communitarian in emphasizing the radical decentering (or death) of the subject vis-à-vis its primary responsibility to the other. By radicalizing existential self-questioning, such deconstructions in turn question the kind of lonely, almost *solipsistic* responsibility for self and other one finds in the writings of classical existentialists like Sartre or the Heidegger of *Being and Time*.

One cannot underestimate the importance of this advance. Many philosophers (including myself) would agree with Nancy that Heidegger's preoccupation with *Jemeinigkeit* (ownness) as an authentic possibility of "being-towards-death" leads to nihilistic subjectivism. This subjectivism, in turn, allows only two possible grounds for "ethical" action: uncritical acceptance of and conformity to the prevailing ethos (tradition), or uncritical acceptance of a resolute Führer who places his own will above all ethics and tradition. A subject so totally centered on its own radically detached, atomic indeterminacy is one that is so lacking in moral principle and character that it is simply incapable of resisting the will of either authority. Perhaps this explains Heidegger's own existential commitment to National Socialism, with its emphasis on the *Führerprinzip* and its glorification of the state as a monolithic, fully integrated, work of art rooted in the equally monolithic, traditional identity of the German people.[3]

Of course, whether the existential dimension of ethos and identity is *best* captured by a deconstructive communitarianism remains to be seen. Does the existential decentration of the monadic subject primarily occur in our *singular* responsibility to the *particular* other (my intimate acquaintance, say), or does it also—and perhaps more fundamentally—occur in our general responsibility to all others in our community? If the latter, then hermeneutics may still provide the key we are looking for. If I am not mistaken, the counterfactual sense of hermeneutical perfectibility defended by Habermas demonstrates precisely this point. By showing how ideal expectations of justice, solidarity, and integrity built into democracy underwrite a radical process of *mutual* self-reflection, it provides an even better explanation of our modern disenchantment with traditional identity—namely, one that doesn't sacrifice critical standards on the altar of existential solipsism.

2.1 Before addressing this democratic feature of our existential identity we must first see how the Derridean conception of language provides a foothold for a kind of criticism that does without any of the rational standards implicit in hermeneutics. Deconstruction differs from more conventional modes of ideological critique in that it denies the existence of any external, nontextual reality from which one might expose the "falsity" of an "ideological" text. It is immanent critique insofar as it shows that the ostensible presuppositions underlying the production of a text's meaning are dependent on and contradict the explicit assertions made within it.

Now the reversal of hierarchies and the breaking down of binary oppositions not only undermine the metaphysical assumptions of identity and semantic wholeness structuring the text. They also deconstruct the assumptions underwriting the critical activity of the reader, so that the autonomy of such activity—its presumed opposition to the text under criticism—is itself inverted. As Derrida never ceases to remind us, "[B]reaks are always, and fatally, reinscribed in an old cloth that must be continually, interminably undone" (Derrida 1981, 22, 66).

Since deconstruction cannot avoid repeating and restoring the oppositions and identities it seeks to undo, it must—if it wants to preserve its own critical intent—resort to new strategies of reinscription. In other words, it must not invoke *différance* as an idea referring to some nonlogocentric meaning, but must itself contribute to the process of differing (or retextualizing) meaning in more radical ways.

This is accomplished by reinscribing the old text in a new one combining different rhetorical strategies and hieroglyphic styles of writing—citation, ideographic supplementation, contamination through juxtaposition of texts, and the deployment of terms *sous rature*, which exploits literal meaning for purposes of communication while simultaneously withdrawing (erasing) it. The important thing to note here is that such supplementary devices ambiguously straddle the space separating the additive from the substitutive, the superfluous from the necessary, the corruptive from the compensatory—in short, the *destructive* from the *redemptive* as Benjamin and Adorno understood it.

Like all forms of immanent criticism, deconstruction simply retraces a real social crisis. However, in this instance the crisis is not specific to particular institutions—such as the contradiction obtaining between private property and democracy—but extends throughout language in general. It thus designates a *permanent* identity crisis besetting all societies in varying degrees.

The implications for communitarianism are clear. Community cannot be a sharing of identity since, as Nancy notes, "what is shared is . . . but the sharing itself and, consequently, the nonidentity of everything, of each with itself and with others, and of the nonidentity of the work with itself, and finally of literature with itself" (Nancy 1986, 164). The weaving of the (con)text is never finished. Consequently, insofar as its identity is necessarily interpellated by the other—continually interrupted and fractured into as many meanings as there are singular contexts—the communal text can never achieve the status of a universal law, or constitution, but must remain illegitimate and without foundation:

> Writing is the gesture which obeys the sole necessity of exposing the limit . . . on which communication takes place. . . . On this limit, the one who exposes himself and to which—if we listen, if we read, if our ethical and political condition is listening and reading—we expose ourselves, does not deliver us to a founding speech *(parôle)*. On the contrary, it suspends and interrupts it. . . . Yet even that speech has something inaugural. Each writer, each work inaugurates a community . . . but the communism here is inaugural, not final. It is not completed. . . . We understand only that there is no common understanding of the community . . . that the sharing creates neither an understanding . . . nor a knowledge nor does it give to anyone or any community itself the mastery of being-in-common. (167–71)

If community lacks the unity of an *opus*, then "it cannot be an object of either an ethics or a politics of community." And yet, as Nancy himself concedes, "[T]his is *prescribed*" (182; my italics). Hence the obvious question: What does this prescription mean precisely? In the next section, we will see that it does indeed implicate a kind of communitarian ethic, but one more originary than any theory of justice or the good.

2.2 Nancy's communitarian ethic bears the trace of deconstruction in its ambivalent appeal to Kant *and* Heidegger. On one hand, he follows Kant in conceiving ethics as addressing a deontological—one might say transcendental—"fact" about our freedom. Such freedom precedes and limits our (communitarian) search for happiness by making us responsible to the other. On the other hand, he follows Heidegger in conceiving freedom as a kind of *contingent,* existential transcendence—one, in his opinion, that exists only as a reaching out (responsibility) to the other.

This latter fact bodes ill for a liberal conception of justice in two senses. First, responsibility to the other cannot ground reciprocal relationships of the sort constitutive of individual rights, since the other to whom one responds must be accorded an unconditional respect. Second, freedom as contingent transcendence renders any legitimation of laws problematic. For no conception of moral self-determination—regardless of how democratic or self-intuitive it may be—is compatible with the asymmetry, alterity, and contingency of responsibility.

According to Nancy, then, our finitude is as much a part of our ethical being as our freedom. Kant said so himself when he argued that freedom involved acting in accordance with the categorical imperative. The latter exists as a *factum rationis* interrupting the causal facticity of natural inclination. As a fact, however, the imperative "does not belong to the nature of a subject, but to that which, even though resembling a subject, exceeds . . . this status." From this premise Nancy draws the very radical—and unKantian— conclusion that to be obligated "does not mean that we give ourselves the law" (Nancy 1983, 24–25). In the words of Lévinas, to whom Nancy appeals, "[T]he freedom of the subject is not the highest or primary value" since "the heteronomy of our response to the human Other, or to God as the absolutely Other, precedes the autonomy of our subjective freedom" (Kearney 1984, 63)

In order to understand the force of the responsibility here commanded, one must pay special attention to the distinction that Nancy, following Lévinas, draws between morality and ethics. Whereas the former concerns the rules of conduct operating "in the sociopolitical order of organizing and improving our human survival," the latter concerns the "vigilant passivity to the call of the Other which precedes our interest in Being . . . [and in] appropriating what is other to itself." Ethical receptivity is the transcendental precondition for moral deliberation about justice and happiness. It therefore cannot "legislate for society or produce rules of conduct whereby society might be revolutionized or transformed" (Kearney 1984, 65). Again, deliberations about the right and the good involve comparing persons and their needs from the detached perspective of an outside observer (or third person); ethics, by contrast, pertains to the asymmetrical encounter (face-to-face) between "I" and "thou."[4] Above all, ethics imposes a prior obligation that has less force as a prescription than as a transcendental (or existential) fact: the question posed by the other must expose (open) us to questioning as such. In the words of Derrida, whom Nancy cites,

> The liberty *of the question* (double genitive) must be stated and protected. A founded dwelling, a realized tradition of the question remaining a question. If this commandment has an ethical meaning, it is not in that it belongs to the *domain* of the ethical, but in that it ultimately authorizes every ethical law in general. There is no stated law, no commandment, that is not addressed to a freedom of speech.[5]

What the categorical imperative commands bears striking resemblance to Nietzsche's cardinal virtue *Redlichkeit* (honesty or truthfulness) in that it involves a task of perpetual questioning that devalues "all morals insofar as they are founded on the representation of an ideal, a value, or an end—which is to say, in Kantian terms, all morals grounded in the regime of the hypothetical imperative" (Nancy 1983, 83). Such questioning implies a fundamental openness toward possibilities of judgment, of disclosing anew the meaningful "identity" (being) of self and other. As Lévinas puts it, this decentered "I" is absolutely subordinated to the Other: "I am defined as subjectivity, as a singular person, as an 'I' precisely because I am exposed to the other" (Kearney 1984, 62).

What are the political implications of this conception of face-to-face responsibility? As the above paragraph clearly attests, the ethical seems as radically detached from the moral and political as the ontological is from the ontic, and the transcendental is from the empirical. But there is the further implication that one's existential singularity and responsibility only fully obtain in those intimate relationships that are not structured by *general* norms or third-person witnesses, such as those involving friendship (Derrida 1988, 641). According to Derrida, it is here, in the *fundamental* "friendship prior to friendships" as *commonly* understood, where real community—in the sense of a prior and *incommensurable* "being together," "sharing of a language," "singularity" (division), in short, *partage*—is to be found (636). Thus, although "there is no friendship without 'respect for the Other' [that is] inseparable from a 'morally good will'," this respect for the Other "should not be simply confused with purely moral respect, the respect owed only to its 'cause', the moral law, of which the person is but an example" (640).

Derrida's reference to friendship as singular and almost selfless devotion to an intimate acquaintance reminds one of Hegel's early criticism of legal alienation. At one level, at least, the truth they convey is undeniable: as feminists like Carol Gilligan remind us, ethics involves more than universal schemes of justice; it also involves applying these schemes in context-sensitive ways and, more importantly, accepting nongeneralizable, nonreciprocal, and context-specific responsibilities with respect to our most significant others, family members, and friends. Yet Derrida *also* remarks that the classical literature affirms a strong bond between friendship and political virtue (justice and reciprocity) that competes with his own ethical analysis (644).

Significantly, at least one feminist theoretician of democracy has challenged the feasibility of linking friendship and politics. Jane Mansbridge (1977) rightly observes that the participatory, egalitarian, and consensual ideals that she (though not Derrida) detects in interaction among intimate friends are transformed in large-scale political associations, from solidarity-preserving bonds to solidarity-destroying rights. Indeed, were this not the case, then friendship would allow a deference to group authority that might smother political responsibility. Hence the wisdom of Mansbridge's compromise, which recommends tying the solidaristic aims of "friendly" small-scale participation to individual rights afforded by more adversarial, representative institutions. Of course, this analysis suggests that the primacy of asymmetry, heterology, and singularity that Derrida and Nancy locate in *legally transcendent,* face-to-face relations *between friends* may need to be deconstructed in turn. As Tom McCarthy (1988, 646) observes:

> [I]t is not only in friendship, but in social interaction generally, that the "singularity of the other" is intimately connected to the law (here normative expectations). And although the individual is related "asymmetrically" to the *generalized* other, which is always "anterior," the socially generalized patterns of behavior the latter comprise are themselves typically structured as relations of *reciprocity* with *individual* Others: the actor is entitled to expect certain kinds of behavior from others in certain situations, and is obligated in turn to meet their legitimate expectations.[6]

As we shall see, this *symmetrical* dimension of responsibility underlies the democratic, communitarian ethics developed by Habermas. But it is one thing to say that social relations are structured by reciprocal expectations based on legitimate norms (or laws), another to legitimate them philosophically.

2.3 This takes us to the heart of Nancy's criticism of liberal justice, namely the inability of legal jurisprudence and philosophy to legitimate themselves. Nancy addresses this problem in an essay entitled "Lapsus judicii," in which reason and legal precedent are themselves shown to be groundless (or fallen). To begin with, all jurisdiction (asserting right) involves circumscribing a domain of propriety on the basis of some rational or traditional precedent. A legal code claiming general validity is applied to a unique set of circumstances in such a way that the contingency and particularity of the latter is "sublated"; the particular set of circumstances is elevated to the rank of a case or redefined as an exemplar possessing universal validity and legitimacy.

This process, however, produces reversal. As Gadamer himself points out, the particular case becomes part of the effective history of the law, and so comes to define and legitimate *it* as well. However, contrary to Gadamer, this by no means bestows authority on legal tradition. The circularity inherent in jurisdiction entails that the very meaning and validity of the law—the fixing of rights and limits—remains undecided at the moment of judgment. "Hard" cases involving unforeseeable—and from the standpoint of literally stipulated legal expectations, recalcitrant—circumstances are necessarily those on which determinate legal traditions remain silent. Yet appeal to abstract moral principles that transcend tradition is of no avail in legitimating adjudication. For infinite applicability is here purchased at the expense of determinacy. Because moral principles are themselves open to endless hermeneutical disputation, their meaning is also a matter of singular discretion. Hence juris-*diction* is juris-*fiction* (Nancy 1983, 41).

Similar arguments for the illegitimacy of law pervade the writings of Derrida and other poststructuralists, where they function to either legitimate *or* delegitimate revolutionary violence.[7] For example, in his tribute to Nelson Mandela, Derrida attempts to explain how the latter's "outlaw" status as a "violent" revolutionary is in some sense more lawful than the illegitimate violence perpetuated by a racist legal system constituted by a white minority. On one hand, no founding act can be legitimate, since "the people" who authorize the act do not exist prior to their own constitution. Attempts to circumvent this vicious circle by postulating an absolute foundation and authority—as in the appeal to divinely sanctioned rights contained in the American Declaration of Independence—illegitimately conflate the constation of a transcendent "fact" with the performance of a contingent political contract (Derrida 1986). On the other hand, "the very logic of the law" implicit within even the South African constitution anticipates the ideal, universal inclusion of all citizens as free and equal. It is this *future anterior* (or present/abyssal) ground of legitimation to which the African National Congress's Charter of Freedom also appeals in justifying *its* violence.

As we shall see in chapter 8, Derrida's treatment of revolutionary violence leaves much to be desired. If the legitimation of violence is justified by the idealism of the ANC's Charter, why wasn't it also justified by the idealism of the Declaration of Independence? After all, both declarations legitimate their rebellion by appeal to a preexisting, sovereign power (the South African People or the American People) that they in turn retroactively authorize and constitute. Perhaps, then, both might be legitimate—their circularity notwithstanding—and only Derrida's own abstract opposition between transcendent ethical violence (revolutionary autonomy) and factual legal violence (institutional coercion) prevents us from realizing it. Of course, liberals like Dworkin and Habermas also explain the illegitimacy of racist legal regimes—and therewith the legitimacy of truly constitutional ones— by appeal to the implicit ideals of justice and integrity informing any system of law. However, unlike Derrida, they attempt to ground law in rational reconstructions of a Kantian variety. This strategy, I shall argue, cannot entirely escape the circle, alluded to by Derrida, at the heart of founding, legislating, and adjudicating. For Derrida, that means it cannot escape the arbitrary violence of facticity, either.

Indeed, was it not Kant himself, Nancy contends, whose extension of the juridical model to philosophy unintentionally bears witness to reason's own groundlessness or facticity? For Kant, dogmatic philosophy, or the metaphysics of pure reason, is illegitimate until it is given its rightful limits (Nancy 1983, 48). But the paradoxical strategy deployed in the *Critique of Pure Reason*—of reason limiting and legitimating itself—seems unprecedented and without any legal standing. To rectify this apparent illegality, Kant turns to geometry as a paradigm of legitimate science, since it constructs figures in intuitions that confirm its own axioms. Yet, as Nancy points out, such construction can but mirror the circular self-legislation of law itself; the case or geometric figure that legitimates the rule of construction is produced by it (53). Indeed, if geometry is illegitimate fiction, then philosophy, or pure reason, is even more so. For it cannot even offer an intuition or schema that would be adequate to its own categories. And to the extent, for example, that a category such as causality *does* find intuitive confirmation in the irreversible succession of sensuous phenomena, its validity is not a priori, but like geometry is limited or conditioned by what happens to appear (54–58).

And so the *myth* of reason interrupts itself, or more precisely, deconstructs its own dogmatic claim to be exempt from the law. Be it making a law without legal warrant—which is what a priori legislation amounts to— or submitting to a law (legal precedent or case) that is not of its own making—which is what (noncircular) legal deduction, justification, or application amounts to—reason betrays its illegitimacy. But this is just to say that reason is itself *myth*: a kind of writing that dangerously straddles the line separating origin and fiction, community and jurisdiction.

This takes us to Nancy's deconstruction of the myth of community, solidarity, and the good. In Nancy's judgment, "nothing is more *common* to the members of a community, in principle, than a myth, or an ensemble of myths. Myth and community define each other at least in part, but perhaps entirely" (Nancy 1986, 104). However, Nancy also believes that the way in which myth and community codefine one another in the modern age is inseparable from the myth of the "suppression and inauguration of myth" (131).

According to this myth, which appears in such diverse streams of thought as the romanticism of Friedrich Schlegel and Nietzsche, the communism of Sorel and Bataille, and the structuralism of Lévi-Strauss, the modern age has suffered a terrible demythologization; the founding narratives of Western civilization have lost their power to inspire, leaving us bereft of meaning, authority, and unity of purpose (i.e., the good). The myth of the loss of community has its provenance in the Christian notion of original sin (expulsion from paradise/separation from God) and redemption (restoration of wholeness/communion with God). In the course of secularization this myth found its way into the millenarian tradition of Rousseau, Hegel, and Marx, whence it influenced the totalitarian movements of the twentieth century.

It is precisely this experience, Nancy contends, that explains the Nazi myth. Weimar Germany lacked a stable national identity and its sociopolitical anarchy contributed even further to disenchantment with rational abstractions such as formal law and procedural democracy (Nancy and Lacoue-Labarthe 1980, 105–7). The myth of Aryan supremacy capitalized on this situation in two ways. First, as a cosmopolitan people who had benefited most from republican reform, Jews—especially assimilated Jews— carried the "stigma" of lacking any identity but that abstract individuality and humanity extolled by liberals and social democrats (121 and 127). Second, since Friedrich Schlegel German romantics had sought a "new mythology" to vent their antirational sentiments, one that would meld the

Greek (the civilization and language most cultivated Germans identified with) with the modern. This required retrieving, as Nietzsche did, both Apollonian and Dionysian aspects of classical myth—the hierarchical classifications of imagination, on one hand, and the xenophobic, in-group attraction and out-group repulsion of ecstatic passion, on the other. The result—celebrated in Heidegger's "The Origin of the Work of Art"—was a new myth having as its aim "the construction, formation, and production of the German people in, by and as a work of art" (Nancy and Lacoue-Labarthe 1980, 116).

In this new ideological configuration, myth was transformed from a classificatory dynamic innate in natural language into an instrument of propaganda. The grandeur of Greek myth ostensibly lay in its constitution of a community of being wherein language and nature mirror one another. *Cosmos* is structured as *logos,* so that the presence and fullness of speech is reflected in an "uninterrupted world of presences"—everything full of Gods, as Thales said (Nancy 1986, 124). However, in our modern conception of mythology, myth functions simultaneously as origin and fiction. *Mimesis* and *poiesis* coincide, but in a manner that remains ambiguous. The Nazis simply capitalized on this ambiguity by clothing their artificial myths in suspect "scientific" genealogies—thereby linking the eugenic social engineering of a pure German *Volk* to the "natural" superiority of the Aryan race (*Blut und Boden*) (Nancy and Lacoue-Labarthe 1980, 119–23).

Of course, attempts to resuscitate the old myths or to invent new ones—the Nazi myth of Aryan supremacy combines both strategies—are doomed to failure. As Nancy notes, the "emptiness of meaning [that] . . . pertains to myth itself" reveals its merely *fictive nature* through being instrumentally manipulated for ideological purposes (Nancy 1986, 121). Although Nancy observes that "the invention of myth is a contradiction in terms"—myth must already be assented to by the community in order for it to "found" community—the very fact that it lives on only in language, as literature or fiction, shows its inherent illegitimacy.

We will have occasion in chapter 8 to discuss further the way in which myths—so essential to our anthropological quest for meaning—inevitably exhaust (or delegitimize) themselves in the course of being passed down as legitimate archetypes for legitimating our otherwise disenchanted scientific worldview. Perhaps even the fateful classifications and *nomoi* of modern science testify to mythic repetition.[8]

This is undoubtedly the case with one such science: psychoanalysis. It is no accident that Freud appealed to myth in unlocking the archaeology of the subject. As we have seen, the subject constitutes its autobiography through repeated "acts" of self-interpretation that are related to the fateful narratives shared by the community at large. Indeed, psychoanalysis legitimates and contributes to the formation of emancipated, narrative identity. At the same time, it problematizes this identity in ways that illuminate the totalitarian undercurrents seething beneath the modern subject.

3. Freud's analysis of the relationships between personal individuation and communal identification, on the one hand, and between narcissistic love and ethical motivation, on the other, is key for understanding the instinctual dynamics underlying patriarchal domination and other authoritarian patterns of legitimation, some of its most significant contributions in this area shedding valuable light on the pathological affinities linking decadent forms of liberalism to totalitarianism. Along with its deconstruction of subjective (conscious) agency, this aspect of psychoanalysis has exercised profound influence over French communitarians like Nancy, who seek to dispel the notion that liberalism and totalitarianism occupy antipodal sides of the political globe, the former postulating the priority of individuality over community, the latter community over individuality. This way of posing the issue, Nancy believes, overlooks the fact that the logic of identity implicit in liberalism, which defines the freedom and personality of the subject as something possessed prior to and in exclusion of any social relation, is the same underlying totalitarianism, which ruthlessly denies this. In both instances identity is conceived in terms of absolute self-determination, or relation to self apart from all reference to difference and otherness. Hence, despite the fact that liberalism and totalitarianism represent opposed ideologies privileging identity of individual and society respectively, their common logic suggests a potential for convergence.[9]

It was Hegel who first articulated this dialectic, Freud and Bataille who extended it to mass psychology. The problem is most incisively formulated in Freud's *Group Psychology and the Analysis of the Ego* (1921), where narcissism—the original condition of the libido-saturated ego—is shown to be the extreme limit of sociality.

Briefly, Freud argued that any attempt to establish a purely libidinal tie between narcissistic individuals inevitably founders on their lack of limitation. Driven on by the pleasure principle, the narcissistic ego necessarily suffers annihilation. Either the other (the libido-object) is only a speculum (or extension) of the ego—in which case the ego collapses into an empty identity—or it is not, in which case it confronts the ego as an opaque limit, *de*flecting its image.

The dilemma, mutual exclusivity or inclusivity, also reveals the paradoxical nature of the "mass individual." Lacking a sense of identity and torn between conformist and rebellious inclinations, the mass individual projects his or her ideal self-image onto an iconoclastic authority figure (the Führer) combining common traits with exceptional charisma.[10] In this instance, the process of identification—for Freud the normal path toward identity-formation—exhibits a pathological characteristic. By transforming genital sexuality into nonpossessive feelings of affection, identification should serve as basis for social bonding and individuation. In other words, what was originally a manifestation of self-love should be transformed into an altruistic vehicle for forming bonds of friendship and respect capable of integrating subjects into higher organic totalities, without degenerating into totalitarianism.

Bataille later used Freud's studies on mass psychology to explain the dynamics of fascism as a reaction to the anomic disintegration affecting modern rationalized society.[11] Following Durkheim, he sought to trace the ethical basis of social solidarity back to a fundamental distinction between sacral and profane spheres of life. The sacral realm—of passion, transcendence, excess (ecstasis) and otherness—circumscribes a domain of unconditioned freedom. Representing a Dionysian principle of attraction, such sovereignty opposes the profane realm of productive labor—of self-objectification, self-limitation, individuation, and unfreedom. However, if the former is not to consume (expend) itself, it must be harnessed to mundane needs of production.

In this respect, Bataille's "general economy" reiterates the same logic of sublimation and repression contained in Freud's diagnosis of civilization. The "reality principle" operant in the process of secularization effectively purges sovereignty of heterogeneous excess—for Freud, the libidinal energy intersected by life and death instincts. What remains—a rational ethic of obligation (respect for others) and responsibility (self-determination)—legitimates a regime of self-limitation, domination, delayed gratification, and forced labor.

As Weber and Durkheim observed, ascetic vocationalism (the Protestant work ethic), passionless consumerism, and individual-familial privatism are but the desiccated, secularized remnants of the sacred. Under the yoke of repression, the abstract ego of material need is no longer driven beyond itself to something higher—the community—that could serve as the basis for its own freedom and identity. Hence the attraction of fascism, which combines the excess of spectacle, sacrifice, and lawless violence with the stability afforded by traditional and charismatic authority rooted in the homogeneous identity of a *Volk*.[12]

If Nancy credits Freud with having perceived the totalitarian logic lurking beneath the surface of liberal society, he does not exonerate him from his complicity in maintaining it. Just as Hegel had sought to resolidify the disembodied—divided and underdetermined—will of civil society in the will of the monarch, so Freud sought to reintegrate the embodied—but anarchic—instincts in the form of patriarchal authority. Whereas the former shatters on the contradiction of a monarch whose personality (identity) and power transcends the ethical relationship too much, the latter founders on the contradiction of a desire that is not transcendent enough (Nancy and Lacoue-Labarthe 1981, 77–79).

Totem and Taboo (1912–13) had already suggested a way to counteract the anarchy of desire in its resolution of the oedipal conflict between father and son over the possession of the mother. Patriarchal authority here functions as the mechanism underlying sexual repression leading to the first form of ethical self-limitation—the incest taboo. On this interpretation, conscience arises from a prior identification with the father by the guilty son—a repetition of what Freud, with his hypothesis of the primal horde, speculated to be an original abrogation of patriarchal dominance culminating in parricide.

According to Nancy, the assumption of original patriarchy, no less than the assumption of original narcissism (subjectivism or egoism), is belied by Freud's own texts. Freud himself realized that the primal horde hypothesis—which explains the elevation of the memory of the slain patriarch to the rank of internalized authority by the remorse of his rebellious sons—is itself question-begging. Unless remorse can be traced back to prior instinctual dispositions—*divided* feelings of love and hatred toward the father that are rooted in *conflicting* life and death instincts (the solution proposed in *Civilization and Its Discontents* (1930)—its emergence following the parricide is not logically compelling (Nancy and Lacoue-Labarthe 1979, 41–43).

It is Nancy's contention that Freud's appeal to a *divided* desire already refutes the notion of primary narcissism as preexisting, integral identity. Only in *Moses and Monotheism* (1939)—the last of Freud's "displacements" of the problem of identity—is patriarchy deconstructed along with narcissistic identity. Here the truth of individuation is properly located in the *mother* as the principle of *nonidentity*. In being removed from her breast and experiencing its absence, the self first experiences itself as *a self*—that is, as *desire*, or *lack of fulfillment (presence)*. The rupture inflicted by the incest taboo—the principle of patriarchal identity—merely *replicates* a primary nonidentity between mother and child. In reinforcing the psychological distance between mother and infant necessary for individuation and self-determination it actually reproduces just the opposite: condemnation of the self to perpetual alienation from its own desire and passion.

It was Lacan, of course, who first appreciated the depths of this alien-ation in his Hegelian analyses of the "imaginary" and "symbolic" stages of infantile development.[13] Lacan initially argued that the infant's fragmented (partial) and dreamlike awareness of its body in the diffuse mother/child dyad gives way to a total *self* image (*imago* or identity) only when it sees—and thus identifies with—its own *alien*, spatially and temporally fixed *reflection* in a mirror (or in its mother's gaze). He later realized that the alterity requisite for subjectivity involved a further—more radical—identification: identification with the other through the normative medium of language. In this symbolic stage the imaginary ego is divided from its integrated images (and desire) by differential sign relations—such as those inscribing kinship. But this only means—in the words of Nancy—that "the other is not first and foremost the identical other, but the withdrawal (*retrait*) of this identity—the alteration of the origin" (Nancy and Lacoue-Labarthe 1979, 52). Thus, for Nancy ethical alterity (guilt), not moral identity (reciproc-ity), remains the ultimate foundation of personality.

3.1 Nancy's psychoanalytic deconstruction of the subject indicates both the limits and possibilities of deconstructive varieties of communitarianism. The positive yield consists in a thoroughgoing critique of SR. The presump-tion of a reason-founding identity that precedes communication and alterity is shown to be both incoherent and ideological—reinforcing domination, patriarchy, and totalitarian closure. Indeed, the Freudian presumption that psychological development proceeds from a condition of dependent, undif-ferentiated, and narcissistic identity to one of autonomous, differentiated, and rational individuality—a presumption criticized as a male bias by Carol Gilligan, Jessica Benjamin, and other feminist psychologists—is also shown to be false. Selfhood is dependent on otherness from the outset, and re-mains so throughout the course of maturation.

The negative yield consists, first, in an incapacity to relate the ideology of SR to empirical processes of socialization, and second, in a manifest failure to appreciate the way in which identity remains structured by *counterfactual*, hermeneutical expectations of reciprocity and integrity. The former complaint raises once again the problem of transcendental and aes-thetic approaches to political philosophy. Deconstructive communitarianism seems to be caught in a bind: [I]t wants to assert the withdrawal of the political as a *historical* development at the heart of Western metaphysics while at the same time denying—on essentialist grounds—that this totalitar-ian logic can ever be realized. Hence the following remark, typical of the kinds of mystification one encounters in Nancy's thoughts on community:

> After all, it is impossible for us to lose [community]. Society can be as little communitarian as possible . . . (but) we cannot not coappear. Only at the limit does the fascist mass tend to annihilate community in the delirium of an incarnated communion. Likewise the concentration and extermination camp—the camp of exterminating concentration—is in its essence the will to destroy the community. But without doubt, even in the camp, the community never entirely ceases to resist this will. (Nancy 1986, 88)

The aforementioned problem—of portraying the historical event of totalitarianism as an illusion masking a "deeper" community—is linked to another one: that of transcendental communitarian criticism. How can essentialist (ontological) analyses of necessary and universal conditions yield prescriptive claims of any kind? Nancy says that communitarian resistance "defines neither a politics nor a writing" but only "a limit at which all politics stops and starts." At the same time, he asserts that "it does not put up with all 'politics' or all 'writing'" (198). Yet if community is "not a work to be made" but a "gift to renew, to communicate anew," how can it also be, in Nancy's words, "a task and a struggle of which Marx had the meaning and which Bataille understood"? And why would such a struggle motivate us if the original and permanent condition of personality is only alienation, loss of integrity—in short, the *divided* self bequeathed to us from liberalism?

I submit that the incapacity of Nancy's transcendental communitarianism to offer convincing empirical and normative arguments rests partially on its failure to transcend metaphysics and—along with it—SR. Why not acknowledge—as Nancy says he does—the breaks and diversity within the tradition of Western metaphysics, thereby *divesting* it of its decisive and determining role in shaping our ontological commitments and sociopolitical destinies? Rather than resurrect Hegel's *Weltgeist* all over again—a mystification that is truly ideological—one could explain how the *multiple* varieties of rationalization inherent in Western culture have been misappropriated in ways that have led to a one-sided emphasis on the cognitive-instrumental. Maybe it is not metaphysics or reason that is to blame for the rise of totalitarian social formations but (following Habermas) the inherent dynamics of a combined economic-administrative system whose provenance—at least in part—resides in a capitalist mode of domination. If so, criticism of this system of alienation would have to begin by hermeneutically appropriating the CR that remains suppressed in social relations—a source of normativity that no amount of deconstruction, focused on the subject-centered writings of Kant and Freud—is likely to reveal.

Thus, it might be more profitable for deconstructive philosophy to overcome its exclusion of political economy in seeking out the causes of totalitarianism. Nancy leaves himself open to just this possibility when he cites with approval Foucault's analysis of the complex interweaving of discourse, power, and knowledge (Nancy and Lacoue-Labarthe 1981, 24). This approach to explaining modern "carceral" societies shows what no amount of transcendental textual deconstruction can: that the self-identical subject of SR, far from being merely a textual construct (or fiction), is a *real* embodied subject constituted by *real* microtechnologies.

4.0 One way to appreciate the difference between Foucault's and Nancy's approaches is by focusing on their relative levels of dissatisfaction with hermeneutics as a whole. Foucault's approach to history is radically nominalistic. Not only is there no deep "subtext" to be deconstructed, but the impenetrable opacity of texts radically incommensurable with our own frames of understanding leaves little room for grandiose metaphysical speculation about the destiny of Being. If anything, Foucault finds the temptation for depth-interpretation—as in the case of the Christian confessional and the psychoanalytic examination of repressed motives—to be an unhealthy preoccupation of our modern, rationalized ethos. Finally, Foucault's initial approach to explaining social action resembles those we have discussed with regard to decision theory and functionalism in its disregard for deeper, background meanings.

This appreciation of strategic power relations and functional constraints no doubt serves as a useful corrective to the textual hermeticism (idealism?) implicit in deconstructive forms of communitarianism. However, its contempt for hermeneutics comes at a steep price: inability to develop a descriptive or normative account of community. Only in Foucault's later work on the history of sexuality do we find a robust sense of the hermeneutical constitution of identity. And only here do we find a theory of the subject that breaks out of the stale mold of SR in a manner conducive to communitarian social critique.

Foucault shares with his counterparts in the Frankfurt School a mutual concern about subjectivity and its relationship to knowledge. This concern is doubly complicated. On one hand, they conceive subjectivity as a social construct. On the other hand, they hold that the *metaphysical* illusion of a self-empowering ego captures a real, *practical* dimension of rational moral agency as it has taken shape in modern occidental culture.

The points of convergence are numerous and striking: Both critiques unmask the universalist pretensions of scientific reason by locating the limits and possibilities of knowing and acting in historically sedimented practices.[14] Both unmask the Cartesian subject, understood as a fixed and universal foundation prior to experience, as incompatible with these practical presuppositions. Both likewise eschew the notion that knowledge is disinterested contemplation of a pregiven object; given the priority of material practice, they assume instead that knower and knowable mutually constitute one another. Both therefore seek to enlighten individuals about the social conditions under which their identities, needs, and interests are historically constituted. Last but not least, both share an awareness of their own problematic relationship to the Enlightenment: The rational discourses of bourgeois science and morality that inform critical theory only emancipate through domination. By investing the self with dangerous drives and energies requiring constant surveillance (self-examination, observation, and interpretation) and rigorous control (technical predictability), they compel the self to subject itself to others as a condition for its own self-empowerment.

Now for the divergence. Critical theorists share Marx's and Freud's belief in a single, *rational* trajectory along which humanity reappropriates its suppressed capacities and instincts. Foucault does not. To begin with, he finds all but fantastic the notion of a universal subject striving to realize its essential nature free from the constraints of power. Arguing that power is more ubiquitous, diffuse, and corporeal than Marxist notions of state-sanctioned class domination suggest, he dismisses any ideological legitimation or delegitimation of domination.

Foucault cites Rusche and Kirchheimer's *Punishment and Social Structures* (1939) as an example of critical theory's failure to grasp this new power. While relating historical changes in punishment to broader changes in political economy, it retained the classical presumption in favor of a vertical distribution of power (in this instance, centered on class domination), thereby overlooking the fact that punishment is a general feature of social conditioning circulating horizontally throughout all areas of life in which the productivity and docility of the body are at stake (Foucault 1977, 24).[15] However, if social conditioning is much less a function of inculcating the "dominant ideas of the ruling class" from the top down than it is of engendering the reciprocal confluence of common desires and corporeal dispositions, it is not, Foucault insists, necessarily more repressive. Freud's hypothesis only explains the *exclusionary* function of power, not its *productivity* in constituting subjects as predictable moral agents who act freely with responsibility (Foucault 1980, 59, 91). Indeed, the stress on productivity is itself a defining feature of those human sciences, such as Freudian psychoanalysis, that have emerged since the classical age. In tandem with the capillary overlapping of such older microtechniques as the religious confessional, the clinical examination, and the military exercise in strategies of *governance*, these *disciplines* increase the economic efficiency of the body politic exponentially. Scientific measurement, classification, and therapy modify strategies of detention, surveillance, conditioning, and spatial partitioning that find increasing deployment in schools and factories as well as in prisons and hospitals. Thus, scientific discipline conspires with strategic technique to create a new hierarchy of knowledge/power that instrumentalizes social relations vertically and horizontally (92).

Foucault does not hesitate to draw what, for a critical theorist, appears to be a damning conclusion: If power insinuates itself into the very discipline constitutive of rational self-identity, then it is impossible to know rationally one's true humanity independently of its distorting effects (96 and 101). Insofar as "ideology" continues to denote a worthy topic of criticism in the Foucaultian agenda, it does so qualifiedly—not as "false consciousness" of genuine emancipatory needs but as blindness with respect to the irrecusable historicity, conditionality, and otherness of one's own subjectivity (118 and 133).

In Foucault's opinion, the logical contradictions associated with humanism are of a different order of magnitude, since it is they, not ideological blindness, that actually motivate the disciplinary rationalization of society. As Foucault conceives it, Kant was the first to have articulated the rational impulse of modern humanism. Kant shattered the classical model of knowledge conceived as passive representation by endowing the knowing subject with new productive powers. "Man" replaced God as the measure and source of all knowledge and action, but only insofar as "He" was conceived dualistically. Subjectivity thus oscillates between two selves: a rational self that thinks its own productive freedom unconditionally, and an empirical self that perceives its own and nature's objective determination through the refracted prism of sensuous (aesthetic) intuition.[16]

For Foucault, the failure of German idealism to resolve this dualism—familiar to us from our examination of liberalism—is mirrored in its pathetic vacillation between subjectivism and objectivism, aesthetic self-reconciliation and ethical self-determination. For, if it is true that the human spirit aspires to total self-reflection, it is truer still that it always finds its limit in the impenetrable opacity of desire, language, and labor. This explains the "will to knowledge" motivating the human sciences. Impelled by emancipatory striving, yet confronted with its own facticity, this will constitutes a humanity whose progressive self-understanding is as infinite as it is elusive. Attempting to penetrate beneath the uneven surface of ethical life to the pristine uniformity and spontaneity of instinctual nature, it ends up dissolving the most intimate expressions of desire and feeling into the most alien objectifications of nomothetic science. The aesthetic redemption of repressed desires, sensibilities, and productive powers sought by Freud and Marx itself contributes to ever greater objectification and repression. Ultimately, hope for a rational reconciliation of ethos and eros unwittingly becomes a pretext for increased domination.

This fact looms large for understanding the precarious no-man's-land in which Foucault situated his own critical theory. Having rejected the inhumanism of humanism as contrary to human liberation, Foucault embraced the antihumanism of positivism as strangely compatible with it (Foucault 1972, 234). This solution, as we shall see, raises more questions than it answers. Can a happy positivism fill the critical void vacated by humanism? And in whose name—if not the rational subject's—can it be justified?

4.1 A brief overview of Foucault's views on action and agency prior to his work on the history of sexuality suggests a negative response to the first of these questions. *Madness and Civilization* (1961) traces the modern understanding of madness back to the rationalization of European society begun in the seventeenth century. Up until that time, Foucault argues, madness had been regarded as a special kind of wisdom; it expressed insight into the tragic secret of humanity's archaic past and its fatal link to atavistic passions. This changed with the advent of the modern nation state. Political absolutism conspired with the nascent medical sciences to create a healthy, productive, well-ordered and uniform citizenry that could truck no relation to madness. Madness was then reconstituted as a mental illness requiring containment and proscription.

If, for Foucault, insanity is now constituted as the diametric antithesis of reason, it is only because reason incarnate—the transparent, self-identical ego—suppresses the unthinkable depths of human existence. This valorization of an aesthetic intuition that precedes clear articulation is doubly paradoxical. First, as Foucault himself conceded, his own attempt to apprehend and articulate the original meaning of madness "in its unfettered state" is self-contradictory. Second, the desire to return to an original truth is symptomatic of the very humanism Foucault later excoriated.

Foucault sought to resolve these paradoxes by bracketing the subjectivity in which self-interpretation moves. The second and third stages of his thought comprise progressive steps in this direction. The second stage deploys an *archaeological* method that brackets both the intentional meaning and the truth (or falsity) of statements. The third stage supplements this procedure with a *genealogical* method that brackets the moral preferability of practices.

The archaeology of knowledge construes meaning in terms of objective structure. The meaning of a statement is defined by the sequence of statements that precede and follow it. This sequence, in turn, is one possible articulation among many alternatives that are permitted by a system of statements. Such a system is not closed, however. Unlike classical structuralism, Foucault does not believe that the determination of semantic elements and the rules governing their possible articulation precede their actual articulation in some transcendental sense.[17] So construed, the system of regularities governing possible speech delimits the range of what can be accepted as a possible true statement, censors unacceptable themes and utterances, and silences "unqualified" speakers *in a continually shifting manner*.

Foucault principally deploys his archaeological method in analyzing just those performative utterances *(énoncés)* that figure in the regimented language games of science. His aim is to articulate the archaeological deep structures that determine the limits and possibilities of knowledge for any given period (Foucault 1972, 191). The systems of language that comprise these formation rules—what Foucault calls *epistemes*—are historically discontinuous. Their analysis ostensibly shows that heterogeneous disciplines within a given period have more in common than disciplines sharing the same subject matter but falling into different periods. Thus, whereas the natural history, general grammar, and the analysis of wealth formed by the classical episteme of the seventeenth century sought to represent and analyze a table of elements, their counterparts in the modern age (biology, philology, and economics) are guided by an altogether different figure: the genetic explanation of visceral functions and productive systems.

The archaeology of knowledge is incapable of providing a coherent account of its own scientific objectivity. From an archaeological perspective, the truth of its statements is but a function of its own groundless formation rules. True, *The Order of Things* suggests otherwise in its assertion that the turn to archaeological science is itself compelled by the humanism preceding it. But, as we shall see in our discussion of Blumenberg in chapter 8, such a dialectical grounding assumes more continuity between epistemes than the archaeological method will allow. Indeed, as Habermas notes, the postulation of radical discontinuity makes it difficult to understand how archaeology—or indeed, any method—could critically check its own objectivity. For here the achievement of objectivity could only occur if the proponents of one episteme (method) could engage proponents of other epistemes (methods) in critical dialogue—a mutual hermeneutics of self-clarification that archaeology forswears (Habermas 1987a, 262).

Aside from this basic difficulty, Foucault's structuralist account of meaning cannot explain actual speech. Structuralism at best accounts for the formal conditions of *possible* syntactic and semantic combinations, transformations, and exclusions *at any given time*. Conditions of possibility, however, do not explain the *actual* selection, or *genesis*, of particular utterances (Foucault 1972, 38, 73, 121). These still depend on subjective intentions and, more basically still, the communicative competence embodied in speaker/listener roles.[18] The latter are learned competencies, acquired through socialization. They comprise capacities for utilizing a know-how— an application of rules—that cannot itself be reduced to mere rule following without generating an infinite regress. To recall Taylor's critique of analytic action theory, the system of language *(langue)* cannot be divorced from *background practices* that generate speech-action*(parôle)*.

The above criticism is related to a deeper problem. As we have seen, Foucault sometimes talks as if his theory of language is really poststructuralist. He cannot maintain a rigid dichotomy between the system of formation rules and actual speech without raising the specter of a transcendental/empirical dualism of the sort he wants to avoid. Instead, he collapses the system into the local and shifting *context* of speech. This strategy, however, creates two difficulties. First, it is unclear how the mere *factual* constellation of dispersed assertoric events can yield regularities of any kind. Context alone—the *open* field of signs externally connected to one another—yields no warrant for distinguishing acceptable from unacceptable sign events.[19] Second, as noted in chapter 2, the rules structuring language games do not function like stochastic regularities; they permit the regular generation of new and wholly unpredictable utterances that often deviate markedly from past practice. Linguistic rules are neither disconfirmed nor violated by such innovations, because they themselves consist of generative competencies rather than mere habits.

Of course, archaeology might avoid this conundrum by simply acknowledging the prescriptive nature of linguistic rules. In fact, while speaking of a unity that resides anterior to the "visible, horizontal coherence of the elements formed" in the "system that makes possible and governs this formation" (Foucault 1972, 72), Foucault notes that the rules of formation "lay down *(prescrit)* what must be related, in a particular discursive practice, for such and such an enunciation to be made, for such and such a concept to be used, for such and such a strategy to be organized" (74). The problem with this acknowledgment of prescriptivity is obvious. Prescriptivity is gained at the cost of reintroducing an *anterior unity*, or transcendental structure, that remains untouched by actual practice.

The archaeology of knowledge thus finds itself impaled on the transcendental/empirical, prescriptive/descriptive dialectic of humanism. The genealogy of power that dominates the third stage of Foucault's thought can be understood as an attempt to overcome the dualism that fuels this dialectic.[20] To begin with, it sees linguistic competence as inextricably bound to actual speech performance. The rules of formation are now conceived as aspects of a *practice* whose normativity is continually contested. In contrast to the relatively static juxtaposition of discontinuous epistemes that one finds in archaeology, genealogy traces the genesis of less global institutions, technologies, and practices across periodic divides. In every instance, their normativity and genesis is conceived as a function of power relations.

Whereas archaeology brackets the truth and intentional meaning of linguistic discourse, genealogy brackets the moral preferability of practices. Like Nietzsche's *Genealogy of Morals*, after which it is patterned, genealogy eschews a universal history of progress or decline. As Foucault puts it in "Nietzsche, Genealogy, History," genealogy shows that "all knowledge rests on injustice (there is no right, even in the act of knowing, no truth or foundation for truth)" (Foucault 1977, 163).

Given statements like these, one cannot but agree with Habermas that Foucault's genealogical criticism, no less than his archaeology of knowledge, succumbs to self-referential paradox. Aside from this obvious defect, it is less clear whether genealogy resolves the problems it inherits from archaeology. Can power relations explain speech action any better than disembodied linguistic structures?

As Habermas points out, "[I]n Foucault's genealogy, 'power' is initially a synonym for this *purely structuralistic activity*; it takes the same place as *différance* does in Derrida. But this power constitutive of discourse is supposed to be a power of transcendental generativity *and* of empirical self-assertion simultaneously" (Habermas 1987, 256). Just as Nancy resolves the tension between his transcendental and empirical accounts of community by conflating ontological and ontic features in his *Seinsgeschichte*, so too Foucault resolves a similar tension by conflating these features in the concept of power.

This conflation is apparent in Foucault's inaugural address, "The Order of Discourse" (1970). The essay distinguishes the peculiar "will to knowledge" characteristic of modern science from "the power of constituting domains of objects" (Foucault 1972, 234). The former is an empirical event traceable to Platonic rationalism and its distinction between true and false, essence and appearance, the latter a kind of ontological generativity.

The conflation of these distinct notions of power results from Foucault's attribution of features to the one that properly belong to the other. What Foucault calls a *dispositive* captures the way in which the will to knowledge inscribed in the technical apparatus of rational society directly creates the rule-governed normativity constitutive of modern, productive subjects. The panoptic objectifications of modern society are thus endowed by him with powers formerly ascribed to transcendental subjectivity. Conversely, power, conceived as a transhistorical condition productive of knowledge and discourse generally, is described in the strategic, objectifying language of the historical a priori appertaining to the modern (subjectless) will to knowledge. Thus the ontic categories of disciplinary power reverberate throughout Foucault's description of ontological power, and vice versa.

This last defect vitiates Foucault's account of subjectivity (Habermas 1987a, 242). Foucault misconceives the constitution of subjectivity as a process of objectification and thus misses the connection between socialization and individuation. On Foucault's reading, socialization constitutes subjects as normal types, whose role behavior is little more than conditioned reflex. So little do they exhibit the critical autonomy, creativity, and individuality of modern subjects that one is continually reminded of Durkheim's segmented tribes (or Garfinkel's "judgmental dopes"), who labor under the mechanical determinism of a monolithic, collective consciousness.

Strangely, the image of a unified functional system that thoroughly dominates its *subjecta membra* is belied by the language of strategic gaming that colors Foucault's characterization of power relations. Instead of the determinism of *habitus*, we are given the anarchism of unregulated clashes between warring forces that—to cite Habermas—"emerge and pop like glittering bubbles from a swamp of anonymous processes of subjugation" (Habermas 1987a, 268).

Foucault's theory thus vacillates between subjectivist (voluntarist) and objectivist (constructivist) conceptions of agency in a manner reminiscent of German idealism. Either the agent is a wholly determined object, in which case individual autonomy is but an illusory mask concealing coercively programmed ethical roles, or she is a strategic subject, whose normatively unbounded gaming creates external relations of domination. The former view predominates in Foucault's "positivistic" writings culminating in *Discipline and Punish* (1979), the latter in his "romantic" panegyric to the "aesthetics of existence" contained in his last interviews and in the second and third volumes of *The History of Sexuality*.[21]

Here, then, we find the rationale underlying Habermas's charge that Foucault is a "young conservative" (Habermas 1981, 13). Foucault's cynicism regarding modern legal ideals undermines the only ground support-ing struggles for freedom and justice. This cynicism, we now realize, lies deeper than Foucault's empirical analysis of biopower in modern society. Even if Foucault were right about this analysis—and it is by no means clear that he is—genealogical criticism could hardly abjure the task of justifying its own norms. But the metatheoretical basis of genealogical critique—above all, its defective conceptualization of the rational subject—makes it virtu-ally impossible for him to do so. The normative reciprocity constitutive of a critical subject is simply absent. Either Foucault conceives norms as sys-temic functions of a disciplinary power that confront the agent as an exter-nal fate to which she must passively submit,[22] or he conceives them as coercive effects of unregulated wars between strategic actors seeking their own subjective advantage. In neither case are they conceived as obliga-tions whose peculiar force derives from their *presumed* satisfaction of genu-ine social needs.

4.2 Foucault's later turn to hermeneutic genealogy can be seen as a be-lated attempt to provide normative justification for his theory. By the late seventies Foucault sought such justification in the unsystematic "subju-gated forms of knowledge" that circulate in the contemporary counterdiscourses of everyday life. In so doing, he adopted a strategy that could be found in the writings of critical theorists dating back to Marx. Here, the justification for criticism is assumed to be immanent in the ordi-nary understanding that oppressed groups have of themselves. Alienated from themselves by the objectifying regimen of scientific management, they nonetheless aspire to freedom and happiness.

If Foucault eventually embraced the subject of commonsense reason, it is not because he thought the latter could be theoretically grounded. Nevertheless, by 1983 he had come to see his own work as a continuation of the enlightenment ethos he had formerly repudiated. He not only openly acknowledged the kinship between his social theory and Habermas's but, in a late interview, ironically observed that he was in "a little more agree-ment" with Habermas than Habermas was with him (Bernauer and Ras-mussen 1988, 18).

Indeed, the last two volumes of the *History of Sexuality* marked some-thing of a watershed in Foucault's understanding of his life's work. For he now admitted that the central preoccupation of his research from the very beginning—the relationship between the subject and truth—could best be approached by way of a hermeneutically enlightened genealogy.[23] Gone is the cold, objective description of functionalist relations. What now occupies center stage in his analysis is ethics or, more precisely, the way in which subjects *voluntarily* and *intentionally* subject themselves to technologies of self-control—technologies that are embedded in specific practices and types of knowledge determinant of a way of life, a manner of self-understanding, an identity, in short, an *ethos* (Foucault 1985, 10).

These practices exhibit their own *continuity* through time. In contrast to Foucault's earlier emphasis on epistemological breaks, his genealogical account of the Christian ethos that has shaped the modern age acknowledges superficial resemblances between its moral codes and those of its Greek and Greco-Roman predecessors. If we think of the moral code as "the set of values and rules of action that are recommended to the individual through the intermediary of various prescriptive agencies," then all three systems are alike in their prescription of sexual abstinence (25).

At the same time, Foucault points out that this continuity conceals deeper shifts in their "ethical substance." The latter refers to "the way in which the individual has to constitute this or that part of himself as the prime material of his moral conduct," that is, the way in which he incorporates the moral code into his conduct (26).[24] Some ethical regimes place greater emphasis on the moral code, its systematicity and inclusiveness. Here adherence to law is decisive in determining the mode of subjection. Others place emphasis on the aesthetics of self-transformation. The Christian ethos and especially its modern, secular equivalent tend toward the former; the Greek and Greco-Roman ethic toward the latter (21 and 31). Transposed over the morality of sexual abstinence, the difference between the three is apparent: whereas the Greek ethos sought to cultivate a moderate use of pleasure for the sake of personal and civic virtue, and the Greco-Roman ethos sought to cultivate a solicitous care over the self for the sake of rationally administering a complex identity, the Christian ethos seeks to cultivate a hermeneutics of desire aimed at discovering the hidden truth of the soul. Its renunciation of a fallen self that is permanently deceived about itself marks the transition to a deontological ethic that privileges dutiful regulation of conduct over aesthetic self-realization.

As we shall see in chapter 8, Foucault's genealogy of ethics complements Blumenberg's legitimation of science in one crucial respect: both regard revolutionary breaks in *practice* as inscribed in continuous patterns of *discourse*. However, there is nothing in the former comparable to the latter's dialectic of provocation that might explain this continuity. For that would involve viewing historical understanding as a kind of dialogue with the past. Instead, Foucault continued to describe the peculiar *hermeneutics of desire* by which modern agents constitute themselves as dutiful subjects in terms of self-objectification rather than intersubjective mutuality (Foucault 1982, 208).

It remains to be seen whether this mode of self-objectification is essential to modernity. Do the Protestant Ethic and its pastoral power comprise our historical a priori, or can we imagine a more emancipated strain of enlightenment? Gilligan's defense of a different—and typically feminine—model of postconventional moral development oriented toward caring for concrete others rather than independent responsibility based on abstract rights suggests the latter possibility. Foucault's own defense of a pagan ethos of aesthetic self-transformation and caring hints in this direction as well: "[I]f one wants to look for a nondisciplinary form of power, or rather, to struggle against disciplines and disciplinary powers, it is not towards the ancient right of sovereignty that one should turn, but towards the possibility of a new form of right, one which must indeed be antidisciplinarian, but at the same time liberated from the principle of sovereignty" (Foucault 1980, 108). This new form of right, as we shall see, can only be legitimated by appeal to a communicative model of ethical socialization of the sort developed by Habermas.

5. Habermas is hardly oblivious to the metaphysical deficiencies of the sovereign subject bequeathed to humanism by way of the "philosophy of consciousness" from Descartes on. Indeed, he agrees with Foucault that the practical implications of subjectivism so conceived are incompatible with the emancipatory intentions of humanism. Contrary to Foucault, however, he thinks these intentions can be redeemed.

According to Habermas, *philosophy of consciousness* departs from the subject-object dualism implicit in Descartes's epistemological problematic. Idealism overcomes the dualism by reducing objectivity to a moment of the reflecting subject. As our discussion of humanism showed, however, this reduction paradoxically entails the rational objectification of the subject. Instead of departing from philosophy of consciousness and its epistemological problematic (SR), as Foucault and first-generation critical theorists do, Habermas turns his attention to the moral foundations implicit in philosophy of social action. Here he observes that the communicative dynamics underlying interaction call forth a distinctly noninstrumental and nonstrategic rationale.

Philosophy of consciousness ignores the fact that the identity of the knowing subject is founded on *intersubjective reciprocity* between free and equal actors. This insight, which forms the cornerstone of Hegel's social thought, is given a peculiar reading by Habermas. Turning to Hegel's early theological writings and the philosophy of spirit contained in the Jena System of 1803 to 1804, he shows how identity is shaped within communicative encounters in which actors mutually exchange the roles of speaker and listener. *Communicative action* foregrounds the internalization of social roles and the acquisition of higher-order competencies for rational argumentation requisite for reflexive forms of learning. Such *discourse*, Habermas believes, is always an immanent possibility for speakers who hold themselves rationally accountable. They must be prepared to justify their utterances if so challenged, and they must do so rationally. This, in turn, implies a commitment to reach an *impartial* consensus on disputed knowledge claims and moral beliefs—a consensus that can be guaranteed only if each interlocutor has equal opportunities to speak, free from the external and internal constraints that distort communication and frustrate mutual understanding (Habermas 1987a, 294).

By retrieving the openness-to-other implicit in CR, Habermas thinks he has found a locus for reason that precedes and conditions the more abstract and derivative forms of *instrumental* (and *strategic*) rationality on which Foucault exclusively focuses. In so doing, he also thinks he has located a space for personal and public expression that securely shelters humanism from the objectifications of SR as well.

First, a theory of communicative action avoids the dialectic of Man as a transcendental-empirical doublet. One aspect of this paradox, we noted, involves the reflexive objectification of a subject whose transcendental activity properly precedes (and thus precludes) empirical representation. The theory of communicative action circumvents the subject-object dualism on which this paradox builds by transferring the transcendental framework formerly ensconced in the isolated subject to the pragmatic assumptions underlying communicative intersubjectivity. Instead of the self relating to itself directly as an observable object—the aporia associated with the transcendental-empirical doubling of the subject—it relates to itself indirectly "from the angle of vision of a second person." Stated somewhat differently, the self relates to the other in the *participatory* mode of performative reciprocity, not in the objectifying mode of cognitive-instrumental domination.

The theory of communicative action ostensibly avoids the other side of this paradox: the self divided into transcendental and empirical aspects. Habermas denies that his theory *is* a transcendental theory. Hewing closely to the interdisciplinary ideal advocated by Horkheimer in the thirties, he maintains that the rational reconstruction of formal competencies of speech and action must cohere with both the empirical findings of social science and the considered normative intuitions of real, historical agents in a manner not unlike Rawls's procedure for achieving reflective equilibrium. Furthermore, the formal conditions underlying communicative competence are not, strictly speaking, transcendentally constitutive of speech action as his colleague-in-arms, Karl-Otto Apel, sometimes argues. Being counterfactual, they regulate, without necessitating, actual speech performance. In any case, such pragmatic norms are not transcendental, if one means by "transcendental" conditions whose necessity and universality can be ascertained with reflexive certainty. Since these norms are regulative for *public* communication, their proper interpretation and confirmation can occur only in actual discourses, not in private introspection. Hence, whatever universality we might be warranted in ascribing to them here and now must be qualified in light of the essential fallibility of *our* critically considered judgments about their meaning and scope (Habermas 1987a, 297).

Habermas claims his theory avoids the other aporias as well. The paradox of a self that is conceived *simultaneously* as thought and unthought vanishes once we realize that language comprises a *background* and a *foreground* for mutual understanding. On one hand, speakers draw from a vast fund of stored meanings, competencies, values, and other shared background assumptions that can be thematized only selectively (299). On the other hand, the most abstract rules regulating communicative competency can be reconstructed in their entirety. Furthermore, contrary to Foucault's pessimistic diagnosis, critical and analytic modes of self-reflection of the sort carried on by psychoanalysis and ideology critique can improve the narrative integrity of an individual's identity. Since biological drives cannot function as motivations apart from being collectively interpreted as socially recognized needs, it no longer makes sense to oppose aesthetic and ethical moments of identity. Reason does not suppress nature; it emancipates it expressively. Once we realize that scientific self-reflection articulates the dynamics and interests of communicative interaction rather than instrumental objectification, we can better appreciate how it eliminates the "pseudonature" of hidden motives that divide us from ourselves and others.

Habermas's theory also seems to vanquish the paradox of the return and retreat of the origin and, along with it, that of the self as creator and created. Habermas insists that communication is neither a unitary "process of self-generation (whether of the spirit or of the species)" nor an alien fate to which we must submit. Communication and its evolutionary logic are themselves contingent on external historical forces, so that "even basic concepts that are starkly universalist have a temporal core" (301).

All of this sounds very good indeed. But how, then, do we explain the dominance of SR and disciplinary power in modern society? Habermas does not deny the carceral malignancy of modern society. Like Foucault, he deplores the extent to which dividing practices and hierarchies of knowledge destroy competencies for critical reflection. The segmentation of the

labor process and the splitting off of specialized forms of technical expertise, he notes, easily lend themselves to the conformist aims of disciplinary
power. He even shares Foucault's conviction that the spread of legal regulation in the welfare democracies of the West embodies a kind of paternalism that hinders freedom.[25]

The colonization of the domestic sphere by welfare provisions exemplifies the kind of bureaucratic domination that Habermas especially finds
interesting. But here he diverges from Foucault. While it is true, for
Habermas, that the pastoral power exercised through welfare law dehu-
manizes recipients of aid by reducing them to faceless case histories classi-
fiable by type, it is also true that it entitles them to social rights requisite for
effective participation in democratic life.

The question of who exercises power over whom and by what authority thus retains its importance in Habermas's analysis of power. For
him, both the modern welfare state and its forerunner, the liberal democratic state, are progressive attempts to satisfy the implicit conditions legitimating constitutional government. But it is precisely here that the irony of
Habermas's defense of liberal democracy shines forth. The constitutional
institutionalization of CR in democratic fora also promotes the establishment of juridical institutions whose emancipatory effects are at best ambiguous. These institutions in turn legitimate self-regulating economic and
administrative systems that constrain and otherwise limit the field of communicative interaction. Yet despite their adverse effects, such strategic power
relations, Habermas believes, are susceptible to *some* democratic control to
the degree that they are publicly debated.

Doubtless Foucault would query many of the points raised in this defense. Can we speak of a communicative normalization of the subject—
including the rational, critical participant of democratic dialogue—free from
the constraints of strategic power? Indeed, is rational, moral discourse capable of adequately articulating the erotic and existential dimension of
human being apart from aesthetic *experience?*

5.1 As I shall endeavor to show below, Foucault's later turn toward
hermeneutic sociology resulted in a major reconceptualization of strategic
power relations that provides a certain supplement and corrective to
Habermas's own theory of communicative action. To see this we need
only turn to Foucault's important essay, "The Subject and Power" (1982),
where he expressly follows Habermas in distinguishing power relations
(or domination) from communicative relations and objective (instrumental) capacities. According to Foucault,

> Power relations, relationships of communication, objective capacities should not therefore be confused. This is not to say that there is a question of three separate domains. Nor that there is on one hand the field of things, of perfected technique, work, and the transformation of the real; on the other that of signs, communication, reciprocity, and production of meaning; finally that of the domination of the means of constraint, of inequality and the action of men upon men. It is a question of three types of relationships which in fact always *overlap* one another, support one another *reciprocally,* and use each other mutually as means to an end. (Foucault 1982, 217–18; my italics)

It might be objected that the convergence between Foucault and Habermas as regards the interdependence of communication, domination, and objective capacity obscures an important difference. In Foucault's essay, power relations are seamlessly assimilated to domination, which in turn is characterized as a "transcendental" on a par with communicative relationships and instrumental capacities. However, in only one of the possible texts to which Foucault might have been referring does Habermas even remotely suggest that power is a transcendental medium of knowledge and action.[26] In *Knowledge and Human Interests* (1968), and in a somewhat later essay on Hannah Arendt, Habermas describes domination *(Herrschaft)* as a wholly contingent and unjustifiable use of a power *(Macht)* whose meaning eludes transcendental categorization (Habermas 1983, 171–87; 1987b, 153–97).

This disagreement between Foucault and Habermas would be decisive were it not for the fact that both eventually came to regard power as a constant, *if variable,* feature of society. For Habermas, the manifestations of power, ranging from relatively innocuous forms of subtle *influence* to overt forms of violent *domination,* vary both structurally and historically. From a structural point of view, power may designate a feature of speech or a mechanism of system integration. As a feature of speech, it specifies the peculiar sanction or authority backing up commands. Although in the *Theory of Communicative Action* (1984) Habermas *categorically* distinguished commands backed by mere threat of force from commands backed by rationally binding moral authority, in a more recent reply to critics he conceded that "a continuum obtains between power that is merely a matter of factual custom and power transformed into normative authority" (Habermas, 1991a, 239). Such a continuum is attested to by the simple fact that *rationally binding* moral platitudes such as "Tell the truth!" are initially learned as commands backed by threat of sanctions.[27]

A similar continuity obtains when power is viewed as a mechanism of social stratification. Here, Habermas notes that in stratified tribal societies the exercise of power in the form of *personal* prestige and influence need not rely on sanctions of any kind. The asymmetrical exercise of power owing to differences in lineage, gender, and/or generation is still interwoven in communicative relations between groups and individuals situated horizontally with respect to one another. Thus the communicative links between these groups and individuals remain bound to symmetrical moral expectations. By contrast, the bureaucratic power exercised in modern organizations depends on *impersonal* legal sanction. Here the *routine* asymmetrical exercise of power is all but sundered from the personal and symmetrical moral consensus critically negotiated in everyday communicative action. Whereas the influence and prestige possessed by technical experts and charismatic leaders in modern society still rely on communicative interaction and, in some sense, condense negotiations with respect to rational and moral accountability, bureaucratic power is exercised *strategically*, without regard to such negotiations (Habermas 1987a, 181–83, 273–81). Indeed, as we shall see below, the exercise of bureaucratic and economic power represents an *extreme*—and by no means typical—case of strategic action, according to Habermas. Yet notwithstanding his identification of *institutionalized* forms of strategic power with the unilateral and hegemonic *repression* of interests, he insists that power "legitimated" through democratic channels retains a *moral* link—however tenuous and ideologically compromised—to a *productive*, communicative consensus on general interests (Habermas 1991a, 254–58).

In a manner that invites comparison with Habermas's taxonomy, some of Foucault's last interviews also distinguish between levels, or degrees, of power: strategic relationships, domination, and governance (Bernauer and Rasmussen 1988, 18–19). Whereas domination involves exercising a unilateral and irreversible *power over* others, governance and strategic relations presuppose reciprocity. Governance implies an unequal relationship that may degenerate into domination under certain circumstances. However, as Gilligan notes, in education or any other kind of nurturing relationship, governance can *empower* the one who is governed, thereby leading to its own transcendence (Gilligan 1982, 168). Strategic relations, by contrast, involve the most reciprocity, since they comprise *games* in which players use *influence* to elicit *free* responses. In all these instances power varies structurally and historically depending on its degree of formal institutionalization. A close examination of Foucault's work would show that he no less than Habermas distinguishes overt from covert, strategic (narrowly construed) from communicative, normative from non-normative, forms of domination, governance, and power.

At this juncture we encounter another obstacle in our attempt to deconstruct the rigid opposition between strategic power and moral reason.

Despite the language of reciprocity, many commentators conclude that Foucault's quasi-transcendental notion of strategic relationship is incompatible with Habermas's notion of communicative interaction. In Habermas's lexicon strategic interaction occurs whenever one or more actors pursue personal aims by influencing the behavior of others through threat of force, covert manipulation, or some other instrumental inducement. Instead of implicitly or explicitly orienting themselves to obligatory norms or other reasons that ostensibly advance common interests and mutual respect, the strategic actor offers incentives calculated to advance his own interest (Habermas 1984b, 273–74). Often, this requires concealing a primary strategic intent behind the facade of communication oriented toward mutual understanding.

Although Habermas's retention of a real distinction between communicative and strategic types of action is, strictly speaking, incompatible with the Foucaultian scheme of mutually overlapping and conditioning aspects, it is more compatible with it than one might expect. Here again, a brief examination of Habermas's distinction reveals structural overlappings and continuities linking strategic and communicative action. For Habermas, the deployment of official power, like the use of money, represents a relatively pure case of strategic action, in that bureaucratic aims can be pursued according to established legal procedure, without regard to moral constraints and communicative rationales circulating in everyday life. However, this *pure* exercise of power represents an atypical case even at the organizational level. As examples of sexual harassment on the job all too frequently attest, superiors are morally accountable to subordinates with regard to personal conduct, if not with regard to choice of policy aims. The situation gets even murkier when considering strategic pursuits in noninstitutional settings. For in the absence of rigid procedures and sanctions, strategic adversaries (from, say, labor and big business) still need to justify their strategic aims in the communicative vocabulary of public interest (Habermas 1991a, 254–59).[28]

The convergence between Habermas and Foucault on the issue of overlapping types of action is perhaps better seen from the latter's vantage point. For, if it can be said that Foucault interprets communicative action strategically, as a game of power, it can also be said that he interprets strategic action communicatively, as a game of dialogue. To begin with, Foucault contests the idea that strategic action—or any action involving game-theoretic calculations aimed at coordinating interaction for purposes of successfully realizing personal goals—is necessarily manipulative, egoistic, or atomistic, as Habermas sometimes suggests. Indeed, egoism and atomism are even less pronounced in his account of strategic relations than in game theories generally, since he repudiates methodological individualism. Indeed, as we shall see below, by emphasizing the normative reciprocity of strategic action, his account of gaming comports with Gadamer's account of the play structure underlying all forms of mutual understanding, in which the action itself conducts the responses of the actors. In both instances we have accounts of communication and *nonmanipulative* exercise of power that seek to influence, through relatively transparent, but literally unannounced, contextual (background) effects.

On the one hand, Foucault says that a strategic power relation is "not simply a relationship between partners, individual or collective; it is a way in which certain actions modify others" (Foucault 1982, 219). This comports with the Gadamerian concept of a free play in which the context (or perlocutionary effect, as Habermas, following Austin, refers to it) elicits a response. To this extent, subjective agency remains beholden to actions that have a meaning (power and efficacy) of their own, independent of consciously intended aims—a condition of ego unboundedness that comes to the fore in *feelings* of mutual caring. On the other hand, he insists that it is not a relationship of violence, but requires "that 'the other' (the one over whom power is exercised) be thoroughly recognized and maintained to the very end as a person who acts" (220). This is to say that "power is less a confrontation between two adversaries or the linking of one to the other than a question of government": the structuration of a field of possible responses (221). According to this latter reading, not only are freedom and power not mutually exclusive, but "freedom may well appear as the condition for the exercise of power" (220). Hence the free play of actions and effects is not entirely independent of rational agency, but presupposes a real—and potentially legal—capacity for initiative and counterinitiative.

Speech act theory provides ample confirmation of this strategic/dialogic interplay in its differentiation between manipulative *strategies*, which aim at domination, and strategic *relations*, which aim at reciprocity. In particular, it shows that the success of the former is dependent on the success of the latter. This dependency obtains even in *nonstrategic actions* such as promising. As Habermas notes, the freedom of the addressee depends on his or her capacity to refuse the promise. The promise offer presents an opportunity for exercising freedom, that is, it opens up a field of possible responses on the part of the addressee. We might say that, by taking the initiative in opening up a determinate field of possibilities, the speaker's offer constitutes a deployment of power whereby the response of the addressee is conducted. This conducting, however, is not a manipulating. Although the field of possible responses is indirectly communicated by the perlocutionary effects stemming from both illocutionary acts and contexts of speech, this determination both presupposes and *enables* a potential refusal. Indeed, the freedom of the addressee is conditional for the addressor's exercise of power; promise making would make little sense if the addressee had no choice but to accept the offer. By contrast, promise *breaking* is parasitic on (and hence secondary to) a normal practice of promise making; as Kant showed, without the assumption of reciprocity that accompanies promise making, the manipulation of the promise breaker would never succeed.

These remarks are important, not only because they suggest that a strategic use of power—prior to strategic manipulation—can comport with communicative aims structured by moral reciprocity, but also because they imply that strategic actors, far from being passive bearers of functional roles and internalized norms, actively and freely contribute to the structuration of the field of possible responses. Here we see how Foucault's contextualist account of discourse as strategic action might be vindicated against Habermas's charge of inconsistency. *From a hermeneutic perspective,* the *regular* and *reflexive* structuration of a field of possible responses implies that the rules governing language games are continually reinterpreted in every new, situation-bound application. This game of reciprocity can become a contest aimed at settling the rules in favor of one of the contestants—a point emphasized by Lyotard in his attack on the primacy of consensual communication and reciprocity. However, if my analysis of promising is correct, then neither agonal self-assertion (Lyotard) nor deferential responsibility (Nancy) supersedes the primacy of communicative reciprocity.

That doesn't exempt communicative reciprocity from qualification. Just as Foucault's account of strategic relationship is more complex and concrete than Habermas's, so too is his account of consensual communication. Foucault seems to accept Habermas's general characterization of consensual communication as foundational for the raising of validity claims and the incurring of general obligations in a modern society. This impression is reinforced by his remark that "In the serious play of questions and answers, in the work of reciprocal elucidation, the rights of each person are in some sense immanent in the discussion" (Foucault 1984, 381).

Elsewhere Foucault takes issue with Habermas's idealization of consensual communication, denying that "there could be a state of communication which would be such that the games of truth could circulate freely, without obstacles, without constraint and without coercive effects" (Bernauer and Rasmussen 1988, 18). Our earlier discussion should alert us to the possibility that Foucault's objection here rests in part on a verbal disagreement. As noted above, both Foucault and Habermas distinguish power from domination, both affirm emancipation from domination as a goal of enlightenment, and both tacitly accept the strategic inducements necessary for initiating and sustaining dialogue. For Habermas, the uncon-strained *force* of the better argument succeeds in persuading only to the extent that the arguer successfully anticipates the reactions of her inter-locutor(s). Thus—to recall our discussion of rational choice theory in chap-ter 2—it is not unreasonable to suppose that a hermeneutically enlightened game theory might shed light on the Prisoner's Dilemma and Free Rider bottlenecks that prevent agents from resolving conflicts consensually.

Thus, despite Foucault's late interest in *parrhesia* (the aesthetic bear-ing-witness-to-truth in one's behavior and demeanor practiced by Greek and Roman ethicists), he never wavered in holding that consensus remains "a critical idea to maintain at all times." On the contrary, he affirmed a parity between communicative, strategic, and expressive action, adding that one must "ask oneself what proportion of nonconsensuality is implied in such a power relationship, and whether the degree of nonconsensuality is necessary or not" so that "one may question every power relationship to that extent" (Rabinow 1984, 379).

Foucault never spelled out the implications of his theory of action for democratic community. However, it is interesting to note that others have. Ernesto Laclau and Chantal Mouffe have argued that the Derridean deconstruction of private and public spheres, coupled with Foucault's cri-tique of essentialism and Gramsci's notion of hegemonic alliance, provides the basis for a radically pluralist conception of democratic politics. Like Taylor, they see democracy as a struggle for identity, or mutual recogni-tion. While many poststructuralists take issue with the Hegelian presup-positions underlying this account—decrying its totalitarian logic—Laclau and Mouffe do not. In their opinion, Hegel justified the radical contingency, particularity, and mutability of identity by introducing contradiction into the relational process of identity-formation (Laclau and Mouffe 1985, 95). The implications for political theory are remarkable: the struggle for rec-ognition is generalized to the point where all sectors of life—political, eco-nomic, cultural, social, familial—are politicized.

Although struggles in these various spheres are not united by over-arching goals, they are, the authors submit, intertwined with one another in loose, hegemonic alliances. Hegemony here rests on an ongoing rearticulation of equivalences (solidarities) and differences (antagonisms). To illustrate the former, one need only recall how the struggle for political equality came to encompass struggles for social, racial, and gender equality as well. Coalitions uniting labor, civil libertarian, civil rights, and women's organizations came to identify with one another in a manner that altered their own internal identities. For example, as white middle-class feminists began to organize alongside welfare activists and women of color in their struggles against racial and class discrimination, many of them began to redefine what their own liberation meant: not merely the freedom to compete with men as equals in the labor market, but abolition of capitalism as a system of patriarchal domination. (One can only hope that, by a similar logic of equivalence, hostile ethnic groups occupying the former territories of the Soviet empire will see that it is in their own economic and political interest to establish national and international—and possibly postnational—alliances of this sort as well.)

Of course, the logic of difference also contributes to the formation of hegemonic alliances. The deceptively simple—but potentially very dangerous—opposition between in-groups and out-groups that occupied so much of the Frankfurt School's analysis of fascism in the thirties and forties is but an extreme example of this logic. Normally, in democratic politics the antagonisms are more complex and muted, owing to the fact that opposed alliances sometimes claim the divided loyalties of their constituent groups, which are themselves irreducibly distinct from one another. Again, to recall our earlier example, workers' interests are not immediately identical to those of consumers, environmentalists, the unemployed, and others joining in their struggle against capitalism. Although it would be heartwarming to think that the tensions currently existing within and between these groups might ease with the passing of such a divisive system, there is no guarantee that they will do so if and when that time comes.

Certainly, Laclau and Mouffe don't think they will. And part of their reasoning stems from their Derridean and Foucaultian framework—or at least one interpretation of it. The interpretation I have in mind, of course, is just the one that emphasizes incommensurable difference. The author's assertion that "the political spaces in which each of [the democratic struggles] is constituted are different and unable to communicate with one another" (182) actually seems too extreme given their intentions. For without communication there could be no hegemony, only the "libertarian logic" and "totalitarian closure" they oppose.

Fortunately, it is clear from the context in which the above citation occurs that the authors do not hold this view. Appealing to the "other" Derrida and Foucault, they rightly affirm the openness and intertextuality of political discourse (112) as well as its regularity, which arises out of "dispersed" relations between contingently—but internally—linked elements, power relations, and practices (105). The question remains, however, whether these accounts of discourse suffice to establish the possibility of hegemonic democratic politics.

Although I have suggested that they do not—mainly because of an absence of any account of normative reciprocity—this judgment should by no means be taken as reflecting poorly on their capacity to extend our understanding of political discourse. What the concept of hegemony captures that Habermas's notion of rational consensus and Rawls's notion of overlapping consensus do not, is just the idea of an alliance that is neither a mere strategic compromise nor an agreement based on univocally understood and agreed-upon terms nor a mystical convergence (or overlap) of incommensurable comprehensive doctrines. The concept of hegemony can capture this notion, because it relies on both a Foucaultian account of discourse that accepts the complementarity of strategic and communicative speech elements and a Derridean account of writing that accepts the metaphorical and metonymical nature of meaning. It is precisely because our isolated struggles function as metonyms symbolizing all struggles, and because the rally cries of all struggles function as metaphors for the shattered dreams and redemptive hopes of all oppressed persons, that democratic alliances are possible. In this sense, democratic politics is simultaneously embodied construction and deconstruction, symbolic strategy and consensual communication.

Is there something unique in this affiliation of modern democratic politics and aesthetic imagery? It may be that all modern political struggles—be they emancipatory or fascist—have symbolically recalled the communal integrity and sovereignty once concretely represented by the body of the monarch. Unlike their fascist counterparts, however, emancipatory struggles cannot represent or reoccupy that position without destroying themselves. Because the locus of sovereignty in a democracy is permanently displaced—"the People" has been replaced by shifting constellations of power—the imagery evoked by emancipatory struggles is less mythical than utopian, less a yearning for some fixed and recountable identity than a hope for the unknown. Perhaps that is why emancipatory politics is symbolic struggle par excellence. For it is nothing less than the sublime yearning to represent the unrepresentable: the community of absolute ends.

Maybe it is this indefinite yearning that Foucault had in mind when he said that the "universalizing tendencies" at the root of Western civilization—"the acquisition of capabilities and the struggle for freedom"—constitute "permanent elements" (Rabinow 1984, 48). Perhaps too that is why he describes "our" freedom as an "ascetic task" of self-production that is also a discipline *and* limit. As he puts it, "[M]odernity does not 'liberate man in his own being'; it *compels* him to face the task of producing himself" (42—my italics). Consequently, since the enlightenment is part of the "historical ontology of ourselves" that has determined *who* we are, it makes no sense to be for or against it (43). At best we are compelled to reinterpret it and by implication ourselves as well.

Here we detect a final convergence between Foucault, Habermas, and the authors of *Hegemony and Socialist Strategy*. At first glance, it seems as though Foucault has no recourse other than to "bodies and pleasures" on which to base his Nietzschean critique of moral rationalism (Foucault 1976, 157). However, if this aesthetic appeal is to avoid any question-begging reference to naturalism, it must rest on the "undefined work of freedom that is condemned to creating its self-awareness and its norms out of itself" (Habermas 1986, 106). Yet this work of freedom cannot be sui generis. As Habermas and the others remind us, the expressive creation of one's personal identity is intimately linked to political struggles in which identity is articulated in juridical terms.[29] If this were not the case, persons could not possibly resist co-optation by the libidinal regime of disciplinary power (Habermas 1987a, 285).

By the same token, it seems as though Habermas has no recourse other than to moral rationalism on which to base his critique of heteronomous aestheticism. If this ethical appeal is to avoid any question-begging reference to transcendentalism, it too must rest on the democratic freedom that collectively determines the legitimate needs of its own subjects. Yet cultivation of aesthetic sensibilities cannot be limited to consensual argumentation about needs or hegemonic discourse. It requires different—*judgmental, intuitive, experiential,* and *affective*—competencies that prescind from the exercise of democratic rights. Indeed, it might require *friendship* and *intimate caring*—democratic virtues that are still inadequately compassed by the abstract social concerns (or solidarity) demanded of speakers who knowingly share a common fate.[30]

To conclude, our examination of deconstructive and genealogical varieties of communitarian thought has uncovered an important dimension of community, namely, that aspect of ethical life that is largely affective, if not instinctual. We respond to—and are responsible for—our situation in ways that are largely beyond our subjective control. Too, we incur nongeneralizable and unreciprocated responsibilities with respect to other persons. Yet our aesthetic receptivity to these and other imaginary communities is but half the story. Our communitarian images and affectations are shaped as much by the exchange of reasoned opinions, whose political locus, as we shall now see, lies at the intersection of politics and law.

PART III

The Legal Rationale of Democratic Community

5

Discourse Ethics and
Democratic Legitimation

My discussion of communitarianism has led to the inescapable conclusion that democracy anchors the hegemonic grounds of modern legitimation. Yet the very notion of democratic community seems problematic. Our survey of democratic theory in chapter 1 suggests that voting seldom if ever generates rational outcomes, or uniquely consistent, maximal rank orderings of preferences of the sort required by a *volonté générale*. Modern pluralism and conflict conspire against it. But if that is so, how can we explain our prima facie obligation to be law-abiding?

Let me reformulate the question. If laws merely express aggregated preferences—or effective demand—and if the latter is a function of social power, then why should "losers" voluntarily submit to winners, if it is *not* in their personal interest to do so? The problem, we noted, touches on the very meaning of practical reason. SR provides no basis for equitably resolving conflicts of interest—unless, perhaps, by recourse to a higher intuition of the public good vouchsafed to judges and administrators. Yet this appeal to rational decision begs the question. If value judgments are subjective, why privilege an expert's intuition over a layperson's?

The introduction of CR as an alternative to SR suggested one way out of this dilemma. In chapters 2 through 4 I sought to show why CR—with its accent on the consensual transformation and validation of interests—provided a richer, more democratic account of practical reasoning than its derivative counterpart. In chapter 2 we saw that the conflict between technological efficiency and democratic legitimation is by no means preordained, since computer technology offers possibilities for egalitarian, democratic learning and deliberation that belie the dominant model of subjective, hierarchical programming. Second, we observed that rational choice accounts of human action, which emphasize the efficient maximization of personal utility, are at best limited and succeed outside a narrow range of economic behavior only if qualified by a deeper understanding of background norms and functional constraints. Indeed, norms anchoring democratic processes enable the discursive revision of preferences in a manner that seems integral to the very idea of rational choice.

In chapter 3, I expanded on this last point with reference to hermeneutical accounts of social identity and agency proffered by Anglo-American communitarians. These accounts raise questions about the relative priority of the good over the right, the relative meaning of the good with respect to different communities, and the relative validity of our interpretation of this meaning. The hermeneutical ideal of coherence and perfectibility implicit in every parochial effort at understanding seemed to mitigate this relativism. Conceived dialogically, this ideal implies a universal notion of CR having implications for democracy as well. To the extent that democratic politics is founded on a certain solidarity with (or openness to) one's interlocutor as coauthor/corecipient of a common destiny, it implies equal rights to question as well as a mutual orientation toward self-realization.

Finally, our discussion of French communitarianism in chapter 4 served to qualify the politics of identity by suggesting that hegemony, rather than conflict or consensus, provides the best model for understanding democratic pluralism. Hegemonic politics affirms the symbolic value of democratic discourse. The metaphors underwriting shifting alliances disrupt group identities by opening them up to—and thus making them responsible to—different interests and values. Not only does this ensure the permanent *decentration of the subject,* but it entails the permanent *absence of a sovereign subject* who monopolizes power. Indeed, democratic politics confirms the inextricable interrelatedness of multiple centers of power and reason, strategic influence and communicative reciprocity.

As I hope to show, the legitimating potential of a democracy premised on this degree of complexity becomes strikingly apparent in Habermas's discourse ethics (DE). On this model, neither moral considerations of justice, communitarian considerations of the good nor strategic success in aggregating and maximizing preferences *taken separately* suffice to legitimate laws. Normally, legitimate laws must be processed through forms of rational discourse that address each of these concerns in unique ways: the pragmatic choice of efficient means, the fair aggregation of interests, the ethical interpretation of collective identities and values, and the moral justification of norms. So construed, the discourse model of legitimation provides a happy medium between liberalism and communitarianism. For not only does it establish the equiprimordiality of civil rights and democratic sovereignty, justice and solidarity, but it shows that the maintenance of tradition-based *identity* valued by Anglo-American communitarians can only be achieved in *modern* society through a process disruptive of traditional *authority*.

I will argue that a properly qualified DE defines the scope of democratic participation more broadly than either Habermas or his critics realize. Habermas's rejection of "simple recipes of workers' self-management" (Dews 1986, 187) in light of the requirements of a government-regulated market economy rests on a questionable distinction between economic and technological efficiency, on one hand, and democratic legitimation, on the other. This distinction—between system and lifeworld, decision and deliberation—seems to contradict the main strand of Habermas's own account of the genesis of rights and sovereignty. In addition to this problem, Habermas neglects the importance of hegemonic discourse, which seems to straddle the line separating strategic bargaining and compromise from consensual communication. Finally, I conclude that a process model of democratic legitimation of the sort proposed by him is not necessarily more egalitarian and libertarian than an account oriented to outcomes.

I begin by discussing the shortcomings of Habermas's original grounding of DE and its failure to adequately distinguish moral and legal discourse from one another and from the principle of DE generally (sec. 1). I then take up Habermas's recent reformulation of the relation between these terms in grounding a democratic system of rights (sec. 2). The last section (sec. 3) defends a notion of workplace democracy that meets Habermas's concerns about "simple recipes" of worker's self-management.

1. In recent years a number of philosophers influenced by Rawls's resuscitation of social contract theory have attempted to reformulate that theory in terms of a model of public dialogue; Charles Larmore (1986), Thomas Scanlon (1982), and Bruce Ackerman (1983) are the most familiar names that come to mind. These reformulations address the problem of motivation noted earlier with respect to Rawls's theory, namely, why one would want to regard oneself as if one were an impartial moral contractor in the original position. Rawls's own stipulation that the contractors in the original position are motivated by rational self-interest begs this question. By contrast, if Rawls had argued from the position in which most of us actually find ourselves—in conversations aimed at resolving disagreements consensually—there would have been no need for him to export moral impartiality into the position from the outside by postulating a veil of ignorance. For, it is argued, an interest in moral impartiality is generated by the very conditions of rational dialogue.

As we saw earlier, even Rawls himself now prefers to justify his principles by appeal to what any person inhabiting a modern democratic society could agree to, so long as he or she were exercising *public reason.* But a problem still remains, as the example of multicultural conflict all too painfully attests. This concept of rational dialogue requires an exercise of bracketing that is almost as unrealistic and without empirical motivation as the hypothetical imposition of a veil of ignorance. For remember, Rawls's concept of public reason requires that we distinguish our *beliefs* from the partial, comprehensive doctrines in which they holistically inhere, and then appeal to only those that other reasonable and rational interlocutors would accept as justificatory grounds for shared principles. This invocation of "conversational constraint," as Ackerman puts it (1983, 375), is also invoked by Larmore, who insists that "each should prescind from the beliefs that the other rejects" (Larmore 1987, 53). Although Scanlon's version of impartial negotiation seems to allow rational interlocutors to express any beliefs and acquire any information they deem necessary for unanimously resolving on a system of rules (Scanlon 1982, 110), it too is formulated as a monological thought-experiment. In the words of Ken Baynes, "[I]t does not require that *real* discourses be carried out, but asks what an *individual* cannot reasonably reject" (Baynes 1992, 117).

The chief accomplishment of Habermas's DE consists in overcoming this residual subjectivism in *social* contract theory. It forges a stronger bond between morality and real discourse than any of the above theories by arguing that impartiality is less a function of monological bracketing of beliefs than a result of mutual dialogical criticism, grounded in fair democratic procedures entailing equal opportunities and resources for public deliberation. Eschewing the deductions and abstract thought-experiments favored by Rawls and others, Habermas argues this point in a way that attests to the very realities conditioning his own moral idealism—social and historical facts whose meaning essentially depends on narrations and interpretations susceptible to dialogic contestation. The most important of these facts is that postconventional systems of morality emerge in response to specifically modern problems of conflict and collective survival. The rule of law (or legal domination, as Weber puts it) thus has a circumscribed range of validity; it applies only to complex societies that have achieved a degree of rational differentiation resistant to regulation by more conventional—sacred, customary, and bureaucratic—types of law (Habermas 1992, 95).

In one sense, modern law marks the intersection of these types of law under new, postconventional headings: natural law, common law, and statutory law, respectively. More importantly, their conventional antecedents already evince a certain complementarity. The oldest forms of law, sacred and customary, anticipate the two main poles around which later legal systems gravitate: transcendent sanction *(legitimacy)* and immanent order *(legality)*. Implicit in the earliest forms of tribal law, sacred law imbues political authority with transcendent binding force. Customary and bureaucratic law, by contrast, give it empirical and rational content—specifically in the form of reliable precedents and effective statutes. In preconventional (tribal) law, normative and positive aspects remain undifferentiated, as is evidenced by the failure to distinguish criminal and civil law, retribution and deterrence, intent and effect, and so on. This shortcoming is later remedied in stratified, centrally organized states whose legal systems have evolved conventional methods for dealing with conflict and deviance. However, coupled with the growing complexity of society, the expansion of a state bureaucracy sets in motion a process of secularization that exacerbates the differentiation of positive and moral aspects, thereby engendering a legitimation crisis (Habermas 1988, 260).

This crisis afflicted the new nation-states that emerged in Europe from the sixteenth century on. The legitimation of bureaucratic law could not be met satisfactorily by appeal to substantive customs, religious traditions, or brute power. Natural law doctrines filled this void by providing an impartial (procedural) basis upon which constitutional law—above all, the separation of powers—could anchor itself. Transcending the vicissitudes of parochial tradition, rational (postconventional) theories of abstract *moral* right at once motivated and reflected the dynamic complexity of a capitalist society composed of heterogeneous and conflicting interests.

To a certain extent, the split between instrumental and moral interpretations of natural law—exemplified in the opposed social contractarian philosophies of Hobbes and Kant—reduplicated the division between bureaucratic and transcendent law at a procedural level (270). It is within *this* context, Habermas remarks, that the tension between moral idealism and social realism surfaces. Here, for the first time ever, a conventional ethic, which assigns personal duties and social roles on the basis of birth, gives way to a postconventional ethic differentiated into complementary moral and legal aspects. As morally autonomous, individuals must critically evaluate the justice of conventional laws against universal standards of right (the principle of self-determination), while freely pursuing their own conception of the good in a lawful manner. This legal freedom, to paraphrase Kant, follows from the demands of moral autonomy while yet being distinct from it. We can observe the law for purely prudential reasons, because it is backed by punitive sanctions; indeed, it exists precisely to regulate conflicts between persons pursuing private ends (Habermas 1992, 124).

The tension between morality and legality becomes apparent when we realize that both aspects need each other. Uprooted from conventional custom and habit, *personal* moral conscience cannot be relied on to assure stable interaction without *public* rules backed by state power. Uprooted from religious and monarchical authority, *state power* cannot become effective without laws that appear *legitimate* (178).

In Habermas's opinion, neither philosophers nor sociologists have appreciated this tension. Over the years moral philosophers have tended to ignore economic and functional constraints imposed by forms of legal domination. The ideals they have intuited or constructed can therefore be criticized as ideological. Conversely, sociologists of law have tended to ignore the efficacy of morality in constituting social reality.

Now, Habermas situates his own position between these extremes. Hence he insists on the importance of morality in legitimating law. Indeed, he defends this insight against the classical sociological tradition of Weber and Durkheim—and he does so in their name. This is nowhere more apparent than in his critique of functionalistic and economistic approaches to law of Weberian provenance.

According to Weber, no form of domination can be sustained unless it is recognized as legitimate by those who fall under it, and only legal domination possesses a rationale that lends the recognition of legitimacy a universally binding force (Weber 1978, 212). Unlike customary law, which is based on shared tradition, and sacred law, which rests on the generally recognized charisma of prophetic legislators, modern law is grounded in impartial *procedures*, the clearest example being voluntary contracts between two or more persons rationally pursuing their own interests (868–69). Yet despite his appreciation of the social contractarian basis underlying voluntary contracts, Weber denies that morality provides a distinctly rational basis for legitimating law, since it is not formalizable to the degree demanded by universal reason. Doctrines of natural law commit a naturalistic fallacy and their derivation from factual or metaphysical grounds infects them with a particularistic, *substantive* content. This happens even when these norms "are obtained through logical analysis of legal or ethical concepts" (868–69). Hence Weber's concern that social legislation targeting select classes undermines legal neutrality.

This repudiation of substantive justice follows from Weber's restriction of reason to SR, which he believed assures maximum predictability requisite for instrumental calculation, economic efficiency, and adaptability. For him technical specialization is but one of the formal attributes legitimating law, alongside generality of form and logical systematicity. Each attribute manifests formal rationality in a morally neutral way. The scientific articulation of law abides by canons of formal logic; the semantic form of law ensures its uniform application to all citizens without regard to social standing, and the technical regulation of adjudicative and legislative procedures establishes predictability, thereby enabling persons to pursue their aims in a calculating, utility-optimizing manner.[1]

The importance Weber attaches to predictability finds its greatest support in economic and functionalist approaches to law. The former seeks to define law in terms of efficiency rather than justice. Efficiency is usually interpreted along the lines of Pareto optimality or some other economic criterion.[2] In the law of torts the assignment of rights by property or liability rules maximizes joint benefits minus joint costs. The determination of damage remedies—correlated with specific performance, expectation, reliance, and/or restitution—authorizes breach of contract on similar grounds. The allocation of resources to crime prevention, as well as the decision regarding what acts are to be criminalized and what sanctions imposed, must likewise be economical.

In calling upon courts to promote efficiency by replicating the outcome of market exchange, economic theories appeal to the Coase Theorem, which encourages civil courts to assign rights to those parties that would have purchased them in an open market under conditions of costless transaction; the litigant who would be *willing* (though not necessarily *able*) to pay more for it should have it. Unfortunately, as an informative account of rational cooperation in the absence of transaction costs, the theorem is patently false; under strategic conditions of game theory, costless transactions need not produce efficient exchanges, let alone agreement.

Other criteria present themselves as candidates for less informative, *hypothetical* strategies for determining legal efficiency. Utilitarians who equate efficiency with preference maximization sometimes appeal to the Kalder-Hicks criterion for this very reason, since it mandates outcomes in which the winners could *(but in fact need not)* compensate the losers in such a way that no one would be worse than he or she was in any other alternative and at least one person would be better off. Yet this criterion lacks the transitivity requisite for establishing comparable utility: two outcomes can be Kalder-Hicks efficient with respect to one another.[3] Only a Pareto superior move optimizes utility in a transitive manner without imposing unfair losses. But Pareto superiority is of no consequence in legal and political disputes involving identifiable losers, who rightfully demand that redistribution of resources accord with standards of justice.

Economically speaking, predictability defines efficiency; functionalistically speaking, it defines legitimacy: to say that a decision is right just means that under certain circumstances it is to be predicted. Predictability is accorded a positive survival value, so that legal behavior can be understood as approximating the stability requisite for efficient social cooperation and adaptation. Predictability is most important in criminal law, where guilty verdicts ideally follow clear proof of violation. It is less so in private law, where such standards would encourage only uncontestable lawsuits, thereby rendering new applications all but meaningless (Dworkin 1986, chap. 4).

Ultimately, efficiency and predictability fail to stabilize legal expectations precisely because law is a dynamic process. Legal proceedings incorporate arguments whose power to convince rests on *normative* assumptions about the truth, justice, and validity of claims, not on diminishing the "surprise-value" of future arguments (Habermas 1988, 254–56). Predictability and efficiency are therefore normative, not instrumental values. The fairness of the procedures—not the mechanical predictability of outcomes—assures the reliability of an ordered process of change. This applies equally to the other formal legal features mentioned by Weber—systematicity and abstract semantic form. The latter guarantees efficiency only when construed as a *moral* precondition for legitimacy, namely, as assuring equal protection under the law.

If sociology of law has suppressed the moral dimension of law as an interpretative practice, philosophy of law, Habermas submits, has failed to reconcile its major terms: the moral and legal freedom of the private subject versus the moral and legal self-determination of the people. This tension can also be formulated in terms of debates between communitarians and liberals, republicans and federalists. In Habermas's opinion, both sides in this debate paradoxically embroil themselves in forms of legal positivism that threaten the very moral autonomy they presuppose. The Kantian liberal wants to ground positive law in some rational version of natural law. The former thus presents itself as a particular instance (copy or implication) of universal morality. However, since there is no *deductive rationale* linking universal and particular, the meaning of positive *and* moral law becomes a matter of personal intuition, or de facto positing (hence the paradoxical reversal of higher and lower, normative and factual, observed earlier by Hegel). This decisionistic line of thinking returns us to Hobbes and the notorious problems of political obligation and moral conscience associated with illiberal command theories of law. The Rousseau-inspired communitarian, by contrast, wants to ground rights in the democratic will of the people, understood as a factual expression of a common ethos and good. This move—which presupposes the transformation of private persons into public (virtuous) citizens—threatens the *private* moral autonomy of individuals no less than its liberal counterpart (Habermas 1992, 130–35).

According to Habermas, liberal and communitarian theories succumb to this dialectic because they reduce law to only one or two of the three rationales underlying modern legitimation—transcendent moral justice (self-determination), concrete ethical solidarity and welfare (self-realization), and personal interest (self-assertion) (137). Moreover, they are led down this reductionist path by their adherence to SR, located in the sovereign individual or the sovereign people (133). The end result is the same in either case: opposition between individual and democratic sovereignty, or, as in the case of poststructuralism, opposition to any normative account of legitimacy.

1.1 DE ostensibly resolves this opposition by grounding private and public autonomy "equiprimordially." Habermas begins his defense of this claim by showing how DE is implicit in (or anticipated by) everyday speech. This mediation of normativity and facticity is repeated in the structure of dialogic justification, which explains how factual agreements entail prima facie obligations. The next step involves applying this model of moral argumentation to law.

You will recall that Habermas defends the first two claims by arguing that the coordination, integration, and socialization of persons inhabiting modern societies depend on communication rather than conventional norms. In speaking of communication he has in mind the sorts of speech acts analyzed by Austin and Searle, which contain a normative (illocutionary) force as well as a propositional (locutionary) reference. The idealism implicit in this mediation of validity and facticity comes to the fore during communication failure or disagreement. In this instance confidence can be restored only through rational argumentation, which embodies postconventional moral reciprocity. He reconstructs this structure by appealing to both the shared—but largely implicit—intuitions of competent speakers and the theoretical hypotheses of philosophers like Stephen Toulmin, who defends a pragmatic, informal account of argumentative validity as a more viable alternative to deductive or inductive approaches.

Viewed from this perspective, conversations, or what Habermas calls *discourses*, replace propositional inferences as the primary concern of logic.

It is axiomatic for Habermas that discourses typically arise whenever the justice of a norm, the sincerity of an expressed intention, or the truth of a cognitive belief is disputed. Claims to justice and truth are of special interest to him since, whenever we assert that something is true or right, we imply that all other persons *would* agree with us after impartial examination of the evidence. Consensus, not deducibility, functions as the touchstone for justification. It is consensus that bridges the gap between *is* and *ought*, and it is consensus that enables us to escape the nihilism plaguing rationalism's insistence on deriving meaningful prescriptions from underivable moral axioms. Just as the principle of induction, applied under controlled conditions, enables scientists to agree on the factual necessity and universality of causal relations, so too, under controlled conditions approximating complete impartiality and fairness, moral discussion enables citizens to reach factual agreement on the rightness of norms in an equally binding—albeit conditional—manner (Habermas 1984c, 165).

Adopting the recommendation of Robert Alexy, Habermas formulates these conditions of discourse as pragmatic rules:

1. Every subject with the competence to speak and act is allowed to take part in discourse.
2. Everyone is allowed to question any assertion whatever ... introduce any assertion into the discourse ... express his attitudes and desires.
3. No one may be prevented, by internal or external coercion, from exercising his rights as laid down in 1 and 2 (Habermas 1990, 89).

Habermas is thus claiming that the *moral point of view* in its most minimal—and *nonprescriptive*—sense is implicit in *any* discourse whatsoever—a claim that harks back to Gadamer's earlier contention that moral reciprocity adheres in any effort at reaching understanding. His defense of this claim has the flavor of a qualified transcendental argument—one that in its own way illustrates the pragmatic bridging of idealism and realism. In particular, the argument owes a great deal to Apel's observation that the relationship obtaining between discourse and moral reciprocity is neither deductive nor inductive, but cogent in a manner that can best be captured by the idea of a *performative contradiction*. Using an argument first articulated by Jaako Hintikka, who noted that utterances such as "I doubt that I exist" involve a *performative* contradiction between a speech act and its pragmatic presupposition, Apel maintained that the skeptic's refusal to acknowledge the claim to universal validity inherent in his factual utterances and moral assertions, as well as his refusal to acknowledge basic speech rights, is belied by his attempt to persuade others rationally. Therefore, basic concepts of universal validity as well as basic notions of freedom and equality are not ideas that participants in discourse *could* elect to reject, without contradicting the pragmatic presuppositions of their own behavior. Although there is no contradiction on the part of the skeptic who refuses to engage in certain justificatory practices, there is a kind of weak inconsistency, *if and so long as* he desires to maintain himself in a rational identity whose stability is maintained through mutual recognition (102). By the same token, the relativist who defends the radical incommensurability of substantive, context-dependent schemes of rationality can only do so by successfully translating them into a common language, which will be governed by higher-order, postconventional procedures of communicative reason.

In Apel's opinion, this demonstration proves that moral reciprocity "belongs to those transcendental-pragmatic presuppositions of argumentation that one must always (already) have accepted, if the language game of argumentation is to be meaningful" (Apel 1987, 277). Habermas favors a weaker interpretation of the argument. Moral reciprocity is not *constitutive* of, but only *regulative* for, argumentation. In failing to live up to the counterfactual expectations implicit in it, one is not necessarily ceasing to argue meaningfully. At the same time, as a "fact of reason," these expectations are at least partially constitutive, since "there are no alternatives to these rules of argumentation" (1990b, 95). Unavoidable presuppositions that they are, they do not have the concrete prescriptive force of moral or political rights. Indeed, because their force is more compelling than the merely obligatory and discretionary sense of the latter, they themselves need not—and cannot—be discursively justified at all. At most, one can debate their *concrete significance* as pragmatic anchors for categories of moral and legal rights.

Here we have the core of Habermas's defense of liberal dialogue as a neutral procedure. Contrary to Rawls and Ackerman, what makes these presuppositions neutral is not that they impose "gag rules" on the expression of particular conceptions of the good. Bracketing such conceptions in order to ensure agreement may actually privilege the particular conceptions that already dominate the discussion. Rather, what makes them neutral is that they are "necessary components of a practice that is without alternatives, or unavoidable"—short of resorting to brute force. Habermas even goes so far as to assert that notions of truth, rationality, justification, and consensus play the same grammatical roles in every culture, despite the fact that speakers from different cultures might interpret them differently.

It might be objected that this concession weakens rather than strengthens Habermas's argument. For it is the unavoidability of the *liberal* interpretation of rational justification, not the unavoidability of rational justificatory procedures as such, that is at stake here. Habermas's attempt to extricate himself from this difficulty by invoking a distinction between the way we explicitly interpret (reconstruct or define) the norms governing our practices—which may be colored by our particular comprehensive ethical and philosophical views—and the purely intuitive way we apply them, does not really address the problem, and in any case seems doomed to failure (1992, 378). If the way we interpret our linguistic rules affects the way we apply them—which it can—then disagreements in interpretation will entail differences in application, or if you will, differences in the very rules being applied. If the way we interpret our rules does not affect the way we apply them—the view Habermas seems to be defending here— then he is invoking a strong form/content distinction that runs contrary to the pragmatic, hermeneutical, and reflexive thrust of his own theory of communicative action. Such a strong distinction would save the universality of speech structures at the cost of reducing them to some ineffable, prediscursive *Ding an sich*. The correct, Hegelian alternative, by contrast, would accept the historicality of speech structures—and along with it, their reflexive indeterminacy—as a necessary price for retaining their interpretability, or meaningfulness.

The third step of Habermas's mediation of idealism and realism, which shows how democratic dialogue and law mutually constitute one another as matters of prescriptive right, acknowledges this indeterminacy. Before proceeding to discuss it, let me briefly note some difficulties with the first two steps. To begin with, postconventional moral reciprocity is not *directly* implicated in rational argumentation. The universal scope of the former enjoins against considering natural and cultural differences in specifying who is permitted to participate in discourse. Yet this does not appear to be a presupposition of argument as such. Socrates, for example, had no difficulty restricting dialogic participation to Greek males. Conceding this point, Habermas now claims that "*of themselves* these normative obligations do not extend beyond the boundaries of a concrete lifeworld of family, tribe, city, or nation." Such boundaries, he adds, "can be broken through only in discourse, to the extent that the latter is institutionalized in modern societies" (Habermas 1989–90, 48).

Habermas, then, acknowledges the necessity of situating the idealism of universal reciprocity within a factual account of social evolution. This attempt to mediate "validity" and "facticity" yields a further difficulty with his argument. Is it possible to defend a homology between social evolution and individual development? Can one abstract a universal typology of moral dilemmas that can be translated from the sociolinguistic context of one culture into that of another? If not, how can the universality of the theory be cross-culturally established? Does it make sense, in general, to talk about increased problem-solving capacity *tout court*, rather than increased problem solving relative to some culturally specific, context-bound set of problems?[4]

Habermas is aware of the magnitude of these difficulties, but he has yet to concede that they are insuperable (Habermas 1990b, 21). The lack of strong evidence confirming Kohlberg's sixth stage of moral development does not, he insists, count against the logical superiority of universalistic moral theories generally. Nor, he believes, does the incidence of moral regression and relativism among test subjects. Ultimately he thinks that these difficulties can be explained away in terms of a disjunction between levels of attained moral consciousness and levels of motivation, or between levels of justification and levels of application (171). Most importantly, Habermas rejects Kohlberg's contention that the highest stages of conflict resolution possess a "hard" or "natural" status (Habermas 1989–90, 33). Lower stages of cognitive and moral development can be empirically confirmed as highly probable, since the competencies in question are organically based. This appears to be the case with respect to the coordination of social perspectives and the ability to perceive objects as invariant through perspectival changes in their aspects. Such is not the case, however, with postconventional moral stages.[5] Empirical psychology alone cannot articulate the different levels of competence that obtain at this stage, since they revolve around a *reflective* capacity to draw distinctions—between the abstract idea of a universalistic morality and various interpretations of it, or between fundamental principles of justice and specific rules and applications—that are themselves *philosophical*. Even neo-Aristotelianism and skepticism (corresponding, respectively, to conventional stages 4 and 4.5 on Kohlberg's scale) find postconventional articulations at the philosophical level. Consequently, Habermas is reluctant to grant postconventional stages a natural status. Instead, he tells us, we have to view utilitarian, social contractarian, and deontological theories as providing different interpretations of a more basic idea: the moral point of view. Which of these ultimately proves most satisfactory in accounting for our moral intuitions is a matter to be decided in practical and theoretical discourses between specialists and test subjects (Habermas 1982, 260).

1.2 Let us leave aside these difficulties in mediating sociology and morality and return to a more basic question: How does Habermas apply DE to morality and politics? As noted above, Habermas concedes that one must distinguish the weak—and pragmatically constrained—reciprocity built into everyday communicative action from the stronger reciprocity built into discourse. Too, he concedes that we must distinguish the postconventional principle *(U)* of universalizability (or universal inclusion) from the kind of moral reciprocity implicit in discourse. Finally, he observes that *U* is a general presupposition underlying any postconventional moral theory, of which DE is but a favored interpretation (and a good candidate for stage 7 in Kohlberg's scheme). As we shall see, DE is favored because, unlike standard deontological and utilitarian theories, it alone allows for the rational transformation of needs in a way that validates autonomy and reciprocity, on one hand, and happiness on the other.

Habermas now insists on viewing DE as a common principle applicable in different ways to morality and law. Initially, however, he identified DE with moral idealism in a way that undercut its applicability to the realities of both moral and political life. This happened in part because of his sharp distinction between deontological questions concerning *universal* right (justice) and teleological questions concerning *personal* and *social* good. To the former he assigned the rational justification of obligatory norms, to the latter the prudent choice of norms. Here practical reason *(Moralität)* is equated with competencies requisite for the discursive adjudication of conflicts, ethical evaluation *(Sittlichkeit)* with the artful know-how *(Klugheit)* requisite for contextual judgment (Habermas 1990b, 104).

Recently, Habermas has softened this distinction in accordance with the realities of practical reasoning. First, he notes that the assessment of moral norms almost invariably involves evaluating—and, if need be, transforming—specific needs, goods, and identities in *ethical* (or existential) discourses. This follows from the fact that the concrete meanings of universal moral principles must themselves be interpreted in light of shared, but parochial, ethical conventions. As embodiments of general goods and values, these conventions are likewise open to multiple interpretations; hence they too will have to be rationally articulated in real ethical discourses. Moreover, standards of taste, as well as the language in which we interpret and express our needs, may also have to be submitted to aesthetic or clinical (therapeutic) critique—discourses that necessarily appeal to historical, aesthetic, or pathological experiences. Second, Habermas allows that speakers in practical discourse combine the roles of prudent actor and impartial spectator, so that they bring with them their own experiences as actors and judges in comparing the potential consequences of norms for hypothetical situations. Actors and judges likewise engage in internally simulated "discourses of application," in which the moral principle of universalizability mandates the consideration of "all relevant aspects of a case" (207). Moral argumentation thus involves balancing principles and conventional responses to situations in a manner approximating a Rawlsian state of reflective equilibrium.

Although these changes anticipate a democratic model of DE, Habermas's general tendency has been to present DE as an alternative to Kantian moral theory. In his opinion, Kant's theory embodies the modern, postmetaphysical insight that the sphere of moral rationality must be restricted to the *justification* of particular maxims of action in light of abstract *procedures* of universalizability. Its weakness, he submits, lies in its reliance on SR. On Kant's account, universalizability resides in a preestablished harmony among isolated agents who possess the same rational faculties. Consistency testing rules out maxims the general application of which, from the subjective standpoint of private moral conscience, is either self-contradictory or incompatible with rational agency.[6] But Kant's bracketing any consideration of consequences, as these bear upon the happiness of those affected, limits and distorts the universalization procedure, so that the latter ends up legitimizing laws and norms that are detrimental to the interests of some persons. This defect is ostensibly remedied by a DE in which "one must be able to test whether a norm or a mode of action could be generally accepted by those affected by it, such that their acceptance would be rationally motivated and hence uncoerced" (Habermas 1990b, 36). Such an ethic shifts the emphasis from what *each* person independent of any consideration of historical interests can will to be a *general law*, to what *all* in agreement with others on such interests can accept as a *universally binding norm*.

This formulation suggests that rational consensus replaces lawful consistency as a *criterion* of moral right, an impression that is reinforced by an early essay of Habermas's published in 1973 *(Wahrheitstheorien)* in which he virtually equates *truth* and *moral validity* with *universal* consensus (Habermas 1984c, 127–83). On closer inspection, however, such an equation seems inconsistent with the democratic thrust of DE. Universal consensus functions as a criterion only if it is conceived as the outcome of a perfectly rational dialogue under ideal conditions, viz., conditions of perfectly transparent communication unlimited by time and space, and by pressures emanating from immediate contexts of action. Since an unlimited community of past, present, and future speakers could reach agreement under constraint-free conditions only if they already possessed complete knowledge of themselves and their world, and were alike in other respects as well, the universalizabilty procedure amounts to nothing more than the question-begging choice of a *single*, ideal "speaker."

That Habermas has not entirely abandoned the *monological* method of ideal role taking is borne out by his recent claim that "when it is a question of examining norms with a genuinely universal domain of validity," consensus functions as a regulative idea in the sense that arguments are "played out in the 'internal forum'" (Habermas 1989–90, 41). This is true in one sense. *Real* moral arguments arise in *contexts of action* and almost invariably concern the justification of *exceptions* to generally accepted rules. This means that universalizability cannot be understood as positively mandating the *general observance* of norms in the manner sometimes asserted by Kant and Habermas (Wellmer 1986, 54–112). Given the fact that there are exceptions to every valid rule, a strict universalizability test could generate only an unconditional obligation to *refrain* from following rules—such as a permission (or obligation) to lie, steal, kill, and so on—the universal compliance with which would be inconsistent, or contrary to what all rational persons could want. This valid but trivial use of the universalization procedure *is* monological in Kant's sense.

Elsewhere Habermas suggests that the advantage of DE over its Kantian counterpart resides in its *intersubjective* account of rational, moral *autonomy*. Individual autonomy does not precede public discourse, since freedom from prejudice is secured only through critical resistance by others. Although Habermas is right about this, it hardly advances beyond Kant's own belief in the importance of communication and public reason in furthering enlightenment and emancipation.

DE, then, is best understood *not* as a *unique* procedure of moral reasoning or a process of moral enlightenment but as an interpretation of *legal* (or political) legitimacy. *The general observance* of *coercive laws* must be justified by a different universalization procedure, one mandating a critical interpretation and revision of personal preferences for the sake of reaching consensus on a common good.

We are back to Rousseau—by way of Kant. Democratic universalization cannot exhaust itself in *voting* procedures that ensure that a *pregiven* agreement on the common good will be passively *represented*. It must also—and more fundamentally—comprise a *discursive* procedure for testing the rationality of this agreement and, if need be, generating a new one. The decisive thing to note here is that the emphasis has shifted from the *hypothetical determination of what universal justice ideally requires* to the *real acceptance or acceptability* of laws regulating the *legitimate* distribution of risks, burdens, and benefits *for a particular society*—a shift, as we shall see, that also safeguards against majoritarian tyranny.

The difference between these discursive procedures is reflected in the criteria of truth and rationality that regulate the conduct and aims of real discourse. In the latter instance justification appeals to truth criteria that are themselves potentially falsifiable. Thus, we might say that the adoption of natural law principles by eighteenth-century political theorists was warranted given their peculiar criteria of rationality and scientific truth, even if it would not be so warranted in light of today's criteria, which prohibit the commission of naturalistic fallacies (Habermas 1982, 273).

Note that a consensus warranting the assertion of fallible truth claims can no longer provide a transcendent criterion for identifying ideological claims. As our example of natural law shows, assertions can be accepted as conditionally warranted only on the basis of truth criteria that, on further reflection, might turn out to be ideological, or the result of partial and constrained thinking subservient to the powers that be. If my analysis of SR in chapter 2 is correct, such reflection is now leading feminists and others to consider the criteria of scientific and technological rationality as equally distorted as the ideology of authoritative expertise perpetuated by mass media.

Now, *if* we directly applied the *ideal* model of DE to a normative theory of legitimacy *without further qualification,* several counterintuitive—not to mention undemocratic—implications would follow. On this model any belief or practice shaped by covert power relations is ideological and hence illegitimate. Since some such beliefs and practices inevitably influence the language in which we reason, no actual agreement—and thus no law—could be truly legitimate.

Moreover, if one insisted on the ideal model, the determination of legitimate norms would seem to imply an undemocratic procedure. The procedure of ideology critique Habermas outlines in *Legitimation Crisis* (1975) suffers from this defect. There Habermas argued that the social critic should hypothetically imagine how the members of a social system "would . . . at a given stage in the development of productive forces, have collectively and bindingly interpreted their needs (and which norms [they would] have accepted as justified) if they could and would have decided on an organization of social intercourse through discursive will formation, with adequate knowledge of the limiting conditions and functional imperatives of their society" (113). As formulated above, the procedure invites us to calculate the consequences of legal institutions for the general satisfaction of needs—a rather uncertain undertaking in light of the limits and paradoxes of utilitarian and rational choice calculations. Although the possibility of calculating a rank ordering of preferences becomes increasingly remote as society becomes more complex and pluralistic, the presumption that there must be *suppressed generalizable interests* could be used to justify the legitimacy of laws that we (the rational elite) hypothesize would or could be accepted by those affected *if they possessed transparent knowledge of their true interests.* Combined with Habermas's claim that the binding character of a norm consists in its validity (104), this presumption could be used to justify the imposition of valid norms on persons against their will—an implication Habermas himself once entertained (Habermas and Luhmann 1971, 243; Habermas 1975, 101).

To summarize: The direct application of DE conceived along the narrow lines of a moral ideal cannot explain the normative legitimacy of laws. To say that one has an obligation to obey laws to which one *could* (ideally) consent is problematic because it suggests that one justifiably might be forced to obey a law against one's will on the grounds that one was mistaken about what one *really* wanted.

2. Habermas's alternative account of DE—which is neutral with respect to morality and law, and stresses the importance of actual discourse in both areas—avoids this precipitous collapse of democratic institutions and moral ideals. Morality and legality are complementary but distinct aspects of modern ethical life. The *moral principle* exists in the form of personal and cultural *competence (knowledge)*; it operates mainly at the level of *argumentation.* The democratic principle, by contrast, exists in the form of social rights and public processes; it operates at the level of legal *institutionalization* (Habermas 1992, 141). Moral norms comprise natural duties; laws comprise artificial rules. The latter relieve us of the cognitive, motivational, and organizational demands placed on us by morality; they stabilize moral and nonmoral expectations, coordinate actions coercively, and provide a collective means for planning and implementing beneficial policies that are beyond the capacity of most citizens acting individually. In short, the irreducibility of democratic legitimation to questions of moral justice reflects the multiple aims of law and the complex system of rights and procedures by which they are discursively processed.

The third step in Habermas's account of the mediation of moral idealism and legal realism demonstrates just this irreducibility. Neither the principle of DE nor the concept of legal form taken separately grounds a system of legal rights (162). By itself legal form establishes a sphere of "subjective" freedom; it coordinates the strategic actions of persons pursuing private aims. It does not guarantee equal protection, due process, citizenship, political self-determination, or material well-being. By itself, the principle of DE establishes an equally abstract orientation to postconventional reciprocity. It does not guarantee concrete liberties.

Habermas thus proposes to undertake a *logical genesis of rights* that involves applying the principle of DE to the notion of private legal autonomy. The argument begins as a Hegelian deduction of the concrete moral and legal presuppositions underlying abstract legal freedom and ends in a Lockean defense of constitutional democracy. The Hegelian argument can be paraphrased accordingly (155):

1. A system of basic rights can be accepted by all affected as participants in rational discourses only if it provides *equal protection* to all, guaranteeing equal rights to everyone.
2. Since enforceable rights fall within the jurisdiction of specific governments, each person has a right to *equal citizenship* compatible with a right to emigration.
3. The rights of citizenship imply rights to *equal treatment before the law* (due process).
4. The validity (legitimacy) of rights presupposes that all persons have *equal rights and chances* to participate in *political* discussions and other democratic processes by which laws as such are legitimated.
5. In order to utilize the rights listed in 1 to 4, each person must have basic rights to the provision of welfare, social security, and a healthy environment protected against social and technological risks.

Numbers 1 through 3 comprise the bare essentials of any legitimate legal code; they are more like abstract legal *principles* than rights, in that they specify only general categories of rights (160). In specifying them further, lawmakers must appeal to the democratic process itself, whose legal basis is spelled out in 4. Whereas abstract categories of right are *theoretically* deducible from the application of DE to the concept of legal freedom, their concrete interpretation and validation as *legal* rights must await the outcome of legally institutionalized forms of democratic *practice*. Stated as a paradox, one might say (following Habermas) that, with the institutionalization of democratic discourse, legitimacy follows from legality and vice versa. Assuming that citizens actively and vigorously exercise their political rights, we can characterize the legal system as a *circular* process that *reflexively* reinterprets and relegitimates itself *and its legitimating conditions*. Thus the *subjective* legal freedom to pursue private ends no longer seems opposed to the *communicative* freedom requisite for morally legitimating it; indeed, both sustain each other (165).

So concludes the first part of Habermas's argument. The second addresses precisely those institutions requisite for effectively realizing the system of rights outlined above. To summarize, the first, Hegelian argument exhibits the mediation of idealism and realism in two senses: law sanctions normative, democratic discussions that ground legitimate rights; and the theoretical reconstruction of rights begins with intuitions drawn from actual historical constitutions. However, unlike Rawls's theory of justice, to which it bears superficial resemblance, Habermas's argument grounds only those universal principles underlying any modern legal system. Since the proper task of political philosophy on this model is limited to rational reconstruction of abstract principles, theory alone cannot determine their substantive content, which instead must be elaborated in democratic discussion.

The second, Lockean phase of the argument delineates in abstract outline the basic institutional structures of that *vertical* organization of state *power* necessary for implementing a system of rights. The constitutional organization of political power replicates the tension between legality and normativity at a higher register. Law does more than simply regulate *conflicts* over scarce goods; it also organizes the *cooperative* pursuit of collective goals. And it is this *political* function that distinguishes law from morality. The legitimacy of laws depends on their normative articulation and pragmatic-strategic satisfaction of public needs and aggregated preferences (173). This means, on the one hand, that the *communicative* power of a public opinion that has been processed through channels of discourse—a power that ostensibly "programs" the legislative, executive, and judicial branches of government with its problem-solving tasks—must remain *relatively* independent of both the *social* power exercised by particular groups strategically pursuing their particular interests *and* the *administrative* power of government functionaries (185). On the other hand, it means that the consensual, egalitarian, libertarian, and spatiotemporal idealizations built into pure discourse have to be qualified considerably in order to accommodate the realities of a complex political system oriented toward decision and compromise.

Law, then, is just the medium through which *communicative power* is transformed into *administrative power.* To accomplish this in a legitimate way it must shield both from the distorting effects of *social power*. Hence the necessity of a constitutional separation of powers. An independent judiciary shorn of legislative responsibilities is needed to monitor the constitutional exercise of administrative power. However, separation of state and civil society is just as important for preserving the autonomy of democratic opinion and will formation.

According to Habermas, the separation of powers—and the priority of democratic lawmaking—ultimately rests on a logical distinction between the different kinds of discourse through which democratic decisions are processed (Habermas 1992, 212). More importantly, it rests on a more complex notion of consensus than that obtaining in discursive models of the social contract advanced by Rawls, Larmore, Scanlon, and Ackerman. The question is this: Can a notion of consensus grounded in discursive rationality explain the possibility of resolving conflicts of interpretation—for instance, between comprehensive doctrines—better than a Rawlsian model of public reason or a Rawlsian model of convergence (or overlap)? If so, can it provide a quasi-transcendental foundation for universal rights that simultaneously accommodates the communitarian vision of a concretely institutionalized form of practical reasoning?

Prior to *Faktizität und Geltung* (1992), Habermas did not distinguish the kind of consensus reached in political discourses from that reached in practical and theoretical discourses. For example, he claimed that semantic consistency was an ideal that all participants in discourse tacitly accept as a condition for reaching consensus (Habermas 1990, 87). But, as our examination of Rawls attests, this assumption—so necessary, perhaps, for *normal* scientific discourses conducted in highly formalized languages—is not necessary for explaining the kinds of overlapping consensus that typically arise in political conversations. Unlike scientists, citizens may agree on principles for sometimes conflicting reasons, and what sometimes passes for common linguistic usage in political debates—as in the invocation of a right to life by advocates on both sides of the abortion controversy—often conceals incommensurabilities rooted in heterogeneous worldviews.

In his more recent work, Habermas pays closer attention to these deeper conflicts of interpretation. However, instead of endorsing Rawls's model of overlapping consensus as the *only* way to resolve them, he argues for a discursive, or transformative, solution that falls somewhere between liberal toleration of difference and communitarian fusion of identity. As a response to Taylor's dilemma, Habermas's proposal shows how fundamental liberties—as distinct from other privileges and immunities—are indirectly implicated in the pragmatic conditions of possible communication. These and other neutral norms of rational discourse unite liberal and communitarian ideals as complementary aspects of a single democratic ideal. Norms of equality, autonomy, reciprocity, and impartiality at least weakly regulate and direct democratic discussion, even while being progressively articulated within them. So construed, democracy reflexively enacts the *institutional* interpretation and realization of its own ideals. This fact is certainly well documented by revolutionary shifts in constitutional paradigms

witnessed in the last 150 years—shifts that were motivated in part by the
republican vision of a more inclusive and emancipatory, yet egalitarian and
solidaristic, democracy.

Rather than undertake a defense of the teleological thrust of this
argument here, I will simply indicate how the reflexive (or democratic)
paradigm synthesizes the demands of liberal autonomy (articulated in the
libertarian paradigm) and communitarian solidarity (articulated in the
welfare paradigm) within a nonpaternalistic, nonproductivist, *pluralistic*
framework. The best way to begin is by noting that the reflexive paradigm distinguishes four types of practical discourse—moral, ethicopolitical,
pragmatic, and applicative—that enter into the process of rational deliberation at various levels of public discussion, legislation, adjudication, and
administration (Habermas 1992, 201).

Public and parliamentary negotiations aimed at reaching fair compromises on nongeneralizable interests do not conform to the consensual model
of moral discourse, since the reasons underwriting the agreement—reflecting as they do competing constellations of power—vary among the consenting parties (205). But the weakly bound representation of conflicting
interest positions in legislative bodies is itself qualified by unmandated, or
unbound, critical reflection on basic values and goals. Of course, representatives—bound or otherwise—should lead their constituents to an informed
understanding of their interests and perhaps even encourage them to modify
them for the sake of all (Pennock 1968, 3–24). However, this level of
reflection must be distinguished from a deeper one that is, or at least ought
to be, more independent of government suasion. Occurring in formal and
informal ethicopolitical discourses, this reflection aims at collectively interpreting a given community's identity (Habermas 1992, 222). Unlike
strategic compromises, such existential discourses are indeed consensual
but in a manner, as we shall see, that is largely sustained by common *experiences* rather than context-independent beliefs. Only when ethical debate
addresses questions that impinge on universal principles of justice and right—
the limits within which all legitimate authority must operate—do the reasons underwriting consensus aspire to something less parochial (200).

In sharp contrast to Rawls, then, Habermas views public reason as a
discursive procedure for testing all relevant reasons—especially those comprehensive doctrines by which we interpret our identities. The constitutional separation of powers reflects this complex web of discourse in the
form of a rational division of labor. Parliamentary discussions generally
take the form of moral and ethical discourses. The aim here is *justification*
of proposed legislation in terms of its moral rightness, satisfaction of general interests, or balancing of competing strategic interests. Courtroom

discussions generally take the form of *application* discourses, which aim at impartial adjudication of concrete cases. Administrative discussions, by contrast, generally take the form of *pragmatic* discourses. Here the aim is to *decide* on strategies for implementing statutes in ways that are technically efficient and utilitarian (or preference-aggregating) (212).

The separation of state and civil society also has a discourse ethical basis. Pragmatic discourses, strategic negotiations aimed at aggregating interests, and moral discourses of legal application are best understood as matters for technical experts and delegated representatives. By contrast, moral discourses aimed at justifying principles and ethical discourses aimed at interpreting collective identity take the form of *inclusive* and *qualitatively informal* discussions. These discourses have their initial locus in the spontaneous associations of an autonomous civil society. Although such discussions are more vulnerable, perhaps, to distortions wrought by inequalities of power, capacity, and motivation than adversarial debates regulated by parliamentary and courtroom procedure—and thus are *formally* less rational—their freedom from the constraints of *decision* make them more suitable for relatively open and unconstrained *deliberation* (374). Thus, whereas parliamentary debates are best suited to the task of *justifying* policies, informal political discussions are best equipped for *discovering* (thematizing and dramatizing) their motivating problems (373).

Leaving aside problems concerning the autonomous generation of public opinion as an effective voice within parliamentary debate, we may tally the gains and losses of this *two-track* division of deliberative politics into formal *decision* procedures and informal *discussion* processes accordingly: Citing Elster's account of strategic negotiation in the American and French constitutional conventions, Habermas notes that rules governing parliamentary and courtroom procedure play the role of "sedimented" virtue, which makes the *actual practice* of public-minded altruism, truthfulness, wisdom, justice, and other moral qualities somewhat dispensable (414). For example, apart from the effects that different voting procedures (for instance, "one person, one vote" instead of "one group, one vote") have on the fair aggregation of preferences, it is well known that the choice between open and secret balloting has a profound impact on the moral quality of voting outcomes. Secret ballots protect against bribes, threats, and other forms of overt and covert pressure; they ensure the (negative) freedom from constraint requisite for voting conscientiously. Open ballots encourage public accountability and (positive) self-determination; they help close the gap between heteronomous choice (self-interested strategic behavior) and autonomous agreement. Secret ballots seem reasonable on the assumption that persons' privately held views correspond to their publicly

stated positions. Without this assumption, open ballots appear more attractive—so long as other controls (for instance, in campaign financing and
disclosure) adequately shield representatives from lobbyists and other pressure groups (Elster 1993, 571).

Finally, and most importantly, procedures allocating time spent on
argument and suasion as opposed to voting and bargaining have a direct
bearing on the moral and ethical transformation of preferences themselves.
Political bargaining no doubt deviates from the ideals implicit in pure,
impartial discourse; but these ideals have a "steering" or "filtering" effect
on the sorts of topics, contributions, information, and reasons that can be
publicly supported. Politicians must mask their assertion of private interest
in the guise of moral scruple. This is a strategy of compromise that cannot
later be abandoned without appearing insincere or inconsistent (Habermas
1992, 414). Since "the very process of open discussion leads people to
adopt moral principles" (Nelson 1980, 170–71), democracy as a discursive
procedure also seems justified by its *long-term* tendency to produce morally
acceptable laws and policies.

To be sure, even a sympathetic supporter of the power of discursive
reason to transform preferences will have to concede that the mere "conceptual impossibility of expressing selfish arguments in debate about the
common good and the psychological difficulty of expressing other-regarding preferences without coming ultimately to acquire them" do not themselves guarantee the promotion of the common good (Elster 1986, 113).
Elster reminds us that an irreducible pluralism of basic values cannot be
ruled out a priori, time constraints may ultimately favor the aggregation
rather than transformation of preferences, not all persons will tolerate the
personal costs of high-level political participation (thereby opening the
door for paternalism and elitism), and adaptive preferences and conformism will continue to plague the psychology of consensual deliberation—at
least as long as the mass media are owned and controlled by the moguls of
Madison Avenue. Aside from these limits to CR, selfish or strictly private
interests may need to be asserted, and will in any case determine how we
conceive and argue for the common good.

Thus, even if formal deliberations do possess a proxy for sedimented
virtue, it by no means follows that such deliberations will necessarily issue
in a rational consensus on common interests. Whether *informal* deliberations also possess a proxy for the virtue sedimented in *formal* debate is
another matter entirely. Given the demands placed on such deliberations—
to foster a solicitous and solidaristic concern for multicultural and postnational differences (Matustik 1993)—it is imperative that average citizens
be *motivated* to engage in precisely the sorts of religious, philosophical, and

ethical discussions that are only reservedly tolerated (if at all) in more formal settings. Yet as the 1992 riots in Los Angeles amply attest, the *economic* and *educational* resources requisite for such motivation are sorely lacking.

Of course, the virtue sedimented in *formal* deliberations is itself partially offset by such *institutional* constraints as traditional precedents, de facto authorities, adversarial relationships, temporal and jurisdictional restrictions, and other "gag rules." While filtering out nonpublicly spirited and uncompromising assertions of self-interest, institutional forms of public reason bracket precisely those *personal life experiences* expressed in the existential languages of religion, art, and literature. Since these experiences underwrite our search for collective identity and common purpose, their entwining—in the form of "literary" public spheres oriented to the *aesthetic* disclosure of a world—with the political public sphere is not a fact to be regretted or dismissed. On the contrary, such experiences are indispensable for sounding the degree of suffering and discontent that signals a legitimation crisis requiring legislative action (Habermas 1992, 443).

The distinction between formal and informal discourses raises certain questions about the separation of state and civil society—or, if you will, the distinction between public and private spheres. On Rawls's and Ackerman's views of the matter, public reason—exemplified in the deliberations of the Supreme Court—requires setting aside strictly personal differences in favor of commonly accepted grounds of argument. By declaring certain topics off-limits, it protects the sphere of private life from public encroachment. Yet Habermas thinks that by relegating conceptions of the good and their corresponding ways of life to a legally protected sphere of personal preference, such exclusions insulate established conceptions of the good from criticism.

As noted earlier, feminists such as Pateman have been quick to point out that established opinion has long regarded domestic life as a sanctioned bastion of privacy, and that this has immunized traditional lifestyles, condoning patriarchal domination and violence, against public oversight. In calling for publicly funded day care, increased financial support for single-parent families, restrictions on the dissemination of pornography, and community and employee control over private industry, they and their allies have gone further in demanding public interference in the private and domestic sectors for the sake of realizing equal democratic inclusion for all. These and other issues pertaining to gender politics—I specifically have in mind the way in which *both* gender-neutral (liberal) and gender-specific (communitarian) statutes governing the workplace have functioned to discriminate against women—impinge on fundamental questions of gender identity and difference that must be treated as matters of collective, transformative interpretation rather than being fixed once and for all in some essentialist manner.

Although, as a good liberal, Habermas insists on maintaining some legal separation of public and private spheres—this is, after all, a prerequisite for nontotalitarian democratic societies—he holds that the precise boundaries separating these spheres are relative to changing contexts. Just how these contexts are to be interpreted is a matter for the community and its representatives to decide—*after rational deliberation*. In response to the objection that this elevation of the public as final arbiter of privacy rights already violates the private/public distinction, Habermas observes that public *discussion* about privacy is distinct from public *intervention* in private lives (Habermas 1992, 381).

Before moving on to an assessment of Habermas's theory in more general terms, let us see how well it resolves the debate between liberals and communitarians. On the liberal model, democracy is limited to *legitimating* the exercise of political power through popular plebiscites that passively register private preferences for parties and candidates. Public reason here approximates the transcendent neutrality of natural law; meanwhile, the state assumes responsibility for aggregating conflicting preferences into rational choices. On the republican model, by contrast, democracy preserves the founding moment by which the people are constituted as a virtuous, ethical community. Public reason here approximates a shared ethos that finds literal expression in the direct presence of a sovereign citizenry exercising its equal and unalienable power to legislate. The republican state—identified with the ruling regime—accordingly functions as a means by which society as a whole is organized into a solidified totality (362).

The discourse ethical model invests democracy with normative expectations that are stronger than the liberal model but weaker than the communitarian alternative. Like the liberal model, it postulates a constitutional separation of powers and a corresponding distinction between state and society, private and public. This reflects the *modern decentration* of society into plural interests and forms of life. So construed, democracy assumes a two-track form in which informal ethical discussions by the people *inform* but do not *decide* policies, and in which formal negotiations by strategic actors and elected representatives decide policies without setting the agendas on which they are based.

Of course, stated in this way it remains unclear how—if at all—Habermas's model of democracy represents a communitarian alternative to the liberal model. In the Habermasian scheme it seems as if consensual democracy reigns in the realm of public opinion—in which case Mill's concerns about the tyranny of public opinion remain in force—while adversarial democracy, with its ever-present danger of bureaucratic usurpation, reigns in the realm of public policy. Yet it is Habermas's belief that in a rational democracy, the two tracks will mediate one another. This mediation of liberal and communitarian features helps mitigate strategic conflicts that aggravate problems of preference aggregation by situating them within a consensus-oriented framework. For, not only do such conflicts occur within larger disputes about moral and ethical questions, but, as we have seen, bargaining itself frames the problem of compromise in consensual terms— at least initially. The implicit orientation to solidarity (social welfare) and justice (individual freedom and equality) that occurs within discourse further explains how liberal and communitarian features might mediate one another. Because individuation and socialization are complementary processes that are dependent on communication, each individual speaker has an interest in preserving the integrity of the life context she shares with others (Habermas 1989–90, 47). Too, individual freedom depends on a vibrant and healthy democratic public as watchdog for government tyranny and locus of collective problem solving.

The problem of virtue and sovereignty must be situated within this context as well. Habermas seems to endorse Ackerman's contention that *normal* democratic politics is largely the way liberalism describes it: apathy on the part of citizens concerned with private matters, strategic bargaining on the part of interest groups and elites, and political initiatives descending from an administration entangled in bureaucratic routine. Under these conditions, the people are neither virtuous nor sovereign in the classical sense: they are simply *absent* (Habermas 1992, 337). Only during periods of moral and ethical crisis is this relationship reversed. Constitutional debates engage citizens in intense, *revolutionary* self-examination of their own historical identity. Consensual politics supplants compromise politics, and the *presence* of "the people" is felt in the form of a moral mandate. If the mandate is *authentic*, the judiciary's resistance to the will of the majority must eventually be rendered moot by amendment or overcome through judicial restructuring. On this liberal republican model, the function of judicial review is confined to defending the gains of successful democratic mandates against the tyrannical whims of transient majorities.

Ackerman's *dual democratic* model—which distinguishes higher (constitutional) from lower (statutory) forms of lawmaking—helps shed light on the dual, liberal-communitarian character of American politics (Ackerman 1991). However, Habermas remains reluctant to characterize the republican moment as a sovereign exercise by the People. Instead, he—like Lefort—locates sovereignty in the impersonal and decentered (subjectless) communication process. Given the plurality of interests—and with it, the "spontaneity," "anarchy," and "wildness" of informal, overlapping public spheres—the procedures and conditions of rational communication must serve as proxy for an antecedent harmony of substantive interests; the general will must be achieved in rational conversation, *if it is to be achieved at all* (Habermas 1992, 365). Only by conceiving democracy in this way—as a medium for the critical formation of opinion and will, hence as a medium in which citizens constitute their own individual autonomy in solidarity with others—can Habermas show how problems pertaining to majoritarian tyranny and the rank ordering of preferences can be mitigated *from within* the confines of discourse, without appeal to antecedent natural rights, rational decision procedures, or ethical virtues.[7]

2.1 Having examined DE from the standpoint of the liberalism/communitarianism debate, let me now return to the question of discourse as a democratic legitimating procedure. Earlier in his career Habermas committed himself to the following definition of legitimacy: "Recommendation X is legitimate" means "recommendation X is in the general (or public) interest" (L1); and "Recommendation X is in the public interest" means "X is accepted by all affected as justified" (L2).[8] Problems immediately jump to mind with these definitions of legitimacy. Take L2, for instance. X might be accepted by the public as justified even if they know that X doesn't satisfy the interests of each person *individually*. Maximizing the greatest happiness for the greatest number (or choosing a policy that will improve the general condition of all citizens present and future), a rich utilitarian might support a soak-the-rich tax statute designed to generate revenue for an egalitarian health care system whose benefits to her, her family, or her immediate circle of associates will not outweigh the costs. Or, to take another example, a community of environmentalists and industrial workers might accept a compromise pollution bill as in the public interest, not because it satisfies either of their particular interests—each party, we will assume, believes that its own interest is identical to the public interest—but because it avoids a public evil (e.g., civil war) or facilitates a mutually beneficial alliance (against capitalists).

Given Habermas's recent acknowledgment that strategic compromises of this sort are the normal outcomes of political negotiations in liberal democracy, it is best to view his insistence on the generalizability of interests as specifying a very weak conception of the common good, one that might be acceptable to all simply owing to the absence of an agreement on some other good that each of the negotiating parties feels is rationally preferable. However, this weaker conception will not save L1. We need only recur to rational choice theory to confirm the theoretical possibility of agreements that fail to produce a consistent—let alone maximal—ranking of preferences.

Paradoxes of rational choice do not speak against a consensus theory of legitimation, so long as the theory allows for compromise *and* stresses rationality of *process* over *outcome.*[9] Of course, if democracy failed to satisfy minimal conditions of instrumental rationality, so that it repeatedly generated inconsistent and/or submaximal preference rankings—thus making goal-oriented politics meaningless—there would be no good reason to prefer it, developmental advantages notwithstanding. Democracy may not be the most economic vehicle for selecting public policy, but it usually satisfies minimal standards of rationality sufficient to justify retaining it as a vehicle of ethical self-realization.

It is now incumbent on me to defend this claim against objections by social choice theorists like William Riker, who argue that democratic self-determination is incoherent and meaningless. In Riker's opinion,

> All elections do or have to do is to permit people to get rid of rulers. The people who do this do not themselves need to have a coherent will.... The liberal interpretation of voting thus allows elections to be useful and significant even in the presence of cycles, manipulation and other kinds of "errors" in voting.... The kind of democracy that thus survives is not, however, popular rule, but rather an intermittent, sometimes random, even perverse, popular vote.... Liberal democracy is simply the veto by which it is sometimes possible to restrain official tyranny. (Riker 1982, 244)

Two points need to be mentioned at the outset in considering this claim. First, as a *description* of current liberal democratic practice, it may well be true, although not necessarily for the reasons advanced in support of it. Second, as a claim that is intended to support the efficiency and meaningfulness of *liberal* democracy as a plebiscitary mechanism for protecting against tyranny—the only aim that liberals in the Benthamite tradition have really felt comfortable in according democracy—it asserts too much. If the vote that vetoes officeholders is as perverse and random as the above quote says it is—as perverse and random, say, as the illnesses that remove them from office, or the aggregation of preferences that brought them to power in the first place—then how can liberal democracy be any more meaningful than populist democracy?

Riker's dilemma stems, first, from a narrow identification of democratic participation with *voting* that is constrained by a *just* and *meaningful* procedure and second, from a narrow view of how voting might be said to express *genuine choice*, or a popular will. According to Riker, the mere fact that democratic procedures satisfy minimal criteria of justice by giving *everyone* an *equal* and *autonomous* vote does not legitimate them apart from their capacity to "organize voting into genuine choice" (5). In other words, the aim of procedural fairness and exclusivity is meaningful only on the condition that it conduce in some unambiguous way to the production of a general will. This is where the second premise kicks in. Riker argues that no voting procedure is meaningful in this sense. To begin with, there are the paradoxes associated with *unstable* majorities that we noted earlier. However, even if these could be circumvented by specifying the requirement of a unanimous majority, limiting admissible choices to two alternatives, or perhaps by admitting larger sets of alternatives through extensions of binary majority rule, the initial choice of alternatives—the legislative agenda—would still have to be winnowed through a larger set involving nonbinary, multiple rankings. Furthermore, the results would suffer from *ambiguity.*

A result is said to be ambiguous when a different outcome would have been obtained by using a different procedure for aggregating votes. A Borda count, in which each individual ranks four alternatives ordinally (for example, assigning four points to the most preferred alternative and one point to the least preferred), may yield different results than a Benthamite count, where each ranks the same alternatives cardinally, depending on their relative utility (for example, by assigning four points to the most preferred alternative, but only two to the second most preferred alternative, if the individual prefers the former alternative twice as much as the latter). Again, the results obtained by using each of these methods may be different if cardinal utility comparisons are multiplied instead of summed, or if alternatives are paired with one another individually.

Riker is deeply impressed by the negative implications of this finding (36), but what do these results really show? As Coleman and Ferejohn (1986, 13) argue, the mere fact that different outcomes result from applying different procedures, all of which are minimally fair and equally plausible, does not entail that these outcomes are inherently meaningless. To use their example, just because we could have scored football games differently—assigning five points instead of six for a touchdown—does not mean that the outcomes reached according to current rules of scoring are ambiguous or unrelated to what happens on the playing field. By parity of reasoning, just because different election results could have been obtained by using different rules for tabulating votes does not prove that the results actually obtained using current procedures are any less meaningful and clear.

The conclusion that they are depends on defining meaninglessness in terms of a *unique* representation of a popular will that is assumed to exist prior to the process of voting itself. However, a populist need not accept this definition. The populist might insist on the existence of such a will for only a certain domain of issues, such as those pertaining to basic constitutional liberties. Even then she might specify the general will in terms of a more loosely defined range of acceptable outcomes. Finally, and most importantly, she can regard voting as less a direct revelation of the general will conceived as a preexisting group sentiment than as an indirect *judgment* about what ought to be the public's proper interest.

This qualified form of populism is still vulnerable to the paradox that the reliability of voting as a method for articulating the general will can only be known independently, by using another method; in which case voting itself could be dispensed with in favor of that other method (17). There are two possible responses to this paradox. The first—defended by Coleman and Ferejohn as well as by Habermas—is that voting need not be the only method for judging the public interest. What recommends voting is not its uniqueness or privileged status as the only or best method for judging the general will, but rather its institutionalization in a system that combines this method with other methods—in particular, with methods that define participation more broadly to include public fora and discussion (17). The second response—offered by Carole Pateman—is that once these methods are deemed to be as good an indicator of the general will—something, she believes, that might occur under a less individualistic and more egalitarian society—voting itself recedes in importance as an essential feature of democratic participation (Pateman 1986, 44). Consequently, while agreeing with Coleman and Ferejohn that a "theory of institutional behavior" is necessary in order to show how the "distribution of preferences" under certain arrangements can moderate voting cycles (Coleman and Ferejohn 1986, 23), I concur with Pateman and Habermas that such distribution itself presupposes, at the very least, a radical overhaul of the behavioral incentives and institutions that currently exist.

However we end up construing populist democracy, we must not make its legitimacy contingent on expressing a *unique*—if discursively generated—general will. Nor, in general, should we make the satisfaction of common interests a necessary condition for a law's legitimacy. But the weaker notion of legitimacy stressing unanimous consent (L2) is no less problematic. I mentioned earlier that such agreement would have to make allowances for compromises, or agreements that none or only some of the parties believed satisfied common interests. But what if some of the parties simply refused to compromise? Could a law be legitimate to which only some persons consented?

Standard democratic theory holds that something less than universal consensus—the preference of a majority or plurality—is sufficient to legitimate laws, so long as those who dissent (the minority) have an equal chance to vote and marshal support against them. In most cases majority rule is morally preferable to rule by unanimous consent, since the latter would give more value to the voice of a lone dissenter than to the combined voice of the majority, thereby violating the principle of equality. If we reject universalization (as I suggest we do), the legitimacy of the results could only be guaranteed by the fairness of the *procedures* regulating the democratic game—contingent, of course, on their capacity to extend equal recognition, equitable treatment, and deliberative responsibility to all citizens (Beitz 1992b, 237).

Habermas himself now suggests that majoritarian procedures are the decisive factors in legitimating laws. If consensus continues to play a role here, it is as a procedural guideline: all parties to the discussion should strive to reach agreement on a common good as disinterestedly as possible—a qualification that by no means precludes the assertion of particular interests. Gone is Habermas's earlier belief that orientation to consensus requires "transfer(ring) subjective desires into generalizable desires"—a formulation that could be construed as hostile to pluralism (Habermas 1975, 109). Since Habermas now declares that "compromises possess a wholly undiminished worth"—indeed, he chides extremists within the Green Party for refusing to compromise with organized labor and the Social Democratic Party on environmental reforms—he must specify procedures by which such agreements may be accepted as legitimate (Habermas 1985, 241; Dews 1986, 182–215). Presumably, such procedures will also explain why minorities accept the legitimacy of laws to which they dissented. For acceptance of the legitimate form of a law, which ostensibly follows from acceptance of the rules of the democratic game, must be distinguished from acceptance of its content.

Habermas thus concedes that fair compromises, or strategic agreements in which conflicting interests are harmonized in a balance of power, may be legitimate without satisfying generalizable interests or being universally accepted by all. However, laws regulating disputes that appear to strike a fair compromise between irreducibly opposed interests might be illegitimate. Habermas claims that such laws can be criticized on the grounds that they reflect *pseudocompromises*. A compromise that emerged out of a discussion slanted in favor of one of the parties (e.g., the wealthier and more powerful) would be invalidated on procedural grounds (Habermas 1985, 111). However, a compromise that concealed a "suppression of generalizable interests" would also be invalid. Indeed, the two defects are closely linked in Habermas's view, since the closer negotiations approximate the conditions obtaining in ideal speech, the less likely generalizable interests will be suppressed. It follows that compromises are valid only if the parties in question have failed to reach consensus on generalizable interests in impartial dialogue.

We noted above how difficult (if not impossible) it is to determine a rank ordering of preferences, even under stringent counterfactual conditions. For this reason, the suppression of generalizable interests is not a useful concept for determining the fairness of a compromise. Therefore we would better off to focus on what Habermas has to say about the procedural requirements for reaching compromise, such as the balance of power requirement (Habermas 1992, 205, 221).

It would be difficult to deny that, in pluralistic societies, some irreducibly particular interests will be more powerful than others—quite apart from the distorting influence of money, power, and ideology. Any compromise balancing the interests of animal experimentation advocates and animal rights activists would likely favor the interests of one of these parties, no matter how fairly it was achieved. Moreover, it is unlikely that controls regulating humane animal experimentation will be regarded by all animal rights activists as fairly balancing their interests against their opponents'.

Habermas's discussion of civil disobedience suggests what his response to this case might be. German peace advocates, he argues, have a right to commit acts of civil disobedience, since strategic decisions have not been processed through democratic channels that present both sides with equal chances for influencing leaders and public opinion. However, he also notes that decisions processed in accordance with fair democratic procedure ought not to be irreversible. Minorities recognize the legitimacy of majority decisions only to the extent that they are reversible and, therefore, only to the extent that they can press for fair compensation or fair compromise.[10]

It may be objected that, in zero-sum games (weapons or no weapons; animal experimentation or animal liberation), the scope for fair compromise or compensation is limited *at least as far as the most militant of interest groups is concerned*. When the majority is not likely to be reversed in the near future (as in the case of animal experimentation) there no longer remains any basis—on Habermas's account—for recognizing the legitimacy of the compromise.

But this result seems counterintuitive. Should winners feel morally compelled to compensate losers in a democratic contest? Perhaps they should if they are indifferent to the outcome (and the losers are not). But perhaps they should not if the losers are extremists who represent views the winners find morally repugnant. Here there is no room for compromise.

We can imagine Habermas's response to this objection: If losers do not have to be compensated, if their views do not have to enter into compromise legislation, and if the decision against them doesn't have to be reversible, how can they be expected to concede the legitimacy of their opponents' law? They can because—as Habermas himself has recently acknowledged—recognition of the legitimacy of the law at most entails a prima facie commitment to abide by it (Habermas 1991, 198). A militant animal rights advocate might agree that the law she refuses to obey was processed in accordance with fair democratic procedure, despite its being morally flawed. The decision for accepting its legitimacy would be based on recognition of the fact that a preponderance of public opinion—a preponderance sufficient to violate Habermas's fair-balance-of-power condition—would likely support at least some animal experimentation for good reasons, quite apart from ideological distortions. Although one's moral convictions should be tempered by the reasonable voice of an opposing majority, the absence of decisive grounds favoring either position will entitle the animal rights activist to question the moral rightness of any compromise favoring the majority, perhaps even to the point of justifying some sort of civil disobedience.[11]

Contrary to Habermas, justifiable acts of civil disobedience need not be directed against illegitimate or undemocratically processed laws. Even when they are, their justification may have less to do with the violation of egalitarian *procedures* narrowly construed than with the failure to achieve egalitarian *outcomes*. Again, recall the examples of congressional reapportionment, supermajoritarian decision procedures, and so on mentioned in chapter 1. Strictly speaking, these examples of substantive due process violate the principle of strict procedural equality by ensuring that minorities will have representation, impact, or influence that, in some cases at least, far exceeds their actual numerical voting strength. Without them, they might not be guaranteed sufficient representation and political clout to protect their interests against majoritarian tyranny.

Indeed, Charles Beitz has convincingly argued that the egalitarian justification of democracy must be sought elsewhere than in either *formal* procedures or *substantive* outcomes taken singly. The principle of procedural equality defended by Habermas and others (that each citizen is to have a fundamental right to an equal opportunity to influence the outcomes of the legislative process) "forbids inequalities in the apportionment of population among legislative districts, even when this is an unavoidable consequence of the effort to realize an ostensibly desirable purpose," such as proportional representation for oppressed minorities (Beitz 1992a, 225). If ideals of equal recognition and equitable treatment of interests do not justify the principle of procedural equality—and in the case just mentioned the principle actually might thwart their realization—then neither does the equal utilitarian weighing of preferences. The problem of using plebiscitary democracy as a means of preference aggregation has been duly noted, but there is no reason to think that a procedure permitting such aggregation would address moral qualms about the rationality of the preferences in question. Inequalities in bargaining power, the existence of an unjust *status quo ante,* and the potential for majoritarian tyranny even suggest that the principle of procedural equality is insufficiently egalitarian when interpreted along utilitarian lines.

Moreover, as Dworkin points out, procedurally fair democracies that *detach* themselves from egalitarian outcomes (involving the distribution of economic resources and opportunities) succumb to the following paradox: Striving to give everyone equality of impact (equal voting or decision power) or influence (equal power in shaping public opinion and policy deliberations) would penalize those political activists who choose to spend their resources on politics while rewarding those who are apathetic—thus undermining the whole aim of participatory democracy. By contrast, in *dependent* democracies oriented to ensuring substantive egalitarian outcomes, resources and opportunities will be distributed so that everyone has *some*—but not necessarily equal—impact and influence. This is not to deny the importance of equality of impact *within* voting districts or of equality of influence *across* districts. Indeed, substantive political equality requires at least reducing the importance of wealth in politics and improving the kind of influence exercised—from advertising to rational argument. Yet the *symbolic* value of according equal *standing* to all citizens may require treating unequals unequally—increasing the leverage and access of targeted minorities relative to their actual numbers, concentration, and resources (Dworkin 1987).

This view is compatible with Beitz's belief that true procedural equality involves a *complex* balancing of three egalitarian interests: in equal recognition, in the equitable treatment of interests, and in deliberative responsibility. These interests, I believe, correspond to basic expectations regulating discourse: equal recognition entails respect for others as autonomous agents;

equitable treatment entails caring about their interests in an attitude of solidarity; and deliberative responsibility entails an orientation toward reaching a rational consensus on common interests. Of course, sometimes these interests clash, as when opponents and proponents of racially based reapportionment appeal, respectively, to formal equality in recognition and substantive equality in treatment. However, the third interest makes possible an impartial and unlimited comparison of competing preferences in a manner conducive to both equal recognition and equal treatment. Seen from this perspective, racially based apportionment can sometimes further all of these interests simultaneously, as long as it is viewed as a stopgap measure to ensure the equitable representation of minorities' interests (which, given a long history of past discrimination, might entitle them to compensatory overrepresentation) and does not deny majorities equal recognition (for example, by stigmatizing them as inferior).

3. Having examined the strengths and weaknesses of a purely procedural model of DE vis-à-vis problems of social choice, majoritarian tyranny, and the like, let us now turn to its more tangible application as a critical model for reform. Although they are too abstract to enable us to infer *directly* the priority of, say, council democracy over other forms of democracy, the system of rights specified by DE and the institutional structures by which it must be implemented might well compel—more strongly than Habermas himself has hitherto indicated—the adoption of some kind of worker democracy (Habermas 1979, 186). This becomes apparent when we reconstruct his deduction of the system of rights in light of the self-transcending logic of procedural justice mentioned above.

Legal freedom means both negative noninterference and positive choice. These two terms condition each other: capacity for choice presupposes both freedom from arbitrary interference, understood as direct physical and mental coercion, *and* freedom from less overt forms of *domination*, rooted in power relations structuring economic, social, and cultural practices. It also presupposes access to material and educational resources that further the cultivation of rational deliberation and the imagination of possible alternatives. Conversely, the capacity to avoid situations in which our freedom will likely be interfered with or constrained is proportional to our access to material and educational sources. Conceived in this way, free action cannot be separated from self-realization, or activity aimed at enhancing the capacity for free action as such. Social interaction and communication are necessary but not sufficient for self-realization. Other conditions include work and consumption activities.

Habermas does not deny that the structuring of the workplace and the social distribution of costs, benefits, and resources impinge on the capacity of individuals to realize themselves as distinct persons and rational agents (despite the fact that he attributes this more to communication than to labor). However, he hesitates to draw what seems to me to be an obvious conclusion from this fact, namely, that each worker (consumer) ought to have an equal prima facie right to determine collectively how his or her work is structured and how benefits, costs, and resources are to be distributed.

One argument for this claim runs as follows: If there is no good reason why one person's freedom should be worth any more than another's, there is no good reason why one person should be more privileged in this respect than another—that is, have fewer arbitrary hindrances to and more positive resources for the exercise of collective choice involving matters that affect him or her. Assuming that all persons ought to have equal rights, it follows that they ought to have equal rights to the conditions for exercising rights. Furthermore, since (a) only citizens can determine *concretely* what these conditions are, (b) such determination generally presupposes democratic discussions regarding the structuring of the workplace and the distribution of benefits and burdens, and (c) the above requirements would be violated if their satisfaction was made contingent on some external authority (e.g., the benevolence of a factory owner), it follows that consumers and producers of goods ought to have a prima facie right to participate in democratic discussions regarding the production and distribution of goods requisite for the maintenance of their own freedom.

Radical critics have conceived the democratic right to participate in decisions about the production and distribution of material resources requisite for full democratic participation in three ways. Some (e.g., Marković) have conceived this right to entail the abolition of an autonomous market as well as the abolition of private ownership of the means of production. On this model democratically structured production units and community associations would elect representatives to central planning boards. Others (e.g., Gould) have conceived participation as functioning within democratically structured productive units that are privately owned (by the workers themselves) and that interact in accordance with relatively autonomous market demands. Finally, some (e.g., Schweickart) have conceived participation along an intermediary path combining council democracy, regulated markets, and public control. I shall argue that discourse ethics requires democratic participation in this third sense.

It is tempting to regard Habermas's skepticism about "simple recipes of workers' self-management" as indicating a general indifference toward, or even dismissal of, all types of workplace democracy. This assessment is premature. First, Habermas's skepticism is directed against romantic conceptions of workplace democracy that envision the abolition of economic markets and/or administrative bureaucracies—an eventuality that seems contrary to rational efficiency and impartial justice. Second, since he believes that abolition of labor markets and cultural privileges associated with class are preconditions for a fully democratic state, he could be expected to favor a decentralized, worker controlled economy (Habermas 1992, 374).[12] Third, Habermas recognizes that segmented labor processes that separate intellectual management from manual labor contribute to a "fragmentation of consciousness" in which "the need for normatively secured or communicatively achieved agreement is decreased and the scope of tolerance for merely instrumental attitudes, indifference, or cynicism is expanded" (Habermas 1982, 281). Finally, Habermas's positive reception of Foucault's insights regarding the local, relational, and strategic manner in which power is exercised suggests a further reason why he would want to institute democracy in the workplace: the critical exposure of power relations that ideologically constrain discursive practices must be undertaken in the first instance at the occupational and domestic level.

Against this line of reasoning one could point out that Habermas designates the public sphere, not the workplace, as the primary locus of radical, participatory democracy. To begin with, Habermas assigns public spheres to a communicatively structured lifeworld and economic units to a media-steered system. Since, as I have argued elsewhere (Ingram 1987, 155), it is better to see the distinction between lifeworld and system on which this assignment is based as reflecting differences in explanatory perspective—between explaining action in terms of agent rationales and explaining it functionalistically—it seems arbitrary to exclude economic units as such from the political sphere of civil society. Habermas, of course, may well be right that political bureaucracies and economic markets are *predominantly* steered by strategic media of power and money, respectively. But, as his own analysis makes clear, they are only *partially* uncoupled from communicative action. Economic entities, no less than the agencies that regulate them, fall under constitutional provisions that draw their legitimacy from democratic input. While falling within the political system, such provisions exercise a "countersteering" influence on the unchecked growth of bureaucratic and economic power (Habermas 1992, 398). For this reason, it is somewhat misleading to say, as Habermas does, that administrators *decide* (or *act*) while the "subjectless" forms of political communication only *deliberate*. Voting, after all, is the penultimate expression of deliberation with intent to decide. Hence there is no good reason not to extend democratic procedures of deliberation and decision to the workplace.

Habermas is no doubt concerned about the *rational efficiency* of utopian forms of industrial democracy that envision the abolition of markets in favor of total community control. But there are other models of democratic socialism we might consider. David Schweickart has convincingly demonstrated the efficiency of a market socialism based on publicly funded worker cooperatives. More importantly, his analysis shows how worker-managed firms meet several conditions of participatory democracy in its classical sense: they tend to be smaller, less competitive, less predisposed to conflict, and thus more predisposed to consensual outcomes than capitalist enterprises.

> *Worker-managed firms, as compared with their capitalist counterparts, do not have the same self-generated tendency to expand.* Under certain rather normal conditions (specifically under conditions of more or less constant returns to scale and/or declining costs), worker-managed firms are not so inclined to grow, nor, when they do grow, are they inclined to grow by qualitative leaps. (Schweickart 1993, 96)

Both capitalist and worker-managed firms respond to market pressures; both will tend to grow with increasing demand (in order to protect or expand their markets) or when there are increasing returns to scale. The reason why capitalist firms are more motivated to expand when returns to scale are constant or costs are cut is—to use the somewhat questionable assumptions of rational choice theory—that worker-managed firms "maximize" *profit per worker* rather than *total profit*. When costs per item are constant, a capitalist can double his profit by doubling his enterprise—two hamburger stands employing twenty people and netting $20,000 each will yield a total of $40,000 profit instead of half that amount. By contrast, a worker-managed firm doubling its operations will not increase profit per worker, since the number of workers for whom the profits will be divided will double as well. Again, when drastic cost-cutting innovations are introduced, capitalist firms will be inclined to cut costs and expand rapidly so as to enlarge market share *aggressively*. Worker-managed firms, by contrast, will be inclined to reap the expanded profit rather than expand production, unless doing so will cost them their current percentage of market shares—a concern in an aggressive, capitalist economy but not in a socialist one (96).

Defensive rather than *offensive* strategies in maintaining market share explain why worker-managed firms will not behave perversely—maximizing individual profits by laying off workers or holding back on expansion in times of steady or increased consumer demand. The objection that worker-managed firms promote too little long-term investment—because members are unable to protect themselves against risk or are unable to reap the full benefit of their investment—applies to capitalist firms as well, and is belied by the actual performance of French producer cooperatives, Yugoslavian cooperatives, and the Mondragon cooperative. The objection that they promote too much *capital* investment is not without some truth; but in a system of economic democracy, in which banks use employment creation as a criterion for loans, this will not be a concern. Finally, in response to the objection that firms in a worker-managed economy will reward equal skills unequally—for example, by not replacing some of their own members with workers who will work for less pay—it can be pointed out that these allocational inefficiencies, which get reflected in differential prices for goods of comparable *real* costs, are in fact so negligible as to be discounted in comparison to questions of justice, and are likely to be much less significant than similar inefficiencies in real capitalist economies, where the marginal contributions of American CEOs, for example, greatly pales in comparison to their bloated salaries.

Thus the dynamics that conduce to democracy-friendly smallness in and cooperation among worker-managed firms under economic democracy are not any less efficient than those influencing their capitalist enterprises. In response to Habermas, we may conclude that decentralized forms of market socialism are not only more democratic than their capitalist counterparts, but are probably more efficient as well.

Although Habermas's location of participatory democracy in the informal associations that comprise the public sphere in no way speaks against the democratization of the workplace, it does speak against privately owned and controlled democratic cooperatives that leave no room for public participation in decisions regarding production and distribution. Regardless of whether the sources for funding cooperatives are private or public, the coordination and planning of a complex economy will require some government regulation, the rationales for specific policies coming from overlapping public spheres (community associations, consumer and environmental groups, etc.).[13] By the same token, since we inhabit overlapping public spheres, enforcement of universal democratic rights will oppose a democratic centralism based exclusively on corporate (i.e., occupational) representation. For Habermas the distinct advantage of a mass democratic system organized along party lines resides precisely in its capacity to provide associative bases that transcend economic, ethnic, and regional boundaries.[14] To offset the disadvantages of the party system—its tendency, as an extension of the government, to manipulate public opinion and obscure social antagonism behind diluted programs—he looks to the spontaneous proliferation of informal, unincorporated, grass-roots associations. This concession to the anarchist and populist tradition, he thinks, provides the only guarantee that the issues and arguments that elected representatives bring to bear in debating the public utility of law will reflect an autonomous—if not wholly rational—set of needs.

To summarize: a political system structured in accordance with discourse ethics must consist of both *participatory* organizations, comprising non-occupational public spheres and economic units, and *formally organized* mass party organizations and state bureaucracies. Democracy and rationality will vary depending on features peculiar to these structures: more orientation toward consensus and procedural equality at the local and occupational level (and hence more social rationality); more compromise and procedural inequality at the level of party politics and administration (and hence less social rationality).[15]

Before concluding this chapter I would like to return briefly to the problem of technology and democracy raised in chapter 2. Experiments in teledemocracy confirm that, by reducing the costs and burdens of participation, communication technologies enhance both its quantity and quality. On one hand, interactive forms of communication—cable television systems equipped with push-button equipment for feedback, videotex systems that link terminals to a mainframe computer, and so on—suggest new possibilities for *plebiscitary* democracy. Although it would be premature to see in these technologies any hope for a return to direct democracy on a mass scale—as Habermas points out, the complexities of legal discourse may well require that elected representatives decide on the formal design of legislative proposals to be voted on or debated—they do afford greater voting access to economically marginalized groups. To compensate for their limited, plebiscitary function, one should supplement these technologies with interactive forms of communication providing a *qualitatively* augmented form of face-to-face, dialogic participation.

The advantages and drawbacks of these different types of interactive communication—in terms of access, reach, effectiveness, agenda setting, diversity of access paths, duration, initiative, costs, educative value, and so on—balance one another (Arterton 1987, 63). Because of their low cost, plebiscitary technologies provide greater access and reach; dialogic technologies, by contrast, provide greater opportunities for initiative, education, and agenda setting for those who are particularly motivated and financially able. Although project designers for plebiscitary experiments have tended to view democracy as an expression of a common will, while project designers for dialogic experiments have seen it as a forum for plural interest group bargaining and compromise, it is clear that these associations are arbitrary. For example, the Alaska LTN project shows that dialogue can often move from confrontation and self-assertion to compromise and even consensus, thereby preempting the sort of reactive, conflictual politics that eventualizes when no dialogue occurs (195–204).

Of course, it is naïve to think that teledemocracy in and of itself will usher in more extensive and better participation. Empirical studies have shown otherwise. Given current inequalities in wealth, education, and motivation—not to mention the prevalence of privatism, consumerism, and manipulation—teledemocracy can at best (and only very unevenly) mitigate inequalities in participation. Nonetheless, without making this technology available to greater numbers of persons at subsidized costs it is hard to imagine how real democracy in today's complex society can be realized.

Let me now summarize the results of this chapter for the remaining portion of my argument. In this chapter I have sought to develop a model of democratic legitimation that draws on Habermas's discourse ethics. The chief advantage of this theory is its ability to ground principles of democratic legitimation in normative expectations that have a real basis in everyday communication. In my opinion, it provides the most promising approach to reconciling the liberal and communitarian, instrumental and expressive, sides of our modern political consciousness. And it does so without succumbing to the moral idealism of natural law theory, the economic realism of rational choice theory, or the ethical traditionalism of conventional, communitarian theory. Indeed, it is even *postmodern* in its acceptance of the irreducible complexity, multivocity, and anarchy of a decentered political rationality that has been shorn of the centripetal, substantive sovereignty of a dominant subject. The remaining chapters will explore this postmodern condition as it bears on our historical and political identity, beginning with the problem of adjudication. Given the conflict of interpretations (libertarian, communitarian, and democratic) and the multivalence of rationales (moral, ethical, strategic, and pragmatic), how can judges decide in a manner both determinate and legitimate?

6

Discourse Ethics and Adjudication

Democracy occupies pride of place in a discourse ethical account of legitimation. Hence the privilege accorded public spheres and legislatures as twin pillars of collective deliberation and decision. These bodies thematize the problems and reasons that, taken together, *justify* laws. The impartial administration of justice, however, involves *applying* laws in ways that are legitimate as well.

In this chapter we will address two interrelated questions that bear on this problem: What are the general grounds of rational adjudication? and, Can disputes about their paradigmatic interpretation be resolved? The first problem recalls the tension between legal facticity and normative legitimacy discussed in chapter 5. Inherent in the concept of legal form is the *principle of certainty*, which defines legal stability in terms of predictability. Factual precedent and procedure provide reliable grounds for strategic action while satisfying moral expectations regarding public forewarning and accountability. However, valid law must not only be interpreted in a manner consistent with its own *internal* history and procedure; it must satisfy *extralegal norms* of rationality as well. Judges must interpret law in light of *moral* principles, *ethical values*, as well as *costs and benefits* (Habermas 1992, 243).

Theories of law often accommodate only one of these grounds. Positivistic theories emphasize the importance of mechanical procedures and unambiguous rules in generating valid outcomes. These rule-generating rules (or secondary rules, to use Hart's expression) ultimately rest on a "rule of recognition" or "basic norm" (Kelsen), such as a constitution, whose validity is simply taken for granted.[1] The principle of rational legitimacy is thus sacrificed in the name of certainty. But if sticking to the literal meaning of dogmatically accepted procedures and rules guarantees certainty, it produces uncertainty when judges are confronted with novel cases falling outside the clearly defined scope of extant law.

Legal realism and its offspring (legal functionalism and the Law and Economics movement) fill this gap by redefining predictability in terms of some criterion of economic efficiency or systemic adaptability. In effect, they abandon the principle of certainty for the sake of some extralegal principle of instrumental rationality. By transforming law into an instrument of policy, subject to the ideological whims of judges, these movements undermine the democratic legitimacy of law as well.

Hermeneutical theories of law of the sort espoused by Gadamer are more successful in accounting for certainty and legitimacy. To be sure, since they presume that the concrete meaning of law varies relative to unforeseeable contexts of application, they allow for the interpretative uncertainty that invariant, mechanical forms of predictability preclude. Nevertheless, it is just this dialectical synthesis of universal and particular that enables such theories to account for the certainty and legitimacy of novel applications not explicitly anticipated in extant law. For, unlike their positivist counterparts, hermeneutic theories do not deny to law any but the most literal meaning; rather, they endow it with a deeper moral truth-content. This rational content, in turn, has its authority vested in effective history, or tradition.

The disadvantage of hermeneutical legal theories—indeed, of all hermeneutical theories—is their parochialism with respect to other traditions and aspects of rationality not justifiable within the legal tradition, however broadly conceived. Fascist legal traditions illustrate the rational illegitimacy of parochialism with respect to morality; religious legal traditions illustrate the same with respect to instrumental and economic considerations (for example in their refusal to weigh costs and benefits in the assignment of rights).

To many, natural law theories—especially deontological varieties—have seemed to be the perfect antidote to the partiality and relativity of imperfect legal tradition. By transcending the vicissitudes of history, the universal decrees of reason, nature, or God have inspired the permanent, critical, and sometimes revolutionary reform of unjust legal systems. Yet the problem with all such theories, of course, is that they run the risk of replacing public laws with the highly personal and unpredictable moral ideologies of judicial prophets.

As we shall see, Dworkin and Habermas are mindful of the shortcomings of each of these four legal approaches. Both attempt to do justice to the full range of reasons contributing to law's legitimacy: procedural, ethical, pragmatic, and moral. Reconciling these different rationales poses obvious problems, and is complicated further by disagreements over competing legal *paradigms*.

To begin with, a general paradigm shift common to all advanced, industrial democracies occurs with the transition from a classical liberal state to a welfare state. The former defines rights as limits to state interference. In keeping with the separation of public and private law requisite for institutionalizing a market economy, the liberal paradigm (LP) places a premium on individual autonomy and responsibility. Hence its preference for highly mechanical, formalistic approaches to adjudication of the sort esteemed by positivists, who seek to maximize predictability. The welfare paradigm (WP), by contrast, defines rights in terms of positive entitlements. In keeping with its weaker separation of private and public law, this paradigm places a premium on communal responsibility, risk sharing, and efficient problem solving. Hence, its preference for flexible approaches to adjudication of the sort esteemed by realists and hermeneuticists.

The limitations of these approaches suggest a third paradigm—which Habermas variously characterizes as procedural, reflexive, or democratic (DP)—that reconciles them in a higher synthesis. It tries to recoup the individual autonomy secured by the liberal paradigm and the equal concern for all secured by the welfare paradigm through the radical institutionalization of democratic rights. To recall Ackerman's remark, the New Deal paradigm compensated for the loss of economic freedom through the expansion of individual rights to privacy, criminal due process, and nondiscrimination; and it did so in ways that augmented individuals' freedom to participate in democratic processes. This extension of democratic rights becomes more urgent in the welfare state, since the potential reach of the public—or rather the state as the agent of public policy—is no longer formally delimited vis-à-vis civil society.

The question remains whether the democratic paradigm *can* succeed in reconciling liberal and welfare paradigms within the present system of law. Can the aim of such a paradigm be limited to *taming* the capitalist economic system by "restructur[ing] it socially and ecologically in such a way that the insertion of administrative power can be simultaneously brought under control," as Habermas says (1992, 494)? Or must capitalism as such be replaced by economic democracy, as argued in the previous chapter?

In answering this question I will begin by exploring the weaknesses of positivistic, realistic, and hermeneutical approaches to law. Relying on Dworkin's theory of law as an embodiment of *integrity*, I argue that none of these *general* theories of law account for the possibility of legitimate adjudication (sec. 1). The latter must satisfy moral and political conditions of *associative community*, based on the kind of egalitarian democracy discussed in chapter 5. Next, I raise familiar objections by CLS advocates to the *idea* of legitimacy (sec. 2). These objections, as we shall see, address the problem of competing paradigms. Although *the stronger version* of these objections fails, a *weaker version* exposes the dilemmatic character of adjudication under capitalism. This latter version, I submit, can be given a discourse ethical grounding of the sort proposed by Habermas (sec. 3). I conclude that Dworkin's tendency to ground the certainty of law in terms of SR does not vitiate his insights regarding the relationship between equality of resources and integrity; these insights, I argue, help justify the sort of transformative democracy both he and Habermas endorse. Conversely, Habermas's failure to appreciate the deep incompatibility of legal integrity with capitalist society ought not detract from his insights regarding the profound changes wrought by a *procedural* paradigm on the nature of legal certainty and the separation of powers—changes that are well illustrated by Ackerman's account of paradigm shifts in American constitutional law.

1.   Dworkin's theory of law provides a convenient place to begin our discussion of legitimacy, since its objections to positivism, realism, and hermeneuticism are, in my opinion, devastating. First, let us examine his critique of positivism. Dworkin does not contest the basic idea that judges remain true to the law as an embodiment of the people's will. But he denies that law's meaning can be fixed by authorial intent or stipulative definition in the manner assumed by positivism. Hard cases cannot be adjudicated absent further consideration of moral principles not *expressly* stated in law. Legal concepts are inherently dynamic and interpretative; their "meaning" encompasses a community's evolving understanding of itself as a "moral personality" possessing rational *integrity*. Such a view comports with democracy. For not only are judges called upon to protect minority rights in the name of democratic fairness, but they are called upon to uphold *principles* that the legislature itself has tacitly endorsed in its enactment of statutes (Dworkin 1985, 22).

Dworkin marshals two arguments in support of his theory. The negative argument shows how fixing legal meaning with reference to authorial intent and formal definition necessarily breaks down. The positive argument shows how legal hermeneutics best comports with our democratic intuition that "force should not be used or withheld, no matter how useful that would be to the ends in view, no matter how beneficial or noble these ends, except as licensed or required by individual rights and responsibilities flowing from past political decisions about when collective force is justified" (Dworkin 1986, 93).

The negative argument begins by showing the insuperable difficulties attendant on any positivistic identification of authors and their intentions. Are the decisive intentions the hopes or expectations of the legislator? Are they the abstract or concrete hopes (expectations)? And what if our legislator intended to delegate the problem of interpreting the meaning of the law to others (Dworkin 1985, 43)?

Given difficulties in specifying a dominant and contemporary intent, it is not surprising to find Judge Bork and other strict constructionists modifying the criterion of authorial intent by introducing *counterfactual* strategies of *interpretation*: either one reasons from the specific beliefs of the Founding Fathers to conclusions about how they would have intended their statements in light of present-day situations *or* one reasons from "the principles the Framers enacted, the values they sought to protect."[2] Unlike the former—counterfactual—strategy, the latter has the distinct advantage of enabling judges to reason from *norms* rather than psychological *facts*. However, the emphasis on norms seems to entail an abandonment of the *originalist* thesis, since their specification can be elaborated at varying levels of generality. Principles are more susceptible to constructive interpretation as their generality increases; but that means that they can be interpreted in ways critical of, or inconsistent with, the original intentions of their authors.[3]

Of course, one can also defend the criterion of authorial intent on a *nonoriginalist* basis that privileges the intentions of legislators. However, aside from the fact that legislative intent may not reflect the current will of the majority of citizens any better than the original intent of the Founding Fathers, there still remain the aforementioned difficulties regarding identification of authorship, specification of intent, and application with respect to unforeseen circumstances.

The second version of positivism—more prevalent in English jurisprudence—attempts to circumvent these difficulties by arguing that, given sufficient analysis, the meaning of law can be fixed definitively, independent of psychological and historical considerations. Semantic versions of positivism hold that the meaning or contextual use of law is clearly defined by shared rules (Hart). Although they allow for the possibility of purely verbal disputes, they disallow any *theoretical* disagreement about the meaning of law. This "plain fact" approach (as Dworkin calls it) is controverted by actual practice. It is also refuted by the *historicity* of language. Dworkin agrees with Hart that all social practices are *rule*-governed language games. Rules regulating the language and behavior of a given social practice enable us to identify the meaning of basic concepts that commonly figure in the language game in question. Unless there were some agreement about the meaning of justice, law, right, and so on, legal discourse would not be possible. This fact explains why Marxists and libertarians can still argue with one another about what justice, in the "thinnest" sense, requires.[4] However, legal disagreements show that no linguistic rule can exhaustively define justice. That explains why Dworkin's equality-in-resources principle is not *logically* entailed by "justice" in the same way that "male" is logically entailed by "bachelor." "Justice" is an interpretative concept; its meaning evolves in the same way that the meaning of a text does (Dworkin 1986, 72).

Agreement on specific interpretations of moral concepts will be weaker than agreement on specific interpretations of legal concepts, which are more closely tied to the peculiar substantive beliefs and concrete practices of a given community. However, contrary to positivists, customary practice in law remains interpretative in a moral sense and so is subject to disagreement. Hence the continuing debate over what constitutes cruel and unusual punishment, voluntary consent, legal personality, and so on.

Dworkin's distinction between abstract concepts and concrete conceptions helps explain the possibility of legitimate adjudication in hard cases. By contrast, positivists hold that law consists entirely of *rules* possessing clearly defined, built-in conditions of application. Whenever such rules collide with one another or whenever the case to be adjudicated is not subsumed under clearly stated conditions of application, judges must have recourse to their own personal values in calculating the assignment of rights.

Dworkin certainly does not deny the importance of policy considerations in legitimate instances of adjudication. However, it is one thing to appeal to policy aims in interpreting statutes, it is another to appeal to them in determining fundamental, abstract rights. Having become a realist charged with the task of adjudicating a novel case, the positivist who now discards legal precedent as a basis for judgment in favor of utilitarian calculations cannot account for the way in which *rights* are at stake. Of course, it often happens that in deciding cases, judges will assign a *concrete right* after weighing costs and benefits to the disputing parties and the community at large. But appeal to policies and cost-benefit analyses in adjudicating conflicts *between* rights is not to be confused with appeal to utilitarian calculations as a substitute *for* rights. In the words of Dworkin, "[I]t follows from the definition of a right that it cannot be outweighed by all social goals" (Dworkin 1977, 92). To deny this claim is to enthrone judges as legislative and administrative tyrants.

Dworkin avoids this impasse by distinguishing legal *rules* from legal *principles.* Unlike rules, principles are abstract *standards* setting forth basic rights. They are either unconditionally valid or conditionally valid in a (general) manner *requiring interpretation.* Most importantly, whenever contradictory rules are at stake, judges can appeal to higher-order principles to help resolve the impasse. Although principles *too* may *compete* with one another in a given case, they cannot contradict one another. For example, the principles of reasonable foreseeability and direct consequence that limit liability against the standards of individual responsibility and actual harm, respectively, yield to one another on a case-by-case basis without invalidating one another.

This concludes the first part of Dworkin's argument: the internal criticism of legal positivism. The second part answers the positivist rejoinder that, whenever principles collide and interpretation is required, rights cease to have an objective foundation. Dworkin's position here is similar to Gadamer's: Interpretation aims at maximizing both the coherence and reasonableness of a text in a way that best *fits* the tradition. The hermeneutical standpoint of the judge is analogous to that of an author who has been assigned responsibility for continuing the plot of a chain novel; his or her creative supplement extends the plot in a way that is objectively constrained by what others have written, but *not* by what they have intended. If several interpretations (or readings) fit the plot equally well, then he or she must choose the one that shows the text (or tradition) in its "best light," as "the best justification of our legal practices as a whole . . . that makes these practices the best they can be" (Dworkin 1986, vii).

Dworkin takes this Gadamerian principle of perfectibility in a decidedly Habermasian direction. Gadamer, you will recall, argues that interpretation involves anticipating the completion of a text's meaning. As he understands it, this principle does not presume a unitary telos, or single right (or best) meaning, toward which interpretation of the text aims. Rather, it entails very nearly the opposite: Because interpretation of the text is guided by the parochial prejudgments of the interpreter, interpretation can never be complete. For Dworkin, by contrast, understanding becomes *fully* interpretative when it is *reflexive*, i.e., oriented toward *rationally justifying* interpretative practices we normally take for granted. With Habermas, he insists that interpretation does not privilege the truth, or validity of tradition as it has been transmitted *unreflectively*—prior to methodical, theoretical justification. Even the jurist who is predisposed to interpreting a legal tradition in its best light will adopt a critical attitude toward it. In seeking to justify his or her decision in light of past precedents, the judge tacitly seeks to find the strongest—and most principled—justification for those precedents. But the process of justification—of finding meaning, purpose, and integrity in the system of law as a whole—necessarily involves a critical and constructive reinterpretation of it that cannot but reject certain precedents and interpretations as false or mistaken (Dworkin 1986, 49-53, 419 n. 12, 422 n. 14). Like Habermas's legal theory, then, Dworkin's theory attempts to mediate universal principles of justice with positive legal tradition. Such principles comprise the implicit telos of law. Hence, to the degree that legal traditions deviate from them they deviate from the rule of law as well.

What are these principles? And what kind of legal community comports with them? For Dworkin, only communities based on shared moral principles—expressing equal concern and respect for all—articulate associative obligations capable of legitimating legal authority (190). Such associative (or fraternal) obligations are distinguished from other responsibilities in four ways: they are *special* (hold for members of a specific group), *personal* (run directly from each member to every other member), express *concern* for the well-being of other members, and do so in a way that is ostensibly in the interests of all *equally* (200). According to this concept of community, neither communities based on accidental circumstance—say, membership in the community of mankind or association based on mutual convenience—nor communities based solely on shared rules (or coordinating conventions) are true communities. The former need not satisfy any of the conditions requisite for fraternal association, and the latter need not exhibit any equal concern for consociates (210).

An associative community, of course, is not automatically just; its "conception of equal concern may be defective or it may violate rights of its citizens or citizens of other nations" (213). Indeed, it is not communitarian, if by this we mean the use of criminal statutes to force persons to conform to a majority's opinions about ethical propriety, as in the court's decision to uphold Georgia's sodomy statute in *Bowers v. Hardwick* in 1986. Liberal community, on Dworkin's reading, is communitarian in an entirely different, *civic republican* sense (Dworkin 1989, 499). The identification with community that it esteems is not identification with a specific conception of the good life, as strong communitarians urge, but identification with the "official political acts"—legislation, adjudication, and enforcement—of the government as embodiments of *justice*. In contrast to the Sandelian caricature of the "detached" liberal reformer whose own personal life remains untouched by the economic inequality, racial discrimination, and social domination he or she combats,

> An integrated citizen accepts that the value of his own life depends on the success of his community in treating everyone with equal concern. Suppose this sense is public and transparent: everyone understands that everyone else shares that attitude. The community will have an important source of stability and legitimacy even though its members disagree greatly about what justice is. (501)

Once we accept that our "fates are linked" (1986, 211) in the reciprocal recognition constitutive of identity, then we must agree with Habermas that justice and solidarity are entwined. Plato was right in this sense: A social system's justice or lack thereof has a direct bearing on the capacity of its citizens to lead just *and* fulfilling lives. Not only is it harder for people to lead just lives in unjust societies, but contrary to Plato, those who manage to do so generally forgo personal happiness (at the very least, they are despondent in contemplating the injustices perpetrated against their fellow citizens). Indeed, according to Dworkin, they are just as internally divided as those who flourish in the midst of injustice. For "when [social] injustice is substantial . . . people who are drawn to both ideals—of personal projects and attachments on the one hand and equality of political concern on the other . . . must compromise one of the two ideals, and each direction of compromise impairs the critical success of their lives" (Dworkin 1989, 504).

Dworkin elaborates the connection between ethical values (the good) and social justice (the right) by noting that, in order to ground stable and legitimate political obligations, communities must embody four distinct political virtues: justice, fairness, due process, and integrity. By *due process* he means procedures for judging whether laws have been violated and by whom, such as rules of evidence, of discovery, and of review. By *fairness* he means an equitable distribution of political power ensuring the accountability and responsiveness of elected officials to all segments of society. As I remarked in chapter 5, the principle of equal concern requires not only that appropriately targeted minorities (for instance, those that have suffered or continue to suffer from discrimination) be given the same formal rights to vote and participate; it also requires that their interests be substantively represented, even if this means augmenting their impact relative to their numerical strength.

From our standpoint justice and integrity merit special consideration because they flesh out certain moral presuppositions that remain undeveloped in Habermas's account of DE. Let us begin with justice. By *justice* Dworkin means *equality of resources* held privately and protection of civil liberties. Stated crudely, on this model "fair shares are those that equalize, so far as this is possible, the opportunity costs to others of the material resources each person holds" (482). Dworkin illustrates the model by means of a hypothetical auction in which a group of immigrants shipwrecked on an island with abundant resources bid for goods (later modified to consist of lifestyles extended over a lifetime). If everyone started out with equal initial bidding power *and* if—through introduction of insurance markets whose premiums were paid through a progressive income tax scheme—due compensation were made for initial and emergent inequalities in handicaps and talents, then no one would envy the lives of others (Dworkin 1981b, 323).

The advantage of this model over equality of welfare, libertarian, and Rawlsian models is striking. Unlike equality of welfare, the model avoids the messy problem—itself requiring massive and continuous bureaucratic intervention—of weighing personal utilities and satisfying preferences; moreover, it holds individuals responsible for the opportunity costs incurred by their choices of lifestyle (with their attendant levels of satisfaction). Unlike libertarian models—including the "starting gate" account that presumes initial equality in resources—Dworkin's model (following Rawls's) treats talents and skills as communal endowments. The differential incomes that result *over time* from such (genetic) endowments (as distinct from cultivated ambitions) must be periodically redistributed through a progressive income tax, itself based on a hypothetical insurance market for underemployment. The latter thus incorporates what is desirable on the libertarian model—the sense that individuals ought to be responsible for assuming the risks that determine their income levels and lifestyles—while rejecting its view that luck (in the form of genetic and environmental lotteries) and communal contribution are irrelevant (309).

Finally, its advantage over Rawls's difference principle consists in the use of income redistribution to compensate specific *individuals* (not confined to the "worst off" *group*) for undeserved handicaps, and in a manner that (unlike Rawls's reliance on primary goods) is sensitive to differences in "ambition, taste, occupation [and] consumption." However, for our purposes what makes the model important is that it explains *why* people would enter into political discourse in the first place. In short, absent an idealized auction, people need to communicate with one another in order to have some sense of the true opportunity costs of their lifestyles *and* attitudes. We are responsible for harms caused by the foreseeable consequences of our actions, no matter how unintended and indirect they might be. Acqui-escence in racist or sexist attitudes, and even failure to exhibit sufficient care about poverty, environmental waste, and injustice in one's daily life indirectly contribute to an atmosphere in which *others* feel free to flaunt their flagrant disregard for others (May 1992). Communication makes us aware of these costs, and if it is not *sufficient* to transform the lifestyles and attitudes that carry them, it is *necessary*. In the final analysis, only a critical transformation of needs, outlooks, and identities will bring about that equal-ity in resources necessary for realizing a more just and happy community (Dworkin 1981b, 338).

We are now in a better position to assess the importance of *integrity* as a communal virtue underlying legitimacy. Integrity is a global virtue infus-ing legislation and adjudication. As a legislative ideal it speaks against "check-erboard compromises" based on unprincipled distinctions. A law that struck a compromise between pro-life and pro-choice advocates by prohibiting women born on odd days from having abortions would be an example of such a compromise. So would a law that held automobile but not motor-cycle manufacturers strictly liable for injuries due to mechanical failure. Justice and fairness also presuppose integrity. The equal protection clause of the Fourteenth Amendment—indeed, the very idea of formal equality under the law—exhibits constitutional integrity, and the latter informs the idea of democratic self-determination, which prevents us from treating ourselves as authors of laws that are incoherent.[5] So construed, integrity is essentially related to communal solidarity, which obligates us to consider a common scheme of justice in resolving conflicts (Dworkin 1986, 64, 176).

Now, Dworkin concedes that the four political ideals underwriting legitimate legal regimes sometimes conflict with one another. Even his ideal judge Hercules knows that "the law is far from perfectly consistent in principle" (268). Dworkin therefore distinguishes *pure* from *inclusive* integ-rity. Pure integrity is the coherence law would possess if it were inter-preted solely in light of the four ideals mentioned above, without regard for precedent. It is at best a regulative idea, since judges are not free to discard whole strands of legal precedent—at least not all at once. Inclusive integrity is the coherence law would possess if it were interpreted against the background of institutional constraints—the judicial obligation to ac-knowledge legal precedent, legislative supremacy, and the priority of par-ticular legal departments over the entire body of law. The legitimacy of these constraints depends on the four ideals mentioned above. However, inclusive integrity can operate within fairly narrow areas of law without necessarily extending to other areas, or requiring deeply principled reflec-tion (405).

Inclusive integrity stops short of rescinding the injustice inherent in the system as a whole; pure integrity, by contrast, seeks "a single, coherent scheme of justice and fairness in the right relation" grounded in a shared communal ideal (219). Whereas the former urges adjudication in the direction of balancing competing—and sometimes conflicting—principles of legitimation and so tolerates compromises that otherwise appear to lack integrity and justice, the latter urges adjudication in the direction of institutional reform, centered around a common vision of justice.

1.1 Obviously, it is Hercules' ability to construct a theory of *pure* legal integrity that—thanks to his ideal knowledge of all the valid elements of extant law and all the relevant facts and policies bearing on specific cases—enables him to declare some past decisions mistakes and to presume a *single right answer* for present and future ones.

Critics have not been remiss in noting the tension between Dworkin's normative idealism—which assimilates interpretation to the rational demands of theoretical unity—and his legal dogmatism, which assimilates interpretation to the parochial demands of traditional precedent. Criticism of his idealism is voiced by Georgia Warnke, who observes that his interpretation of the way Hercules would have resolved two hard cases—*McLaughlin v. O'Brian* and *Brown v. Board of Education*—relies more on philosophical reasoning about what is or is not a principled theory of rights than on understanding the way the Founders of the Constitution, subsequent constitutional lawyers, or current Americans view issues of liability and equality. The danger of such a philosophical approach, Warnke submits, is that it lands us back in the kind of foundationalist, natural law tradition Dworkin himself criticizes. For the SR implicit in this tradition operates without the hermeneutical constraint of critical dialogue (Warnke 1993, 81). Hence, she concludes that Dworkin's appeal to principles in deciding in favor of *Brown* is every bit as uncritical as Justice Brown's majority opinion in *Plessy v. Ferguson* in 1896, which ruled that "equal but separate" accommodations for blacks and whites accorded with the Fourteenth Amendment's equal protection clause (Brown presumed that "legislation is powerless to eradicate racial instincts or to abolish distinctions based on physical differences ... [since one] race cannot but be inferior to the other politically"—quoted in Arthur 1989, 219).

Warnke's concern about the potentially reactionary implications of natural law theory do not, of course, speak to the potentially reactionary implications of a purely hermeneutical approach—a problem of which she herself is fully aware. In this context one could reverse Warnke's charge by pointing out the way in which Dworkin's subjectivistic approach approximates conventionalism and positivism. This conservatism is evident in the way Dworkin distinguishes two phases of adjudication. In the first phase we narrow our range of possible interpretations to those that "fit" established law equally well; in the second phase we select the one that best coheres with our (substantive) moral evaluations.[6] This division replicates positivism all over again, in which the element of moral interpretation appears subjective and arbitrary in comparison to the formal interpretation of objective fit (Hoy 1987, 341–44).

The suspicion that Dworkin is a positivist in disguise is not dispelled by his acknowledgment that formal considerations of fit may be "actually soldered to and driven by more substantive ones" of value (Dworkin 1986, 237). Are these values primarily conventional or transcendent? Unlike Habermas, Dworkin does not attempt to ground his principle of equal respect and concern in necessary presuppositions of postconventional communicative action. Hence the validity of basic rights is either taken for granted or at best justified by appeal to the moral conventions of Anglo-American jurisprudence. Although I would argue that Dworkin is best understood as balancing positive convention and philosophical reason through a Rawlsian procedure of reflective equilibrium, his insistence that in most cases there is a single right answer to every legal conflict privileges the former of these authorities.

Let me explain. Dworkin imagines that those who deny the single-right-answer thesis are positivists who hold that, in hard cases, there are no plain legal facts that would establish the truth or falsity of a legal proposition. (For the positivist a statement ascribing a constitutional right to abortion and one ascribing a constitutional prohibition of it would both be false (Dworkin 1985, 131).) However, if one abandons the positivist definition of "legal fact" and accepts "facts of narrative consistency" as well as facts of "normative consistency," then, Dworkin argues, with the sole exception of legal systems possessing few settled rules or treating only a limited range of conduct, the chances of legal indeterminacy (in which two dispositive propositions are equally true or equally false) will be remote (138 and 142). For in "modern, developed, and complex" systems it seems inconceivable that two competing interpretations of the general principle underlying rights—that of equal respect—would be equally right, unless this is due to "some more problematic type of indeterminacy or incommensurability in moral theory" (144). However, in order to rule out the likelihood of this latter moral and theoretical indeterminacy, Dworkin would have to abandon his interpretive approach to law's meaning. What guarantees a single right answer to every legal conflict cannot be philosophical and moral interpretations, since these are by their very nature indeterminate, and are in any case more contentious than settled opinions. What guarantees a single determinate outcome can only be the settled system of law.

Dworkin must therefore accord legal positivism more respect than he does if he wants to retain his strong determinacy thesis. However, legal positivism itself implies indeterminacy with respect to unpredictable cases. Recourse to principled philosophical reflection is necessary for overcoming indeterminacy in these instances, but only at the cost of reintroducing another kind of indeterminacy; consequently, as CLS scholars point out, incommensurability in moral theory *cannot* be discounted. Dworkin might follow Habermas by appealing to a developmental history of legal paradigms in delimiting the scope of "true" interpretations. But, as we shall see, the historical record—as philosophically reconstructed—is notoriously ambiguous: "Individualist" and "altruistic" conceptions may be complementary in principle, and formal justice may demand substantive justice for its realization, but they can never be completely harmonized within the dilemmatic structure of social welfare law.

1.2 Before addressing the CLS critique and the dilemmas facing the liberal and welfare paradigms, let us see how a discourse ethic might resolve the contradiction between SR and CR, idealism and conventionalism, inherent in Dworkin's theory. Following Klaus Günther's discourse ethical analysis of law (1988, 268), Habermas shows how the subjectivistic limitations of this model present problems for reconciling factual certainty and normative legitimacy. Reiterating Gadamer's observation that norms and their contexts of application mutually determine one another, Habermas argues that both the concrete meanings of norms *and* the system of law and principle with which they cohere *change* from case to case. This "ripple effect" secures the determinate, certain, and legitimate (single right) application of law in any given case, but only at the expense of introducing *theoretical* uncertainty (Habermas 1992, 269).

Habermas draws several lessons from this radical contextualization of Hercules' theoretical interpretations. First, the classical (formalist or positivist) conception of certainty must be abandoned. There can be no certainty of *outcome* because no legal norm has the status of a fixed, well-defined rule capable of mechanical (i.e., interpretation-free) application. Second, it follows that the only certainty to be had under these conditions is *procedural;* one can expect that only relevant reasons—filtered through valid procedures—will decide a case. Third, the scope of relevant reasons will be *substantively* limited by *shared paradigms* of the sort mentioned at the outset of this chapter. To the extent that such paradigms find a consensus in the legal community, they secure additional certainty (270).

The need to secure certainty and legitimacy through formal procedures and substantive paradigms requires abandoning the monological standpoint of an ideal judge in favor of a discourse ethical one (273). Paradigms are shared, normative backgrounds; they ossify into inflexible ideologies when not discursively tested against one another. The same can be said of professional standards, maxims of interpretation, rules for submitting evidence, procedures separating the treatment of legal matters from factual matters, and the like.

As I remarked in chapter 5, Habermas distinguishes the kinds of application discourses that occur in judicial contexts from the justification discourses that occur in legislative contexts. Whereas the latter aim to justify norms as satisfying generalizable interests, the former aim to justify applications of such norms—that is, the proper choice of norms and their concrete determination vis-à-vis different interpretations of a situation. Impartiality here means integrating all relevant perspectives—including, for instance, those of the litigants, affected parties, and so on—into a coherent description of the situation (266).

As in the case of political discourses, legal discourses in the narrow sense should not be construed as a subset of moral discourses. Rather, legal discourses compensate for the fallibility and uncertainty of parliamentary discourse and decision by institutionalizing procedural laws governing review and appeal. Although they, too, allow moral as well as pragmatic and ethical reasons to figure in legitimate arguments—indeed, civil and even criminal proceedings incorporate adversarial contests involving the strategic assertion of particular interests—there is a unique sense in which they exhibit a *higher* level of rationality than parliamentary debates (282).

Yet, as Stephen Toulmin has shown, the adversarial structure of legal arguments deviates strongly from an impartial search for truth. Moreover, such arguments are constrained by precedents and statutes whose validity is largely taken for granted and by the imperative to reach a timely decision. At the same time, it is clear that legal arguments contain "essential elements that can be grasped only on the model of moral argument, generally of discussion regarding the rightness of moral standards" (Habermas 1984, 35).

To begin with, Habermas notes that the adversarial structure of legal debates conduces even more favorably to the discovery of truth (or justice) than does the adversarial structure of parliamentary or constitutional debates. It allows both sides—prosecution and defense in criminal proceedings, plaintiff and defendant in civil ones—*equal* chances to present evidence (in criminal trials the separation of legal from factual matters contributes toward this end as well). Furthermore, it better secures the *public* impartiality of the proceedings by introducing the "neutral" intermediary of a judge and by subjecting decisions to higher levels of appeal and review. It is the responsibility of the judge to ensure that all relevant perspectives that bear on the interpretation of a disputed situation be "transformed" or integrated into each other in a fair and coherent manner (1992, 280).

Legal *procedures* thus retain at least an indirect connection to the impartial, consensual presuppositions of DE, while legal *deliberations* assume the form of a cooperative procedure for theory formation—a feature that is most evident in appellate and Supreme Court discussions between judges. Under these conditions certainty and legitimacy take on a new teleological meaning. The ideal, unconditional demand for the "single right answer" can no longer be understood in the way Dworkin assumes: as a substantive *deduction* from a theoretically *closed legal system* possessing inclusive or pure integrity. Rather, since pragmatic, substantial arguments never compel in any conclusive sense but only motivate the mutual acceptance of claims relative to inherently fallible reasons, we can at most speak of their *procedural* force. Thus the rationality gap between *factually* uncertain, fallible, and inconclusive *deliberations* and the *normative ideal* of a single right, conclusive *decision* is partly closed by the *idealizations* built into the procedural norms of discourse itself: we assume counterfactually that, to the extent that these idealizations are in fact approximated, the "chain of arguments approaching an ideal limit like a straight line" will reach "the vanishing point Peirce called the 'final opinion'" (278).

In summation, we can give a procedural sense to the directional idea of "law working itself pure" (Dworkin, 1986, 400). However, that idea still presumes that the conflicting paradigms by which we interpret law can be reconciled at a higher level. Speaking against this possibility is the very fact of conflict itself. It can be argued that in capitalist societies the range of institutional conflict is such that the quest for justice will always be compromised. If the pursuit of pure integrity becomes a battleground for different ideals of the good—as Dworkin notes, communitarian, utilitarian, and libertarian ideals all have a foothold in the tax laws and welfare statutes that currently prevail in the United States—imagine how much more elusive the pursuit of inclusive integrity must be. The scope for internal and external institutional conflict is magnified even further when the social fabric is torn by economic division.

2. In recent years a renegade group of lawyers and legal scholars has argued that liberal theory and practice is fundamentally incoherent. The founder of this movement, Roberto Unger (1975), argued that the nominalist attack on philosophical essentialism inaugurated by Hobbes issues in fundamental antinomies that render liberalism—qua theory of knowledge, self, and society—incoherent. The most basic antinomy—between theories (concepts) and facts (particulars)—implies a use of reason that is strictly formal (procedural) and instrumental. If we accept this notion of reason, then, Unger maintained, values and substantive goods will necessarily appear subjective, and public reason will oppose private autonomy.

To better situate Unger's Hegelian-Marxist critique—the essentials of which have been dealt with in my treatment of SR in chapters 1 and 2—we must briefly review the rise of legal formalism in common law adjudication. In effect, Unger is claiming that Hobbes's assumptions about the instrumental nature of rationality justified a mechanical, formalistic approach to law that later prevailed in nineteenth-century Anglo-American jurisprudence, long after social contractarian legal theories had lost their appeal.

Rejecting Aristotle's virtue-based conception of distributive justice, Hobbes argued that one's desert (worth) amounted to what others were willing to pay for one's services (Hobbes 1929, 67). This was a clear anticipation of the *will* theory of contract that would emerge at the beginning of the nineteenth century. Although eighteenth-century natural law doctrines stressing equity (Rousseau, Paine, and Locke) were just as irrelevant to actual jurisprudence as their classical predecessor, they at least conformed to the common law at that time.[7]

In truth, eighteenth-century social contract theory mirrored a contradiction between libertarian and communitarian conceptions of rationality—a contradiction poignantly illustrated by the debate between federalists and republicans discussed in chapter 1. On one hand, the legitimacy of the legal order depended on public consent. This consent ostensibly issued from rational knowledge of the common ends served by the state—a knowledge made possible by the basic equality and autonomy of citizens. On the other hand, possession of these moral attributes was made contingent on ownership of private property (Habermas 1989, 89). Thus, to put matters bluntly, although the scope of rational consent was presumed to be inclusive and universal, in practice it was not. A subjective conception of economic rationality qualified one to participate in what was in principle an unconditional discussion about the public good.

This contradiction—which finds exemplary expression in Kant's legal philosophy—had its analogue in English common law, which at once protected and limited contractual freedom in the name of equity. As articulated in Blackstone's *Commentaries* and practically implemented in eighteenth-century common law, contracts primarily served to transfer title of property, enforcing performance in accordance with customary standards of equity. This requirement—that properties exchanged be of equal value—still resonated in the writings of political economists (Smith, Say, Ricardo) on whom Marx's own labor theory of value relied. However, with the expansion of capitalism this concept became untenable in practice. Contract law ceased to be subsumed under property law once the *market value* of goods became the standard for determining damages.

The will theory of contract that came into being in the early nineteenth century dispensed with equity considerations altogether. Under the title theory of exchange, law exhibited a substantive concern for equity that made it an imperfect vehicle for capital accumulation. Not only were sellers not assured of the market value of their goods when payment was finally—and often belatedly—received, but the values exchanged had to be equivalent to one another according to pregiven standards. By interpreting contracts as "meetings of minds" or voluntary conjunctions of arbitrary wills, in which it was assumed that the contracting parties were seeking their own advantage, the will theory succeeded in detaching contract law from property law and whatever moral constraints the latter still contained. Courts now rewarded damages due to breach in accordance with the seller's or buyer's market-based expectations rather than on the basis of terms originally negotiated. Once "consideration" was received, even the most unfair bargain became irrevocable.

Whatever difficulties attended the will theory of contract stemmed from a residual reliance on local customs and merchant laws in determining the intent of the contracting parties. This, in turn, had a corrosive effect on the predictability of adjudication so necessary for efficient market calculations. Consequently, the will theory—with its focus on subjective intent—gave way to a formalist theory that defined the meeting of minds objectively, in terms of "the strict letter of contract" or other overt acts.

Its objectivism notwithstanding, formalism represents the clearest example of a jurisprudence founded on SR. The transparent nature of legal facts as indisputable "overt signs" mechanically determines judicial decisions in a manner both unambiguous and replicable by any judge whatsoever. Such logic, in turn, establishes a predictable legal universe necessary for strategically rational, game-theoretic calculations on the part of legal subjects. The price paid for this formalism is the elimination of any substantive interpretation of a contract's reasonableness, or justice.[8]

This trend would be reversed with the advent of the welfare paradigm.

The doctrine of unconscionability, good faith, and reliance informing twentieth-century contract law reintroduces standards of equity—albeit more for the purpose of strategically balancing private interests than for the sake of moral justice *simpliciter*.[9] Unger explains this shift away from formalism as a function of a dialectic internal to the logic and epistemology of liberal jurisprudence. Formalism—or the idea that civil rights have a rationally intuitable, perspicuous meaning prior to and independent of politics and personal morality—presumably solves the problem of order that arises in any liberal regime tolerant of freedom and diversity. However, in Unger's opinion, rights are not transcendent with respect to conflicting private aims, and therefore are not inherently impartial. This caveat applies equally to legislation and adjudication.

Legislative neutrality is impossible for reasons mentioned in chapter 1: Formal democracy encourages the aggregation of conflicting interests in ways that favor the most dominant and powerful interests. Public law is inherently political, but the politics are such that no rational, legitimating consensus ever emerges. Adjudicative neutrality is likewise impossible because any well-defined rule will serve multiple purposes and so must be interpreted in light of vague subjective standards of public welfare. However, without shared *and* well-defined conceptions of good there will be no consensus regarding the meaning of laws. Once adjudication ceases to be formally limited by clear precedent, the constitutional separation of an impartial judiciary and a partisan legislature collapses. A judiciary whose autonomy is regarded as integral to the containment of majoritarian attacks on fundamental rights now reveals itself as personal domination (Unger 1976, 180; 1975, 83–100).

Unger argues that the blurring of legislation and adjudication is propelled by the logic of law itself. The demands of legal impartiality require that formal equality give way to substantive equity. In contrast to the formal jurisprudence of the nineteenth century, the "procedural equality" enforced by the Realist School in the thirties mandated equity in bargaining power, thereby preventing workers from "freely" assenting to formal agreements that were deemed coercive.[10] Substantive justice would rectify bargaining inequities further, for, in the words of Unger, equity lies "in the control of unjust enrichment, in the justification of a policy of income distribution, and in the definition of a criterion of public interest for the control of administrative agencies" (Unger 1975, 187).

Without procedural safeguards and equity considerations protecting against economic duress, contract law would fail to *formally* distinguish a *voluntary* "meeting of minds" from coercive agreement. Thus courts are now responsible for interpreting indeterminate, open-ended standards and general clauses of legislation designed to police unconscionable contracts, to void unjust gain, to regulate economic concentration, and to ensure that government agencies act in the public interest. However, this responsibility can only be discharged by adopting *policy-oriented* forms of legal reasoning that undercut any formal appeal to abstract permissions and entitlements. Courts and administrative agencies must balance conflicting interests in light of changing circumstances, thereby making it increasingly difficult to sustain rigid categories of classification and criteria of analogy. In private law the determination of whether a contract was negotiated in good faith will require entering into the practices and belief systems of specific social groups. In public law the determination of criminal liability will require balancing the judgments of trained specialists against the background of the defendant's life history and the peculiar circumstances of his crime (Foucault 1979). In both cases instrumental considerations—moral, political, and economic—involving the advancement of public good may override any formal appeal to "inalienable" rights.

Simply stated, Unger's critique of formalism asserts that all appeals to the transparent meaning of right are either circular or patently political. The distinction between public and private law founders on the shoals of SR. Does driving a hard bargain—in which, for example, a company offers destitute workers the opportunity to sign a "yellow dog" contract prohibiting them from joining a union—involve coercion? Common law clearly outlaws agreements made under duress, and so distinguishes offers from threats. But what constitutes duress is partly a function of accepted practice—and *that* is a matter of some political dispute. When *Coppage v. Kansas* was decided in 1915, Americans still saw themselves as living in a semi-agrarian society with a vast frontier of opportunity. Under these conditions one could plausibly argue, as Justice Pitney did, that the fact that parties to a contract "are not equally unhampered by circumstances" does not discriminate against the weaker party's freedom to seek his or her fortune elsewhere. In today's complex world, this argument seems less plausible. Yet despite the New Deal's rejection of *Coppage*, the question of what counts as duress is far from being settled. To recall our earlier discussion of the Walzer/Dworkin debate, the problem of interpreting the finer discriminations underlying our institutionalized practices of bargaining (as Taylor puts it) must itself be negotiated politically—as is well-illustrated by pending congressional debate on legislation that would prohibit companies from hiring temporary laborers as permanent replacements for striking workers.

Regardless of what one thinks of this critique of *formalist* jurisprudence, it does not establish the strong claim that *liberal* jurisprudence is torn between incompatible paradigms. Rather, it shows, first, that the liberal paradigm in its *classical* formulation is unworkable for the welfare state, and second, that formalistic (or positivistic) theories of jurisprudence are internally incoherent. The first point is uncontroversial; the second point is less so, but does not *ipso facto* contradict Dworkin's own optimistic assessment that politically sensitive interpretations of law are capable of being rationally and coherently ordered into a system possessing both legitimacy and integrity.

Duncan Kennedy attempts to disprove Dworkin's optimism by arguing that liberal jurisprudence is torn between two *antithetical* moral visions, roughly corresponding to the liberal and welfare paradigms mentioned above. The *"formalist"* jurisprudence espoused by the former vision is *individualistic;* (negative) freedom implies absence of restraint favoring a market allocation of goods and limited liability in commercial law. The *substantive* jurisprudence espoused by the latter vision is *altruistic;* (positive) freedom implies access to resources favoring government redistribution and extended liability. The former is implicated in modes of reasoning that appeal to well-defined *rules*; it assures maximum predictability (fair warning) and limited judicial discretion in ways that promote self-reliance. The latter is implicated in modes of reasoning that appeal to vague *standards;* it ensures inclusiveness and flexibility in ways that promote the spreading of burdens for the sake of the common good. The result of this split is familiar to us from our earlier discussion of Marx in chapter 1: "[W]e are divided, among ourselves, and also within ourselves, between irreconcilable visions of humanity and society and between radically different aspirations for our common future" (Kennedy 1989, 36).

In order to show that equally rational (legitimate) but *contradictory* judgments are possible in any given case, Kennedy must show three things: (1) for any pair of principle and counterprinciple applicable to a given area of law, each member of the pair is defensible solely on the basis of one model (or rule) of reasoning; (2) these models are contradictory, and (3) in at least some cases, both principle and counterprinciple are equally applicable (Altman 1990, chap. 4). One version of this argument asserts that liberal legal culture is an unprincipled "patchwork" of formal and substantive, individualistic and altruistic, norms (Kennedy 1983, 15). If this means only that the distinction between form and substance is relative, so that some principled appeal to general standards—coupled, perhaps with a consideration of policy aims—enters into even the most mechanical and unproblematic decisions, then, once again, we have not gone much beyond radicalizing Dworkin's own view that law is interpretative. If the patchwork thesis means that any subcategory of law consists of rules and standards that overlap one another, this, too, need not generate contradictions. Again, to recall Dworkin's point, general principles at most compete with one another. Even were we to assume, as Kennedy does, that both principles are somehow logically (and biconditionally) connected to *rule*-governed forms of reasoning that contradict one another, contradictions would only arise if the principles in questions were *equally* applicable to the case in question.

Kennedy's distinction between "core" and "periphery" actually seems to minimize the problem of contradiction by suggesting that, within the current capitalist regime, the individualistic paradigm and its formalistic decision procedure "trump" the altruistic paradigm and its interpretative or policy-driven decision procedure. Thus, although "there are no overall unifying principles of law which . . . give the subject an internal necessity," there is "a deep level of order and structure to the oppositions between competing conceptions of doctrine and of policy and of everything else" (16). Elsewhere, however, Kennedy argues that "what distinguishes the modern situation is the breakdown of the conceptual boundary between the [individualistic] core and the [altruistic] periphery, so that all the conflicting positions are at least potentially relevant to all issues" (Kennedy 1989, 46).

In Dworkin's opinion, the problem with Kennedy's position is that it never establishes that "all the conflicting positions are at least potentially relevant to all issues." He voices this objection most convincingly when addressing Allan Hutchinson's version of Kennedy's argument. Hutchinson argues that liability rules based on reasonable foreseeability and those based on direct consequences are incompatible in that the former reflects an individualistic vision of democratic order, the latter a collectivist one.[11] However, as Dworkin convincingly points out, Hutchinson never shows that the individualistic principle, which bases liability on reasonable foreseeability, and the collectivist principle, which bases it on direct consequences, are contradictory rather than *competing*.

> These principles are inevitable aspects of any decent response to the world's complexity . . . [and] it is implausible to suppose that someone who makes that choice differently in different kinds of circumstances, fixing the loss on the actor in some and on the victim in another, is morally schizophrenic. . . .These principles are sometimes competitive but they are not contradictory. (Dworkin 1986, 444)

Finally, even Kennedy concedes that altruism and individualism are sufficiently abstract—formal in the context-independent sense—to permit the derivation of either a standards or rules approach. Fraud and unconscionability standards can follow from altruistic principles disallowing advantages based on misinformation, incapacity, duress, and so on, but they can also be derived from individualistic principles requiring voluntary consent. Moreover, some altruistic legal schemes—progressive income tax laws, for example—will be fixed by rules rather than standards.

To conclude, the argument proving the rational incoherence of liberal jurisprudence fails, since formal and substantive modes of reasoning are compatible with both individualistic and altruistic principles, and these principles do not contradict one another but at most compete with one another. Nevertheless, if it could be shown that competition between complementary principles of the sort adduced by Dworkin is not merely incidental to context but is systematically generated within capitalism, then the CLS claim that modern law is dilemmatic will be partially redeemed. To see how this might be possible we must turn to Habermas.

3. Despite its merits, the CLS critique of law overestimates the irrationality of liberal doctrine. The liberal attempt to ground law in basic rights possessing a general—if not strictly universal—validity need not founder on the shoals of the form/content distinction. Contrary to Unger, liberal theory is not committed to the subjectivity of all values. In particular, those values that specifically revolve around the most abstract ideas of right are generally regarded as objectively valid by liberal theorists, even if there is disagreement among them regarding their precise interpretation. These values are indeed formal, but not in the way that legal formalism demands— as specifying precise rules that can be applied in a mechanical manner. Rather, they are formal in the sense of specifying *relatively* indeterminate *standards* or *principles*.

Now, Habermas's appreciation of the deeper procedural norms underlying legal discourse places him in a unique position to assess the peculiar strengths and weaknesses of the CLS movement. The rationalist in him cleaves to liberal ideals of autonomy and democracy even while criticizing their ideological content. In this respect he and Unger are alike. By opposing individualist principle and collectivist counterprinciple, liberal paradigm and welfare paradigm, he and Unger hope to devise modes of social organization in which individual freedom and democratic solidarity complement, instead of oppose, one another. But Habermas and Unger differ on one important point. Unger's "deviationist" strategy is "limited solely by institutional arrangements lacking any higher authority" and so "lays claim to no privileged status capable of distinguishing it clearly from ideological dispute."[12] Habermas's, by contrast, is underpinned by a theory of communicative action that provides independent standards for assessing the ideological content of just these very institutions (Rasmussen 1988, 155–70).[13] These standards—implicit in rational argumentation—function at a deeper level than the formal procedures attacked by CLS advocates.

Habermas eschews Unger's historicism, arguing that these procedures culminate a moral and legal evolution whose separation of morality and legality, state and civil society, public and private spheres, and legislative, judicial, and administrative functions is unidirectional, *if not entirely irreversible*. That means, however, that the infusion of substantive political aims into legislation and adjudication diagnosed by Unger poses a problem. At the very least, it threatens to *deformalize* law in ways that reverse its rational evolution, namely, by undermining the separation of competencies, action spheres, and powers. This tendency, in turn, vitiates law's impartiality and transforms it into a medium destructive of the very individual autonomy it ostensibly secures.

This problem is compounded by the fact that tendencies toward deformalization may be inherent in the institutionalization of law. In order to better grasp this dynamic, let us recall the role played by legal paradigms in structuring the meaning of law. Following Kuhn, Habermas conceives a legal paradigm as a shared *background* understanding, consisting of *exemplary* decisions, practices, and maxims of interpretation that coalesce with a specific conception of social reality, human agency, and so forth (Habermas 1992, 472). Legal paradigms thus disclose, interpret, and contribute to the construction of a social world. Although they normally function as a kind of background knowledge, once they become problematic—as has happened in the case of the liberal and welfare paradigms—they lose their taken-for-granted status and become matters of intense theoretical reflection.

It is Habermas's contention that neither liberal nor welfare paradigms suffice to *describe* the complexity of social reality in the modern state; and neither, he believes, accounts for the *normative legitimacy* of modern law. To see why this is so we must briefly survey the history of these paradigms.

The liberal paradigm fully emerged within the compass of the *constitutional state*. The latter arose in response to the contradiction between legal absolutism and capitalist economy. Accordingly, in this paradigm "right" means (negative) freedom from the intrusive interference of government. On this model, *formal* laws are rules for coordinating interaction; they solve the problem of preserving social order amidst conflict (525).

The breakdown of laissez-faire capitalism and heightened awareness of the *functional* constraints and *collective* contributions in sustaining social order led to the emergence of the welfare paradigm. Furthermore, the democratic principle underlying the legitimation of the constitutional state demanded the universal provision of educational, medical, and other resources requisite for exercising political rights. Stated differently, the welfare paradigm emerged in response to the tension—inherent in the libertarian paradigm—between having legal *permission* to do something (abstract or formal right) and being entitled to resources requisite for doing it (effective or substantive right); it assumes, as I argued in chapter 5, that even negative rights to noninterference can be violated, and unfair privileges granted, by *withholding* provisions as well as by *limiting action* (500). Hence, it defines the meaning of rights in terms of the *positive freedom* to participate in democratic processes and the system of material entitlements requisite for doing so equally. On this model, laws are also *substantive* policies for realizing collective goals; they solve the problem of social inequality (480 and 490).

Two transformations in law exhibit the strengths and weaknesses of this paradigm. On one hand, formal legal approaches give way to more substantive ones. Unger's analysis of formal contractual freedom serves as a reference point for this "materialization of law," as Habermas puts it. Other examples include the "institutionalization of quasi-political bargaining processes" that replace normal channels of legislation and adjudication (corporatism and reflexive law); the marginalization of civil and criminal codes rendered inoperable due to social and political change; and the instrumentalization of law for purposes of social policy (Habermas 1988, 231).

On the other hand, whole new categories of entitlements emerge that compensate for market disadvantages and other contingencies. The danger involved in these transformations consists of two forms of freedom-denying tendencies. First, as Unger notes, the materialization of law shifts responsibility for interpreting the meaning of general policy statutes to judges and administrators, thereby endowing them with an illegitimate legislative authority that undermines the separation of powers. With the transition to the *security state*, which assumes responsibility for insuring against long- and short-term *group risks* posed by nuclear energy, biogenetic engineering, and other scientific technologies, greater leeway is allowed for expert planning, oversight, and decision—free from the cumbersome procedures of parliamentary oversight. *Regulatory laws* leave even more room for unilateral interpretation and implementation than other policy statutes (Habermas 1992, 521).

Second, welfare entitlements foster dependency in trying to secure autonomy. Of course, social entitlement is no more unambiguously dehumanizing than is market entitlement unambiguously liberating. However, what makes unemployment compensation, welfare, and child custody specifically dehumanizing is not their bureaucratic form as such—formal media generally facilitate the regular and efficient transaction of economic and administrative business—but their bureaucratic integration of family, education and other areas of life constituted, integrated and coordinated on the basis of shared norms. A *power relationship* treating the client as a *general case* subject to economic calculation and manipulation replaces a *communicative* relationship predicated on individuality (autonomy) and solidarity (equal respect and care), and does so in the latter's name (490).

In chapter 1, I argued that the demands of economic efficiency—embodied in contractual relations between provider and client of the sort esteemed by Weber—undermine the moral conditions for the possibility of their own legitimacy. Now we are in a better position to appreciate the dilemmatic structure of this dynamic. It seems that the altruistic principle of substantive justice necessary for actualizing the individualistic principle of formal autonomy has to be instrumentalized in ways that end up violating the freedom and solidarity regulative for communicative action generally.

Feminist critics of labor law write a particularly damning expose of this *paternalistic* altruism. Among other things, they focus on the *normalizing* function of safety regulations that prevent women—especially pregnant women—from working in so-called "hazardous" jobs. Until recently, laws excluding women from certain occupations made no pretense about the "natural and proper timidity and delicacy which belongs to the female sex," whose divinely ordained "destiny and mission" is "to fulfill the noble and benign offices of wife and mother" (*Bradwell v. Illinois* [1873]—cited by Arthur 1989, 256). In some cases, exceptions to general job exclusions designed to protect women from situations in which they might be morally compromised (e.g., bar tending) were allowed if oversight by the father or husband were guaranteed (*Goesaert v. Cleary* [1948]). If they did not exclude women from occupations, they limited their manner of employment. To cite the Court's 1908 opinion in *Muller v. Oregon:* "[T]he two sexes differ in structure of body, in the function to be performed by each, in the amount of physical strength, in the capacity for long-continued labor, particularly when done standing, the influence of vigorous health upon the future well-being of the race, the self-reliance which enables one to assert full rights, and in the capacity to maintain struggle for subsistence" (Arthur 1989, 38).

To be sure, if the welfare paradigm can be accused of exaggerating biological differences and fixing gender identities in accordance with traditional roles, the liberal paradigm can be faulted for neglecting gender differences altogether. For example, prior to the passage of the 1993 Family and Medical Leave Act, women and men who chose to leave their jobs temporarily in order to care for newborns, indigents, or other members of their family were subject to dismissal. Even with the protection provided by this law—which, after all, only allows up to twelve weeks of unpaid leave—single parents (typically women) face special obstacles in competing in the job market.

According to Habermas, neither liberal nor welfare paradigm adequately protects private autonomy. This is indeed ironic, given the fact that both paradigms privilege private autonomy over democratic self-determination. Both "share the *productivist image* of a capitalist industrial society" in that they define the problem of justice in terms of the distribution of economic rights and goods to individual actors (Habermas 1992, 491, 505). By construing rational agency, equality, and freedom in terms of the conditions requisite for sustaining *individual purposive action*, they lose sight of the vital connection between such action and democratic communication.

Only the third, *procedural* paradigm, which shows how justice and legitimation are functions of CR (more precisely, democratic self-determination) rather than SR, grasps this connection. For only it conceives questions of justice *reflexively*. In the words of Iris Marion Young (1990, 25), whom Habermas cites, "[R]ights are not fruitfully conceived as possessions. Rights are relationships, not things; they are institutionally defined rules specifying what people can do in relation to one another." As such, their legitimacy depends on democratic processes that are themselves institutionally secured through rights. This *reflexive law* establishes discursive *procedures* by which all other kinds of law—formal civil liberties, substantive welfare entitlements, policies, administrative regulations—are legitimately generated (Habermas 1992, 493–96, 499, 528).

According to Habermas, the *procedural* paradigm establishes a *legal* basis for implementing feminist reforms. If one examines what is at stake in labor law, for example, it becomes apparent that the decisive issues revolve around the question of equal treatment. Better still, they revolve around the question of treating women with equal respect and concern—a principle that requires taking into account *relevant differences* between men and women in securing equal resources and opportunities for employment (507). However, treating different persons differently (or unequals unequally) can further equal concern and respect for all *only if* the relevant differences are not naturalized into *essential* differences. Unless the question of *identity*—or, if you prefer, of basic, morally relevant needs—is treated as a political matter to be deliberated on and decided by all who are directly affected, the continued presence of patriarchal domination and sex discrimination based on rigid, essentialist classifications will remain (513).

Thus, the question is not merely whether women are alike or unlike men with respect to satisfying the conditions of a particular job description. More important is whether the occupation in question can be redefined to accommodate biological differences, or "gender as a social construct can be redefined to make those differences less occupationally relevant" (Rhode 1989, 97).

The feminist critique of labor law bears indirectly on the separation of powers problem associated with the materialization of law. Feminists appeal to the full panoply of rights—formal civil liberties (e.g., rights to privacy and abortion) substantive entitlements (rights to state-funded day care, income transfers in the form of wages, not welfare, etc.), and reflexive procedures (rights to fair political representation, economic inclusion, and so on)—in securing equal dignity for all women. This mediation of the three paradigmatic legal forms is itself a defining feature of the *procedural* paradigm. The latter does not change the basic meaning of rights as expressions of mutual agreements. It does not replace formal and substantive rights securing *private* autonomy. Rather, it changes the *context* in which such rights are realized—not the free market or client-provider relationship but the civic sphere wherein *public* autonomy is exercised (Habermas 1992, 483).

This change in context renders the meaning of the separation of powers more abstract (528).[14] The materialization of law, the infusion of policy-oriented statutes into law, and the emergence of welfare and regulatory law not only undermine the classical separation of public and private spheres, they endow judicial and executive branches with quasi-legislative powers. However, just as political discourse functions as the medium in which citizens collectively define and distinguish their private and public identities, so too discourse functions as the medium by which governmental branches mutually define and distinguish their own powers.

According to the procedural paradigm, *each* branch of government deploys types of reasoning characteristic of the other branches. In Habermas's opinion, not only should legislative bodies incorporate more specific directives about the application and implementation of legislation—indeed, he thinks they should have their own constitutional watchdog committees—but executive agencies should open themselves up to citizen participation (e.g., through public hearings, citizen advisory boards, etc.), and courts should concern themselves with maintaining the integrity and justice of the democratic process.

This last point merits special consideration. Sometimes Habermas (following Günther) defines the scope of judicial discourses narrowly, so as to exclude questions about the normative justification of legislation (284).

However, as Dworkin points out in his discussion of checkerboard compromises, the integrity of statutory legislation—not just the integrity of democratic procedure—has a direct bearing on the possibility of rational adjudication. Habermas himself concedes as much when he says that "to the extent that statutory policies *(Gesetzesprogramme)* depend for their realization on further concretization, so that decisions falling in the gray zone between legislation and adjudication devolve on the judiciary (cautelary restrictions notwithstanding), juristic discourses about application must be supplemented in a recognizable manner by elements taken from justificatory discourses. . . . The additional burden of legitimation could be satisfied by the necessity of providing justifications before an enlarged judicial-critical forum" (530). This branch-specific mediation of discourses finds parallel expression at the level of the administration as well: "In the modern administration that is actively geared toward securing public welfare *(Leistungsverwaltung)* . . . problems pile up that require the weighing of collective goods, the choice of competing goals, and the normative evaluation of individual cases. These can be treated rationally only in discourses of justification and application that explode the framework of a normatively neutral fulfillment of tasks" (530).

Here we see how the problem of judicial review is reconfigured in procedural terms. If we agree with Ely, Sunstein, and Ackerman that the main function of constitutional courts no longer involves protecting private citizens from public interference but instead requires safeguarding the democratic process—that is, protecting the exercise of communicative power from economic, social, and administrative power—then this can only mean, to cite Frank Michelman, the "inclusion of the other, of the hitherto excluded—which in practice means bringing to legal-doctrinal presence the hitherto absent voices of emergently self-conscious social groups."[15] Thus, the courts should be taking a more active role in encouraging legislators to apportion districts on the basis of ensuring minority representation rather than protecting parties and incumbents. In Habermas's opinion it would be wrong to give this "reasoned analysis requirement" (Sunstein) too strong a republican spin, as if the constitutional court were nothing more than—in the words of Ackerman—the "representation and trace of the People's absent self-government." To grant the courts this *paternalistic* power of oversight presupposes an "ethically constricted" notion of democracy that underestimates the sedimented virtue implicit in political bargaining (Habermas 1992, 341). Nevertheless, it can be argued that a more egalitarian and inclusive democracy incorporating the economic. educational, technological, and electoral reforms defended in earlier chapters of this book would have to be realized in order to transform this *weak* virtue into the kind of solidaristic force capable of uniting concern for the unique interests of others with concern for the common good. A program of judicial review oriented to the aggressive defense of this model of democracy would be neither ethically constrained nor paternalistic, since its very success would undermine its own raison d'être as "the people's absent self-government" (345).[16]

With this sober reminder of the daunting task facing would-be reformers, we return to Habermas's own problematic exclusion of workplace democracy from the critical agenda. After having declared that existing forms of class domination are incompatible with realizing the procedural paradigm, one would have thought that he would be more enthusiastic about embracing some market-based conception of economic democracy of the sort defended in chapter 5. Indeed, the problems he himself mentions in connection with collective bargaining—the sacrifice of the private autonomy of rank-and-file union members on the altar of public interest negotiations between high-powered officials—would suggest an obvious procedural solution. But this solution would extend beyond the democratization of union and labor relations boards to include the democratization of the workplace itself (498).

Having pointed out one of the glaring omissions in Habermas's substantive recommendations for democratic reform, let me conclude by indicating his positive contribution to the remainder of my argument. First, both Habermas and Dworkin appreciate the reflexive nature of adjudication as a *synthesis* of different ideals and rationales. Habermas, in particular, conceives this synthesis on the model of communication. Ultimately, the reflexivity of communication requires opening up formally institutionalized legal discourses to informally organized ethical, strategic, and moral discourses. As if to reemphasize the *postmodern*—incomplete and continually deferred—nature of this mediation, Habermas speaks of the "precautionary *interruption* of an otherwise self-referentially closed circle of legitimation" by the judiciary (318).

In the remainder of this chapter I would like to illustrate the tension—alluded to in this last remark—between inclusive integrity, which requires synthesizing disparate legal paradigms into a "self-referentially closed circle of legitimation," and pure integrity, which requires "interrupting" this circle with principled moral mandates emanating from "the People." I can think of no better place to begin than with Ackerman's Kuhnian account of revolutionary paradigm shifts in American constitutional law.

You will recall that Ackerman's model of dual democracy attempts to walk a fine line between Burkean traditionalism and Jacobin republicanism. During periods of *normal* democracy, when the majority of Americans are too lost in mundane pursuits to take much of an active interest in politics, the function of the court is mainly conservative: preservation of hard-fought constitutional freedoms against the tyrannical whims of unrepresentative legislatures dominated by extremists. This reflects the *liberal* cycle of American democracy. However, during periods of *revolutionary* upheaval, when the majority of Americans are intensely engaged in reexamining their constitutional identity, the proper function of the court—after it has appropriately resisted the majority mandate for a new republic—is to acquiesce to it. Thus, contrary to both Hartz's view of the Constitution as a "Lockean consensus" and Pocock's view of it as a modern ideal of republican self-government, Ackerman sees it as neither and both (Ackerman 1991, 25, 201).[17]

The *republican* cycle is of special interest to Ackerman, for it determines the basic track along which higher (constitutional) lawmaking ushers in a new, revolutionary regime. Especially noteworthy for the argument set forth in this chapter is that the cycles ushering in the Reconstruction and the New Deal (the Middle and Modern Republics) revolutionized the *procedures* for higher lawmaking as well (44–50). Both abjured the procedure for ratifying amendments set forth in Article 5 of the Constitution, which placed primary control over initiating and ratifying amendments in the state legislatures. (Congress or the president assumed primary responsibility for the Civil War amendments; in the case of the New Deal, presidential leadership claiming a popular mandate succeeded in persuading a skeptical court to accept revolutionary statutes.) This entailed a corresponding revolution in the constitutional separation of powers. Although Ackerman's discussion of this *procedural* revolution resonates with much that Habermas himself has to say about the transformation in the separation of powers, I shall suggest another point of comparison. These *seemingly illegitimate* deviations from constitutional procedure exemplify the tension between inclusive and pure integrity and in just this sense: In order to legitimate a new regime (or paradigm) claiming a revolutionary moral mandate, the courts must somehow integrate it with the old regime.

According to Ackerman, such a synthesis involves a two-step process. Initially, the new constitutional paradigm is interpreted narrowly. It is less a revolutionary change in *global* principles than a minor revision in *particular* applications. For example, if we see how the Reconstruction amendments were initially interpreted by the Supreme Court—as "superstatutes" to use Raoul Berger's expression—it becomes apparent that their synthesis with the Bill of Rights and the Constitution was not deeply intrinsic, comprehensive, and generalizing, but supplementary, fragmentary, and *particularizing* (Ackerman 1991, 86–90). The due process clause of the Fourteenth

Amendment was first interpreted narrowly, as incorporating the Civil Rights Act of 1866 into the Constitution. This narrowness is reflected in the Court's decision in 1873 in the *Slaughterhouse Cases,* where it ruled against white butchers who claimed that a Louisiana law requiring them to pay a fee to a state-licensed meatpacking company violated their "privileges and immunities as citizens of the United States." In the words of Justice Miller, the only purpose of the Civil War amendments was to protect the "freedom of the slave . . . from the oppression of those who had formerly exercised unlimited dominion over him" (Arthur 1984, 31).

It was not until 1905—thirty years after the particular events motivating its ratification had faded from living memory—that the Fourteenth Amendment's guarantee of equal protection would be interpreted in a more universal, principled light—as radically limiting the statutory power of states vis-à-vis all *national* citizens. Thus, no matter how morally obtuse the majority opinion in *Lochner v. New York* (1905) may seem to us today, it cemented the comprehensive, *revolutionary* meaning of the Fourteenth Amendment as a principle that radically reversed the relationship between the federal government and the states, and between the states and individual citizens (Ackerman 1991, 99–103).

The Middle Republic confronted a single—and from our perspective, relatively simple—problem of synthesis: extension of the Constitution and Bill of Rights to formerly autonomous state and municipal jurisdictions. This revolution did not extend to the most important substantive provisions of the Early Republic, namely freedom of contract—and for good reason. That was the only domain of individual action that the early courts *had* singled out for federal protection. By contrast, the Modern Republic confronted three problems of synthesis. It needed to integrate the "superstatutes" of the New Deal with the constitutional legacy of the Early and Middle Republics *taken separately* and *jointly.*

Once again, the modern court began its synthetic task in a particularistic manner. The first paragraph of the footnote to *Carolene Products* accomplished this in two strokes. First, in addressing the Early-Modern Republic synthesis, it redefined the Bill of Rights as a "list of specific prohibitions." Then, in addressing the Early-Middle Republic and Middle-Modern Republican syntheses, it selectively incorporated those prohibitions ensuring freedom of speech, press, association, and religion into the due process clause of the Fourteenth Amendment. Significantly, none of these rights had been accorded the same degree of protection as contract and property rights under the Early and Middle Republics. But the Modern Republic did more than merely elevate the constitutional standing and scope of older provisions. It diminished the standing and scope of property and contract rights.

It is important to understand how the first step in this synthetic process—the reduction of the Bill of Rights to a list of specific prohibitions—paved the way for the second step. By leveling all prohibitions to the status of *particular* applications of more fundamental principles, *Carolene Products* diminished the status of those prohibitions pertaining to private property and contractual freedom while enabling the possible elevation of others (Ackerman 1991, 121–27).

The three syntheses outlined above could only be completed in the generalizing phase of interpretation, since it was that phase which redefined what was now to be regarded as a paradigmatic right. Unlike the generalizing synthesis effected by the Middle Republic, that effected by the Modern Republic was begun in the very same footnote that detailed the particularizing synthesis. The generalizing synthesis worked out in the concluding paragraphs of the footnote, which I described in chapter 1, took advantage of the latter's leveling achievement by selecting out just those specifics pertaining to *procedural* and *democratic* rights as paradigmatic, universal rights. It did not eliminate contractual and property rights, but it did deny them their fundamental moral and constitutional status. More importantly, it compensated for this loss of former basic rights by inventing new basic rights, to privacy and due process, out of a wholly new conjunction of the Bill of Rights and the Fourteenth Amendment (127–30).

Our all too perfunctory summary of the revolution inaugurated by the Middle and Modern Republics thus confirms Habermas's own hypothesis about the logical progression and synthesis of legal paradigms. The progression from liberal to reflexive paradigms illustrates the way in which the people's moral sovereignty can interrupt the normal legitimation of law. And yet the revolutionary sovereignty of the people remains an elusive notion. What hegemonic alliance stands in for the people is as much a matter of circumstance as any other accession of power, normal or revolutionary—all of which is summed up in Habermas's concluding gloss on Lefort: "[T]he symbolic location of discursively fluid sovereignty remains *empty*" (Habermas 1992, 534).

Unquestionably, just as it had surpassed the corporeal sovereignty of the monarch, the national sovereignty of the people has been surpassed in turn by the sovereignty of an even more abstract idea—democracy—that is itself but a symbol of something even more abstract: reason. No single power of government and no single hegemonic alliance can claim to represent democratic community. Yet thanks to the symbolic imagery of democratic life, all can claim a share in it.

In the concluding chapters we will see that reason, as the idea behind the idea, comprises its own community—and one that is no less political than democracy itself. This community—composed of rationalization complexes, rational values, and rational discourses—must likewise be protected from tyranny. The tribunal responsible for protecting it—the tribunal of reason—has its own judge, the faculty of judgment itself. This faculty, which adjudicates boundary disputes between competing spheres of rationality, must, like any judge, compare and synthesize heterogeneous perspectives, and it must do so analogically. Mediating diverse discourses but determined by none, it is the perfect symbol for a democratic sovereign that is empty, indeterminate, and utterly ideal.

PART IV

The Aesthetic Rationale of History and Politics in a Postmodern Age

7

A Postmodern Legitimation
of Community and Judgment

So far I have argued that reason is communitarian in a distinctly communicative sense. This way of conceiving it enables us to resolve liberalism's legitimation crisis. The model of CR grounds democratic community and individual liberty equiprimordially. Moreover, it does so without sacrificing the complexity of rational society on the altars of unity and opposition. Individual and democratic rights complement one another, so that freedom from noninterference and orientation toward public welfare comprise twin aspects of a CR capable of legitimating laws. The same applies to the separation of powers. The judicial system properly functions to secure the integrity of a democratic process, which in turn reflexively redefines the constitutional scope of legitimate law.

The symbolic imaginary of democracy thus permeates all aspects of economic and domestic life, bringing into play a dialogue between private and public spheres that transforms our most basic needs and identities. But the aesthetic dimension of democratic legitimation penetrates further than the transformation of needs and the symbolic hegemony of deliberative politics. Society as a felicitous balance, interpenetration, and mutual realization of spheres of justice (Walzer), legal integrity (Dworkin), and rationality

(Habermas) implies a kind of aesthetic harmony and integrity as well, the discernment of which is a matter of critical judgment.

But what are the presuppositions underlying this kind of aesthetic judgment? And how do considerations of *taste* enter into our political and historical judgments generally? My answer begins with Kant's seminal account of aesthetic judgment. The past decade has witnessed an extraordinary resurgence of interest in Kant's writings on aesthetics, especially as they pertain to politics and history. On the Continent much of this interest has centered around the debate between modernism and postmodernism. Both sides of the debate are in agreement that Kant's differentiation of cognitive, practical, and aesthetic domains of rationality anticipated the fragmentation of modern society into competing if not, as Weber assumed, opposed lifestyles, activities, and value spheres, and that this has generated a crisis of *judgment*. Tradition is deprived of its authority as a common reference point for deliberation; judgment appears to be all but submerged in the dark void of relativism. Yet, having accepted Kant's differentiation of reason as emblematic of modern complexity, modernists and postmodernists remain divided over its implications. Habermas, Blumenberg, and Arendt appeal to transcendental notions of unity or community to mitigate conflict and fragmentation. This solution recalls Kant's own grounding of judgments of taste in a *sensus communis*. By contrast, postmodernists such as Lyotard embrace conflict and fragmentation with a vengeance—a position that draws from Kant's analysis of the *sublime* as an experience of *incommensurability*. Whereas the modernist emphasizes the capacity of rational agents to rise above the parochial limits of local community in aspiring toward an autonomous perspective, the postmodernist denies the possibility of impartiality altogether, thus binding judgment to traditional contexts.

This way of viewing the debate, I shall argue, neglects the fact that the postmodernist, no less than the modernist, must acknowledge a higher community of discourse. The rational reflexivity of our modern condition may foster indeterminacy and conflict. But it does so only within the compass of a community whose members actively embrace their mutual differences, thanks in part to an exercise of judgment that mediates between plural (and possibly incommensurable) perspectives—a view, as we shall see, that finds ample support in the writings of Arendt (sec. 1), Habermas (sec. 2), and Lyotard (sec. 3).

1. It is vexing to expositors of Kant that he left unclarified what is arguably the most important concept in his philosophy: judgment. Doubtless he meant many things by this term: a "faculty of thinking the particular as contained under the universal" common to cognitive, practical, and aesthetic modes of experience; a capacity for finding analogical passageways linking these disparate modalities; a distinct faculty of taste. The most detailed discussion of judgment occurs in the *Critique of Judgment*, where it is introduced in conjunction with two problems. The former concerns the need to bridge the "immeasurable gulf" separating "the sensible realm of nature and the supersensible realm of the concept of reason." This "gulf" was a by-product of Kant's famed resolution of the free will/determinism problem in the *Critique of Pure Reason*. Since understanding (the faculty that subsumes nature under the law of causality) and reason (the faculty that subsumes volition under the law of freedom) have their source in the subject, it is entirely possible, Kant concluded, that they exercise "two distinct legislations on one and the same territory of experience without prejudice to each other" (Kant 1951, 12). However, if "the concept of freedom is meant to actualize in the world of sense the purpose proposed by its laws," nature, Kant reasoned, "must be so thought that the conformity to law of its (causal) form at least harmonizes with the possibility of the purposes to be effected in it according to laws of freedom" (11–12). Somehow we have to imagine the possibility of a supersensible ground of freely willed purposes producing causal effects in nature. Though such production is beyond our ken, Kant insisted that it is presupposed whenever we try to explain a complex event in terms of natural or historical teleology, or judge nature to be beautiful.

In teleological explanations and aesthetic evaluations we find a species of judgment whose reference to a quasi-objective purpose (or purposiveness) is based on a curious analogy with our own subjective agency. Despite their differences—Kant's own interest in the sublime as a figure of historical progression suggests that they are not always clearly distinguishable—these two types of comparative (or reflective) judgment have a speculative ground in both reason *and* feeling. This is most apparent in aesthetic judgments, whose ground is nothing other than pleasure itself.

The tendency to conclude that judgments of this type are merely arbitrary opinions is fiercely resisted by Kant, who follows Shaftesbury and Burke in defending their presumption of intersubjective validity. It would be folly, Kant notes, to reprove another person's judgment of what is gratifying in an immediate, nonreflective way, since "as regards the pleasant . . . the fundamental proposition is valid: everyone has his own taste [the taste of sense]." Thus "he is quite contented that if he says 'Canary wine is pleasant,' another man may correct his expression and remind him that he ought to say, 'It is pleasant to me.'" It is otherwise in the case of pure aesthetic judgments. A person "judges not merely for himself, but for everyone, and speaks of beauty as if it were a property of things"; hence when he says that something is beautiful "he does not count on the agreement of others . . . because he has found this agreement several times before, but he *demands* it of them" (46–47).

Judgments of taste, then, are at once evaluative and cognitive to the degree that they refer a subjective feeling to an object in a manner conducive to bringing about an expectation of universal agreement. However, unlike judgments of the good or of knowledge, which produce similar expectations, the ground of aesthetic judgments cannot be conceptually represented and objectively demonstrated; one cannot show that a painting is beautiful in the same way that one can show that a saw is useful, a square perfect, an action worthy, or an end universalizable. For to say that something is beautiful is to say nothing at all about its possible utility, worthiness, perfection, or purposiveness with respect to any conceivable end.

But how can judgment lay claim to universal validity if its source is subjective pleasure? One might suppose that an appeal to transcendental grounds would help here, for on Kant's reading of the matter, transcendental judgments attributing categorical properties to objects have their origin in the subject too. The appeal can be made but not, Kant adds, without encountering difficulties arising from the peculiar reflexivity that distinguishes aesthetic from categorical judgments. The categorical properties predicated of objects of knowledge, such as causality and substance, can be proven to be universally and necessarily valid as a priori conditions for experiencing natural or historical events. Ascriptions of this sort are instances of what Kant calls *determinant (bestimmend)* judgment, or predication that subsumes a particular under a *pregiven* universal. Judgments of taste clearly do not determine their object in this way; one does not judge this diamond to be beautiful because it has been universally established in advance that all diamonds are beautiful. Rather, one judges it so only after associating its particular formal attributes with feelings of pleasure. Stated differently, such *reflective (reflektierend)* judgments discover the universal (the beautiful, the sublime, etc.), which best captures our *subjective* response to a given particular.

For Kant, it is the *disinterested* contemplation of an object solely in regard to its *pure form* alone independent of any purpose it might serve (be it subjective gratification of the senses or objective conformity to some concept) that suggests a way out of the grounding dilemma. Might there not be a priori formal conditions of aesthetic pleasure analogous to the formal unity of cognitive faculties underlying the possibility of objective knowledge? The deduction of such a ground cannot, of course, aspire to rigorous demonstration in accordance with concepts or other determinate criteria, since we are here talking about the *exemplary* necessity and universality of certain subjective states of pleasure—our general feeling that all persons of disinterested mind ought to agree in matters of taste—not the apodeicticity of categories of possible objective knowledge. What is at issue here is the existence of a common sense *(sensus communis)* that enables feelings to be communicated as universally as cognitions.

According to Kant, there would be no agreement in persons' feelings or cognitions unless they shared the same cognitive faculties and the same "state of mind" affected by acts of judgment (75–76). In the case of cognitive judgments, a sensible intuition is schematized by the faculty of imagination in *prior conformity* to the laws of the understanding. In aesthetic judgment, however, this formal unity is not predetermined by understanding. Instead, the imagination, representing only the mere form of a particular intuition apart from any sensuous or conceptual content, harmonizes with the understanding spontaneously (128–32).

The feeling of pleasure arising from the *free play* of cognitive faculties permits us to judge the subjective purposiveness, or beauty, of an object in a manner that leads Kant to formulate a new solution to the conflict of faculties. Not only is the imagination in its freedom harmonized with the understanding in its conformity to law, but as Kant later notes, beauty—especially natural beauty—can also be said to *symbolize,* and thereby harmonize with, morality. For Kant, symbols function as indirect representations and, more specifically, as concrete *analogues* or metaphors of rational ideas to which no direct sensible intuition corresponds. In his opinion, nature in the wild, independent of any conceptual or utilitarian associations, excites those pure aesthetic feelings whose underlying formal structure—implicating, free, immediate, universal, and disinterested pleasure—is analogous to the feeling of respect accompanying our fulfillment of moral duty. Hence there is a sense in which the symbolizing of moral ideas such as freedom and the kingdom of ends by means of aesthetic "ideas" implies a supersensible ground (sometimes referred to as *Geist*) identifiable with neither nature nor freedom taken singly (96–99).

Nowhere is this reflective comparison with moral reason more evident than in judging the sublime. Like judgments of beauty, judgments of sublimity are grounded in shared feeling or, more precisely, experience of pleasure arising from the free (playful) harmony *(Zusammenstimmung)* of incommensurable faculties, in this case between imagination and *reason.* The pleasure associated with the sublime is mixed with pain, owing to the peculiar complexity of the judgment in question. Unlike judgments of beauty, in which the imagination apprehends a formal representation in a way that harmonizes with the *understanding,* the imagination here apprehends a representation as so *unlimited* and *exceeding all form* that it discloses not the harmony but the utter inadequacy *(Unangemessenheit),* of intuition with respect to Idea. In the case of the *mathematical* sublime, the imagination's attempt to completely represent an infinite *magnitude* discloses a *disharmony* between imagination and *theoretical* reason. In the case of the *dynamical* sublime, the imagination's attempt to entertain the infinite *power* of raw nature or divinity reveals a disharmony between imagination and *practical* reason. Yet judgments of sublimity also reflect a *harmony* between our finite capacity to resist nature and our infinite, rationally destined empowerment over nature in a manner analogous to the painful /pleasurable feeling of moral respect *(Ehrfurcht)* (82).

As we shall see, this tension between harmony and disharmony, unity and disunity, in judgments of sublimity is emblematic of the kind of *metaphorical* complicity linking incommensurable languages and genres of reasoning—in this instance, those of aesthetics and morality—that Lyotard finds at the heart of all critical conflict. Such complicity also explains the possibility of Habermas's own clinical judgment regarding the integrity (or lack thereof) of modern societies, which depends on a nondemonstrable analogy between aesthetic evaluations, moral prescriptions, and cognitive truth claims. Finally, as I shall now endeavor to show, it undergirds Arendt's own linkage of judgments of taste with the political and historical capacity to "think from the standpoint of everyone else" enjoined by "common human understanding" (136–37).

1.1 The reader who has some familiarity with the modernism/postmodernism debate can now begin to see the relevance of Kant's aesthetics for a nonfoundationalist account of political rationality. To begin with, the conflict between theoretical and practical reason motivating much of Kant's discussion of judgment crops up again in the postmodernism debate. The terms may be different, yet the issue of fragmentation and conflict—in this case involving domains of discourse and action—is the same.

Two questions arise concerning this fragmentation: What place does philosophy occupy in this scheme, and to whom can the political actor appeal in deciding what is right? Lyotard and Habermas are interested principally in the former question, viz., they are concerned about the legitimacy of a discipline that aspires to the status of an impartial tribunal regulating the rightful boundaries of heterogeneous language games, types of rationality, and spheres of justice. In particular, they wonder whether it makes sense to appeal to a transcendent (or transcendental) notion of reason, or community, in defending philosophy's right to judge in these matters. Perhaps a universal ideal of community is operational here, but if so, what kind—one conforming to the harmonistic model underwriting judgments of beauty or one conforming to the transgressional aesthetics of the sublime?

The second question—concerning the questionable authority of traditions that undergird the historical legitimation and identity of political and scientific communities—is addressed primarily by Arendt and Blumenberg. Can political agents whose vision—however revolutionary—is essentially limited by the past aspire to an impartial, spectatorial (or aesthetic) distance on life capable of securing an overarching sense of purpose, meaning, and progress for the future?

I shall begin with Arendt's answer to this second question, which recalls the importance of narrative understanding in constituting the meaning, identity, and purpose of political action. Let us begin with her transcription of Kant's system in *The Life of the Mind* (1978). After treating the *vita activa*—the life of labor, work, and political action—in the *Human Condition* (1958), Arendt returned to some of her earlier concerns pertaining to thinking, willing, and judgment—the triad comprising the *vita contemplativa*, or life of mind, modeled on Kant's three critiques. Kant's distinction between *Vernunft* and *Verstand* is preserved in her distinction between *thought*, which "deals with invisibles, with representations of things that are absent" (the combined capacities of abstraction, critical reflection, and imaginative reproduction and synthesis) and *intellect*, which concerns the necessary conditions for cognition (Arendt 1978, 1:193). Thinking endows life with meaning by weaving experience into a coherent narrative; cognition, which depends on thinking, aims at demonstrable truth. The other, noncognitive faculties of mental life—willing and judging—are also dependent on (but irreducible to) thinking.

It is Arendt's contention that intellect—whose characterization approximates the kind of abstract reasoning I have hitherto designated by SR—has come to dominate and suppress thinking, whose dialogic mode of understanding corresponds to the model of CR. Initially, Arendt proposes to frame this problem as an opposition between modernity—or rather, science and technology—and culture. She begins by conceding the devastating impact the Industrial Revolution had on premodern societies "held together only by customs and traditions" (Arendt 1953, 385). This impact was immediately registered in the degradation of cultural goods to the status of exchange values serving the social aspirations of philistine *parvenus*. With the advent of mass society, artful fabrication of meaningful, enduring culture (work) gave way to the functional production of entertainment and other evanescent consumer goods (labor). Absorption of culture into the life process was not without political implications, since the public sphere—the stage on which the drama of political life is acted out and recorded before an audience of spectator-judges—is itself constituted by the narratives, artistic images, and cultural artifacts that lend it the permanence of *beauty*.

> Culture indicates that art and politics, their conflicts and tensions notwithstanding, are interrelated and even mutually dependent.... [T]he fleeting greatness of word and deed can endure in the world to the extent that beauty is bestowed upon it. Without the beauty, that is, the radiant glory in which potential immortality is made manifest in the human world, all human life would be futile and no greatness could endure. (Arendt 1980, 218)

Inasmuch as political action depends for its enduring appearance, meaning, and purpose on the sound judgment and judicious understanding of a public, the "crisis in culture" is a political crisis as well. Gone is the man of action, replaced by a mass man whose "capacity for consumption [is] accompanied by inability to judge, or even to distinguish" (199).

Symptomatic, too, of the crisis in culture is the widespread dissemination of scientific and technological modes of thought. The rational questioning of traditional authority has had the further consequence of depriving judgment of reliable standards. In conjunction with the rise of state bureaucracy devoted to global economic management, the demise of community based on shared values and common sense is the main culprit in Arendt's account of totalitarianism. Having "clearly exploded our categories of political thought and our standards of moral judgment," totalitarianism challenges not only the capacity of the actor to discern right from wrong, but also the capacity of the historian to understand (Arendt 1953, 379).

Arendt must be credited for bringing to our attention the aesthetic, "democratic imaginary" underwriting the politics of identity and hegemony. At the same time, however, it must be conceded that her own differentiation of political action from labor and cultural fabrication (work) as distinct spheres—a distinction, be it noted, that still survives in a more attenuated, if equally obstructionist, form in Habermas's own assignment of workplaces and public spaces to system and lifeworld, respectively— oddly limits and undermines this notion. Indeed, both she and Habermas segregate worker self-management of businesses from worker self-determination in councils, both holding, apparently, that the latter involves political discussion concerning ethical *ends* while the former only involves technical decisions concerning instrumental *means*. My earlier critique of Habermas's distinction between political discussion and strategic (instrumental) decision, as well as my more general uneasiness with his categorical bifurcation of sociocultural space into science and technology, on one side, and ethical life and communication, on the other, suggests the limits to this way of thinking about democracy. For the time being, it suffices to note that, in the opinion of Arendt and Habermas, such distinctions were necessary in order to provide an ontological or transcendental basis for resisting the hegemonic—and for Marcuse and other members of the early Frankfurt School, potentially totalitarian—ideology of science and technology. Arendt herself believed that totalitarianism arises when ideologies offering solutions to "the social question" (that is, poverty, class conflict, and so on) insinuate themselves into politics in the form of socially engineered recipes of distributive justice. Her preference for Madisonian pluralism over Robespierre's dogmatic insistence that "il faut une volonté UNE"—to which I will return in chapter 8—can be understood in this light as well (Arendt 1973, 76). It reflects her conviction that the "republic of virtue" inevitably degenerates into a "republic of terror" in substituting the certain and methodical engineering of a homogeneous race of harmonious and happy people for the indecisive, self-interested, faction-torn, legislative gridlock of politics.

Again, Arendt's attempt to define the autonomy of the political by extruding transcendental moral aims and virtues from its purview seems just as unwarranted and problematic as her purgation of its economic preoccupations. If the democratic imaginary of modern politics has extended its reach to include workplace and home—indeed, all of society—it is due in no small measure to the role of universal moral rights in constituting the political sphere, a fact about which I shall have more to say in chapter 8. Although it is true that the transformation of public education into moral indoctrination that has been so vigorously advocated by right-wing fundamentalists in recent years poses a certain threat to a system of rights founded on tolerance and motivated by skepticism, it can be argued that it is precisely concern over *economic* justice that has served to counteract this hegemonic agenda. And if it is also true that instrumental approaches to politics reflected in the party system and government bureaucracy suggest the dangers to which Arendt adverts, it is not because they are wholly detached from a realm of pure communicative action. Contrary to Arendt, the political struggle for recognition and identity is also an economic struggle for justice, just as the bureaucratic implementation of policies designed to procure general well-being is also a matter for public oversight and political action.

Despite her anachronistic fondness for the *classical* republican segregation of private (socioeconomic) and public (political) spheres, Arendt
succeeded in diagnosing the crisis of judgment at the heart of modern
nihilism and totalitarianism, a crisis, as we shall see, that eventually led her
to appreciate the *interdependence*—not separation—of moral, political, aesthetic, and historical judgment. The trajectory of this line of thought began
with her reflections on the Eichmann trial in the sixties. Not Eichmann's
diabolical nature (if he possessed one) but his banal thoughtlessness, his
failure to engage in responsible judgment by blindly obeying the orders of
others, was the root cause of his evil. Consequently, Arendt felt that it was
all the more imperative that we ascribe to each and every one "an independent human faculty, unsupported by law and public opinion, that judges
anew in full spontaneity every deed and interest whenever the occasion
arises."[1] But how can one judge or understand the unprecedented inhu-
manity of totalitarianism? What gives the historian the right to judge actions whose circumstances are so novel as to defy comprehension? Isn't
the actor better qualified to judge than the historian?

This question was raised by Gershom Scholem with regard to Arendt's
harsh judgment of those Jewish elders who had urged compliance with
Nazi authorities. Had she not presumed firsthand knowledge of their plight?
While conceding that it might be too early for a "balanced judgment,"
Arendt replied that "the argument that we cannot judge if we were not
present and involved ourselves seems to convince everyone, although it
seems obvious that if it were true, neither the administration of justice nor
the writing of history would be possible" (Arendt 1965, 295–96). The
moral of this story is that if the historian must judge, the actor must understand, or insert his or her own judgments into the broader framework of a
community of persons united by common narratives, meanings, and goals.
Eichmann was evil because he lacked the imagination to take into account
other persons' interests save those limited to his own chosen company.[2] In
the words of Arendt, "[U]nderstanding becomes the other side of [politi-
cal] action" engaged in making a new beginning, for one must "eventually
come to terms with what irrevocably happened and to what unavoidably
exists," including, one would think, the provenance of one's own identity
and that of the community to which one belongs (Arendt 1953, 391).

A crisis of meaning and judgment likewise clouds political action aimed
at initiating fundamental change. The freedom to initiate fundamental
political change imposes a responsibility—the need to legitimate the new
order—that can only be accomplished by situating the founding act within
a historical narrative connecting it to a prior foundation in the past. It was no
accident that the new secular (or worldly) orders founded by the framers

of the Declaration of Independence and the Declaration of the Rights of Man sought legitimation in the civic ideals of classical antiquity. Yet, as we shall see in chapter 8, Arendt—like Blumenberg—denies that the modern age is a simple continuation of the past. Indeed, she believes that the essential freedom and "natality" of world-constituting political action implies a radical break with the past (Arendt 1973, 195–215).

Of course, the break cannot be absolute, lest it deprive itself of the legitimating rationales and meanings provided by the tradition against which it is reacting. Like Hegel, one is tempted to recount a story of progress in which the revolutionary event is justified as inevitable or necessary. But, Arendt notes, this kind of totalizing history, which labors under humanity's *need* to achieve material fulfillment and spiritual (ideological) self-certainty, cannot be written without tacitly denying freedom of the will. Two alternatives remain: one resigns oneself to nihilism or redeems the meaningfulness of the past (along with hope in the future) without any appeal to ultimate ends.

Nietzsche, of course, tried to do both—and failed. He believed that in order to affirm nihilism as a positive expression of its freedom and power willing would have to deny the past—that residue of congealed meaning weighing upon the present and future like a "stone." "Powerless against what has been done," the will, Nietzsche tells us, "is an angry spectator of all that is past."[3] Short of denying time itself (which would usher in the extinction of the will), Nietzsche can only affirm its inherent purposelessness—the "innocence of all Becoming"—in the doctrine of Eternal Recurrence (Arendt 1978, 2:170). A better solution—one that accords with the temporal openness necessary for freedom—would require redeeming each moment of the past by disinterested judgment.

At this juncture Arendt turns to Kant. She here notes two ways in which he sought to apply the concept of judgment in order to retrieve meaning out of political chaos, each demarcating distinct philosophies of history. The first departs from the central tenets of the *Critique of Practical Reason*: We are enjoined by practical reason to strive for moral perfection; such a state presupposes the realization of a universal kingdom of self-legislating agents regarded as ends in themselves, an ideal condition that cannot be attained by imperfect, mortal beings; yet "ought" implies "can"—we can only be obligated to strive for what we have reasonable hope of attaining; hence, we must postulate as regulative ideas the immortality of the soul and divine providence.

The pursuit of moral perfection on earth is taken up further in Kant's miscellaneous writings on history, where he argues that the achievement of a cosmopolitan federation of republics in a state of "perpetual peace" is a precondition for the free exercise of practical reason (Kant 1951, 284). The question is posed whether we have any reason to hope that such a state can be brought about by a species naturally inclined to pursue its own selfish interests. For the moral agent caught up in the vicissitudes of action, the answer would appear to be negative (Reiss 1975, 90). However, from the vantage point of the spectator-judge surveying the totality of human history, the situation is quite different. The basis for this optimism (following the strategy outlined above) resides in the Idea of nature as a supersensible realm of final ends. In response to the question raised in the second half of the third *Critique*—Why is it necessary that man should exist at all?—Kant defends the view that humanity, like any other class of living things, must ultimately be accounted for in terms of teleology, since "absolutely no human reason . . . can hope to explain the production of even a blade of grass by mere mechanical causes" (Kant 1951, 258). On this reading, our natural self-interestedness is judged to be so providentially designed as to force us out of a state of nature (which Kant, following Hobbes, conceives as a state of war) and into a political condition compelling lawful behavior culminating in "a moral predisposition." Man's natural "unsocial sociability" is here understood as causally effecting the progressive advent of an unnatural (i.e., moral) state of peace and harmony in accordance with an Idea of reason. It is this teleologically based interpretation of natural history, then, that perhaps explains how Kant could wax enthusiastic over the sublimity of the French Revolution as a symbol of eternal moral progress while yet condemning the lawlessness of its leaders (Reiss 1975, 182).

The appeal to reason notwithstanding, Arendt finds this use of teleological judgment in resolving the nature/freedom dilemma and explaining the superior insight of the philosopher-historian questionable, since it relegates moral agents to the undignified status of means in attaining prior ends (Beiner 1982, 18, 31). Elsewhere, however, the aesthetic strain prevails in Kant's conceptualization of historical judgment, and it is here, she believes, that the core of Kant's political thought resides. The "wishful participation that borders closely on enthusiasm" that Kant detects in his positive judgment of the French Revolution is described as consisting in "the attitude of the onlookers as it reveals itself *in public* while the drama of great political changes is taking place; for they openly express universal, yet disinterested sympathy for one set of protagonists against their adversaries, even at the risk that their partiality could be of great disadvantage to themselves" (Reiss 1975, 182).

Implicit in this description is an aesthetics of judgment that Arendt characterizes as essentially imaginative, dialogical, and communitarian

(Beiner 1982, 66–67). To begin with, there is the idea that the aesthetic attitude of the spectator is superior to the moral attitude of the actor. From the standpoint of the actor revolution "is at all times unjust," since its success would involve violating the principle of publicity. As Kant puts it, a "maxim which I may not *declare openly* without thereby frustrating my own intention, or which must at all costs be *kept secret* if it is to succeed, or which I cannot *publicly acknowledge* without thereby inevitably arousing the resistance of everyone to my plans, can only have stirred up this necessary and general (hence a priori foreseeable) opposition against me because it is itself unjust and thus constitutes a threat to everyone" (Reiss 1975, 126). This perspective seems to clash with that of the spectator-judge for whom the *sublimity* of the ends takes precedence over the ignominy of the means—in this regard, at least, war is by no means a handmaiden to the "commercial spirit . . . low selfishness, cowardice, and effeminacy" wrought by a successful peace (Kant 1951, 102). Arendt goes on to say, however, that insofar as "publicness is already the criterion of rightness in [Kant's] moral philosophy," the opposition between the practical and aesthetic standpoints and with it "the conflict of politics with morality" is partially resolved (Beiner 1982, 19). The "political moralist," whom Kant sees as forging "a morality in such a way that it conforms to the statesman's advantage" is the one who takes the narrow view of history as a "mere mechanism of nature." The "moral politician," by contrast, is capable of viewing history, if not as a natural process progressively striving to realize a final end, then at least as a theater of moral purposes in which his or her own freedom is tested and affirmed (Reiss 1975, 116–17). In this instance the possibility of taking up the moral standpoint, far from opposing the aesthetic distance of the spectator-judge, actually presupposes it. Publicity not only becomes the great regulator of moral action; it also anticipates an ideal public of spectators who, in *transforming* their solitary perspectives by *communicating* with one another, reach an understanding about the moral sublimity of what is otherwise—when viewed from the moral point of view of the isolated actor—a crime that ought not to have seen the light of day.

Arendt proceeds to unpack the meaning of this ideal in terms of the disinterestedness of the spectator. Of the three maxims of common human understanding mentioned by Kant—think for oneself; think from the standpoint of everyone else; and think consistently—it is the second, the maxim of "enlarged thought," that specifically applies to the disinterestedness of the spectator's judgment. A person of enlarged mind "detaches himself from subjective personal conditions of his judgment, which cramp the minds of so many others, and reflects upon his judgment from a universal standpoint (which he can only determine by shifting his ground to the standpoint of others)" (Kant 1951, 136–37). The importance of enlarged thought for the problem of judgment hinges on the role of imagination. In her earlier essay, "Understanding and Politics," Arendt writes:

> Imagination alone enables us to see things in their proper perspective, to put that which is too close at a certain distance so that we can see and understand it without bias or prejudice, to bridge abysses of remoteness until we can see and understand everything that is too far away from us as though it were our own affair. (Arendt 1953, 392)

Imagination enables one to "represent something to oneself that is no longer present"; thinking subjects the representation to the critical dialogue of the mind. Judging, by contrast, does not deal with representations (universal or otherwise) but "always concerns particulars and things close to hand." Nonetheless, it is "the by-product of the liberating effect of thinking" and "realizes thinking, makes it manifest in the world of appearances" (Arendt 1978, 1:192–93). The thoughtful distancing of imagination "cannot arise unless we are in a position to forget ourselves, the cares and interests and urges of our lives, so that we will not seize what we admire but let it be as it is, in its appearance" (Arendt 1980, 210).

As Ernst Vollrath and Ronald Beiner have pointed out, the kind of impartiality intended here should not be confused with scientific objectivity.[4] It is rather kindred to phenomenological openness; things are to be judged afresh in all their phenomenal richness and inexhaustible particularity without being subsumed in advance under conventional universals or habitual modes of classification. Still, without some mediation of universal and particular neither perception nor judgment would be possible. In the case of phenomenological description particular appearances are elevated to the rank of exemplary universals (essences) through a process of imaginative variation and eidetic intuition. Something similar happens to particular events when judged; brought into relief with the aid of narrative understanding and imaginatively interpreted with an ideal audience in mind, human actions come to exemplify what is best or worst in us, what should or should not be emulated. This is how "redemptive" judgment resolves the antinomy of freedom and necessity, willing and thinking; reconciliation with the past is made possible by endowing the contingent particular with intrinsic meaning and worth.

But surely not all redemptive judgments are legitimate. In the next chapter we will see how judgments of historical progress might be redeemed as imaginary exemplars—not as *cognitive* or developmental-logical schemes. For our present purposes it suffices to emphasize that the *idealization* im-

plicit in the exemplifying (or universalizing) work of aesthetic and historical imagination is *also* captured by Kant in terms of an ideal community, or
audience of interpreters who are thought of as striving to reach impartial
agreement and mutual understanding:

> [U]nder the *sensus communis* we must include the idea of a sense com-
> mon to all, i.e., of a faculty of judgment which, in its reflection, takes
> into account *a priori* the mode of representation of all other men in
> thought, in order, as it were, to compare its judgment with the collec-
> tive reason of humanity. . . . This is done by comparing our judgment
> with the possible rather than the actual judgments of others, and by
> putting ourselves in the place of any other man, by abstracting from
> the limitations which contingently attach to our own judgment. (Kant
> 1951, 136)

Implicit reference is here made once again to the maxim of publicity. In
Kant's opinion, it is not enough to possess a right to the private use of one's
reason, for even the most conscientious exercise of judgment will be biased unless it is exposed to public examination. Hence, even the private
moral judgment of the *actor* needs to be qualified by the public judgment of
the aesthetic spectator, whose imaginative figuration of *possible* perspectives and situations indirectly depends on freedom of speech and press
(Beiner 1982, 74–75).[5] In this sense, Kant's understanding of the complementarity of reflective and determinant (specifically, moral and legal) judgments anticipates Habermas's notion of CR.

If the postmodern condition renders reason and tradition equally suspect as authoritative reference points for judgment, then what can be the
basis for saying that the standpoint of the spectator is any better than that
of the actor? A more congenial way of conceiving their relationship is to
acknowledge their mutual interdependence. Interestingly, some of Arendt's
earlier writings do just this in their anticipation of a postmodern rapproche-
ment between the conventional, casuistic moral judgment of action favored
by the ancients and the rational, distantiated judgment of taste favored by the
moderns. In "The Crisis in Culture," for example, Arendt discusses the
role of *phronesis* in judgment:

> That the capacity to judge is a specifically political ability in exactly
> the sense denoted by Kant, namely the ability to see things not only
> from one's own point of view but in the perspective of all those who
> happen to be present, even that judgment may be one of the funda-
> mental abilities of man as a political being insofar as it enables him to
> orient himself in the public realm, in the common world. . . . The

Greeks called this ability *phronesis*, or insight, and they considered it
the principal virtue or excellence of the statesman in distinction from
the wisdom of the philosopher. (1980, 221)

The juxtaposition of Aristotelian and Kantian motifs is quite surprising
given Kant's own conviction that prudence, or *prudentia* (following Aquinas's
Latin translation of *phronesis*), ought to be excluded from the moral-politi-
cal realm as a "heteronomous" exercise of will. This decision rests on
narrowly interpreting the prudence of the "political moralist" as a purely
theoretical (or technical-practical) skill involving the calculation of means
for efficiently bringing about desired ends, such as "exercising an influence over men and their wills" for the sake of advancing interests of state
(Kant 1951, 8). Aristotle, however, was careful to distinguish *phronesis* from
techne and *episteme*, and accorded it the title of practical wisdom, by which
he meant deliberation over ends as well as means. This activity clearly has
certain features in common with Kant's notion of reflective judgment; it is
"concerned with particulars as well as universals," not simply in order to
subsume the particular under the universal (application), but to discover
the universal, or rather, the proper mean, appropriate to a given situation;
and its exercise involves considering the good of the community as well as
one's own.[6] One reflects on the particular situation and the opinion of
one's fellow citizens in qualifying the universal, and in this regard, at least,
prudence is more open to the particular and less rigidly determined by the
universal than Kant's "law-testing" approach to moral judgment (as Hegel
referred to it). Still, it is quite opposed to Kant's notion of reflective judgment in its focus on the substantive qualifications of statesmanship—experience, cultivation of virtuous character, formation of sound habits, and so
on—which, presupposing active membership within local political communities bound by common customs, cannot fulfill ideal conditions of
impartiality, universalizability, and autonomy (Arendt 1980, 220–21).[7]

One wonders why Arendt ever abandoned this classical conception of
judgment, since it comports much better with the presumed truthfulness
of political opinion—a presumption whose basis admittedly resides in the
shared convictions of a community rather than in the hypothetical
contractarian constructions of moral theorists. Yet, for a civilization whose
identity has become so abstract as to verge on total disintegration, the only
community capable of serving as touchstone for judgment may well be
that disinterested ideal mentioned by Kant. Thus, despite formalistic shortcomings, the "aestheticization" and concomitant "depoliticization" of *sensus
communis* for which Gadamer rebukes Kant is possibly a better gauge of

how things really stand with us than he or any other neo-Aristotelian would care to admit.

In sum, Arendt correctly sides with Kant in grounding political judgment in reason rather than tradition. Even if Gadamer is right about the role that traditional prejudgments play in guiding and constraining everyday practice, the *exercise* of judgment properly comes into its own during those occasions when traditional *habitus* no longer avails us—for example, when we have to choose between competing norms applicable to a given situation. In these instances, we must compare what otherwise appear to be incommensurable criteria or perhaps even incommensurable ways of interpreting the situation at hand, ways of world-disclosure that in turn reflect competing traditional and cultural outlooks. Cognizant of this dissonance, the judge must at least try to rise above the partial perspective of the actor as much as is humanly possible, and adopt an impartial stance encompassing (ideally) all relevant viewpoints. But this requires real communication—or discourses of application, to recall Habermas's account of adjudication.

Still, there remains a profound difference between Arendt and Habermas with respect to the cognitive significance of aesthetic rationality in communicative action and judgment. Arendt denies that aesthetic rationality has a rationally demonstrable basis. From this fact, however, she concludes that *both* aesthetic rationality *and* communicative rationality deal with opinions, not with assertions claiming to be true or false in the strict sense. Of course we cannot presume that our aesthetic judgments will meet with the same universal acceptance as our scientific propositions and deontological moral prescriptions. But surely that cannot mean that they are mere opinions. If they were, we could hardly be expected to take them seriously.

Arendt thus tends to succumb to the kind of aestheticism we diagnosed earlier in our discussion of Rorty. This was not the case in some of her earlier writings. In her essay, "What is Freedom," she spoke of a "judgment *of the intellect* which precedes *action*" (1980, 156; emphasis added). However, in her unpublished lectures delivered in 1965 and 1966 she wavered, first identifying judgment with the "arbitrating function" of the will and then, in her last lectures, aligning it with the noncognitive *vita contemplativa*. Perhaps there are good reasons after all for severing aesthetic judgment from the kinds of pragmatic claims and cognitive functions associated with communicative action. As we shall see below, Habermas himself has followed this path—without, however, relinquishing the unique truth-function of aesthetic rationality (Habermas 1977, 184). Indeed, by openly acknowledging the complexity of political deliberation and judgment in a way that was never fully countenanced by Arendt, he shows even more forcefully why such a path must now be taken, and why it must lead to a more egalitarian, multicultural cultivation of judgmental competencies in us all. However, the *political* relevance of Kant's account of aesthetic judgment—as a largely *intuitive* and *spontaneous* faculty of *mediation*—only becomes fully apparent when examining the way in which *aesthetic experience* critically enlightens our *clinical evaluations* of social pathology.

2. The aforementioned problem of mediation and integrity touches on the first question I posed with respect to Kant's aesthetics, namely, the question concerning the idea of community underlying social critique. We first raised this question in our discussion of Walzer and Taylor. Now we shall attempt to answer it by examining the debate between Habermas and Lyotard.

It is surprising that Habermas mentions Lyotard only once in *The Philosophical Discourse of Modernity* (1987a, xix). After all, Lyotard *is* the leading exponent of the postmodernism Habermas criticizes, and his objections to Habermas's own project confirm this. Simply stated, Lyotard wonders why the pluralizing effects of self-reflexive, self-transcending reason underwrite—rather than undermine—the autonomy and identity of persons living in late modern societies. This objection, in turn, directly challenges the legitimacy and justice of those enlightenment ideals defended by Habermas. For Habermas, justice consists in permitting all persons to participate freely and equally in conversations aimed at reaching consensus on norms regulating their conduct. So construed, norms are legitimated by a universal consensus whose own legitimacy is demonstrably grounded in conditions of rational speech. Taken together, these ideals of justice and legitimation anticipate a democracy whose citizens shape their mutually intertwined identities through collective deliberation on common ends. Lyotard, by contrast, denies the necessity or desirability of unconstrained consensus as a goal of rational speech. He holds that consensus is only one of the possible goals of rational speech and opposes other goals, such as the invention of deviant vocabularies and the assertion of differences. For him, dissensus wrought by invention is preferable to consensus, since it alone subverts the modern trend toward totalitarian homogeneity and majoritarian tyranny.

Rather than disputing the disagreement between Lyotard and Habermas over the justice and legitimacy of rational speech, I propose to use it as a basis for exploring their deeper understanding of the preconditions underlying a more fundamental kind of rationality: the *clinical* judgment of philosophers and political agents engaged in bringing about conditions of global well-being suitable for fostering autonomous agency and integral identity. Such judgment requires drawing essential distinctions between different types of rational comportment, deliberation, and discourse. Its guiding idea is not political justice narrowly conceived but the idea of a community in which distinct spheres of rational comportment—such as those operant within science, economics, politics, law, morality, and aesthetics—communicate with one another in a *just* or nonhegemonic manner.

The problem of bad hegemony indicated here—which opposes the good hegemony discussed in chapter 4—becomes important when we recall the dialectic of enlightenment that comprises the background of their respective philosophies. Like Arendt, both philosophers hold that the pluralizing dynamics of social rationalization encourage forms of specialization that threaten to impoverish laypersons' capacities for autonomous moral reflection. Habermas thinks there are countervailing tendencies within modern culture that offset this inequality; Lyotard does not—unless, of course, this culture is seen as transcending its own logic. However, regardless of their stance on this issue, both believe that the dynamics of postindustrial capitalism exacerbate the problem of a one-sided cultivation of rational competencies in that it encourages the growth of one aspect of rationality—the scientific and technological—at the expense of the moral and expressive. The economic and administrative expansion that fuels this growth in turn disrupts the biopolitical integrity of environment and community requisite for autonomous selfhood.

Criticism of such rational one-sidedness necessitates clinical judgment; discrimination of the proper harmony and felicitous interaction between types of rationality must be guided by an idea—at once descriptive and normative—of their unity. For reasons that will become clear, Lyotard and Habermas eschew the strongly dialectical (or conceptual) solution to this problem developed by Hegel, preferring instead the aesthetic solution provided by Kant's account of reflective judgment.

Our examination of this feature of their thought will require revising certain misconceptions about their respective views of rationality. Contrary to the assumption—held by Habermas among others—that Lyotard is a radical contextualist (or conservative?) who rejects universal ideas of justice, I will argue that the *agreement to disagree* that he appropriates from Kant represents an idea that he and Habermas both find compelling (Lyotard 1984, 73).[8] Habermas's recent concession that "there are no metadiscourses" and no definite criteria of rational unity governing our clinical judgment about pathological forms of rationalization suggests that the idea of community informing such judgment is regulative, not prescriptive. Likewise his staunch opposition to a "dialectics of reconciliation" and his support for a "plural, nonintegral and yet nonseparatist" concept of reason suggests that the kind of communal integrity he endorses is far removed from the harmonistic totality that Lyotard criticizes (Habermas 1991a, 222, 226).

In conclusion, I argue that neither Lyotard nor Habermas provides us with a wholly satisfactory account of the legitimacy and justice of reason qua integral phenomenon. Lyotard fails because of his extreme deference to the anarchism of communication, Habermas because of his equally extreme deference to its idealism. Indeed, it may well be that the grand narrative that they inherit from Kant and that forms the backdrop to their problematic—the dialectic of enlightenment—is incapable of any resolution one way or the other. Yet even if we reject this narrative as an unsatisfactory interpretation of modernity, we still confronted with the problem of cultural hegemony and the problem of reasonably adjudicating spheres of justice, as Michael Walzer puts it. Judgment here necessarily involves *metaphorically* commensurating what appear to be incommensurable types of distributive criteria or—to borrow a phrase from Habermas and Lyotard— incommensurable types of reasons. Given that the judgment in question mediates between conflicting types of criteria instead of being determined by any one of them separately, it cannot be—as Kant correctly observed— discursively demonstrated. At best, it can be indirectly shown—by appeal to more global intuitions and "ways of seeing" that *feel* authentic to us.

Thus, contrary to Habermas, the postmodern critic's refusal to offer propositional support in lieu of narrative interpretation or aesthetic representation does not ipso facto involve commission of a performative contradiction. Moral and expressive judgments combine *determination* of particular instances along with *reflexive* articulation of the rules under which they are subsumed. Thus they mediate indeterminate ideas of reason and determinate contexts of experience in ways that undermine both the modernist's and postmodernist's insistence on rational incommensurability and purity.

2.1 Habermas's critical philosophy seeks to justify modernity in the face of Weber's paradoxes. This defense hinges on rejecting philosophy of consciousness in favor of philosophy of communication. Habermas's appeal to communicative intersubjectivity apparently enables him to avoid the most serious implications of Weber's paradox—the equation of reason with instrumental domination and the equation of social rationalization with capitalism.

Yet residual problems concerning the unity of communicative rationality have not been satisfactorily answered.

First, even if we accept Habermas's claim that there are *exactly* three validity claims that *necessarily* accompany *every* speech act and that these correspond to recognizable types of rational argumentation—theoretical and practical with respect to truth and moral rightness, evaluative and therapeutic with respect to aesthetic appropriateness, sincerity, and authenticity—there remain significant discrepancies between these types of argumentation concerning the *scope* of the anticipated consensus and the moral symmetry of the interlocutors. For instance, Habermas concedes that participants in evaluative discourses raise claims that are not strictly universal, as in the case of practical and theoretical discourse. And he concedes that the relationship of transference binding analyst and analysand in therapeutic discourse deviates from dialogic assumptions of mutual equality and freedom (Habermas 1984, 15).

Second, as noted in chapters 5 and 6, Habermas subtly distinguishes moral types of practical discourse from more complex types associated with political deliberation and adjudication. Along with the first set of considerations, this fact renders the procedural unity of CR even more enigmatic. Not only do different types of reasoning differ from one another procedurally, but no overarching procedure accounts for their complex integration. Since Habermas insists that the core of CR is formal, or procedural, it appears that either no rational unity exists—in which case Weber's paradox has not been dissolved—or that such a unity must be conceived substantively, as a matter of reflective judgment. As the reader will recall from our discussion of Beitz's notion of complex proceduralism in chapter 5, it is the latter disjunct that is here affirmed. For politicians must exercise judgment in contextually harmonizing multiple egalitarian interests in ways that maximize substantively legitimate outcomes in the long run.

The need to harmonize competing—if complementary—ideals and interests becomes more apparent when we turn to the problem of reification, that a critical theory of rationality is supposed to diagnose. Now, social reification occurs whenever the proper balance between cognitive and moral rationalization within society favors the former more than it should, and whenever rational specialization has gone too far in empowering experts and impoverishing lay critics. On Habermas's understanding of the matter, criticism of reification involves a clinical judgment of *health*, or of the right mixture of cognitive, practical, and aesthetic competencies requisite for cultivating happy—well-integrated and evenly developed—moral identities

(73–74). Unfortunately, he nowhere shows that health is a rationally defensible value on a par with truth, justice, and sincerity, all of which find a secure niche in communicative action. Since he says that critical theory must limit its assessments of society to those aspects of reason that *do* find such a niche, he can ground *at most* ideology critique, which derives its standard of truth from the notion of a just, unconstrained consensus (Habermas 1987b, 383). Yet Habermas now thinks that the critique of reification should be the proper task of critical theory (345).

Thus far I have argued that Habermas's account of the procedural unity of rational discourse fails both as a description of the possible integrity of rational comportment and as a normative ground for criticizing reification. However, some of Habermas's tentative remarks about the entwining—or, if one prefers, impurity—of aspects of validity and rationality within so-called purely differentiated types of rational discourse suggests a rather different set of possibilities. The same applies with respect to his speculative pronouncements on aesthetic truth.

The question of impurity can best be approached by recalling a difficult section of *The Theory of Communicative Action* where Habermas argues that different aspects of validity complement one another in grammatically articulated speech. On the one hand, locutionary, illocutionary, and expressive functions are *logically* irreducible. For example, you cannot infer that a person sincerely believes something from the mere fact of her having asserted it to be true; nor can you infer that she ought to do something from that fact that she has factually promised to do it. On the other hand, intermodal transitions between first-, second-, and third-person perspectives clearly reveal structural linkages between locutionary, illocutionary, and expressive functions. First-person expressions of intent or obligation ("I promise you that *p*") are in principle convertible into third-person ascriptions ("He promises him that *p*"). Thus, the asymmetrical conversion of first-person expressives and performatives into third-person assertions implies a *nonreductive structural unity* that makes possible the rational preservation and criticism of context-independent claims. However, such conversion possibilities say nothing about the potential rationality of everyday speech since, on Habermas's interpretation, such speech still manifests a certain disregard for logical distinctions (Habermas 1987b, 62). Thus, we infer that persons believe what they assert to be true and that they incur obligations in factually uttering promissory oaths.

Rational argumentation disallows such leaps in logic. In addition to excluding the metaphorical conflation of validity claims (taking truth-claims as claims for truthfulness), it regiments both type and sequence of reasoning in accordance with a logic specially adapted to a *dominant* validity claim. However, as Habermas notes, the capacity to reflect on the *practical* presuppositions underlying *theoretical* knowledge, the capacity to reflect on the *theoretical* presuppositions underlying *practical* self-understanding, and the capacity to reflect *therapeutically* on the viability of our language as a medium of discourse unconstrained by ideological distortion, suggests that specialized discourses are no less impure when taken to radical extremes (Habermas 1984c, 174). Even when not taken to such extremes, specialized discourses, he observes, typically implicate the full range of validity claims and discursive logics. For instance, moral arguments aimed at justifying general principles frequently raise factual and evaluative questions about the adequacy of case descriptions and the probable satisfaction of genuine needs; and aesthetic critiques aimed at evaluating the authenticity of works of art similarly raise issues pertaining to appropriate descriptions and moral values (Habermas 1987b, 398).

These impurities are even more pronounced in the case of those specialized discourses, such as philosophy and art criticism, that serve to communicate the highly technical insights of the arts and sciences in a more colloquial language accessible to the layperson. This potential for mediation can serve to mitigate one of the pathological tendencies associated with the diremption of modern reason: the splitting off of elite subcultures. The resolution of this problem requires not only disseminating technical knowledge relevant to democratic decision making but also restoring to ordinary citizens critical competencies that have been lost in the culs-de-sac of specialized discourses. If citizens cannot become experts, they can at least acquire the knowledge and critical skills necessary for holding them accountable. Philosophy and literary criticism can facilitate the critical mediation of technical expertise and everyday language, because they are at once discursive (specialized with respect to single validity aspects, like expert discourses) and colloquial (deploying rhetorically and metaphorically charged expressions that violate the cognitive demand for clarity and semantic consistency) (Habermas 1987a, 209).

The use of metaphorical language in mediating aspects of validity and rationality assumes even greater importance in Habermas's discussion of the critical power of art to illuminate social reification resulting from the colonization of a communicative lifeworld by the economy and the administrative system. Indeed, works of art represent a specially significant illustration of the intermeshing of validity claims and rationality aspects inasmuch as they function simultaneously as arguments and as idealized anticipations of integral experience.

2.2 In order to appreciate the political significance of Habermas's aesthetic theory—especially its attribution of a critical, enlightening function to modern works of art—one must situate it against the backdrop of his defense of modernity against Weber's paradox. Modernity, as he understands it, is preeminently an aesthetic phenomenon. Although previous epochs dating back to the fifth century may have understood themselves as modern relative to a superseded past, they did so in the name of a renewal (or imitation) of the past. What distinguishes the *aesthetic modernity* that arose in the course of the nineteenth century from, say, the classicism of the Renaissance or romanticism of the early nineteenth century was the former's "abstract opposition between tradition and present." According to Habermas, this opposition designates *both* a "changed consciousness of time" (the "anticipation of an undefined future . . . the experience of mobility in society, acceleration in history, of discontinuity of everyday life") *and* a "principle of unlimited self-realization" ("the demand for authentic self-experience") (Habermas 1981, 3–4).

As we shall see, this account of modern *cultural* consciousness resonates with the postmodern account given by Lyotard. Significantly, both Habermas and Lyotard relate these cultural changes to socioeconomic ones. While modern, industrial capitalism "commodified" spatiotemporal relationships in the form of rigid bureaucratic routines (the mechanical segmentation and quantification of labor in terms of abstract, sequential units) and spatial landscapes (the mechanical division of labor functions and urban sites), postindustrial capitalism *compresses* them. David Harvey and others have observed that the new regime of "flexible accumulation" has shortened the time-space gap between production and consumption thanks to new systems of transportation and telecommunication. Enabling the exploitation of cheap, Third World labor and the rapid "mobilization of all the artifices of need inducement," global changes in financing and speculation have produced economic instabilities, as reflected in extreme fluctuations in currency exchange rates, a rising number of bank failures, and so on. These instabilities, in turn, have had profound cultural effects, ranging from an experience of transiency and contingency to a feeling of superficiality, anarchy, and meaninglessness.[9] Hence Harvey's symptomatology of postmodern culture as a pathological expression of bourgeois decadence.

Conservative critics such as Daniel Bell view these developments with dismay, often citing a familiar litany of pathological symptoms—"hedonism, the lack of social identification, the lack of obedience, narcissism, the withdrawal of status and achievement competition"—that ostensibly confirm the pernicious effects of aesthetic modernity on the traditional ethos of family and work (5–7). By contrast, radical critics—and here Habermas

chiefly has in mind French poststructuralists of Nietzschean provenance—
embrace aesthetic modernity as an antidote to the freedom-denying aspects of modern economic and administrative life (13–14).

Although his sympathies are with the radicals, Habermas looks askance
at their antimodernism, which he believes reflects an abstract opposition
between modern art and modern, rationalized culture. Habermas distinguishes four main periods in the development of modern art that conform
very closely to Weber's analysis of rationalization (9–10). The *Renaissance*,
he claims, marked the removal of art from the public domain of religious
cult into markets for private consumption. The beautiful is now constituted
as a distinct value, complex stringed and wind instruments are invented,
and scientific and mathematical principles are deployed in the pictorial
representation of linear and atmospheric perspective, the engineering and
construction of new architectural forms, and in the development of musi-
cal notation and harmony. Next, Habermas notes that toward the end of
the eighteenth century popular literature, music, and other fine arts were
publicly institutionalized—outside of courtly and religious life—in museums, theaters, concert halls, and literary magazines. The use of culture for
purposes of popular moral enlightenment is here accompanied by the
appreciation of the sublime as a distinct aesthetic value. The next wave,
late romanticism, gave birth to aestheticism (art for art's sake) and a corresponding hedonistic counterculture which encouraged the separation of
artistic production and critique from the popular demands of the marketplace. This resulted in a redirection of artistic aims away from representation and moral enlightenment toward expression. It was accompanied by
the rise of an avant-garde whose reflections on the media and techniques
of production show how "the enhanced instrumental rationality of an art
that makes its own production processes transparent enters into the service
of enhancing aesthetic value" (Habermas 1984b, 178). Finally, according
to Habermas, the present century witnessed the introduction of dynamic
mechanisms of artistic reproduction such as film, radio, television, and so
on, which revolutionized perception and "completed" the process of
artistic deritualization. Accompanying this development were new art
movements such as surrealism and dadaism which challenged the right of
art to exist and questioned the separation of art and life, fiction and praxis,
appearance and reality. These movements were later superseded by
"postmodern" or "post-avant-garde" countermovements announcing the
"end of art." Conceptual art, earth art, pop art, computer video art, photo-
realism, and neo-Expressionism are just some of the examples mentioned
by Habermas that illustrate this trend.

What chiefly interests us about the above account is its *dialectical* characterization of aesthetic rationalization. On one hand, art has become *worldly*. Having been emancipated from religion and courtly life, it now functions as a vehicle for popular enjoyment. On the other hand, art—above all, avant-garde art—has become *transcendent*. This *countermovement*, which Habermas characterizes as a splitting off of *high* culture from *popular* culture, is attributed to both external and internal factors. The desire to cultivate art for its own sake that emerged toward the end of the nineteenth century arose, he notes, in opposition to the growing *commodification* of popular culture. Yet in order to remain faithful to art's intrinsic values of expressive authenticity avant-garde artists were driven to purify it of those cognitive and moral accretions that normally accompanied its popular reception.

It was with the advent of surrealism and dadaism, Habermas maintains, that the avant-garde showed its profoundly ambivalent and dialectical nature. The radical exploration of subjectivity undertaken by surrealists led them beyond subjectivity in the direction of the unconscious and its hidden relationship to life (Freud). This *return to life*, however, marked a return to a reality that conflicted with the *objectified* and *commodified* reality of everyday life. It was less secularization than *profanation*, less affirmation than negation. As Habermas puts it: " The *purification* of the aesthetic from *admixtures* of the cognitive, the useful, and the moral, is mirrored . . . in the surrealistic celebration of *illumination* through shock effects with its ambivalence of attraction and repulsion, of *broken continuity*, of the shudder of profanation, of agitated disgust: in short in the reflection on those moments in which the bewildered subject 'transgresses his boundaries,' as Bataille puts it" (Habermas 1984a, 200–201).

The surrealist revolt was directed against both the quasi-sacral transcendence of *high* culture *from* everyday life and the assimilation of *popular* culture *to* everyday life. In Habermas's opinion it failed to deliver on either account. The attempt to mediate art and life failed because it ended up collapsing the aesthetic and the practical, but not in a way that produced emancipatory effects. The desublimation of meaning that follows from the destruction of aesthetic *form*—for Habermas and Adorno the unifying feature that sets *autonomous* art *above* everyday life—"can just as easily signify the degeneration of art into propagandistic mass art or into commercialized mass culture" (Habermas 1975, 86). The attempt to overcome the transcendence of high culture likewise failed: it "gave new legitimacy, as an end in itself, to appearance as the medium of fiction, to the transcendence of the art work over society, to the concentrated and planned character of artistic production as well as to the special cognitive status of judgments of taste" (Habermas 1981, 10).

If Habermas remains skeptical of attempts to mediate art and life it is not because he doubts their *inherent rationality*. An avant-garde aesthetic that has become so entrenched in the specialized language of personal expression that it no longer *communicates* in any meaningful way with the moral aspirations and cognitive orientations of everyday life is *irrational*. This ambivalence in Habermas's attitude toward aesthetic rationalization is reflected in his mixed assessment of both the *technical* achievement of avant-garde art and the *autonomy* of aesthetic *form*. To begin with, Habermas believes that advances in artistic technique make "transparent" the production process in a way that promotes the clarification of basic aesthetic experiences (Habermas 1984b, 177–78). At the same time, however, he agrees with Weber and Adorno that advances in technique do not necessarily issue in advances in value (Habermas 1975, 161, 177). With regard to value enhancement in the aesthetic domain "the idea of progress fades into that of renewal and rediscovery, an innovative revivification of authentic experiences." Such renewal is placed in doubt by the technical realization of art itself. The technique of automatic painting deployed by surrealists, for example, gave free play to unconscious impulse in a way that frustrated the *conscious, self-critical* renewal of authentic experience. The *formation* of free subjectivity that bourgeois art formerly accomplished was thus negated in the Dionysiac profanation of *formal* limits.

Yet Habermas also harbors reservations about the value of autonomous art. To understand why this is so one must turn to his analysis of the critical role that autonomous art played in shattering the humanistic illusion of reconciliation contained in *pictorial or representational* forms of bourgeois art. According to Habermas, the bourgeois art of the nineteenth century was able to have an impact in shaping the identity of citizens as free, integrated persons only positively, or *ideologically* (78). It could not fully succeed in advancing *critical enlightenment* because it had not yet attained full independence from everyday life. This *incomplete rationalization*, or *partial* separation of art from the moral and cognitive values of everyday life, enabled art to *affirm* existing reality as *ideally* (i.e., harmonistically) depicted, thanks in part to the quasi-religious authority accruing to it in virtue of its enshrinement in museums. It was only in this way that the commodity owner could encounter himself in solitary contemplation as a fulfilled human being. With the deritualization of art—above all, in the passing away of representational art in favor of purely *formal*, abstract art— there arose "a counterculture, arising from the center of bourgeois society itself and hostile to the possessive-individualistic, achievement- and advantage-oriented lifestyle of the bourgeoisie" (85).

Adorno believed that "after the destruction of the aura, only the

formalist work of art, inaccessible to the masses, resists the pressures toward assimilation to the needs and attitudes of the consumer as determined by the market." Habermas, however, remains unconvinced by
Adorno's appeal to modernism, citing in support of his disbelief the dialectical reversal of an *autonomous* art that has removed itself from everyday
life:

> Adorno's thesis can be documented with examples from literature
> and music only insofar as these remain dependent on techniques of
> reproduction that prescribed isolated reading and contemplative lis-
> tening (the royal road of bourgeois individuation). In contrast, for arts
> received collectively—architecture, theater, painting—just as for popu-
> lar literature and music, which have become dependent on electronic
> media, there are indications of a development that points beyond mere
> culture industry and does not *a fortiori* invalidate Benjamin's hope for a
> generalized secular illumination. (Habermas 1983, 142)

It is thus in the spirit of defending a secular art that might proffer both
critical and *popular* enlightenment that Habermas affirms the intention underlying the surrealist revolt. Questioning Marcuse's own ambivalence with
respect to autonomous art and popular counterculture he remarks: "I'm
not sure whether Marcuse does justice to the experimental logic of the
artistic avant-garde, which in the wake of surrealism, using extreme means
(even to the point of demonstrative muteness), lays bare the petrified forms
of speech and interaction, i.e., negates them up to the very threshold of a
self-negating art" (167).

No doubt the ambivalence that Habermas finds in Marcuse is a reflection of his own. He too is torn between two types of modernist aesthetic:
the formalism of the one establishing a *critical distance from*, the antiformalism
of the other a *relationship to*, everyday life. As the above passages indicate, it
is Benjamin who (despite his defense of surrealism) provides a way out of
this dilemma. For Habermas, the *post*-avant-garde work of art deploys techniques of artistic (re)production (Benjamin) that render its own form problematic in a manner that critically illuminates the reification of everyday
life. At the same time, however, he believes that such "Brechtian" techniques might also serve the task of *positive enlightenment*—the projection of
something like a *reconciled* life.

I shall return to Habermas's resolution of the dialectic of aesthetic
rationalization. What presently concerns us is the charge by neo-
conservatives that aesthetic modernity is responsible for the degradation
of culture to commodity fetish, instrumentalized for hedonistic and narcissis-

tic purposes. What distinguishes their critique of modern art from Habermas's is their attribution of these symptoms to cultural and social rationalization. In this respect they reiterate Weber's analysis of the adversarial relationship obtaining between cultural value spheres and their antagonistic embodiment in scientific, moral-juridical, and artistic-erotic forms of life.

Habermas's attempt to rescue aesthetic modernity from the clutches of Weber's paradox defies summary description. However, a few remarks may suffice to indicate the general outlines of his strategy. Habermas claims that selective rationalization occurs when "(at least) one of the three constitutive components of cultural tradition is not systematically cultivated *(bearbeitet)* or when (at least) one cultural value sphere is insufficiently institutionalized without a structure-building effect for the whole society or when (at least) one sphere of life prevails so far that it subordinates other orders of life under its alien form of rationality" (Habermas 1984b, 240). A society would not be fully rational if it allowed scientific and technological values to occlude or otherwise prevent moral and aesthetic values from having a structure-building effect for *society as a whole;* nor would it be fully rational if economy and state absorbed communicative lifeworld.

Of course, persons are free to adopt, say, either a scientific or a moral point of view in their dealings with society. For Habermas this means that conflicts between overlapping "rationality complexes" are unavoidable. There is no easy way, for example, to resolve the dispute between functionalistic and interpretative sociology, except perhaps to insist upon the equal (but limited) rights of both. Fortunately, conflicts between rationality complexes are limited, Habermas claims, by the fact that not all points of view are susceptible of being converted into rational learning processes furthering the progressive accumulation of knowledge. Habermas does not think that a scientific orientation toward the subjective world of desire (a hedonistic calculus) can succeed as a rationalizable endeavor. The same, he feels, applies to moral and aesthetic orientations toward nature and society respectively.

What is important here is the *exclusion* of a domain of aesthetic "learning" by which societies might evolve more sophisticated, or "enhanced," visions of their own collective good, health, and happiness. Habermas asserts that "expressively determined forms of interaction" (e.g., countercultural forms of life) "do not form structures that are rationalizable in and of themselves" (328). This view—which seems so antithetical to the remarks he made in conjunction with Marcuse's ambivalence toward popular avant-garde countercultures—deprives society of perhaps the only medium capable of communicating aesthetic discoveries gained in rational discourse to social agents engaged in everyday moral conversation. In doing so, however, it also appears to sanction a kind of selective rationalization. The interplay of value spheres, rationalization complexes, and lifestyles that instantiates a collective vision of global well-being is *cut off* from potential sources of aesthetic enlightenment. That being the case, it is all the more incomprehensible how Habermas might appeal to reason in adjudicating the aesthetic conflict between form and function that continually resurfaces in public policy making in general and urban planning in particular.

2.3 The path leading from this impasse to a critical theory of aesthetic rationality was already prepared in Habermas's break with his predecessors in the Frankfurt School. If we are to believe Habermas, the single most important difference between his aesthetics—indeed, his philosophy generally—and theirs is his relinquishing of philosophy of consciousness for communication theory. Habermas anchors aesthetic value in an expressive claim to truthfulness *(Wahrhaftigkeit)* that (along with claims to truth and rightness) is tacitly raised by speakers oriented toward reaching mutual understanding. In assuming the truthfulness of a speaker one not only takes for granted that the *feelings, desires,* and *tastes* she implicitly and explicitly expresses are those she actually has, but also that they are the ones she would have upon deeper reflection. In other words, we assume both that the speaker is truthful to us *and* truthful to herself, that is, that she has not deceived herself regarding her true feelings, desires, and tastes.

Now, it is unclear how the presumed truthfulness of speakers oriented toward reaching agreement for purposes of coordinating action has anything whatsoever to do with art and aesthetic enlightenment. Not only is everyday speech utterly prosaic and utilitarian, but the language of art seems to be highly subjective—hardly the sort of thing that one associates with the raising of universal claims.

The problem can be stated thus: Assuming that art communicates anything at all, it does not communicate in the way that everyday speech action communicates. This difficulty can be approached from the standpoint of Habermas's attempt to explain poetic language. In an early study "What Is Universal Pragmatics?" Habermas did not distinguish poetic language or aesthetic critique from his general theory of communication. This lent the impression that poetic language no less than everyday speech raises validity claims to truth, normative rightness, truthfulness, and comprehensibility. Fiction, comedy, theater of the absurd, nonsense poetry—not to mention art exhibitions, concert performances, and dances (which

Habermas [p. 41] regarded as unintentional behavior rather than speech action)—are all instances that refute this view.

Owing in part to criticisms by J. B. Thompson, Jonathan Culler, and others, Habermas has recently thought it necessary to distinguish poetic, fictive, and other aesthetic "languages" from everyday speech.[10] This has been accomplished in three strokes. First, he has expanded the repertory of linguistic functions to include a "poetic" disclosure of the world. Second, he has enriched the concept of a validity claim to include nonpragmatic expressive and evaluative claims. Finally, he has elaborated a notion of aesthetic *critique* that deviates in important respects from the standard model of argumentative rationality.

Habermas discusses poetic language at some length in *The Philosophical Discourse of Modernity*. He contends that poetry and fiction are *parasitic* on everyday discourse without being reducible to it. His main support for this thesis comes from the work of Roman Jakobson and Richard Ohmann, for whom "a literary work creates a world . . . by providing the reader with *impaired* and incomplete speech acts which he completes by supplying the appropriate circumstances."[11] This view runs contrary to some of Habermas's earlier opinions about poetry. In "A Reply to My Critics" (1982) he said that poetry as well as jokes and games were parasitic on communicative action in that they involved a deliberate *conflation* of validity claims to truth, rightness, and so on. He now describes the parasitic relationship and corresponding impairment as an *uprooting* of speech acts from their normal context of use (Habermas 1982, 270)

This is not to deny that poetic elements inhere in everyday language. Habermas approvingly cites the research of Mary L. Pratt (1977), who uses the sociolinguistic studies of W. Labov to show that normal language is permeated with fiction, narrative, metaphor, and rhetoric. Yet these studies, Habermas claims, do not "speak against the attempt to explain the autonomy of the linguistic work of art by the bracketing of illocutionary forces." For, "what grounds the *primacy* and the structuring force of the poetic function is not the deviation of a fictional representation from the documentary report of an incident, but the exemplary elaboration that takes the case out of its context and makes it the occasion for an innovative, world-disclosive, and eye-opening representation in which the rhetorical means of representation depart from communicative routines and take on a life of their own" (Habermas 1987a, 203).

Habermas's attempt to explain the poetic bracketing of communicative validity claims by appeal to "an innovative, world-disclosive, and eye-opening representation" points to a fundamentally different function of language—one similar to Arendt's own stress on the redemptive features of judgment and culture, but distinct from the world-founding function attributed to art by Heidegger (98–99), which it superficially resembles. Yet it is not quite accurate to say (as Habermas does) that the poetic use of language in fiction involves bracketing all illocutionary (normative) forces. For as he himself points out, such uses also raise validity claims, albeit for purposes having nothing to do with coordinating action. Unlike the expressive function of speech action, in which Habermas initially sought to ground the aesthetic, the poetic function is not dependent on a claim to sincerity. It is, however, dependent on a claim to worthiness: "before a text can lay claim to the patience and discretion of the audience, it also has to satisfy certain criteria of relevance: it *has to be worth telling*" (Pratt). In particular, "tellability has to be assessed in terms of the manifestation of some significant exemplary experience. . . . [that] reaches beyond the local context of the immediate speech situation and is open to further elaboration" (203). Habermas adds that, besides the claim to *exemplary validity*, literary texts also raise claims to *artistic truth, aesthetic harmony (Stimmigkeit), innovative force*, and *authenticity* (207).

The inclusion of authenticity in the list of claims attached to poetic functions raises an interesting problem. Might there not be aesthetic validity claims, such as authenticity, that are sometimes expressively raised in communicative action? Might the poetic function of art serve to *enlighten* speakers as to their *true* (authentic) interests *so as to further facilitate the pragmatic function of coordinating action around shared values?* The answer for Habermas is clearly yes: "[A]ctions regulated by . . . expressive self-presentations and also evaluative expressions supplement constative speech acts in constituting a communicative practice . . . oriented to achieving, sustaining, and renewing consensus . . . that rests on the intersubjective recognition of criticizable validity claims" (1984b, 17).

Of the two sorts of expressions mentioned above, *evaluative* expressions are the ones that directly impinge upon the aesthetic. They can either refer to works of art (in which poetic claims are raised) or to needs, interests, and so forth that refer to *practical* values and even norms. As Habermas points out, their status is somewhat murky. Evaluations "are not simply expressive—that is, manifesting a merely private feeling or need— nor do they lay claim to be normatively binding." Nevertheless—and this is the important point—they can be rationally justified in terms of standards of value by means of which a *given* historical community interprets its needs.

A person who makes an aesthetic judgment does not presume that any and all rational persons would consent to it:

> Cultural values do not appear with a claim to universality, as do norms of action. At most values are *candidates* for interpretations under which a circle of those affected can, if occasion arises, describe and normatively regulate a common interest. The circle of intersubjective recognition that forms around cultural values does not yet in any way imply a claim that they would meet with general assent within a culture, not to mention universal assent. For this reason arguments that serve to justify standards of value do not satisfy the conditions of discourse. (20)

Habermas's defense of the rational nature of aesthetic evaluation owes a great deal to Kant. Like Arendt, Habermas clearly wants to retain Kant's subsumption of the aesthetic under a kind of communicative (or communitarian) rationality linked to the redemption of evaluative judgments claiming *exemplary validity*, but without the transcendental or psychological "baggage." This retention, however, is problematic. Habermas claims that what is at stake in the redemption of aesthetic claims is "the application of a standard of value as *appropriate (angemessen)* or *inappropriate* (1984b, 39). But appropriate (or adequate) to *what*? On one hand he suggests that the basis for rational agreement must be the shared value standards that already find acceptance by members of a particular cultural community: "Anyone who is so privatistic in his attitudes and evaluations that they cannot be explained and rendered plausible by appeal to standards of evaluation is not behaving rationally" (17). Now if someone has a *good reason* for indulging an unusual appetite (Habermas cites Richard Norman's example of a person wanting a saucer of mud because he or she enjoys its rich river smell), others might still "recognize in these descriptions their own reactions to similar situations." However, in the case of idiosyncratic expressions ("the spectrum ranges from harmless whims, such as a special liking for the smell of rotten apples to clinically noteworthy symptoms, such as a horrified reaction to open spaces") such understanding, Habermas claims, will be lacking (16–17).

On the other hand, Habermas recognizes that community standards cannot be the last court of appeal in defending the rationality of one's value preferences, since the former may in fact be perverted or otherwise irrational. Thus we "call a person rational who interprets the nature of his desires and feelings *(Bedürfnisnature)* in the light of culturally established standards of value, but especially if he can adopt a reflective attitude to the very value standards through which desires and feelings are interpreted" (20). Once again, we are reminded that persons who are truthful to others must be truthful to themselves; the needs and values that they profess to have should be *authentic*, or reasonable (appropriate) given their situation.

Aesthetic learning thus occurs in a medium of critical reflection in which "the adequacy of value standards, the vocabulary of our evaluative language generally, is made thematic." Art and its criticism create and disseminate *new* standards of value; they authentically express *exemplary experiences*. To repeat what has been said before, they function *poetically* in revealing possibilities of world-disclosure. Like all learning processes such reflection involves rational dialogue in which only the force of the better argument prevails. However, unlike theoretical and practical discourse, the form of aesthetic argumentation is *indirect*, if not *experiential*, or *prediscursive*:

> In this context reasons have the peculiar function of *bringing us to see* a work or performance in such a way that it can be perceived as an authentic expression of an exemplary experience, in general as the embodiment of a claim to authenticity. *A work validated through aesthetic experience can then in turn take the place of an argument and promote the acceptance of precisely those standards according to which it counts as an authentic work.* In practical discourse reasons or grounds are meant to show that a norm recommended for acceptance expresses a generalizable interest; in aesthetic criticism grounds or reasons serve to guide perception and to make the authenticity of a work of art so evident *that this aesthetic experience can itself become a rational motive for accepting the corresponding standards of value.* (20; emphasis added)

Aesthetic critique thus differs both quantitatively and qualitatively from theoretical and practical discourse: quantitatively insofar as an evaluative claim to validity cannot claim universal assent; qualitatively in that some of the "reasons" that "bring us to see" a work or performance as "an authentic expression of an exemplary experience" are themselves aesthetic experiences. In a note to the above passage Habermas suggests that what guides perception in these instances is the *perlocutionary*—or nonexplicit and prediscursive—effect attached to what are otherwise simple, nonevaluative descriptive statements such as "The drawing X is particularly balanced." Unlike discourse, a perfectly appropriate aesthetic "reason" might consist of emphatic pointing (perhaps accompanied by perlocutionary inducements of the form "Just see here!" or "Just feel [imagine] it!"), a deconstruction of meaning or—as in the case of someone confronted with the sublime incommensurabilities of a chain of heterogeneous speech acts (Lyotard)—silence.

2.4 The reader who has followed the argument thus far may well wonder what the preceding discussion of aesthetic language and critique has got to do with the problem stated at the outset. Recall that Habermas sets out to defend modern rationality (including the aesthetic variety) against Weber's paradox. Rationality, he claims, is not inherently irrational; it does not lead to a loss of freedom, meaning, and value. Weber was wrong to think that all values were grounded in particular religious convictions. Truth, rightness, and truthfulness are *formal* value orientations necessarily implicated in speech. Moreover, the "irrational" relegation of art to connoisseurs cut off from mainstream life, as well as its degradation to hedonistic entertainment, is not necessitated by the "inner logic" of aesthetic rationalization, but by its subsumption under the commodity form.

Now, I concluded my summary of the above defense by noting a residual problem: Habermas's proposal to limit the conflict between differentiated value spheres involves depriving artistic counterculture of any rationalizing effect on society as a whole. Without such an effect it remains unclear how social agents might come to be enlightened as to their common good. This problem is partially remedied by Habermas's treatment of aesthetic rationality. Persons in everyday life confront one other with opposing needs and interests—visions of the good, if you will—that can be rationally argued in aesthetic critique. Moreover, outside the framework of communicative action persons exposed to art can *experience*—in communion with others but also alone—the poetic illumination of their world, and this illumination can also effect a transformation of their needs and interests.

As early as 1980 Habermas, following the advice of Albrecht Wellmer, developed the notion of poetic illumination in a manner that underscored the differences between aesthetic critique specialized with respect to expressive claims to authenticity and aesthetic reception. The bourgeois sought to relate aesthetic experiences to everyday life problems but in an affirmative manner that confused the specialized role of the professional critic with the everyday mode of aesthetic experience. These two sides cannot be collapsed, for, as Habermas points out, the "exclusive concentration on one aspect of validity alone, and the exclusion of aspects of truth and justice, breaks down as soon as aesthetic experience is drawn into an individual life history and is absorbed into everyday life" (Habermas 1981, 12). More specifically, "as soon as such an experience is used to illuminate a life-historical situation and is related to life problems, it . . . not only renews the interpretation of our needs in whose light we perceive the world" but it also "permeates as well our cognitive significations and our normative expectations and changes the manner in which all these moments refer to one another" (12).

Still, it can scarcely be denied that the sort of rational "problem solving" engaged in by artists and professional critics regarding technique, formal unity, expressivity, and so on seems far removed from the day-to-day concerns of the average citizen. There seems to be, in other words, a tension between aesthetic critique as a *rationalizable* undertaking and *popular* aesthetic *reception*. Unlike the former, the latter is not specialized with respect to expressive values only, but encompasses all aspects—cognitive, moral, and aesthetic—of *experience*.

Indeed, as we noted above, Habermas's own treatment of aesthetic critique—in which experience itself functions as a reason for accepting an artwork's claim to exemplify authentic values—already blurs the distinction between critique and experience. If this blurring seems unproblematic, it is because experience is here narrowly correlated with *subjective* feelings, desires, and needs. However, in discussing the capacity of art to illuminate a life-historical situation, Habermas equates experience with a holistic preunderstanding, or illumination of a world, in which cognitions, moral expectations, and needs interpolate one another. In speaking of *this* experience, Habermas contrasts the rational *specialization* of the aesthetic in artistic countercultures—that is, its restriction to the interpretation and expression of subjective needs—with the rational *dissemination* of popular aesthetic enlightenment. This creates a problem, however. For although he is willing to weaken the distinction between *subjective* experience and rational critique, he is not willing to weaken the distinction between rational critique and *holistic* experience. Weakening the latter distinction would violate the concept of rational discourse, which always remains specialized with respect to a single validity claim referring to a single world modality—either subjective, objective, or social. But if holistic experience is so strongly segregated from rational critique, wherein lies its rationality?

As we shall see, even if the narrow specialization of rational discourse makes some sense within the context of science and possibly morality, within the context of aesthetic critique it does not. For here the insinuation of holistic (and not merely subjective) experience requires a form of rational discourse that metaphorically mediates cognitive, moral, and expressive validity claims. Consequently, however much professional art criticism differs from popular aesthetic reception, it does not differ from it the way Habermas thinks it does.

Given this, it is important to note that as Habermas's awareness of the difference between pragmatic communication and poetic language grew, so did his insistence on distinguishing specialized from nonspecialized forms of aesthetic critique. Formerly Habermas had believed that art could be understood as raising *pragmatically functional, purely expressive* claims to *authenticity* that might influence the reinterpretation of *subjective needs*. Now, however, he argued that works of art raise *purely aesthetic* claims that are not subordinate to *pragmatic communicative functions* but refer entirely to *experience*.

> The aesthetic "validity" or "unity" that we attribute to a work of art refers to its singularly illuminating power to open our eyes to what is seemingly familiar, to disclose anew an apparently familiar reality. This validity claim admittedly stands for a *potential* for "truth" that can be released only in the whole complexity of life-experience; therefore this "truth-potential" may not be connected to (or even identified with) one of the three validity-claims constitutive for communicative action, as I have previously inclined to maintain. The one-to-one relationship which exists between the prescriptive validity of a norm and the normative validity claims raised in speech acts is not a proper model for the relation between the potential for truth of works of art and the transformed relations between self and world stipulated by aesthetic experience. (Habermas 1984a, 203)

The introduction of poetic language creates new difficulties for Habermas's account of aesthetic rationalization. Originally this notion was tied to the emergence of *a discourse specialized with respect to pragmatic expressive claims to authenticity*. Now it appears to be related to a claim to truth, which, if it is not to be regarded as irrational, must imply a *different conception of CR*. For this claim arises in and through the reception of the work of art, that is, in *experience*. Hence it implies a notion of rationality that is in some sense intuitive—compelling in a metaphoric-rhetorical rather than purely discursive way. Habermas thus approvingly cites Wellmer's claim (1984–85) that

> Neither *truth* nor *truthfulness* may be attributed unmetaphorically to works of art, if one understands "truth" and truthfulness in the sense of a pragmatically differentiated everyday concept of truth. We can explain the way in which truth and truthfulness—and even normative correctness—are *metaphorically* interlaced in works of art only by appealing to the fact that the work of art, as a symbolic formation with an aesthetic validity claim, *is at the same time an object of the lifeworld experience, in which the three validity domains are unmetaphorically intermeshed.* (Habermas 1984a, 203; emphasis added)

The reasons given in support of a work of art's *symbolic* embodiment of a metaphorical unity of experience cannot be *reduced* to objective claims regarding formal properties, normative claims regarding moral content, or expressive claims regarding pleasurable feelings. As Kant noted, the reference to conceptually specifiable properties alone cannot be decisive in aesthetic judgments; at most they can lead us to *feel* or *experience* the work of art in a way that validates its instantiation of experience in its integrity—something like Kant's notion of a nonrepresentable, supersensible Idea of Nature. Thus, for Kant, what is ultimately decisive is the achievement of *rational experience*, or the cultivation of disinterested contemplation.

I shall return to the importance of this new conception of aesthetic rationality for Habermas's critical project as a whole. Suffice it to say, the salutary acknowledgment of a prediscursive rationality (whose practical implications I discuss below) is not without problems of its own. For the cultivation of rational experience can no more be severed from rational critique than can the cultivation of subjective experience.

No one has demonstrated this more clearly than Martin Seel, who draws on the hermeneutic—and above all, communicative—insights of Habermas and Gadamer in developing a distinct notion of aesthetic rationality. Seel relies on a phenomenological description of experience to build a strong case against two polarities toward which contemporary aesthetic theories lean. One extreme identifies the aesthetic with an immediate experience or subjective reaction to sensed properties that resist conceptual or discursive articulation. Since this ineffable experience is held to be radically distinct from cognitive descriptions and moral evaluations about the perceived object, it is effectively deprived of any relationship to the rational. The other extreme commits the opposite error of building too much rationality into the aesthetic, in effect transforming it into a kind of global (philosophical or speculative) knowledge about certain ideal (or utopian) states of experience. In this instance the aesthetic takes on the meaning of a higher "truth" regarding a perfected experience in which moral, cognitive, and affective aspects of individual and social life achieve felicitous harmony. Paradoxically, by assimilating the aesthetic to the cognitive in a way that allows for no differences, this view ends up with exactly the same result as its counterpart. The aesthetic is again dissociated from rationality. If the kind of unified, speculative knowledge provided by art transcends conceptual distinctions between truth, goodness, and beauty, it cannot but resist articulation in the form of argumentatively justifiable descriptions and evaluations. The "supersensible idea" of a reconciled nature or humanity is just as indeterminate and ineffable as the spontaneous feeling of aesthetic pleasure.

Seel's approach to resolving this antinomy involves scrupulously attending to the logic of aesthetic experience. In a nutshell, he shows how aesthetic experience must be conceived as encompassing three distinct elements: a subjective reaction, a reference to specific objective properties, and a critical (corrective) discursive "synthesis" of subjective confrontation and objective commentary. Basically, these three elements refer to one another in a circular manner. Objective commentary initially situates aesthetic experience by describing what sorts of properties persons of a given culture might agree are relevant for negative or positive evaluations. Yet commentary can only become aesthetically relevant by integrating ascriptive *metaphorical* interpretations with evaluative judgments. Whereas the former relate the objective properties of the artwork to aesthetic functions, the latter relate the subjective interests of the perceiver—for instance, in achieving freedom—to experiences capable of being reflectively, that is, holistically *cultivated*.

The import of Seel's analysis for Habermas's aesthetics can be summarized as follows. Seel argues against Habermas that the tendency toward radical specialization typical of cultural rationalization—in other words, the radical segregation of cognitive, ethical, and aesthetic modes of argumentation—does not entail the radical purification of such modes of discourse from claims and arguments extraneous to them (Seel 1985, 30, 64, 292, 321–26). Aesthetic critique exemplifies this impurity, although moral and cognitive arguments also testify to it. Aesthetic experience completes itself in rational critique in which descriptive and ascriptive statements claiming to be true, ethical evaluations claiming to be appropriate (and moral judgments claiming to be right), and subjective expressions claiming to be sincere, authentic, and truthful are argumentatively tested and corrected against one another. Thus, if there is a global rationality *(Vernunft)* and "truth" of aesthetic experience, it is one that is founded on the differences (diremptions or *Entzweiungen*) between distinct types of rationality *(Rationalität)* and their complementarity.

Although Seel's analysis of the impurity and complexity of rational discourse clearly anticipates Lyotard's own account of the unresolvable and unreconciled tensions, or differences, between regimens and genres of discourse, it is not as opposed to Habermas's theory as he thinks. For over a decade now Habermas has acknowledged that the "radically differentiated moments of reason" point to a kind of unity that "might be established *this side* of expert cultures, in a nonreified communicative everyday practice" (Habermas 1987b, 398). And as we have seen, his most recent account of political and judicial deliberation emphasizes the integration of distinct types of discourse. Significantly, these deliberations, which connect existential discourses regarding authentic forms of collective *identity* with clinical judgments regarding exemplary ways of living free and fulfilled lives, integrate moral questions about rights and cognitive questions about economics around ethical questions of the good. However, it is no accident that Habermas turns to post-avant-garde (realistic and engaged) art to illustrate the free play of cognitive, moral, and expressive "moments." For what distinguishes holistic aesthetic criticism and its peculiar type of experiential rationality from other forms of integrated reasoning is that it alone involves a presentative reflection on the ways of seeing (Danto), or world-making (Goodman) that globally delimit the scope of possible cognitions, evaluations, and sensibilities.

Despite its uncertain vacillation between the polarities of expressivism and cognitivism, Habermas's aesthetic seems to aspire to the sort of presentative reflection, or secular illumination, that Seel (following Benjamin) finds exemplary. As he puts it, modern art

> reaches into our cognitive interpretations and normative expectations and transforms the *totality* in which these moments are related to one another. In this respect, modern art harbors a utopia that becomes a reality to the degree that the *mimetic powers* sublimated in the work of art find resonance in the *mimetic relations of a balanced and undistorted intersubjectivity of everyday life.* (1984a, 202; emphasis added)

The above passage bears a striking resemblance to Taylor's discussion of the importance of *epiphanic experience* in grounding a communitarian critique of social reification—a concept, you will recall, that Habermas elsewhere criticizes for being overly transcendent and prerational. In this context, however, he himself indicates the need for an aesthetic, secular illumination in grounding the critique of social reification. Not surprisingly, he and Taylor both turn to Schiller's social and political transformation of Kant's aesthetics to illustrate this possibility.

The subjectivism of Kant's aesthetics—in particular, his inability to resolve the oppositions in his system between individual and society, freedom and nature, private moral duty and public life—was seen by Schiller as symptomatic of real class divisions within bourgeois society. The separation of mental activity and physical labor, moral universalism and cognitive egoism, he believed, results in *self*-alienation.

Schiller's diagnosis of a separation *within the individual*—between a rational impulse striving for moral freedom *(Formtrieb)* and a sensuous impulse seeking natural happiness *(Stofftrieb)*—undoubtedly influenced Marx's own diagnosis of alienated labor and parallels my diagnosis of the split individual that is of concern to liberals and communitarians alike. Following Kant's own lead, Schiller gives this diremption an aesthetic interpretation: In the naïve artist of antiquity these impulses are naturally and spontaneously harmonized in accordance with the sensuous principle of *beauty*; in the sentimental artist of modernity, such unity is posited as an infinite ideal to be freely striven for, and is thus registered in the moral incommensurability of thought and imagination characteristic of the *sublime*. For Schiller, the aim of aesthetic education is to reconcile these impulses in a higher play impulse *(Spieltrieb)* without doing violence to the modern division of labor and differentiation of faculties. The exchangeability of functions within the division of labor, he speculated, would make possible the harmonious realization of faculties instead of their antagonistic frustration (thus looking ahead to Marx). Likewise, morality would cease being a function of isolated conscience; ethical judgment would be enhanced by judgment of taste, and the latter would be cultivated through public exposure to art.

It is here, in Schiller's synthesis of Aristotelian and Kantian senses of judgment, that the relation between art, communication, and common sense becomes apparent. As against the dissolution of art into life called for by surrealism, Schiller clings "to the autonomy of pure appearance." Yet art is not without impact on social life: "[T]he emancipation of consciousness must be rooted in the emancipation of the senses." With this reference to Marcuse's reading of Schiller Habermas concludes that

> an aestheticization of the lifeworld is legitimate only in the sense that art operates as a catalyst, as a form of communication, as a medium within which separated moments are rejoined into an uncoerced totality. The social character of the beautiful and of taste are to be confirmed solely by the fact that art "leads" everything dissociated in modernity—the system of unleashed needs, the bureaucratized state, the abstractions of rational morality and science for experts—"out under the open sky of common sense." (Schiller 1984, 139; Habermas 1987a, 50)

It is precisely at this juncture, where Habermas's aesthetics joins up with Schiller's, that the concept of communicative rationality—now universalized to encompass even the poetic and metaphorical function of art—loses its discursive rigidity. This derigidification of communication is not limited to art, however. Recall Habermas's contention that cognitive, normative, and expressive elements "communicate" with one another in the post-avant-garde work of art in a particularly felicitous, aesthetically harmonious manner. Recall, too, that his distinction between aesthetic critique and aesthetic reception threatened to undermine any *communication* between avant-garde art movements and everyday life. Lacking such mediation, the former retreats into the obscure oblivion of lifeless formalism (or worse, aformal expressionism) while popular reception remains parochial and uncultivated. The result is a truncated process of aesthetic rationalization in which both sides are impoverished and rendered irrational (or uncritical). Recently, however, Habermas has taken note of the way in which art (literary) criticism as well as philosophy mediate between specialized disciplines (art and science, respectively) and everyday life. The key to this communication is the extension of poetic, metaphoric, and rhetorical uses of language in the domain of rational discourse itself. According to Habermas, while philosophy and art criticism are primarily specialized with respect to claims to truth and expressive authenticity, they can communicate these claims in ways that affect the totality of life—and in much the same way as art itself, namely, "by rhetorically expanding and enriching their special languages to the extent that is required to link up indirect communications with the manifest contents of statements, and to do so in a deliberate way" (Habermas 1987a, 209). Thus, if philosophy is not exactly literature (as Derrida would have it), it is nonetheless literary, that is, rhetorical and aesthetic—operating at least partially by means of expressive perlocutionary effects.

In the final analysis, Habermas—like Seel—leaves us with two very different views about the critical function of aesthetic enlightenment: *poetic* illumination of the ideal unity of experience or *profane* illumination of its actual fragmentation. Habermas's appeal to aesthetic truth no doubt explains the possibility of reunifying aspects of validity and rationality that his own critical philosophy has shown to be conceptually incommensurable. In this respect it follows the same logic as Kant's third *Critique*. But Kant, of course, understood that aesthetic ideas can symbolize sublime incommensurability as well as beautiful harmony. Hence, the question-begging nature of Habermas's appeal to aesthetics—an appeal aptly queried by Lyotard:

> What Habermas requires from the arts and the experiences they provide is, in short, to bridge the gap between cognitive, ethical, and political discourses, thus opening the way to a unity of experience. My question is to determine what sort of unity Habermas has in mind. Is the aim of the project of modernity the constitution of sociocultural unity within which all the elements of daily life and of thought take their places as in an organic whole? Or does the passage that has to be charted between heterogeneous language games—those of cognition,

of ethics, of politics—belong to a different order from that? And if so, would it be capable of effecting a real synthesis between them? The first hypothesis, of a Hegelian inspiration, does not challenge the notion of a dialectically totalizing *experience*; the second is closer to the spirit of Kant's *Critique of Judgment;* but must be submitted, like the *Critique*, to that severe reexamination which postmodernity imposes on the thought of the Enlightenment, on the idea of a unitary end of history and of a subject. (Lyotard 1984, 72–73)

We have already answered part of Lyotard's query: Habermas's modernism places him squarely on this side of the Kant/Hegel divide. But the "completion of modernity" he and Kant propose as a practical task remains questionable from the standpoint of postmodernism. If, as Lyotard maintains, discourse is always potentially in a state of crisis, if it is always on the verge of transcending its "own" internal logic and unitary end—literally losing its determinate identity by becoming a different kind of discourse—then would it not be more accurate to talk about its disintegration into conflicting norms (goals) than about its harmonization in accordance with a dominant one?

3. These last reflections take us to the heart of Lyotard's postmodern alternative. The fluidity and complexity of this alternative defy easy translation into fixed philosophical categories. Lyotard is a thinker who finds equal merit in the biologism of Nietzsche and Freud, the contextualism of Aristotle and the Sophists, the anarchism of Feyerabend, *and* the idealism of Kant. Moving freely across boundaries separating rationalism from antirationalism, universalism from particularism, idealism from materialism, his "critical rationalism" owes more to Adorno's "micrologies" than to Kant's tribunal of reason (Lyotard 1986, 97, 107, 114).

The way to Kant as a postmodern thinker—for Lyotard, postmodernism is but the "nascent" and "constant" state of a modernism that has become aware of its own self-disruptive reflexivity—was prepared, oddly enough, by Lyotard's early disenchantment with structuralist rationalism. Influenced by the anti-intellectualism of Merleau-Ponty's phenomenology of perception, the culminating fruit of Lyotard's early phenomenological phase, *Discours, figure* (1971), criticized Lacan's structuralist reduction of the unconscious—indeed, all sense and intuition *(figure)*—to the rational law of the signifier *(discours)*. This dualism of spontaneous, polymorphous desire and systemically determined, linguistically articulated reason resonated nicely with his ultraleft affiliation with *Socialisme ou barbarie*. Indeed, the investment of artistic fantasy with subversive political effects paralleled the "Great Refusal" espoused by Blanchot, Marcuse, and others who extolled the anarchistic, countercultural interventions of avant-garde artists. However, by the time he wrote *Économie libidinale* (1974), Lyotard had abandoned the dualism of discourse and figure so central to a disruptive politics. Inspired by Deleuze and Guattari's critique of Freud, *L'Anti-Oedipe* (1972), he propounded a libidinal monism that reduced the "great ephemeral theatre" of consciousness, discourse, and socioeconomic structure to the dissimulation of fluid energies along a single surface, not unlike that of a Möbius strip. By eliminating the Freudian dualism of life-and-death instincts and replacing the teleological notion of desire as lack striving for fulfillment with the nonteleological notion of desire as energetic drive issuing in discharge, Lyotard was compelled to embrace a Nietzschean aestheticism far removed from that entertained by Marcuse. Since no desires—including even the polymorphous intensities of consumer capitalism—were beyond redemption, the libido-driven economy ultimately entailed a metaphysics of force, as Lyotard himself later characterized it. Not surprisingly, his more recent turn to Kant and the question of justice can be understood as a reaction to and partial reversal of the subsumption of discourse and reason to figure and force.

No contemporary thinker of repute has capitalized on the postmodernism of Kant's thought to the extent that Lyotard has. The aestheticization of science and politics that his philosophy proclaims is clearly descended from that great fragmentation of value spheres animating German thought since Kant. Indeed, what one normally associates with postmodernism is a reaction to functional unity in all its manifestations. This reaction takes the form of a kind of *aesthetic* eclecticism, or stylistic pastiche, whose most enduring monuments—pop art and the new architecture—satirize the modernist suppression of regional and traditional modes beneath the cold surfaces of functional design. Like other currents of poststructuralism, postmodernism inveighs against the totalitarian impulse toward social homogeneity and its attendant marginalization of dissident subcultures, which it blames on the rational demand for unity, purity, universality, and ultimacy.

Yet it is precisely this demand that ostensibly informs our modern understanding of legitimacy. In thinking of the latter, we invariably fix upon the idea of valid authority vested in universal consent. Lyotard's attempt to develop an alternative account of legitimacy, beginning with *La condition postmoderne* (1979), thus merits special consideration.

The key assumption in this work is that there is an isomorphism between science, on the one hand, and ethics and politics on the other. The grand narratives *(grands récits)* that legitimate science are the same that legitimate the state even if "the statements consigned to these two authorities differ in nature" (Lyotard 1984, 8). This linking of knowledge and power is especially evident in today's information society. The right to decide in the political sense is more and more a function of possessing the right type of credentials, the right type of expertise. Communication here ceases to be a medium of impartial dialogue and increasingly assumes the status of an exchange system in which the ledger sheets of informational capital are balanced out. The "general transformation" in the way in which scientific research is conducted and transmitted in the cybernetic age goes hand in hand with the "mercantilization" of knowledge. Knowledge has for some time been accorded the value of a productive force; with the advent of postindustrial capitalism, it has emerged as a commodity whose possession determines the economic fate of nations. One of the questions raised by this new economy of knowledge and language is whether the technical capacity to enhance the functional adaptability of the state, for instance, by augmenting productivity through increased informational input, is capable of justifying demands for legitimacy. Can efficient adaptation be a substitute for justice, or does the incommensurability of "ought" and "is" refer the concept of legitimacy to a purely normative category, such as free universal consent? If the latter no longer seems adequate to express the dynamic *bricolage* we call modern society, what is?

Lyotard proceeds to answer these questions by examining what it is about scientific knowledge and its legitimation that bears upon the issue of the state. Since Plato, philosophers have been accustomed to viewing knowledge as an important ingredient in the legitimation of power, but only recently have they sought to relate the legitimation of knowledge to politics. Unlike earlier metaphysical narratives, the narratives of the Enlightenment presupposed that science directly institutionalized rational discourse and that politics mirrored science. Two distinct but overlapping narratives reflected this change, one liberal, the other conservative (27–31).

The liberal legitimation of science asserted that technically useful knowledge was the key to individual and social emancipation. The educational policy appropriate to this narrative, which found its supreme expression in the French Third Republic, emphasized primary over secondary schooling. By contrast, the conservative legitimation of science promoted self-understanding above emancipation. The educational policy that it embodied reflected less the utilitarian bent of the French and English schools than the moralizing spirit distilled in Humboldt's proposal for the founding of the University of Berlin. Philosophy is here called upon to provide the speculative means for integrating the knowledge of the various disciplines and recovering the moral purpose animating the nation (31–37).

In Lyotard's opinion, these narratives now stand discredited, and for good reason. The speculative philosophy of the German school could only legitimate the positive sciences by denigrating their knowledge as partial, abstract, and wholly incapable of grasping the higher truth of living spirit. The subsequent decline of German idealism brought home the utter contingency of the separate spheres of knowledge and ushered in a positivistic phase that also discredited its French and English counterparts. Since it was now taken for granted that prescriptions for achieving political emancipation and statements of scientific fact were logically irreducible, truth and justice lost whatever value their former association had once accorded them (37–41).

If we no longer look to science and political life as legitimating one another, it is just as true that the time is long past for thinking of science as truthfully representing reality in itself and politics as justly mirroring the ideal conditions of emancipation. The two rival models of legitimation mentioned by Lyotard that dominate the contemporary scene attest to this nihilistic self-awareness in radically different ways, and both do so even while maintaining the formal unity of science and politics. On one hand, there are those systems theorists such as Parsons and Luhmann who claim that knowledge must be justified performatively. Efficiency here replaces truth as the criterion of validity. This substitution, it seems, is dictated not only by the methodological connection between verifiability, predictability, and technological control, but also by the functionalistic imperatives of the modern state. As a cybernetic system, the state requires fresh inputs of information in order to adapt itself to a capricious environment. Its legitimation is guaranteed by maintaining efficient administration and economic growth. Although consensus is still taken to be an important index of social stability, it is deprived of antecedent validity. The freedom to make informed administrative decisions, Luhmann tells us, requires manipulating democratic input from above, if not scaling it back altogether. Because it would be impractical and dangerous to implement an interdisciplinary liberal arts curriculum, higher education should properly confine itself to the business of proffering technical and vocational instruction. On the other hand, there are those, such as Habermas and Apel, who claim that cognitive and prescriptive judgments must be justified on the basis of their universal acceptance by persons in rational dialogue. Unconstrained consensus provides a touchstone for truth and justice that favors democracy. Accordingly, the critical theory of legitimation views society as a communication network in which social conflict, not functional equilibrium, is the norm. Nevertheless, by advocating the view that society ought to reflect unity, it too stands in close proximity to the legitimating narratives of the Enlightenment, for which knowledge is seen as dispelling ideology and ensuring collective emancipation.

Lyotard sometimes speaks as if this latter theory of legitimation were distinctly modern in its articulation of an ideal of rational autonomy. If we turn to *Au juste* (1979) we find him contrasting the kind of free, mutual recognition intrinsic to modern justice with the heteronomy of its pagan counterpart. For the Greeks, the legitimacy of the state is proportional to its imitation of an ideal harmony (or mean) inscribed in the cosmos—a proper distribution known by theoretical reason or observation to be conducive to social and individual well-being. With the advent of modern science, forms of naturalistic, teleological reasoning are replaced by more abstract, formal conceptions of calculating and consistency reasoning. What ought to be no longer stands in any logical relation to what is. By the same token, no combination of existing passions, desires, or conventional habits is sufficient to ground moral practice.

It is principally out of a modern and fundamentally Kantian distaste for moral heteronomy that Lyotard denies the possibility of any scientific, or functionalistic, legitimation. Morality presupposes a spontaneous initiation of action that emanates solely from individual practical reason. This supposition is also the cornerstone of those modern social contract theories of legitimation about which Lyotard himself feels ambivalent. Since it is incumbent upon any government aspiring to the title of legitimacy to satisfy the common interests of its citizenry and to do so by their free consent, it follows as a matter of course that the best government will be democratic. Legitimate states, we believe, ought to advance rational, universalizable interests. And this conviction remains even if these interests extend no further than endorsing the most basic rules of the democratic game (Lyotard and Thébaud 1979, 41–50).

It is just this assumption of a shared discourse, or agreement over the rules of a universally binding game, that Lyotard challenges. The rise of multinational corporations, the decline of nation-states as global administrative agencies, the logistics of information gathering and transmission, the need for self-regulating systems to avoid informational overloading and bureaucratic entropy, and the unpredictable nature of social displacements in response to new data seem to undermine the functionalistic conception of the state and its performative legitimation. The state is no longer in control of the technical apparatus necessary to guarantee efficient administration and economic growth. And it is not just because the databanks are in the hands of hostile corporations. To the contrary, the absorption of information itself proves dysfunctional when it outstrips the capacity of the system to make decisions (Habermas and Luhmann 1971). This undecidability penetrates to the heart of modern science itself. Antinomies revolving around the formal and pragmatic limits to the derivation of consistent and complete systems of axioms (Gödel), the establishment of independent criteria of verification or falsification (Popper and Kuhn), and the imprecision built into the prediction and measurement of subatomic particles (Heisenberg), testify to the inherent instability of modern science (Lyotard and Thébaud 1979, 53–60). The need to ground knowledge and moral obligation in logically incommensurable language games would already render a functionalistic legitimation of the state suspect were it not for the fact that science itself is just as impure as it is ungrounded. Indeed, the composite descriptive/prescriptive nature of scientific principles seems to fracture any claim to rationality, thus bearing witness to the irrationality of social life itself. The schizophrenic fragmentation of persons and institutions into so many atomic roles and language games continually undermines the formation of a unitary political culture based upon principles of consistency and personal sovereignty. Summoning the spirit of the late Wittgenstein along with the specter of deconstruction, Lyotard writes, "The social subject itself seems to dissolve in this dissemination of language games. The social bond is linguistic, but is not woven with a single thread. It is a fabric formed by the intersection of at least two (and in reality an indeterminate number of) language games obeying different rules" (1984, 40).

In the next chapter I will argue that Lyotard's account of the incommensurability and fragmentation of scientific and social community is somewhat exaggerated. For our present purposes it suffices to note that the aforementioned futility of attempting any scientific, or argumentative, grounding of theory would seem to have the paradoxical effect of rendering his views on this matter "illegitimate" were it not for the fact that he develops an alternate theory of legitimation. Despite their impurity, all forms of scientific legitimation strive to maintain the logical separation of descriptive, prescriptive, and expressive language games. Such is not the case with the "small narratives" underwriting everyday practice, which Lyotard likens to "a monster formed by the interweaving of heteromorphous classes of utterances" (Lyotard 1984, 65). The idea that knowledge and practice must be argumentatively justified is foreign to them. The knowledge guiding our conduct appears to be more a matter of pragmatic "know-how" than propositional "know-that." According to Lyotard, what is important about this so-called "narrative knowledge" is that it is passed down through ritual imitation and oral recitation. Because the authority of these narratives, and to a lesser extent, their scientific counterparts, ultimately lacks a privileged past, they are legitimated, "by the simple fact that they do what they do" (18–23). Of course, all theories, including scientific ones, must have recourse ultimately to storytelling in order to legitimate their practical worth in the grand scheme of things. Indeed, the Kuhnian interlocking of politics and epistemology in the twin figures of scientific paradigm and scientific revolution testifies to this very fact. Hence, such global rationalizations of institutionalized practices that answer the question "Why should there be science at all?" are at least indirectly interwoven with the myths and everyday practices defining our membership in local and multicultural communities. The legitimacy of Lyotard's own theory thus resides in its retelling at a higher register one of the many mundane stories we moderns share—a story of alienation and loss of self-identity but also of an expanded horizon of future possibility.

If the postmodern condition fosters an incessant search for the new, the unknown, the anomalous, the subversive, the eclectic, in short, dissent from dominant conventions and decentration of subjectivity, then only a "legitimation by paralogy" can satisfy "both the desire for justice and the desire for the unknown" (65–67). But what could this amalgamation of the political and the aesthetic amount to?

3.1 The problem of legitimation becomes more acute in *Le différend* (1983), where the contrast between Habermas and Lyotard is particularly striking. As in his earlier theory, Lyotard follows Habermas in rejecting philosophy of consciousness in favor of a theory of speech action based on Wittgenstein's model of language games. However, the result is more consistent with Wittgenstein's own dismissal of his earlier attempt to found language on truth-functional logic. For the late Wittgenstein, postulation of a transcendental metarule governing the application of rules succumbs to Russell's paradox—if the metarule is a member of the class it regulates, it ceases to be ultimate; if it is not, then it ceases to be a rule. Lyotard and Wittgenstein avoid this antinomy by conceiving linguistic rules as local practices subject to continual reinterpretation (Lyotard 1984, 10).

Where Lyotard differs with Wittgenstein is over the primacy of consensus and convention. Lyotard stresses the unconventional, agonistic inventiveness of "moves" *(coups)* within language games. Like another philosopher with whom he has much in common—Donald Davidson—he pushes this principle of linguistic *uncertainty* to the point of endangering the very concept of rule-governed language. Yet, unlike Davidson, Lyotard vigorously protests the *literal* translatability of different language games. In his opinion, language games may share rigidly designating names (as Kripke puts it) and metaphorical complicities that ease transitions between them, but they are at bottom essentially incommensurable.

At the same time, the nominal and metaphorical links between language games infect them with external impurities. The difference between Lyotard and Habermas on this score is striking. Although Habermas concedes linguistic impurity up to a point—he says, for example, that the ideal constraints implicit in consensual speech are superimposed over success-oriented aims; that the hortatory rhetoric of political discourse combines consensual and strategic orientations; that the opening up and preservation of communicative interaction often depends on the unannounced power, or indirect influence, of *perlocutionary effects*; and that different orientations toward validity are metaphorically interlaced in discourse as well as in everyday communication—he insists that such impurity is mostly contingent and contained by the dominant consensual orientation (Habermas 1991a, 245, 254). In principle, such impurities could be eliminated from theoretical discourse entirely and from practical discourse to the extent that action constraints are bracketed or kept subordinate.

Lyotard disagrees. Although he shares Habermas's view that scientific discourses, strictly speaking, are oriented toward consensus and abide by canons of logic in a way that distinguishes them from everyday conversations, he denies that consensus orientation and logic exhaust their function and structure. Of course, the logical distinction between object language and metalanguage disqualifies badly formed—but colloquially acceptable—sentences of the sort "This statement is false" from science. But, as we saw in chapter 2, scientific discourse allows for practical, aesthetic, and therapeutic reflections on the core concepts regulating accepted paradigms that violate this distinction. This possibility resides in its mixing of meta-prescriptives (rules of logic), prescriptives (paradigmatic axioms), denotations (observations), and heteromorphous combinations of prescriptive and denotative assertions (laws). In Lyotard's opinion, such reflexivity and impurity conspire to generate "paralogies" (Heisenberg's Uncertainty Principle, Gödel's Theorem, etc.) as well as anomalies and surprises. Thus, conflict, dissensus, "the winning strategy," and novelty are as much a part of the aim of science as consensus (Lyotard 1984, 64).

As in *La condition postmoderne*, the view of language presented here has ominous consequences for the idea of subjectivity. What we have is not the decentration of a transcendentally unified subject of speech, as in Habermas's model, but the dissolution of a subject caught in the midst of a chain of speech acts and positioned with respect to multiple and sometimes conflicting roles, realities, and expectations (40). According to Lyotard, the referent, meaning, addressor and addressee "presented" by any phrase (speech act) are determined by the phrase following. Now phrases belong to different *regimens* (or language games), such as ostension, description, prescription, and interrogation. Regimens are *not* commensurable; you cannot translate prescriptions into descriptions; and the former cannot be offered in lieu of the latter *when* the game in question is just describing. However, different regimens can be linked to one another in more complex language games called *genres*. For example, it is normally acceptable in scientific discourse to link a description to an act of ostension (denoting its spatiotemporal location). The ostensive phrase, in turn, might be offered in response to a question, command, or request for information. In any case, the universe of a descriptive phrase P varies depending on subsequent phrases. It could be a response to a question; but it could also be a warning, a command, or a request. Most importantly, its sense at least partially depends on the response it elicits; proclaimed authorial intent does not always carry final authority in these matters. My intended use of P as a signal for assistance can be overridden by my interlocutors, who understand it as an offhand remark, a description awaiting further qualification, and so forth.

This last point is decisive for understanding the sorts of conflicts that arise in everyday communication. Unlike the rules governing regimens, the rules governing genres do not determine a specific response. What they determine is an overall aim: truth in the case of science; unconditional obligation, in the case of morality; and so forth. A problem arises, however, inasmuch as phrases provide occasions for linking heterogeneous regimens *and* genres. Thus, a certain injustice, or *différend*, occurs whenever the aim of a phrase is suppressed and superseded by that of its successor.

More precisely, a *différend* occurs "whenever a plaintiff is deprived of the means of arguing and by this fact becomes a victim," as in the case where the settling of a conflict between two parties "is made in the idiom of one of them in which the wrong [*tort*] suffered by the other signifies nothing" (Lyotard 1983, 24–25). As distinct from litigation, "a *différend* would be a conflict between (at least) two parties that cannot be adjudicated equitably for lack of a rule of judgment applicable to the two arguments" (9). A *différend* occurs, for example, when the silence of Holocaust survivors—say, in response to a revisionist historian's "scientific" demand that evidence be given to prove the existence of death camps—is interpreted as a denial of such evidence. Indeed, the very existence of Holocaust survivors—which the historian's cognitive discourse demands as proof—seems to undermine the proof itself. Here the survivor is deprived of the means of argumentation and reduced to silence.

Although historian and survivor seem to be communicating with one another rationally—they both use the same names (Auschwitz, Treblinka, etc.) to rigidly designate a simple (empty) referent, and they both have equal opportunities to make and rebut arguments pertaining to this referent—they have positioned themselves in different universes of discourse.[12] The names mean something different to the survivor; they do not designate determinable, historical facts about which one could argue and on which one could reach consensus. Rather, they signify suffering of such indeterminable, inhuman magnitude that they can only be thought in silence.

The contractualist language of market exchange marks the site of another *différend*, in this case between labor and management. The legal terms specified in the contract require that laborers define their labor as alienable exchange value (remunerable in terms of some monetary equivalent)—not as the living expression of their very personality. If it were defined as a power of expression and self-actualization, its articulation would carry us into the moral and political discourse of democratic self-determination—a sphere of discourse whose criterion of justice would require nullifying the split between labor, management, and (perhaps) ownership presupposed in the labor contract.

The example of the labor contract illustrates how one kind of discursive process (bargaining)—which necessarily tends toward a definition of terms—issues in exclusion, suppression, hegemony, and ultimately political domination. Yet despite whatever sympathy we might feel for the workers, it would be wrong to think that this kind of *différend* is merely incidental to the process of communication, and could be eliminated in a just democratic order. Indeed, for Lyotard, all political discourse—including democratic dialogue—suffers from a profound legitimation crisis centering around innumerable *différends*. For, he tells us, the latter "is not a genre; it is the multiplicity of genres, the diversity of ends"—the very "threat of the *différend*" itself (200).

Like Habermas, then, Lyotard departs from the premise that democratic political reasoning comprises a complex web of pragmatic, ethical, moral, and juristic genres of discourse that qualify one another in various ways. Although his specific account of the typology and connection of genres differs from Habermas's in minor details, what is important for us to note is the antithetical way in which this "unity" is described: not as a relatively coherent and hierarchically ordered process, but as a symmetrical chain of suppressions and injustices.

In Lyotard's model, the genre initiating democratic discourse is ethical, and its characteristic interrogation begins by asking: What should we be? (213). In this phrase the "we" that is obligated might be "humanity," if what is enjoined upon us is realization of our universal personality as bearers of certain fundamental rights. Or, it might be "we Americans (Germans, French, etc.)," if what is enjoined upon us is the realization of our national identity. In any case, the question of what legitimates this obligation already suggests a kind of *différend*. If it is just ourselves—we authorize (democratically) the authority (constitution, idea of humanity, nation) that authorizes us—we produce a vicious circle, a point, we noted, that poststructuralists like Derrida and Nancy frequently make.[13] Morally speaking, the one who authorizes (addressor) and the one who is authorized (addressee) cannot be identical. Otherwise the *limits* imposed on the one who is authorized by the one authorizing are no longer limits (i.e., normative obligations), and injustices (*différends*) in the name of The People against the people will occur. Hence, the idea of democratic *self-determination* (the absolute sovereignty of the people) ought to be qualified by a healthy respect for prepolitical rights (206).

Perhaps this can be achieved by grounding, as Habermas does, the idea of a democratic constitution in something preceding the will of the people: practical discourse. However, this strategy, Lyotard suggests, again involves the commission of a *différend*. A universal, *indeterminate idea* (of humanity, nation, etc.) is thought to be binding in some *determinate* way. But this can happen only if certain persons (e.g., the Founding Fathers) presume to speak on behalf of the universal—a clearly illegitimate and paradoxical usurpation of authority that effectively silences political opposition (209).

Let us momentarily leave aside the *différend* that occurs at the founding moment. Once the supreme ethical question is answered the next asks: What should we do? The prescribers of determinate policies (laws) act in the name of indeterminate ideas, but the abyss between prescription and idea cannot be bridged without doing violence to the latter. The bureaucrat's prescription usurps the Founder's idea. Moreover—as paradoxes of collective choice amply attest—since "The People" simply does not exist as a representable or realizable phenomenon, Habermas's hope that an amorphous, popular consensus on ethical identity can be translated without loss into legislative proposals, and that these, in turn, can be translated without loss into concrete policies and judgments, appears to be without foundation. The impersonal form of the law conceals the partisan nature of its prescriptive content (214).

This *différend* is followed by another, which involves the trumping of the moral genre by the cognitive. Since "ought" implies "can," the addressee of an unconditioned command—the expert delegated the task of implementing the policy—is now required to consider it as factually conditioned and potentially revocable. However, actuality does not exhaust possibility. So, cognitive discourse must be trumped, in turn, by the "irreal" narrative of imaginable achievements. The appeal to speculative history

returns us to the Arendtean question of political ends. At this point, someone must "adjudicate" between conflicting ends. But who has the right to
judge and by what authority?

It should be clear by now that everyone has the right to judge, yet no
one has the authority to do so. To begin with, judgment is not legitimated
by consensus on universal interests. Nor is it legitimated by consensus on
the rules of the game; the latter remains subject to shifts in signification
and authorization that accompany *différends* in political discourse. Indeed,
Lyotard fears that, by linking legitimation to the consensual regularization
of moves within a language game rather than to their agonal contestation,
Habermas comes dangerously close to abetting the kind of systemic closure he himself opposes. The danger is only magnified by his talk of a
universal subject of history (humanity, or the human species) whose emancipation remains linked to a universal consensus on true needs. Like all
grands récits of the Enlightenment, Habermas's appeal to universal history
(or developmental psychology as analogue for social evolution) regresses
behind the contingent standpoint of decentered dialogue to the speculative standpoint of *Geist*-centered dialectic. To cite Lyotard: "The cause is
good, but the argument is not" (1984, 66).

A better argument, Lyotard thinks, links legitimation to popular justice ("give the public free access to the memory and data banks") and to
the paralogical creation of new moves—a view that reflects the fact that
systems are always on the verge of breaking down under the weight of
their own internal complexity. Of course, such crises are not inevitable. By
seeing the contestable *communicative* network in which "autonomous" subsystems interact with their environments as part of their internal complexity, Lyotard and Habermas open a space for critical interventions aimed at
theoretically enlightening functionaries within those systems about the
practical limits of the cognitive regime under which they labor (Lyotard
1984, 61–63; Habermas 1992, 74).

We are back to our original problem: critically judging the rightful
boundaries separating cognitive from moral discourse. In the Thébaud
interview Lyotard offered what appeared to be a "modern" response to
this problem (Lyotard and Thébaud 1979, 182). Determination of the fairness of moves relative to the rules of a particular language game (the multiplicity of justices) was said to presuppose determination of the autonomy
of incommensurable language games (the justice of multiplicities). The
problem arises concerning the status of this latter justice: What entitles
philosophy to adjudicate boundary disputes between other language games?
Indeed, can there be a judgment that doesn't arbitrarily impose order—and
commit a *différend*—in the name of some partial law?

Nancy, for one, thinks not—and alludes to the dialectic of abstract pluralism to which Lyotard's own position succumbs (Lyotard 1983, 60). Defending an Aristotelian perspective, Lyotard denied any possibility of grounding judgments claiming universal validity. This would perhaps explain the inconsistency of many of his own judgments in the Thébaud interview about the rightful boundaries separating moral and scientific discourse. Depending on the context of his own reasoning, Lyotard argued both that prescription should be left out of science and that scientific discourse is and even should be impure and undecided. That the logical status of a scientific law or a rule of language hovers somewhere between the prescriptive and the descriptive is something to be at once praised as "paralogical" and condemned as "terroristic." The resulting *lack of centeredness* and discrimination conveys precisely the impression of sophistry Lyotard so assiduously seeks to cultivate.

Accepting much of Lyotard's thesis concerning the postmodern condition, Nancy still prefers to read Kant through the eyes of Arendt and Heidegger. Judgment is not an arbitrary game of reversal or a mere play of phrases, but presupposes some relationship to the disclosure of being and world. This disclosure, as Heidegger would say, is *already centered* (enclosed or located) within a linguistically determined horizon of possible meaning and for that reason must be distinguished from the sort of cognitive truth expressed in propositional or categorical judgments. Contrary to Kant—but in agreement with Arendt—the synthesis of concept and intuition constitutive of a meaningful reality presupposes a deeper disclosure of world, self, and community involving reflective, not determinant, judgment.

Of course, Lyotard's self-acknowledged willingness to play "the great prescriber" who judges the proper limits governing all language games from the detached perspective of the spectator seems to suggest that he is not the relativist that Nancy makes him out to be. Indeed, it may well be that Nancy's own appeal to the relatively centered nature of judgment is itself question begging, resting as it does on an ontological conception of language. But here the problem with Lyotard's account of judgment lies elsewhere. By *prescribing* very determinate boundaries to the language games of morality and science he may have confused (so Nancy argues) determinant and reflective judgment (Nancy 1985, 13–14). On this reading, Lyotard overstepped the limits of aesthetic judgment. The latter may well be guided by an indeterminate idea of community, but if so this universal is not of the order of something that can be prescribed as a definite purpose to be striven for. Having thus succumbed to a kind of transcendental illusion, Lyotard became entrapped in a totalitarian logic of his own making—that of absolute pluralism.

3.2 Lyotard's response to this quandary hinged on finding an *aesthetic* rationale for philosophical criticism that avoids the paradox of the "great prescriber": the presumption of judicial authority that acts in the name of law at once determinate (local) and transcendent (universal). His point of departure, not surprisingly, is Kant's notion of reflective judgment in general, and judgment of the sublime, in particular. The notion of reflective judgment captures the problem of moral uncertainty in a dynamic, modern age; in the absence of reliable conventional criteria—above all, in the face of ever recurring "hard cases" that are not subsumed in advance by determinate rules—judgment cannot involve merely applying rules and subsuming cases. More often, it is called upon to discover the right rule—and in extreme instances, to invent a new rule (or new interpretation of an old rule)—for problematic cases. Such judgment seems to obey the logic of the sublime, since it involves an ambivalent feeling of pain and pleasure: pleasure in harmonizing a particular case with a universal rule, pain in the awareness of incommensurability between infinite Idea (of justice, integrity, etc.) and finite decision. Here, the limits determining *prescriptive* judgment are violated as soon as they are imaginatively reinterpreted in light of an indefinite horizon of possible situations. This spectatorial horizon is likened by Lyotard to a regulative idea that postulates neither the convergence of all possible judgments nor the universalizability of any standard, but only the autonomy of judgment—its capacity to "maximize opinions," or generate new possibilities of interpretation (Lyotard 1979, 146–53).

The *différend*, however, designates yet another site of incommensurability. In addition to the unavoidable incommensurability between types of phrase regimens noted above, that is, between determinate prescriptions of a local (conventional) nature and reflective judgments about their ideal (universal and indeterminate) scope and validity, we note the incommensurability between opposed—and not merely competing—standpoints and idioms. Unless one wants to deny *in principle* the possibility of trenchant moral dilemmas or *différends*, one must concede that genuinely tragic choices will have to be made even under the best of circumstances. In the face of current economic *différends*—for instance, between the liberal idiom of contractual freedom and the republican idiom of communal self-determination and self-realization—any hope of adjudication must await the advent of new idioms and institutions of the reflexive variety described in chapters 5 and 6. Absent such institutions and idioms, the appropriate response of the critical theorist who is called upon to justify his or her judgment can only be one of hesitation or vacillation between unknown and known, future and past, ideality and reality—in short, between what is unsayable and sayable. In the final analysis, the silence of sublime agitation aroused by yearning for the unrepresentable Idea can only find its proper voice in a new narrative that frames the rhetorical power of judgment within the context of our ever evolving self-understanding.

But don't these *différends* preclude precisely that community that grounds the possibility for judgment? Yes and no. Clearly the concept of subjectivity, of the collective "we," must be reelaborated—a task that, Lyotard claims, involves "abandoning from the outset the communicative linguistic structure (I/you/it) that the moderns, consciously or not, have accredited with being an ontological and political model" (Lyotard 1986, 51). But in that case, how can the Ideas of community and justice still be retained? At this juncture of Lyotard's argument one detects a divergence from the earlier account of judgment presented in *Au juste* that explains just this possibility. There judgment meant either the application of conventional rules requiring specification (Aristotle) or the reflexive discovery of rules in light of Ideas (Kant). In neither case was it explained how pagan heterogeneity might be compatible with modern universality or community. In the work presently under consideration, the community, or bond of communicability, without which the partisans of consensus, or beautiful harmony, and the partisans of conflict, or sublime incommensurability "would not even be able to *agree* that they are in *disagreement*," is rephrased in terms of the conflict of faculties elaborated by Kant in his later writings (Lyotard 1983, 243).

In *The Strife of the Faculties* (1798), Kant no longer conceived critical philosophy as a neutral tribunal that delivers final verdicts (prescriptions) without incurring new wrongs. We find instead the notion of a guardian who, while not a litigant in the dispute, intervenes indirectly on behalf of the weaker party by judging what is "just," or conducive to an agreement to disagree. The dispute in question is the conflict of faculties—in the first instance, between the "higher" university faculties of theology, law, and medicine and the "lower" faculty of philosophy, and in the second, between opposed cognitive and practical mental faculties laying claim to the same territory, human nature. One cannot regulate the various injustices (or *différends*) that arise when conflicting "discourses" range over the same territory; at most, one can expose them by defending the equally valid claim of the weaker party, the advocate of freedom, against the apparently stronger claim of the dogmatist. The basis for this peculiar judgment would thus appear to be that the conflict of mental faculties—indeed, the very sickness of the distracted subject—may yet be conducive to the health of the soul. Lyotard's preferred symbol for the disputed territory traversed by these overlapping jurisdictions is the archipelago:

The faculty of judging would be at least in part like a ship owner or an admiral who would launch from one island to another expeditions destined to present to the one what they have found (discovered in the old meaning of the term) in the other, and who could serve up to the first some "as-if" intuition in order to validate it. This force of intervention, war or commerce, hasn't any object, it has no island of its own, but it requires a milieu, the sea, the archipelago, the principal sea as the Aegean Sea was formerly named. (190)

Recall that the third *Critique* takes note of symbolic or analogical passages *(Übergänge)* linking what are otherwise heterogeneous moral, aesthetic, and cognitive faculties. Lyotard curiously finds in this "oceanic" simile something like a higher ground on which to base the critical judgment of the philosopher—a common place (the sea) in terms of which competing islands of discourse can be relativized (located) with respect to their particular domains of validity—though he characteristically interprets it in a manner that brings into relief an underlying tension.

For Lyotard the kind of critical judgment exercised by the philosopher is not restricted to any given locale (or discursive regime) but ranges over an entire "archipelago." Nor is it guided in advance by any theoretical or practical notion of finality. What guide this judgment are aesthetic considerations pertaining to the integrity of a whole whose parts achieve harmonious equilibrium only through conflict. This is not a judgment of beauty in Kant's sense, but a judgment of the sublime. Sublime for Kant are those experiences of formlessness, boundlessness, and lack of finality such as political revolutions, which paradoxically arouse enthusiasm in us because they manage in spite of themselves to signal the finality and community they empirically deny (240–43). Sublime, too, is the lack of finality evident in the *différend*, since it symbolizes a community in which conflict is the basis for integrity, harmony, and justice.

With the appeal to the oceanic it would appear that Lyotard's thought once again slips back into the dark void of the singular, the fluid, and the prediscursive. Transcending the stable, background consensus on traditional norms and values supportive of communicative interaction, the free-floating idea of community to which his judgment appeals lacks sufficient ground *(Grund)* for discrimination. Hence Nancy's suspicion that his judgment amounts to little more than an unprincipled, sophistical rhetoric of provocation, forever mutable with respect to context—aesthetic performance rather than reasoned criticism.

Yet perhaps there is another way to read Lyotard here. His postmodern patchwork of paganism (Aristotle) and modernism (Kant) suggests that *determinant* and *reflective* judgments are abstractions of a single movement of deliberation (52). Judgments determine the regulative content of ideas by applying them to particular cases, while prejudgments—originating in tradition—determine the process of judging itself, apart from *thematic* reflection. This process, however, is not deterministic. Both instances engage a prethematic reflection in which particular and universal, judge and (pre)judgment, interpret one another dialogically—*not* discursively. Only in the course of this inner and more or less unconscious dialogue do the identity of the judge, the criteria on which he or she relies, and the facts on which he or she judges acquire mutual definition. Yet as our discussion of Arendt and Habermas indicated, this private, aesthetic dialogue can only acquire rationality by being inserted into public discourse. Only in this way can the historical community requisite for sustaining legitimate expectations over time and the rational community requisite for criticizing illegitimate prejudices *determine* one another in a manner conducive to judgment. If judgments presuppose agreement in contextual sensibility—to paraphrase the early Lyotard, *discours* is no substitute for *figure*—they nevertheless remain rationally free and indeterminate with respect to an ideal, open-ended future (150).

Contrary to Habermas, we may conclude that refusal to offer standard sorts of reasons in ethicopolitical discourse need not entail commission of a performative contradiction. Since discourse in this instance involves getting one's interlocutor(s) to enter the hermeneutic circle in which one's own highly situated life's experience is intimately implicated, the reasons offered in support of a judgment will not be exhausted by illocutionary claims to truth, justice, and the like, but will necessarily include such things as experiences, which we indirectly indicate through perlocutionary acts. And if—after all is said and done—no such common experience emerges, we might then rightly choose to remain silent.

3.3 The endless spectacle of *différends*—indeed, of boundless formlessness—cannot arouse the sort of sublime enthusiasm and sense of rational finality that Kant, as disinterested historical spectator, managed to feel about the French Revolution, despite all its injustices. It cannot do so because unity and finality—humanity progressing toward perpetual peace—are alien to it. But can we rest satisfied with a response that amounts to little more than the modest demand that "politics cannot have for its stake the good, but would have to have the least bad" (Lyotard 1983, 203)?

Answering this question would require adjudicating the *différend* between Habermas and Lyotard—an impossible task, no doubt, and one that

I myself have undertaken only with the greatest reservation. Instead I propose an immanent criticism of their respective views. I have already noted the tensions in Habermas's modernism. *Within* the logical and semantical limits of practical discourse as Habermas sees it, one cannot infer a procedural idea of justice without committing certain fallacies: the fallacy of inferring a normative phrase from a transcendental one, and the fallacy of inferring a transcendental phrase from a factual one. Habermas's attempt to account for the *quasi*-transcendental, *quasi*-prescriptive nature of rules of argumentation that are neither strictly compelling (necessary) nor strictly discretionary (susceptible to violation without performative contradiction) shows that he is cognizant of the former difficulty. His attempt to ground rational reconstructions in the considered judgments reached by philosophers, social scientists, psychologists, and test subjects in a reflectively equilibrated dialogue shows that he is cognizant of the latter. Contrary to Lyotard, neither difficulty speaks against the possibility of practical discourse per se but only against the possibility of a discourse that insists on suppressing the metaphoricity of reason behind the rigid exterior of logical incommensurabilities. Neither do they preclude the raising of *fallible* truth-claims so long as their meaning and validity are not assumed to be finally determined (Habermas 1990, 93).

Finality would make sense *only if* we could purify a unitary form of the multiplicity of local contents. Habermas's own "fudging" of boundaries separating *literally* incommensurable phrasal regimens and genres amply testifies to the impossibility of such purification. The integrity of reason can be conceived only if its contextual *impurity* and *metaphoricity* are factored in. Habermas's account of the integrity of both specialized and everyday discourse—as well as his recent claims about the *informal* (intuitive and aesthetic) rationality governing judgment—are compatible with this position (Habermas 1987b, 398); his insistence on the finality and—above all—procedural rationality of justice is not.[14] For, if Habermas's idea of democratic procedural justice intentionally lacks the institutional specificity that Lyotard, fearing totalitarian democracy, thinks it does not lack, it also intentionally lacks the utopian feel for integral happiness that Habermas, fearing social reification, wishes it might have.

This last point brings us to similar tensions in Lyotard's account of the *différend*. The *différend* presupposes incommensurability between different genres and regimens. This all too modern presumption of pure, rational types threatens to degenerate into a atomistic plurality of unrelated phrases whose external interaction cannot even begin to explain the mere possibility of communicative linkage. In order to account for the latter, Lyotard must qualify the extent to which phrases and genres are literally incommensurable, without abandoning the idea entirely. Like Habermas, he does this by introducing the notion of aesthetic judgment, which reflects the metaphorical commensurability of literally incommensurable language games. In effect, both philosophers concede that the strict opposition between rational argumentation and aesthetic judgment falls to the ground.

Now, I shall argue that Habermas's idea of rational community is preferable to Lyotard's, if for no other reason than that it explains why one ought to resist hegemonic injustice. Put simply, health (integrity) is a more attractive aesthetic idea to fight for than sublimely endless distraction.

The preference for Habermas becomes clearer when we examine the limits of the *différend* as a cipher for justice. Lyotard nowhere clearly distinguishes the *différend* that occurs between the camp survivor and the revisionist historian from the *différend* that necessarily occurs in any speech. Although the former plainly constitutes a wrong, the latter does not. (Indeed, does it not seem bizarre to describe as *injustice* a condition whose continual interruption of hegemonic closure supposedly redeems our faith *in* justice?) In fact, Lyotard takes great pains to show that the *différend* is a class of injustice totally *unlike* our customary notions of political injustice.

At this juncture I feel compelled to raise an objection that goes directly to the heart of the problem Lyotard and Habermas inherit from German idealism: the problem of choosing between total(itarian) unity or total(itarian) anarchism. I am sympathetic to Richard Rorty's suspicion that these thinkers are scratching where it does not itch. Surely, the source of hegemony—if indeed there is hegemony—is nothing as murky as the diremption or selective cultivation of reason. At first blush, it seems closer to the kind of injustice Michael Walzer talks about when he criticizes the wrongful hegemony of one sphere of goods over another—a hegemony without which political injustice (class domination, or monopoly over dominant goods) would not be a problem in the first place. Like Walzer, Lyotard argues that questions of justice must be resolved in accordance with the "common understandings" that persons in a given society share regarding the distribution of specific types of goods. Specific *criteria* of justice are thus validated with respect to the popular narratives (or *petit récits*, as Lyotard puts it) that persons of specific societies recount to one another about these goods even if we concede, with Lyotard, that these narratives are open to continual disputation and interruption.

Since the dominance of money in capitalist democracies threatens the autonomy of the other spheres of justice and violates what Lyotard calls "the justice of pluralities" and what Habermas, under the very different rubric of health, designates the "integrity of a form of life," its influence must at least be curtailed or confined more thoroughly to the sphere of commodity exchange than it presently is. Here it should be noted that Lyotard's call for universal access to information in "non-zero-sum" democratic games confronts the hegemonic pretensions of business and administrative elites with a demand for *political* justice that is no less urgent than Habermas's (Lyotard 1984, 67).

Yet as our examination of Lyotard and Habermas has shown, one could hardly justify democracy as a *universal* and *pure* type of political rationality. Even if the *structural* combination of ethical, moral, and pragmatic criteria underwriting political discourse comprises an integral whole and not a *différend*, something of the latter still persists in the mediation of more substantive ethical and moral interpretations. Contrary to Walzer and Habermas, our "common understanding" of the *concrete* meanings of distributional criteria vis-à-vis specific assortments of goods is, if anything, uncommon. Being grounded neither in *the* reason of things (Habermas) nor in stable, coherent traditions (Walzer), its sense fluctuates depending on the conflicting "stakes" intersecting our political discourse.

This tension must be borne in mind when considering Lyotard's alleged hostility to democracy. Given his fear of manufactured consensus in mass democracy ("majority does not mean large number, but great fear" [Lyotard 1979, 188], it is no accident that some commentators have seen his postmodern call for political justice as centering on "neo-liberal, interest group pluralism," and "free, flexible, contractual arrangements."[15] Yet Lyotard's federalist suspicion of majoritarian tyranny is consonant with the spirit of dualist democracy, as Ackerman understands it. If it is also more radical than dualist democracy, this is because Lyotard thinks that no dual democratic vision "harmonizing" republican and federalist aims can overcome all injustice. No single criterion of justice—be it procedural (pertaining to decision rules), structural (pertaining to distributive rules), or libertarian (pertaining to civil rights)—suffices to legitimate legal institutions. At best, appeal to such criteria in proper combination serves to mitigate the injustices perpetrated by each separately (Fishkin 1979)

Having momentarily strayed into the dense thicket of postmodern political justice, we can now safely assert that the problem of judging hegemony remains even after we jettison the dialectic of enlightenment as our point of reference. These same considerations suggest that judgment can never achieve the rational integrity toward which it aspires. Habermas's acknowledgment of the "tortuous routes along which science, morality, and art communicate with one another" reminds us that judgment here may well be mixed with tinctures of the kind of sublimity attested to by Lyotard (Habermas 1987b, 398). The metaphorical link between the "truth" of a poem as an event of secular illumination, the "truth" of its moral content, the "truth" of our description of it, and the "truth(fulness)" of its expression of authentic experience comprises a syndrome that is as compelling to literary critics as it is to laypersons. But the syndrome by no means eliminates the literal incommensurabilities (disanalogies) separating these distinct senses of truth. That sublimely infinite gap reflects critically on the *felt* disparity between our *presentiment* of a vibrant life lived with full integrity (Dewey) and the *reality* of a life dispersed into opposed moments.

Unlike Lyotard, Habermas refuses to exaggerate this dissonance. In his opinion, the inability to "link meaning and validity, meaning and intention, and meaning and accomplished action," as well as the inability to effect "intermodal transfers" of validity within a communication setting, is nothing less than pathological (Habermas 1991a, 226).[16]

Certainly, contrary to some of Lyotard's more extreme formulations, there must be some integrity in our capacity to *judge*. The *manner* in which we switch from one mode of argumentation to another within a specific type of discourse, from one phrasal regimen to another within a mode of argumentation, and from one perspective (modality) to another within a phrasal regimen, must be regulated in advance by the logic of the discourse in question, even if the transition (or translation) between otherwise incommensurable modalities is metaphorical, not logical. As Habermas puts it, "*[W]hether* and *when* we are supposed to accomplish it depends on the faculty of judgment inherent in communicative action itself" (226). If this is the case—and all our previous inquiries suggest that it is—then the rationale guiding this faculty must be intuitive, aesthetic, and prediscursive. Again, to cite an earlier example, one might question my judgment that P sincerely believes what she says, but whether or not my inference is a good one surely depends on my experience in dealing with her. At some point it becomes silly for me to offer any further reasons in support of my judgment, a view amply confirmed in my ultimate retort: "You don't know P the way *I* do!" The ensuing silence once again marks the *rational* limits of reasoned justification. No one better states the case for it than Habermas himself when he reminds us that "there are no metadiscourses for this (judgment)"—indeed "no metadiscourses whatsoever"—since "every discourse is . . . equally close to God" (226).

With this reference to the day of redemption I leave the reader with one final note—an anticipation of things to come, as it were. Despite its intuitive nature, judgment—at least as I have here presented it—is also, in the final analysis, indistinguishable from the character and autobiography of the judge, and that means situated with respect to the narratives he or she shares with others. These narratives, we saw, essentially anticipate their

own completeness and perfectibility, be they ever so personal or monu-
mental. As for the latter—and here I include Habermas's own epic analogy
between individual moral development and social evolution—I propose
that we think of them as transcendental illusions possessing a rationale
more broadly aesthetic than narrowly cognitive. Such "myths" enable us
to *think as if* "we" decentered subjects are progressing in the direction of a
community, and therein lies their legitimacy. This latter assertion merits a
more detailed discussion than can be marshaled here, but two points are
worth noting. First, grand narratives are indispensable for engaging in debates about the larger questions of justice raised by Lyotard, Walzer, and
Habermas. The struggle against totalitarianism is conducted on multiple
fronts, each centered on some specific lingua franca. The meanings and
distributive criteria attached to these goods change, as do the boundaries
delimiting the language games in which they are staked. Interpreting them
therefore requires engaging a grander narrative about who we are—whence
we have come and whither we are going—as part and parcel of a more
encompassing community of judgment.

The second point qualifies the first. In contrast to the guardedly optimistic, problem-solving orientation of progressive, modernist narratives,
Lyotard's *différend* reminds us of the inherent limits and unavoidable injustices that come with trying to impose any simple *or* complex schema of
justice. Indeed, it reminds us of the peculiarly *tragic* nature of our dirempted
(post)modern condition; the aims of truth, honesty, equality, freedom, and
happiness that enter into our complex reasoning are not reconcilable in a
way that could do justice to them all. Such a reminder entails conservative
cynicism just as much (or as little) as its opposite—optimistic idealism—
entails revolutionary totalitarianism. Should it perchance encourage
piecemeal amelioration of suffering and injustice in the name of liberal compassion, so much the better. If this is the price we democrats must
pay for justice, then *silence*—or the "great refusal"—may well be as justified
as unremitting participation in a "dialogue" whose promise for redemption, however illusory, still remains our only hope.

The Legitimacy of the Modern Age
Toward a Metaphorology of
Revolution, Myth, and Progress in
Science and Politics

History is the subject of a structure whose site is not homogeneous, empty time, but time filled by the presence of the now. Thus, to Robespierre ancient Rome was a past charged with the time of the now which he blasted out of the continuum of history.
— Walter Benjamin, *Theses on the Philosophy of History*

there is the question of this ungraspable revolutionary instant that belongs to no historical, temporal continuum but in which the foundation of a new law nevertheless plays, if we may say so, on something from an anterior law that it extends, radicalizes, deforms, metaphorizes, metonymizes. . . .
— Jacques Derrida, *Force of Law: The "Mystical Foundation of Authority"*

The major part of this study has been devoted to clarifying the communitarian grounds of legislation and adjudication. After rejecting SR as an unsatisfactory account of rationality in part 1 and defending an alternative account predicated on communication in part 2, I proceeded to argue in part 3 for a complex theory of legitimation. The theory holds that legitimate laws are laws that have been processed in accordance with procedures that instantiate egalitarian criteria. Aside from being anchored in formal conditions of CR, what makes such procedures legitimate is their long-term production of substantively just results. This happens only when the particular institutional forms that concretely articulate them are sensitive to the peculiar historical circumstances of the society they regulate. Judgment is here called upon to evaluate what justice in its integrity requires in any given situation and to weigh the values most conducive toward bringing it about.

In examining the communicative conditions for judgment in part 4, we confronted a new legitimation crisis centering on the dialectic of enlightenment. That reason lacks unity and integrity, and so both permits and promotes the one-sided growth of instrumental reason to the detriment of communicative rationality, undermines the traditional and communitarian authority on which judgment depends for its legitimate exercise. This dialectic, however, appears less inevitable once we realize that capitalism, rather than reason as such, is the primary cause of reason's disintegration. Reason's internal differentiation into distinct formal values and rationalization complexes need not preclude its harmonious integration. However, what is most needed to offset disintegration—judgment—is also what is most endangered by it. For what makes integration possible is the aesthetic reflection that judges similarities between distinct aspects of experience. We exercise this faculty whenever we spontaneously shift from one modality of discourse to another and, more importantly, whenever we critically evaluate the health of a form of life, the integrity of a system of justice, or the beauty (or sublimity) of an experience.

If the dialectic of enlightenment were the only crisis affecting modernity, our task would be finished. However, things are not quite that simple. We have taken the historical inevitability and progressiveness of modernity for granted, without attending to the legitimacy of its revolutionary repudiation of authority. I have already appealed to Kuhn's conception of scientific revolution to explicate paradigm shifts in constitutional authority, specifically as regards the authorization of amendments. Now I will reexamine the communicative preconditions underlying that notion as a constraint on scientific authority. However, before doing so it will be useful to clarify the legitimation problems besetting political revolutions, since they illuminate similar problems affecting scientific revolutions. If I am not mistaken, Arendt's account of the secular legitimation of modern political revolutions parallels Kuhn's—and especially Blumenberg's—accounts of modern scientific revolutions, and all three underscore the importance of progress and authority as complementary categories without which—contra Derrida and Lyotard—revolutions and epochs, in short history as a theater of change, would be meaningless.

1. While ruminating on Abbé Sieyès's celebrated appeal to national sovereignty in legitimating the Constituent Assembly, Hannah Arendt mentions two problems that appear to render all revolutions necessarily illegitimate:

> the problem of the legitimacy of the new power, the *pouvoir constitué*, whose authority could not be guaranteed by the Constituent Assembly, the *pouvoir constituant*, because the power of the Assembly itself was not constitutional and could never be constitutional since it was

prior to the constitution itself; and the problem of the legality of the new laws which needed a "source and supreme master," the higher law' from which to derive their validity. (Arendt 1973, 163)

Let us call the first problem the problem of *preconstitutional* legitimation. Formulated as a paradox, it says that all constitutional assemblies authorize their own historical authority; they constitute the people in whose name they act. The only way out of this circle, it seems, is to argue, as Sieyès did, that the authority vested in the assembly exists outside the act of constitution, in some transcendent moral law (such as Sieyès's national will). This generates the second problem of *prepolitical* legitimation. Equally paradoxical, this problem concerns not the historical title but the radical autonomy of equals who freely contract with one another to constitute a new political foundation: The free consent that morally binds the contractors can break from the constraints of conventional law only by deriving its authority from a higher, more universal law; but this law, in turn, apparently emanates from an *external*–naturally or divinely preordained–force that imposes itself on the contractors independently of their free consent. Thus in the modern era revolutionaries have justified their acts on two problematic grounds: one referring to the historical authority of a particular people whose sovereignty has been violated and is now being reconstituted; the other referring to the metaphysical authority of a universal subject, be it humanity or God, whose sovereignty limits free consent even while limiting historical authority.

This "modern" solution to the problem of legitimation has recently come under attack by "postmodernists," who argue that the attempt to circumvent circularity is itself illegitimate–and for two reasons. First, it commits a kind of naturalistic fallacy; it involves inferring a prescriptive utterance (that certain rights *ought* to be freely accepted) from a descriptive one (that they *must* be accepted). Second, in conflating politics and metaphysics in this manner, it conceals the inherent partiality and violence of any legal regime, thereby encouraging imperialism under the banner of universal, manifest destiny.

Although I do not deny that attempts by revolutionaries to justify their acts in terms of universal principles have often had the consequences described by postmodern critics, I doubt that these consequences are necessary. In particular, I will argue that they are not necessary, so long as the principle appealed to is understood as a procedural rule for agreeing on rights rather than as a direct prescription of them.

My argument will be framed in terms of a confrontation between Jacques Derrida and Jean-François Lyotard, on one side, and Hannah

Arendt, on the other. Although Arendt shares Derrida's opinion that the American Declaration of Independence cannot avoid appealing to "absolute" foundations in its declaration of inalienable rights, she argues that this absolute can refer to legitimate, nonmetaphysical principles as well as to illegitimate, metaphysical ones. Thus, while sharing Lyotard's concern about the imperialistic (or absolutist) implications of collapsing politics and metaphysics in the way the French Declaration of the Rights of Man and Citizen did, she observes that the Declaration need not have had these implications had its underlying principle been understood as a constitutive rule regulating the "grammar" of free political deliberation about ends rather than as a natural imperative dictating a single aim (namely, welfare) realizable solely through sovereign state power. In her opinion, procedures of democratic fair play implicit in this grammar not only adhere in the higher law of human nature—the pluralistic constitution of meaningful and perduring identity through free and open communication among equals—but such procedures augment *this* law in turn. They enhance political freedom only to the extent that they are translated into *positive* law, specifically, in the form of a durable constitution providing for a separation of powers. Far from being vicious, the circularity implicit in this mediation of principle and practice is legitimate in a hermeneutical, if not logical, sense.

2. We noted that postmodern critics like Derrida and Lyotard are skeptical about philosophical legitimations of any sort. It therefore comes as no surprise to find them deconstructing the revolutionary documents of the Enlightenment. Their intent is not to impugn revolutions or revolutionary actions, much less universal responsibilities with respect to fellow human beings. It is rather to expose the nonsense of confusing the latter with the former. In their opinion, the ethical command to respond to others respectfully is akin to an existential presupposition. This universal idea ought not to be confused with any concrete declaration of political rights, since doing so, they tell us, is not only fallacious but ideological—endowing contingent and partial laws with the sanctified aura of a timeless justice. Since every modern constitution commits this fallacy when it enjoins universal human rights, none, according to postmodernists, are truly legitimate. Hence revolutionary action is justified simply because no legal system can be legitimate for all.

The fact that all constitutions are partial in their protection and advancement of political interests would seem to make them easy targets for revolutionaries bent on realizing justice for all. Yet, ironically, postmodernists have discarded a critical distinction—between morally just and unjust political regimes—that revolutionaries routinely deploy in justifying their actions. Construing justification on the model of logical inference, post-modernists argue that there is a rational distinction, or logical incommen-surability, between descriptive (constative) and prescriptive (performative) speech acts, speculative and political language games, and so on, such that revolutionary initiatives, which are framed as prescriptions of political rights, cannot be justified on philosophical grounds, which are framed as descrip-tions of essential moral laws. However, they then go on to argue that po-litical discourse inevitably violates this injunction anyway, by eliding, smoothing over, or collapsing the logical gap separating political prescrip-tion from speculative constation. This fallacious equivocation immunizes such discourse against more conventional political criticism, unless that criticism takes the form of a radical deconstructive critique of legitimating discourse in general.

The clearest example of this kind of critique is contained in a public lecture that Derrida delivered at the University of Virginia in 1976, where he argued that the "meaning and effect" of the Declaration of Independ-ence depended on masking its own historical contingency and political partiality. It ostensibly accomplished this by conflating two kinds of speech acts, constative and performative, and then concealed this fallacy behind an appeal to God as the highest authority—"the last instance" and "ultimate signature" of the Declaration (Derrida 1986, 12).

Derrida initially raises the question of authorization in conjunction with the problem of circularity mentioned above. The signers of the Dec-laration claim authorization from the very people whose sovereignty their Declaration authorizes. The signers state that they are acting "in the name and by the authority of the good people of these colonies" when they declare that "these united colonies. . . ought to be free." According to Derrida, by simultaneously asserting and enjoining the sovereignty of the American people, they do not represent so much as create this people. In the words of Derrida,

> This people does not exist. They do *not* exist as an entity, it does *not* exist, *before* this declaration, not *as such*. If it gives birth to itself, as free and independent subject, as possible signer, this can hold only in the act of the signature. The signature invents the signer. . . . In signing the people say—and do what they say they do, but in differing or deferring themselves through *(différant par)* the intervention of their representa-tives whose representativity is fully legitimated only by the signature, thus after the fact or the coup *(après coup)*—henceforth, I have a right to

sign, in truth I will already have had it since I was able to give it to myself. I will have given myself a name and an "ability" or a "power," understood in the sense of a power- or ability-to-sign by declaration of signature. (10)

In this passage Derrida alludes to the postmodern, future-anterior modality of the Declaration; that is, the unstated assumption that each representative *will have had* the right to sign the Declaration upon signing it. The signature supposedly creates the people that are presumed to authorize the signing.

Stated in such bald terms, this postmodern reading of the Declaration seems false. Surely the American people existed before the signing; indeed, as Arendt points out, the signing of the Declaration merely reenacted prior political compacts that the colonists believed had been violated by the Crown. And yet, there is a sense in which this new Declaration can be said to officially ratify and authorize the sovereignty of the American people for the first time, namely, in its appeal to a *universal* right to self-determination.

In fact, a closer reading of Derrida's deconstruction of the Declaration shows that he is aware of both possibilities: the American people already possess the sovereign title to authorize the declaration of their independence *and* this title is only first authorized by the signers. According to Derrida, the power of the Declaration actually depends on collapsing these two possibilities; on the one hand, the Declaration *does* something; it *makes* the American people free (i.e., it normatively constitutes a fact, the sovereign being of the United States). On the other hand, it reasserts a fact; it alludes to the historical and metaphysical freedom of Americans. So construed, the Declaration seems to commit the "is-ought" fallacy first discussed by David Hume in the *Treatise;* it infers a prescriptive (or performative) utterance of the form, "There ought to be...," from an assertoric (or constative) utterance of the form "There is (must) be ..."

Derrida's suggestion that the Declaration commits such a fallacy appears at the conclusion of a long commentary in which he seems to be saying several things. First, he seems to be saying that the Declaration's circular authorization of its own authority is problematic, at the very least. Interpreted in its most charitable light, the circularity, he suggests, would entail two qualifications that severely limit the legitimating potential of the Declaration: only those who actually signed would be bound by it and only provisionally, since they or their descendants would once again have to retroactively authorize the authority of the Declaration. Second, even if we dismiss the temporal circularity of the Declaration and limit its binding scope to the actual signers, we still have the problem of explaining how a prescription—even one addressed exclusively to oneself—can follow from an historical or metaphysical fact.

Let me clarify these points further by returning to the passage cited above. Derrida seems disturbed by the circularity implicit in the act of legitimation, which constitutes a future sovereign by the authority vested in its prior existence. Is he disturbed because of the partiality of the signatories, who do not, after all, represent—not even "virtually"— all Americans? If so, one might counter that there is at least nothing ideologically dangerous in retroactively taking moral or legal possession of one's own de facto sovereignty (the signers of the Declaration, we know, never deluded themselves into thinking that they spoke for African-American slaves). Derrida himself does something analogous to this when he observes that, through being shaped in response to others, his own self-determination and identity impose a corresponding obligation on him (Derrida) to behave responsibly toward these very same others (Kearney 1984, 118–21).

If the patent circularity of the Declaration were construed in this way, as a performative representation, ratification, or reenactment of a *personal* fact about oneself, the Declaration's legitimacy would be quite limited. It would be clear that the only people the representatives might declare independent—as a matter of *political* as opposed to *ethical* fact, right, and duty— would be just themselves, in which case they would cease to be representing anyone else. From this perspective, the circularity inherent in constitutional acts *does* undermine absolute—unconditional and unlimited—claims to representation and legitimacy, and for two reasons. Stated in Rousseauean terms, it shows that no one can be under an obligation to which they could not have personally consented, and that whatever obligation a person consents to cannot be binding on future generations without their express consent. More radically, it undermines *re*presentation as such, since what is supposedly represented was never fully present in the first place but is at best a promise, or idea, whose conditions of satisfaction are forever deferred.[1]

I will have more to say about the deferred nature of authorization later. Suffice it to say, the delegates intended to speak on behalf of persons other than themselves—not just the American people but all "men." In doing so they over-extended their "rightful" power; indeed, they presumed an *absolute* power to endow humanity as such with *inalienable* rights. Lyotard's reading of the Declaration of the Rights of Man confirms this assessment. For him, the appearance of absolute rectitude is achieved by collapsing different genres of discourse that possess incommensurable scopes of validity. Like Derrida, Lyotard takes note of the future anterior circularity of the Declaration but finds nothing shocking in it (Lyotard 1988, 146)

Indeed, if the above analysis is correct, this circularity—inherent in the preconstitutional act of legitimation—is incapable of legitimating anything as impersonal and timeless as the "rights of man." Rather, what supposedly legitimates the rights of man is the linkage of a *political* declaration of specific obligations owed to French citizens by their state with a phrase—about the universal necessity of rights, generally—belonging to a very different, *metaphysical* or *speculative,* genre of discourse. These incommensurable discourses, which respectively address the French citizen and humanity, are collapsed in Article 16's assertion that "The representatives of the French People, organized in National Assembly . . . have resolved to set forth in solemn declaration the natural, inalienable, and sacred rights of man. . . ." (145). The overall effect is striking: the representatives of the French people, with their limited temporal authority and geographical power, seem to be divinely legislating for all humanity—a sure recipe for imperialism if there ever were one:

> The splitting of the addressee of the Declaration into two entities, French nation and human being, corresponds to the *equivocation* of the declarative phrase: it presents a philosophical universe and copresents a historical-political universe. The revolution in politics that is the French Revolution comes from this *impossible passage* from one universe to another. Thereafter, it will no longer be known whether the law thereby declared is French or human, whether the violence exerted under the title of freedom is repressive or pedagogical (progressive), whether those nations which are not French ought to be French or become human by endowing themselves with Constitutions that conform to the Declaration, be they anti-French. This *confusion* permitted by the Constituent Assembly and assured its propagation throughout the historical-political world will turn every national or international conflict into an *insoluable différend* over the legitimacy of authority. (147; my italics)

Thanks to its equivocation, the Declaration of Rights set in motion a world revolution whose effects are still being felt two hundred years later. But was this revolution progressive or simply destructive? Were the revolutionary wars that continued through the Napoleonic era wars of liberation—attempts to extend the blessings of divinely sanctioned natural right to all of humanity—or were they wars of imperial expansion—attempts to extend the dominion of the French government over its neighbors? Even if we regard the revolution in more benign terms, as a cultural revolution that spread the emancipatory blessings of the Enlightenment throughout the world, it still remains unclear whether this should be called progress.

In Lyotard's opinion, we are confronted with a *différend,* or situation where the injustices perpetrated on non-European peoples as a result of emancipatory enlightenment and the injustices perpetrated on them by their own dogmatic tradition cannot be fairly balanced against one another for lack of a neutral legal language. Absent any impartial litigation, the "universal" language of the Declaration of Rights will inexorably "legitimate" the forceable imposition of "free" constitutions everywhere—albeit only in conformity with the French model.

Perhaps it is this conflation of universal and particular discourses that ultimately explains Derrida's concern about the appeal to inalienable rights contained in the Declaration of Independence. If so, it is because this conflation rests on a more fundamental fallacy involving the inference of prescriptions from constations. For him, too, such a confusion explains why "the coup of writing, as the right to writing"–which is simultaneously the "coup of force [that] makes right" (Derrida 1986, 11)–must appeal to God as the final authority.

One need only recall the salient and all too familiar passages of the Declaration to see Derrida's point. The appeal to absolute power is fully apparent in the Declaration's opening reference to the "laws of nature" and "nature's God"; in its closing reference to Divine Providence "for support of this declaration"; and, of course, in the famous second paragraph of the preamble, which begins with the words, "We hold these truths to be self-evident, that all men are created equal; that they are endowed by their creator with certain inalienable rights." Like Lyotard, Derrida insists that the appeal to God as absolute power and authority is not merely gratuitous. In claiming that "these united colonies are and of right ought to be free and independent states," the representatives violate a logical distinction between "the to be and the ought to be, the constation and the prescription, the fact and the right." But only God, who is at once "creator of nature and judge, supreme judge of what is (the state of the world) and of what relates to what ought to be (rectitude of our intentions)" (13) has the power and right to violate the laws of logic. For it is he who "founds natural laws and thus the whole game which tends to present performative utterances *as* constative utterances" (11).

Notice that Derrida assumes that performative and constative utterances comprise logically heterogeneous classes of utterances. This supposedly entails the illegitimacy of inferring the former kind of utterance, an "ought" statement, from the latter, an "is" statement. Is Derrida right about this? John Searle–one of Derrida's chief critics–wrote a compelling paper some years ago showing how an "ought" statement, such as "Jones ought to pay Smith five dollars," might follow in some nondeductive way from a factual statement asserting that "Jones uttered the words 'I hereby promise to pay you, Smith, five dollars'" (Searle 1970). Simply put, Searle used speech act theory to show how the institution of promising is both factually constituted and normatively regulated by certain sorts of practices. Without entering into a detailed discussion of this demonstration, we can see that certain words such as "promise" are both normative and descriptive; in uttering this word in the appropriate circumstances one has in fact promised; and having promised, one is (all things being equal) normatively bound to satisfy the behavioral expectations attendant on promising.

The power of Searle's argument is hard to resist. Indeed, both Habermas and Taylor have been convinced by it. As we shall see shortly, something like it also underlies Arendt's own take on the performative character of the Declaration's promise. Before proceeding to that discussion, however, I would like to touch briefly on another difficulty with Derrida's constation/ performance distinction—one that seems to undermine the credibility of his own ethical standpoint.

Besides failing to explain the valid inference of prescriptions from descriptions of performative speech acts, the logical incommensurability between "is" and "ought" renders an important class of philosophical utterances illegitimate as well, namely those essentialist claims about human nature that implicitly enjoin the perfectibility of the essential quality they assert. Again, recall the assertion/prescription that persons ought to act responsibly toward one another because they are (necessarily) responsible to and for one another. Since Derrida himself subscribes to this declaration, would he not be compelled to concede *its* illegitimacy (Kearney 1984, 118–21)? There is reason to think that he would. After all, he himself notes how hard it is for speakers to resist the "metaphysical" illusion that the language they speak represents rather than constitutes reality (Derrida 1981, 58–59). And since he has made much of the inherent undecidability of performance and constation in all language—especially deconstructive language—he would doubtless accept the logical verdict that all language is illegitimate and nonsense to some degree.[2] Whether this makes his own work an ironic exercise in self-refutation is for the reader to decide. Yet, regardless of how one resolves this issue, one thing remains abundantly clear: Derrida's apparent belief that *all* language *must* conflate performance and constation, use and mention, in a foundationalist manner reveals more about the metaphysical cast of his own thought than it does about the representational mystifications of language.[3] Suffice it to say, in the interpretation of the Declaration to which we will now turn, Arendt provides us with a very different account of the secular grounds of legitimation—

one that construes the unity of constation and performance, facticity and freedom, in terms of historical understanding.

In summation, then, Lyotard and Derrida argue that whatever political freedoms revolutionaries seek to promulgate cannot legitimately claim title to universal right, because the languages and speech acts in which politics and philosophy find expression are just too incommensurable to allow it. Legitimate revolutions—if there are any—must rest content with that limited and local authority befitting self-referential acts. But can an authority so limited in scope suffice to legitimate a modern, revolutionary constitution or international charter of rights?

2.1 Let us grant for the sake of argument that the languages of philosophy and politics, constation and performance, are *logically* incommensurable, so that you cannot infer a phrase belonging to one of them from a phrase belonging to another. Does it then follow that these different kinds of speech cannot supervene on one another without commission of a fallacy? Can we conceive the circle of legitimation in a nonvicious, *hermeneutical* way, so that appeal to a past authority does not collide with the free constitution of a future, and the latter does not collide with constraints imposed by timeless principles?

My reading of Arendt, whom I see as responding positively to this question, will doubtless strike many as odd given the favorable reception accorded her writings by Derrida, Lyotard, and other French postmodernists.[4] Yet, despite the fact she too denounced political ideologies based on metaphysical absolutes, she found nothing inherently objectionable in founding universal rights on secular grounds. The grounds she had in mind were constitutive rules or procedures of common deliberation, among them being the obligation—proclaimed by Derrida among others—to respond openly to one's interlocutor as a singular person. But this obligation, she insisted, was more than an abstract ethical command. It was a principle that could only realize itself in a democratic constitution, that is, in a contingent political act that retroactively secures the principle's own meaning and efficacy—and with it, the autonomy of the actor—through historical interpretation.

Arendt frames her discussion of this peculiar circle in terms of an interesting contrast between premodern and modern revolutions. The *premodern*, astronomical sense of revolution as a recurrent cycle still survived in the "Glorious Revolution of 1688," which understood itself to be "a restoration of monarchical power to its former righteousness and glory"

(Arendt 1973, 43). By contrast, the first *modern* revolutions—the American Revolution of 1776 and the French Revolution of 1789—not only restored ancient liberties, they refounded them on a totally new, universal order. Between past and future, they revolved back to the republican models of Greek and Roman antiquity in order to revolve ahead to a final, lasting, constitution of freedom. Hence their need for some higher, absolute authorization beyond the transient realm of politics.

The idea of revolving back to a past in legitimating the present and future is hardly novel. More interesting is the idea of revolving ahead to a future to redeem, or legitimate the past. This idea, which we encountered earlier in our examination of Derrida's account of the future anterior status of the Declaration of Independence, will be the topic of a later discussion. Of more immediate concern is the problematic absoluteness by which modern revolutions distinguish themselves from their premodern counterparts.

A superficial reading of her "deconstruction" of the Declaration of Independence suggests that Arendt is in basic agreement with the postmodern critics in criticizing the philosophical appeal to absolutes.

> Jefferson's famous words, "We hold these truths to be self-evident," combine in a historically unique manner the basis of agreement between those who have embarked on revolution, an agreement necessarily relative because related to those who enter it, with an absolute, namely with a truth that needs no agreement since, because of its self-evidence, it compels without argumentative demonstration or political persuasion. (192)

In this passage Arendt seems to agree with Derrida that political and philosophical modes of speech are incompatible. Indeed, she makes the case more strongly by suggesting that philosophical assertions about necessary and universal laws contradict human freedom: "By virtue of being self-evident, these truths are prerational—they inform reason but are not its product—and since their self-evidence puts them beyond disclosure and argument, they are in a sense no less compelling than 'despotic power' and no less absolute than the revealed truths of religions or the axiomatic verities of mathematics" (192). The impression that philosophical language has no legitimate place in the Declaration is further reinforced by another curious remark. As if to get Jefferson off the hook, she adds that if he had solely intended to justify his claim that "all men are created equal" philosophically, he would have dispensed with the performative (or practical) speech act "We hold . . ." and simply asserted: "These truths are self-evident" (193).

From this last remark it is apparent that Arendt agrees with Derrida that Jefferson's declaration illegitimately conflates performative political speech and constative philosophical speech but disagrees with him about whether *this* particular conflation was necessary in order to procure the declaration's universal authority. For unlike him, she thinks that its rhetorical effect is entirely secured by the performative act alone. The appeal to absolute authority was redundant, she submits, since what really legitimated the declaration was its *reenactment* of the sorts of social contracts that had been made by the colonists dating back to the Mayflower Compact, and its *reassertion* of the kinds of rights that typically entered into such agreements (170).

But surely that can't be the whole story, for Arendt herself insists that what was truly modern about the American Revolution was not its restoration of local and contingent rights, but its declaration of their universality. Indeed, it is possible to understand her as saying that the appeal to a secular, praxis-immanent absolute was both historically and philosophically necessitated, but in a manner sustained by free acts of interpretation. Instead of the image of an imperious will (or nature) imposing its dictates unilaterally (and illegitimately) against our free consent, she substitutes the image of an unconstrained dialogue oriented toward consensus—a collective but pluralistic sort of willing wherein the performative presuppositions of dialogue itself become an object of democratic interpretation and constitution (204, 212, 214).

Let me begin by briefly recapitulating Arendt's argument for the historical necessity of absolute legitimations, since this argument has considerable bearing on their philosophical necessity as well. For Arendt, "no revolution is even possible where the authority of the body politic is truly intact" (Arendt 1977, 115). So, faced with the dilemma of having to invoke an old authority in violation of their emancipatory ideal or relinquish any historical title to their newly acquired power, the revolutionaries compromised: they filled old bottles with new wine. They not only justified their acts as *restorations* of ancient liberties that had been illegitimately suppressed under absolutist government. They did so in an absolutist manner that mimicked the very power and authority they were rebelling against. For, "Just as the old concept of liberty, because of the attempted restoration, came to exert a strong influence on the interpretation of the new experience of freedom, so the old understanding of power and authority, even if their former representatives were most violently denounced, almost automatically led the new experience of power to be channelled into concepts which had just been vacated" (155).

According to Arendt, the revolutionaries could scarcely avoid appealing to absolutes given the fact that preceding generations of monarchs had solved the problem of authority "within the given frame of reference in which the legitimacy of rule ... had always been justified by relating them to an absolute source. . . ." (160). Indeed, they did so even while breaking with that same frame of reference. For they argued that the absolute power and authority presumed by the monarchs usurped the power and authority of God's messengers along with the power and authority of political agents engaged in radical acts of self-determination.

> The specific sanction which religion and religious authority had bestowed upon the secular realm could not simply be replaced by an absolute sovereignty, which, lacking a transcendent and transmundane source, could only degenerate into tyranny and despotism. The truth of the matter was that when the Prince "had stepped into the pontifical shoes of the Pope and Bishop," he did not, for that reason, *assume the function* and receive the sanctity of Bishop or Pope; in the language of political theory, he was not a successor but a usurper, despite all the new theories about sovereignty and the divine rights of princes. (159–69; my italics)

For the revolutionaries, then, the illegitimacy of absolute monarchy consisted in transferring a spiritual conception of power and authority into public life, with the result that the *proper functions* of both religion and politics—the absolute relationship between private moral conscience and God and the contingent, social contract between political equals—were violated.

Clearly, if the legitimacy of modern revolutions depended on historically appropriating the absolutist framework of authority and power, it could only be the bare *form* or *function* of that framework, not its specific *substance*.[5] In fact, there was a profound substantive difference between the deistic God of the revolutionaries, who allows human beings to interact freely and equally in accordance with their own rational natures, and the paternalistic God of the monarchs, who assigns their governance to His divinely anointed trustees.

By attenuating divine intervention in human affairs, deism brought about a profound reversal. It transferred the final authority and absolute power that had formerly been vested in God to human beings acting in accordance with their secular principles. That might explain why Arendt held that the inalienable rights proclaimed by Jefferson "were in principle independent of religious sanction" (171), deriving from principles *inherent* in promising and common deliberation. Contrary to Arendt, performative acts like these both enact and constate their a priori conditions of possibility. They constitute substantive—that is, contingent and political—rights in a manner that accords with universal procedural rights. In promising and dialogic deliberation we both *factually* assume the equality, autonomy, and mutual openness of our fellow interlocutors *and* we *normatively* enjoin it. The "entirely new concept of power and authority" (166) revealed by the Declaration of Independence is thus not based on a "homogeneity of past and origin" (that is, on a particular language community bound by common traditions), but on practices that are virtually identifiable with the possibility of human society as such. If, as Benjamin and Derrida insist, we look to the past of a particular culture for guidance, it is a past that, in the words of Arendt, exemplifies something universal. This *timeless* past can be invoked by revolutionaries to liberate the present from an *oppressive* and *parochial* past. And if the "self-evident truths" and norms that inform such timeless exemplars of practical reasoning are not themselves the product of reasoning, it is not because they are axioms from which we might *logically* derive substantive political conclusions; rather, as abstract procedures of reasoning their own substantive meaning and institutional concretion unfolds in reasoning, viz., in discursive reflection and interpretation. This Habermasian reading of Arendt's text is confirmed in those passages where she says that the principle of "open discussion" (268) regulating "argumentative demonstration and political persuasion" (192) comprises the very "grammar of political action" (173). From remarks like these it would seem that, far from infringing on the ethical autonomy of political actions as postmodernists and their supporters maintain, principles of procedural justice actually constitute their possibility (204, 212, 214).

Arendt's argument that the American revolution succeeded where the French failed also confirms this reading. As she points out, "The most obvious and the most decisive distinction between the American and French Revolutions was that the historical inheritance of the American Revolution was 'limited monarchy' and that of the French Revolution an absolutism which apparently reached far back into the first centuries of our era and the last centuries of the Roman Empire" (155). The legacy of absolutism that burdened both revolutions was philosophical and theological. However, in the case of the French Revolution the legacy in question equated freedom with a united will (Robespierre's "Il faut une volonté UNE"). That legacy proved useful to revolutionaries confronting the daunting task of saving Europe's starving masses, just as the latter's need for material security proved useful in endowing the former's Declaration of Rights with a *natural necessity* that was lacking in the American prototype. Yet it was Arendt's belief that the appeal to natural necessity as a substitute for real freedom could not but prove disastrous for politics. This explains why, for her, the French Revolution betrayed its emancipatory promise and degenerated into a caricature of the very absolutism it had overthrown. The French revolutionaries could not have allowed their revolution to congeal into a permanent constitutional democracy without consenting to the lawful disruption of their own dictatorship through the regular election of new majorities. To have done otherwise would have frustrated the achievement of their own transcendent aims. Their Rousseauean equation of democratic polity with an absolutely united and sovereign people (or general will that can never bind itself) also serves to explain why the totalitarian descendants of the French Revolution in our present century manifested themselves as *movements* whose centers of power, Arendt observed, could reside only in the secret police, not the state.

For Arendt, nothing more clearly attests to the greater success of the Founding Fathers in breaking with the absolutist legacy than the durable authority of their accomplishments. Unburdened by the thought of starving masses, slaves, and general wills, their aim was to fashion a lasting constitution that would safeguard and augment the freedom they already enjoyed.[6] Their belief—inherited from Montesquieu—that power is augmented through its constitutional division and opposition—testifies to the inherent plurality of the human condition. More importantly, it mirrors the principle of the social contract—agreement based on a free and equal exchange of opinions—that in turn evinces the universal grammar of human action, communication, and identity.

In a nutshell, then, Arendt suggests that universal rights are legitimated by the universal political grammar in which they *indirectly* inhere. This enables her to avoid the paradox of prepolitical legitimation as well as the naturalistic fallacy that ostensibly accompanies it; for the conditions that determine and constrain political acts partially derive their force from these very same acts. The laws that citizens voluntarily give themselves interpret and constitute the moral presuppositions underlying lawmaking as such. As we shall see, without constitutional acts like these, the force of that moral imperative so extolled by postmodernists—the obligation to respect others—would be indeterminate and weak. Arendt's solution to this paradox also enables her to avoid the imperialistic implications that follow whenever political acts are logically (albeit fallaciously) identified with philosophical absolutes. Once we admit that our constitution is but one of many possible interpretations of that universal grammar regulating human communication, we will not be so imperious in imposing it on other people. Only one question remains to be answered. How does this hermeneutical circle shed light on the postmodern, future-anterior paradox of progress: that because those who have benefited from a constitutional tradition are freer than those who founded it, the real legitimation of a revolution is never finally completed?

2.2 Let us reformulate the question: Does Arendt's appeal to the hermeneutical circle effectively meet postmodern objections regarding the ethical illegitimacy of legislation and adjudication? Does interpreting our ethical grammar progressively realize or violate it? In order to answer these questions we must take a closer look at what it might mean to legitimate a revolution. For Arendt, the legitimacy of a revolution descends from both a prior claim entitling (or *empowering*) it and a subsequent success *authorizing* it. These temporal dimensions recall her earliest "transcendental" reflections on the nature of freedom, which is not surprising, since, in her judgment, revolutionaries not only act in the name of freedom, they exemplify it.[7] In beginning something radically new and unpredictable, revolutionaries reveal the extent of their own undetermined "natality." Conversely, in founding a democratic constitution providing for its own permanent emendation, they continue their revolution into the future, bringing about a greater freedom than they themselves enjoyed (Arendt 1977, 152).

Herein lies the tension, however. The freedom to initiate a radical beginning—to create one's legal identity ex nihilo—comes into conflict with the democratic freedom that has its legal identity preconstituted. But that is not the only problem. Radical foundings also need to legitimate themselves with respect to a prior law, power, and authority. Hence they cannot be the unprecedented acts of *self*-determination that they purport to be.

The reader will recall that Arendt frames these problems in terms of two circles. The conflict between revolutionary freedom and its constitutional augmentation recalls the postmodern, future-anterior circle of legitimation; it is we, the citizens of a democratic polity, who retroactively confer legitimacy on the constitutional foundation, since thanks to that constitution, our political assent is in some measurable sense freer than that given by the Founders and their constituents. But even "we the people" do not have final authority to confer legitimacy, for our own sovereign rights are always in the process of being constituted by the constitution. In Derrida's words, the legitimacy of the founding act remains indefinitely deferred.

The conflict between revolutionary freedom and its prior warrant recalls the other circle, discussed in the previous section. Because the founding act is never self-contained but always inherits its title from preexisting republican traditions and secularized absolutes, its freedom and legitimacy is indefinitely diminished in comparison to these original foundations.

Extrapolating from Arendt's distinction between historical and philosophical *levels* and originary and final *temporalities* of legitimation, there appear to be *four* legitimation problems. Using the distinction alluded to above (between power and authority) as our basal reference point, we detect, first of all, two problems involving the legitimation of power. The legitimation of power raises the following question: In whose name and by what right was the act originally undertaken? Suppose we try to give a historical answer to this question. In that case we are caught in the following double bind. Either the new regime accepts as legitimate the basic concepts and institutions of the political tradition it opposes, in which case it can claim to be a legitimate heir—but not a revolution; or it does not, in which case it seems arbitrary and without apparent reason or cause. If we try to give a philosophical answer to this problem we encounter a different kind of legitimation problem, one revolving around the concept of self-determination. Either revolutionaries act in the name of some absolute principle that constrains the mutual assent of all humanity—in which case neither they nor their acts exemplify spontaneous self-determination; or they do not, in which case, being unprincipled and conditioned by arbitrary circumstance, they remain as unfree as before.

A similar dialectic applies to the legitimation of authority, which concerns the end rather than the origin of revolutionary acts. In inquiring into the authority backing a revolution we ask: Why revolt? For what purpose? Suppose we give a historical answer to this question: We revolt for the sake of progress, to establish an enduring constitution in which people will be freer than they are *now*. If the revolution succeeds, it will have violated its own principle of self-determination. For how can it be progressive to deny subsequent generations the opportunity to exercise real—that is, revolutionary—self-determination? To reiterate Jefferson's concern, how can they be legitimately bound by an act they could not have possibly authorized? The democratic self-determination that they enjoy is not of their own making; and its institutional framework may even frustrate constitutional emendation. Of course, if the revolution does not succeed, then there will be plenty of opportunities for the people to reconstitute themselves freely. But a revolutionary dead end cannot be said to have legitimately realized its stated purpose.

The double bind is somewhat different if we give a philosophical answer to the question. Suppose I say I am revolting for the sake of realizing some transcendent, absolute ideal. If the end is truly final, then no constitution will be able to embody it. But short of actually doing so, no constitution will be legitimate, and our revolution will have been declared a failure. The alternative to this kind of utopian anarchism is a more qualified, immanent idealism, which identifies the purposes to be achieved with what was resolved and realized, once and for all, by the concrete articles set forth in the constitution itself. But in that case success is again purchased at the cost of legitimacy. Having no other purpose but to be itself, the revolution cannot progress, and, indeed, seems pointless—another dead end.

Does Arendt's understanding of the relationship between absolute ethical principle and contingent political action help us to "resolve" these paradoxes better than the postmodern alternative? First, it is well known that Derrida often celebrates the aporetic nature of language and philosophy in many of his writings. However the playful tone of his deconstructions seldom overshadows the political earnestness with which they're offered. Derrida wants to affirm the "deconstructibility" of law as "a stroke of luck for all politics, for all historical progress" by linking deconstruction to the open-ended imperative to be just (Derrida 1992, 15). He observes that this transcendent ethical imperative supervenes on law from the outside (14–15). Presumably, it is the continual interruption of business as usual by ethical conscience that explains inventive deviations from standard legal practice. This inventiveness, in turn, supposedly makes "progress" possible.

But does it? Because, in Derrida's account, transcendent justice commands openness vis-à-vis the Other, he can only conceive the interface between ethical principle and legal precedent as a catastrophic moment. In its deconstructive capacity interpretation is destructive; the judge decides as if he or she "invented the law in every case" (23). But as Derrida points out, such inventiveness is no more legitimate than mechanical application.

> [I]f the rule guarantees [the decision] in no uncertain terms, so that the judge is a calculating machine, which happens, and we will not say that he is just, free and responsible. But we also won't say it if he doesn't refer to any law, to any rule or if, because he doesn't take any rule for granted beyond his own interpretation, he suspends his decision, stops short before the undecidable or if he improvises and leaves aside all rules, all principles. It follows from this paradox that there is never a moment that we can say *in the present* that a decision *is* just (that is free and responsible), or that someone *is* a just man—even less, "I *am* just." (23)

In this passage Derrida poses—without resolving—the four paradoxes of legitimacy mentioned above. First, he tells us that ethical responsibility requires acting in the name of justice, not the law. However, in elevating private moral conscience above legal precedent, jurists act irresponsibly, without the guidance of established criteria of reasonableness. Yet mechanically adhering to the strict letter of the law is equally unreasonable when the matter to be decided is unprecedented and recalcitrant to legal calculation (or subsumption). Second, Derrida insists that the ethical imperative remain open-ended and indeterminate. But then it will not be able to move judgment in any determinate direction. This movement will be effected by the force of law. Third, in Derrida's anarchistic universe, the rebellious reinvention of the constitution in every legislative and adjudicative act ensures that the constitution does not ossify into an oppressive force constraining the freedom of future generations. However, its fleeting legitimacy will be purchased at the expense of liberties that might otherwise have had the protection of standing law. Fourth, consonant with their lack of authority, Derrida quite rightly concludes that legal systems cannot possibly realize the utopian ends of justice: "[I]n the founding of the law or in its institution, the same problem of justice will have been posed and violently resolved, that is to say buried, dissimulated, repressed" (23).

Needless to say, the antipodes of permanent (legal) repetition and permanent (ethical) revolution do not leave much room for that historical progress so sought after by Derrida. Indeed, if Blumenberg is right, they do not leave much room for historical change as distinct from mere succession. In this dichotomous universe, progression of the past that progresses beyond the past remains essentially enigmatic.

I submit that, by not opposing political action and transcendental principle, freedom and necessity, and particular and universal in the way that Derrida and Lyotard do, Arendt is able to resolve the aporias of legitimation. The reader will recall that, in her opinion, the absolute principles that legitimate a revolutionary undertaking are not external laws emanating from some transcendent, sovereign power but immanent conditions for the possibility of genuine action. Persons act freely to the extent that they have rationally entertained all possible options, checked their own biases, and coordinated their behavior with other people. Only in unlimited rational communication regulated by a desire to reach unconstrained agreement under conditions of mutual reciprocity, equality, autonomy, sincerity, and solidarity can such deliberation occur. Indeed, here we find an impartial procedure by which "incommensurable" languages can enrich one another, narrow horizons of experience can mutually interpenetrate and expand one another, and legitimate decisions can be reached in a manner agreeable to all.

Once we see that ethics and politics, regulative idea and historical reality mediate each other, the other problems of legitimation shed their aporetic guise. The problem of historical empowerment, which presumes that principled acts of genuine self-determination must be unconditioned by extant political and legal traditions, is dispelled once we see that principles free actors from mundane routines only when they provide alternative reasons for behaving differently. Their efficacy as a source of rational motivation depends on their concrete connection with familiar modes of reasoning.

Revolutionaries, then, could not have understood their own actions as reasonable responses to the provocations of a failed political tradition had they not done so in terms of the categories and expectations of that very same tradition. And this explains why the destructive repudiation of the past by the present—or perhaps what amounts to the same thing, the repudiation of the present by a past pregnant with the future and a future pregnant with the past—has the character of a determinate negation, or reversal that synthetically reapplies and progressively reappropriates what has been rejected.

Of course, the kind of progress that builds on the hermeneutical appropriation of past precedents need not involve a revolutionary reversal of meaning. More typically, it involves eliminating anachronism and expanding meaning. The successful reinterpretation of a constitution generally preserves and augments its authority, that is, it demonstrates its "timeless" and "universal" validity. In that case the authoritative meaning and legitimacy of a revolutionary act is never finally determinable. Indeed, it is not inconceivable that a constitutional tradition might exhaust its meaning and validity for future generations faced with a new revolutionary crisis. But as we have seen, under more felicitous circumstances of the sort surrounding the American Founding, provision for constitutional amendment can enable the original act of self-determination to be carried forward in ways that are quite revolutionary, even to the point of redefining the institutional mechanism authorizing amendment as such.

However relative it might be to changing circumstances, progress in the field of law would have been all but inconceivable had the American Constitution and Declaration of Independence not been inspired by universal principles. The hermeneutical circle in which human understanding moves explains why the ideal demands of justice can never be absolutely transcendent and opposed to the legal traditions that give them concrete force and meaning, just as it explains why these same traditions must expand and generalize their meaning in the course of repeated application, or else perish.

2.3 Ackerman's Kuhnian interpretation of American dual democracy illuminates both the normal legal synthesis that progressively occurs within a legal paradigm and the revolutionary progress and synthesis that occurs between legal paradigms. But as we have seen, the comparison between science and politics extends much further than that. Arendt herself alludes to one such comparison in her comment that "the strange pathos of novelty, so characteristic of the modern age, needed almost two hundred years to leave the relative seclusion of scientific and philosophic thought and to reach the realm of politics" (46). She later notes another effect that science had on political life in the eighteenth century: the *permanent* revolutions already underway in the arts and sciences made the desire for absolute political foundations and enduring institutions all the more urgent.

Significantly, nowhere does Arendt explain how revolutionary developments in one area of life (science, say) spread to other areas. This poses a number of interesting questions, which I hope to answer in the remainder of this study. To wit: How did it come to pass that science and astronomy became metaphors for revolutionary politics? For that matter, how did one astronomical event in particular, the Copernican Revolution, become a metaphor for scientific paradigm in general? And how many revolutions has that revolution undergone as metonym and metaphor for modernity?

Our study of legitimation will not be complete until we answer these questions. For the time being, it suffices to note that any such incendiary talk about revolutions spreading from one domain of life to another is challenged by no less a revolutionary than Kuhn, whose own metaphorical comparison between scientific and political revolutions suggests a far greater degree of sovereign authority within science than one might otherwise expect:

> Like the choice between competing political institutions, that between competing [scientific] paradigms proves to be a choice between incompatible modes of community life.... As in political revolutions, so in paradigm choice—there is no other standard higher than the assent of the community. (Kuhn 1970, 94)

Kuhn's assertion that each scientific community "is its own exclusive audience and judge" seems to imply a kind of monadic insularity and incommensurability that would render any historical judgment about the legitimacy of revolutions inexplicable. However, he also points out that scientific communities are far from stable; in the course of dogmatically applying a shared paradigm in their normal research—that is, in exercising the *determinant judgment* characteristic of *phronesis*—practitioners of the paradigm force the *reflective* disclosure of anomalies in ways that proliferate new problems, threaten the coherence of the paradigm, and give rise to revolutionary dissension from within the established research tradition. Indeed, it is only against the dogmatic background of ever "precise and far-reaching" expectations that anomalies first appear. That is why "normal science, a pursuit not directed to novelties and tending to suppress them, should nevertheless be so effective in causing them to arise" (64).

Here, then, resides the *aesthetic rationale* for Lyotard's postmodern interpretation of what otherwise appears to be a *dogmatically* rational, consensus-oriented form of problem solving. But if scientific revolutions—including the revolution that inaugurated the beginning of modern scientific culture—are *not* rationally motivated in a manner that can be *determinately* judged by appeal to univocally understood values and criteria, how can we judge them to be the *progressive* advance beyond tradition we normally associate with revolution?

The problem of rational motivation addresses the causes underlying scientific revolutions. Are the causes *internal* or *external* to science, that is, do they emanate from scientists' beliefs about the rational inadequacy of the dominant scientific paradigm in comparison to the proposed new paradigm? Or do they emanate from economic, political, and cultural factors that indirectly influence the acceptance of the new paradigm in ways that are largely covert? The problem of progress addresses the comparability of scientific paradigms. Are competing paradigms commensurable with one another, that is, can they be *translated* into each other or to some other common language for purposes of evaluative ranking?

Questions about causation and commensurability are no doubt distinct. However, if we believe that an adequate explanation of a scientific revolution consists of reasons internal to science, so that *some* reasons that function in scientific explanations in one paradigm function in scientific explanations in its successor, then we must also hold that successive paradigms are at least partially commensurable.

It is at this juncture that the historiographical writings of Hans Blumenberg become pertinent. Blumenberg's discussion of the *epochal break* that initiated modern science reveals conceptual problems attending Anglo-American debates about commensurability. Those, like Larry Lauden, who defend the commensurability of paradigms tend to assimilate the conceptual scheme of the old paradigm to that of the new in ways that obscure their differences. This approach not only suppresses the distinctive feature of premodern epochs, it obscures the originality of the modern age, thereby undermining the latter's *own* unique claim to legitimacy.

Conversely, sociologists of science such as David Bloor and Barry Barnes and postmodern critics like Steve Fuller and Joseph Rouse who defend the radical incommensurability of paradigms tend to fragment the historical process to such an extent that they cease writing history at all, or do so in a manner contrary to their own stated assumptions.

Blumenberg's critique of Kuhn suggests a third path between these alternatives. Kuhn's notion of a scientific revolution, he argues, underestimates the deep continuity between premodern and modern epochs. However, this continuity is poorly captured by the notion of commensurability presupposed in most internal explanations of paradigm change. For Blumenberg, the rationale for the paradigm change that inaugurated post-Copernican science is only fully explicated by reasons that lie outside the narrow scope of medieval physics and astronomy. The progressiveness of modern science consists in its satisfaction of certain *expectations* internal to Scholastic *theology* that the latter could no longer meet. Yet the existence of a common matrix of needs, expectations, and questions conjoining medieval theology and modern science, Blumenberg cautions, should not mislead us into thinking that these conceptual schemes are *literally* commensurable.

As we shall, Blumenberg's rejection of the internal history of science as purely rational and absolutely progressive has at least this much in common with the sociologists and postmodernists: a Hegelian (or Marxian) insistence on the largely unconscious making of a "history" motivated by diverse factors whose "continuous" meaning only emerges in retrospective, metaphorical interpretation. In this respect it hews closely to the mediation of incommensurable rationales emblematic of aesthetic judgment generally.

That Blumenberg is *not* defending a commensurability thesis is often neglected by commentators, but the *illusion* that he is cannot be easily dispelled. As we shall see, his own argument against *radical* incommensurability is structurally isomorphic to Donald Davidson's well-known argument against incommensurability in general. I submit that this isomorphism conceals an important different between the two arguments: whereas Davidson's position hinges on the possibility of *radical translation* as a condition for *literal interpretation*, Blumenberg's hinges on the possibility of *functional reoccupation* as a condition for *metaphoric understanding*.

3. When Kuhn first introduced his notion of a scientific paradigm over three decades ago it was unclear how, if at all, it related to his thesis about scientific revolutions. To begin with, much confusion reigned over the precise meaning of the concept *paradigm*.[8] On one hand, "paradigm" meant something like a normal scientific tradition of continuous puzzle-solving. On the other hand, it meant an ontological and epistemological worldview. The fact that Kuhn failed to distinguish these two senses of paradigm, and also failed to distinguish the notion of a theory-independent world (comparable to Kant's *Ding an sich*) from the multitude of phenomenal worlds constituted anew by each successive paradigm, made it appear that he was defending two incompatible theses about paradigm change. This was apparent in his account of the Copernican reform. While stressing the experimental and theoretical *continuity* between Ptolemaic and Copernican traditions of astronomy, he insisted that Copernicus had inaugurated a revolution in worldview. Yet, how could Kuhn argue that the Copernican system was better at solving the problems of its predecessor (or explaining more of the observable phenomena it conceptualized), if the problems each system addressed pertained to phenomena relative to distinct worldviews as conceptualized by distinct paradigms?

Since the appearance of *The Structure of Scientific Revolutions* in 1962, Kuhn has devoted much energy toward resolving this problem. In order to appreciate his refinements, however, we must reexamine the conception of scientific paradigm as a tradition of problem solving. When Kuhn was working at the Center for Advanced Studies in Behavioral Sciences at Stanford from 1958 to 1959, he was struck by the lack of consensus that prevailed among his colleagues in the social sciences regarding scientific methods and problems. The concept of a paradigm, which he developed from Wittgenstein's account of practical examples in language acquisition, articulated what he believed to be essential to *normal* scientific research and *progressive* problem solving: a disciplinary matrix consisting of shared generalizations, heuristic models, scientific values, and exemplary solutions.

The difficulty in using this conception of scientific paradigm to explain scientific revolutions is apparent in Kuhn's account of the Copernican reform. Critics have pointed out that the Copernican reform did not significantly expand the problem-solving range of currently existing astronomy. Indeed, unless one defines the very proliferation of ad hoc hypotheses as inherently critical, there was no problem-solving crisis in Ptolemaic astronomy that precipitated its abandonment. Kuhn cites as evidence for a "classic description of a crisis state" the famous passage in *De Revolutionibus Orbium Coelestium* (1543) where Copernicus—sounding very much like a Lyotardian *avant la lettre*—likens the current astronomy to a "monster" composed of wonderfully designed but mutually disproportionate limbs (Kuhn 1970b, 69). Presumably, the modernist in him sought to resolve this "crisis" by replacing an incoherent set of hypotheses with a coherent theory.

However, the various theories of longitude, of latitude, and of distance whose combination Copernicus found monstrous yield an incoherent whole only if one tries to fashion a *realistic*, three-dimensional picture of the universe out of them—something that no Scholastic astronomer save Copernicus would have thought to do. In any case, the putative incoherence of Ptolemaic astronomy did not impair its problem-solving capacity, since its observational computations were roughly equivalent to those generated by the Copernican model (Heidelberger 1976).

Kuhn's characterization of the Copernican reform as a paradigm shift would lead one to expect more novelty in its mathematical generalizations, models, scientific values, and exemplars than is actually borne out by the evidence. Not only did Copernicus use the same mathematical tables used by Ptolemy, but he found scientific value in the latter's observations, inherited his model of uniform circular movement, and accepted Aristotelian-Platonic physics as an exemplar of what astronomy *should be*.[9]

If there is an explanation for the emergence of Copernican astronomy, it may well have to do with factors that are less pertinent to the conduct of science as a predictive enterprise than to the cultural conditions that led to the revaluation of science as a method for progressively revealing nature's secrets. As Pierre Duhem pointed out, Copernicus's synthesis of two incompatible research paradigms—the pragmatic (instrumentalist, or problem-solving) tradition of mathematical astronomy and the realist (qualitative, or essentialist) tradition of Aristotelian-Platonic (meta)physics—managed to create a new astronomy whose theoretical structure was both simpler and capable of greater explanatory power (Duhem 1969, 69). Kuhn himself mentions the capacity of the Copernican system to explain the retrograde motions of the planets in terms of their distance from the sun. What he does not explain is the process by which Copernicus's mathematical realism itself became an exemplar, or *metaphor*, for the newly emergent modern attitude that arose out of nominalist and humanist reactions to an *internally related*, albeit *prescientifically reasoned, theological* crisis.

To appreciate how this extrascientific crisis bore *internally* on the emergence of modern science, one must turn to Blumenberg's explanation of the Copernican reform. As things presently stand, Kuhn's attempt to defend a Copernican paradigm shift founders on the shoals of his own narrow *internalist* position. On one hand, by focusing on Copernicus's explicit understanding of his accomplishment as it relates to medieval astronomy and physics, Kuhn has failed to demonstrate the occurrence of a paradigm shift. On the other hand, by not adequately attending to the broader theological framework that covertly motivated Copernicus's reform and made possible its eventual reception as an exemplar of a new scientific attitude toward nature, Kuhn has failed to provide any convincing rationale for its lasting impact.

I conjecture that Kuhn's narrow internalist explanation, which mainly addresses Copernicus's objections to the tradition as *literally* formulated, has made it easier for critics like Davidson and Putnam to argue against the very idea of incommensurable conceptual schemes. Kuhn held that incommensurability implied either untranslatability or *imperfect* literal translatability.[10] Putnam and Davidson found this position incoherent. Putnam noted that if terms used in another culture could not be equated in meaning and reference with any terms we use, we could not translate them, in which case it would be meaningless to say that they meant something radically different from the terms we use. Davidson formulated Kuhn's position as a paradox: "We are encouraged to imagine we understand massive conceptual change . . . by legitimate examples of a familiar sort. . . ." (Davidson 1985a, 183–84).

Davidson and Putnam actually raise *three* objections to Kuhn's incommensurability thesis. First, it is incoherent to express the content of an untranslatable language within a language into which it is untranslatable. Second, ideas expressed in an untranslatable language are incomprehensible, so claiming to understand them is incoherent. Third, as Wittgenstein argued, it is incoherent to conceive the speaker of an untranslatable language as having a language at all (Wittgenstein 1958, 82e, #207).

Now the first objection applies only to cases in which the meaning of the example cited is supposed to be untranslatable in the *argument* language as well as in the object language of the contrasted paradigm. Kuhn, however, only claims that "a small group of (usually interdefined) terms" localized in each incommensurable theory resists mutual translation (Kuhn 1983, 670–71). Furthermore, he concedes that this group of terms *might* be translatable into the larger (natural) language in which their untranslatability is argued for.

The idea of "local incommensurability" also enables us to understand the conceptual continuity existing between succeeding traditions of normal science as well as the comparability of their respective problem-solving capacities. In particular, Kuhn argues that proponents of the old paradigm can *learn* the intension and extension of revolutionary concepts by reference to the old concepts.

The second and third objections bear on just this possibility. That is, they assume that learning (or interpreting) a new language involves translating it literally into the home language of the interpreter. Such an assumption is contested by Kuhn, who argues that "acquiring a new language is not the same as translating from it into one's own" (Kuhn 1983, 672–73).

Moreover, it can be argued against the third objection that, as a matter of fact, fragments of a dead language (e.g., Linear B) or foreign expressions can be recognized as evidence of linguistic behavior without being understood (Wittgenstein 1958, 82e, #207).

Now one might suppose that Davidson's formulation of these objections is immune to such commonsense rebuttals. After all, his objections are aimed at the purported impossibility of translation, not at the *empirical* or practical limits of actual translation.

In this respect Davidson's argument invites comparison with Kant's transcendental refutation of skepticism. Both are premised on the assumption that it makes no sense to talk about objective reality apart from the way that reality is subjectively experienced (Kant) or linguistically specified by speakers (Davidson). However, Davidson is more radical than Kant in his rejection of any form/content distinction whatsoever. Since reality (content) can be nothing other than what can be meaningfully communicated by means of some linguistic conceptual scheme (form), it makes no sense to talk about it (reality) as something that the latter must somehow fit or externally classify (Davidson 1985a, 187–90).

Having established the meaninglessness of nonlinguistic facts, Davidson goes on to argue that a necessary condition for the possibility of linguistic understanding is a Tarski-style theory of truth. However, instead of using semantics to define truth as Tarski does, he uses truth to define semantics: the meaning of an utterance, he submits, is bound up with its truth-conditions. Davidson here expressly invokes an extensionalist theory of meaning as a minimal prerequisite for interpretation on the grounds that we could have no other access to the intentions of speakers using a radically unfamiliar language apart from their linguistic behavior. However, since Davidson accepts Quine's thesis about the indeterminacy of radical translation (and, hence, the inscrutability of reference) he must make additional assumptions to show how we as interpreters can move from facts about behavior to facts about belief.

Davidson's truth-conditional semantics entails an important fact about the beliefs of speakers of an alien language: they hold their sentences to be true. Now, in order to use this assumption to infer the meaning of alien utterances, Davidson must introduce an additional transcendental condition: the principle of charity. A precondition for interpretation is agreement: we cannot understand alien utterances without making them reasonable (true) by our standards. So interpretation proceeds by assigning truth-conditions, formulated in the interpreter's language, to the speaker's utterances (196–97).

Following Tarski's Convention T, Davidson states that knowledge of the truth conditions for an utterance S is equivalent to translating S into a comparable set of sentences in one's own language; S is true if and only if *p*, where *p* is itself a statement in the interpreter's language. Given the fact that truth is inseparable from translatability, the aim of radical interpretation is to compose a truth theory of the target language, consisting of a *coherent*—if also changeable and contextual—system of T-sentences (194–96).

The astute reader will note the parallel with Kant's First Analogy of Experience. Just as Kant had argued that there must be a minimum of identity (substantial sameness) in our experience as a constant frame of reference for distinguishing difference (temporal change), so too Davidson argues that there must be a minimum of agreement (translatability) in our understanding of alien languages in order for us to precisely determine, over time, differences in meaning (extension) that resist translation.

If Davidson's argument shows only that there must be substantial translatability between languages in order to determine the small core of locally untranslatable utterances distinguishing them, then it poses no problem for Kuhn's incommensurability thesis. Furthermore, Kuhn need only concede that *nonliteral interpretation* is a prerequisite for determining local incommensurability. As he puts it, a "theory of translation based on extensional semantics" overlooks intensional aspects of meaning that "are what a perfect translation would preserve" (Kuhn 1983, 680).

The difference between Davidson and Kuhn thus revolves around what is to count as evidence for meaning. For a Quinean like Davidson, who restricts meaning to overt behavior, many different, but equally correct, translations of an alien language are possible (Quine 1960, 27; 1987, 9). For Kuhn, no translation is possible, and for reasons with which we are familiar. First, meaning is intensional; we cannot infer why someone believes that an utterance is true from merely knowing that he or she holds it to be true. Second, knowing why someone believes that an utterance is true involves participating in the *tacit know-how* underlying the language game in which the utterance functions. But this *practical* understanding resists propositional articulation (Kuhn 1989, 11).

As Kuhn had already pointed out in his reply to Popper many years ago, scientific paradigms specify exemplary practices whose meaning cannot be literally defined—at least not entirely (Kuhn 1970b, 267). Perhaps, we should think of them as traditions of practical understanding embodying a kind of *phronesis*, or judgmental competency (art) implicated in the character of the researcher (Bernstein 1983, pt. 2). In that case, there would always be a residue of semantic obstruction frustrating *rational* communication between proponents of incommensurable paradigms. For, regardless of the extent to which some divergent cognitive values might be clearly articulated and critically debated, there would be other such values (or perhaps aspects of these very same values) that could not be, simply owing to their embeddedness in a dense totality of practical habits and competencies.

Having examined the strength of Kuhn's defense of paradigmatic incommensurability, let us assess its weakness. If a scientific paradigm delimits a specific language whose meaning can be practically understood only by participating in it, then what sense can we give to its being even partially commensurable (and communicable) with a different paradigm?

Now there are two ways to interpret this question. The first way problematizes the possibility of learning a new paradigm. To reiterate an objection formulated earlier with respect to MacIntyre's account of cross-cultural understanding, how could a Ptolemean convert to the Copernican reform simultaneously participate in two distinct language games—literally inhabit two distinct lifeworlds—without experiencing something like a split identity, dispersed over distinct practical, epistemic, and ontological roles? The second problematizes the possibility of writing the history of a new paradigm. How can the contemporary historian of science give an internal account of the Copernican reform that shows how it constituted both a revolutionary break *from* an age with which it has a great deal in common and a revolutionary foundation *for* an age with which it still had too little in common?

Kuhn is chiefly interested in answering the first question, Blumenberg the second. However, their answers are remarkably similar, in that they appeal to the way paradigms instantiate metaphors whose exemplary import extends both backward and forward in time.

Accepting Black's interaction theory of metaphor, Kuhn argues that metaphors play a *constitutive role* in theory change and transmission (Kuhn 1979, 409). According to Black, metaphors create new similarities by relating a "system of commonplaces," associated with the metaphorical word, to the subject of the metaphor. Like the reflexive modus operandi of aesthetic judgment, the interaction between the literal meaning of the metaphor (the system of commonplaces associated with it) and the subject of the metaphor does not merely function comparatively (i.e., it does not draw our attention only to apparent similarities between the conjoined terms); it illuminates a wealth of new similarities whose cognitive content resists literal paraphrase. As Black puts it, "[T]he relevant weakness of the literal paraphrase is not that it may be tiresomely prolix or boringly explicit; it fails to be a translation because it fails to give the insight that the metaphor did" (Black 1962a, 46).

Black distinguishes the merely heuristic function of a paradigm qua exemplary instance of a correct application from the similarity creating function of a metaphor. However, he adds that the "exemplary instance . . . functions as a prototype for the derivative uses" by relying on metaphors: "We continue to model descriptions of cases remote from the prototypes upon the simpler cases, often by using metaphors literally applicable only to these simpler cases" (Black 1962b, 158). Kuhn has precisely this metaphorical function in mind when he talks about paradigms (models) as constitutive of a new way of seeing the world.

> "Metaphor" refers to all those processes in which the *juxtaposition* either of terms or concrete examples calls forth a network of similarities which help to determine the way in which language attaches to the world. . . . Metaphor plays an essential role in establishing links between scientific language and the world. Those links are not, however, given once and for all. Theory change, in particular, is accompanied by a change in some of the relevant metaphors and in the corresponding parts of the network of similarities through which terms attach to nature. The earth was like Mars (and was thus a planet) after Copernicus, but the two were in different natural families before. . . . (Kuhn 1979, 415–17; my italics)

This passage underscores two of the most important aspects of Black's interaction theory of metaphor. First, there is no defining feature shared by all metaphors. Not only is metaphoricity primarily a function of contextual usage rather than semantics, but metaphorical *processes* play a constitutive role in literal discourse as well. Hence, a literal use of a word whose meaning appears well defined, such as "planet," is capable of conjoining (or condensing, to use Freud's expression) heterogeneous frames of reference (415). Second, all metaphors—even the heuristic metaphors that serve as paradigmatic examples—constitute a new way of seeing the world. Bohr's model of the atom, which represented electrons and nucleus by tiny bits of matter that behaved like billiard or Ping-Pong balls instead of like a solar system, was not taken literally as a description conformable to all laws of mechanics and electromagnetic theory; but it was taken seriously as a hypothesis about some billiard (or Ping-Pong) ball types of behavior that would have to be discovered and eventually described.

Kuhn follows this point with a reaffirmation of the incommensurability thesis: "There is no neutral language into which (incommensurable) theories as well as the relevant data may be translated for purposes of comparison." This allusion to Black's thesis about metaphoric untranslatability, however, directly recalls the problem of dual participation mentioned above:

either one participates exclusively in a single paradigm, in which case there exists no communicative basis for comparing incommensurable paradigms, or one participates in several of them simultaneously, in which case there exists cognitive and semantic dissonance.

Kuhn's response to this problem, like Arendt's response to the problem of rational motivation, invokes the idea of a nominal continuity in the *function*, but not *meaning*, of metaphors spanning incommensurable paradigms: "I take metaphor to be essentially a higher-level version of the process by which ostension enters into the establishment of reference for natural-kind terms" (415). More specifically,

> The techniques of *dubbing* and of *tracing lifelines* permits astronomical individuals—say, the earth and moon, Mars and Venus—to be traced through episodes of theory change, in this case the one due to Copernicus. The lifelines of these four individuals were continuous during the passage from heliocentric to geocentric theory, but the four were differently distributed among natural families as a result of the change.... Eliminating the moon and adding the earth to the list of individuals that could be *juxtaposed* as paradigms for the term 'planet' changed the list of features salient to determining the referents of that term. That sort of redistribution of individuals among natural families or kinds, with its alteration of the features salient to reference, is, I now feel, a central (perhaps the central) feature of the episodes I have previously labeled scientific revolutions. (417; my italics)

The continuity underlying the metaphoric process that enables "planet," "earth," "moon," "sun," and so on to retain their identity through changes in their extension and intension is explained in terms of a causal theory of reference of the sort developed by Kripke in his theory of proper names as rigid designators (Kripke 1972, 253–55). The advantage such a theory has over the Russellian view of names as definite descriptions is that it specifies a continuous criterion (function) for applying a given name independently of any contingent feature (description) we attribute to it. Kuhn simply takes this insight one step further. Not only names, he holds, but also natural kinds, like planets, have a *primary* reference (causal *identity*, or history) fixed in this manner. A natural *kind*, then, denotes a class of ostensively determined referents that remains unchanged throughout its reassociation with different natural *families* in the course of scientific revolutions. Thus, the formal identity of a term (its identity-maintaining function for purposes of primary reference) is distinct from its *content*, or secondary reference, which is distributed over distinct natural families and the features (descriptions) ontologically constitutive of them (Kuhn 1979, 410–13).

As I remarked in chapter 1, Kripke's theory of names can at most presume a *relative* independence of reference and meaning, form and content, *if* it is to withstand the Hegelian critique of nominalism as an incoherent account of identity. However, by assuming only that the primary referring function is relatively more free of descriptive content than the secondary one, we can account for the kinds of cognitive, practical, and aesthetic dissonance analyzed by Lyotard under the rubric of *différends*, in which opposed conceptual schemes or rationales legitimately claim equal title to a disputed domain of experience. Conversely, Kuhn's reference to the identity-preserving function of metaphoric *processes* in scientific revolutions provides one way to account for incommensurability (literal untranslatability) *without discontinuity* or conflict. As an answer to the problem of dual linguistic participation, it implies that converts to new language games participate only virtually in incommensurable conceptual schemes. That is, they temporarily suspend the literal meanings of the terms they deploy in favor of their fluid, metaphoric meanings and (more importantly) their primary referential functions, which remain continuous across changes in meaning. Thus, the scientific and culture-specific identity of the convert, which is grounded first and foremost in primary referring practices, secondarily in metaphoric comparisons, and only partially in literal meaning, withstands the dissonance caused by simultaneously participating in incommensurable language games.

Now this answer will not satisfy all critics of the incommensurability thesis. Indeed, the attempt to specify metaphoric meaning apart from literal meaning has come under attack by none other than Davidson, who argues (against Black and others) that "we must give up the idea that a metaphor carries a message, that it has a content or meaning (except, of course, its literal meaning)" (Davidson 1985b, 261).

Kuhn, I think, need not be too concerned about this objection. First, Davidson's conclusion only follows if one accepts his peculiar truth-conditional semantics. (Our earlier discussion of Rorty counsels against doing so.) Second, Davidson does not dispute the *function* of metaphors to effect *new ways of seeing (or constituting) the world*. Third, Davidson's argument applies only to metaphors *strictu sensu*, not to the metaphorical processes that underlie the generation and acquisition of all linguistic terms. Fourth and finally, it's unclear how Davidson's argument applies to nonlinguistic metaphors, such as the models, exemplars, and paradigms that are Kuhn's major concern.

More important than Davidson's disagreement with Kuhn is their mutual belief that the metaphoric *function* is specifiable apart from the generation of continuous *meaning*. As we shall see below, the concept of *juxtaposition* that appears in Kuhn's account of metaphoric processes has its analogue in Blumenberg's notion of a *reoccupation of positions*, conceived as a purely *formal* (or functional) condition of identity. Here functional continuity will serve a different purpose: not the explication of dual linguistic participation in the process of conversion but the explication of epochal novelty from the disinterested, aesthetic standpoint of the judge who interprets history retrospectively. The latter, in turn, will provide a transcendental historiographical framework in terms of which the rational, scientific progress heralded by modernity and first intimated by Copernicus appears legitimate.

4. Blumenberg's scattered references to Kuhn suggest two major points of contact between them. First, Blumenberg, like Kuhn, is interested in the historiographical conditions that make possible a rational, internal account of radical scientific change. However, instead of focusing on changes within science, he addresses the broader epochal break that marked the birth of modern, scientific culture generally. Second, the concept of paradigm plays roughly the same role in Blumenberg's historiography as it does in Kuhn's, namely, it designates the moment of incommensurability in the history of science (broadly speaking). Citing Kuhn's remark that "scientists work from models ... often without quite knowing ... what characteristics have given these models the status of community paradigms" (Kuhn 1970b, 46), Blumenberg writes,

> The concept of paradigm thus represents in a certain respect a moment of discontinuity in the schema of the history of science. The *violations of expectations* are possible and consequential precisely only when a consolidated continuous tradition *(Bestand)* is capable of being endangered. The paradigm is a latent complex of premises which need not at all be expressly formulated as implications of scientific praxis, but which rather already enter into methods and modes of questioning *(Fragestellungen)*. . . . For this reason scientific progress is therefore not like a process that can be comprehended as a sequence of additions; the spontaneity that emerges in it has much more the character of a *technique for producing surprises.* (Blumenberg 1981b, 157–58)

Kuhn repeatedly emphasizes that paradigms do more than enable "normal" problem solving. The latter, which is exclusively a feature of *mature* science, is disrupted, if not absent, during the phase leading up to a paradigm shift. What practitioners of "immature" and revolutionary paradigms share is an *expectation* that their models will generate new problems and hypotheses (Kuhn 1970b, 178). Hence, contra Popper and others, the acceptance of a new paradigm is not motivated primarily by empirical reasons pertaining to successful problem solving. Proponents of the old and the new paradigms may agree on minimal criteria of theory choice, such as "accuracy, simplicity, fruitfulness, and the like," but there is no neutral algorithm that can persuade adherents of the old to accept the new (199). As Kuhn himself makes quite clear, the 'conversion experience' leading to the acceptance of a new paradigm is largely one of learning a new language and, above all, accepting its metaphors (Kuhn 1970b, 184, 196, 202).

For Blumenberg, Kuhn's concept of paradigm is thus "nothing but a 'consensus,' which is able to stabilize itself not, indeed, exclusively, but partly by means of the rhetoric of the academies and the textbooks" (436). The rhetorical consensus Blumenberg has in mind recalls Kuhn's contention that paradigms are "constellations of group commitments" that are ultimately irreducible to a unified body of rules explicitly shared by a community of researchers. They comprise a *network of loosely overlapping models of concrete problem solving* whose "family resemblances," as Wittgenstein put it, resist explicit definition (Kuhn 1970a, 45). The appeal to family resemblance, of course, underscores the metaphorical process by which classifications are formed and terms are applied.

As noted above, the conceptual opacity, or untranslatability, of metaphors indicates the moment of incommensurability in the history of science. However, metaphors also create new resemblances by which incommensurable paradigms can be linked to one another. Indeed, the capacity to condense conceptually and phenomenally disparate things is the very essence of metaphor. However, in contrast to the identity of subsumption characteristic of determinant judgment, metaphor dialectically alters the meanings of the terms it reflexively compares. As Blumenberg remarks, "[I]f the limiting case of judgment is identity, the limiting case of metaphor is symbol; here the other is entirely other, which delivers nothing but the pure possibility of putting something that is at our disposal in the place of something that is not" (Blumenberg 1987a, 439–40).

Here Blumenberg retrieves Lichtenberg's insight into the metaphorical nature of the Copernican reform as a paradigm for all other disciplines. Writing two decades after Kant's Copernican Revolution, the famous astronomer and biographer of Copernicus argued that the reform provided something like a grammatical paradigm for the declination of all future discovery whatsoever. In thinking of the reform in this way, he not only had in mind the methodological simplification it brought about in the field of astronomy—a simplification he found lacking in the chemistry of his time—but he also had in mind its symbolic import as reflected in the Kantian decentration of the knowing subject.

In Blumenberg's opinion, Kant had taken the Copernican reform well beyond its author's humanistically inspired realism when, in the second preface to the first *Critique*, he compared it to the transcendental elevation of reason as lawgiver to nature. Indeed, the subsequent dubbing of this *idealistic reversal* of Copernicus's standpoint as a "turning" or "revolution" showed how far the reform had become a metaphor for the revolutionary progress embedded in scientific method generally (Blumenberg 1987b, 595). Despite whatever modernist misunderstanding might be occasioned by the use of "progress" here, it is clear to Blumenberg that the only attitude compatible with science is postmodern resignation to the utter contingency of finite human understanding in the face of the indefinitely many vistas—literally, worlds—opened up by ceaseless rational inquiry. As Lichtenberg so aptly put it, we never get beyond the mere surface of things.

To see how Blumenberg's Lichtenbergian interpretation of the Copernican "paradigm shift" fits into his historiographical concerns we must turn to *The Legitimacy of the Modern Age*, where he explicitly takes issue with Kuhn's notion of scientific revolution:

> "Scientific revolutions," if one were to choose to take their radicalness literally, simply cannot be the ultimate concept of a rational conception of history; otherwise that conception would have denied to its object the very same rationality it wanted to assert for itself. . . . The theory of "scientific revolutions" describes, for the most part correctly, the breakdown of dominant systems as a result of their immanent rigorism, the "pedantic" disposition of every school-like mode of thought, which leads with fateful inevitability to the self-uncovering of the marginal inconsistencies from which doubt and opposition break into the consolidated field. This conception of what historians have been pleased to call "downfalls" may be capable of generalization to a high level in relation to historical phenomena. But in relation to the new foundations called for afterward, to the preference given to the new "paradigm," this schema has no explanation whatever to offer. (Blumenberg 1983, 467)

At issue here is not Blumenberg's misreading of Kuhn—for it is Kuhn, after all, who insists against Lakatos and Popper that the "replacement theory" does not arise by pure coincidence, but "is usually conceived in response to, and is often shaped by, particular difficulties encountered in the development of its predecessor." It is rather Blumenberg's far more interesting claim that *identifying* scientific revolutions in the first place involves understanding how they are *rational* responses to problems and questions posed by older paradigms. More specifically, his account represents a transcendental deduction of the kind of narrative unity that has to obtain in order for *any* history of science to be written. The argument explicitly appeals to Kant's First Analogy, and hence bears a striking resemblance to Davidson's own critique of Kuhn. The argument can be summarized accordingly:

1. The capacity to experience history presupposes a capacity to distinguish old from new.
2. The capacity to distinguish old from new entails a constant frame of reference.
3. The constant frame of reference must consist of basic needs, expectations, and questions that provoke new responses.

The first premise is directed against so-called "secularization theorists" like Karl Löwith, who see the modern age as a mere culmination of ancient or medieval tendencies. These philosophers bury the novelty requisite for distinguishing radical, epochal changes beneath a continuous flow of subtle changes whose fundamental significance remains unchanged. Whether one sees the modern age as just another response to a timeless question or as just the fulfillment of a timeless need makes little difference here. For, without some sense of "progress beyond," little remains to be narrated; the conclusion is reached before the story has even begun.

One might object to Blumenberg's depiction of secularization theories as neglecting the narrative progression requisite for writing history. However, the point remains that the modern age saw itself as radically breaking with the past in a way that no other "age" had done before. If we accept Blumenberg's reading, late medieval Christianity was the "belated elaboration" of its own failed attempt to overcome its Gnostic past. The contradictions in the great schools of Hellenistic metaphysics that culminated in Gnostic resignation were only "resolved" with the advent of modern self-assertion, which rejected any transcendent fatalism (467–68). Indeed, history itself only comes into full view with the birth of a modern consciousness aware of its own historical (i.e., epoch-making) contingency.

Of course, as Blumenberg's second premise indicates, consciousness of historical contingency cannot be the last word on the possibility of experiencing historical novelty. The Enlightenment's claim to have effected a radical break with past tradition was hyperbolic. Indeed, for Blumenberg this very rejection of the past carries the past within itself. The Cartesian belief in a rational self-grounding, the Promethean faith in "Man" as the conscious maker of history, and the Providential idea of universal scientific progress were themselves (paradoxically) nothing more than "an attempt to answer a medieval question with the means available to a postmedieval age" (48).

According to Blumenberg, however "illegitimate" these answers may appear to be from the perspective of the antimetaphysical attitude of scientific self-assertion, they were nonetheless necessitated by an anthropological compulsion to preserve a sense of continuity with the past, understood as a primary reference system for meaningful identity and legitimacy. But anthropological requirements for self-justification and identity maintenance over time do not yet explain the transcendental necessity of a constant frame of reference for the possibility of writing history. Again, to cite Blumenberg:

> All change, all succession from old to new, is accessible to us only in that it can be related—instead of to the "substance" of which Kant speaks—to a constant frame of reference, by whose means the requirements can be defined that have to be satisfied in an identical "position." That what is new in history cannot be arbitrary in each case, but rather is subject to a rigor of expectations and needs, is the condition of our being able to have such a thing as "cognition" *(Erkenntnis)* of history at all. The concept of "reoccupation" designates, by implication, the minimum of identity that it must be possible to discover, or at least to presuppose and to search for, in even the most agitated movement of history. In the case of systems of "notions of man and world" *(Welt- und Menschenansicht*: Goethe), "reoccupation" means that different statements can be understood as answers to identical questions. (466)

Blumenberg's transcendental argument implies that successive epochs (and paradigms) must be commensurable up to a point, since it is inconceivable how one could satisfactorily explain the birth of the new apart from its being internally motivated by the expectations, needs, and questions of the old. If one takes the Copernican reform as a "systematic point of reference" for the epochal threshold that bisects both medieval and modern systems, it is only because it can be regarded as a logical response (or evaluative comparison) *within the Ptolemean paradigm* to broader questions raised by medieval theology that are not fully compassed by Ptolemean astronomy. In other words, it makes possible an evaluative comparison between, for instance, the medieval worldview of Nicholas of Cusa and the modern worldview of Giordano Bruno that also "makes obvious the impossibility of exchanging their historical positions" (479).

The Copernican comparison, then, suggests a kind of cross-epochal incommensurability, or untranslatability, which brings us to the concluding statement in Blumenberg's argument. The questions that constitute the common frame of reference are not "anthropological constants." As Blumenberg notes, "[I]n the new organization, certain questions are no longer posed." Today we no longer feel compelled to address the question of immortality that dominated Western thought "from its entry into the biblical text after the Babylonian exile all the way to Kant's postulate" (467). However, more important than the relative durability of questions is their reinterpretation from one epoch to another:

> The reoccupation of systematic functions during the change of epoch conditions linguistic constancy in a variety of ways. Not only the great questions but also the great words require historical "preparation." This process resembles more than anything else the process of ritualization: An ingrained traditional mode of activity has lost its motivating content of ideas and thus also its intelligibility, so that the schema of the activity is available for a retrospective interpretation and integration into a new context of meaning, which in the process makes use of and secures, above all, its sanctioned status as something that is beyond questioning. (78)

It is here that we detect illuminating parallels between Blumenberg's and Arendt's approaches to the problem of revolutionary continuity and those of Kuhn and Davidson to the problem of semantic incommensurability. For Blumenberg, historical identity is not one of "contents," or *intensional* meanings—as it is for Gadamer—but of "functions." To say that "totally heterogeneous contents . . . take on identical functions in specific positions in the systems of man's interpretation of the world and himself" is tantamount to saying that a question from an older system can impose itself on a new system in such a way that it loses its original meaning entirely. A tradition may continue to affect us and its questions may continue to provoke responses in ways that are not always legitimate, reasonable, and truth-preserving in Gadamer's sense. Appropriated by the new system in abstraction from the concrete, *practical,* and theoretical totality of relationships that constituted its original, lived meaning, it assumes the status of mere dogma. Its validating application interrupted (Nancy), tradition lives on as a dead metaphor.

This is precisely what happened to the older theological question

regarding salvation. Proponents of scientific enlightenment initially answered it with their own secular—but unscientific—philosophies of history.
It would have been more consistent—more meaningful and legitimate—
had they done so with scientific concepts of piecemeal, methodological
progress. Consequently, if theological attributes such as infinity continue
to live on in modern notions of space, time, matter, and progress, they, no
less than the questions that provoked them, do so at the expense of their
original meaning. Today, the concept of infinite progress has been stripped
of its teleological import and instead signifies the indefinite and meaningless task by which human curiosity ceaselessly adapts to changes its own
technology has wrought (83–85).

This *legitimate* appropriation of an old metaphor reinvests it with new
life, but only by radically destroying its original legitimacy. As Kuhn himself notes, "[W]hen paradigms change, there are usually *significant shifts* in
the criteria determining the legitimacy both of problems and of solutions"
(Kuhn 1970b, 109). Situated within a different classificatory system, terms
and questions carried over from an incommensurable paradigm take on a
new identity and truth-function along with their change of meaning. Thus,
"though much of Newton's work was directed to problems and embodied
standards derived from the mechanico-corpuscular world view, the effect
of the paradigm that resulted from his work was a further and partially
destructive change in the problems and standards legitimate for science"
(105). To use Davidson's language, the metaphorical carryover of terms
from one system to another preserves extensional, but not intensional,
identity. In radical translation, the capacity to match sentences of the
speaker's language to our own preserves truth (as *we* understand it) without rendering secondary reference any less inscrutable. The same applies
to Blumenberg's account of functional reoccupation; historians engaged in
radical translation can tell that the questions that reappear in different epochal and paradigmatic systems occupy identical positions in those respective systems, regardless of what these questions might have meant to the
actual historical agents positioned along the epochal divide.

Despite superficial similarities between Blumenberg's argument for
functional reoccupation and Davidson's argument against radical incommensurability, it is Blumenberg who insists with Kuhn that the cross-para-
digmatic translation effected by the historian of science is metaphorical
rather than literal. Yet, just as Blumenberg's historical sweep is broader
than Kuhn's, so too is his understanding of the metaphorical process. For
Blumenberg, it is not enough to show how particular terms and questions
get carried over from one paradigm to another. One must show how an
entire paradigm—in this case, the Copernican reform—functions as a meta-

phor for something its author could not possibly have envisaged: the radical, anthropocentric decentration implicit in modern self-assertion.

By expanding the range of metaphoricity to include whole paradigms, Blumenberg ironically expands the frame of functional positions to include anthropological constants. The "absolute metaphors" that he finds instantiated by entire systems address the most basic questions concerning the limits and possibilities of the human condition. In "Paradigmen zu einer Metaphorologie" Blumenberg had argued that the attempt to "represent the totality of reality" implicit in absolute metaphors was something to be resisted (Blumenberg 1960, 20). Since then he has gradually modified his position to the point that metaphor itself has become the master (absolute) concept governing all modes of activity by which human beings seek to preserve their life and identity (cf. Adams).

In order to understand how the Copernican reform functions as an absolute metaphor for the human—and above all, modern—condition, we must turn to Blumenberg's account of its relationship to medieval theology. To begin with, Blumenberg notes the difficulty we alluded to earlier in Kuhn's attempt to consider the reform as a paradigm shift within medieval astronomy and science proper. Although Kuhn approvingly cites Alfred North Whitehead's claim that "faith in the possibility of science, generated antecedently to the development of modern scientific theory, is an unconscious derivative from medieval theology" (Whitehead 1925, 19, in Kuhn 1957, 122), he himself never undertook to explain the Copernican reform as a fundamental revolution in the broader "system" of existential worldviews. However, without explaining the *epochal* shift inaugurated by the reform—the metaphorology of its revolution—no sense can be made of its *paradigmatic* novelty.

For Blumenberg, Copernicus's transformation of astronomy from an *art*, dealing with mere hypotheses concerned with the prediction of appearances, into a *science*, dealing with truths concerned with a unified, homogeneous reality, constituted the real beginning of its revolutionary history. However, this transformation cannot be adequately explained by reference to Copernicus's synthesis of philosophy (or physics) and astronomy, as Duhem suggested. It is true, of course, that it cannot be explained *without* reference to this synthesis. The Aristotelian-Platonic metaphysical tradition claimed to offer true knowledge of real essences, as opposed to the phenomenal hypotheses of astronomy. However, this system also presupposed a dualistic ontology that frustrated the development of a unified science of reality. So long as the earth and its elements were the focus of a qualitative (Aristotelian) physics, while the heavens were the object of a mathematical (Platonic) physics, no basis existed for elaborating an

Chapter 8

experimental, quantitative method for the discovery and explanation of physical events generally.

Now, Copernicus himself could not have anticipated the emergence of a strictly quantitative, nonteleological science. Yet his faith in a mathematically knowable universe certainly paved the way for its eventual acceptance. According to Blumenberg, this faith stems from Copernicus's synthesis of two other, seemingly incompatible traditions: nominalism and humanism (Blumenberg 1987a, pt. 2, chaps. 3–4). Copernicus's faith in God's goodness reinforced his faith in humanity's capacity to know the ultimate reality of the cosmos. However, his belief in a purely theoretical, mathematical access to this reality was influenced by his nominalist skepticism vis-à-vis *intuitable*, qualitative essences.

The originality of Blumenberg's account of the Copernican Revolution resides in its demonstration of the complementarity of these traditions. Humanism and nominalism, he argues, were logical outgrowths of Scholastic theology (Blumenberg, 1983, pt. 2, chap. 3; pt. 3, chaps. 5–7). That theology had inherited the Gnostic problem of evil and Augustine's unstable resolution of it.

Now, Augustine overcame Gnostic dualism by investing God with absolute power. On the one hand, theological absolutism required both divine predestination and human responsibility for sin—an intolerable contradiction that Renaissance humanism resolved by implicating the goodness and power of God in the highest of his creations. On the other hand, theological absolutism undermined the Aristotelian belief in a uniquely rational cosmos. The Paris Condemnation of 1277 that established the absolute freedom of God to create infinitely many worlds enabled philosophers to speculate about alternatives to Aristotelian physics and cosmology.

The theory of impetus and the doctrine of *appetitus partium* were *only* speculative attempts to repair the old system, and did not lead to new ideas that directly anticipated modern, quantitative methods of experimental research. The other consequence of the Paris Condemnation—and the one most decisive for the Copernican Revolution—was the nominalists' rejection of essentialist realism and its assumption of a hierarchy of being created by an external prime mover. This rejection, which resonated in their belief that everything exists for God without distinction, ironically harmonized with an empiricist realism, *once it was assimilated to the anthropocentric assumptions of Renaissance humanism*. The result, in Copernicus's case, is a realism that privileges mathematical insight rather than vision as the *via regia* of a *unified* science of nature.

We can now understand how the Copernican reform "reoccupied" an important position in the medieval system of functions: It reaffirmed the traditional teleological conception of the cosmos in basing its faith in man on the absolute goodness and power of God. However, this reoccupation already anticipates a new answer to (reoccupation of) a more fundamental question (position) posited by the anthropological system of functions: namely, the meaning of history and progress. The Judeo-Christian tradition explained the problem of suffering by situating humanity within a history of progress bounded by a *creatio ex nihilo* and a *dies irae*. The history of progress configured humanity as the largely passive subject of God's power and redemptive love. By elevating man to the level of God, Copernicus anticipated the later substitution of man for God as the agent of his own revolutionary creation and redemption.

This Promethean vision—or reoccupation—no doubt explains the hyperbolic foundationalism and teleological optimism informing the Age of Enlightenment from Descartes through Kant. However, it masks the deeper metaphorical significance of the Copernican reform, suggested by Copernicus's comparison of Ptolemean astronomy to a "monster." Monstrousness is a metaphor for the archaic chaos that continually threatens the self-preservation and identity of the human species. In Blumenberg's lexicon, it is an *absolute metaphor* that functions as a *limit concept*, or cipher, for the most basic problem confronting the human condition: the *absolutism of reality*. Like the state of nature introduced by social contract theorists, the absolutism of reality refers to a hypothetical state in which "man came close to not having control of the conditions of his existence and . . . believed that he simply lacked control of them" (Blumenberg 1985, 3–4).

The absolutism of reality refers to man's existential condition as a creature of deficiency *(Mangelwesen),* a fact that underscores the centrality of metaphor as *the* decisive mechanism for adaptation:

> Man's deficiency in specific dispositions for reactive behavior vis-à-vis reality—that is, his poverty of instincts—is the starting point for the central anthropological question as to how this creature is able to exist in spite of his lack of fixed biological dispositions. The answer can be reduced to the formula: by not dealing with this reality directly. The human relation to reality is indirect, circumstantial, delayed, selective, and above all, "metaphorical." (Blumenberg 1987a, 439)

More important than the metaphorical naming and classification of hostile natural forces for purposes of control—a function common to myth and science that Blumenberg characterizes as "a piece of high-carat 'work of logos'"—is the metaphorical ascription of roles necessary for defining our social and personal identities (441). The most distinctive feature of our modern identity—a feature already implicit in the anthropological conception of man as a creature of deficiency—is the antinomic relation to self and world announced by the Copernican reform.

> Man is defined by what he lacks *or* by the creative symbolism with which he makes himself at home in worlds of his own. He is the observer of the universe, in the center of the world, *or* he is (literally) "eccentric," exiled from Paradise on an insignificant dust speck called Earth. Man contains in himself the stored-up harvest of all of physical reality, *or* he is a creature of deficiencies, left in the lurch by nature, plagued by residues of instincts that he does not understand and that have lost their functions. (429)

The metaphorical significance of the Copernican reform resides in its expression of both sides of the human antinomy. Its immediate motivation was anthropocentric—by elevating man to the level of God, it placed him in the center of the universe, in a position analogous to the divine creator. However, its mediate significance for later science was just the opposite. By devaluing visual intuition, it denied humanity any direct access to reality. Condemned to eccentricity, circling about a nature of which it is and is not a part—at least insofar as its knowledge remains indirect and metaphorical—science approximates neither an absolute truth nor a summum bonum. The relative progress within normal science, as well as the relative progress within the history of science, achieves its purpose by suppressing (or transforming) old questions and generating new ones. Given this eccentricity, it is hardly surprising that the Promethean self-assertion extolled in German idealism would exhaust itself in Nietzsche's postmodern *Übermensch*, whose heroic self-creation and life affirmation in the face of *eternal recurrence* perfectly mirror the interminable self-overcoming indigenous to the nihilistic Age of Science.

4.1 Blumenberg's reference to the shipwreck metaphor with its implication that we are adrift in a sea of metaphor—metaphors, incidentally, that resonate with the oceanic metaphors proposed by Lyotard—is no doubt intended to mitigate our modern dyspepsia (Blumenberg 1979). If scientific reason continually threatens our security and identity by ceaselessly questioning our taken-for-granted institutions, myths, and metaphors, it can only do so by reinvesting these very same institutions, myths, and metaphors with new life. In the final analysis, science needs *meaning* in order to legitimate itself.

With this assertion we find ourselves back where we started: the question of scientific progress and its relationship to historiography. I noted that the defense of scientific progress—however relative it might be—depends on the possibility of some kind of rational comparison between what are otherwise incommensurable paradigms. Furthermore, if Blumenberg is correct, historiographical considerations necessitate the adoption of this perspective as well. We cannot write the history of science without reference to epochal breaks, and these only make sense within a system of reoccupations, in which successive paradigms and epochs progress in resolving some of the outstanding problems of their predecessors.

Defenders of the Strong Program in the sociology of science such as David Bloor and Barry Barnes, as well as critics sympathetic to postmodern approaches (Steve Fuller, Joseph Rouse, et al.), vigorously contest these assumptions. Either they repudiate an internalist account of history or they question the values of periodization and unicity implied in the concepts of paradigm and epoch. Conversely, defenders of stronger notions of scientific progress—among whom Kuhn himself must be included—find any hint of transepochal relativity discomfitting.

In my judgment, what makes Blumenberg's narratology so attractive is its avoidance of familiar difficulties associated with these extremes. In asking historians of science to "switch their exemplars from Gadamer to Kuhn," Steve Fuller demands an end to the humanistic tendency "to use evidence, usually extended textual quotation, either to make narrative transitions or to provide occasions on which to speak authoritatively on the events surrounding the evidence" (Fuller 1991, 162, 166). Joseph Rouse takes the invitation to Foucaultian archaeology even further. Citing with approval Lyotard's postmodern devaluation of the grand legitimating narratives of science, he comes close to replacing the history of science with micronarratives of scientific *cultural* practice (Rouse 1991).

The postmodern critics of science, of course, are right—up to a point. Fuller and Rouse describe a central weakness in the internal history of science as it is written by many modernists: the assumption that 'it must be possible for the same *content* to be transmitted and preserved through varying formulations in different contexts' (Fuller 1991, 158; 1989, 1–4). Their view that "knowledge exists only through its embodiment in linguistic and other social practices" is affirmed by Kuhn and Blumenberg against semanticists like Davidson and Putnam. Blumenberg, in particular, endorses their critique of absolute progress and its assumption of a purely rational, internal account of history. As he never ceases to remind us, history is not made consciously by people; rather, it comprises the unintended and collateral effects of diverse internal and external factors, some of which, as in the case of science, are revealed ex post facto through interpretative and metaphorical processes.

On the other hand, we have seen that the kind of extreme historicism endemic to Foucaultian archaeology (to cite one example) is simply incompatible with the writing of history. As Arthur Danto incisively observed, a pure chronology of events as described from the standpoint of the historical agents that participated in them (or, by parity of reasoning, a pure archaeological documentary) would lack the narrative unity *and* progression inherent in any history (Danto 1964). Indeed, given our anthropological need for continuous meaning and identity, it is no accident that Dilthey and other radical historicists resort to *ahistorical* universals in their vain attempt to recover a semblance of historical unity (Blumenberg 1983, 462). However, what is needed is the decontextualization and recontextualization of meaning in a way that preserves differences in content (or perspective) along with a continuity of function—whether it be through "narrative sentences" (Danto), reinterpretations of the intentional fabric of action (Olafson), or through metaphorical reinscriptions of linguistic experience. If I am correct in my reading of Blumenberg, this is precisely what his interpretation of the Copernican reform achieves.

4.2 By permitting us to talk about radical discontinuity and external complexity in the same breath with continuity and internal rationality, Blumenberg's achievement illuminates the minimal conditions any historical narrative must satisfy. But what does it tell us about the legitimacy of the modern age? What distinguishes legitimate from illegitimate reoccupations of (or answers to) traditional functions (or questions)? Unlike Arendt, Blumenberg insists that the "accomplishments of reason" are irrelevant to its legitimation. But he himself has precious little to say about what counts in this area, other than that "a program of self-assertion against transcendent uncertainties . . . had become necessary" in the face of "difficulties on which the medieval/Scholastic system had run aground" (Blumenberg 1983, 468). Since he also says that the illegitimate reoccupation of medieval notions of absolute beginnings and ends—in the form of modern foundationalism and teleological progression—is just as necessary, this criterion of legitimacy is simply useless.

Indeed, Blumenberg himself seems to succumb to illegitimate teleological speculation when he adds that the modern reoccupation of medieval positions was "irreversible," moving "in a single, unambiguous direction" (468) So perhaps legitimation *is* a matter of accomplishments after all! As we shall now see, this impression is both confirmed—and disconfirmed—

by Blumenberg's more recent fascination with natural selection as a metaphor for the historical process.

Blumenberg insists that the natural selection of culture implies that "there is objective progress" and that "history, whatever else it might be, is also a process of optimization" (Blumenberg 1985, 165). Two problems arise here. The first concerns the standard for determining progress. As I noted earlier, one cannot assume that the questions (problems, needs) addressed by a "new" organization are the same ones addressed by the "old" one. In some sense, the new system reinterprets the old problems by integrating them into a different problem context. Thus the problem of spiritual and physical survival we moderns "inherited" from antiquity and medieval Christianity is really our problem, not theirs.

Sometimes, however, Blumenberg sounds more like an old-fashioned traditionalist who finds legitimation in de facto authority rather than in progress. Here "optimization" and "natural selection" just refer to the durability of an institution (as Gehlen puts it). To cite Blumenberg: "What the heading 'institutions' covers is, above all, a distribution of burdens of proof. Where an institution exists, the question of its rational foundation is not itself urgent, and the burden of proof always lies on the persons who object to the arrangement the institutions carry with it" (166). With this passage we are led to understand that the model of progressive enlightenment—of radical questioning—cannot be extended to the domain of everyday practice without undermining the habits, customs, and institutions that provide the preconditions and resources for understanding and acting. Demand for rational justification in this context is legitimate only when it is selectively aimed at specific traditions whose problem-solving capacity is placed in doubt.

This is where Blumenberg's "Darwinism of words" makes its entry. The durability of tradition supposedly provides ample justification of its problem-solving capacity. Indeed, culture in general can be seen as an adaptive response to a biological shortcoming. Since "reason means just being able to deal with something," any manner of successful coping—discursively justifiable or not—is rational. True, Blumenberg's use of myth to illustrate rationality appears to contradict his earlier account in *The Legitimacy of the Modern Age*. In that work, the defense of rational self-assertion is staked on the historiographical necessity of drawing epochal boundaries between modernity and its subrational precursor. Now, however, Blumenberg seems to be saying—much like the secularization theorists he formerly criticized—that modern self-assertion is but a variant of a larger process of rational adaptation that includes mythmaking. Just as for Vico myth is a metaphorical interpretation of and compensation for the body, so for Blumenberg reason is a metaphorical interpretation of and compensation for myth. Myth and reason complement each other: the former survives because it fulfills a need that neither science nor morality can satisfy: the need for some higher meaning and purpose.

Perhaps this explains why the Book of Nature metaphor continues to haunt modern biology, where RNA molecules are said to "read" genetic codes written in the DNA alphabet, and why the myth of eternal recurrence survives in the death instinct postulated by Freudian psychoanalysis and the second law of thermodynamics (the principle of entropy) postulated by physics (Blumenberg 1981a, 381–403). If so, it might also explain why Blumenberg's appeal to natural selection succeeds in legitimating our *modern* traditions only to the extent that it incorporates a rational account of progress embedded in a mythic account of recurrent and originary struggle—a feature it shares with Marx's historical materialism.

Today, myth is overshadowed by reason, so that work on myth, i.e., the reception of myth, labors under the imperative of finality. Congruent with Nancy's analysis of myth, Blumenberg reminds us that mythicizing that "brings myth to an end" and "fully exploits and exhausts" the form of a given myth through extreme deformations of its "original figure" functions to "present the subject's responsibility to himself and for himself," but in a manner that liberates the decision to act from temporizing rationalization and future uncertainty (Blumenberg 1985, 266). The Prometheus myth has furnished today's existentialists with the heroic model requisite for the modern age; the reincarnation and recurrence myths in Schopenhauer and Nietzsche offer a kind of metaphysical ground (and comfort) for the otherwise contingent and indefinite strivings of the will. Blumenberg's myth of adaptation and progress merely reinstantiates these themes at the level of science.

If Blumenberg's account of the adaptive function performed by final myths in the modern age enables us to appreciate their rationality, it does so only in the truncated, instrumental sense of SR. The "old *consensus gentium* (consensus of all)," he tells us, "is no longer the criterion of truth . . . in view of the particularism of interests and convictions" (Blumenberg 1983, 96). Consequently, in the modern age of existential self-assertion "theory that can no longer be anything but hypothesis has already lost its immanent value, its status as an end in itself; thus the functionalization of theory for arbitrarily chosen ends, its entry into the role of technique, of a means" (200). With this dismal prognosis we return to the Lyotardian position that the truly rational (i.e., workable) moral myths we moderns possess— excluding the unworkable *grands récits* of the Enlightenment—are "legitimated by the simple fact that they do what they do" (Lyotard 1984, 23).

But is the mere fact that a given institution satisfies the need for meaning and purpose a sign that it is working, or advancing society's true well-being? Doesn't suspicion of ideology warrant testing our beliefs in discourse, as Habermas says? And doesn't the CR constitutive of such discourse imply some grander narrative about our moral destination as emancipated and fulfilled beings?

If optimization only implied satisfaction of subjective needs, it could not blunt rational questioning in the way Blumenberg thinks. Indeed, the problem today seems to be that too much of our lives has been sacrificed on the altar of functional adaptation (narrowly construed to mean mere self-preservation and durability). Even Blumenberg concedes that "one does not have to deny that there can be inconsistencies in the system of the objectifications produced by selection, inconsistencies that impair the overall result" (Blumenberg 1985, 165–66). Here he has in mind those reifying tendencies diagnosed by Habermas: "the isolation and rendering autonomous of partial subsystems in the historical process; the history of science and technology—both severed from the continuity of life as a result of unavoidable specialization—is an example of this" (165–66).

The question arises: When do such inconsistencies render a system suboptimal? When does scientific objectivism "progress" to the point where it becomes regressive, or illegitimate in light of modern demands for self-determination? To pose this question *as* a question of legitimation, namely, as a "modern" demand for rational justification, we would have to possess an objective standard of need satisfaction. We have mentioned Habermas's model of undistorted communication as one such possibility. Oddly enough, despite his own criticism of unreasonable demands for rational justification, Blumenberg himself is drawn to this possibility as well. He writes, for example, that "the possibility of giving rational arguments for behavior" (234) underlies mutual cooperation in modern societies, and that rational communication contributes to the "objectivity" of myth and, therewith, the objectivity of values and norms constitutive of identity (168).

As I just remarked, a teleological account of moral evolution seems to be implied in CR. Hence, it is plausible to think that it might provide some cognitive or theoretical criterion for criticizing social reification as well as ideology. Habermas—whose attempt to address Blumenberg's concerns regarding modern social pathology we earlier examined—certainly thinks it does. But as we have seen, this view cannot be easily sustained. Even if one could develop a *testable* theory of moral development for individual and society—a prospect that seems doomed from the outset—clinical judgments about pathological crisis states would convince in an aesthetic, not strictly cognitive, manner.

In the final analysis, natural selection can explain neither the necessity nor optimality of cultural institutions.[11] Seen from this Darwinian standpoint, modern rationality emerged as a random mutation that proved successful at solving certain problems—period. Whether it was the only solution possible at the time and whether it presently conduces to the optimal well-being (survival) of society cannot be answered: Success is no substitute for self-realization and fulfillment. This conclusion is echoed by Stephen Jay Gould, who has devoted much effort to documenting the often discontinuous and nonprogressive nature of adaptive change in the realm of biology.[12] Even Blumenberg in his more sober moments concedes that "reason would not be the summit of nature's accomplishments . . . [but] would be a risky way around a lack of adaptation; a substitute adaptation; a makeshift agency to deal with the failure of previously reassuring functional arrangements and long-term constant specializations for stable environments" (Blumenberg 1987b, 683).

If we can still speak of legitimating the modern age—and there is considerable doubt whether even Blumenberg thinks we can—it would have to be a postmodern legitimation.[13] Such a mode of legitimation, to paraphrase Foucault and Lyotard, would accept the critical rationalism of the Enlightenment heritage minus its foundationalism (universalism). At the same time, it would acknowledge the role that *petit récits*—myths and parochial narratives—play in lending purpose and meaning, in short, legitimacy, to our lives.

The conjunction of modern self-assertion, which opens up an indefinite space for innovative questioning vis-à-vis the merely possible, and parochial tradition and habit, which stabilize and delimit the range of the possible, is not, to be sure, a consistent or harmonious mix. Indeed, it is far from obvious what this mélange of modern and premodern narratives concretely achieves. Lyotard relishes the schizophrenic dissolution of the modern subject implicit in the conflictual politics of the everyday. Blumenberg, on the contrary, thinks that "final myths" provide a kind of regularity and groundedness to our lives that enables us to accept the ideal—but empty—demands of modern self-determination. Uprooted from the past and shorn of higher purpose, modernity cannot be legitimated. At best, its legitimacy would depend on encouraging the *democratic* dissent, heterogeneity, and novelty necessary for *discursively* solving its own problems.

We have finally arrived at the end of our journey. If it is indeed true that the three-pronged legitimation crisis mentioned at the outset of our quest—of scientific means and ends, of political values and norms, and of historical precedents and purposes—has its source in modern rationality, it is just as true that it finds its redemption there as well. The functional imperatives of domination informing existing forms of capitalism and socialism have dictated the truncated cultivation of reason in the form of SR. Any future revolution ought to reverse this trend by capitalizing on the eminently democratic potential of CR already implicit in science, law, and artistic-literary culture.

SR renders the rationality—and therewith the legitimacy—of values and norms meaningless. Reducing them to arbitrary preferences generates a democratic legitimation crisis that rational choice critics and their allies in government have been quick to seize upon. Similarly, it has affected the very function and structure of scientific research and technology, which has hitherto reflected the control hierarchies and bureaucratic compartmentalizations characteristic of society as a whole. Technologies geared toward decision and control (prediction) in turn lend themselves to managing the crisis of political administration. If history here *is* understood to be *more* than a random collection of meaningless events susceptible to ideological manipulation—and Francis Fukuyama's premature declaration (1989) of the final victory of capitalist democracy reminds us how often it is not—it is only in the most conservative sense, as a body of ostensibly authoritative precedents and policies requiring mechanical implementation.

By mitigating the conflict of needs and interests through consensus-oriented discussion and by providing a fair procedure for doing so, CR also mitigates the conditions that give rise to democracy's legitimation crisis. To the extent that cybernetic and telecommunications technologies incorporate CR, they too enter into the administration of political affairs *as efficacious instruments of collective learning* rather than as mere tools of managerial domination.

But CR would not be able to mitigate political conflict and tendencies toward unitary, hierarchical domination were it not for the aesthetic modus operandi of reflective judgment—and in two senses. First, contrary to formal logical canons of semantic consistency, speakers would not be able to reach rational consensus on most important issues unless their everyday language permitted a great deal of metaphorical flexibility and ambiguity. So something like Rawls's overlapping consensus does indeed carry the greater burden in our democratic negotiations, be they aimed at consensus or compromise. Second, the judgmental capacity to think and speak metaphorically (i.e., comparatively), also involves a reflective capacity to think creatively. Contrary to Rawls, the overlapping consensus is not a convergence of otherwise dissociated comprehensive doctrines but a dialogical fusion of horizons that transforms these doctrines into internally related rationales—a community of belief, if you will.

To be sure, the peculiar class divisions and technological hierarchies of capitalism produce their own crisis of judgment that severely restricts the scope for communication and imagination presupposed in efforts to reach consensus. As our examination of Dworkin's legal hermeneutics amply attests, the capacity to judge with inclusive integrity presupposes that the Constitution, the common law, and the entire body of democratically legislated statutes exhibits integrity as well. CLS critics have demonstrated that this is not the case.

Since the legitimacy of laws depends on the integrity of the combined legislative, judicial, and administrative system, and since the latter in turn depends on the approximate realization of what Dworkin calls associative community, we seem confronted with an uncomfortable fact: short of establishing economic democracy, the democratic-procedural paradigm heralded by Habermas as a solution to our legitimation crisis will not be realized. And yet paradoxically, the capacity to envision such a state of pure integrity and democratic solidarity—a state, incidentally, that would reconcile our liberal and communitarian identities—already presupposes some capacity to judge with integrity.

This takes us back to the problem of clinical and historical judgment. If my reading of Kant's reflexive aesthetic is not mistaken, political actors no less than social scientists and historians must enlarge their thinking in two directions—the one vertical (or temporal), the other horizontal (or spatial). On the horizontal plane, actors must gain a deeper understanding of the values and interests they share with others as well as a deeper understanding of the unintended consequences of their actions for society as a whole. As noted earlier, the very dynamics of interpretation compel us to expand our participatory, first-person horizon of understanding in the direction of a disinterested (or distantiated) third-person perspective. This spectatorial perspective opens up the latent, functional meaning (purpose) served by various action systems in maintaining or realizing an optimal goal state—a state that can be characterized as a felicitous (or healthy) equilibrium of freely interacting rationalization complexes. One necessarily taps into this latent stratum of meaning in clinically judging the current state of social pathology as reflected, for example, in the "colonization" of the lifeworld by economy and administration, and in the hierarchical organization and scientific management of the workplace.

This clinical judgment, however, must be expanded in a vertical direction as well. The capacity to feel the disharmony of a disintegrated society no doubt depends on experiencing aesthetically, with full integrity. But the secular illumination afforded by works of art needs supplementation from a speculative imagination that draws inspiration and hope from insight into the past. Something like this occurred on a lesser scale when Copernicus was confronted with the monstrous disunity of Ptolemean astronomy. If we follow Walter Benjamin in extending the idea of secular illumination to history, we realize that Copernicus, too, had to enlarge his horizon of understanding to encompass incommensurable traditions within a radically visionary perspective. What the critical theorist writing epochal history does on a grand scale—adopt a functionalist perspective with respect to the totality of the historical process—Copernicus did on a modest scale: he drew from the past in order to explode it. It goes without saying that today's political revolutionaries will have to do the same in exploding the monstrous hegemony of disorganized capitalism.

Notes

Introduction

1. While my use of *subjective reason* accords with Horkheimer's (1973, 3–57) pioneering use of the term in many respects, there are notable differences as well. Horkheimer identifies SR with Weber's notion of formal rationality and contrasts it with objective (teleological or substantive) rationality. By contrast, I follow Habermas in opposing SR to communicative rationality.

2. Kant criticized popular sovereignty unchecked by constitutional separation of powers. However, since he grounded the legitimacy of legislation in "the united and consenting will of all," he could not but support representative democracy. That he did so inconsistently can hardly be denied. On the one hand he insisted that "passive" citizens, who are "under the orders or protection of other individuals"—such as women, servants, and wage earners—be denied voting privileges. On the other hand he declared that the state should tax the wealthy to provide for indigents, orphans, and the poor, and actively foster the rational autonomy of all its citizens. The latter view comports with a more interventionist and inclusive democracy. It should be noted further that Kant's conception of the general will as a regulative idea, grounded in rational *procedure,* allowed him to embrace the pluralism and individualism associated with liberal polity in a way that Rousseau's

more traditional and substantive conception did not (Kant 1965, 79, 93). Cf. Riedel 1981.

3. The class of nontrivial claims includes negative statements, counterfactual assertions, generalizations, and so on.

4. For further discussion of the metaphorical dimension of political action, see Oakeshott 1962, especially "The Voice of Poetry in the Conversation of Mankind"; and Ricoeur 1977 and Dallmayr 1984, 174–83.

5. Obviously not all forms of communication are marked by reciprocal openness, and even those that are need not instantiate anything like universal rights and obligations. Interestingly, in denying the universality of civil and political rights but not the universality of economic rights, the Bangkok Declaration supported by many delegates at the first U.N. World Conference on Human Rights seems, on one reading at least, inconsistent. While it can hardly be denied that the satisfaction of basic needs is a prerequisite for the exercise of civil and political rights, and that chaos caused by severe economic shortages sometimes justifies their temporary, partial suspension, the notion of *legitimate rights*—as distinct from merely legal permissions and prohibitions generally applicable to everyone—hardly makes sense apart from institutions guaranteeing both freedom from arbitrary constraint and freedom to participate in democratic government. See chapter 5.

Chapter 1. Reason and Liberal Theory: A Communitarian Critique

1. Cf. L. Strauss, *Natural Right and History* (Chicago: University of Chicago Press, 1953).

2. See Plato's scathing caricature of democracy in book 8 of *The Republic* and Aristotle's preference for restricting participation to "husbandmen and those of modest fortune" (*Politics* 4.6:1292b).

3. In 3.19 of the *Second Treatise of Government* (1689), the state of nature is contrasted with the state of war, but in 3.21 and 9.123 it is not. At 8.111 Locke claims that it was only after the introduction of a money economy and its attendant social inequalities that ambition and luxury entered people's minds. Also see *Some Considerations of the Consequences of the Lowering of Interest and Raising the Value of Money* (1691).

4. Rawls's first principle of justice (the Principle of Equal Liberty) asserts that "each person has an equal right to a fully adequate scheme of basic liberties which is compatible with a similar scheme of liberties for all." These basic liberties consist of "political liberty (the right to vote and be eligible for public office) together with freedom of speech and assembly; liberty of conscience and freedom of thought; freedom of the person along with the right to hold (personal) property; and freedom from arbitrary arrest and seizure as defined by the concept of the rule of law" (Rawls 1971, 61). The second principle of justice (the Difference Principle) provides a framework for evaluating the distribution of those goods whose possession, from a moral point of view, need not be strictly equal. It asserts, first, that "social

and economic inequalities must be attached to offices and positions open to all under conditions of fair equality of opportunity"; and second, that such inequalities "must be to the greatest benefit of the least advantaged members of society." As Rawls puts it, "[A]ll social primary goods are to be distributed equally unless an unequal distribution of any or all of these goods is to the advantage of the least favored" (303).

5. Cf. N. Daniels, "Equal Liberty and the Unequal Worth of Liberty," in N. Daniels, ed., *Reading Rawls* (New York: Basic Books, 1975).

6. Bentham began by advocating a franchise limited to educated men of independent means (*Principles of Parliamentary Reform*, 1818 ed., in Bentham 1931, 40n, 127). By 1817 he had come around to accepting universal suffrage for all except those who were under age and illiterate, and possibly except women, but conceded that "for the sake of *union* and *concord*, many exclusions might be made" (35–37 and 41n). In 1820 he declared that he could support a more limited householder franchise but doubted that this would satisfy the "majority of adult males," who would be excluded (*Radicalism Not Dangerous*, in Bentham 1838–43, 3:599). Although Bentham acknowledged that women were entitled to the vote, he feared that the "confusion" generated by proposing this reform would "engross the public mind, and throw improvement, in all other shapes, to a distance" (*Constitutional Code*, in Bentham 1838–43, 9:109). James Mill's defense of "one person, one vote" as a safeguard against tyranny in *An Essay on Government* (1820) likewise vacillates between endorsing universal suffrage and supporting (on practical grounds) a franchise limited to the wealthiest two-thirds of all males over forty years of age (roughly a sixth of the adult population). His reasoning seems to have been that the interest of women "is involved in either that of their fathers or that of their husbands"; the "great majority of old men have sons, whose interest they regard as their own"; and "the benefits of good government accruing to all, might be expected to overbalance ... the benefits of misrule" that would accrue to the wealthiest two-thirds (Mill 1937, 45–47, 49–50).

7. Arguing that "every body of man ... is governed altogether by its conception of what is its interest, in the narrowest and most selfish sense of the word interest: never by any regard for the interest of others," Bentham concluded that "with the single exception of an aptly organized democracy, the ruling and influential few are enemies of the subject many: ... and by the very nature of man ... perpetual and unchangeable enemies" (*Constitutional Code*, in Bentham 1838–43, 9:102–43).

8. As James Mill put it, "[T]he business of government is properly the business of the rich, and that they will always obtain it, either by bad means or good" ("On the Ballot," *Westminster Review*, July 1830).

9. *On Liberty*, chap. 3, in vol. 18 of J. S. Mill 1963–65.

10. J. S. Mill, *Principles of Political Economy*, bk. 4, chap. 7, secs. 1 and 2; in J. S. Mill 1963–65, 761–63.

11. Mill did not think that social inequality was a necessary consequence of capitalism and attributed existing disparities to past oppression (*Principles of Political*

Economy, bk. 2, chap. 1, sec. 3, p. 207). Indeed, he believed that the rise of cooperatives in which workers are their own capitalists would bring a "moral revolution to
society" promoting "the healing of the standing feud between capital and labour"
and "the transformation of human life, from a conflict of classes struggling for
opposite interests, to a friendly rivalry in the pursuit of a good common to all" (bk.
4, chap. 7, sec. 6, p. 792).

12. Since Mill, unlike Bentham, believed that pleasures associated with the
intellect were superior to those of the body, he could not accept the view that the
aim of government was to optimize production and consumption. However, he
was afraid to extend the franchise to the working class prior to their having developed their collective intelligence, for this would lead to a class legislation every bit
as debilitating as the one existing. In his *Thoughts on Parliamentary Reform* (1859),
Mill believed that the numerical advantage of the working class would be offset by
a system of plural voting without having recourse to a limited franchise. So construed, an unskilled worker would receive one vote, a skilled worker two, a fore-
man three, a farmer, manufacturer, or trader three or four, a professional, an artist,
a writer, a public functionary, a university graduate five or six. However, in his
Considerations on Representative Government (1861) he thought it wise (in addition to
a plural voting provision) t o exclude those on poor relief, those who had experienced bankruptcy, those who could not pay a direct head tax, and those who could
not read, write, and reckon. See *Thoughts on Parliamentary Reform* (Mill1963–65,
19:324–25); and *Considerations on Representative Government* (19:445–46, 470–76).

13. For one of the earliest and most influential discussions of the role of political elites in democracy, see R. Michels, *Political Parties* (1911; New York, 1962).

14. Arrow (1951, 51–59, 75–80) proved that if there are more than two alternatives, any democratic decision procedure preserving transitivity in reasoning will,
under certain circumstances, require the imposition of decision from the outside.
The theorem holds for individual and group decision. Given three individuals (A,
B, C), three alternatives (x, y, z) and the following distribution:

> A prefers x to y, y to z, and x to z
> B prefers y to z, z to x, and y to x
> C prefers z to x, x to y, and z to y

each alternative is preferred by a combination of two individuals, hence no solution to the problem of sovereignty is possible. Translated into group choice involving 101 individuals, the following distribution

> 1 individual prefers x to y, and y to z
> 50 individuals prefer z to x, and x to y
> 50 individuals prefer y to z, and z to x

yields the paradoxical result that 51 prefer x to y, 51 prefer y to z, and *assuming
transitivity of choice,* 51 prefer x to z, while 100 individuals prefer the opposite. In this
case, the rational principle of transitivity requires that a decision be imposed by

one person against the preferences of all others. Only if we abandon the requirement of transitivity (or assume that the possible orderings of individual choices be "single-peaked") can the paradox be avoided.

15. A number of "chaos theorems" have been adduced regarding the problem of agenda control. Unless a proposal is a Condorcet winner—that is, unless it defeats all plausible alternatives in a series of pairwise equations—it will not merit a unique priority as a candidate for discussion. However, the problem of generating such proposals is exacerbated by the fact that the pool of plausible candidates is seldom well-defined. Proposals in one area of policy impact proposals in other areas (public health, employment, international trade, and so on). As a result of this indeterminacy, voting cycles in one policy domain can be used strategically to create voting cycles in other domains that otherwise might not have suffered from them. Cf. Richard McKelvey, "Intransitivities in Multidimensional Voting Models and Some Implications for Agenda Control," *Journal of Economic Theory*, vol. 12 (1976).

16. In the words of Dahl, "With all its defects [the American political system] does nonetheless provide a high probability that any active and legitimate group will make itself heard effectively at some stage in the process of decision . . . so long as the social prerequisites of democracy are substantially intact in this country. It appears to be a relatively efficient system for reinforcing agreement, encouraging moderation, and maintaining social peace in a restless and immoderate people operating a gigantic, powerful, diversified, and incredibly complex society" (Dahl 1956, 150–51).

17. Schumpeter observes that the assumption of perfect competition underlying the neoclassical economic theory of equilibrium does not obtain and he adds that "what we are confronted with in the analysis of political processes is largely not a genuine but a manufactured will" (1977, 263). For a defense of voter apathy in maintaining stability, see Berelson et al. 1954, chap. 14. For recent discussions of class differential in political participation, see Sidney Verba and Norman H. Nie, *Participation in America, Political Democracy, and Social Equality* (New York: Harper & Row, 1972); and Richard A. Cloward and Francis Fox Piven, *Why Americans Don't Vote* (New York: Pantheon, 1987).

18. Alan Ware, "Political Parties," in Held and Pollitt 1986.

19. Rational choice theorists disagree on this point. David Gauthier argues that theorems of economic choice suffice to justify impartial (moral) constraints on utility-maximizing behavior (cooperation being more maximizing than noncooperation). But his contractualist approach appears to exclude those who, for whatever reason, lack sufficient bargaining strength, and it nowhere speaks to the virtues of democracy as a vehicle of political rationality. Jon Elster, by contrast, has shifted his thinking to the point where he now defends the rationality of participatory democracy on the grounds that it is reasonable, when faced with uncertain consequences, to forgo maximizing utility in favor of pursuing justice. Cf. Gauthier 1986 and Elster 1989.

20. Pluralism deviates from classical liberal assumptions in its postulation of the primacy of groups over individuals as the agents of political action. However, it continues to evince the logic of SR, viewing groups as possessing fixed, subrational

preferences. In general, it ignores individual differences within groups, and it neglects the internal, communicative relations between individuals and groups by which they constitute their own identities in the form of shared (consensual) understanding. Hence pluralism affirms conflict-oriented democracy as the norm, in spite of its irrationality as a mechanism for aggregating preferences. For a good critique of pluralist ontology, see Gould 1988, 97–100.

21. Madison's use of the concept of checks and balances primarily applied to a bicameral legislature, not the whole constitutional system. The constitutional use originally derived from the classical notion of "mixed government" designed to guarantee each class of persons—the monarch, the aristocracy, and the people—a special institutional power or office. Madison's use, by contrast, appears to be partially motivated by concern for efficiency with regard to the application of distinct democratic values. Yet in keeping with the older theory (qualified by his belief in legislative supremacy), he also defended the principle as a check on both the institutional concentration of power and majoritarian tyranny (*Fed. Pap.* nos. 10, 51). As Dahl rightly notes (see below), the constitutional separation of powers has not been particularly successful in checking majoritarian tyranny, but then, neither has the conflictual dynamics of pluralistic democracy (polyarchy). Moreover, these dynamics have also encouraged bureaucratic interventions that increasingly undermine democracy.

22. J. Madison, "Vices of the Political System of the United States" (1787), in M. Meyers, ed., *The Mind of the Founder: Sources in the Political Thought of James Madison* (Hanover, Mass.: Brandeis University 1981), 64.

23. Brutus, "Essays," in H. Storing, ed., *The Anti-Federalists* (Chicago: University of Chicago Press, 1985), 114–15.

24. *Muller v. Oregon* (1908) is one of the more glaring examples of denying women and children contractual freedom out of respect for their supposed weakness and dependency.

25. Karl E. Klare, "Judicial Deradicalization of the Wagner Act and the Origins of Modern Legal Consciousness, 1937–41," in Hutchinson 1989, 229–55.

26. Karl E. Klare, "Critical Theory and Labor Relations Law," in Kairys 1982, 65–88.

27. *First National Maintenance Corp. v. NLRB,* 101 S. Ct. 2579–81 (1981).

28. Cf. Barbara J. Nelson, "Women's Poverty and Women's Citizenship: Some Political Consequences of Economic Marginalization," *Signs: Journal of Women in Culture and Society* 10, no. 2 (Winter 1984): 209–31; and Nancy Fraser 1989, chap. 7.

29. Rand E. Rosenblatt, "Legal Entitlements and Welfare Benefits," in Kairys 1982, 262–75.

30. For a fuller treatment of the historical circumstances underlying Marx's stance on the Jewish question, especially as it pertains to his critique of Bruno Bauer, see Ingram 1988.

31. Tucker 1972, 529–30. Marx's comment about political rights merits a separate discussion. Under socialism, the "dictatorship of the proletariat" could assume a nondemocratic form in which the state would still be a coercive instrument of

proletarian class domination (*The Communist Manifesto,* in Tucker 1972, 490). Elsewhere Marx suggests that if the proletariat is in the majority, the state would be democratic (*The Civil War in France,* in Tucker 1972, 632). Whether such a state would still be a political state standing over and against civil society is unclear; it would not be representative in the parliamentarian sense, and those empowered to govern would be employed by the people directly. In any event, it is clear that the democratic association that would prevail in Communist society would no longer issue exchange or labor certificates, would no longer be founded upon bourgeois right, and, therefore, would be no political state at all. Hence, political emancipation and formal democracy as functions of political representation, as institutions for adjudicating social conflict through compromise or consensus, would be rendered otiose.

32. See George G. Brenkert, "Marx and Human Rights," *Journal of the History of Philosophy* 24, no. 1 (January 1986): 55–77.

33. Richard Miller, *Analyzing Marx* (Oxford: Oxford University Press), 15–96.

34. Rawls (1980) argues that the range of socially regulated good must be selected in advance of the hypothetical deliberations in the original position. In *A Theory of Justice* the list of primary goods is drawn up with reference to general psychological assumptions regarding the prerequisites for carrying out a rational plan of life. However, in "Social Unity and Primary Goods" (1982) they are justified as those that "are necessary for realizing the powers of moral personality." The change in emphasis from a relatively neutral justification of primary goods in terms of rational choice to a justification based on a definite conception of moral autonomy—what Rawls, in reference to a *model conception* of the person, calls the *reasonable*—is not inconsequential. For one thing, it shows that conditions of rational choice in the original position are already circumscribed by moral presuppositions, even if the economic rationality of the participants is not. For another, since personality traits now take over the burden of grounding justice formerly assumed by the ideal procedures underwriting the original position, it now appears—as Habermas argues—that Rawls has abandoned a cognitivist philosophical justification of morality in favor of a politically oriented ethics founded on a partisan view of a "thick" conception of the good (Habermas 1991, 128).

35. For a discussion of Rawls's recent accommodation of certain communitarian tenets, see Doppelt 1990, Baynes 1990, Gutmann 1985, and Kymlicka 1988 and 1989.

36. The following discussion of Hegel represents a highly simplified and compressed analysis of key arguments in books 1 and 2 of the *Science of Logic.* For a more detailed commentary of these and other related texts by Leibniz and Kant, I refer the reader to Ingram 1985.

37. See P. F. Strawson, *Individuals* (Garden City, N.Y.: Doubleday, 1963) and R. Rorty, "Strawson's Objectivity Argument," *Review of Metaphysics* 24 (1970): 218.

38. See C. Taylor, "The Opening Arguments of the Phenomenology," in A. MacIntyre, ed., *Hegel: A Collection of Critical Essays* (Garden City, N.Y.: Anchor Doubleday, 1972), 151–87, for an account that compares Hegel's critique of *sinnliche*

Gewißheit with Wittgenstein's refutation of ostensive definition in the *Philosophical Investigations.*

39. See R. Aquila, "Predication and Hegel's Metaphysics," *Kant-Studien* 64 (1973): 231–45, and R. Pippin, "Hegel on Contradiction," *Journal of the History of Philosophy* 16, no. 3 (1978): 301–12, for a detailed examination of these issues.

40. The *Logik* is neither descriptive nor normative. It comprises a transcendental deduction of categories arranged in ascending order in which those that are the most abstract and least penetrating are shown to presuppose those that are progressively richer and deeper in meaning. The nisus toward greater concreteness and semantic coherence corresponds to the realization of categorical rationality, conceived as the comprehensive grounding and reconciliation of opposed moments of reality.

41. See H. F. Fulda, *Unzulängliche Bemerkungen zur Dialektik,* in R. P. Horstmann, ed., *Seminar: Dialektik in der Philosophie Hegels* (Frankfurt: Suhrkamp, 1978). Fulda considers the dialectic of the *Logik* as preeminently one of progressive meaning modification whereby abstract philosophical categories, which lack an ordinary linguistic referential context, have their *vagueness* reduced through rational reconstruction of their meaning. However, he notes that some basic transitions cannot be interpreted as attempts to eliminate semantic ambiguity. Becoming, for example, is not part of the meaning of Being, but rather denotes a necessary condition for specifying a range of successful, nonantinomial application.

42. Hegel's analysis of contingency *(Zufälligkeit)* in the final section of book 2 is relevant to the question of individuation, because a thing's identity only unfolds in the course of its interaction with an environment, a process that Leibniz's system of monads cannot comprehend. Insofar as they are truly self-related, finite things display their *Selbstständigkeit* and rational groundedness in the form of a well-defined identity. The richness of variable content that accompanies their individuation is simply the intense concreteness of the totality concentrated in an Archimedean point. Conversely, insofar as finite things are dependent upon conditions that remain bound to an indefinite horizon of possible interaction, individuation is contingent, or permanently ambiguous and indeterminate. The scope of possible change is groundless because each successive event actuates a further alteration in the contextual *mise-en-scène,* thereby generating new possibilities of identity that continually frustrate any determinate closure (Hegel 1969, 542–47). See G. Giovanni, "The Category of Contingency in the Hegelian Logic," in *Art and Logic in Hegel's Philosophy* (London: Humanities Press, 1980).

43. For Tocqueville's discussion of the "immense and tutelary power" of the democratic state, see Tocqueville 1945, 2:318–19.

Chapter 2. Science and Technology as Practical Reason

1. See Carl Hempel and Paul Oppenheim, "Studies in the Logic of Explanation," *Philosophy of Science,* vol. 15 (1948); and Karl Popper, *The Logic of Scientific Discovery* (London: Hutchinson, 1959).

2. Von Wright has argued that statistical explanations only show that something was to be expected and therefore do not explain anything. See von Wright 1971, 13–15.

3. See R. Chisholm, "The Contrary-to-Fact Conditional," *Mind,* vol. 55 (1946); and N. Goodman, "The Problem of Counterfactual Conditions, *Journal of Philosophy* 44 (1947): 113–28.

4. Cf. H. L. A. Hart and A. M. Honoré, *Causation and the Law* (Oxford: Oxford University Press, 1959).

5. Ibid., 195. See B. Fay, "General Laws in Explaining Human Behavior," in D. R. Sabia, Jr., and J. T. Wallulis, eds., *Critical Theory and Other Critical Perspectives* (Albany: State University of New York Press, 1983), 103–28.

6. C. S. Peirce, "The Doctrine of Chance," in M. Cohen, ed., *Chance, Love, and Logic* (New York: Harcourt, Brace, 1923), 69.

7. One version of the indeterminacy principle asserts that it is impossible to obtain *simultaneously* precise measurements for *both* position and momentum coordinates of subatomic particles; at best, precise determination of one coordinate enables us to calculate the *probability* value of the other. In support of this claim Heisenberg adverted to the fact that "the interaction between observer and object causes uncontrollable and large changes in the system being observed" (Heisenberg 1930, 3). He continues by noting that "a direct result of the indeterminateness of the concept 'observation'" is the indeterminateness of a process in which "the wave and corpuscular pictures both possess the same approximate validity." On Bohr's reading, however, the paradoxical dual nature of subatomic phenomena is mitigated somewhat once we realize that these competing pictures complement one another in describing the full range of phenomena across different experimental contexts. The impossibility of assigning precise simultaneous values to position and momentum coordinates thus follows from the fact that each coordinate might be interpreted differently—as corpuscular or wave phenomenon—depending on context. For a good discussion of this issue as it bears on the problem of causation, see E. Nagel, *The Structure of Science: Problems in the Logic of Scientific Explanation* (New York: Columbia University Press, 1961), 302.

8. S. Toulmin, *The Uses of Argument* (Cambridge: Cambridge University Press, 1958).

9. C. S. Peirce, "The Logic of 1873," in C. Hartshorne and P. Weiss, eds., *Collected Papers of Charles Sanders Peirce* (Cambridge: Cambridge University Press, 1931–35), 7:340.

10. The failure of the reductionist program was well documented in a series of essays by Carnap. In "Testability and Meaning," *Philosophy of Science,* vol. 3 (1936) and vol. 4 (1937), Carnap conceded that the attribution of dispositional predicates such as "soluble in water" to phenomena such as sugar cubes is inextricably linked to general laws, such as the law that sugar will dissolve in water. In a later paper, "The Methodological Character of Theoretical Concepts," *Minnesota Studies in the Philosophy of Science,* vol. 1 (1956), he allowed that many theoretical terms are only indirectly and incompletely linked to observation terms by means of theoretical postulates and correspondence rules. By appealing to such postulates and rules, it

was shown that theoretical expressions such as "temperature of X" could be correlated with the standard calibrated thermometer reading of X. However, in order to eliminate the ambiguity of theoretical expressions linked to nonequivalent measuring procedures, later operationalists demanded that theoretical terminology be made more precise, so that ambiguous terms like "temperature" would be replaced by "mercury thermometer temperature," "gas thermometer temperature," and so on down the line. The main difficulty with this approach is that it controverts the function of theoretical abstraction, which is to unify and generalize—not fragment and contextualize—our understanding of reality. Radical instrumentalists have thus rightly concluded that scientific theories do not purport to picture reality at all, but merely provide context-specific tools for prediction and technological control. For further discussion of this issue, see Barry Hindness, *Philosophy and Methodology in the Social Sciences* (Sussex, England: Harvester, 1977), 129–33.

11. See Popper 1959; *Conjectures and Refutations* (London: Routledge and Kegan Paul, 1963), and *Objective Knowledge* (Oxford: Clarendon Press, 1972).

12. According to Kuhn, only when scientists agree on a paradigm does progressive problem solving occur. For Paul Feyerabend, on the contrary, progress consists in innovation, or disagreement. A middle position is defended by Lakatos, who situates Feyerabend's scheme within a broader tradition of research. See Lakatos and Musgrave 1970.

13. Feyerabend's entire argument presumes that learning to speak a first language, which involves no interlinguistic translation, and learning to speak a second language are structurally indistinguishable. He later concedes, however, that "in the absence of commensurable alternatives" refutations based on the internal contradictions of a given theory "are quite weak." Cf. *Against Method* (London: Verso, 1975), 85–90; and chapter 3 below.

14. Cf. D. Haraway, *Primate Visions* (New York: Routledge, 1989); and S. Harding, *The Science Question in Feminism* (Ithaca: Cornell University Press, 1986). On the topic of racism and sociobiology, see A. Rosenberg, *Sociobiology and the Preemption of Social Science* (Baltimore: Johns Hopkins University Press, 1980).

15. The view expressed here *resembles* the view propounded by Rorty when he correctly argues, against Charles Taylor, that natural and social science both involve explanation and interpretation, and *for that reason* do not differ methodologically. However, Rorty's recognition that understanding and explanation serve different aims—critical reflection versus instrumental control—does not acknowledge the extent to which *only* understanding and explanation in social science (as opposed to understanding and explanation in natural science) serve uniquely emancipatory critical ends. Cf. R. Rorty, "Method, Social Science and Social Hope," in *Consequences of Pragmatism* (Minneapolis: University of Minnesota Press, 1982), 191–210.

16. Admittedly, even formal logical and verificationist principles have been successfully invoked by positivists to critique ideologies based on false generalizations, category mistakes, inconsistent and ambiguous usage, and so on. Moreover, Elster and others have shown how rational choice theory—which I take to be a variation of, if indeed an advance beyond, the empirical approach espoused by

positivism—can be deployed to critique ideologies (including that of rational choice theory!). On the other hand, the limitations of such approaches in explaining human action attest a fortiori to their limitations as methods of ideology critique.

17. K. Popper, *The Poverty of Historicism* (New York: Harper & Row, 1957), xi.

18. For further discussion of this ambiguity, see Apel 1984, 111–42.

19. R. Martin, "Explanation of Understanding in History," in Manninen and Tuomela 1975, 310.

20. The ensuing discussion of rational choice theory follows closely the criticism developed by James Bohman (1991).

21. H. Simon, *Models of Man, Social and Political: Mathematical Essays on Rational Human Behavior in a Social Setting* (New York: Wiley, 1975).

22. A. Sen, "Rational Fools," in F. Han and M. Hollis, *Philosophy and Economic Theory* (Oxford: Oxford University Press, 1979).

23. J. Elster, "Arguing and Bargaining in Two Constituent Assembles," The Storrs Lectures, Yale Law School, 1991, ms., p. 4.

24. D. Lewis, *Convention: A Philosophical Study* (Cambridge: Harvard University Press).

25. T. Abel, "The Operation Called Verstehen," in Dallmayr and McCarthy 1977, 81–92.

26. M. De Certeau, *L'Invention du quotidien* (Paris: UGE, 1980). Cited in Feenberg 1991, 85.

27. For a discussion of the temporal experience of dispersed and integrated identity, see J. Dewey, *Art as Experience* (New York: Putnam, 1934), 35–37; and M. Heidegger 1962, para. 65.

28. See L. Hirschhorn, *Beyond Mechanization : Work and Technology in a Postindustrial Age* (Cambridge: MIT Press, 1984).

29. See F. Varela and H. Maturana, *The Tree of Knowledge* (Boston: Shambhala, 1987). Drawing from existential phenomenology and gestalt psychology, Hubert Dreyfus convincingly argues that the unavoidable absence in computer design of any corporeality—and hence the absence of any context (background or field) of practical involvement constituted by such corporeality—designates the outer limits of what computers can do. See H. Dreyfus, *What Computers Can't Do: The Limits of Artificial Intelligence* (New York: Harper & Row, 1979), esp. pp. 256–80.

30. Rorty 1979, 315–16, 377; Bernstein 1987 and Ingram 1985b.

31. Cf. Rorty 1989, 87–95; and Nancy Fraser's critique of this distinction in "Solidarity or Singularity? Richard Rorty between Romanticism and Technocracy," in Fraser 1989, 99–110.

Chapter 3. Anglo-American Communitarianism and the Dilemmas of Social Critique

1. It is true that MacIntyre distinguishes between the ways in which liberal and traditional societies resolve such conflicts. However, his claim that only the latter confront the tragic experience of having to choose between equally binding,

objective goods seems unconvincing. After all, liberals too find themselves confronted by conflicting claims possessing equal authority (Galston 1991, 75).

2. Carol Gould (1994, 350–51) notes three aspects of an ethic of care that can be extrapolated to the larger context of democratic community: specific concern for the individuality and differences of others, which is a necessary condition for reciprocal respect; familial concern for the common good, which is a necessary condition of reciprocal cooperation; and nurturing concern for "the sick, the aged, the unemployed, and the otherwise dependent members of the community," which as a benign form of nonreciprocity" is necessary for bringing about inclusive equality and reciprocity among all citizens. She also notes, however, three limits to such extrapolation: citizen relations are primarily reciprocal, based on impartial rather than preferential treatment, and nonaltruistic.

3. Jane Mansbridge argues against the gender-specific view in "Feminism and Democratic Community," in John W. Chapman and Ian Shapiro, eds. *NOMOS 35: Democratic Community* (New York: New York University Press, 1993). For a parallel argument, see my discussion of Habermas and Benhabib, respectively, in chap. 6 below and Ingram 1990b, 207–11.

4. A. Gutmann, *Democratic Education* (Princeton: Princeton University Press, 1987), 30–31.

5. A. Ferrara, "Universalisms: Procedural, Contextualist, and Prudential," in Rasmussen 1990, 11–38.

Chapter 4. French Communitarianism and the Subjugation of Identity

1. C. Lefort, "The Question of Democracy," in Lefort 1988, 9–20.

2. J. Derrida, *Of Grammatology,* trans. G. C. Spivak (Baltimore: Johns Hopkins University Press, 1976), 49.

3. Cf. R. Wolin, *The Politics of Being: The Political Thought of Martin Heidegger* (New York: Columbia University Press, 1990), and my review essay, "Wolin on Heidegger and the Politics of Being," *Praxis International* 18, no. 2 (July 1992): 215–28.

4. Lévinas, of course, resists using Martin Buber's nomenclature because of its implicit formalism and symmetry. See E. Lévinas, *Totality and Infinity,* trans. A. Lingis (Pittsburgh: Duquesne University Press, 1969), 68.

5. J. Derrida, "Violence and Metaphysics: An Essay on the Thought of Emmanuel Lévinas," in Derrida 1978, 8.

6. For a vastly different assessment of the strengths of Derrida's political philosophy, see Martin 1992.

7. J. Derrida, "The Laws of Reflection: Nelson Mandela, in Admiration," trans. Mary Ann Caws and Isabelle Lorenz, in J. Derrida and Mustafa Tlili, eds., *For Nelson Mandela* (New York: Holt & Co., 1987), 20–22.

8. This is the thesis advanced in Adorno and Horkheimer 1972. For further

discussion of Schlegel and romanticism, see J.-L. Nancy and P. Lacoue-Labarthe, *L'absolut littéraire* (Paris: Seuil, 1978).

9. Nancy 1986, 13–15. Rousseau was perhaps the first philosopher who succumbed to this dialectic. For a fascinating examination of the logic and politics underlying his liberal/totalitarian proclivities, see Julia Simon-Ingram 1995, chap. 2.

10. See Nancy and Lacoue-Labarthe 1979 and Adorno's analysis in "Freudian Theory and the Pattern of Fascist Propaganda," in Ingram and Simon-Ingram 1991, 84–102; and *The Authoritarian Personality* (New York: Harper Brothers, 1950).

11. G. Bataille, "The Psychological Structure of Fascism," in Bataille 1985.

12. This diagnosis resonates with that of Max Horkheimer, for whom fascism represents "a satanic synthesis of reason and nature." See M. Horkheimer, *Zur Kritik der Instrumentellen Vernunft* (Frankfurt a.M.: Suhrkamp, 1967), 119.

13. Lacan 1977, esp. chaps. 1 and 3. Also see J.-L. Nancy and P. Lacoue-Labarthe, *Le titre de la lettre* (Paris: Galilée, 1972).

14. These points of convergence are duly noted by Foucault in a 1978 interview. Cf. *Remarks on Marx: Conversations with Duccio Tombadori,* trans. R. James Goldstein and James Cascaito (New York: Semiotexte, 1991), 115–29.

15. However, Foucault adds that Rusche and Kirchheimer "were right to see [public tortures and executions] as the effect of a system of production in which labor power, and, therefore, the human body, has neither the utility nor the commercial value that is conferred upon them in an economy of an industrial type" (Foucault 1979, 54). He also shares their view that formal notions of retributive justice foundational for criminal law during the liberal phase of capitalism have since been replaced by more substantive approaches aimed at evaluating, reforming, and preempting future behavior rather than rectifying past acts. This restoration of judicial discretion on a large scale has been abetted by the introduction of psychology into the judicial process—an event that coincides with the decline of bourgeois notions of individual responsibility (17–19).

16. Among critical theorists, Adorno (1973) comes closest to Foucault in his analysis of this dialectic. Cf. my "Foucault and the Frankfurt School: A Discourse on Nietzsche, Power and Knowledge," *Praxis International* 6, no. 3 (Fall 1986): 311–27.

17. "Whereas grammatical construction needs only elements and rules in order to operate . . . there is no statement in general, no free, neutral, independent statement; but a statement always belongs to a series or a whole" (Foucault 1972, 99). This contextualist view of language is further reinforced by Foucault's assertion that "the regularity of statements is defined by the discursive formation itself" so that "the fact of its belonging to a discursive formation and the laws that govern it are one and the same thing" (116).

18. Charles Taylor, "Foucault on Freedom and Truth," in Hoy 1986, 68–102 and Putnam 1981, 162–63 reiterate this objection.

19. These difficulties also vitiate Ernesto Laclau and Chantal Mouffe's attempt to define social hegemony on archaeological principles (1985, 105–7). For further

discussion of their position, see 5.1 below and Barry Smart, "The Politics of Truth and the Problem of Hegemony," in Hoy 1986, 157–73.

20. For commentaries that stress the incompatibility of archaeology and genealogy, see Richard Rorty, "Foucault and Epistemology," in Hoy 1986; and Dreyfus and Rabinow 1982. For commentaries that stress their compatibility and complementarity, see Arnold Davidson, "Archaeology, Genealogy, and Ethics," in Hoy 1986; and Ian Hacking, "The Archaeology of Foucault," in Hoy 1986.

21. Foucault's romantic side mirrors the antirealist view of science he inherited from Georges Canguilhem and Gaston Bachelard. See M. Foucault, "Gaston Bachelard, le philosophe et son ombre: Pieger sa propre culture," *Le Figaro* 1376 (30 September 1972): Litt. 16; and his introduction to Georges Canguilhem's *On the Normal and the Pathological,* trans. C. Fawcett (Boston: Reidel, 1978), ix–xx. For critical treatments of Canguilhem's influence, see Gary Gutting, *Michel Foucault's Archaeology of Scientific Reason* (Cambridge: Cambridge University Press, 1989), and Walter Privatera, *Stil-probleme: Zur Epistemologie Michel Foucaults* (Frankfurt: Athenaeum, 1990).

22. For similar criticisms of Foucault's functionalism, see Michael Walzer, "The Politics of Michel Foucault," in Hoy 1986, 51–68; and Charles Taylor 1986, 68–102. For a defense of Foucault (especially of the later Foucault) against the charge of reductive functionalism, see Dreyfus and Rabinow 1982; and David Hoy 1986, 1–25.

23. Whether these theoretical and methodological shifts in Foucault's thought constitute radical changes or just refinements is a matter of some dispute. In one retrospective summation of his life's work, Foucault reiterated his abiding interest in the relationship between the subject and truth, but acknowledged that his analysis of this relationship over the years stressed different angles: the role of the theoretical human sciences in constituting the image of man, the role of coercive practices and institutions (penology, medicine, and psychology) in normalizing behavior, and the role of ascetic practices in constituting the ethical subject (Bernauer and Rasmussen 1988, 1–2). Elsewhere he said that his aim had been the creation of a history of the different modes of objectification of the subject in linguistics, economics, medicine, and so on; the coercive objectification of the self in exclusionary and disciplinary practices; and the self-objectification of the subject in the hermeneutics of desire (Foucault 1982, 208). Again, in the introduction to *The Use of Pleasure* Foucault describes these "theoretical shifts" as expanding the scope of genealogy, on the one hand, while specifying more precisely its method and goal, on the other (1985, 6, 9). For further discussion of the question of continuity in Foucault's thought, see Davidson 1986; Hoy 1986, introduction; Garth Gillian, "Foucault's Philosophy," in Bernauer and Rasmussen 1988, 34–44; and James Bernauer, "Foucault's Ecstatic Thinking," in Bernauer and Rasmussen 1988, 45–82.

24. More precisely, the ethos depends on the *mode of subjection* (the way in which the individual recognizes his obligation), the *form of ethical work* (the way in which the individual transforms himself into an ethical subject), and the telos of the ethical conduct (Foucault 1985, 27).

25. First, Habermas notes that the welfare state has succeeded partially in un-

coupling its own legitimacy from the classical ideal of democratic self-determination in the manner suggested by Foucault. Voter apathy is partly symptomatic of a widespread belief that the proper business of government is to ensure long-term economic growth and prosperity for all. Second, he shows how the spread of bureaucratic regulation in all its forms implies a more subtle detachment from legitimating ideals. The spread of commercial law is one example of this.

26. J. Habermas, "Knowledge and Human Interests: A General Perspective," in Ingram and Simon-Ingram 1991, 263.

27. According to Habermas, one must distinguish between normative expectations that accompany the acceptance of *meaningful* utterances (illocutionary force in the narrow sense) from normative expectations that accompany the acceptance of *morally binding* obligations (illocutionary force in the broad sense). Even borderline cases involving *immoral* demands such as a bank robber's "Hands up!" accord with *norms* of correct speech *as a condition for their being successfully understood.* However, since the conditions of pragmatic (illocutionary) meaningfulness *ultimately* include the conditions for successful interaction as well (illocutionary meaning broadly construed), Habermas says that the bank robber's demand remains *parasitic* on the structure of mutual moral obligation inherent in voluntary speech action. As we shall see, Habermas's characterization of the rules of discourse as a "fact of reason" perfectly illustrates the sense in which a generalized, *customary* practice of communicative action *within the historical context of Western rationalized culture and society* also assumes the status of a normatively binding authority (ibid.).

28. For Habermas, actors resort to communicative action *precisely in order to coordinate the pursuit of personal aims.* Here, however, the orientation toward personal success is subordinated to the orientation toward reaching mutual agreement. Only when strategic and communicative orientations are pursued on the same level, as it were, does contradiction occur. However, Habermas also recognizes that there are borderline cases, such as the hortatory rhetoric of the politician, that mix orientations. Here, the orientation toward reaching mutual understanding is pursued reservedly, at best (Habermas 1991a, 291 n. 63). In this regard it bears noting that Habermas by no means neglects the subordination of strategic speech acts to communicative aims that occurs whenever one "gives another to understanding something" indirectly. The opening up and preservation of communicative interaction often depend on such nonverbalized *perlocutionary* effects. The unannounced power, or indirect influence, that stems from the (relatively independent) meaning of the speech act and/or its context of deployment cannot be conceived merely as a strategic accretion *in the narrow sense,* as Habermas once thought. Rather, it constitutes, as he himself now realizes, an indirect communication in its own right, one that is perhaps best captured by the very different notion of strategic action alluded to by Foucault (Habermas 1991, 239).

29. See Habermas 1987b, 40, 57, where Habermas appeals to Mead's account of the relationship between "me" and "I" to explain the complementary of moral individuation and autonomy, on one hand, and aesthetic self-realization and creativity, on the other.

30. Habermas's own (1989–90)—and in my opinion, not entirely adequate—response to Gilligan on this point underestimates the way in which abstract ideas of solidarity draw support from concrete feelings of intimate caring.

Chapter 5. Discourse Ethics and Democratic Legitimation

1. As David Kairys puts it, classical jurisprudence appeals to a formal decision procedure that assumes that "(1) the law on a particular issue is preexisting, clear, predictable, and available to anyone with reasonable legal skill; (2) the facts relevant to disposition of a case are ascertained by objective hearing and evidentiary rules that reasonably ensure that the truth will emerge; (3) the result in a particular case is determined by a rather routine application of the law to the facts; and (4) except for the occasional bad judge, any reasonably competent judge will reach the 'correct' decision" (Kairys 1982, 1–2).

2. A social state Y is Pareto superior to another, X, if and only if no one is worse off in Y than in X, and at least one person is better off in Y than in X. A social state is Pareto optimal if and only if there exists no social state Z such that Z is Pareto superior to Y. Note that the problem of interpersonal comparability besetting utilitarianism does not arise, since Pareto optimal states are the eventual product of Pareto superior moves, and Pareto superior moves increase utility without making anyone worse off.

3. The paradox to which the Kalder-Hicks theorem succumbs (the Scitovsky paradox) may be stated as follows: suppose there are two social states, X and Y, two persons P and Q, and two commodities, a and b, distributed in X and Y between P and Q according to the following matrix:

	X		Y	
	a	b	a	b
P	2	0	1	0
Q	0	1	0	2

Given the following preference orders for a and b and by P and Q,

P: 1,1;2,0;1,0
Q: 1,1;0,2;0,1

one can show that X and Y are Kalder-Hicks efficient to one another. In going from X to Y, P is made worse off, Q better. Q could compensate P one unit of b, so that P would attain his most preferred state while Q would be no worse off than before. In going from Y to X, P could compensate Q with one unit of a, so that Q would attain his most preferred state and P would be no worse off than before.

4. Cf. P. R. Dasen, ed., *Piagetian Psychology: Cross-Cultural Contributions* (New York: Halstead, 1977).

5. See T. McCarthy, "Rationality and Relativism: Habermas's 'Overcoming' of Hermeneutics," in Held and Thompson 1982, 72–73.

6. R. M. Hare links universalization to the semantic principles requiring consistent usage of predicates in similar cases. Applied to morality, it requires that a rule or obligation applying in situation X to person P apply to all others in situations comparable to X. Habermas argues that consistency requirements like this fail to capture the meaning of impartiality. Only when universalization is linked to public defendability (Gert) and equality of treatment (Singer) does it approximate the meaning of impartiality. Cf. Habermas 1990b, 64; R. M. Hare, *The Language of Morals* (Oxford: Oxford University Press, 1952); Bernard Gert, *Moral Rules* (New York: Harper & Row, 1976); and Marcus Singer, *Generalization in Ethics* (London: Eyre & Spottiswood, 1963).

7. J. Habermas, "Ist der Herzschlag der Revolution zum Stillstand gekommen? Volkssouveranität als Verfahren. Ein normativer Begriff der Öffentlichkeit?" in *Die Ideen von 1789 in der Deutschen Rezeption* (Frankfurt a.M.: Suhrkamp, 1989), 7–36.

8. J. Habermas, "Legitimation Problems in the Modern State," in Habermas 1979, 204.

9. Cf. J. Bohman, "Communication, Ideology, and Democratic Theory," *American Political Science Review* 84, no. 1 (March 1990), 93–109.

10. Habermas adopts Rawls's view that justifiable civil disobedience must (a) not endanger the constitutional order through acts of violence, (b) have as its aim the conscientious correction of an egregious injustice, and (c) be undertaken only after all legal remedies have been exhausted (1985, 83). Moreover, he follows Dworkin in conceiving civil disobedience as an indispensable device—along with judicial review—for adjusting legal requirements to the demands of changing political interests in cases where the will of the people (and its constitutional embodiment) is not adequately represented (88). As such, civil disobedience symbolizes a potentially universalizable (legitimate) interest that supersedes the legality of parliamentary decision, especially when the decision does not reflect public opinion, or effects changes that are irreversible, that is, that create permanent minorities or bind the democratic sovereignty of the people for an indeterminate duration, as in the case of German-based American missile installations (94). It is interesting to note that neither Habermas nor Rawls acknowledges justifiable acts of civil disobedience that protest laws that appear to satisfy ideal as well as real (legal) procedural constraints, for neither understands that procedural fairness alone cannot legitimate laws in the absence of substantively fair outcomes. Cf. Rawls 1971, paras. 55–59; and R. Dworkin, "Civil Disobedience," in Dworkin 1977.

11. In the essay on civil disobedience mentioned above, Habermas argues that democratic procedures at most warrant recognition of the *legality* of a law, not its legitimacy, which (he argues) still appeals to a hypothetical general will.

12. Habermas does not talk about abolishing labor markets per se, but he does mention the elimination of unemployment as basic to the socialist ideal he defends. See J. Habermas, "Nachholende Revolution und linker Revisionsbedarf: Was heißt Sozialismus heute?" in Habermas 1990a, 199.

13. Despite Habermas's claim that "the argument about forms of ownership has lost its doctrinal significance" (Habermas 1990a, 198), that argument remains central to discussions of democracy. As Gould notes, a prima facie case for private worker ownership (qualified by public oversight) can be made on the grounds that such ownership is needed to safeguard worker self-management rights against arbitrary bureaucratic interference. Schweickart argues, to the contrary, that public ownership is required to ensure even development and to protect against the potential for exploitation inherent in private financial markets.

14. The idea that mass democratic parties are functionally requisite for procuring the loyalty of the modern state has its moral justification in Habermas's argument that ego development involves an expansion of role identity beyond occupations to embrace more abstract principles, and in his further claim that this sets in motion a certain decentration and fluidity in one's perspectives and loyalties.

15. Cf. Jean Cohen, "Discourse Ethics and Civil Society," *Philosophy and Social Criticism* 14, nos. 3 and 4 (1989): 315–37.

Chapter 6. Discourse Ethics and Adjudication

1. Of course, the legal positivism advanced by Hart and Kelsen must be distinguished from the earlier command theory advanced by John Austin in its insistence on the *normative* grounds of constitutional authority. However, it remains positivistic insofar as these grounds are located in parochial custom and convention. Cf. Hart 1961, 107; H. Kelsen, *Pure Theory of Law* (Los Angeles: University of California Press, 1967), 351–52; and J. Austin, *The Province of Jurisprudence Determined* (London: Weidenfeld & Nicholson, 1954).

2. R. Bork, "Original Intent and the Constitution," *Humanities,* February 1986, 22, 26.

3. Cf. R. Bork, foreword to McDowell, *The Constitution and Contemporary Constitutional Theory* (1985), xi; Michael Perry, *Morality, Politics, and Law: A Bicentennial Essay* (Oxford: Oxford University Press, 1988); and R. Dworkin, "From Bork to Kennedy," *New York Review of Books,* 17 December 1987, 36–40. For an excellent critique of the normative originalism advanced by Bork and Perry, see David Hoy, "A Hermeneutical Critique of the Originalism/Nonoriginalism Distinction," *Northern Kentucky Law Review* 15, no. 3 (1988): 479–98.

4. Dworkin 1986, 75–77. Marxism, however, may not be a theory of justice on Dworkin's interpretation, since whether a doctrine has a theory of justice depends on how closely it agrees with the accepted liberal "paradigm." For a critique of Dworkin's conventionalism, see D. Brink, "Legal Theory, Legal Interpretation, and Judicial Review," *Philosophy and Public Affairs* 17 (1988): 106–16.

5. Legal equality as Dworkin and I understand it does not require that citizens be treated the same way. However, it does require that they be treated with equal respect and concern. The civil, political, and social rights accorded to all (out

of equal respect for their autonomy) must be embodied in legal institutions that also provide for an equitable considerations of interests (out of equal concern for their well-being). Progressive tax schedules, affirmative action programs, and the like, do not necessarily violate citizens' equal standing before the law, so long as these schemes are necessary for securing the effective civil, political, and social rights of poor citizens and oppressed minorities and they do not stigmatize other classes of citizens as inferior.

6. Compare Dworkin's claim that "no theory can count as an adequate justification of institutional history unless it provides a good fit with that history" (1977, 340) with his claim that fit is tied to political morality (1986, 410). Rolf Sartorius and C. L. Ten both contest Dworkin's claim that moral adequacy, rather than logical fit with settled law, provides a better description of the ultimate aims underlying judicial practice. See R. Sartorius, *Individual Conduct and Social Norms* (Encino, Calif.: Dickenson, 1975), 196–97; and C. L. Ten, "The Soundest Theory of Law," *Mind* 88 (1979): 535.

7. E. Mensch, "The History of Mainstream Legal Thought," in Kairys 1982, 18–39.

8. M. Horwitz, "The Triumph of Contract," in Hutchinson 1989, 1187–19.

9. P. Gabel and J. Feinman, "Contract Law as Ideology," in Kairys 1982, 172–84.

10. To be sure, *Post v. Jones* (1856), which ruled that *exploitative* agreements between distressed shippers of endangered goods and opportunistic buyers were unconscionable, shows that substantive considerations of equity still supervened. However, it was not until the twentieth century that such considerations would enter into the determination of *coercive* agreements. Since these—and not exploitative—agreements are the main concern of legal formalists, they will occupy the center of my analysis.

11. A. Hutchinson, "Of Kings and Dirty Rascals: The Struggle for Democracy," *Queens Law Journal* 9 (1984): 273–92.

12. Unger 1989, 325–33. Unger's historicism is somewhat mitigated by his appeal to human nature. Although plasticity of personality is the only immutable feature he endorses, he interprets it against the background of four convergent images that recur in history, thereby endowing it with normative significance. The tension between solidarity and autonomy that they mark out supposedly justifies the *immunity, destabilization, market,* and *solidarity* rights Unger adduces in his article. However, it also belies the plasticity of human nature. See R. Unger, *Passion: An Essay on Personality* (New York: The Free Press, 1984); D. Cornell, "Toward a Modern/Postmodern Reconstruction of Ethics," *University of Pennsylvania Law Review* 133 (1985): 1066, 1077; and R. A. Belliotti, "Radical Politics and Nonfoundational Morality," *International Philosophical Quarterly* 29, no. 1 (March 1989): 43–48.

13. Belliotti, "Radical Politics and Nonfoundational Morality," *International Philosophical Quarterly* 29, no. 1 (March 1989): 43–51) claims that the CLS advocate can acknowledge the basic irrationality and ungroundedness of his/her political

commitment without embarrassment. By refusing to "play the mainstream game" of argumentation the advocate need no longer be accused of relativism, nihilism, or inconsistency. In this he follows Rorty, who now repudiates his earlier endorsement of "the conversation of mankind." Belliotti is theoretically right but practically wrong. Although he wants to "start from our concrete *experiences* of love, truth, and power" (the "politics of everyday life") that validate the desire for solidarity and "dialogue without ahistorical conclusions" (Rorty)—he ignores the fact that these experiences only make sense in conversations about the truth or rightness of claims.

14. Cf. Habermas 1988, 235, 276. Habermas once argued that "separation of powers and democracy are not of equal rank as political ordering principles," since the former is justifiable only after it has been democratically determined whether the particular interests protected under such a separation are, in fact, nongeneralizable (1975, 111). Today he emphasizes the need for "*another* kind of separation of powers" (Dews 1986, 186).

15. F. Michelman, "Law's Republic," *Yale Law Journal* 97 (1988): 1529.

16. C. R. Sunstein, "Interest Groups in American Public Law," *Stanford Law Review* 38 (1985): 38, 48, 59.

17. Cf. C. Beard, *An Economic Interpretation of the Constitution of the United States* (New York: Macmillan, 1913); L. Hartz, *The Liberal Tradition in American Political Thought Since the Revolution* (New York: Harcourt, Brace, 1955); and J. G. A. Pocock, *The Machiavellian Moment: Florentine Thought and the Atlantic Republican Tradition* (Princeton: Princeton University Press, 1975).

Chapter 7. A Postmodern Legitimation of Community and Judgment

1. H. Arendt, "Personal Responsibility under Dictatorship," *The Listener,* 6 August 1964, 185–87.

2. Course at Chicago: "Basic Moral Propositions," Seventeenth Session, Hannah Arendt Papers, Library of Congress, Container 41, p. 024560.

3. F. Nietzsche, *Thus Spoke Zarathustra,* in W. Kaufmann, trans. and ed., *The Portable Nietzsche,* (New York: Viking Press, 1968), 251.

4. Cf. Beiner 1982, 111; and Ernst Vollrath, "Hannah Arendt and the Method of Political Thinking," *Social Research* 44 (1977): 163–64.

5. "We do admittedly say that, whereas a higher authority may deprive us of freedom of *speech* or of *writing,* it cannot deprive us of freedom of *thought.* But how much and how accurately would we *think* if we did not think, so to speak, in community with others to whom we *communicate* our thoughts and who communicate their thoughts to us!" (Reiss 1975, 247).

6. *Nicomachean Ethics,* bk. 6, chaps. 2–4, 7–9.

7. Substantive considerations, however, do enter into the account of judgment and social taste presented in Kant's *Anthropology.* There judgment ("the fac-

ulty of discovering the particular, so far as it is an instance of a rule") is similar to Aristotle's golden mean in that it involves correct understanding, which "maintains the properness of concepts necessary for the purpose for which they are used." Such discrimination "cannot be taught, but only exercised" and "does not come for years" (Kant 1974, 93). Elsewhere Kant talks about the "goodness of soul ... around which the judgment of taste assembles all its judgments" as the "pure form under which all purposes must be united." But "greatness of soul and strength of soul relate to the matter (the tools for certain purposes)" (144). Finally, Kant remarks that "to be well-mannered, proper, polite, and polished (by disposing of crudeness)" is a condition of taste, albeit a negative one (147).

8. Habermas links Lyotard's more recent work, *Le différend* (1983), to Rorty's own "radical contextualism," which rescues from idealism "moments of the non-identical and the non-integrated, the deviant and heterogenous, the contradictory and conflictual, the transitory and accidental." Lyotard's contrary opinion of his work as *rationalisme critique* may be found in Lyotard 1986a, 114. See Habermas 1988, 153.

9. David Harvey 1989, 156. Also see A. Giddens, "Modernism and Postmodernism," *New German Critique* 22 (1981): 15–18.

10. See J. Culler, "Communicative Competence and Normative Force," *New German Critique* 35 (Spring/Summer 1985), 133–44; and J. B. Thompson, "Universal Pragmatics," in Held and Thompson 1982, 116–33.

11. Richard Ohmann, "Speech-Acts and the Definition of Literature," *Philosophy and Rhetoric* 4 (1971): 17.

12. There are other paradoxes pertaining to the functionistic reduction of meaning, truth, and legitimacy to efficiency that, owing to his suspicion of hermeneutics, Lyotard does not acknowledge. For a discussion of these, see Habermas and Luhmann 1971, 187–95.

13. I discuss Derrida and Lyotard's deconstruction of this "vicious" circle in more detail in chapter 8.

14. Habermas thinks that speech-act theory ought not sacrifice *universal* typifications on the "altar of contextualism" (1991a, 236). But when speaking of the "heterological" impurity of everyday discourse (263), he concedes that "argumentational games do not form a hierarchy" that would enable us to adduce "final reasons." This option would entail "freez[ing] the context in which we here and now consider a certain type of reason to be the best"—in effect, prematurely closing an inherently open process of dialogue (248).

15. Cf. S. Benhabib, "Epistemologies of Postmodernism: A Rejoinder to Jean-François Lyotard," *New German Critique* 33 (Fall 1984): 124; and White 1991, 136.

16. Habermas discusses varieties of systematically distorted communication affecting disturbances in personal identity that bear a striking resemblance to the sorts of *différends* mentioned by Lyotard. One such variety involves covertly switching the context and meaning of an argument, so that, for example, it ceases to be about a cognitive assertion and becomes a justification for a moral prescription (Habermas 1984c, 255–56, 267–69).

Chapter 8. The Legitimacy of the Modern Age

1. Arendt reaches a similar conclusion by a somewhat different train of reasoning. She thinks that the problem of political representation permits no solution, since either representatives are messengers—bound to convey their constituents' interests and hence replaceable by plebiscites—or they are independent judges of the common good—rulers rather than representatives. Since plebiscites require the administrative aggregation of interests, both instances amount to "elective despotism" (1973, 237). Given this paradox, Arendt could only endorse representative government with the gravest of reservations. Although she conceded that representation enabled poor people and others "exclusively given to their personal interest" to control their rulers without having to directly participate in political debate (133), she firmly denied that it enabled them to present themselves in a free, publicly recognizable way.

2. See, for example, the section subtitled "Beyond the Speech Act," in J. Derrida, "Psyche: Inventions of the Other," in W. Godzich and L. Waters, eds., *Reading De Man Reading* (Minneapolis: University of Minnesota Press, 1986).

3. For a concise but sympathetic critique of Derrida on this point, see D. Hoy, "Philosophemes," *London Review of Books,* 23 November 1989.

4. There are strong postmodern resonances in Arendt's political philosophy, the most obvious being her antifoundationalism, privileging of plurality over sovereignty, and aestheticism. But even defenders of a postmodern reading of Arendt have to acknowledge the modern—and distinctly enlightenment—mentality of *On Revolution.* For example, Dana Villa ("Beyond Good and Evil: Arendt, Nietzsche, and the Aestheticization of Action," *Political Theory,* May 1992) concedes that there is a tension between the agonal, aesthetic conception of action developed in *The Human Condition* and the dialogic, deliberative model developed in *On Revolution.* However, he argues that the latter conception, especially as interpreted by Habermas, cannot account for the former in the way that the former can account for the latter (279). I must demur, if only because a Nietzschean reading that places Arendt's agonal conception of action beyond good and evil flies in the face of her own critique of evil as a failure to act and judge politically (in Arendt's opinion, Eichmann's inability to speak was symptomatic of his inability to think). The same applies to Villa's contention that Arendt's conception of action is largely devoid of teleological and instrumentalist features. I am not sure whether it makes sense to talk about political action as an end in itself—pure performance and display unmotivated by political aims; in any case, Arendt herself sometimes contrasted utilitarian common sense with totalitarian ideology. Villa's intriguing attempt to show how Arendt's later turn to Kant's theory of judgment avoids "the antipolitical tendencies encountered in the actor-centered version of agonistic action" is qualified by his conclusion that, in light of the fragmentation of contemporary life, which renders the idea of a common feeling for the world more paradoxical, something like a Habermasian "legislation of proceduralist rationality" might be more viable, after all (301). In her interesting comparison of Derrida's and Arendt's readings of the

Declaration of Independence, Bonnie Honig also seems to read Arendt as a postmodern *avant la lettre.* Although she astutely notes that Arendt grounds the authority of the Declaration in general conditions of promising, she suggests that even she had to have recourse to something outside of action—namely, retrospective narrative—to provide for the stabilizing function of constation. Hence she concludes that "in every system (every practice)" there are placeholders that enable the system, "but are illegitimate from its vantage point" (Honig 1991, 106). I'm frankly puzzled by this conclusion. If a condition (e.g., mutual openness) establishes the possibility for a practice such as argumentation, that shows that it *is* legitimate from the vantage point of that practice.

5. The distinction between form and substance is not absolute, of course. As our discussion of Hegel, Kennedy, and others has confirmed, the function of a category of meaning—be it in science, law, or any other discipline—is itself a function of its substantive interpretation. For further clarification of this matter, see the following discussion of Blumenberg and Kuhn.

6. Arendt is closer to the mark when she suggests that the long histories of despotism preceding the French and Bolshevik Revolutions—rather than any compassion for the needy—predetermined their antirepublican course. On the other hand, an assessment of the American Revolution more balanced than hers would show that its deviation from the republican course was not *simply* caused by the "rapid and constant economic growth . . . of a constantly expanding private realm" (252) or the absence of constitutional provisions for local forms of participatory government (such as Jefferson's "wards"). More basically, it is also traceable to a constitutional neglect of the most pressing social question at the time of the Founding: slavery.

7. According to Arendt, the complementarity obtaining between power and authority reflects the complementarity obtaining between action (the power to initiate) and judgment (the authority to retroactively redeem). The distinction between action and judgment in turn is incorporated into the constitutional separation of the legislature from the judiciary.

8. M. Masterman (in Lakatos and Musgrave 1970, 59–89) lists twenty-one different senses of paradigm found in *The Structure of Scientific Revolutions.*

9. More precisely, Copernicus argued that "although consistent in the numerical data," the planetary theories of Ptolemy "were not adequate unless certain equants were also conceved," which equants made it appear "that a planet moved with uniform velocity neither on its deferent nor about the center of its epicycle." Hence a system of this sort, he concluded, "seemed neither sufficiently absolute nor sufficiently pleasing to the mind" (Copernicus [1514] 1971, 57).

10. In the 1969 postscript to *The Structure of Scientific Revolutions,* Kuhn said that "what the participants in a communication break-down can do is recognize each other as members of different language communities and then become translators" (202). However, more recently he has emphasized the untranslatability (or partial, imperfect translatability) of incommensurable paradigms. As he now puts it, "[T]here is no language, neutral or otherwise, into which both [of two incommensurable]

theories, conceived as sets of sentences, can be translated without residue or loss" (Kuhn 1983, 670).

11.   Although Wallace presents the "Darwinism of culture" as a middle alternative to the rationalism of Habermas and the traditionalism of Gadamer, Blumenberg's account of it seems rather to vacillate between these extremes. Cf. R. Wallace, "Blumenberg's Third Way, between Habermas and Gadamer," in Flynn and Judovitz, *Dialectic and Narrative* (Albany: SUNY Press, 1993), 183–95.

12.   See Stephen Jay Gould, *Hen's Teeth and Horse's Toes* (1983) and *The Flamingo Smile*, published by Norton and Company (New York).

13.   This point is overlooked by critics who ignore his insistence on "the separation of cognitive achievement and the production of happiness" (Blumenberg 1983, 404). See R. Pippin, "Blumenberg and the Modernity Problem," *Review of Metaphysics* 40 (1987): 535–57; B. Yack, "Myth and Modernity," *Political Theory* 15 (1987): 244–61; M. Jay's review of *The Legitimacy of the Modern Age* in *History and Theory* 24 (1985): 183–97; and Ingram 1990.

Bibliography

Ackerman, B. 1983. "What is Neutral about Neutrality." *Ethics* 93:372–90.

———. 1991. *We the People,* vol. 1, *Foundations.* Cambridge: Harvard University Press.

Adams, David. 1991. "Metaphors for Mankind: The Development of Hans Blumenberg's Anthropological Metaphorology." *Journal of the History of Ideas* 52, no. 1:152–66.

Adorno, T. W. 1973. *Negative Dialectics.* New York: Continuum.

Adorno, T. W., and Max Horkheimer. 1972. *Dialectic of Enlightenment.* Translated by J. Cumming. New York: Herder & Herder.

Altman, A. 1990. *Critical Legal Studies: A Liberal Critique.* Princeton: Princeton University Press.

Apel, K. O. 1984. *Understanding and Explanation: A Transcendental-Pragmatic Perspective.* Translated by G. Warnke. Cambridge: MIT Press.

———. 1987. "The Problem of Philosophical Foundations in Light of a Transcendental Pragmatics of Language." In *After Philosophy: End or Transformation,* edited by K. Baynes, J. Bohman, and T. McCarthy, 250–90. Cambridge: MIT Press.

Arendt, H. 1951. *The Origins of Totalitarianism.* New York: Harcourt, Brace.

———. 1953. "Understanding and Politics." *Partisan Review* 20, no. 4:377–92.

———. 1958. *The Human Condition.* Chicago: University of Chicago Press.

———. 1965. *Eichmann in Jerusalem: A Report on the Banality of Evil.* New York: Viking Press.

———. 1973. *On Revolution.* New York: Viking Press.

———. 1978. *The Life of the Mind.* Edited by Mary McCarthy. New York: Harcourt, Brace, Jovanovich.

———. 1980. *Between Past and Future.* New York: Viking Press.

Arrow, K. 1951. *Social Choice and Individual Values.* New York: John Wiley & Sons.

Arterton, F. C. 1987. *Teledemocracy.* Beverly Hills, Calif.: Sage.

Arthur, J. 1989. *The Unfinished Constitution: Philosophy and Constitutional Practice.* Belmont, Calif.: Wadsworth.

———, ed. 1992. *Democracy: Theory and Practice.* Belmont, Calif.: Wadsworth.

Barnes, B., and D. Bloor. 1982. "Relativism, Rationalism and the Sociology of Knowledge." In *Rationality and Relativism,* edited by M. Hollis and S. Lukes. Oxford: Basil Blackwell.

Barry, B. 1979. "Is Democracy Special?" In *Democracy: Theory and Practice,* edited by J. Arthur, 59–66. Belmont Calif.: Wadsworth.

Bataille, G. 1985. *Visions of Excess: Selected Writings, 1927–1939.* Edited by A. Stoekl. Minneapolis: University of Minnesota Press.

Baynes, K. 1990. "The Liberal/Communitarian Controversy and Communitarian Ethics." In *Universalism vs. Communitarianism: Contemporary Debates in Ethics,* edited by D. Rasmussen, 61–82. Cambridge: MIT Press.

———. 1992. *The Normative Grounds of Social Criticism: Kant, Rawls, and Habermas.* Albany: State University of New York Press.

Baynes, K., J. Bohman, and T. McCarthy, eds. 1987. *After Philosophy: End or Transformation.* Cambridge: MIT Press.

Becker, G. 1976. *The Economic Approach to Human Behavior.* Chicago: University of Chicago Press.

Beiner, Ronald, ed.. 1982. *Hannah Arendt: Lectures on Kant's Political Philosophy.* Chicago: Chicago University Press.

Beitz, C. 1992a. "Procedural Inequality in Democratic Theory: A Preliminary Inquiry." In *Democracy: Theory and Practice,* edited by J. Arthur, 223–35. Belmont Calif.: Wadsworth. Originally published in *Liberal Democracy: NOMOS 25,* edited by J. R. Pennock and J. W. Chapman (New York: New York University, 1983), 59–91.

———. 1992b. "Complex Proceduralism." In *Democracy: Theory and Practice,* edited by J. Arthur, 236–47. Originally published in C. Beitz, *Political Inequality: An Essay in Democratic Theory* (Princeton: Princeton University Press, 1989).

Benhabib, S. 1992. *Situating the Self.* New York: Routledge.

Bentham, J. 1838–43. *The Works of Jeremy Bentham.* 11 vols. Edited by J. Bowring. New York: Russell & Russell, 1962.

———. 1931. *Bentham's Theory of Legislation.* Edited by C. K. Ogden. London. Routledge and Kegan Paul.

Berelson, B. R., P. F. Lazersfeld, and W. N. McPheee. 1954. *Voting.* Chicago: University of Chicago Press.

Bernauer, James, and David Rasmussen, eds. 1988. *The Final Foucault.* Cambridge: MIT Press.

Bernstein, R. 1983. *Beyond Objectivism and Relativism.* Philadelphia: University of Pennsylvania Press.

———. 1987. "One Step Forward, Two Steps Back." *Political Theory* 15, no. 4 (November): 538–63.

Black, M. 1962. *Models and Metaphors.* Ithaca: Cornell University Press.

Blumenberg, H. 1960. "Paradigmen zu einer Metaphorologie." *Archiv für Begriffsgeschichte* 6:7–142.

———. 1981a. *Die Lesbarkeit der Welt.* Frankfurt am Main: Suhrkamp.

———. 1981b. *Wirklichkeiten in denen wir leben.* Stuttgart: Reklam.

———. 1983. The *Legitimacy of the Modern Age.* Translated by R. Wallace. Cambridge: MIT Press.

———. 1985. *Work on Myth.* Translated by R. M. Wallace. Cambridge: MIT Press.

———. 1987a. "An Anthropological Approach to Rhetoric." In *After Philosophy: End or Transformation,* edited by K. Baynes, J. Bohman, and T. McCarthy, 429–58. Cambridge: MIT Press.

———. 1987b. *The Genesis of the Copernican World.* Translated by R. Wallace. Cambridge: MIT Press.

Bohman, J. 1991. *New Philosophy of Social Science.* Cambridge: MIT Press.

———. 1992. "The Limits of Rational Choice Explanation." In *Rational Choice Theory: Advocacy and Critique,* edited by J. Coleman and T. Fararo, 207–27. Los Angeles: Sage.

Chomsky, N., and E. S. Herman. 1988. *Manufacturing Consent: The Political Economy of the Mass Media.* New York: Pantheon.

Cohen, J., and J. Rogers. 1983. *On Democracy.* Harmondsworth: Penguin.

Coleman, J., and J. Ferejohn. 1986. "Democracy and Social Choice." *Ethics* 97:6–25.

Coleman, J., and J. Murphy. 1990. *Philosophy of Law: An Introduction to Jurisprudence.* London: Westview.

Copernicus. [1514] 1971. *Commentariolus.* In *Three Copernican Treatises,* edited by E. Rosen. New York: Octagon Books.

Dahl, R. 1956. *A Preface to Democratic Theory.* Chicago: University of Chicago Press.

———. 1982. *Dilemmas of Pluralist Democracy: Autonomy versus Control.* New Haven: Yale University Press.

———. 1985. *A Preface to Economic Democracy.* Berkeley: University of California Press.

Dallmayr, F. 1984. *Language and Politics: Why Does Language Matter to Politics?* Notre Dame, Ind.: University of Notre Dame Press.

Dallmayr, F., and T. McCarthy, T., eds. 1977. *Understanding and Social Inquiry.* Notre Dame, Ind.: University of Notre Dame Press.

Daly, M., ed. 1994. *Communitarianism. A New Public Ethics.* Belmont, Calif.: Wadsworth.

Danto, A. 1964. *Analytical Philosophy of History.* Cambridge: Cambridge University Press.

Davidson. D. 1968. "Actions, Reasons, and Causes." In *Readings in the Theory of Action,* edited by C. Landesman and N. S. Care, 179–198. Bloomington: Indiana University Press.

———. 1985a. *Inquiries into Truth and Interpretation.* Oxford: Oxford University Press.

———. 1985b. "What Metaphors Mean." In *Inquiries into Truth and Interpretation.* Oxford: Oxford University Press.

———. 1985c. "On the Very Idea of a Conceptual Scheme." In *Inquiries into Truth and Interpretation.* Oxford: Oxford University Press.

———. 1986. "A Nice Derangement of Epitaphs." In *Truth and Interpretation.* Edited by E. LePore. Oxford: Basil Blackwell.

Derrida, J. 1978. *Writing and Difference.* Translated by A. Bass. Chicago: University of Chicago Press.

———. 1981. *Positions.* Translated by A. Bass. Chicago: University of Chicago Press.

———. 1986. "Declarations of Independence." *New Political Science* 15:7–15.

———. 1988. "The Politics of Friendship." *The Journal of Philosophy* 85:632–45.

———. 1992. "The Force of Law: The Mystical Foundation of Authority." In *Deconstruction and the Possibility of Justice,* edited by D. Cornell, M. Rosenfeld, and D. G. Carlson, 3–67. New York: Routledge.

Dewey, J. 1962. *Individualism: Old and New.* New York: Capricorn.

———. 1963. *Liberalism and Social Action.* New York: Capricorn.

Dews, P. 1986. *Autonomy and Solidarity: Interviews with Jürgen Habermas.* London: Verso.

Doppelt, G. 1990. "Beyond Liberalism and Communitarianism: Towards a Critical Theory of Social Justice." In *Universalism vs. Communitarianism: Contemporary Debates in Ethics,* edited by D. Rasmussen, 39–69. Cambridge: MIT Press.

Downs, A. 1957. *An Economic Theory of Democracy.* New York: Harper & Row.

Dray, W. 1957. *Laws and Explanation in History.* Oxford: Oxford University Press.

Dreyfus, H. 1985. "Holism and Hermeneutics." In *Hermeneutics and Praxis,* edited by R. Hollinger, 227–47. Notre Dame, Ind.: University of Notre Dame Press.

Dreyfus, H., and P. Rabinow. 1982. *Michel Foucault: Beyond Structuralism and Hermeneutics.* Chicago: University of Chicago Press.

Dreyfus, H., and S. Dreyfus. 1990. "What Is Morality? A Phenomenological Account of the Development of Ethical Expertise." In *Universalism vs. Communitarianism:*

Contemporary Debates in Ethics, edited by D. Rasmussen, 237–64. Cambridge: MIT Press.

Dworkin, R. 1977. *Taking Rights Seriously.* Cambridge: Harvard University Press.

———. 1981a. "What Is Equality? Part 1: Equality of Welfare." *Philosophy and Public Affairs* 10, no. 3:185–246.

———. 1981b. "What Is Equality? Part 2: Equality of Resources." *Philosophy and Public Affairs* 10, no. 4:283–345.

———. 1983. Review of Walzer's *Spheres of Justice.* In *Communitarianism: A New Public Ethics,* edited by M. Daly, 110–14. Belmont, Calif.: Wadsworth.

———. 1985. *A Matter of Principle.* Cambridge: Harvard University Press.

———. 1986. *Law's Empire.* Cambridge: Harvard University Press.

———. 1987. "What Is Equality? Part 4: Political Equality." Marshall P. Madison Lecture. *University of San Francisco Law Review* 22, no. 1:1–30.

———. 1989. "Liberal Community." *California Law Review* 77, no. 3:479–504.

Elster, J. 1983. *Sour Grapes.* Cambridge: Cambridge University Press.

———. 1986. "The Market and the Forum: The Varieties of Political Theory." In *Foundations in Social Theory,* edited by J. Elster and A. Hylland. Cambridge: Cambridge University Press.

———. 1989. *Solomonic Judgments: Studies in the Limitations of Rationality.* Cambridge: Cambridge University Press.

———. 1993. "Constitutional Bootstrapping in Philadelphia and Paris." *Cardozo Law Review* 14:549–75.

Feenberg, A. 1991. *A Critical Theory of Technology.* Oxford: Oxford University Press.

Feyerabend, P. 1975. *Against Method.* London: Verso.

Fishkin, J. 1979. *Tyranny and Legitimacy: A Critique of Political Theories.* Baltimore: Johns Hopkins University Press.

Foucault, M. 1970. *The Order of Things: An Archaeology of the Human Sciences.* New York: Random House.

———. 1972. *The Archaeology of Knowledge and the Discourse on Language.* Translated by A. M. Smith, A. Sheridan, and Rupert Swyer. New York: Pantheon.

———. 1973. *Madness and Civilization.* New York: Random House.

———. 1977. *Language, Countermemory, Practice: Selected Essays and Interviews by Michel Foucault.* Edited by D. Bouchard. Ithaca: Cornell University Press.

———. 1978. *The History of Sexuality,* vol. 1, *An Introduction.* Translated by R. Hurley. New York: Random House.

———. 1979. *Discipline and Punish: The Birth of the Prison.* Translated by Alan Sheridan. New York: Pantheon.

———. 1980. *Power/Knowledge: Selected Interviews and Other Writings, 1972–1977.* Edited by Colin Gordon. New York: Pantheon.

———. 1982. "The Subject and Power." In *Michel Foucault: Beyond Structuralism and*

Hermeneutics, edited by H. Dreyfus and P. Rabinow, 208–26. Chicago: University of Chicago Press.

———. 1984. "What Is Enlightenment." In *The Foucault Reader*, edited by Paul Rabinow, 32–50. New York: Pantheon.

———. 1985. *The History of Sexuality*, vol. 2, *The Use of Pleasure.*. Translated by R. Hurley. New York: Random House.

———. 1986. *The History of Sexuality*, vol. 3, *The Care of the Self.* Translated by R. Hurley. New York: Random House.

Fraser, N. 1989. *Unruly Practices: Power, Discourse, and Gender in Contemporary Social Theory.* Minneapolis: University of Minnesota Press.

Fukuyama, Francis. 1989. "The End of History." *The National Interest* 16:3–18.

Fuller, S. 1989. *Philosophy of Science and Its Discontents.* Boulder, Colo.: Westview Press.

———. 1991. "Is History and Philosophy of Science Withering on the Vine?" *Philosophy of the Social Sciences* 21, no. 2 (June): 149–74.

Gadamer, H.-G. 1960. *Wahrheit und Methode. Grundzüge einer philosophischen Hermeneutik.* Tübingen: J. C. B. Mohr.

———. 1967. "Über die Planung der Zukunft." In *Kleine Schriften.* Tübingen: J. C. B. Mohr.

———. 1971. "Replik." In *Hermeneutik und Ideologiekritik*, edited by H.-G. Gadamer et al., 283–317. Frankfurt am Main: Suhrkamp.

———. 1975a. "Heremeneutics and Social Science." *Cultural Hermeneutics* 2:307–16.

———. 1975b. *Truth and Method.* Translated by G. Barden and J. Cumming. New York: Seabury Press.

———. 1976a. "On the Scope and Function of Hermeneutical Reflection." In *Philosophical Hermeneutics*, edited by D. Linge, 18–43. Berkeley: University of California Press.

———. 1976b. *Vernunft im Zeitalter der Wissenschaft.* Frankfurt am Main: Suhrkamp.

Galston, W. 1991. *Liberal Purposes.* Cambridge: Cambridge University Press.

Gauthier, D. 1986. *Morals by Agreement.* Oxford: Oxford University Press.

Gilligan, C. 1982. *In a Different Voice: Psychological Theory and Women's Development.* Cambridge: Harvard University Press.

Gould, C. 1988. *Rethinking Democracy. Freedom and Social Cooperation in Politics, Economy, and Society.* Cambridge: Cambridge University Press.

———. 1994. "Feminist Theory and the Democratic Community." In *Communitarianism: A New Public Ethics*, edited by M. Daly, 344–53. Belmont, Calif.: Wadsworth.

Guinier, L. 1991. "The Triumph of Tokenism: The Voting Rights Act and the Theory of Black Electoral Success." *The Michigan Law Review* 89:1077–1154.

Günther, K. 1988. *Der Sinn für Angemessenheit.* Frankfurt am Main: Suhrkamp.

Gutmann, A. 1985. "Communitarian Critics of Liberalism." *Philosophy and Public Affairs* 14:308–22.

Habermas, J. 1975. *Legitimation Crisis.* Translated by T. McCarthy. Boston: Beacon Press.

———. 1979. *Communication and the Evolution of Society.* Translated by T. McCarthy. Boston: Beacon Press.

———. 1981. "Modernity versus Postmodernity." *New German Critique* 22:3–22.

———. 1982. "A Reply to My Critics." In *Habermas: Critical Debates,* edited by D. Held and J. B. Thompson, 219–83. Cambridge: MIT Press.

———. 1983. *Philosophical-Political Profiles.* Translated by F. Lawrence. Cambridge: MIT Press.

———. 1984a. "Questions and Counter-Questions." In *Habermas and Modernity,* edited by R. Bernstein, 192–216. Cambridge: MIT Press.

———. 1984b. *The Theory of Communicative Action,* vol. 1, *Reason and the Rationalization of Society.* Translated by T. McCarthy. Boston. Beacon Press.

———. 1984c. *Vorstudien und Ergänzungen zur Theorie des kommunikativen Handelns.* Frankfurt: Suhrkamp.

———. 1985. *Die Neue Unübersichtlichkeit: Kleine politischen Schriften V.* Frankfurt: Suhrkamp Verlag.

———. 1986. "Taking Aim at the Heart of the Present." In *Foucault: A Critical Reader,* edited by David Couzens Hoy, 103–8. Oxford: Basil Blackwell.

———. 1987a. *The Philosophical Discourse of Modernity: Twelve Lectures.* Translated by Fred Lawrence. Cambridge: MIT Press.

———. 1987b. *The Theory of Communicative Action,* vol. 2, *Lifeworld and System: A Critique of Functionalist Reason.* Translated by T. McCarthy. Boston: Beacon Press.

———. 1988. "Law and Morality: Two Lectures." In *The Tanner Lectures on Human Values,* edited by S. McMurrin, 8:217–79. Salt Lake City: University of Utah Press.

———. 1988. *Nachmetaphysisches Denken.* Frankfurt am Main: Suhrkamp.

———. 1989. *The Structural Transformation of the Public Sphere: An Inquiry into a Category of Bourgeois Society.* Translated by T. Burger and F. Lawrence. Cambridge: MIT Press.

———. 1989–90. "Justice and Solidarity: On the Discussion Concerning 'Stage 6.'" *The Philosophical Forum* 21, nos. 1–2 (Fall/Winter): 31–53.

———. 1990a. *Die Nachholende Revolution: Kleine Politischen Schriften VII.* Frankfurt am Main: Suhrkamp.

———. 1990b. *Moral Consciousness and Communicative Action.* Translated by C. Lenhardt and S. Nicholsen. Cambridge: MIT Press.

———. 1991a. "A Reply." In *Communicative Action,* edited by A. Honneth and H. Joas, 214–64. Cambridge: MIT Press.

———. 1991b. *Erläuterung zur Diskursethik.* Frankfurt: Suhrkamp.

———. 1992. *Faktizität und Geltung: Beiträge zur Diskurstheorie des Rechts und des demokratishen Rechtsstaats.* Frankfurt: Suhrkamp.

———. 1994. "Struggles for Recognition in the Democratic Constitutional State." In *Multiculturalism: Examining the Politics of Recognition,* edited by A. Gutmann. Princeton: Princeton University Press.

Habermas, J., and N. Luhmann. 1971. *Theorie der Gesellschaft oder Socialtechnologie: Was Leistet die Systemforschung?* Frankfurt: Suhrkamp.

Hamilton, A., J. Madison, and J. Jay. 1982. *The Federalist Papers.* Edited by G. Wills. New York: Bantam.

Hart, H. L. A. 1961. *The Concept of Law.* Oxford: Oxford University Press.

Harvey, D. 1989. *The Condition of Postmodernity.* Oxford: Basil Blackwell.

Haverkamp, Paul. 1987. "Paradigma *Metapher,* Metapher *Paradigma*—Zur Metakinetic hermeneutischer Horizonte (Blumenberg/Derrida, Kuhn/Foucault, Black/ White." In *Epochenschwelle und Epochenbewußtsein: Poetik und Hermeneutik 12,* edited by R. Herzog and R. Koselleck. Munich: Fink.

Hegel, G. W. F. 1952. *Hegel's Philosophy of Right.* Translated by T. M. Knox. Oxford: Oxford University Press.

———. 1969. *Science of Logic.* Translated by A. V. Miller. New York: Humanities Press.

———. 1975. *Natural Law.* Translated by T. M. Knox. Philadelphia: University of Pennsylvania Press.

———. 1977. *Phenomenology of Spirit.* Translated by A. V. Miller. Oxford: Oxford University Press.

Heidegger, M. 1962. *Being and Time.* Translated by John Macquarrie and Edward Robinson. New York: Harper & Row.

———. 1978. *Nietzsche, Vol. 4: Nihilism.* Translated by F. Capuzzi. New York: Harper & Row.

Heidelberger, M. 1976. "Some Intertheoretic Relations between Ptolemean and Copernican Astronomy." *Erkenntnis* 10:323–36.

Heisenberg, W. 1930. *The Physical Principles of Quantum Theory.* New York: Dover.

Held, D., and C. Pollet, eds. 1986. *New Forms of Democracy.* Beverly Hills, Calif.: Sage.

Held D., and J. B. Thompson, eds. 1982. *Habermas: Critical Debates.* Cambridge: MIT Press.

Hempel, C. 1965. "The Function of General Laws in History." In *Readings in Philosophical Analysis,* edited by H. Feigl and W. Sellars, 459–71. New York: Appleton-Century-Crofts.

Hobbes, T. 1929. *Leviathan.* Edited by W. G. Pogson Smith. Oxford: Oxford University Press.

Hollinger, R., ed. 1985. *Hermeneutics and Praxis.* Notre Dame, Ind.: University of Notre Dame Press.

Honig, B. 1991. "Declarations of Independence: Arendt and Derrida on the Problem of Founding a Republic." *American Political Science Review* 85:97–113.

Horkheimer, M. 1973. *The Eclipse of Reason.* New York: Continuum.

Hoy, David Couzens. 1987. "Dworkin's Constructive Optimism versus Deconstructive Nihilism." *Law and Philosophy* 6:321–56.

——, ed. 1986. *Foucault: A Critical Reader.* Oxford: Basil Blackwell.

Husserl, E. 1970. *The Crisis of European Sciences and Transcendental Phenomenology.* Translated by D. Carr. Evanston, Ill.: Northwestern University Press.

Hutchinson, A., ed. 1989. *Critical Legal Studies.* Totowa, N.J.: Rowman and Littlefield.

Ingram, David. 1985a. "Hegel on Leibniz and Individuation." *Kant-Studien* 4:420–35.

——. 1985b. "Truth and Hermeneutics." In *Hermeneutics and Praxis,* edited by R. Hollinger, 32–53. Notre Dame, Ind.: University of Notre Dame Press.

——. 1987. *Habermas and the Dialectic of Reason.* New Haven: Yale University Press.

——. 1988. "Rights and Privileges: Marx and the Jewish Question." *Studies in Soviet Thought* 35:125–45.

——. 1990a. "Blumenberg and the Philosophical Grounds of Historiography." *History and Theory* 29:1–15.

——. 1990b. *Critical Theory and Philosophy.* New York: Paragon House.

Ingram, David, and Julia Simon-Ingram, eds. 1991. *Critical Theory: The Essential Readings.* New York: Paragon House.

Kairys, David, ed. 1982. *The Politics of Law.* New York: Pantheon.

Kant, I. 1927. *Critique of Pure Reason.* Translated by N. K. Smith. Oxford: Oxford University Press.

——. 1951. *Critique of Judgment.* Translated by J. H. Bernard. London: Macmillan.

——. 1965. *The Metaphysical Elements of Justice.* Translated by J. Ladd. Indianapolis: Bobbs-Merrill.

——. 1974. *Anthropology from a Pragmatic Point of View.* Translated by M. J. Gregor. The Hague: Martinus Nijhoff.

Kearney, R. 1984. *Dialogues with Contemporary Continental Thinkers.* Manchester: University of Manchester Press.

Kennedy, D. 1983. "The Political Significance of the Structure of the Law School Curriculum." *Seton Hall Law Review* 14:1–16.

——. 1989. "Form and Substance in Private Law Adjudication." In *Critical Legal Studies,* edited by A. Hutchinson, 36–55. Totowa, N.J.: Roman and Littlefield.

Kripke, S. 1972. "Naming and Necessity." In *Semantics of Natural Language,* edited by D. Davidson and G. Harmon, 253–355. Dordrecht: Reidel.

Kuhn, T. 1957. *The Copernican Revolution: Planetary Astronomy in the Development of Western Thought.* Cambridge: Harvard University Press.

———. 1970a. "Reflections on My Critics." In *Criticism and the Growth of Knowledge,* edited by I. Lakatos and A. Musgrave, 231–78. Cambridge: Cambridge University Press.

———. 1970b. *The Structure of Scientific Revolutions.* 2d ed. Chicago: University of Chicago Press.

———. 1977. *The Essential Tension: Selected Studies in Scientific Tradition and Change.* Chicago: University of Chicago Press.

———. 1979. "Metaphor in Science." In *Metaphor and Thought,* edited by A. Ortony, 409–19. Cambridge: Cambridge University Press.

———. 1983. "Commensurability, Comparability, Communicability." In vol. 2 of *PSA 1982,* edited by the Philosophy of Science Association, 669–88. East Lansing, Mich.: Philosophy of Science Association.

———. 1989. "Possible Worlds in History of Science." In *Possible Worlds in Humanities, Arts and Sciences,* edited by S. Allen. Berlin: Walter de Gruyter.

Kymlicka, W. 1988. "Liberalism and Communitarianism." *Canadian Journal of Philosophy* 18:181–204.

———. 1989. "Liberal Individualism and Liberal Neutrality." *Ethics* 99:883–905.

Lacan, J. 1977. *Écrits: A Selection.* New York: Norton.

Laclau, E., and C. Mouffe. 1985. *Hegemony and Socialist Strategy: Towards a Radical Democratic Politics.* London: Verso.

Lakatos, I., and A. Musgrave, eds. 1970. *Criticism and the Growth of Knowledge.* Cambridge: Cambridge University Press.

Larmore, C. 1987. *Patterns of Moral Complexity.* Cambridge: Cambridge University Press.

Lefort, C. 1988. *Democracy and Political Theory.* Minneapolis: University of Minnesota Press.

LePore, E., ed. 1986 *Truth and Interpretation: Perspectives on the Philosophy of Donald Davidson.* Oxford: Basil Blackwell.

Lindblom, C. E. 1977. *Politics and Markets: The World's Economic and Political Systems.* New York: Basic Books.

Locke, J. 1960. *Two Treatises of Government.* Cambridge: Cambridge University Press.

Lyotard, J.-F. 1983. *Le Différend.* Paris: Les Editions de Minuit.

———. 1984. *The Postmodern Condition: A Report on Knowledge.* Translated by B. Massumi and G. Bennington. Minneapolis: University of Minnesota Press.

———. 1986. *Le Postmoderne expliqué aux enfants.* Paris: Editions Galilée.

———. 1988. *The Differend: Phrases in Dispute.* Translated by Van den Abbeele. Minneapolis: University of Minnesota Press.

Lyotard, J.-F., and J.-L. Thébaud. 1979. *Au Juste.* Paris: Christian Bourgeois.

MacIntyre, A. 1975. "Causality and History." In *Essays on Explanation and Understanding,* edited by J. Manninen and R. Tuamela, 137–58. Dordrecht: Reidel.

———. 1981. *After Virtue.* Notre Dame, Ind.: University of Notre Dame Press.

———. 1988. *Whose Justice? Which Rationality?* Notre Dame, Ind.: University of Notre Dame Press.

———. 1994. "Is Patriotism a Virtue?" In *Communitarianism: A New Public Ethics,* edited by M. Daly, 307–18. Belmont, Calif.: Wadsworth.

Macpherson, C. B. 1962. *The Political Theory of Possessive Individualism: Hobbes to Locke.* Oxford: Oxford University Press.

Manninen, J., and R. Tuomela, eds. 1975. *Essays on Explanation and Understanding.* Dordrecht: Reidel.

Mansbridge, J. 1977. "The Limits of Friendship." In *NOMOS: Participation in Politics,* edited by J. R. Pennock and J. Chapman, 16:246–66. New York: New York University Press.

Martin, B. 1992. *Matrix and Line: Derrida and the Possibilities of Postmodern Theory.* Albany: State University New York Press.

Marx, K. 1975. *Marx: Early Writings.* Harmondsworth: Penguin.

Matustik, M. 1993. *Postnational Identity: Critical Theory and Existential Philosophy in Habermas, Kierkegaard, and Havel.* New York: Guilford Press.

May, L. 1992. *Sharing Responsibility.* Chicago: University of Chicago Press.

Mill, J. 1937. *An Essay on Government.* Edited by E. Barker. Cambridge: Cambridge University Press.

Mill, J. S. 1963–65. *Collected Works of John Stuart Mill.* Edited by F. E. Mineka and J. M. Robson. Toronto: University of Toronto Press.

Mitchell, W. C. 1983. "Efficiency, Responsibility, and Democratic Politics." In *NOMOS: Liberal Democracy,* edited by J. R. Pennock and J. Chapman, 25:246–66. New York: New York University Press.

Nancy, J. L. 1982. *Le partage des voix.* Paris: Galilée.

———. 1983. *L'impératif catégorique.* Paris: Flammarion.

———. 1985. "Dies Irae." In *La faculté de juger,* edited by J. Derrida et al., 9–54. Paris: Les Editions de Minuit.

———. 1986. *La Communauté désoeuvrée.* Paris: Christian Bourgeois.

Nancy, J.-L., and P. Lacoue-Labarthe. 1979. "La panique politique." *Confrontations* 2.

———. 1980. "Le mythe nazi." In *Les mécanismes du fascisme.* Strasbourg: Colloque de Schiltigheim.

———, eds. 1981. *Rejouer le politique.* Paris: Galilée.

———. 1983. *Le retrait du politique.* Paris, Galilée.

Nelson, W. 1980. "Open Government and Just Legislation: A Defense of Democracy." In *Democracy: Theory and Politics,* edited by J. Arthur, 156–74. Belmont, Calif.: Wadsworth.

Noble, D. 1984. *Forces of Production.* New York: Oxford University Press.

Nozick, R. 1974. *Anarchy, State, and Utopia.* New York: Basic Books.

Oakeshott, M. 1962. *Rationalism in Politics and Other Essays.* New York: Basic Books.

Olafson, F. 1979. *The Dialectic of Action: A Philosophical Interpretation of History and the Humanities.* Chicago. University of Chicago Press.

Pateman, C. 1970. *Participation and Democratic Theory.* Cambridge: Cambridge University Press.

———. 1985. "Feminism and Democracy." In *Democratic Theory and Practice,* edited by G. Duncan, 204–17. Cambridge: Cambridge University Press.

———. 1986. "Social Choice or Democracy? A Comment on Coleman and Ferejohn." *Ethics* 97:39–46.

Pearce, D. 1979. "Women, Work, and Welfare: The Feminization of Poverty." In *Working Women and Families,* edited by Karen Wolk Feinstein. Beverly Hills, Calif.: Sage.

Pennock, J. R. 1968. "Political Representation: An Overview." In *NOMOS: Representation,* edited by J. R. Pennock and J. Chapman, 10:3–24. New York: Atherton.

Popper, K. 1959. *The Logic of Scientific Discovery.* New York: Basic Books.

Pratt, M. L. 1977. *Speech Act Theory of Literary Discourse.* Bloomington: Indiana University Press.

Putnam, Hilary. 1981. *Reason, Truth, and History.* Cambridge: Cambridge University Press.

Quine, W. V. O. 1960. *Word and Object.* Cambridge: MIT Press.

———. 1963. "Two Dogmas of Empiricism." In *From a Logical Point of View.* New York: Harper & Row.

———. 1987. "Indeterminacy of Translation Again." *Journal of Philosophy* 84:5–10.

Rabinow, Paul, ed. 1984. *The Foucault Reader.* New York: Pantheon.

Rasmussen, D. 1988. "Communication Theory and the Critique of Law." *Praxis International* 8:155–70.

———, ed. 1990. *Universalism vs. Communitarianism: Contemporary Debates in Ethics.* Cambridge: MIT Press.

Rawls, J. 1971. *A Theory of Justice.* Cambridge: Harvard University Press.

———. 1980. "Kantian Constructivism in Moral Theory." *Journal of Philosophy* 77:515–72.

———. 1982a. "The Basic Liberties and Their Priority." In vol. 3 of *The Tanner Lectures on Human Values,* edited by S. McMurrin. Salt Lake City: University of Utah Press.

———. 1982b. "Social Utility and Primary Goods." In *Utilitarianism and Beyond,* edited by A. Sen and B. Williams, 159–85. Cambridge: Cambridge University Press.

———. 1993. *Political Liberalism.* Cambridge: Cambridge University Press.

Rehg, W. 1994. *Insight and Solidarity: A Study in the Discourse Ethics of Jürgen Habermas.* Berkeley: University of California Press.

Reiss, H., ed. *Kant's Political Writings.* Cambridge: Cambridge University Press.

Rhode, D. L. 1989. *Justice and Gender.* Cambridge: MIT Press.

Ricoeur, P. 1977. *The Rule of Metaphor: Multi-Disciplinary Studies of the Creation of Meaning in Language.* Translated by R. Czerny. Toronto: Toronto University Press.

Riedel, M. 1981. "Transcendental Politics? Political Legitimacy and the Concept of Civil Society in Kant." *Social Research* 48:588–613.

Riker, W. 1982. *Liberalism Against Populism: A Confrontation between the Theory of Democracy and the Theory of Social Choice.* San Francisco: W. H. Freeman & Co.

Rorty, R. 1979. *Philosophy and the Mirror of Nature.* Princeton: Princeton University Press.

——. 1989. *Contingency, Irony, and Solidarity.* Cambridge: Cambridge University Press.

Rouse, J. 1991. "Philosophy of Science and the Persistent Narratives of Modernity." *Studies in History and Philosophy of Science* 22, no. 1:414–62.

Rousseau, J.-J. 1987. *The Basic Political Writings.* Indianapolis: Hackett.

Russell, B. 1966. "Logic as the Essence of Philosophy." In *Twentieth-Century Philosophy: The Analytic Tradition,* edited by M. Weitz, 127–44. New York: The Free Press.

Sandel, M. 1982. *Liberalism and the Limits of Justice.* Cambridge: Cambridge University Press.

Scanlon. T. M. 1982. "Contractualism and Utilitarianism." In *Utilitarianism and Beyond,* edited by A. Sen and B. Williams, 103–28. New York: Cambridge University Press.

Schiller, F. 1984. *On the Aesthetic Education of Man in a Series of Letters.* New Haven: Yale University Press.

Schrag, C. 1992. *The Sources of Rationality: A Response to the Postmodern Challenge.* Bloomington: Indiana University Press.

Schumpeter, J. 1947. *Capitalism, Socialism, and Democracy.* London: Allen & Unwin.

Schweickart, D. 1993. *Against Capitalism.* Cambridge: Cambridge University Press.

Searle, J. 1970. "How to Derive 'Ought' from 'Is'." In *Readings in Ethical Theory,* 2d ed., edited by J. Hospers and W. Sellars, 63–72. New York: Appleton-Century-Crofts.

Seel, M. 1985. *Der Kunst der Entzweiung: Zum Begriff der ästhetischen Rationalität.* Frankfurt am Main: Suhrkamp.

Shaw v. Reno, U.S. Supreme Court Reports, 125L Ed 2d, no. 1 (6 August 1993): 520–36.

Simon-Ingram, J. 1995. *Mass Enlightenment: Critical Studies in Rousseau and Diderot.* Albany: State University of New York Press.

Sunstein, C. 1991. "Preferences and Politics." In *Communitarianism: A New Public Ethics,* edited by M. Daly, 291–307. Belmont, Calif.: Wadsworth.

Taylor, C. 1977. "Interpretation and the Sciences of Man." In *Understanding and Social Inquiry,* edited by F. Dallmayr and T. McCarthy, 101–31. Notre Dame, Ind.: University of Notre Dame Press.

———. 1985. "The Nature and Scope of Distributive Justice." In *Philosophical Papers.* vol. 2, *Philosophy and the Human Sciences.* Cambridge: Cambridge University Press.

———. 1989. *Sources of the Self: The Making of the Modern Identity.* Cambridge: Cambridge University Press.

———. 1992. *Multiculturalism and the Politics of Recognition: An Essay by Charles Taylor.* Princeton. Princeton University Press.

———. 1994. "The Modern Identity." In *Communitarianism: A New Public Ethics,* edited by M. Daly, 55–71. Belmont, Calif.: Wadsworth. Originally published as "Alternative Futures: Legitimacy, Identity. and Alienation in Late-Twentieth-Century Canada," in A. Cairns and C. Williams, eds., *Constitutionalism, Citizenship, and Society in Canada* (Toronto: Toronto University Press, 1985).

Tocqueville, A. de. 1945. *Democracy in America.* 2 vols. New York: Alfred A. Knopf.

Tucker, R. C., ed. 1972. *The Marx-Engels Reader.* New York: Norton.

Unger, R. 1975. *Knowledge and Politics.* New York: The Free Press.

———. 1976. *Law in Modern Society.* New York: The Free Press.

———. 1989. "The Critical Legal Studies Movement." In *Critical Legal Studies,* edited by A. Hutchinson, 325–33. Totowa, N.J.: Rowman and Littlefield.

von Wright, Georg. 1971. *Explanation and Understanding.* Ithaca: Cornell University Press.

Walzer, M. 1977. *Just and Unjust Wars.* New York: Basic Books.

———. 1983. *Spheres of Justice: A Defense of Pluralism and Equality.* New York: Basic Books.

———. 1989–90. "A Critique of Philosophical Conversations." *The Philosophical Forum* 21:182–96.

———. 1990. "The Communitarian Critique of Liberalism." *Political Theory* 18, no. 1:6–23.

Warnke, G. 1993. *Justice and Interpretation.* Cambridge: MIT Press.

Weber, M. 1958. *The Protestant Ethic and the Spirit of Capitalism.* New York: Scribner.

———. 1969. *From Marx Weber.* Edited by H. H. Gerth and C. R. Mills. Oxford: Oxford University Press.

———. 1978. *Economy and Society.* 2 vols. Edited by G. Roth and C. Wittich. Berkeley: University of California Press.

Wellmer, A. 1984–85. "Truth, Semblance, and Reconciliation." *Telos* 62:89–115.

——. 1986. *Ethik und Dialog: Elemente des moralischen Urteils bei Kant und in die Diskursethik.* Frankfurt am Main: Suhrkamp.

White, S. 1991. *Political Theory and Modernism.* Cambridge: Cambridge University Press.

Whitehead, Alfred North. 1925. *Science and the Modern World.* New York: Macmillan.

Winch, P. 1958. *The Idea of a Social Science and Its Relation to Philosophy.* London: Routledge & Kegan Paul.

Wittgenstein, L. 1953. *Philosophical Investigations.* London: Macmillan.

——. 1961. *Tractatus Logico-Philosophicus.* London: Routledge & Kegan Paul.

Young, I. M. 1990. *Justice and the Politics of Difference.* Princeton: Princeton University Press.

Index of Names

150, 235; on legal interpretation, 243–76, 394

Eichmann, A., 418n. 4
Ellul, J. 98
Elster, J., 36, 90, 96, 110, 118, 223–24, 401n. 19, 406n. 16
Ely, J. H., 271

Fay, B., 405n. 5
Feenberg, A., 98–103
Feinman, J., 415n. 9
Ferejohn, J., 230–31
Ferrara, A., 408n. 5
Feuerbach, L., 50
Feyerabend, P., 82
Fichte, J. G., 48, 59
Fishkin, J., 340
Foucault, M., 17–18, 98, 101, 153–54, 174–97, 262, 392; on archaeology, 178–81; on communicative and strategic action, 193; on ethics, 184–85; and Frankfurt School, 175–76; on genealogy, 181–85; on Habermas, 193; Habermas's critique of, 179–83, 188; on humanism, 177; on power relations, 136, 192–94, 238; on the subject, 175, 183–84. Works: *Discipline and Punish*, 182; *History of Sexuality*, 182–83; *Madness and Civilization*, 178; *Nietzsche, Genealogy, History*, 181; *Order of Discourse, The*, 181; *Order of Things, The*, 179; *Subject and Power, The*, 188
Fraser, N., 402n. 28, 407n. 31
Frege, G., 62
Freud, S., 169–74, 176, 178, 373. Works: *Civilization and its Discontents*, 172; *Group Psychology and the Analysis of the Ego*, 170; *Moses and Monotheism*, 172; *Totem and Taboo*, 172
Fukuyama, F., 393
Fulda, H. F., 404n. 41
Fuller, S., 366, 387

Gabel, P. 415n. 9
Gadamer, H.-G., 16, 22, 93, 111–12, 123–24, 129–34, 140–41, 147,

149–50, 152, 154, 166, 192, 210, 244, 256, 394–95, 316, 387, 394–95, 420n. 11; and deconstruction, 158–60; and Dworkin, 249; and Habermas, 132–33, 150; *Truth and Method*, 130–31
Galileo, 29
Galston, 117–18, 408n. 1
Garfinkel, H., 182
Gauthier, D.: 30, 401n. 19
Gehlen, A., 389
Gert, B., 413n. 6
Giddens, A., 417n. 9
Gillian, G., 411n. 23
Gilligan, C., 116, 127, 165, 173, 185, 190, 412n. 30
Giovanni, G., 404n. 42
Gödel, K., 326, 328
Goodman, N., 76, 81, 318
Gould, C., 237, 402n. 20, 408n. 2, 414n. 13
Gould, S. J., 392
Gramsci, A., 194
Green, T. H., 33
Guattari, F., 322
Guinier, L., 44–45
Günther, K., 256, 270
Gutmann, A., 118, 403n. 35
Gutting, G., 410n. 21

Habermas, J., 16, 18–20, 37, 55–56, 90, 102, 112–114, 122, 124, 126, 129, 132, 137–38, 140, 149, 153, 155, 159, 161, 174, 179–94, 196–97, 201–42, 245–46, 249, 251–52, 254, 256–57, 259, 265–66, 270–73, 275, 280, 293, 337–42, 352, 391, 394
on aesthetics and judgment, 146–47, 284, 295–96, 302–21
on Apel, 211
on communicative action, 185–88, 209, 328
on democracy, 150, 286–87, 324, 331–32, 340
on discourse ethics, 209, 214–16, 297–301
on Dworkin, 256–58
on Foucault, 179–83, 188
Foucault's disagreement with, 193

Index of Subjects

abortion, 253

absolutism: moral, 126; political, 355, 357–58, 365; of reality, 385; and theology, 356–57, 384

action, 30, 65, 72–74, 202, 216, 236, 238, 269; Arendt on, 285–89, 356–58, 362–63; communicative, 14, 17, 68, 98, 185–86, 191, 212, 255, 266, 268, 295, 300–301, 309–10; coordination of, 209, 218, 266, 309–10; grammar of, 357; Habermas on, 185–86, 191–94, 309–10; instrumental, 14; intentional, 73–74, 84–97; moral, 291; political, 285–89; purposive, 269; rational, 72–74; social, 72; strategic, 14, 191–94, 218, 243

adjudication. *See under* law(s)

administration, 3, 222, 227, 241, 271; bureaucratic, 13, 28, 34, 36, 37, 45, 49, 57, 67, 99, 238; complexity of, 20; overloading of, 325

aestheticism, 120, 295, 303, 322, 418n. 4

aesthetics, 13, 376, 391, 393–94; Arendt on, 285–86; and form, 304–5; of Frankfurt School, 304–7; Habermas on, 296–321; and integrity, 16; Kant on, 280–84, 316, 318, 320; Lyotard on, 320–22, 334, 336; and reception of art, 314; and secular illumination, 306, 318; as source of identity, 22; and world disclosure, 146–48, 309–10, 312–14. *See also* art; judgment, aesthetic; judgment, of beauty; judgment, of sublimity

aestheticization of lifeworld, 322

AFDC, 46–47

affirmative action, 43–45, 134, 138–39, 415n. 5

African Americans, 43–45

agency, 98, 175–76, 182, 269

Alaska LTN Project, 241

alienation, 28, 50–53, 140; consumer, 67; of labor, 51–52, 66–67, 99–100; Marx on, 50–53, 66–67, 99–100

Cartesianism, 8, 21, 98, 152, 176, 185
categorical imperative, 163–64
causality, 15, 63, 65, 70, 75–80; 84–88, 92–96, 210, 365; Humean concept of, 76–77; as synthetic accomplishment, 2;
causation: in law, 78; and linguistic meaning, 123;
chaos theorems, 401 n. 15
checks and balances, 136
child custody, 268
Christian millenarianism, 168
citizen advisory boards, 270
citizenship, 218
civic republicanism, 251
civil disobedience, 233–34
civilization, 172; Western, 196
civil rights. *See under* rights
Civil Rights Act of 1866, 274
civil rights movement, 119
Civil War amendments, 273
class, economic and social, 32–34, 38, 44, 138, 207, 400n. 11
classification, 377
client–provider relationship, 46–48, 268, 270
Coase Theorem, 207
cognition, serial v. parallel process of, 101. *See also* artificial intelligence; knowledge
collective choice: paradoxes of, 5, 18
colonization, 136; of lifeworld, 301
commodity: fetishism, 115; form, 313
common sense. See *sensus communis*
communication, 44, 58, 149, 252–53, 272, 343, 358, 370, 394, 398n. 5; consensual, 203; cross–cultural, 63; Foucault on, 189–93; Habermas on, 133, 185–86, 191–94, 209, 214–15, 227, 236–38, 241, 262, 269, 298; and interpretation, 103; Kant on, 216, 293; and labor process, 100, 103–4; Lyotard on, 193, 323, 327–29; metaphorical, 82, 124; Nancy on, 193; poetic dimension of, 103, 121; pragmatic dimension of, 103, 220; public, 187, 293; rational, 9, 12, 17, 21, 34, 90, 124, 228, 362; reflexivity of, 272; undistorted, 122,

191, 193, 391. *See also* action, communicative; speech
communicative reason (CR): as aesthetic, 315, 319; in Arendt's thought 285; and French poststructuralism, 152, 154, 174, 186; as regards historical narrative and progress, 390–91; in Kant's theory of judgment, 293; as regards law and adjudication, 256, 269, 343; as regards law and democracy, 201, 211, 223, 279, 343; as regards liberal society and liberal theory, 33, 36–37, 53; as regards the liberalism/communitarianism debate, 111–12, 120, 148; in the sciences and in philosophy of science, 69, 71, 81, 83, 90; versus subjective reason (SR), 1–3, 8, 10, 12, 14, 17, 285, 397n. 1; as regards technology and the labor process, 98–99, 101–3; unity of, in Habermas's philosophy, 299. *See also* action, communicative; discourse; rationality; reason
communism, 52–53
communitarianism, 4–11, 15–19, 33, 37–38, 48–53, 64, 201, 203, 208, 220, 226, 250, 343; Anglo–American, 7–9, 15–16, 53–58, 107–53, 202; and democratic procedural justice, 45; Dworkin on, 250–52; French, 9–10, 16–18, 151–197, 202; French compared with Anglo–American, 151–53; genealogical, 17; Habermas on, 144–45, 209, 226; and MacIntyre, 112–14, 120, 124, 127–30, 152; postmodern, 10, 20; and Rawls, 108–11; and Sandel, 53–58; and science, 103; and Taylor, 114–16, 140–49, 152; and Walzer, 116, 120, 134–40
community, 3–6, 8–9, 13–17, 19–22, 39, 56–58, 67, 102–3, 110–11, 246, 394; democratic, 3, 41, 53, 100, 116, 194, 201; Dworkin on, 250–52, 279; Habermas on, 140, 215, 222–25, 228–29; instrumental view of, 56; legal, 257; Rawls on, 108–11; of reason, 14, 67; scientific, 2, 15, 71,

integration, 59, 112; of action, 209; bureaucratic, 268; of personality, 12, 54; system, 189

integrity, 10–11, 14, 16, 19–20, 37, 68, 112, 150, 251, 263; Dworkin on, 253–54, 258, 271; of experience, 2; inclusive and pure, 253–54, 272–73; of life context, 227; of the political system, 39, 250, 270; of the self, 49, 55; of society, 145–49; Taylor on, 145–49

intellect, 285

intentionality, 121, 158

interest groups, 18, 34, 233

interests, 37, 91, 118, 393, 399 n. 7; aggregation of, 203; class, 33; commercial, 37, 50; common, 5–6, 18, 231, 235; conflicting, 205, 261; egalitarian, 235; equitable consideration of, 415 n. 5; generalizable, 217, 232–33, 257; historical, 215; particular, 18, 44–45, 48–49, 54, 220; plural, 36, 228; public, 228, 261–62, 272; rational and public, 3–5, 7, 40, 42, 49; transformation of, 202; true, 218; validation of, 202

interpretation, 366, 371, 394; in Ackerman's account of constitutional history, 271–75; and communication, 103–4; conflicts of, 11, 16, 47–48, 72, 134, 138–39, 145, 149, 221, 242; constitutional, 28, 39–46; critical, 94; and democracy, 221; and Dworkin's theory of law, 246–50, 254–57, 263–65; and experience, 8, 102; Gadamer on, 130–34; Habermas on, 132–33, 204; incommensurability of, 10; in judgment, 9–11, 15–16, 19–20; legal maxims of, 266; metaphorical, 317; and relativism and indeterminacy of, 16, 72, 103–4, 210; transformative, 226; in science, 15; Taylor on, 145–48. *See also* hermeneutics

intuition, 5, 126; eidetic, 292; sensible, 283

investment, 239–40

is-ought fallacy. *See* naturalistic fallacy

Jews, 168

Jewish Question, 51

Judeo–Christian worldview, 115

judgment, 10–11, 343–44. *See also* jurisprudence; laws, adjudication of; law(s), Dworkin on; law(s), Habermas on
aesthetic, 82, 150, 280–84, 290–91, 295–96, 316–19, 333, 336, 339, 366
Arendt on, 284–95, 333
of beauty, 283
categorical, 282
clinical, 297, 318, 394
cognitive, 282–83
communicative condition for, 343
community of, 342
contextual, 214
critical, 103, 150, 336
in Derrida's account of law, 362
determinant, 282, 293, 333, 337, 364, 377
faculty of, 276, 280–84
Habermas on, 284, 295–321, 338, 341
of health, 299–300
historical, 280, 290, 394
integrity of, 341
as intuitive, 341
Günther on, 256, 270
Kant's theory of, 280–84, 292–96, 316, 333–37
Lyotard's theory of, 317, 332–38, 341
moral and practical, 86, 94, 97, 298
and Nancy's account of law, 167–68
political, 20, 280, 295
prescriptive, 334
redemptive, 292, 311
reflective, 14, 20, 281–82, 293–94, 297, 299, 333–34, 337, 393
rule of, 329
of sublimity, 283–84, 336
of taste, 280–82, 284, 304, 319
transcendental, 282
value, 201

judicial review, 271–72; and democracy, 6, 19, 40–41,

jurisprudence: Anglo–American, 255; English, 247; formalist, 262–63;

spirit *(Geist)*, 152
Stalinism, 152
standards, 263, 264–65
state, 28, 47, 62, 226; centrally orga-
    nized, 205; and civil society, 49–51,
    66–67, 220, 223, 266; constitu-
    tional, 266; as cybernetic system,
    324; democratic, 55; Greek theory
    of, 324; Hegel's conception of, 13,
    33, 48–50, 52; liberal, 245; Marx's
    conception of, 48, 50–53; Mill's
    conception of, 33; modern, 266;
    republican, 226; security, 267. *See
    also* welfare state
state of nature, 29–30, 59, 398n. 3
statesmanship, 294
status, 135
strategic media, 238
strategies, 192
strict constructionism, in law, 247
strong program, in sociology of science,
    387
structuralism, 180
subcultures, splitting off of, 301
subject: decentration of, 202; sovereign,
    202
subjective reason (SR): as regards
    Blumenberg's theory of history,
    390–91; versus communicative
    reason (CR), 1–3, 8, 10, 12, 14, 21,
    397n. 1; in French poststruc-
    turalism, 152, 154–55, 173, 174–75,
    185–87; in Hegel, 67; as regards
    law and adjudication 246, 254, 256,
    259–260, 262, 269; as regards law
    and democracy, 201, 215; in liberal
    society and liberal thought, 27–28,
    33–37, 48, 50, 55; as regards the
    liberalism/communitarianism
    debate, 108, 120, 148; in science
    and philosophy of science, 69–71,
    74–76, 80–81, 83, 88, 91, 95; as
    regards technology and the labor
    process, 98–99, 101–3. *See also*
    rationality, instrumental; rationality,
    strategic
subjectivism, 120, 126–27
subjectivity, 97; transcendental, 70
subject–predicate, 64

sublimation, 171
sublime, the, 280, 283–84, 303, 319,
    334; dynamic and mathematical,
    284
substance, 282, 371, 379
suffrage, 399n. 6, 400n. 12
supersensible ground, 281
supplementarity, 162
Supreme Court, 225, 258, 273
surrealism, 303–4, 306, 319
symbols, aesthetic, 283
synthetic a priori proposition, 63, 75–76
system(s): administrative, 324; adapta-
    tion, 324; causal, 76; crisis, 325; of
    decision, 89; formal, 75; functional-
    ist, 95–97; of law, 250; and life-
    world, 203, 238; of interpretations
    of self and world, 281; media-
    steered, 238; political, 220; as self–
    regulating, 325; of signifiers, 65–66;
    social, 217, 251

Taft–Hartley Act, 42
taste, standards of, 214
Taylorism, 53; and assembly line, 99
tax, 252
tax exemptions, 119
technique(s): disciplinary, 17; of social
    engineering, 3; as distinct from
    technology, 98
technology, 3, 69–71, 74, 241; computer,
    4, 12, 15, 18, 53, 74, 101–4, 202;
    and democracy, 15, 18, 53; design,
    98; and domination, 1–3, 12;
    theories of, 98
teledemocracy, 241
teleology: in history, 125, 290; in nature,
    29, 125, 290
television entertainment, 119
tellability, as validity claim in literature,
    310
theater, 303
theism, 145–46
theory, democratic, 201
theory and practice, 108
thermodynamics, second law of, 390
thought (thinking), 285; enlarged, 291–
    92
tolerance, 20, 112, 117–18, 121, 143